Every serious student of the Bible should own a copy of Dr. Patterson's excellent commentary on Revelation. It's an invaluable resource I reach for often whenever I prepare to teach on the glorious return of Jesus Christ.

Dr. Robert Jeffress
Senior Pastor, First Baptist Church
Dallas, TX

There are many commentaries available on the book of Revelation, but not many that cover all the bases of solid hermeneutics, exegesis, theology, and are written in such a way as to be serviceable to both the pastor and scholar. Paige Patterson's volume succeeds in all categories. Written from a premillennial perspective, I consider Patterson's commentary on Revelation to be the best overall commentary on the market. I have used it many times and found it to be a reliable guide to the Apocalypse. I am happy to commend this work with my highest recommendation from a mentor and friend whom I have known for fifty years.

David L. Allen
Distinguished Professor of Practical Theology
Dean, Adrian Rogers Center for Biblical Preaching
Mid-America Baptist Theological Seminary
Memphis, TN

Anyone who seeks to do a study of the book of Revelation should read this book carefully. Paige does not back away from the interpretive difficulties that arise from studying the Apocalypse. With his high view of Scripture and knowledge of history, we come away from this book with a deep appreciation for the marvelous future that awaits all believers! Read *The Lion is a Lamb* to be both instructed and blessed!

Erwin W. Lutzer
Pastor Emeritus, Moody Church
Chicago, IL

It takes both knowledge and courage to embark on such pivotal work. I do not know too many theologians who have done it, and there were many attempts, for sure. Anyone who knows Dr. Paige Patterson recognizes his academic abilities and consistent courage, which have proven sufficient to write this monumental work after many years of research. What we have within these pages is an amazing tool in this biblical commentary on what Dr. Patterson calls the Apocalypse.

Dr. Ilie "Elijah" Soritau
Professor of Homiletics & Missions/Evangelism
Emanuel University of Oradea, Romania

This study of the Revelation is the sharpest of exegetical swords! This weapon has a balance that affords it to be wielded by every soldier in the Lord's service who would dare to explore the last book of the Bible. A must study in these changing times is the Revelation of Jesus Christ. The best companion for that study is *The Lion is a Lamb*!

This Christmas, every preacher in our church will be receiving *The Lion Is a Lamb: An Exegetical and Theological Exposition of the Book of Revelation* as their gift from their pastor.

Thomas E. Hatley
Pastor of Immanuel Baptist Church at the Global Outreach Center
Coordinator of Global Ministries of the Conservative Baptist Network
Rogers, Arkansas

Of the entirety of the Bible the book of the Revelation may be one of the most difficult to understand, and at the same time the book most people are interested in. Also, any pastor worth his salt wants to know what John the Revelator was talking about. What are the meanings of the Four Horsemen, the Beast, the Seven Seals, the Trumpets? What does it mean to have the mark of the beast? Who are the 144,000? What is the great tribulation? Readers ask these questions and so many more. They want to know what it means. In this volume, Dr. Paige Patterson makes that possible for the everyday layman and even for new believers. Every Pastor, Evangelist, Professor, Missionary, Sunday School teacher and anyone that has an interest in biblical prophecy should own this book! In full disclosure, Dr. Patterson is a dear friend of mine. There are a few friends that I would fight a buzz saw for and make no mistake, he is among those friends.

Tim Lee
Evangelist
Chairman of the Board
Liberty University
Lynchburg, VA

Serving as the President of Northeastern Baptist College has afforded me the opportunity to teach through The Revelation in intensive studies on both the bachelor's and master's level. In addition, it has been my joy to preach or teach through the last book of the Bible numerous times over the last 45 years. In my own education, it was my privilege to study the book with W. A. Criswell and Charles Ryrie, as well as to engage the book in an intensive doctoral seminar.

All this has afforded me opportunity to read many books on the Revelation. Though there are many good commentaries, none compare to Paige Patterson's *The Lion is a Lamb*. Dr. Patterson's book demonstrates a knowledge of the book and its contents that are second to none. The book lives up to its sub-title. It is truly *An Exegetical and Theological Exposition* of the book. Following the Grammatical-Historical approach to interpretation, Dr. Patterson leaves no stone unturned. The reader will gain a thorough understanding of the various interpretative approaches, the key issues of discussion, and gain an understanding of the structure, content, and application of the Revelation. Whether the reader is a faithful church member, a pastor, or a seasoned theologian, reading this commentary will prove both instructive and encouraging in your daily walk with Jesus.

Mark H. Ballard, PhD
President, Northeastern Baptist College
Publisher, Northeastern Baptist Press
Bennington, VT

In the ever-growing field of commentaries on the Book of Revelation, few contributions achieve the rare combination of exegetical precision, theological coherence, and pastoral accessibility. The Lion is a Lamb by Dr. Paige Patterson is one such work. In this second edition, Patterson offers more than a scholarly analysis of the Apocalypse—he presents a theologically rich, spiritually edifying, and textually faithful exposition that invites both the mind and the heart into the majestic vision of the glorified Christ.

Dr. Patterson's decades-long service to the church—as a theologian, president of Seminaries, biblical scholar, and preacher of the Gospel—has produced a legacy that few can rival. Thousands of students have sat under his teaching, and his preaching has reached millions across the globe. His engagement with the text of Scripture has never been detached from its ecclesial and evangelistic purpose. That integrated vision is profoundly evident in this commentary.

The Lion Is a Lamb is marked by a rigorous treatment of the Greek text, sensitive attention to intertextual references—particularly to Daniel, Ezekiel, and Zechariah—and a deep awareness of the theological structures that undergird John's prophetic vision. Patterson consistently situates his interpretation within a futurist framework, but without the excesses of speculative eschatology. Instead, he offers a sober, reverent, and hermeneutically sound approach that reflects a high view of biblical authority and the unity of redemptive history.

Theologically, the commentary is distinguished by its unwavering christocentrism. Patterson rightly recognizes that the Book of Revelation is not first and foremost a code to be cracked, but a revelation of Jesus Christ himself. The juxtaposition of the Lion and the Lamb—power and sacrifice, judgment and redemption—is not merely a literary device, but the theological center of the Apocalypse. Patterson draws this out with clarity and conviction, allowing readers to see how divine sovereignty and suffering love coalesce in the person of Christ.

Moreover, this is a commentary that refuses to remain abstract. Patterson's exposition consistently moves from interpretation to implication, from text to transformation. His aim is not only that readers would understand the visions of Revelation, but that they would live in light of them—with renewed hope, persevering faith, and reverent worship. In that sense, the commentary becomes not only a tool for the classroom or the study, but also a resource for the pulpit and the counseling room.

Particularly noteworthy is Patterson's pastoral concern for those who read Revelation amid trial or confusion. Far from fostering fear or fascination with disaster, this work calls the church to confidence in Christ and fidelity in witness. In an age often characterized by theological shallowness or apocalyptic sensationalism, The Lion is a Lamb stands as a model of exegetical depth wedded to spiritual clarity.

In sum, this commentary offers what few do: academic credibility, theological integrity, pastoral usefulness, and devotional warmth. Dr. Patterson has given the church a resource that not only explains the last book of the Bible, but also models how the Word of God is to be read, preached, and lived. I recommend it without hesitation to pastors, students, and scholars who desire to encounter the Revelation not only as text, but as testimony to the risen Christ, the Lamb who reigns.

Dr. Heinrich Derksen
President, Bibel Seminary Bonn (Germany)
Deputy Chairman, Association of Evangelical Seminaries in Germany, Austria,
and Switzerland (Konferenz bibeltreuer Ausbildungsstätten e.V.)
Gießen, Germany

The first commentary I ever owned was Patterson's *The Troubled Triumphant Church*. In it, I discovered a storyteller who presented scholarly information in a way accessible to the new believer that I was, while not watering it down. Every day I read it, I was lifted up to a new level of knowledge and passion for God's word. Revelation achieves the same goal for a NT book which few have the proficiency and prowess to teach. Rooted in decades of research, in his exposition, Patterson presents a plethora of views of the text, interspersed with à propos excursuses on important issues, and then humbly shares his conclusions, all with the ultimate goal to equip and embolden preachers and bible scholars to interact seriously with this difficult prophetic epistle, so that they can boldly teach the Apocalypse to the next generation of believers. I have been requiring the previous edition of this book for over a decade in my General Epistle-Revelation class at Truett McConnell University, and I would highly recommend it to any student of the Apocalypse.

Maël L. D. S. Disseau
Vice President for Academic Services
Charles F. Stanley Endowed Chair of Theology
Associate Professor of Biblical and Theological Studies
Truett McConnell University
Cleveland, GA

THE LION IS A LAMB

AN EXEGETICAL AND THEOLOGICAL EXPOSITION OF THE BOOK OF REVELATION

Paige Patterson

Second Edition
Edited by Matt Queen

THE LION IS A LAMB

AN EXEGETICAL AND THEOLOGICAL EXPOSITION OF THE BOOK OF REVELATION

Paige Patterson

Second Edition
Edited by Matt Queen

NEBP ACADEMIC

BENNINGTON, VT

TABLE OF CONTENTS

DEDICATION

This commentary on the Apocalypse is dedicated to my son Armour Patterson of Melissa, Texas. No one has been a more consistent encourager than Armour. In life's most discouraging and intimidating moments, Armour has challenged me to stand strong for the Lord and for the faith. Typical of his support is the following poem, which appeared beneath the picture of an Indian warrior. Armour sent it to me when I was experiencing great sorrow and challenge. How can one exhibit a lack of courage in the face of a challenge like this?

THE WARRIOR

For a warrior who stood alone,
Who spilled his own blood,
And never feared for his own life,
Who rode boldly through the storms,
Stood unwaveringly in winds of strife,
And withstood lonely winters and long nights,
Who was undaunted by threat and attack,
Willing to lead when others would not follow,
And loyal and caring always to his own,
The war goes on always.
But though the flesh weakens,
The spirit and the heart remain strong.
When the storms come again,
The wounds sting and the blood spills,
And the valley of the shadow of death is at hand,
It is only the beginning.
The good fight has been fought.
The war's end is nigh.
The sun sets in its splendor of this earthly battlefield;
Peace flows in the whispers of the night's wind,
And joy comes in the morning.

Armour Patterson
Father's Day, 1994

PREFACE TO THE SECOND EDITION

The biblical doctrine of salvation is incomplete without a consummation. To have God's forgiveness and fellowship in this life is exquisite; but if the onslaught and inevitability of physical death is the conclusion of salvation, then Satan clearly has prevailed. However, because the resurrection of Christ and His promise to raise the righteous dead to life, indeed to make of them "a kingdom of priests," is reliable, then salvation is realized and Satan is forever defeated. Hence the Bible, particularly the New Testament, presents a vivid doctrine of eschatology—the essential concomitant of soteriology. The Revelation of John, inscribed from the stone quarries of the horseshoe-shaped island of Patmos, is one entire book largely devoted to an explanation of God's enduring plan for believers in eternity and His eternal punishment for the devil in hell.

Perspectives on the interpretation of the Apocalypse differ widely. For all of Christian history, Revelation and its interpretation has charmed and often befuddled its multiple interpreters. No one could begin to read all the commentaries penned over the 1900-year history of New Testament interpretation. Yet in preparation for the writing of this volume, I read what frequently seemed like a whole library of them. Profoundly do I respect the efforts and products even of many with whom I differ radically. Sometimes I found treatments with which I generally agreed but found their exegesis uncompelling. I saw little need to revisit the same terrain traversed by hundreds of others before me.

I envision and desire that this commentary benefits the busy pastor caring for the sheep of his pasture, comforting hurting souls, winning the lost, and attempting to preach through the Apocalypse to deliver a message of Christian hope to the saints living in a troubled world. To accomplish this task, I envisioned a relatively short treatment designed for the overworked pastor, which would be fair to the five classical interpretive options, while embracing a futurist perspective for the majority of this prophecy. I hoped to provide an interpretation that would lend itself naturally to the pastor's sermon preparation. Some pastors have encouraged me by suggesting that I have succeeded. John F. Evans, in his authoritative *A Guide to Biblical Commentaries and Reference Works*, has deemed it a significant "contribution to scholarship," as well as "a leading commentary, influential for evangelical scholarly discussion." I can only pray that the Spirit of God will use my feeble efforts.

The first edition followed the *New International Version* text. While I encountered no problems, working as I did primarily from the Greek manuscripts, I chose to employ the *New King James Version* (NKJV) for this second edition. As an advocate of the inerrancy of the autographs of Scripture, I did not select the NKJV because I found it preferable in every case, rather because I grew up memorizing Bible verses in the *King James Version* (KJV) and, therefore, developed a love for much of the Elizabethan English of the KJV. Recent days have revealed a return of many to a form of this translation, so I thought it appropriate to invoke it again.

Reading the Revelation provides remarkable preparation for triumphal living in troubled times. Hope is engendered with the sullen hearts of discouraged saints. Confidence is engendered by the promises of God. Please do not miss the centrality of the Person of Jesus the Christ on virtually every page of Revelation. He is the Lion of Judah, but the Lion of Judah is also the sacrificial Lamb of God, providing atonement for the sins of all who seek Him. May the Lord add His benediction to your reading of this sacred Book of hope.

Until He Comes,
Paige Patterson
Sandy Creek Foundation
Parker, Texas

ACKNOWLEDGEMENTS

Writing a commentary is never solely the work of the author. In fact, in this case, there are so many who have helped that adequate acknowledgement is circumscribed by my own memory. My parents, long since with the Lord, Thomas Armour and Roberta Mae, taught me to love Jesus, his Word, and the lost. They believed that God would use me when few had that faith. My children, Armour and Rachel, Mark and Carmen, my granddaughters, Abigail, her husband Aaron, and Rebekah, and my great grandchildren, J. J. and Lizzie Joy have provided almost constant inspiration and encouragement. The granddaughters never knew a time in their lives when PawPaw was not working on the first edition of this commentary!

In the writing of this volume's first edition, *Revelation*, Jimmy Draper stirred me up continually to good works; and was far more long-suffering with me than he had reason to be. Advice, encouragement, and prayer came from my colleagues, the faculties at Southeastern and Southwestern Baptist Theological Seminaries. The former staff in the president's office and at Pecan Manor deserved combat pay for their faithfulness and assistance. Jason Duesing, Kelly King, Marissa Yanaga, Preston Atwood, Candi Finch, Neal Batman, and Justin Williams all assisted in too many ways to remember, as did Chris Thompson and Bobbi Moosbrugger at Magnolia Hill. Keith Ninomiya helped begin the research while working with me at the Criswell College. Richard Land, president of the Ethics and Religious Liberty Commission and a friend since seminary, gently but continually implored me to get it done even though he more than most knows well the stress of two seminary presidencies on my efforts to produce such a volume. Chuck Kelley, president at New Orleans Baptist Theological Seminary and my brother-in-law, never ceased insisting on how important he believed it was for me to do the commentary. Jerry Vines was less gentle but never ceased the pressure, and for him I am grateful. Also, for three churches in which I either preached or taught the Apocalypse—Bethany Baptist in New Orleans, Louisiana; First Baptist, Fayetteville, Arkansas; and First Baptist, Dallas, Texas—I express gratitude for their long-suffering. Vern Charette and Tamra J.

Sanchez receive a special measure of gratitude for assisting with the typing of the original manuscript and location of sources.

This second edition would have never happened without the intervention of Mark Ballard, the publishing and marketing efforts of Northeastern Baptist Press, the dependable assistance of Lauren Cook, and the patient editing of Matt Queen. Most of all, to my wife Dorothy, I express eternal thanks for believing in me, encouraging me, reading and editing this manuscript as well as many others. I depend on her knowledge and wisdom to edit. Her spiritual reservoir seems never to be depleted—her faith legendary among those who know her. Without her this book would never have become a reality. For everyone's support, I offer my eternal gratitude.

ABBREVIATIONS

Gen	Isa	Luke
Exod	Jer	John
Lev	Lam	Acts
Num	Ezek	Rom
Deut	Dan	1, 2 Cor
Josh	Hos	Gal
Judg	Joel	Eph
Ruth	Amos	Phil
1, 2 Sam	Obad	Col
1, 2 Kgs	Jonah	1, 2 Thess
1, 2 Chr	Mic	1, 2 Tim
Ezra	Nah	Titus
Neh	Hab	Phlm
Esth	Zeph	Heb
Job	Hag	Jas
Ps (pl. Pss)	Zech	1, 2 Pet
Prov	Mal	1, 2, 3 John
Eccl	Matt	Jude
Song	Mark	Rev

AB	Anchor Bible
ABR	*Australian Biblical Review*
ACCS	Ancient Christian Commentary on Scripture
ACNT	Augsburg Commentaries on the New Testament
ANF	*Ante-Nicene Fathers*, American reprint of the Edinburgh edition. Grand Rapids: Eerdmans, 1973.
AUSS	*Andrews University Seminary Studies*
BDB	Brown, F., S. R. Driver, and C. A. Briggs. *A Hebrew and English*

NIGTC	New International Greek Testament Commentary
NJBC	*The New Jerome Biblical Commentary.* Edited by R. E. Brown et al. Englewood Cliffs, NJ: Pearson, 1990.
NovT	*Novum Testamentum*
NPNF¹	*Nicene and Post-Nicene Fathers*, Series 1
NPNF²	*Nicene and Post-Nicene Fathers*, Series 2
NTG	New Testament Guides
NTL	New Testament Library
NTS	*New Testament Studies*
OCD	*Oxford Classical Dictionary.* Edited by S. Hornblower and A. Spawforth. 3rd ed. Oxford, 1996.
ODCC	*The Oxford Dictionary of the Christian Church.* Edited by F. L. Cross and E. A. Livingstone. 3rd ed. New York: Oxford University Press, 1997.
OED	*Oxford English Dictionary.* Edited by J. A. Simpson and E. S. C. Weiner. Oxford: Clarendon Press, 1989.
OTG	Old Testament Guides
SBLMS	Society of Biblical Literature Monograph Series
SBLSymS	Society of Biblical Literature Symposium Series
SNTSMS	Society for New Testament Studies Monograph Series
SP	Sacra Pagina
TDNT	*Theological Dictionary of the New Testament.* Edited by G. Kittel and G. Friedrich. Translated by G. W. Bromiley. 10 vols. Grand Rapids: Eerdmans, 1964–1976.
TNTC	Tyndale New Testament Commentaries
TWOT	*Theological Wordbook of the Old Testament.* Edited by R. L. Harris, G. L. Archer, Jr. 2 vols. Chicago: Moody, 1980.
WBC	Word Biblical Commentary
WUNT	Wissenschaftliche Untersuchungen zum Neuen Testament

INTRODUCTION

OUTLINE

1. Authorship
2. Date
3. Genre
4. Text and Canonicity
5. History of Interpretation
6. Theology and the Apocalypse
7. The Key to the Book
8. Symbolism
9. Premillennialism
10. Pretribulationism
11. Preaching the Apocalypse
12. Outline

Peering through the early morning mist over the azure waters of the Aegean Sea from a prominence on the island prison of Patmos on the Lord's Day morning, the centenarian apostle John may have found himself nursing a plethora of apparently contradictory notions. The forty-five miles of water that separated him from his beloved disciples in Ephesus may as well have been a vast ocean. Further, exile on Patmos could not have been a Club Med experience. Given his age and circumstances, the sense of his own mortality must have pressed on him. Somber reflections, however, may have been mitigated by precious memories. The water may have summoned vivid mental portraits of those early, heady days on the Sea of Galilee when he with incredulity observed the miracles of Jesus, felt his heart quickened by the authority of the teachings of Jesus, and reveled in the fellowship of the motley crew of fellow-fishermen, a hated agent of Roman taxation, and an assortment of other unlikely inhabitants of Galilee who followed the One whom they believed to be the long-awaited Messiah of Israel.

The pirouette of these contemplations, accompanied only by the music of the breakers on the eastern beach of Patmos and the occasional rustling of the prevailing southeasterly breeze, on this Sunday morning was destined for divine interruption as John describes in Rev 1:9–11. "In the Spirit" on the Lord's Day, John's relative serenity was shaken by a loud voice that was "like a trumpet." The voice was intelligible, instructing the aging apostle to write all that he was about to see and cede the contents to seven congregations in Asia Minor. The inclination to look in the direction of this phonic mandate rewarded the islander not only with a vision of seven golden lampstands but also with a startling revelation of one "like a son of man" regally displayed against the backdrop of an unforgettable heavenly landscape. The series of visions, which followed like a Mongol hoard, constitute the book of the Revelation. Frequently John needed assistance to understand the vision. And if John was sometimes baffled by his own book, little wonder that the intervention of more than 1,900 years and the often contradictory interpretations of hundreds of commentators leave contemporary exegetes with a formidable task of attempting to provide insight into that which is generally acknowledged to be one of the most difficult books of the Bible.

Although these themes have been visited frequently, an introduction to the commentary sets the stage to understand the nature and direction of the commentator. Attention will now be focused on those introductory matters affecting the interpretation of the Revelation.

1. AUTHORSHIP

Conjectures about the authorship of the Apocalypse do not proliferate as with some books. The four suggestions include John, the brother of James and son of Zebedee, one of the "sons of thunder," who was one of the most intimate of the Lord's original circle of disciples; a certain John the Elder, who lived at Ephesus well into the second century; another John about whom nothing is known, the name itself most probably being a pseudonym; or, more recently, John the Baptist. The vast majority of energies expended relate to arguments maintaining or opposing the authorship of John the apostle.[1]

---

1   Even though the present author disagrees with the conclusions of R. H.

Among the more interesting postulates is the proposal of J. Massyngberde Ford in her Anchor Bible commentary. She posits John the Baptist and the prophetic community associated with him as the probable author. Noting that John of the Apocalypse makes no claim for apostleship, Ford prefers to believe that the origins of the book should be traced to the community surrounding the fiery prophet, John the Baptist, and that at least a portion of the book dates to the time of Christ.[2] This view blends well with the perspectives of those who find strong similarities with John the Baptist and the Qumran sect and find Revelation not dissimilar from the apocalyptic emphases of the Dead Sea documents.[3]

Ford's proposal lacks historical precedence but has greater plausibility than most historical-critical reconstructions. Ford notes in the preaching of John the Baptist theological themes, such as the emphasis upon the Lamb of God, which are reduplicated in the Apocalypse. In the end, lack of earlier testimony of such involvement, the presence of more developed ecclesiology in the Apocalypse, and the developed opposition to the early Christian movement on the part of both Rome and the Jewish community all seem devastating to Ford's idea. The possibility of another unknown John or someone using this name as a pseudonym seems even less likely than the Ford proposal.

Charles, writing in the ICC, advances the thesis that a second presbyter from Ephesus, also called John, was the author of the Apocalypse. This individual Charles calls John the Elder. The suggestion is based on the testimony of Papias, the bishop of Hierapolis on the mountain overlooking the cities of Laodicea and Colossae in the valley below. Since Papias was a contemporary of Polycarp of Smyrna, though he denied, according to Eusebius, having heard firsthand from any of the apostles, he is located in time close to the writing of the Apocalypse. Therefore, Charles's attribution of the Revelation to John the

---

Charles, the most comprehensive discussion of the question is still found in his *A Critical and Exegetical Commentary on the Revelation of St. John*, ICC (Edinburgh: T&T Clark, 1920), 1:xxix-l.

2   J. M. Ford, *Revelation: Introduction, Translation, and Commentary*, AB (Garden City, NY: Doubleday, 1975), 28–37.

3   For extensive discussions on the eschatology of Qumran, see C. A. Evans and P. W. Flint, eds., *Eschatology, Messianism, and the Dead Sea Scrolls* (Grand Rapids: Eerdmans, 1997); L. H. Schiffman, *The Eschatological Community of the Dead Sea Scrolls: A Study of the Rule of the Congregation*, SBLMS 38 (Atlanta, GA: Scholars Press, 1989); W. W. Fields, *The Dead Sea Scrolls: A Full History: Volume One, 1947-1960* (Leiden and Boston: Brill, 2009); J. VanderKam and P. Flint, *The Meaning of the Dead Sea Scrolls: Their Significance for Understanding the Bible, Judaism, Jesus, and Christianity* (San Francisco: HarperCollins, 2002).

Elder is not insignificant. Charles also cites the work of Dionysius of Alexandria as sharing this view.[4] Eusebius specifically reports,

> This confirms the truth of the story of those who have said that there were two of the same name in Asia, and that there are two tombs at Ephesus both still called John's. This calls for attention: for it is probably that the second (unless anyone prefer the former) saw the revelation which passes under the name of John. The Papias whom we are now treating confesses that he had received the words of the Apostles from their followers, but says that he had actually heard Aristion and the presbyter John.[5]

Charles buttresses his view by noting that the author of the Apocalypse claims to be a prophet and not an apostle. Furthermore, Charles sees strong stylistic and thematic similarities between John's Gospel and the First Epistle of John but thinks that he discerns significant dissimilarities between these and the Revelation.[6] Charles also sees the hand of an editor in the existing version of the Apocalypse.[7]

The arguments of Charles, in the end, are insufficient to dislodge the majority opinion of antiquity that Revelation is the work of John the apostle. Stylistic and thematic differences are easily accounted for based on the circumstances that called for the different books as well as the genre of the books. The testimony of Papias, though important, is anything but compelling for several reasons. First, Eusebius did not harbor a high view of Papias, considering him of little consequence. He found the chiliasm of Papias particularly repugnant. So one should not place too much confidence in the judgments of Eusebius. Further, the testimony of Papias, with few supporters, is relatively unimpressive. Papias apparently denied any direct association with any of the apostles, removing him a generation from the writing of the Apocalypse, thus increasing the possibility of error.

Evidence favoring John the apostle as the author of Revelation begins with the testimony of Irenaeus of Lyon. Irenaeus, bishop of Lyon in southern Gaul, was born in Asia Minor and as a boy had listened to Polycarp, the bish-

---

4   Charles, *Critical and Exegetical Commentary*, 1:xl–xli.
5   Eusebius, *The Ecclesiastical History*, trans. Kirsopp Lake, LCL 153 (Cambridge, MA: Harvard University Press; London: William Heinemann, 1980), 1:293.
6   Charles, *Critical and Exegetical Commentary*, 1:xliv–xlv.
7   Ibid., 1:l–lv.

op of Smyrna, who as an old man was martyred, possibly as early as AD 155. Polycarp had heard John the apostle perhaps in Ephesus.⁸ Polycarp's influence on Irenaeus plus the latter's familiarity with the history of Christianity in Asia Minor establish him as a significant voice in determining both the authorship and the meaning of the Apocalypse of John. As to the authorship of Revelation, Irenaeus writes of John the apostle as the author almost as a matter of recognized fact. Describing the passing of the earth and heavens, he writes,

> When these things, therefore, pass away above the earth, John, the Lord's disciple, says that the new Jerusalem above shall [then] descend, as a bride adorned for her husband; and that this is the tabernacle of God, in which God will dwell with men.⁹

Or again, Irenaeus observes,

> And if any one [sic] will devote a close attention to those things which are stated by the prophets with regard to the [time of the] end, and those which John the disciple of the Lord saw in the Apocalypse, he will find that the nations [are to] receive the same plagues universally, as Egypt then did particularly.¹⁰

In another place, the bishop of Lyon mentions this same John as the author of the Apocalypse:

> John also, the Lord's disciple, when beholding the sacerdotal and glorious advent of His kingdom, says in the Apocalypse: "I turned to see the voice that spake with me."¹¹

---

8   "But Polycarp also was not only instructed by apostles, and conversed with many who had seen Christ, but was also, by apostles in Asia, appointed bishop of the Church in Smyrna, whom I also saw in my early youth, for he tarried [on earth] a very long time, and, when a very old man, gloriously and most nobly suffering martyrdom, departed this life, having always taught the things which he had learned from the apostles, and which the Church has handed down and which alone are true." See Irenaeus, *Against Heresies* [AH] 3.3.4, trans. A. Roberts and W. H. Rambaut, *ANF* 1:416.

9   Irenaeus, *AH* 5.35.2, *ANF* 1:566.

10   Irenaeus, *AH* 4.30.4, *ANF* 1:504.

11   Irenaeus, *AH* 4.20.11, *ANF* 1:491.

Additional support for Johannine authorship comes from Justin, who lived in Ephesus about AD 135, placing Justin in the location where John ostensibly was living only forty years earlier. In declaring that John the apostle was the author of Revelation, he is joined by Melito of Sardis (c. AD 165), another of the cities addressed by the apocalypticist, as well as by Tertullian, Origen, Hippolytus, and the Muratorian Canon. Origen's student, Dionysius, does not follow the lead of his teacher in this matter.[12]

Attempts to determine authorship based on style, syntax, and vocabulary are intriguing but in the end not determinative. Charles cites examples such as John's use of *mē* ("not") with the participle (eleven times), whereas no cases of this occur in the Apocalypse, and the prevalence of *alla* ("but") and *gar* ("for"); 100 and sixty-five respectively in John's known writings versus the author of the Apocalypse, who uses the terms only thirteen and sixteen times).[13] But as frequently noted, such differences can be accounted for in various ways and do not strike anything close to a knock-out punch against the possibility of John the apostle as author. Many strong similarities, especially of a theological nature, are sufficient to offset these observations.

In the end, as is the case with most books from antiquity, establishing proof of authorship is not possible. What may be safely affirmed is that the cases for all other proposed authors are so unimpressive that there appears to be no substantial reason to reject the nearly universal confidence of the church through the ages that the Revelation is the final, preserved written scroll of John the apostle. This conclusion will be assumed in the remainder of the commentary.

2. DATE

While a few have suggested a date for the Apocalypse during the reign of Trajan (AD 98–117), since the patristic era only two serious possibilities have been perpetuated in the race for an acceptable date of writing. The first, the early date hypothesis, suggests that the Apocalypse was written during the reign of Nero (AD 64–68). Epiphanius even suggested a date under Claudius (AD 41–54). Hort, Lightfoot, and Westcott support a date between Nero's death and the fall of Jerusalem in AD 70. John A. T. Robinson notes J. Massyngberde Ford's ar-

---

12 Charles, *Critical and Exegetical Commentary*, 1:xxxix–xl.
13 Ibid., 1:xxix–xxx.

gument for John the Baptist and an early date, pronouncing it "eccentric" but recognizing B. W. Henderson's monograph on five Roman emperors as "powerfully argued."[14]

One of the more detailed, fascinating, and convincing defenses of the early date for the Apocalypse is that of Robinson in *Redating the New Testament*. The argument is multifaceted and complex but central to the discussion is the relative paucity of evidence from Roman sources for serious persecution of Christians during the reign of Domitian. Revelation seems to be penned against the backdrop of serious persecution and impending threats. Robinson attempts to demonstrate that this circumstance fits snuggly in the context of the Neronian era, but that no substantive case can be presented for a similar situation during the reign of Domitian.[15]

However, Robinson's position is based on an essentially preterist reading of Revelation, an interpretation unimpressive at best to this commentator. If the book of the Revelation is intended as prophecy or the revelation of a future trajectory for the people of God, then the threats of impending persecutions are both understandable and accurate. Further, more recent writers like Hemer have called attention to the black clouds gathering on the Christian horizon and signaled by such events as the issuing of the curse of the Minim (a Jewish curse against Christians) and the growing estrangement of the church from Judaism.[16]

Upheaval within the Roman Imperium, social and economic pressures, efforts to prop up the decadent religions and gods of the empire, and the irresistible spread of the new faith called Christianity were clearly working together to set the stage for serious persecutions for Christians at the end of the first century—even if these did not fully materialize during the reign of Domitian. References to the "temple" in the Apocalypse, though with no mention of the destruction of the Jerusalem temple, are not sufficient grounds to establish an early date. In fact, the absence of the destruction may actually be strong evidence for a date of AD 95. An event, however cataclysmic, that took place 25 years earlier may not have merited mention but could certainly explain the apocalypticist's interest in future temples.

Robinson has presented the best case possible for a date prior to AD 70. But in the end even Robinson's theorizing is inadequate. The widely accepted

---

14   J. A. T. Robinson, *Redating the New Testament* (Philadelphia: Westminster, 1976), 225.

15   Ibid., 232–35.

16   C. J. Hemer, *The Letters to the Seven Churches of Asia in Their Local Setting*, JSNTSup 11 (Sheffield, England: Sheffield Academic Press, 1986; reprint, 1989), 4.

date of approximately AD 95, placing Revelation as the last book of the New Testament, still appears to have better support. The first evidence for this arises from the virtual unanimity of the earliest witnesses. Charles notes, "The earliest authorities are practically unanimous in assigning the Apocalypse to the last years of Domitian."[17] He proceeds by appealing to Mileto of Sardis, Irenaeus, Clement of Alexandria, Origen, Victorinus, Jerome, and Eusebius.

This argument is buttressed by Charles when he notes that the AD 95 date best accounts for the apparent familiarity that John exhibits for early New Testament books.[18] The enforcement of the imperial cult was unknown until the days of Domitian, and the possible appearance of the Nero Redivivus myth form other lines of evidence for the later date.[19]

G. K. Beale provides one of the more complete summaries of the case for the late date. He claims that AD 95 is "the consensus among twentieth-century scholars."[20] He proceeds to point to some evidence for significant persecution under Trajan around AD 113. He further notes the condition of the churches in Asia Minor as a measure of development reflecting a date in the last decade of the first century. Beale cites the fact that the use of Babylon as a descriptor for Rome did not occur until after AD 70 as perhaps "the strongest internal evidence for a post-70 AD date."[21]

---

17 Charles, *Critical and Exegetical Commentary*, 1:xcii.

18 Ibid., 1:xciv. Charles notes, "Our author makes most use of the prophetical books. He constantly uses Isaiah, Jeremiah, Ezekiel, and Daniel; also, but in a less degree, Zechariah, Joel, Amos, and Hosea; and in a very minor degree Zephaniah and Habakkuk. Next to the prophetical books he is most indebted to the Psalms, slightly to Proverbs, and still less to Canticles. He possessed the Pentateuch and makes occasional use of all its books, particularly of Exodus. Amongst others, that he and his sources probably drew upon, are Joshua, 1 and 2 Samuel, and 2 Kings" (1:lxv). Or again: "From an examination of the passages given below in §8, it follows quite decidedly that our author had the Gospels of Matthew and Luke before him, 1 Thessalonians, 1 and 2 Corinthians, Colossians (or else the lost Ep. To the Laodiceans, which presumably was of a kindred character), Ephesians, and possibly Galatians, 1 Peter, and James. Our author shows no acquaintance with St. Mark" (1:lxv–lxvi). This concluding observation about the absence of reference to the Gospel of Mark is not helpful for those who wish to argue for the priority of Mark's Gospel in the synoptic development.

19 Ibid., 1:xcv–xcvii.

20 G. K. Beale, *The Book of Revelation: A Commentary on the Greek Text*, NIGTC (Grand Rapids: Eerdmans; Carlisle, UK: Paternoster, 1999), 4.

21 Ibid., 18. Other helpful discussions of date are in G. R. Osborne, *Revelation*, BECNT (Grand Rapids: Baker Academic, 2002), 6–11; R. L. Thomas, *Revelation 1–7: An*

The preponderance of the evidence favors the date for the composition of the Apocalypse to be AD 95. Majority acceptance of this view in every era of church history bears testimony to the paucity of evidence supporting the earlier Neronian date. Certainly, acceptance of the date at the end of the first century eases the hermeneutical task and provides insight into the interpretation of a number of texts.

3. GENRE

Commonly, the book of Revelation is called "The Apocalypse." This title is correct but also partially misleading. The derivation of the title "Apocalypse" is a transliteration of the first word of the book, which is *Apokalupsis*. The word itself means "reveal" or "unveil" (see commentary discussion of 1:1). In this sense the book is accurately called an "apocalypse." However, another nuance of the word describing a particular genre of literature developed from the second century BC to the second century AD. The Apocalypse Group of the Society of Biblical Literature's Genres Project adopted the proposal of John J. Collins as a working definition:

> "Apocalypse" is a genre of revelatory literature with a narrative framework, in which a revelation is mediated by an otherworldly being to a human recipient, disclosing a transcendent reality which is both temporal, insofar as it envisages eschatological salvation, and spatial insofar as it involves another, supernatural world.[22]

H. H. Rowley focused on the nature of the confidence of apocalyptic writers in the divine initiative of God in history:

> Their faith goes beyond the faith in the divine control of history, indeed. It is a faith in the divine initiative in history for the attainment of its final goal. Such a belief is fundamental to the Christian view of God and the world.[23]

Exegetical Commentary (Chicago: Moody, 1992), 20–23; and the best recent discussion in Hemer, *Letters*, 2–20.

22 M. G. Reddish, ed. *Apocalyptic Literature: A Reader* (Nashville: Abingdon Press, 1990), 20; J. J. Collins, ed., *Apocalypse: The Morphology of a Genre, Semeia* 14 (1979): 9.

23 H. H. Rowley, *The Relevance of Apocalyptic: A Study of Jewish and Christian Apocalypses from Daniel to the Revelation*, rev. ed. (Greenwood, SC: The Attic Press, 1963), 168.

An extensive list of books and fragments that qualify as apocalyptic liter-ature can be found in D. S. Russell's *The Method and Message of Jewish Apocalyp-tic*.[24] Russell also discusses the decline of prophecy in Israel as it gradually gives rise to the apocalyptic. Citing the work of J. Lindblom, Russell provides the following characteristics of apocalyptic literature. These include transcenden-talism, mythology, cosmological survey, pessimism about human history, dual-ism, numerology, pseudo-ecstasy, pseudonymity, cosmic history, and conflict between the kingdoms of darkness and light, to name a few.[25] When compared to the book of the Revelation, apparently the book lacks some of these elements noted and also displays additional elements normally absent in the apocalyptic. As Schüssler Fiorenza remarks,

> The epistolary framework of Rev. [Revelation] is not an artificial and acci-dental setting for John's mythopoeic vision. John derives the authority of his work not from pseudonymity and fictional timetables, but from the rev-elation of Jesus Christ which he must communicate as prophetic address.[26]

The apocalyptic elements contained in the Revelation, on mature reflec-tion, are distinct from those found in most books of apocalyptic genre. For ex-ample, the author identifies himself, and the context suggests that the recipients would know precisely who he is. But in addition to the absence of pseudonym-ity, the book purports to be a circular letter providing not only information about the seven churches on the circuit but also preparing the recipients of those historic congregations for the unfolding of God's plan of redemption. Consequently, the genre of the Revelation is epistolary.

Revelation is also literature of prophetic genre. In David Aune's extensive evaluation of prophecy, he notes the interesting absence of references to local ecclesiastical officials. Aune says, "Although the author addresses his prophetic book to seven Christian communities in western Asia Minor, not once does he be-tray the existence of such local officials as bishops, presbyters, and deacons."[27] Or

---

24 D. S. Russell, Appendix 1: "Christian Lists of Jewish Apocryphal Books," in *The Method & Message of Jewish Apocalyptic: 200 BC–AD 100* (Philadelphia: Westminster, 1964), 391–95.

25 Ibid., 105.

26 E. S. Fiorenza, *The Book of Revelation: Justice and Judgment* (Philadelphia: For-tress, 1985), 23. Also note Fiorenza's section on the linguistic and theological affinities of Revelation and the fourth Gospel, 93–108.

27 D. E. Aune, *Prophecy in Early Christianity and the Ancient Mediterranean World*

again, "John the prophet intentionally ignored the officials of the local churches because his role as a mediator of divine revelation transcended petty local concerns and because his message was directed to the communities at large, not just to their leaders."[28]

The best conclusion for understanding the nature of the Revelation of John is to see it as a prophetic circular letter which not infrequently makes use of apocalyptic imagery and device. Clearly, the author understood his role as that of prophet. On the other hand, he lived in a day of conflict with imperial authorities and had learned the value of the apocalyptic as a mode of communication to the faithful. Having much in common with the biblical books of Daniel and Ezekiel and citing or alluding to massive amounts of Old Testament prophecy, the author of Revelation has provided a genuinely unique treatise.

4. TEXT AND CANONICITY

The text of Revelation is less well attested than some earlier written books of the New Testament, yet attestation is adequate for us to be confident of its contents. Beale notes,

> As we assess here the most valuable manuscript witnesses, it must be recalled, first, that the textual history of the Apocalypse is significantly different from that of the other New Testament books. The most important manuscripts for Revelation are often different from those for other books of the NT.[29]

He also provides a helpful assessment in five categories of the relative importance of the quality of the various texts. He lists the manuscripts together with the contents of each and the probable dates for each. Early papyri, p18, p24, and p47, all date to the first four centuries but are only fragments, with p47 being the largest, containing portions of eight chapters. Sinaiticus and Alexandrinus contain the whole of the book and are apparently the earliest such manuscripts of the full text. Concerning the textual history of the Apocalypse Osborne notes,

---

(Grand Rapids: Eerdmans, 1983), 205.

    28 Ibid.

    29 Beale, *The Book of Revelation*, 70.

While scholars feel more confident than ever that we can get close to the original text of Revelation, it is not an easy task due to the nature of the manuscripts. The student must watch closely not only the quality of the manuscripts and the internal criteria for evaluating the strength of a reading but also scribal tendencies in trying to harmonize the difficult grammatical constructions.[30]

Beale joins other commentators in the conviction that only in the book of Revelation does the Majority Text have greater weight than that of the earlier witnesses.[31]

As to the canonicity of the book of Revelation, its position has never been seriously challenged in the West. In addition to Irenaeus, Papias, the *Epistle of Barnabas*, Justin Martyr, Tertullian, Clement of Alexandria, and Origen, though representing diverse interpretive traditions, all seem to acknowledge the book. It also appears in the Muratorian Canon (c. AD 200).

However, the canonical list of the Council of Laodicea (AD 360) does not contain the Revelation, and several Eastern fathers had doubts. Eusebius of Caesarea denied canonical authority to the Apocalypse. Cyril of Jerusalem, John Chrysostom, and Theodore of Mopsuestia also had their doubts about it.[32] However, by the time of the Council of Constantinople (AD 680), even the East acknowledged its canonicity.

5. HISTORY OF INTERPRETATION

Commonly noted is the similarity between Revelation and the prophecies of Daniel, Ezekiel, and Zechariah. Almost unnoticed is the shared hermeneutical circumstance of the Revelation with *Shir Hashirim* or the Song of Solomon and perhaps with the book of Job. Both Revelation and the Song share a sharp contrast between literal and allegorical interpretive frameworks, beginning with a commentator's assumptions that determine in advance many of the conclusions to which he will be drawn. Literalists typically see the Song as a beauti-

---

30 Osborne, *Revelation*, 23. For those interested in extensive examination of textual issues in the Apocalypse, see H. C. Hoskier, *Concerning the Text of the Apocalypse*, 2 vols. (London: Bernard Quaritch, 1929), for a monumental discussion.

31 Beale, *The Book of Revelation*, 72.

32 Osborne, *Revelation*, 23–24.

ful poem depicting the sanctified affections of Solomon for the Shulamith.[33] Others, wondering how a book of the Bible could possibly devote itself to such mundane and perhaps carnal considerations present the book as an allegory of Christ's love for the church.[34] But the point to be made is that the exegete makes a decision about whether to treat the book as a literal poem or as a magnificent allegory, and this decision determines how individual passages will be viewed. An approach to understanding the Apocalypse is the same.

Accordingly, there are four historical approaches to understanding the Revelation. In addition, a fifth position has emerged in contemporary scholarly circles. The *preterist* perspective sees the book as an assessment of circumstances and the perceived threat of persecution in the era in which John lived and composed the Apocalypse. Acknowledging that there are references to a future eschatological hope, the view, nevertheless, suggests that most of the material in Revelation is about events taking place in the first century, often prior to the destruction of Jerusalem, in AD 70. As Kenneth Gentry states the matter:

> "Preterism" holds that the bulk of John's prophecies occur in the *first century*, soon after his writing of them. Though the prophecies were in the future when John wrote and when his original audience read them, they are now in *our* past.[35]

Patrons of this view according to Osborne include Charles, Sweet, Roloff, Yarbro Collins, Krodel, Gentry, and Chilton.[36] Gentry adds Jay Adams as an advocate.[37] These and others stake their position in part on the Revelation's

---

33 J. C. Dillow, *Solomon on Sex: A Biblical Guide to Married Love* (Nashville: Thomas Nelson, 1977); T. Nelson, *The Book of Romance: What Solomon Says About Love, Sex, and Intimacy* (Nashville: Thomas Nelson, 1998); P. Patterson, *Song of Solomon*, Everyman's Bible Commentary (Chicago: Moody, 1986); T. Longman III, *Song of Songs*, NICOT (Grand Rapids: Eerdmans, 2001); S. C. Glickman, *A Song for Lovers* (Downers Grove, IL: InterVarsity, 1976).

34 C. H. Spurgeon, *"The Most Holy Place" (On the Song of Solomon)* (Pasadena, TX: Pilgrim Publications, 1974); R. Ellsworth, *He Is Altogether Lovely: Discovering Christ in the Song of Solomon* (Darlington, England: Evangelical Press, 1998); Bernard of Clairvaux, *On the Song of Songs III: Sermons 47–66*, trans. K. Walsh and I. M. Edmonds, Cistercian Fathers Series 23 (Kalamazoo, MI: Cistercian Publications, 1979).

35 K. L. Gentry Jr., "A Preterist View of Revelation," in *Four Views on the Book of Revelation*, ed. C. M. Pate, Counterpoints (Grand Rapids: Zondervan, 1998), 37.

36 Osborne, *Revelation*, 19–20.

37 Gentry, "A Preterist View of Revelation," 37.

promises that suggest that "the time is near" (Rev 22:10) or concerning prophecies that "must soon take place" (Rev 1:1). The argument is that John himself seems to anticipate a near fulfillment of the prophecies of the book.

Another approach has been called *historicism*, although the preterist view also focuses on history at least from the contemporary reader's vantage point. This fact led Thomas to speak of the historicist view as the "continuous-historical" approach, treating the book as a panorama of church history from John's time to the second advent.[38] Beale says of historicist advocates that they "generally see Revelation as predicting the major movements of Christian history."[39] Concerning this view, Marvin Pate writes,

> Although there have been many esteemed advocates of the historicist approach in the past (e.g., Wycliffe, Knox, Tyndale, Luther, Calvin, Zwingli, Wesley, Edwards, Finney, Spurgeon), there are very few today. Historicism was extremely popular during the Protestant Reformation as reformers identified the Antichrist and Babylon with the pope and Roman Catholicism of their day.[40]

According to Osborne, the origins of this perspective are to be found in Joachim of Fiore in the twelfth century.[41] The Franciscans followed this view and so eventually did most of the Reformers, except the Anabaptists.

An earlier perspective is called the *idealist* view or, as Thomas prefers, the "timeless-symbolic" approach.[42] Pate traces the DNA of the interpretation to the Alexandrian church fathers.

> The origin of the idealist school of thought can be traced back to the allegorical or symbolic hermeneutic espoused by the Alexandrian church fathers, especially Clement (second century) and Origen (third century).[43]

---

38 Thomas, *Revelation 1–7*, 30.

39 Beale, *The Book of Revelation*, 46.

40 C. M. Pate, *Reading Revelation: A Comparison of Four Interpretive Translations of the Apocalypse* (Grand Rapids: Kregel, 2009), 9. For a comprehensive look at the literature and positions on Revelation from 1940-1996, the serious student should consult R. L. Muse, *The Book of Revelation: An Annotated Bibliography* (New York and London: Garland Publishing, 1996).

41 Osborne, *Revelation*, 18–19.

42 Thomas, *Revelation 1–7*, 31.

43 Pate, *Reading Revelation*, 12.

This interpretation arose out of the influence of Hellenism and the allegorical interpretation, which surfaced under Philo. Clement and Origen rejected what they saw as the primacy of the literal interpretation of Revelation in favor of understanding the various symbols in the text as allegories of spiritual truths. In turn this became a form of eschatology espoused by such notables as Augustine and Jerome.[44]

The idealist view is not much interested in chronological issues but rather understands the Revelation to depict the cosmic struggle of good and evil while forecasting the eventual triumph of God's purpose. Examples of advocates of this perspective in recent times include Hendriksen, Hoekema, P. Hughes, and Ray Summers.

The *futurist* position can also be discovered early in Christian history represented by Papias, Irenaeus, Justin, Hippolytus, and others. The virtual triumph of Augustinian theology suppressed the literal understanding of the Apocalypse for more than a thousand years. Osborne credits its revival to Franciscus Ribeira, a Spanish Jesuit who wrote in the late sixteenth century.[45] But truthfully among the Radical Reformers, relatively early in the sixteenth century, various concepts of futurism were already accepted.[46]

The futurist view of Revelation is that chaps. 4–22 form a prophecy of John focused almost entirely on the eschaton. While acknowledging some difficulties in the futurist position Ramsey Michaels nevertheless concludes,

> Another interpretation, the *futurist*, is that the book of Revelation has to do with the future of the world—not what was future to John and is now past or present to us, but what was future to John and is *still* future to us. It is as if time has stood still, as if the "prophetic clock" set to go off at the end of the world shut itself off right after John finished his book and is only now ready to start ticking again—after nineteen hundred years! Such an interpretation can never be proven wrong, for when events in the

---

44 Pate, *Reading Revelation.*

45 Osborne, *Revelation,* 20.

46 For a description of eschatology among Anabaptists, see T. N. Finger, *A Contemporary Anabaptist Theology* (Downers Grove, IL: InterVarsity, 2004), 512–61. Finger summarizes, "In my view, eschatological expectations among historic Anabaptists were too diverse and functioned too differently to shape their core vision as consistently and explicitly as salvation's personal, communal and missional dimensions. Nevertheless, eschatology pervaded Anabaptist awareness thoroughly enough that without it, Anabaptism's salvific vision could not have been what it was" (513).

world do not match the scenario of John's visions, the answer is that the events John prophesied have not yet begun to happen.

The futurist view has its detractors, yet there is much to be said in its favor. Above all, it has the virtue of immediacy in confronting the modern reader with precisely the same promises, the same threats and the same choices that the book's original readers faced.[47]

Adela Yarbro Collins acknowledges that the future is in view in much of the Apocalypse even though she finds its significance elsewhere.

To a large extent, the visions concern the future, but they were written down in order to illuminate the present experience of the author and the first readers and to evoke a particular response to that experience. The author, probably the prophet himself, made use of traditional images in describing his visions. He did so in such a way that they express a view of reality which is still powerful today.[48]

Positions ranging from self-acclaimed *historic premillennialism* to *dispensationalism* all view the book as essentially prophecy and hence a promise of the cosmic conflicts of the last days as well as the conquering conquest and judgment of the returning Christ at the end of the age. This view, that the Revelation is essentially a prophecy of the end times to be fulfilled principally in the future, is the perspective that will be developed in this commentary.

The four views outlined thus far represented the spectrum of approaches until relatively recently. Beale presents what he calls *eclecticism*.

A more viable, modified version of the idealist perspective would acknowledge a final consummation in salvation and judgment. Perhaps it would be best to call this fifth view "eclecticism." Accordingly, no specific prophesied historical events are discerned in the book, except for the final coming of Christ to deliver and judge and to establish the final form of the kingdom in a consummated new creation—though there are a few exceptions to this rule. The Apocalypse symbolically portrays events throughout history, which is understood to be under the sovereignty of the Lamb as a result of his death

---

47   J. R. Michaels, *Revelation*, The IVPNTCS (Downers Grove, IL: InterVarsity, 1997).

48   A. Y. Collins, *The Apocalypse*, New Testament Message 22 (Wilmington, DE: Michael Glazier, 1979), x.

and resurrection. He will guide the events depicted until they finally issue in the last judgment and the definitive establishment of his kingdom. This means that specific events throughout the age extending from Christ's first coming to his second may be identified with one narrative or symbol. We may call this age inaugurated by Christ's first coming and concluded by his final appearance "the church age," "the interadventual age," or "the latter days." The majority of the symbols in the book are transtemporal in the sense that they are applicable to events throughout the "church age."[49]

While this view is eclectic, attempting to borrow insights from all of the other perspectives, notice must be given to Beale's confession that the view in the end is only a modified expression of the "idealist" persuasion. The erudition of Beale's commentary in The New International Greek Testament Commentary series, together with the decline of interest in dispensational thought, has created substantial interest in the eclectic view. But while "eclecticism" seems always to have a pleasing sound to the contemporary ear, and while valuable insights are to be gained from gifted commentators from all positions, the essentially prophetic nature of the Apocalypse is too well established from Irenaeus until the present to be seriously doubted.

6. THEOLOGY AND THE APOCALYPSE

Because the Revelation has been so vigorously debated, glamorized as popular eschatology, or completely avoided as a book too difficult to comprehend, the rather remarkable insights into theology have often been given short shrift. Yet these intensely theological avowals, in part, form one of the most significant differences between Revelation and other Jewish apocalypses, thus making it difficult to categorize John's book as apocalyptic literature per se.

Eschatology may be the prevalent theme, but a robust Christology together with a doctrine of atonement repeatedly emerges from the pages of this prophecy. As Charles cogently remarks,

The chief theme of the Apocalypse is not what God in Christ has done for the world, but what He will yet do, and what the assured consummation will be. It is therefore the Gospel of faith and hope, and seeks to inspire

---

49 Beale, The Book of Revelation, 48.

the Churches anew in these respects; for that the end is nigh. As it sets forth its theme, it instructs, though incidentally, and its teaching is always fresh, and in some respects unique.[50]

Charles continues by observing that the Christology of the Apocalypse is "very comprehensive," and that "nowhere in the N.T. is the glory of the exalted Christ so emphasized."[51] Blended with the eschatology of Revelation, the Christology of the prophecy is the recurring theme. Charles discovers in the text that Jesus is presented as the historical Christ, the exalted Christ, the unique Son of God both preexistent and divine, and finally as the Great High Priest, the Lamb of God.[52] As the Jesus of history, he has twelve apostles (Rev 21:14); he was crucified in Jerusalem (11:8); he rose from the dead (1:5,18) and ascended to heaven (3:21; 12:5). He is the Root of David (5:5), the Lion of Judah, and the Lamb of God (5:5, and mentioned as Lamb twenty-eight more times).

As the exalted Christ, he is the center of the throne room vision of chap.1. He is the object of the worship of heaven in chap. 5. Seated on his heavenly white steed, he is the judge of all in chap. 19. Jesus is the unique Son of God, while others through God's special provision may become the sons of God (21:7). Jesus, as in John's Gospel, is the Word of God (19:13) and is identified as "Sovereign Lord" (6:10).

The concept of the atonement of Christ is periodic in this prophecy. The white-robed multitude "have washed their robes and made them white in the blood of the Lamb" (7:14). In perhaps the most exquisite verse in the entire book, Satan has been overcome "by the blood of the Lamb / and by the word of their testimony" (12:11). The appearance of the Lion of the tribe of Judah turns out to be a Lamb bearing the marks of sacrifice in chap. 5. The reader is further informed that with the blood of the Lamb men have been "purchased . . . for God" from every tribe, language, people, and nation (5:9).

While the concept of the Trinity is not developed as precisely as in the baptismal narrative of Jesus or in the introductory passages of some Pauline letters, even a cursory reading of the Apocalypse reveals that its author was a trinitarian. The Lord God is the one "who is, and who was, and who is to come, the Almighty" (1:8). He is the Judge who has as one of his attributes wrath against sin (15:7). Regarding the Holy Spirit, John was "in the Spirit," almost certainly a reference

---

50 Charles, *Critical and Exegetical Commentary*, 1:cix.
51 Ibid., 1:cx–cxi.
52 Ibid., 1:cx–cxiii.

to the Holy Spirit (1:10). At the conclusion of the Apocalypse, "the Spirit and the bride" issue an invitation to the lost (22:17). The reference to "the seven spirits before his throne" (1:4) is believed by many to be a reference to the Holy Spirit as he makes himself available to each of the congregations addressed.

Eschatology is the subject of the prophecy and will be developed in the commentary that follows. Likewise, soteriology is specific (22:14 and elsewhere) and is the underlying *raison d'être* for the consummation of the plan and purpose of God. Ecclesiology is not developed in the Apocalypse so much as it is assumed. While no information is provided about church government, officers, baptism, or the fellowship meal of the church, spiritual aspects of church life both positive and negative are provided in the letters to the seven churches in chaps. 2 and 3, providing rich insights into ecclesiastical life at the close of the first century.

All the doctrines of the faith once delivered to the saints are not developed in the Revelation. Some are given extensive development while all seem to be implicitly endorsed. Suffice it to say, the prophecy of Revelation is replete with theological significance. Atypical for an apocalypse, the work is clearly a Christian work focused on the consummation of salvation in Christ.

7. THE KEY TO THE BOOK

"Write, therefore, what you have seen, what is now and what will take place later" (1:19).

Commentators differ sharply about the significance of 1:19. Charles observes,

> These words summarize *roughly* the contents of the Book. The ἃ εἶδες [*ha eides*] is the vision of the Son of Man just vouchsafed to the Seer: ἃ εἰσίν [*ha eisin*] refers directly to the present condition of the Church as shown in chaps. ii.–iii., and indirectly to that of the world in general; ἃ μέλλει γίνεσθαι μετὰ ταῦτα [*ha mellei ginesthai meta taûta*] to the visions from chap. iv. onwards, which, with the exception of a few sections referring to the past and the present, deal with the future.[53]

Smalley sees 1:19 as more "wide ranging" but acknowledges that the phrase "the things which are after these things" essentially focuses on the fu-

---

53 Charles, *Critical and Exegetical Commentary*, 33.

ture.[54] Chilean priest and theologian Pablo Richard identifies "the things that come after" as the content of Rev 4 to the end of the book.[55] Thomas adds,

> The interpretation that understands a three-part division of 1:19 sees the past vision of the glorified Christ (chap. 1, esp. vv. 11–18) pointed out by *ha eides* as the first part, the present condition of the churches (chaps. 2–3) indicated in *ha eisin* as the second part, and the third part, the future happenings (chaps. 4–22) represented by *ha mellei genesthai meta tauta*. This position is represented in the words, "Write, then, the things which you have seen and the things which are and the things which will happen after these things."
>
> The threefold division is the most natural understanding of the symmetrical grammatical construction of 1:19 and fits the contents of the Apocalypse quite well. *Eides*, an aorist tense, is best explained as looking back to the vision of Christ that is now past (contrast *blepeis*, present tense, in 1:11). "The things which are" (*ha eisin*) is accurate as a description of the messages to the seven churches that detail specific conditions in the churches of John's day and throughout the period until the events foretold in 4:1 ff. begin to unfold. The similarity of *ha mellei genesthai meta tauta* to *ha dei genesthai meta tauta* of 1:1 (see earlier discussion at 1:1) and 22:6 and to *ha dei genesthai meta tauta* of 4:1 is strong evidence that the third relative clause of 1:19 points to chapters 4–22, which constitutes the main body of the book (Swete; Charles; Smith). It is natural that this is the longest of the three sections.[56]

W. A. Criswell, in his three-year preaching journey through the Revelation, is more emphatic and certain about this interpretation than most. Appealing to Aristotle in a single sermon on 1:19, Criswell finds similar constructions and utilizes them to argue for a threefold division of the apocalypse.[57]

Aune admits the formula arises from widespread tripartite prophecy but concludes that it probably actually means only the present and the future.[58] Caird

54   S. S. Smalley, *The Revelation to John: A Commentary on the Greek Text of the Apocalypse* (Downers Grover, IL: InterVarsity, 2005), 56–57.

55   P. Richard, *Apocalypse: A People's Commentary on the Book of Revelation* (Maryknoll, NY: Orbis Books, 1995), 52.

56   Thomas, *Revelation 1–7*, 115.

57   W. A. Criswell, *Expository Sermons on Revelation: Five Volumes Complete and Unabridged* (Grand Rapids: Zondervan, 1969), 1:181–83.

58   D. Aune, *Revelation 1–5*, WBC 52a (Dallas, TX: Word Books, 1997), 105.

thinks this approach is a "grotesque oversimplification."[59] Blount acknowledges the three divisions but sees "what will take place later" as pertaining

> to the certain reprisals that will come when Christ-believers "out themselves" as Christ-believers by testifying demonstrably to his lordship. The "after this" that closes the verse, then does not refer as much to "this apocalyptic age" as it does to the specific circumstances surrounding the aftermath of John's visions of Christ's lordship and the people's testimony to it.[60]

Beale, always in heavy pursuit of eclecticism, attempts to have a little of both ways. He accurately links the idea of the apostle to Dan 2:28 and the revelation of what must take place in the latter days. After a lengthy discussion he arrives at what he calls the "new view," which, while acknowledging the general futurist intent of the Apocalypse, pleads for a position that evaluates the whole prophecy, and hence 1:19 also, in the now popular "already—not yet" formula. Accordingly, he would hold that all three aspects of the verse reflect that understanding.[61]

This commentator acknowledges the "already—not yet" character of the kingdom of God and of the eschaton. That stated, the location of the affirmation of 1:19 and natural sense of the verse seem strongly to favor seeing the verse as the logical division of the contents of the book. While the material in chaps. 4–22 contains flashbacks to historical events (12:7–9) and contemporaneous events (John's frequent participation in his own visions), the essential information concerns the future. In fact, since chaps. 1–3 focus on the churches and the word *church* never occurs after chap. 3, there is good reason to believe that chap. 4 initiates an era following the "times of the Gentiles" (Luke 21:24) or the age of the church.

For John to write what he had *seen* is logically the vision of the Christ in chap. 1. The things that *are* clearly represent the church scene in which the prophet was a participant. Looking beyond that era introduces God's plan for the last days. Hence 1:19 may be viewed as the general outline for the Apocalypse.

---

59   G. B. Caird, *The Revelation of St. John the Divine*, HNTC (San Francisco: Harper & Row, 1966), 26.

60   B. K. Blount, *Revelation: A Commentary*, NTL (Louisville, KY: WJK, 2009), 47.

61   Beale, *The Book of Revelation*, 153–70.

8. SYMBOLISM

As is typical in apocalyptic literature, Revelation abounds in rich, colorful symbols. Threatening dragons, intimidating beasts, a scarlet woman of ill repute, a radiant but righteous woman, conquering horses and horsemen, and a plethora of other symbols parade in view of the reader. From the outset of the book, John makes clear that much of his message is delivered through this medium. The unveiling of Jesus Christ was made known to him through angels that were given the mission of "making known by signs" (Gk. *esēmanen*, 1:1) the message of God for the end times.

These symbols, like all symbols, point to a reality beyond themselves. The "great red dragon" of chap. 12, for example, is a symbol for Satan, explicitly stated in 12:9. "Great" points to the fact of his significance in the cosmic struggle. "Red" denotes violence in character and deed while "dragon" carries a sense of the ominous danger of such creatures in the ancient mythologies of most civilizations.

While the symbols suggest picture language, they represent real persons and events. The picture in 19:11–16 of the triumphant, returning Christ, with sharp Roman broad sword protruding from his mouth, is manifestly grotesque if the sense intended is one-to-one correspondence. But if the intent of the author is to convey that the word of the triumphant Christ is sharper and more penetrating than a Roman sword, then the symbol is a picturesque method of pointing to a literal truth (Heb 4:12).

The apostle's use of numerical symbolism is more complex. Just as the number thirteen carries negative connotation in the West, in the East many numerical values also featured social or philosophical significance. Ray Summers discusses this use of extended significance of numbers. "One," he avers, stands for unity or independent existence. "Two" symbolizes strength or confirmation. "Three," Summers suspects, is a symbol of the divine. "Four" became the number for the world while "five" is the number for the human, which when doubled to ten represented human completeness. The number seven, which includes the addition of the divine represented by three and of the cosmos represented by four, expresses completeness. But when three is multiplied by four, resulting in twelve, organized religion in the world is in view. "Six," falling one short of "seven," boasted a sinister meaning.[62]

---

62 R. Summers, *Worthy Is the Lamb: Interpreting the Book of Revelation in Its Historical Background* (Nashville: B&H, 1951), 19–25. For a similar discussion from a totally different perspective, see Criswell, *Expository Sermons on Revelation*, 1:71–84.

The complication arises when the interpreter faces the question of when to assign only numerical significance and when to look behind the number to discover an idea of more profound significance. In fact, there are times when the numerical value and the symbolism may be mutually in view. The suffering church at Smyrna is told that she will have tribulation for ten days (Rev 2:10). Probably the interpreter should look behind this number and see indication of all-encompassing, thorough persecution. When two beasts arise out of the land and sea in chap. 13, the emphasis is more likely on the number of beasts, which happens to be two. Whereas, in Rev 20, when the reader is introduced to the 1,000 years (multiple of ten), the anticipation of a utopian era by Old Testament prophets alerts the reader to a situation in which the 1,000 years may ostensibly be an actual era, while the number symbolizes the nature of that period. As always, the interpreter must have contextual awareness.

9. Premillennialism

The perspective advocated in this commentary is that of premillennialism. However, certain acknowledgments seem incumbent upon the author. First, orthodox Christianity requires a literal return of Christ. The angel who greeted the disciples at the ascension stated with crystal clarity, "This same Jesus, who has been taken from you into heaven, will come back in the same way you have seen him go into heaven" (Acts 1:11). Jesus promised that after going to prepare a place, he would return to receive the disciples to himself (John 14:3). This is a first-order truth that must be embraced to claim orthodoxy.

Second, the precise nature of what transpired in history is often notoriously difficult to discern. How much more difficult to ascertain the future—that which has not yet happened. This accounts for vast differences in the understanding of biblical prophecy. The church can and must affirm the truth of prophecy but at the same time have the humility to admit that one often cannot say for certain what the truth entails. When Francisco Vásquez de Coronado's men first viewed the Grand Canyon, they assured him that the river running through the canyon was no more than about six feet across. And so it appeared from 7,000 feet above on the canyon rim. They must have been astonished to discover a raging torrent averaging more than 300 feet of water cascading through the canyon.[63] So anyone

---

63 See chap. 1 in T. R. Berger, *It Happened at Grand Canyon* (Guilford, CT: The Globe Pequot Press, 2007); and D. Lago, *Grand Canyon Trivia* (Helena, MT: Riverbend

who does not anticipate some surprises in the ultimate fulfillment of prophecy must not be paying attention.

The incontrovertible fact that gracious and godly interpreters of the Bible have differed widely over the details of prophecy should astonish no one. Alert Christians, as this author, can profit from most of them. And how the Apocalypse is interpreted is a second-order issue. Though this author has difficulty seeing the prophecies of Scripture in amillennial or postmillennial constructs, he acknowledges that those holding such views, if they also endorse a literal return of Christ at the end of the age, must be considered orthodox brothers and sisters in Christ (assuming the other first-order doctrines).

However, this commentary is written from the premillennial perspective. Following are some of the reasons that view holds such sway in my own mind.

1. The earliest view of the post-apostolic church reflects a premillennial perspective. George Eldon Ladd writing in 1956 against the prospect of a pretribulation rapture, nevertheless demonstrated at some length that the faith of the earliest church was premillennial. Citing the Didache, the Epistle of Barnabas, the Shepherd of Hermas, Justin Martyr, Irenaeus, Tertullian, Lactantius, and Hippolytus, Ladd demonstrated that the earliest postapostolic Christians looked for a literal reign of Christ at the end of the age.[64] If this were the hope of the church in the earliest era and a hope endorsed by those closest to the apostle John, there appears little rationale for embracing another perspective.

2. More important is the witness of the Old Testament. Passages abound concerning a kingdom age. Isa 2:1–5 forecasts a day of worldwide peace when the word of the Lord goes out from Jerusalem. Isaiah 4 anticipates a great cleansing for Israel. One day the domesticity of animal life will develop when the "Branch" arises (Isa 11). A highway will track from Egypt to Syria, and all people will belong to God (Isa 19:23–25). Israel will be restored as a light to the Gentiles (Isa 49:6). Israel will no longer be forsaken but rather married (Isa 62:1–7). God will accomplish the revival of Israel (Ezek 37), and he will do

---

Publishing, 2009), 33.

    64   G. E. Ladd, *The Blessed Hope* (Grand Rapids: Eerdmans, 1956), 20–31.

this for his holy name's sake. In Joel 3, God promises peace and incredible productivity. In Amos 9, Israel will again be planted in their own land amid great prosperity. Micah prophesies of a coming day when the nations shall flow into Zion in the last days (Mic 4:1–4). These passages provide only a sampling of numerous texts of promise.

An author of a biblical text may certainly disclose truth that reaches to insights given by the Holy Spirit transcending even what the prophet himself comprehended. But to insist that the text meant something entirely different from that which the author understood is asking far too much. Further, a fair reading of these texts will reveal that the prophets anticipated literal fulfillment—an actual fulfillment that included and focused on Israel as the recipient of the promises of God to Abraham.

3. If Jewish apocalyptic literature turned out to be indecisive as a genre for Revelation, at this point one may find help from these books. Certainly the style of apocalyptic writings was known and employed by John. And if one thing is clear about most apocalyptic writings, including Qumran, they look to the end times and a glorious triumph on earth for righteousness. And those ideas are clearly found also in the Apocalypse. The possibility that John intended his work to be understood in some other way remains highly unlikely.

4. The postmillennial option appears to have at least two virtually insurmountable flaws. First, the rather obvious sense of Rev 19–20 is that sequentially Christ returns to earth inaugurating his reign over the earth. There is no evidence of an agency (i.e., the church) through which this is accomplished, and clearly Christ himself is enjoying hegemony over the millennial earth.

Further, while premillennialists differ widely among themselves about how some symbols and texts should be understood, postmillennialists (whether preterists or historicists) differ so broadly about the details as to render even mild consensus a remote goal. In the end the actual interpretation of the Apocalypse by postmillennialists has never inspired much confidence and by default has yielded the historical high ground to either amillennialism or premillennialism.

5. Amillennialism, as a coherent interpretive structure, fares better than postmillennialism but encounters serious difficulties that also render it highly unlikely. The first and primary difficulty is found in the way New Testament authors evaluate Old Testament prophecy. As Pentecost notes,

> Inasmuch as God gave the Word of God as a revelation to men, it would be expected that His revelation would be given in such exact and specific terms that His thoughts would be accurately conveyed and understood when interpreted according to the laws of grammar and speech. Such presumptive evidence favors the literal interpretation, for an allegorical method of interpretation would cloud the meaning of the message delivered by God to men. The fact that the Scriptures continually point to literal interpretations of what was formerly written adds evidence as to the method to be employed in interpreting the Word. Perhaps one of the strongest evidences for the literal method is the use the New Testament makes of the Old Testament. When the Old Testament is used in the New it is used only in a literal sense. One need only study the prophecies which were fulfilled in the first coming of Christ, in His life, His ministry, and His death, to establish that fact. No prophecy which has been completely fulfilled has been fulfilled any way but literally.[65]

Micah prophesies that Messiah will be born in Bethlehem and the prophecy is literally fulfilled. If such prophecies have literal fulfillment, it becomes difficult for the amillennialist to justify the switch to allegorical methods when the subject is eschatology. The symbolic nature of the Revelation is apparent to all, but such symbolism does not negate actual events and persons that lie in the bosoms of the symbols. That Satan is imaged as a great red dragon in chap. 12 does not mask his real identity, nor does it prevent the

---

65 J. D. Pentecost, *Things to Come: A Study in Biblical Eschatology* (Findlay, OH: Dunham Publishing Company, 1958), 10–11.

reality of his assault on heaven or his loss of status there. In the end amillennialism defaults to premillennialism because of the natural reading of Scripture employed by the latter.

6. Premillennial interpretation commends itself on the basis of the faithfulness of God in the keeping of his promises to Israel. Promises made to Abraham (Gen 12:1–3; 22:18), to David (2 Sam 7:11–16), and to Israel as a whole (Jer 31:31–40) were never abrogated. This is corroborated by Paul's testimony in Rom 9–11, indicating that God is faithful to his promises to ethnic Israel and has plans for her in the last days. God's faithfulness to his promises to Israel becomes the ground for the broken branches of Israel to be "grafted into their own olive tree" (Rom 11:22–24).

7. This conclusion now focuses on the treatise of Paul in Rom 9–11. While there is a sense in which believers constitute the true Israel, concentration on ethnic Israel is apparent from the first. Paul is concerned about his own people (Rom 9:1–5). He is sufficiently concerned as to wish their salvation even if it meant that he would be accursed (Rom 9:3). He knows them to be zealous for God, but this zeal is not based on knowledge (Rom 10:1–2). But God has not rejected his people whom he foreknew (Rom 11:2). A day is coming when all living Israel will be saved (Rom 11:25–27). Since this development corresponds with other Old Testament millennial prophecies as well as the Jewish recognition of Jesus as Messiah, to understand this as belonging to the kingdom age after Christ's return is most natural.

8. In Acts 1:6 the disciples query Jesus about Israel by asking, "Lord, are you at this time going to restore the kingdom to Israel?" If there is no intent to do this, if this is ill-conceived theology, there could not have been a more propitious moment for a correction. That Jesus did not set straight the matter of a visible, earthly kingdom is not merely an argument from silence. To the contrary, his answer, "It is not for you to know the times or dates" is a de facto acknowledgment that their expectation was correct, though the timing lay in the counsels of God. This

appears to be a confirmation from the lips of Jesus that such an age lay yet ahead.

9. Matt 19:28 constitutes one of two places in the New Testament where the word "regeneration" occurs. In Titus 3:5 *palingenesia* refers to personal regeneration. But the discussion of Matt 19 is a promise of Jesus to the apostles. "I tell you the truth, at the renewal (*paliggenesia*) of all things, when the Son of Man sits on his glorious throne, you who have followed me will also sit on twelve thrones, judging the twelve tribes of Israel." This could be construed as a heavenly promise, but the most natural reading would be a confirmation of the kingdom era that these disciples were clearly anticipating. If so, again we have an anticipation of a kingdom age preceded by the return of the Messiah.

10. The extended passage in Rev 20:1–10 mentions a period of 1,000 years, not once but five times. Chronicled as events to occur in that time period are the binding of Satan, the reign of Christian martyrs with Christ, and the temporary release of Satan following the 1,000 years. All of this transpires sequentially after the victorious return of Christ in chap. 19.

After referring to Rev 1:1 as a naïve answer to the nature of the Revelation, Ramsey Michaels goes on to insist that Revelation is about a conflict happening in John's day. But he goes on to warn,

There have always been futurists, whether called enthusiasts, pietists, charismatics, millenarians, or fundamentalists. Before discarding their "naive" approach too quickly, the student should consider carefully whether such an approach might actually be closer to the mind of John than are some of the other options.[66]

Once again, the exegete is responsible for determining first what the author intended. The Holy Spirit, the ultimate author, may indeed have had the author say more than the writer himself understood, but no case can be made among evangelicals for the Holy Spirit's leading an author to write about that which he did

---

66 J. R. Michaels, *Interpreting the Book of Revelation*, Guides to New Testament Exegesis 7 (Grand Rapids: Baker, 1992), 50; see also 13–14.

not comprehend at all. The *locus classicus* for this is found in 1 Pet 1:10–12 where Peter spoke of prophets who wrote concerning salvation (a concept that they understood) but searched themselves to determine the time of the unfolding of these events. And as Michaels confesses, John's view may well have been the futurism that is found among the much-ridiculed "fundamentalists."[67] Rev 20:1–10 seems to suggest that John anticipates a millennial reign following the return of Jesus to the earth.

The above provide some of the reasons for the author's confidence in a futurist interpretation of the Apocalypse. This approach commonly called the premillennial perspective allows for divergent interpretation of many passages but does establish a general framework for the book. In so doing, the author follows the earliest stream of the thinking of the church.

10. PRETRIBULATIONISM

The commentary is not only composed from a premillennial perspective but also from a pretribulational view, a conviction that the church will not be left in the world during the seven years of the tribulation. While it is the personal conviction of this author, I recognize that if a millennial position is a second-order doctrine, the relationship of the church to the tribulation period is even less certain. Texts can be marshaled and interpreted to support pretribulationism and posttribulationism, and there are also proponents of midtribulationism, partial rapturism, and prewrath rapturism. Whatever the view adopted, a measure of humility and grace toward others is warranted.

Pretribulationism is often associated with dispensationalism. Two important notes should be observed. First, the word *dispensation* is a translation of the word *oikonomia*, referring literally to the "law of the house" or how things operate. Of the seven occurrences in the New Testament, four are translated "dispensation" in the King James Version (KJV), but none are rendered by that translation in the New International Version (NIV). Eph 3:2, where the term is rendered "administration" by the NIV, is the most critical instance where KJV renders the word "dispensation of grace." In any event the word became associated with dispensational theory.[68] This perspective identifies seven periods or

---

67 Michaels, *Interpreting the Book of Revelation*, 50.
68 For a discussion of dispensationalism, its history and nuances, see C. Ryrie,

dispensations in which God varies his methods of dealing with the human family. Second, not all millenarians are dispensationalists. In fact, not all pretribulationlists are dispensationalists. My own position is that the dispensations are notoriously difficult to identify. They constitute an imposed grid that has no specific support from Scripture.

Certainly there are differences between the ways by which God deals with humans under the law and after the advent of Christ. But salvation itself was always mediated by grace through faith (Gen 15:6; Rom 4:3) and that always on the basis of the work of Christ on the cross (Rev 13:8). In the end the concept of dispensations is not really determinative for any of the views.

There are, however, good reasons to believe that the church will be taken out of the world prior to the tribulation.

1. The rationale for a posttribulation rapture of the church is hard to establish. The saints of God are said to reign with Christ on the millennial earth. But if the church is in, though not the object of, the tribulation, and if true believers alive at the Lord's coming are caught up to Christ at the *parousia* (1 Thess 4:15–18), what could be the purpose of this rapture when they return immediately to the earth? If, on the other hand, the church is removed from the earth prior to the tribulation and returns with Christ at the outset of the millennium, then the exodus of the church makes sense. First, the church is not left to suffer the outpouring of God's wrath on the earth. Second, events such as the *bema*, the judgment seat of Christ, and the marriage of the Lamb have time to take place in heaven.

2. An even more comprehensive problem arises if a posttribulation rapture is envisioned. The New Testament is clear that when Christ is revealed and Christians are caught up to him, both those who "sleep" in Jesus and those alive at

---

Dispensationalism Today (Chicago: Moody, 1965); and M. J. Vlach, *Dispensationalism: Essential Beliefs and Common Myths* (Los Angeles: Theological Studies Press, 2008). For a recent discussion on progressive dispensationalism, see C. Blaising and D. Bock, *Progressive Dispensationalism* (Grand Rapids: Baker, 1993); and R. Saucy, *The Case for Progressive Dispensationalism* (Grand Rapids: Zondervan, 1993). For an adverse treatment of the topic, see V. Poythress, *Understanding Dispensationalism* (Grand Rapids: Academie Books, 1987); and C. Bass, *Backgrounds to Dispensationalism* (Grand Rapids: Eerdmans, 1960). For a recent assessment favoring dispensationalism, see Vlach, *Dispensationalism: Essential Beliefs and Common Myths.*

his coming will be glorified (1 Cor 15:50–53; 1 Thess 4:13–18). Insofar as is possible to know, Jesus seems to indicate that glorified or resurrected bodies, while infinitely superior to sin-ravaged physical bodies, will not have the capacity for reproductive acts or results (Matt 22:29–30). Such would not be needed in the heavenly kingdom.

Therefore, if every true believer is glorified at a posttribulation rapture and if only believers enter the millennium (Matt 25:31–46), how is the millennial kingdom repopulated? Following the devastating results of the great tribulation with the decimation of the largest part of the world's population, repopulation during the millennium is essential. In fact, when Satan is released at the conclusion of the millennium for a short time (Rev 20:1–9), he has an immediate following. How is this possible if the millennial kingdom consists only of glorified believers? How is it possible for him to have a following?

In contrast, pretribulationism easily accounts for these events. The church is caught up to Christ and glorified at the beginning of the tribulation. During the tribulation period, 144,000 Jews and a considerable number of Gentiles come to faith (Rev 7:1–9). Those not martyred by the man of sin (i.e., the prince to come) will be alive (Dan 9:26), living in their physical, though fallen, bodies at the Lord's return; and they will become the initial inhabitants of the kingdom age (Matt 25:31–46). Since they are in their as yet unglorified bodies, they can and do repopulate the earth during the millennium. Of course, their progeny must also repent and exercise faith in Christ to be saved. Though all will confirm outwardly to the millennial reign of Christ, the loosing of Satan at the conclusion of the millennium (Rev 20:7–8) will provide opportunity for those whose hearts are in rebellion to manifest themselves as unbelieving.

If some suggest that the salvation of people during the tribulation constitutes a second chance, they are faced with facts that are otherwise. Those, after all, are still living an initial lifetime, and "man is destined to die once, and after that to face judgment" (Heb 9:27). Should one object that following the exodus of the church, those remaining would have greater evidence, one needs only to acknowledge and also note that all men had considerable increase in evidence following the incarnation of Christ. Besides, along with greater evidence, those living in the tribulation period also experience much greater deceit (Matt 24:24).

Pretribulationism, then, best explains how these diverse concepts of last-day events coalesce one with the other. This ability of pretribulation premillennialism to make reasonable sense of the diversified eschatological events is significant.

3. The first three chapters of the Apocalypse mention the churches extensively. But beginning with chap. 4, the explicit mention of the church never occurs again in the Apocalypse. Unquestionably, one can argue that the church appears under other symbols or expressions, and a case can be made for that view. This does not change the unusual shift from frequent mention to total absence. If, however, the plan of God moves back to a distinctly Jewish focus for the events of the tribulation (also called the time of Jacob's trouble, Jer 30:4–7), then for the church to be absent from the events of the period, which constitutes the majority of the text of the Revelation, is not surprising.

4. In Rev 3:10, a remarkable promise is made to the church in Philadelphia. "Since you have kept my command to endure patiently, I will also keep you from the hour of trial that is going to come upon the whole world to test those who live on the earth." Several important features of this verse merit attention. First, there is an hour of trial that will come on the entire world. Jesus himself spoke of such a time saying, "For then there will be great distress, unequaled from the beginning of the world until now—and never to be equaled again. If those days had not been cut short, no one would survive, but for the sake of the elect those days will be shortened" (Matt 24:21–22). A great distress unequaled from the beginning of the world and never to be equaled again, from which none would survive if the time were not limited, presents a concept that only the most tortured exegesis can assign to the fall of Jerusalem. The time of which Jesus spoke has to be synonymous with the coming trial to the whole earth.

Second, the promise to Philadelphia is exemption from that trial. While the church at Philadelphia is addressed, in the messages to the seven historic churches, a universal applicability has often been noted. The problems addressed are visible in churches of every era. So, too, are the accomplishments of the churches. The promises to the seven churches are also applicable not just to these historic congregations but to all of the church in every age. Just as believers in every age are exempt from the horrors of the second death (Rev 2:11), are dressed in white purity (3:4), will sit with Christ on his throne (3:21), so they will be protected from the great hour of trial. The promise "I will also keep you from the hour of trial" implies absence from the scene and hence the taking away of the church before the tribulation.

5. The New Testament seems unanimous in its proclamation of the imminent return of Christ. Numerous passages illustrate this point, including Phil 3:20; Col 3:4; 1 Thess 1:10; Jas 5:8; Rev 3:3; and especially Titus 2:13. Few contest this doctrine of the imminency of Christ's return. But such a view, posing no problem for either amillennialism or pretribulation premillennialism, introduces a significant conundrum for all other perspectives of the relationship of the church to the tribulation.

If, for example, posttribulationism is invoked, then it is possible to count from the beginning of the reign of Antichrist and know that seven years later Christ will return, thereby nullifying the doctrine of the imminency of Christ's return. Or, to be even more precise, from the moment when the prince that shall come (Antichrist) defiles the temple (Dan 9:27) after precisely 1,260 days, Christ will return to the earth. This not only eliminates the possibility at the imminent return of Christ but also has the unfortunate result of rendering Jesus mistaken when he said that no one knew the time of Christ's return (Matt 24:36,42,44)! All views of the relationship of the church to the tribulation, except that of pretribulationism, face this same difficulty.

6. Few texts in the Bible present as much difficulty for interpreters as the prophecy of Daniel's seventy weeks in

Dan 9:20-27.[69] However, the decision about the *terminus a quo* and the *terminus ad quem* of the sixty-nine weeks is determined; the final or seventieth week of the prophecy corresponds to the seven-year period of the great tribulation. A ruler arises in the seventieth heptad, or week of years, who immerses the world in war, destroys Daniel's city (Jerusalem) and the sanctuary (temple). He does this only after making a covenant with Daniel's people of seven years (the seventieth week). But at the halfway point, he breaks this pact and desecrates the temple, bringing great desolation. All of this concerns Daniel's people Israel and the holy city, which is Jerusalem. Thus the prophecy of the seventieth week concerns ethnic Israel and is broken from the sixty-ninth week by an interval of time (the times of the Gentiles or the church age, Jer 30:4-7). While it is conceivable that this seventieth week is somehow contemporaneous with the era of the church, no convincing argument has been marshaled in favor of such a view; and to see the prophecy as relating specifically to Israel in the absence of the church, which has been transported to heaven, is more logical.

7. Rev 7 records the sealing of the 144,000. These are declared to be Jews, 12,000 from each of the twelve tribes of Israel. Their Jewish heritage seems further established by John, who distinguished them from a great multitude that by contrast arises out of every nation, tribe, people, and language. This event is precisely what the pretribulationist anticipates but poses serious problems for all other views. Amillennialists must arrange for some symbolic interpretation that designates these 144,000 as another way to speak of the church or of God's people generally. Of course, this is not what the text says, and the view leaves unexplained why the author went to so much trouble to list the tribes, especially as they are listed. The question of authorial intent also

---

69 For careful analysis of the particulars of this prophecy of the seventy weeks, see R. Anderson, *The Coming Prince* (Grand Rapids: Kregel, 1975); H. W. Hoehner, *Chronological Aspects of the Life of Christ* (Grand Rapids: Zondervan, 1977), 115–39; and P. Patterson, "Israel and the Great Tribulation," in *The Return of Christ*, ed. D. Allen and S. Lemke (Nashville: B&H Academic, 2011), 62–74.

surfaces again, and John, a Jew, seems to have understood these to be Jews.

The posttribulationist faces similar difficulties. If the church is still present on the earth at the time of this sealing, why are these Jews not assimilated into the church as was the case for John, Peter, and Paul? Nothing in the further discussion of the 144,000 in Rev 14:1–5 lends any evidence for the presence of the church, suggesting that once again the age of the Gentiles has past, the church has been removed, and once again the focus is on Israel during the great tribulation.

8. Rev 12 introduces the reader to a radiant woman who gives birth to the Messiah. As will be argued in the discussion of chap. 12, properly identifying this woman constitutes a major key not only to that chapter but also to the whole book of Revelation. The woman gives birth to the one who is to rule all nations. She has to flee from the dragon to a place where she is protected for 1,260 days. That time is later given as "time, times and half a time" (Rev 12:14; see also Dan 7:25; 12:7) or three and one-half years.

Reasons for identifying the woman as Israel are provided in the exegesis of chap. 12. Suffice it to say that by understanding the woman to be Israel, the passage agrees with the understanding of Daniel's seventieth week offered above. This places the chapter in the last half of the great tribulation and once again reflects a Jewish era from which the church is absent.

Again, there are many other reasons to find that the church is not present in the seven-year period of the tribulation. Altogether a case cannot be built with finality or scuttled for this view or others. The church must be prepared for suffering and persecution because she was promised that inevitability (John 16:18–20). But there is evidence for the intervention of Christ on behalf of his bride, taking her from the wrath that will surely come.

11. Preaching the Apocalypse

In 1962 the first of five volumes of sermons on Revelation was published by W. A. Criswell, far-famed pastor of the First Baptist Church of Dallas, Texas.[70] Criswell, after preaching through the entire Bible in a 16-year series, took a six-month "sabbatical" to prepare for the series on the book of Revelation, which then occupied his attention and that of his parishioners for more than three years. Attendance increased, Bible knowledge proliferated, and the church grew in the mid-1960s to become the largest evangelical church in America—and all that on the back of expository preaching coupled with evangelism.

Yet, aside from a few journal articles and fewer monographs, few homiletical adventurers have evidenced the moxie to enter the eschatological lists and take on this book in the pulpit.[71] This remains the case even though curiosity abounds in many congregations where parishioners fervently wish that their respective pastors would explain the book to them. Among those who embark on this adventure, most sail no further than the messages to the seven churches in chap. 3, thus missing the grandeur of the promises that proliferate in chaps. 4–22. As I noted elsewhere:

> Evangelical preaching from the Apocalypse gyrates wildly as it caroms off walls of neglect only to settle into theological opium fields where enthusiastic illusions inhaled from the fertile poppies of human imagination are passed on to bewildered congregants as insights into the minute details of the last days. Attempts to identify the Antichrist by means of numerics may smack of cabalism, but Christian interpreters have, nevertheless, wearied themselves and embarrassed the faith with relentless efforts to sort out Antichrist's identity whether it be Nero, Henry Kissinger, or Saddam Hussein. Prophetic calendars, discoveries of contemporary weaponry from helicopters to missiles, and gross literalisms of an almost infinite variety have all been part of the mishandling of the Apocalypse by its most ardent admirers.
>
> If there is something more regrettable than the treatment of the Revelation by enthusiastic friends, it is its abject neglect by most evangelical

---

70 Criswell, *Expository Sermons on Revelation*. In 1966 all five volumes were consolidated into one volume.

71 Aside from a few journal articles and one dissertation, D. Russell's *Preaching the Apocalypse* (New York: Abingdon Press, 1935) is one of the few books published on the subject. See also P. Patterson, "Interpreting the New Testament for Preaching—The Apocalypse," *Faith and Mission* 12, no. 1 (Fall 1994): 67–79.

preachers. Partly as a reaction to the unbridled sensationalism of reckless interpreters and partly as a result of intellectual and exegetical laziness, the average evangelical pastor just never gets around to the Apocalypse. If he should decide to venture into such "foreign territory," he is most likely to bring a few messages on the seven churches or at most expound the first three chapters. As everyone quickly learns, there may be some hermeneutical mountains to climb in the first three chapters, but at least there are no Gordian knots awaiting some special interpretive sword which was never released from the seminary armory!

Did I say seminary? Ah yes, the scene is seldom any better there. Many professors secretly dread the prospects of encountering students who are sure to have some halfbaked views about the Apocalypse—just enough knowledge to ask a battery of questions that are calculated to reveal cavernous lacunae in the doctor's knowledge and induce the most intolerable form of academic humiliation. Consequently, the rule in New Testament Survey or, even in a narrower focus on the epistles, is to have so much material that the semester "regrettably" expires before the class gets to the Apocalypse. Or if one must encounter the Apocalypse, at least he can spend several days lecturing on Apocalyptic genre in Judaism, 200 B.C. to A.D. 100, drag out the first three chapters as long as possible, and pray for spring rains to bring a gully washer and wipe out enough class days to realize the universal salvation of graduation.

Both tragedies can be easily avoided by the pastor or professor who is willing to tackle the text of Revelation and, like Jacob's encounter with the angel at the Jabbok River, hang on until he gets a blessing. Following long-accepted hermeneutical basics, coupled with an awareness of the prophetic and apocalyptic genres, the preacher or professor can grasp this book and expound it fruitfully. Furthermore, he may discover a hunger among his sheep that is more than just endtimes curiosity. And in the satiation of that hunger he may also see an increase and ingathering. My thesis is that people want to know what this Bible means and how its message makes a difference. The Revelation is a book that makes an enormous difference![72]

Here are several reasons such feats should be attempted:

1. Revelation is the only book in the Bible that publishes a beatitude for all those who read, who hear what is read, and

---

72 Patterson, "Interpreting the New Testament for Preaching," 67–68.

who take to heart the words written (Rev 1:3). Of course, evangelical Christians believe this is true even if unstated about every book in the Bible, but with the promise of this book made so specific, how can our pastors and congregations risk neglecting it?

2. In the face of charlatans, unbridled eschatological enthusiasts, and sensationalists, the careful and humble exposition of eschatological themes and particularly the Apocalypse is needed in every generation.

3. Preachers need the challenge of vigorous study in an endeavor that is challenging. Preaching through Revelation will provide this challenge.

4. Attendance will almost always be bolstered and the interest of parishioners in understanding the text of the Bible will be strengthened.

5. The promise of the Lord's triumphant return is profoundly needed by the anemic churches of our time. Confidence and resolve develop in those situations where pastors assist their parishioners in understanding the discouragements and sorrows present in light of the promises of God for the future.

From a previous article I would add:

Remember that all the tested rules of hermeneutics apply to the Apocalypse. Couple this with awareness of major features of apocalyptic literature, and the preacher is ready to embark on his assignment. Add to this the following final observations:

1. In initiating the study of the Apocalypse for preaching, read the book as a unit—as it was written. Continue doing this until the perspective of John and his first century readers can be grasped in its larger sphere.

2. Watch closely for Old Testament parallels and allusions, and allow them considerable weight as guides to understanding the book.

3. Treat the Revelation as end-time prophecy designed to engender faith, hope, and courage for the church in every era.

4. Squeeze the symbols gently for every drop of the nectar of significance they will give, but do not squeeze so hard that

you get seeds instead of nectar. Your listeners often will intuitively know when you do not support an interpretation adequately. They will also note the difference between exegesis and speculation. The latter is not offensive unless such speculation is passed off as exegesis or used to excess.

5. In the process of explicating prophetic events, do not overlook the moral mandates and the rich insights into the doctrinal verities that abound in the Apocalypse.

6. Few Bible books are as focused on worship as Revelation. Be certain the texts are presented in such a fashion as to culminate in worship.

7. Above all, exalt Jesus as you preach the Apocalypse. After all, John himself did!

8. Finally, if you are preoccupied with preaching the Apocalypse and dwell on prophetic themes to the relative neglect of Exodus, John, Romans, Galatians, and Hebrews, then you are probably in danger of becoming unbalanced, and you are almost certainly failing to preach the whole counsel of God. On the other hand, if the Revelation is forbidding and difficult for you to preach, then perhaps you need to change your presuppositions to ones that allow you not only to see the grandeur of the book but also to interpret the book successfully and meaningfully for your flock.[73]

12. OUTLINE

There are almost as many outlines for the Apocalypse as there are commentaries. The strength of an outline is in its attempt to demonstrate that a book or treatise has a structure and development. The weakness is that such outlines are external and later impositions on the Bible books and as a result do not always reveal much about the mind of the author. As applied to the Apocalypse, the broad outline is relatively clear, but little is certain beyond that. In 1979, this author prepared an outline (as well as annotations) for the Apocalypse, which appeared in the *Criswell Study Bible*. Since I remain essentially unchanged in my general perspective of the book, I have chosen to reproduce that outline here.

---

73 Patterson, "Interpreting the New Testament for Preaching," 77.

INTRODUCTION
1:1-3

The prologue to the Apocalypse, though brief, is nonetheless laden with information critical for both its initial recipients and modern interpreters. Three groups crucial to the book are described: the author, the intermediaries, and the auditors. The human author discounts his ownership of the book's content and claims that the message originated with God, who first gave to Jesus a revelation unveiling events, which, at the moment of disclosure, were predominantly yet future.[1] Possessing this knowledge would subsequently make it possible for the churches addressed not merely to grasp unfolding events but also to be prepared and even blessed in the midst of what would emerge as a time of incredible global upheaval.

> [1]**The Revelation of Jesus Christ, which God gave Him to show His servants—things which must shortly take place. And He sent and signified *it* by His angel to His servant John, [2]who bore witness to the word of God, and to the testimony of Jesus Christ, to all things that he saw. [3]Blessed *is* he who reads and those who hear the words of this prophecy, and keep those things which are written in it; for the time *is* near.**

"Revelation" (*apokalupsis*) refers to something formerly hidden but now unveiled.[2] In this case the revelation is said to be "of Jesus Christ," which is a geniti-

---

1   The appearance of δεῖ (present, imperative of δέω, meaning "to bind"), translated here as "must," emphasizes the inevitability of the unfolding events that John will describe. Those events "must" soon take place.

2   ἀποκάλυψις has an interesting history in the Greek language. It described the receding of the Nile, the disclosure of the mind's thoughts, the discovery of true motives, and the uncovering of a head or body. Only gradually did cultic or religious usages for the term evolve. Oepke, acknowledging that the word was used as a technical term for "soothsayers," argues that this concept imported from the East is alien to Greek theology and philosophy. He even ventures that nonbiblical, religious usages of the term may well owe their origin to the Greek Bible. For a full discussion, see LSJ, 201. Also note A. Oepke, *TDNT* 3.556–92. Apringius of Beja, one of the earliest to write a commentary on the Apocalypse, notes: "From this we learn that this [book] is called an Apocalypse, that is, 'revelation,' which manifests those secrets which are hidden and unknown to the senses, and that unless [Christ] himself reveals them, he who perceives [the revelation]

1

val construction in Greek grammar. This could mean either that Jesus was being revealed (objective genitive) or that Jesus was the mediator revealing the Father's message (subjective genitive). Most commentators have agreed that the latter is the correct grammatical understanding.[3] In a sense Jesus himself is revealed in the book as he is (1:12-16; 5:1-6; 12:5; and 19:11-16). Twenty-eight times in the book of Revelation, Jesus is referred to as "the Lamb." This metaphor alone reveals much about the nature and purpose of the Christ. His awesomeness as the glorified Christ is revealed (1:12-16). Christ's relationship to the world and his sacrifice and worthiness are the subjects of 5:1-6. In 12:5, his destiny is established, and in 19:11-16 Jesus is observed returning in triumph and judgment.

But much more than the glorified Christ emerges from these visions. The rise and fall of kingdoms, the four series of judgments on the earth, the visions of final judgment, and the glimpses of the eternal state all await the reader. Furthermore, the same construction takes place in 1:2, where the book is identified as the testimony of Jesus . . . and Jesus apparently is the one giving the testimony. In fact, the testimony of Jesus is equated with the "word of God" (1:2), giving biblical authority to the testimony of Jesus and even hinting at the deity of Jesus.

Divine authority and origin is twice emphasized in the prologue when John avers that "God gave [it to] him" (1:1) and that this testimony of Jesus was "the word of God" (1:2). God then is the source of all contained in the book, while three intermediaries—one divine, one angelic, and one human—collaborate in the communication of the material. Angelic involvement is common in Jewish apocalyptic literature, more so in fact than in the Revelation.[4] John restricts himself to the role of the servant, or in some translations—"slave," to whom the angel signifies or reveals by signs those things that must soon take place.

---

will not have the strength to understand what he sees" (*Tractate on the Apocalypse*, cited in *Revelation*, ACCS [Downers Grove, IL: InterVarsity, 2005], 2).

3   S. Thompson observes, "Under this heading a conjecture will be put forward which, if accepted, would resolve a puzzling, if not particularly troublesome, v[erse]. Apc. 1:1 is traditionally rendered 'The revelation of Jesus Christ, which God gave him, to show his servants what must take place' (RSV). The versions, ancient and modern, do not stray from this, and indeed it is the only way to understand the present text. The relative clause 'which God gave him' is the heart of the puzzle, though. How could the Seer write of God giving a disclosure *of* Jesus Christ *to* Jesus Christ?" (*The Apocalypse and Semitic Syntax*, SNTSMS 52 [New York: Cambridge University Press, 1985], 112).

4   See, for example, *1 Enoch 1:2*; *The Apocalypse of Zephaniah B:8*; and The Greek Apocalypse *of Ezra 1:5*, in *Apocalyptic Literature & Testaments*, vol. 1 of *The Old Testament Pseudepigrapha*, ed. J. H. Charlesworth (Garden City, NY: Doubleday, 1983), 13, 508, 571.

Here the author is claiming that this "Revelation [from] Jesus Christ" is a direct word from God, an unveiling of his plan and purposes. This claim excludes the possibility that this prophecy is human speculation or mere religious reflection. Contemporary interpreters must make a decision. Either John is conveying to his readers precisely what God said, or else he is guilty of prevarication. Any patronizing suggestion that John was mistaken, though sincere in thinking that he heard from God, is inadequate.[5]

While the ultimate recipients of the vision await more thorough identification (1:11), the prologue simply denominates them as "his servants" (1:1). And those servants of Jesus are given a promise, which constitutes the first of seven beatitudes in the Revelation (1:3; 14:13; 16:15; 19:9; 20:6; 22:7,14). A benediction is pronounced on those who read, hear, and take to heart the words of this prophecy.

Two features of this benediction are noteworthy. In the continuing discussion as to whether Revelation should be viewed as apocalyptic, prophetic, or epistolary genre (see Introduction), interestingly John speaks of the entire work as "prophecy."[6] The "one who reads" refers to the person who publicly reads the letter to the congregations as is indicated by the extension of the blessing to those who hear it read and "keep those things which are written in it."

The "blessedness," which is to benefit both readers and hearers alike, arises from the fact that they are hearing the words of God, the testimony of

---

5   For example, M. G. Reddish notes that "John, like all other apocalyptic thinkers was wrong in tying the events of his day so closely to the end of the world. His mistaken expectation of the imminent end of the world does not invalidate his message for the church, however" (*Revelation*, Smyth & Helwys Bible Commentary [Macon, GA: Smyth & Helwys, 2001], 33). For a similar view see M. E. Marty, "M.E.M.O.: A Revelation," *The Christian Century*, 114 (14 May, 1997): 495. For Marty, the Revelation is a "dream" that almost did not make the canon.

6   The aorist, active, indicative ἐσήμανεν in v. 1 means "show by means of a sign or symbol." The word, however, does not suggest that the author of the book intended his readers to hear the "symbols" as indications that actual historical events are not in view. Anticipated events are merely portrayed in apocalyptic symbols. Suggestions as to why the author of the Apocalypse chose to write a circular letter, which he calls a "prophecy," in the genre of the apocalyptic, range from the necessity of disguising the contents for protection to merely choosing the apocalyptic imagery as a vehicle of expression popular at the time of writing. Since any immediate, serious danger arising out of the dissemination of written epistles is difficult, if not impossible, to demonstrate, John probably borrowed in part a popular apocalyptic style especially employed when discussing future events (see Introduction).

Jesus. They are thus made privy to the continuing plan and purpose of God for the future, which would otherwise have remained hidden in the providences of God. Further, the readers, as they encounter anticipated tribulations, are blessed by the reassurance that Christ not only reigns supreme but also guides history to his designed climax, at which time good conquers forevermore.

The most problematic expressions in the prologue relate to the phrases "what must shortly take place" (v. 1) and "for the time is near" (v. 3). As other commentators have noted, essentially four possibilities for the meaning of these expressions may be considered.[7] (1) They may indicate that the author anticipated immediate fulfillment of the prophecies. If anything more than a highly spiritualized, or allegorical, interpretation of the book is endorsed, this imminent anticipation was tragically in error. (2) Those who adhere to preterist or historicist interpretations (see Introduction) advocate an immediate beginning for the fulfillment of the prophecies but see full realization of the prophecies after about a decade (preterists) or only at the culmination of the church age (historicists). (3) Futurists have generally found the expressions troubling and have sought to explain them as carrying the sense of "certainty," meaning that the prophecies must certainly take place. (4) Another approach is to find the significance of the expression "soon take place" (*en tachei*) to be "quick" in the sense of "suddenly." When least expected and with minimal warning, these events will occur.[8]

---

7   D. Chilton presents a view of Revelation as a "covenant lawsuit" of God's wrath on Jerusalem, suggesting that the book contains primarily those events that John expected his readers to see immediately (*The Days of Vengeance* [Fort Worth, TX: Dominion Press, 1987], 51). For a variation of the idea that the expression is intended to mean that the events of the Apocalypse were expected to take place immediately, including the return of Christ and the consummation of the age, see G. B. Caird, *A Commentary on the Revelation of St. John the Divine* (New York: Harper and Row, 1966), 12. M. E. Boring agrees with Caird but goes further by saying, "Does this mean he was wrong? Yes, Christians . . . ought not to hesitate to acknowledge that its author made errors" (*Revelation*, IBC [Louisville, KY: Westminster John Knox, 1989], 72–73). As usual, no criteria are offered for distinguishing between reliable and unreliable data. G. E. Ladd joins Caird and Boring in their conclusions and then attempts to soften the reality of John's expectation by explaining that in prophecy both near and distant perspectives form a single canvas (*A Commentary on the Revelation of John* [Grand Rapids: Eerdmans, 1972], 22).

8   Advocates of one or the other of these last two views include J. F. Walvoord, *The Revelation of Jesus Christ* (Chicago: Moody, 1966); Henry Alford, *The Greek Testament*, vol. 4 (Chicago: Moody, 1958); W. A. Criswell, *Expository Sermons on Revelation: Five Volumes Complete and Unabridged* (Grand Rapids: Zondervan, 1969); R. H. Mounce, *The Book of Revelation*, NICNT (Grand Rapids: Eerdmans, 1977); and R. L. Thomas, *Revelation 1–7:*

Perhaps the best solution is to recognize some truth in each of these positions. The thesis of this commentary is that the early church believed in the imminency of Christ's return. If that assessment has merit, the two phrases can be read as possibility rather than as time-specific indicators. Furthermore, without endorsing the conclusions of historicist or preterist interpretations, even the most determined futurist sees that some of the prophecies specifically addressed to the seven churches in chaps. 2 and 3 were shortly fulfilled while other prophecies were set in motion to gather momentum until finally fulfilled in the eschatological consummation.

R. Summers takes issue with the futurists, who translate *en tachei* as "certainly" instead of his preferred translation "immediately," which he supports in this way:

> The prepositional phrase translated "shortly" means just what it says—shortly, quickly, hastily. Two or three thousand years will be too late . . . any attempt to make this phrase mean no more than "certainty" fails to meet the situation which is confronted by the churches.[9]

But Summers has surely overstated his case since the precise interpretation that futurists suggest, namely, that "shortly" (NKJV) or "soon take place" (NIV) can sometimes mean "certainly," is found in Rom 16:20. Paul promises the Roman church that God will crush Satan's head "shortly" (*en tachei*), the precise wording of this text. Since that final crushing has yet to transpire, the apostle must have intended *en tachei* to mean "certainly." Consequently, that an element of promised certainty is involved in both of these expressions is not at all improbable. And who can fail to appreciate the rapidity of movement in the Apocalypse? The idea of "suddenly" is also entirely credible.

Those writers who wish to argue that the church must anticipate the experience of the great tribulation face one of their most difficult dilemmas at this point. These expressions are hard to explain as anything other than another rehearsal of the pristine church's belief in the imminency of Christ's return. That expectation of the early church may be observed in such passages as John 14:2-3;

An Exegetical Commentary (Chicago: Moody, 1992). All of these cite passages where ἐν τάχει seems to mean "suddenly," such as Luke 18:8 and Rom 16:20. Criswell adds Jas 5:8, in which the coming of the Lord "draws near" (ἐγγίζω), a form of the expression translated in v. 3, "the time is near."

9   R. Summers, *Worthy Is the Lamb: Interpreting the Book of Revelation in Its Historical Background* (Nashville: B&H, 1951), 99.

Acts 1:11; 1 Cor 15:51–52; Col 3:4; 1 Thess 1:10; 1 Tim 6:14; Jas 5:8; 2 Pet 3:3–4; 1 Thess 5:6; Titus 2:13, and Rev 3:3. Credulity is strained if Christians are supposed to be looking for the "blessed hope" when, in fact, such an event cannot transpire until the ominous events of seven years of tribulation come and go.

This idea of the imminency of the return of Jesus is further enforced by the warning of the Lord that believers are to be watchful "because you know neither the day nor the hour" (Matt 25:13). Furthermore, in answer to his followers' inquiry about the restoration of the kingdom to Israel, Jesus cautioned, "It is not for you to know the times [chronos] or seasons [kairos] which the Father has put in His own authority" (Acts 1:7). If some portion or all of the tribulation is to take place before the return of Christ for his church, then these statements of Jesus are false and misleading. The time of the Lord's return could be calculated almost to the day simply by beginning with the Antichrist's revelation and covenant with Israel (Dan 9:26–27), adding 1,260 days (midtribulationism) or 2,520 days (posttribulationism) to the covenant with Israel and arriving at just about the precise moment of his return. Amillennialism and pretribulation premillennialism avoid this impasse by positing the imminency of the coming of Christ. Unfortunately, amillennialism does so at the cost of jettisoning all natural understandings of both the great tribulation and an earthly manifestation of the kingdom.

Whatever else may be said about the two phrases, urgency oozes from the Johannine injunction to hear and to take to heart the words of the glorified Christ and a benevolent God who has, as an act of his grace, rolled back the curtain to reveal a broad outline of the end times. Because those times will embrace both cataclysmic judgment and costly witness, the message revealed is vital. Both phrases, "what must shortly take place" and "for the time is near" underscore the urgency motif and suggest that the servants of Christ assess this prophecy immediately.

I. A Vision of the Glorified Christ
1:4-20

1. Triunitarian Greeting (1:4-6)

⁴John,

To the seven churches which are in Asia:

Grace to you and peace from Him who is and who was and who is to come, and from the seven Spirits who are before His throne, ⁵and from Jesus Christ, the faithful witness, the firstborn from the dead, and the ruler over the kings of the earth. To Him who loved us and washed us from our sins in His own blood,

⁶and has made us kings and priests to His God and Father, to Him *be* glory and dominion forever and ever. Amen.

The human author now discloses more fully the identity of the recipients. Beginning with "servants" (1:1), the focus narrows to seven churches in Asia (1:4); and those seven will be specifically identified (1:11). The author also repeats his own name. He is John, the beloved disciple of the Lord. As noted in the Introduction, the similarities and dissimilarities of language in the Apocalypse, when compared with the Gospel of John and the Johannine epistles, are notable. The combined consideration of the content of the book, the probable rush of production, and the nature of the genre sufficiently account for the differences. Irenaeus, the co-laborer and friend of Polycarp, who knew John in Ephesus, bore testimony that favored John, the fisherman son of Zebedee, as the author of the book.[10] "The province of Asia" is a reference to what has been

---

10 Irenaeus, *Against Heresies*, 4.20.11, trans. A. Roberts and W. H. Rambaut, *ANF* 1:491.

called Asia Minor in the ancient world or in modernity the Asian portion of the country of Turkey.

A benedictory prayer expresses the bestowal of grace and peace from God. Noteworthy is the order: Lasting peace is only found in the wake of grace. Both radiate from him "who is, and who was, and who is to come."[11] Since both grace and peace can only come from God and since John's identifying phrase carries overtones of the Tetragrammaton,[12] only God could be said to exist contemporaneously with John, while at the same time being a person who always was and still was one yet to come. However, if the first and third sources of this message are the Father and the Son, the author left much for discussion when he spoke of "the seven spirits before his throne." Efforts to explain the expression can be classified essentially in five categories. (1) Some interpreters are confident that the reference is to angels. Specifically, the seven prominent angels of Jewish apocalyptic literature are in view.[13] (2) Other scholars prefer to see Babylonian astrological influence in the text with the seven spirits representing the five known planets plus moon and sun.[14] (3) A third perspective assigns the refer-

---

11   This expression has been subject to criticism in part due to its grammatical construction, which violates conventional Greek grammar. Mounce provides an excellent analysis of these allegations and demonstrates that the grammar of the sentence does not arise out of ignorance but is rather a purposeful construction designed to provide an exact reproduction of the Hebraism (*The Book of Revelation*, 68, n.13). R. H. Charles goes so far as to suggest that "the Seer has deliberately violated the rules of grammar to preserve the divine name inviolate from the change it would necessarily have undergone if declined" (*A Critical and Exegetical Commentary on The Revelation of St. John*, ICC [Edinburgh: T&T Clark, 1920], 1:10). Boring calls attention to Pausanus's similar identification of Zeus as "Zeus was, Zeus is, and Zeus will be" (*Revelation*, 75).

12   See the discussion of יהוה in BDB, 217–18. R. L. Thomas notes that the entire expression ἀπὸ ὁ ὢν καὶ ὁ ἦν καὶ ὁ ἐρχόμενος is to be regarded as "an undeclinable [sic] proper name" (*Revelation 1–7*, 65).

13   Boring says, "This tripartite formula is not the developed Trinitarianism of later theology: the seven spirits are the seven angelic beings said by John to be under the authority of both God and Christ" (*Revelation*, 75). Charles thinks it "highly probable" that these seven spirits are to be identified with the seven archangels (*Critical and Exegetical Commentary*, 1:13). In this they sustain the judgment of Oecumenius, one of the earliest commentators (*Revelation*, ACCS, 4).

14   A. Y. Collins sees no connection at all to the Holy Spirit. She is positive the reference is to seven ranking angels who were regarded as heavenly beings and were related to the seven planets that were known to exist in John's day. See *NJBC*, 1000. See also 1 Enoch 90:21; Tob 12:15; Sibylline Oracles 2:215–20. In Pseudepigraphal literature, more extensive lists of angelic names, both of good angels and of fallen angels, are found

ence to the Holy Spirit, based on a reading of Isa 11:2–3, where the promised Branch will be endowed with the Spirit, including the Spirit of wisdom, understanding, counsel, might, knowledge, and fear of the Lord.[15] (4) A fourth view, along with advocates of the third approach, agrees that the appropriate understanding of the phrase is "the Holy Spirit" but disagrees that the background for the passage is Isaiah. Rather, Zech 4:2–6 is identified as the Old Testament backdrop for the language.[16] (5) The final view, adopted by R. H. Charles, sees the difficult phrase as an interpolation—even though his view is void of any significant textual support—and therefore dismisses the problem.[17]

The view of R. H. Charles is based solely on the presupposition that the author of the Revelation could not have penned this. He makes no case for the position but proceeds to attempt an exegesis of this "late interpolation." In so doing, he opts for the first view, namely, that angels are intended. He goes so far as to conjecture that the theory of seven archangels is probable. Indeed, the Bible does speak of angels as spirits (Heb 1:7,14). But John's pattern is to identify angels plainly in the text (see Rev 8:2). Furthermore, internal relationships in the text render another view more likely.

The view that John has been influenced by Babylonian astrology has little to commend it other than the supposition that discoveries of zodiac signs in some synagogues and references to astrology in histories, such as that of Josephus, prove that Jews of the period were enamored with such things. The idea that the Jewish menorah, or seven-branched lamp, represented the seven planets and was of astrological significance is an ancient idea dating at least to Philo. But such a view is foreign to the text. More popular has been the aforementioned third view, which identifies the "seven spirits" as a cryptic reading for Holy Spirit with the background for this interpretation in Isa 11:2–3. But Revelation speaks

---

than what is provided in the biblical canon. In 1 Enoch 20:1–8 the archangels are said to be Uriel, Raphael, Raguel, Michael, Gabriel, Remiel, and Saraqael. See also J. M. Ford, *Revelation: Introduction, Translation and Commentary*, AB (Garden City, NY: Doubleday, 1975), 377.

15   See W. E. Biederwolf, *The Millennium Bible* (Grand Rapids: Baker, 1964), 544.

16   See Ladd, *Commentary on the Revelation of John*, 25; Leon Morris, *Revelation*, TNTC (Grand Rapids: Eerdmans, 1988), 49; J. P. M. Sweet, *Revelation* (Philadelphia: Westminster, 1979), 63; and Alford, *The Greek Testament*, 4:549. R. Stefanovic finds a way to place views three and four together and arrives at the same conclusion (*Revelation of Jesus Christ: Commentary on the Book of Revelation* [Berrien Springs, MI: Andrews University Press, 2002], 61).

17   Charles, *Critical and Exegetical Commentary*, 1:11.

of the "seven spirits," while Isaiah technically alludes to only six virtues in addition to "the Spirit of the Lord," which will rest upon the Branch.

The best approach seems to be identifying the background of the passage as Zech 4:2–6, where the prophet saw a solid gold lampstand boasting seven lamps. Zechariah inquired as to the meaning of the vision. After the usual humiliation suffered as a result of the angel's evident astonishment at Zechariah's ignorance, the prophet is informed that the vision is "the word of the LORD to Zerubbabel: 'Not by might nor by power, but by my Spirit,' says the LORD Almighty." The revelator is thoroughly familiar with the Old Testament and uses this verse as the ideal identification for the Holy Spirit. Zechariah has provided the author of the Apocalypse with the perfect picture of the ministry of the Holy Spirit to the seven congregations to whom the prophecy is addressed. While there is but one Holy Spirit, he does not invest himself incrementally in the churches but is always available simultaneously, in his fullness, to all seven congregations.

This interpretation is strengthened by the references to God and to Jesus, the faithful witness. Highly unlikely is the possible insertion of a reference to angels in the midst of references to deity.[18] Almost certainly, then, this phrase is a trinitarian greeting at the inception of the Apocalypse. However, in keeping with the apocalyptic language employed by John and with a view to connecting the work of the Spirit to the churches and to the seven angels of the churches, John speaks of the Holy Spirit as the seven spirits before the throne. As Morris notably states, "John never uses the expression 'the Holy Spirit' in this book, . . . he uses the word 'Spirit' in a variety of ways; 'the Spirit' is found in 22:17, etc., so John clearly knows of the Holy Spirit."[19]

Finally, the prophecy is from Jesus, who is described in three ways. He is the faithful witness, the firstborn from the dead, and the ruler over all earthly kings. Witnesses abound, but only One is ultimately, absolutely dependable. He is faithful both in the sense that he will appear to testify and in the sense that he will speak only that which is factual. His witness concerning the condition of man and the nature of salvation is true. His witness concerning himself is true. His testimony concerning the unfolding events of the future and his assessment of the seven churches is also fully reliable.

Death is the tyrant that threatens all creation with irreplaceable loss and ultimate meaninglessness. But the One who brings this prophecy has dealt with death and rendered death helpless by becoming the firstborn from the dead

---

18 Mounce, *The Book of Revelation*, 69.

19 Morris, *Revelation*, 49.

(i.e., the first to be born out of the matrix of the penalty for sin). This metaphor is particularly arresting since normally life can only emerge from existing life. But here the witness is from One born not out of life or even out of nothingness but out of death. Jesus is the firstborn from the dead, implying that many others will be resurrected as a result.[20]

Jesus is also the ruler of the kings of the earth. All terrestrial authorities are subject to him and can continue their reigns only as he sovereignly permits. There is a sense in which Jesus may be observed here in his three ministries as prophet (faithful witness), priest (conquering for man the wage of sin exacted against man through his victory over death), and king (ruling all other kings).

Contemplation of the Lord and his majesty evokes a benediction, an act of worship, a doxology from John. Ascribing to him both glory and power forever, John focuses on the redemptive work of Christ in its application to the saints of God. Christ is said to have acted on the basis of his love for the world by freeing the saints from their sins by means of his blood.[21] Here the author of

---

20 G. K. Beale notes that "'Firstborn' refers to the high, privileged position that Christ has as a result of the resurrection from the dead (i.e., a position with respect to the OT idea of primogeniture, especially in the context of royal succession [Ps. 89:27–37 develops this idea from 2 Sam. 7:13–16 and Ps. 2:7–8]). Christ has gained such a sovereign position over the cosmos, not in the sense that he is recognized as the first-created being of all creation or as the origin of creation, but in the sense that he is the inaugurator of the *new* creation by means of his resurrection" (*The Book of Revelation: A Commentary on the Greek Text*, NIGTC [Grand Rapids: Eerdmans, 1999], 191). B. Witherington III notes the assurance of this avowal for suffering Christians, saying, "Put another way, John is reassuring his audience that the major factor that they might fear at this juncture, namely a shameful death at the hands of their own rulers, will be overcome, as it was for Christ" (*Revelation*, NCBC [Cambridge: Cambridge University Press, 2003], 76). Chilton relates the declaration to the similar statement in Col 1:18 (*Days of Vengeance*, 62). Aune notes the same parallel with Colossians; but, while acknowledging the statement as striking, he, predictably, does not think that it originated with John. "ὁ πρωτότοκος τῶν νεκρῶν, 'the firstborn from the dead.' This striking title is an instance of paradox, for the notions of birth and death are obviously antithetical. In all probability, the writer did not formulate this title, for the title ἀρχή, πρωτότοκος ἐκ τῶν νεκρῶν, 'the beginning, the firstborn from the dead,' occurs earlier in Col 1:18 (in the context of a hymn incorporated into that letter). Since Colossians was circulated in the Roman province of Asia, including Laodicea (Col 4:16), one of the seven churches to whom Revelation was addressed, the title may have become part of the Christological tradition in the region" (D. Aune, *Revelation 1–5*, WBC 52a [Dallas, TX: Word Books, 1997], 38).

21 Verse 5 provides a classic case of a textual variant. Some texts read λούσαντι or "washed us from our sins in His own blood." Others read λύσαντι or "released us from our sins in His own blood." Favoring this latter reading are p18, א, A, C, and assorted

the Apocalypse voices an atonement doctrine thoroughly compatible with that found in Paul. Passages of such profound Christological and soteriological content are among the reasons many scholars have found Revelation, in a number of ways, distinct from Jewish apocalyptic genre.

The picture is of those formerly shackled by sin but now liberated on the basis of a transaction, the currency for which is the blood of Christ.[22] Familiarity with the Old Testament is again paramount in John's thinking as he recalls Lev 17:11 and its prohibition against the eating of blood since "the life of a creature is in the blood," and blood has been authorized as the appropriate sacrifice upon the altar. Precisely because the author sees the shed blood of Christ as the life of Jesus poured out in substitution, he understands that sacrifice as providing liberation from sin and death.

However, liberation is only half the story. The saints are not only forgiven but also are vested with significance. They are made into a kingdom of priests. This priesthood is not a rugged individualism boasting of its "right" to do or to think whatever the individual desires. Rather, there exists a kingdom of priests, and to have a kingdom, there must be a king. To discover the meaning of this priesthood of believers—these believer-priests who exist and exercise priesthood to serve God the Father—is no surprise.[23] As priests they have access to

---

other sources. However, as is often the case, the majority of the variant readings favor the former reading. The NASB translators have chosen to follow "released" while the NKJV employed "washed." The author of this commentary suspects that the NASB is correct. However, like most variant readings, the conclusion reached is a technical matter that has no real effect on its theological understanding. Either rendering is theologically true. The blood of Christ is said to "cleanse us from all sin" (1 John 1:9); hence we are "washed" in his blood. But we are also "loosed" from our sins as a consequence of his atoning death. Either way the passage places hope for forgiveness precisely in the shed blood of Jesus as an atonement for our souls.

22   On the significance of the blood of Christ as a propitiatory sacrifice for sin, see A. M. Stibbs, *The Meaning of the Word "Blood" in Scripture* (London: Tyndale Press, 1954); J. R. Stott, *The Cross of Christ* (Downers Grove, IL: InterVarsity, 1986); Leon Morris, *The Apostolic Preaching of the Cross* (Grand Rapids: Eerdmans, 1965); P. Patterson, "Reflections on the Atonement," *CTR* 3 (1989): 307–20; and id., "The Work of Christ" in *A Theology for the Church* (Nashville: B&H, 2007), 545–602.

23   The priesthood of believers is mentioned five times in the New Testament (1 Pet 2:5; 2:9; Rev 1:6; 5:10; 20:6). Only two of the passages provide much insight into the significance of the idea. The "privilege" in the doctrine is the unimpeded, direct access to God with no need for the intervening of a special cadre of human priests. The emphasis of the New Testament is more on the responsibility of this priesthood.

God individually, but they are engaged in subservient service to the king. The "amen" appended to the end of the doxology represents John's approval and affirmation of the ascription.

The benediction seems to trigger what might be termed a paean of eschatological hope in anticipation of the return of Christ. The author declares that he will come "with the clouds," a statement doubtless reflecting the fact that the initial promise of Christ's return after his ascension was made by angels just after Jesus was received up into heaven. The message of the angel was that Jesus would return "in the same way you have seen him go" (Acts 1:11). However, John may also have had in his mind the mysterious *shekinah* glory of God, which, in the history of Israel, had sometimes manifested itself as something of a visible effulgence of God at moments marked with profound spiritual significance, such as the completion of the tabernacle and the temple.[24] These manifestations were viewed in the form of a luminous cloud of such intensity that the work of the priests could not continue. Perhaps the apocalypticist anticipates the same type of experience in connection with the return of Christ.

2. The Promise of Christ's Return (1:7–8)

[7] **Behold, He is coming with clouds,**
   and every eye will see him,
even they who pierced him.
   And all the tribes of the earth will mourn because of Him.
Even so, Amen.
[8]**"I am the Alpha and the Omega, *the* Beginning and *the* End," says the Lord, "who is and who was and who is to come, the Almighty."**

Believer-priests are to "proclaim the excellencies of Him who has called you" (1 Pet 2:9 NASB). They are also "to offer up spiritual sacrifices acceptable to God through Jesus Christ" (1 Pet 2:5 NASB).

24 *Shekinah* [Heb. שכינה], meaning "that which dwells," is not a term found in the Old Testament. Appearing in the Targums, it was used in the Talmud to describe both the Word of God and the glory of God. For discussion of *shekinah*, see H. L. Drumwright Jr., "Shekinah," in *The Zondervan Pictorial Encyclopedia of the Bible* (Grand Rapids: Zondervan, 1975), 5:388–91. Regarding the various nuances of *glory* [Gk. δόξα] see the extensive discussions by Kittel and von Rad in *TDNT* 2.232–55. Especially interesting is von Rad's observation that "glory" was used "to define that which is intrinsically impressive in the being of God" (2:239).

In addition to such phenomena, his return will be missed by no one. "Every eye will see him" (Rev 1:7) constitutes a remarkable affirmation in light of the physics of the earth. Elaborate contemporary explanations as to how this might unfold are unconvincing. The explanation belongs to the imponderables of God. Clearly the majority of the inhabitants of the earth will be less than excited about his appearing. The fact that "those who pierced him" will also see him introduces the interesting information that his coming will be known even to those long since deceased. Attempts to suggest that this statement is an anti-Jewish threat are unworthy of the Jewish author who has so saturated himself in the Old Testament Scriptures.

The universal response of mourning is explicable in light of the rejection and crucifixion of God's anointed and as a consequence of the failure of most people in the world to receive the Messiah even after his incarnation and atonement. The situation is tantamount to an apartment owner returning unexpectedly as the tenants are trashing the premises. In this case not only has the world failed in its stewardship of God's grace in creation, but also the world has overwhelmingly rejected his grace in forgiveness. To this John adds not just the approving "amen" but also the simple Greek word *nai*, rendered by the NJKV "even so." The response would be more naturally rendered with a simple, emphatic "Yes!" As though to say, "Yes, this is that for which we have patiently waited. Yes, this is the triumph of justice."

As if to set the whole prologue in perspective, the writer concludes with a declaration of God's immutability. First, God is prior to all creation, and last he is the only One who can bring to consummation the purpose of the cosmos. The declaration is made by attributing to God the initial and ultimate letters of the Greek alphabet—alpha and omega. Further, this One who is Alpha and Omega is the One who continually exists (present active participle of the "to be" verb), who always was (imperfect of the same verb), and the One who is himself yet coming (a present middle participle). The term translated "Almighty" is a reference to the idea of the supremacy of God over all things. Some commentators suspect that John uses the word *pantokratōr* in contrast to the Roman emperors who spoke of themselves with the word *autokratōr* ("one's own master, absolute ruler").[25]

---

25 See W. J. Harrington, *Revelation*, SP 16 (Collegeville, MN: Liturgical Press, 1993), 67.

3. The Glory of Christ (1:9–18)

[9]I, John, both your brother and companion in the tribulation and kingdom and patience of Jesus Christ, was on the island that is called Patmos for the word of God and for the testimony of Jesus Christ.[10]I was in the Spirit on the Lord's Day, and I heard behind me a loud voice, as of a trumpet, [11]saying, "I am the Alpha and the Omega, the First and the Last," and, "What you see, write in a book and send *it* to the seven churches which are in Asia: to Ephesus, to Smyrna, to Pergamos, to Thyatira, to Sardis, to Philadelphia, and to Laodicea."

[12]Then I turned to see the voice that spoke with me. And having turned I saw seven golden lampstands, [13]and in the midst of the seven lampstands *One* like the Son of Man, clothed with a garment down to the feet and girded about the chest with a golden band. [14]His head and hair were white like wool, as white as snow, and His eyes like a flame of fire; [15]His feet *were* like fine brass, as if refined in a furnace, and His voice as the sound of many waters; [16]He had in His right hand seven stars, out of His mouth went a sharp two-edged sword, and His countenance *was* like the sun shining in its strength.

[17]And when I saw Him, I fell at His feet as dead. But He laid His right hand on me, saying to me, "Do not be afraid; I am the First and the Last. [18]I *am* He who lives, and was dead, and behold, I am alive forevermore. Amen. And I have the keys of Hades and of Death.

The apocalypticist next describes a moving personal encounter, which results in the writing of the book of the Revelation. In a sense the first eight verses of the initial chapter provide the rationale and the theological basis for the book, while vv. 9–18 recount the existential milieu that actually gave rise to the writing of the book. In this latter section John describes his location at the time of the heavenly visitation as well as the reason for his presence there. The precise identity of the recipients is clarified, and an astounding theophany introduces the reader to the experience of John, which provided the authority for his writing.

1:9–11 Heretofore John has identified himself only as the human transcriber (v. 4) and as a servant (v. 1). Now he indicates a certain intimacy with the readers, whom he clearly anticipates will know him. He is a brother and a companion in suffering. The use of "brother," a frequent metaphor, follows the familiar understanding of the people of God as the family of God throughout Scripture. God is the husband of his wife Israel in the Old Testament (Isa 54:4–6; 62:4–5; Hos 2:16–20). He is the Bridegroom coming for his bride in the New Testament (John 3:29; Eph 5:25–27; Rev 21:2). One of the facets of salvation is that the redeemed are adopted by God (Rom 8:15; 9:4; Gal

15

4:5; Eph 1:5), which makes them heirs and joint heirs with Christ (Rom 8:17). As such, they are the children of God (John 1:12), who is now both Creator and Father. As part of this family, they are brothers and sisters in Christ (Phlm 16; 1 John 3:13). Because John maintains such intimacy with his readers, he does not here appeal to his role as a disciple but rather to his status as a "brother." This familiarity suggests that John both knew and was well known by his intended readers, even though he almost certainly ultimately anticipated a far more extensive audience (Rev 10:11).

The term "companion" is a translation of *sugkoinōnos*, which combines the word *koinōnia* or "fellowship" with the preposition *sun* or "with." The word *koinōnia* refers literally to something held in common. Three specific items that John shared with his readers are mentioned; their suffering (*thlipsei*) or tribulation, the nature of the kingdom, and their patient endurance (*hupomonē*). All three of these come to believers as a result of being "in Jesus."

The linking of the three experiences shared by John and his readers is an interesting construction. G. E. Ladd is convinced that tribulation is the lot of the church in every age. Then follows the kingdom, which is gained by endurance. Ladd cites Acts 14:22, which indicates that one must enter the kingdom of God through many tribulations.[26] R. Mounce follows with confidence, citing Ladd's conclusion that "tribulation here includes all the evil which will befall the church, but especially the great Tribulation at the end, which will be only the intensification of what the church has suffered throughout history."[27] But surely this is difficult to square with the words of Jesus in Matt 24:21–22. There Jesus speaks of a great tribulation that exceeds any previous tribulation and even provides the guarantee that it will never be equaled thereafter. In fact, Jesus suggests that if the days were not shortened, no one would survive. This hardly sounds like mere intensification of what the church has always experienced. Furthermore, it fails to account for the fact that the overwhelming majority of sufferings described in chaps. 5–19 afflict the world as distinct judgments of God. The tribulations that John shares with his readers are the persecutions directed at the church, specifically by Jews and Romans. John, for example, is suffering nothing here as a judgment of God but is marooned on Patmos as an act of Rome. The localized sufferings of Christians, as in the case of John, are in strong contrast to the global, catastrophic upheaval chronicled by John in Rev 5–19.

---

26 Ladd, *Commentary on the Revelation of John*, 29–30.
27 Mounce, *The Book of Revelation*, 74–75.

A better approach to the passage is to understand that for those committed to Jesus, three experiences inevitably await them. First, they share in the kingdom of God. Already as indicated in 1:6, believers constitute a kingdom of priests. A future manifestation of the kingdom awaits, and they will share that also. But now during the inaugural phase of the kingdom, the church will also share in tribulation precisely as stated by Paul, who said, "Everyone who wants to live a godly life in Christ Jesus will be persecuted" (2 Tim 3:12). Kingdom citizens are expected to face these tribulations with patient endurance worthy of those who belong to the retinue of heaven.

In John's case, enduring tribulation for the sake of the kingdom translated into exile on the Aegean island of Patmos, where felons and enemies of Rome mined the quarries for the stone that satiated the Roman urge to build.[28] John's offense, in his own mind, was his devotion to the word of God and to the testimony of Jesus Christ. Here evidently the author believed that there is such a thing as the "word of God." Indeed, he believed that his own exile had resulted from his determination to share that word of God. A portion of that word was the testimony or witness of Jesus.[29]

The author suggests that he became "in the Spirit" on the Lord's Day (v. 10). Some interpreters suggest that the Lord's Day is synonymous with the Day of the Lord, to which John is escorted in the Spirit.[30] More likely this literary phrase, which became common parlance among believers in the second century, is first used here. Because of the Lord's resurrection on the first day

---

28 G. B. Caird notes two kinds of banishment that were practiced in the Roman Empire. The first, *deportatio in insulam*, involved confiscation of property and loss of civil rights. The second, *relegatio in insulam*, was more lenient and did not involve confiscation or loss of civil rights. While only the emperor could prescribe *deportatio*, a provincial governor could invoke *relegatio*, if he had a suitable island within his jurisdiction. Tertullian, trained in jurisprudence, records that this latter penalty was exacted against John (*A Commentary on the Revelation of St. John the Divine* [San Francisco: Harper & Row, 1966], 21–22). See also A. Y. Collins, *Crisis and Catharsis: The Power of the Apocalypse* (Philadelphia: Westminster, 1984), 102–4.

29 Some interpreters have not taken the expression "because the word of God" to be the reason for John's exile but rather the consequence of the exile in the providence of God. In other words, what emerges from the experience of exile is the word of God. But the emphasis of the whole text is that of tribulation. Almost certainly John's residency on Patmos was coerced and probably difficult. And this exile was doubtless result of the apostle's faithfulness to the word of God and to the testimony of Jesus.

30 See discussion in Charles, *Critical and Exegetical Commentary*, 1:22–23. Charles argues that this reference to the Lord's Day is the first mentioned in Christian literature.

of the week, the church hallowed that day, designating it as the Lord's Day and thereafter assembling together as a congregation regularly on that day. Though separated from his congregation at Ephesus by forty miles of Aegean water, John apparently sought the Lord on the Lord's Day.

Adventism has insisted that worship should be held on the Sabbath in keeping with the fourth commandment. While this is not the place to dwell at length on the arguments for the church's observance of the Sabbath, two observations can be safely ventured. First, there can be little doubt that John's reference to "the Lord's Day" is a reference to the first day of the week, the day of the resurrection of Jesus. By the same token, John felt the urge for special worship on that day, presumably a habit in the churches. Second, the early churches apparently often gathered more often than one day per week, suggesting that corporate worship is appropriate on any day. This is perhaps the intention of the exhortation of Heb 10:25 to assemble "all the more" as the day of Christ approached.

The text declares that John became *en pneumati*, "in the Spirit." The phrase seems to suggest something more than just a time of spiritual meditation. However, the usual Greek word employed to depict a trance (*ekstasis*) is not employed here. Efforts to find in this passage some equivalent to the popular practice of being "slain in the Spirit" will go begging. For one thing, there is no intermediary. The apostle's experience involves only God and him. For another, the language is chaste and unspectacular. The image evoked is of a man seeking the face of God in profound meditation, meeting God in an unaccustomed fashion such that a consciousness of time and other objects is transcended; and God begins to reveal in a rapid succession of stimulating visions a message to be wafted to the churches.

In this trance-like state, John heard a great voice, which had the clear tone and strong sound of a trumpet. But for all of its strength, the voice was intelligible; and John was instructed to write all that he would see on a scroll, which, in turn, would be sent to seven churches.[31] Now those previously identified only as servants (v. 1) and as seven churches (v. 4) are given specificity. These churches are located in seven cities in Asia Minor or southwestern Turkey. Ephesus and Pergamos were prominent, while Thyatira and Laodicea were

---

31   While the NKJV translators render the word βιβλίον as "book," the NIV translators render it as "scroll" and are right to do so. The term has its origin in the word βίβλος, a loan word from Egyptian, denoting the shrub of the papyrus and later its bark. "βιβλίον" is a diminutive of βίβλος. Eventually, it was employed in reference to almost any surface. Often the term is rendered "book," but only as regards content. The scroll was the usual way of preserving and transporting a text in John's day. See *TDNT* 1:615-20.

less well known. But each boasted a congregation of believers in Jesus, and the prophecy is addressed to them.[32]

1:12–16 Curiosity as to the source of such a mega voice induces John to turn in search of the speaker. Having turned, he is faced with seven golden lampstands and one like the Son of Man, who holds seven stars in his right hand. The tabernacle and temple claimed a seven-branched lampstand, so the idea was well known (Zech 4:2). These oil lamps were the principal source of light after sundown or in otherwise dark places, such as the tabernacle. These lamps are not accompanied by two olive trees, as in Zechariah, but rather by a remarkable figure who resembled the Son of Man.

Many contemporary Christians have seen or even purchased examples of these lamps from the Middle East. In some Bible lands, genuine ancient lamps, as well as a fair number of recently manufactured "antiquities," are available. The oil lamp has a long history, and the shapes and the kinds of clay used in construction often assist archaeologists in assigning a temporal period to a site of "ruins." Coming in varied sizes, some held enough oil to burn for twenty-four hours without refill. Others were small and needed to be refilled every hour or so. At least two apertures allowed the pouring of oil through the larger opening and the placement of a wick in the smaller. John notes seven of these golden lampstands. Whether each lamp had its own stand or was a part of what would later be called a "menorah," in which each lamp is connected to the others with a common stand, is not clear from the text.

Though the "son of man" title has been much debated as to both its origin and its significance, clearly Jesus used the term to describe himself (Matt 8:20; 9:6; Mark 2:28; Luke 21:27). Undoubtedly John, through his use of that terminology here, intends to identify this Son of Man he now beholds as the resurrected, glorified Christ. Furthermore, the similarity of what follows as a description of the "son of man" with Daniel's rehearsal of his own encounter with the Ancient of Days (Dan 7:8–14) is arresting. The author of the Revelation is giving notice of an exalted Christology, which is the warp and woof of the book of Revelation.[33]

---

32 C. J. Hemer, *The Letters to the Seven Churches of Asia in Their Local Setting*, The Biblical Resource Series, JSNTSup 11 (Sheffield, England: Sheffield Academic Press, 1989), offers the most thorough recent account of the historical and cultural milieu of the seven host cities. As for the order of the listing, see Thomas, *Revelation 1–7*, 93–94.

33 Discussions of the meaning of the "son of man" terminology and its selection by Jesus as his preferred self-designation are extensive. For an excellent older account, see G. P. Gould, "Son of Man," in *A Dictionary of Christ and the Gospels* (Edinburgh:

The exalted Christ is clad with a floor-length robe accented by a golden sash around the chest instead of the usual belt at the loins (v. 13b). His head and hair are like wool, as white as snow, and are testimonies to his hoary age, clearly suggesting his existence prior to the incarnation. The white color is probably an attestation to purity and holiness. In the earliest known commentary on Revelation, Victorinus of Petovium says, "By the 'whiteness of the head' is shown antiquity and immortality, and the source of his majesty, for 'the head of Christ is God.'"[34] John noted among his facial features only the hair and the eyes, the latter of which are described as "like blazing fire" (v. 14). The intention of the author is to depict the Son of Man as perceptive, even omniscient, able at a glance to see, comprehend, and judge even the most hidden mysteries. Later the same theme will be harnessed as a picture of unavoidability (Rev 19:12).[35]

Focus is next directed to the feet of the Son of Man, which are "like fine brass, as if refined in a furnace" (v. 15). The precise intent of the term *chalkolibanon* is not known. Sometimes the word is rendered "copper" or "brass" or even "bronze." The latter meaning is probable here.[36] Bronze was made by smelting copper and tin ores together with charcoal. This material boasted greater hardness than copper, while retaining some of the latter's characteristic gold color.[37] Here the writer seems to suggest irresistible strength.

T&T Clark, 1908), 659–65. For a more contemporary assessment, note I. H. Marshall, "Son of Man: Gospels," in *The IVP Dictionary of the New Testament* (Downers Grove, IL: InterVarsity, 2004), 1043–49. Clearly here Jesus is probably relating himself, as a messenger from God, to the preeminent use of the term in both Ezekiel and Daniel. Further, the reference to Dan 10:16 and Daniel's vision of the radiant ruler of the cosmos is probable in John's mind also. In addition, Aune's section addresses the technical subtleties of the issue (Aune, *Revelation 1–5*, 38).

34   *Revelation*, ACCS, 13.

35   B. Witherington III observes, "Upon analysis of the rhetoric of this section of Revelation, it becomes clear that it is the rhetoric of display, where the more hyperbolic and fantastic the image, the better. John cannot find words big enough to describe the awesome reality he saw, and so he is reduced to saying 'it was like' over and over again. The visual images are intended to be stunning, with the audience reacting similarly to the way John reacted. If this work was performed, meaning read aloud in dramatic and rhetorical fashion, one can only imagine the impact when first heard—vivid descriptions followed by loud sayings from heaven. There is not a syllogistic logic to Revelation, but there is a narrative logic, and later in this study I will talk about the story that John seeks to tell" (*Revelation*, 83).

36   LSJ, 1973.

37   D. R. Bowes, "Metallurgy of Copper," in *The Zondervan Pictorial Encyclopedia of the Bible*, (Grand Rapids: Zondervan, 1975), 4:208–9.

The voice, which before had been noted for its penetrating crescendo (like a trumpet), is now likened to the sound of rushing waters. Anyone who has ever stood near to a great cataract, such as Iguaçu Falls or Victoria Falls, has been impressed not only with the scenic grandeur but also with the roar of the falls, which drowns out every other sound. The resonance of the voice of the Son of Man is like one of these torrential falls.

The hand, the mouth, and the general effect of the face remain to be described (v. 16). In the hand of the glorified Son of Man, the author observes seven stars, while the opening of his mouth reveals a sharp, doubled-edged, broad sword. This last image, grotesque if reduced to canvas and paint, is intended by John to describe the effects of every spoken word of the Son of Man. His word is piercing, cutting, separating, revealing (Heb 4:12), and absolutely irresistible. As John gazed into the face of the figure, he could only describe the effect as being similar to an attempt to gaze directly at the radiance of the noonday sun.[38]

1:17-18 This description of the Son of Man demonstrates John's advocacy of high Christology, closely identifying Jesus with the Ancient of Days in Daniel. The Son of Man is regally attired, presented in holiness and awesomeness. John's response was to fall in awe before the feet of this kingly figure. This reaction, which seems to be the rule for response to appearances of God or of the glorified Christ (Isa 6:5; Dan 10:7–9; Luke 5:8), is in rather stark contrast to many contemporary expressions of those who claim to be in God's presence. With the same right hand, which only a moment before had cradled the seven stars, the Son of Man gently touches John and assures him that there is no need for fear. Fear is unnecessary because of the identity of the Son of Man. He precedes all, follows all, lives after having died, and now lives eternally. In addition, he holds the remedy for death and for the grave.

The instruction not to fear forbids the continuation of something already in progress. This is indicated in the grammar of the Greek New Testament by the use of the present imperative with the negative particle *mē*. To claim to be the first and the last is certainly a claim appropriate only for deity and explains why John needs to fear no longer. Christ describes himself as One who is living continually, though he "was dead," only to live again into the ages of the ages, the Greek way of saying "forever." Possessing keys is to guarantee entrance, which in this case is for liberation of those held captive. The captors are death and Hades. "Hades" is one of the more difficult concepts in the New Testament,

---

38 Victorinus of Petovium identifies the two edges of the sword as the Law of Moses and the Gospel (*Revelation*, ACCS, 15).

even though its broad sweep is fairly obvious. Joachim Jeremias shows the development of the Hebrew concept of *sheol*, which is translated in the Septuagint as *hadēs*. He further traces the various nuances of *hadēs* as found in the New Testament.[39] Here it is enough to say that *hadēs* represents the unseen, shadowy world of departed spirits and may be rendered "grave" only if the reader knows that this is not the same as "tomb" or "earthen grave" but more the state of being continually dead. Christ, through his atoning death and triumphant resurrection, has shown that he holds suzerainty even over the archenemy of the race and that he will unlock the prison doors for those who follow him.

4. The Mandate and the Key (1:19-20)

[19]**Write the things which you have seen, and the things which are, and the things which will take place after this.** [20]**The mystery of the seven stars which you saw in My right hand, and the seven golden lampstands which you saw are the seven churches.**

1:19-20   The mandate now given by the Son of Man constitutes the outline for the Apocalypse.[40] The servant is asked to write three things. He is to inscribe what he has seen. He is further to record "the things that are" and then to write of "the things that will take place after this." "Which you have seen" is a transla-

---

39   J. Jeremias surveys the lexical uses of *hadēs* in a succinct but perceptive article in *TDNT* 1:146–49.

40   Those who interpret v. 19 as an outline of the Revelation and also a grid for chronology include Criswell, *Expository Sermons on Revelation*, 1:181–82; Walvoord, *The Revelation of Jesus Christ*, 47–49; W. Scott, *Exposition of the Revelation of Jesus Christ* (Westwood, NJ: Revell, 1968), 50–51; Ladd, *Commentary on the Revelation of John*, 34; Charles, *Critical and Exegetical Commentary*, 1:33; Caird, *A Commentary on the Revelation of St. John the Divine*, 26; Morris, *The Book of Revelation: An Introduction and Commentary*, TNTC (Grand Rapids: Eerdmans, 1987), 56; and others. What is worth noting here is that dispensationalists are not alone in seeing this significance in the phrase. Aune is typical of these who find this position unconvincing (ibid.). He concludes, "Therefore it is best to take this verse as a modification by John of the widespread Hellenistic tripartite prophecy formula in which he appears to refer to the past, present, and future, but in actuality means to emphasize only the present and the future" (Aune, *Revelation 1-5*, 105). Beale finds this view of the book to be the "least plausible" but admits the importance of the verse, noting that, "The meaning of v. 19 is crucial since it is usually understood to be paradigmatic for the structure and content of the whole book" (Beale, *The Book of Revelation*, 216).

tion of the aorist active indicative of *eidō*, a Greek verb meaning "see." Though the essential sense of the Greek aorist tense is indeterminate as to the time of action, here clearly the command is to write the vision that the author has just experienced.[41] The readers in Asia will need to know the source and the reason for the book, and both are stated in chap. 1, the initial vision.

Next, the seer is to pen "the things that are." What logically follows in chaps. 2 and 3 is the message to seven historical congregations of believers. While the verses contain universally applicable truths for church life in every era, the assessments, promises, and warnings in the letters to these churches were addressed to specific situations in churches with which John was almost certainly familiar. Thus, these chapters have to do with "the things that are," that is things contemporary to the time of John's writing.

Then John is to record "the things which will take place after this," a translation of the Greek expression *meta tauta*, which the NKJV renders "after this." But to what does the expression refer? First, the book itself obviously references all the material after chap. 3 and the messages to the churches in Asia. How one handles the expression beyond this depends entirely on presuppositions as to the nature of the book (see Introduction).

If the book is viewed as allegorical in nature, then the *meta tauta* is nothing more than a division in John's outline, and the information belonging to that section is merely a highly stylized picture of the perpetual warfare between good and evil throughout the course of the present age.[42] Preterists and historicists treat the expression the same way except that they make some attempt to find historical substance in the remainder of the book.[43] However, both groups still see the events as an unfolding of the history of the church either in the time of John or else in the succeeding centuries. Many futurists share this perspective, preferring to interpret the events of the prophecy as the expectation of the church.[44] They differ, however, from the allegorical, preteristic, and historical

---

41 For the meaning of the aorist, see F. Stagg, "The Abused Aorist," *JBL* (1972): 222–31.

42 R. Bratcher, *A Translator's Guide to the Revelation of John* (New York: United Bible Societies, 1984), 17; Sweet, *Revelation*, 73.

43 D. Chilton, *Days of Vengeance*, 78–79.

44 Mounce (*The Book of Revelation*, 81–82); and R. H. Gundry (*The Church and the Tribulation* [Grand Rapids: Zondervan, 1973], 64–66) provide a thorough discussion from this perspective. S. Kistemaker holds the same view but with a different twist: "The seven lampstands are the seven churches. Notice the difference with respect to the first part of the explanation: the seven stars are angels of the seven churches. They are not called 'seven angels,' and in the Greek they are merely called 'angels' without the

methods in viewing the rest of the book as belonging to an end-time scenario. Meanwhile some futurists take *meta tauta* even more literally and understand the meaning to be "after the things of the churches." These interpreters believe chaps. 4–22 reflect a period after the church has been taken into heaven.

Interpreting the Apocalypse is in a sense simply a matter of identifying the various symbols. The first chapter leaves no doubt about the source of the scroll (Jesus) or its intermediaries (the angels and John). The recipients (seven churches) are apparent. But what is one to make of the seven golden lampstands and the seven stars in the right hand of the Lord? To see them is one thing. To identify their meaning in the text is a mystery (*mustērion*). A mystery in the New Testament refers to something that does not yield to any form of investigation. The meaning is discernible only as a direct act of God's revelatory will. Hence, the author is now informed that the seven lampstands represent the seven churches, and the seven stars are the "angels" of the seven churches.[45]

Possible meanings for the "angels," while numerous in their manifestations, are essentially two. Perhaps each of the seven churches in Asia (maybe all New Testament churches) have an angel assigned to the church as a part of God's providential oversight of the assemblies. Favoring such a concept is the fact that this view preserves the most natural reading of the Greek *aggeloi*, especially in light of the frequency with which such spirit beings appear in the Apocalypse.[46] Furthermore, the idea of angels assigned specifically to certain

---

definite article. The emphasis, therefore, falls not on the number of angels or the entire class of angels but on their capacity as being representatives. Pastors come and go but the pastoral responsibility remains." *Exposition of the Book of Revelation*, New Testament Commentary (Grand Rapids: Baker Academic, 2001), 103.

45   For a discussion of the concept of "mystery," see R. L. Saucy, "The Church as the Mystery of God," in *Dispensationalism, Israel and the Church: The Search for Definition* (Grand Rapids: Zondervan, 1992), 127–55.

46   Boring represents the view that these angels are actual angels relating to the churches at least for the purpose of the vision. He admits that the word sometimes references humans but finds such an interpretation here to be "pedestrian" (*Revelation*, 86–87). Reddish has a variation: "John says that the stars are the angels of the churches, the heavenly counterpart to the Christians. Thus the image of Christ holding the stars in his hand portrays Christ holding the churches" (*Revelation*, 47). S. S. Smalley sees the argument for angels being understood to be pastors, but he is unsure: "Since ἄγγελος (*angelos*) means 'messenger,' and the word is used in the Old Testament in relation to human as well as heavenly intermediaries (e.g. Gen. 19.1–23; Judg. 13.6; Zech. 4.1–6), it could be argued that the 'angels' in this context are the responsible leaders of the churches around John the apostle, authorized by the congregations themselves (cf. SB 3, 790–92).

tasks on earth is not entirely foreign to the New Testament. For example, women who pray or prophesy in the church are to have authority on their heads "because of the angels" (1 Cor 11:10). This suggests the presence of heavenly visitors in the worship of the congregations. Care is to be taken with children since their angels "do always behold the face of [the] Father" (Matt 18:10 KJV). While not supporting the popular idea of guardian angels, this latter passage does at least lend support to the heavenly assignments of angels.

Against this interpretation is the difficulty of discerning exactly how all this develops. If John is the last of the intermediaries receiving the message of the risen Christ assisted by angels, what is the purpose for John's writing the message from angels to give to other angels? And how, in turn, do these angels of the churches ferry John's words to their congregations? No precedent appears in the Bible for either writing or addressing churches by angels.

This point has led other interpreters to suggest that the older meaning of the Greek noun *aggelos* is in view, giving the word no more meaning than "messenger." Hence the "messenger" or "angel" of the church could refer to another person, a delegate from John, or perhaps even the pastor of the church. Since the pastor is the most likely to read the letter to the congregation, a certain logic supports the idea. Further, in classical Greek the word originally denoted a messenger. This interpretation might suggest a kind of augury, a nightingale or a loquacious person. Only in later Greek philosophy does the term seem to refer to what Liddell and Scott call "a semi-divine being."[47]

Dogmatism is not appropriate on the point and, fortunately, is not necessary to grasp the full intent of the text. While the author of this commentary leans toward the latter view, to observe that the "angels," whoever they may be, are providentially protected in the hand of the Son of Man is sufficient. Furthermore, these angels are pivotal links in the transfer of the Revelation to the churches.

The last identification in the chapter is that of the seven lampstands, which are now plainly said to represent the seven churches of Asia. A more appropriate symbolism for the church is scarcely imaginable. The church is like a lamp, a receptacle that is to give light in darkness. However, like a lamp, the church is helpless to fulfill its mission without fuel. Oil, throughout the Old

---

Nevertheless, . . . the seven letters of Rev. 2 and 3 are addressed to Asian communities as a whole, and not first to their presiding officers. Moreover the term 'angel' in Revelation, beyond Chapters 1–3 (59 times), is regularly used in association with heavenly—not human—beings." See S. S. Smalley, *The Revelation to John: A Commentary on the Greek Text of the Apocalypse* (Downers Grove, IL: InterVarsity, 2005), 58.

47 LSJ, 7.

Testament is used for anointing. Priests, kings, prophets, tabernacle furnishings, and books were anointed. Particularly in the case of Saul, the meaning of this anointing was that of the empowering for an assignment by the Spirit of God (1 Sam 10:1–11). Oil then had become a symbol for the Holy Spirit, a concept observable in the New Testament in James 5:14–15. When the church is filled with the Spirit of God, then she is able to give light to the world. Minus such presence and anointing, despite outer appearances, a church has no real possibility of fulfilling her Great Commission mandate.

II. A Message to the Churches
2:1–3:22

The messages to the seven churches, which occupy the focus of chaps. 2 and 3 in the Apocalypse, have received the most intense homiletical attention. While that may be regrettable in terms of the remainder of the book, even the casual reader would have to recognize the remarkable applicability of these letters to the postmodern church. In fact, pastors in every age of the church seem to have recognized the value of this congregational counsel.

To grant this pastoral value to the letters to the seven churches is to recognize something of a universal quality to the messages contained here. First, almost any church—even a contemporary congregation—has more in common with one of these historic congregations than with the others. For example, in some parts of the world, churches are Smyrnan churches, suffering almost overwhelming persecution and yet remaining true to their witness to Christ. Other churches are Philadelphian churches with an open door of missionary effectiveness. Other churches are Ephesian churches, busy but with misplaced priorities and thus not functioning out of a pure love for Christ. Others are Sardian congregations with a reputation for vitality but largely ineffective in what they do. There are Pergamian churches, married to the world with moral virtue fading or nonexistent. Thyatiran churches have delved deeply into heretical doctrines, while Laodicean churches are neither hot nor cold but just lukewarm.

Even within each local church one can find these same problems and virtues. For example, some Christians are Ephesian Christians, having lost their first love, while others are Philadelphian Christians before whom God has placed an open door, and so forth. In addition, some interpreters have purported to observe the history of the church in the messages to these seven churches. For example, one interpreter would see the Ephesian church as representing the church at the end of the apostolic era, continuing to function with a certain militancy but with a receding of its first love. The Smyrnan church is the era of the Roman persecution, beginning approximately with Trajan (AD 98) and continuing to the reign of Constantine (AD 313). The Pergamian congregation is thought to represent the church in the period immediately following Constantine's embracing of Christianity when the church became married to the world and then theologically and morally apostate. The church at Thyatira is usually viewed as the church of the Middle Ages, immersed in heretical teaching and moral turpitude. The church at Sardis is considered the church of the Reformation when some are found who have not defiled their garments, even though the majority of the church is still dead. The church at Philadelphia is pictured as the church of missionary expansion, beginning with the work of William Carey (1792) and continuing until the contemporary period. Finally, the church at Laodicea, which is merely lukewarm, is almost inevitably applied to the present period. From this application of the church through the ages, one may deduce that the coming of Christ must be near at hand, since the church is in the Laodicean age and in all probability nearing the conclusion of that age.[48]

Although many respected interpreters have held to such a church age view of the messages, there appears to be little evidence to commend such a view. These interpreters, who have often been premillennial in their theology, in fact, have adopted a page from the historicists but simply limited the application of those ideas to chaps. 2 and 3 rather than proceeding with an application to the whole book. Furthermore, they never exactly agree among themselves as to which church represents exactly which era. The lack of precision in this interpretation alone is enough to render it suspect.

Beyond that, as mentioned above, the universal value of the two chapters resides in the fact that people and churches remain much the same throughout history. What might be a bit disturbing to the interpreter is to note that five of the seven churches receive rather harsh critiques from the Lord of the lampstands, while only two of them are relatively free from such assessment. Unquestionably,

---

48 W. A. Criswell, *Expository Sermons on Revelation: Five Volumes Complete and Unabridged* (Grand Rapids: Zondervan, 1969), 2:34–44. For a more cautious defense of this idea, see J. Walvoord, *The Revelation of Jesus Christ* (Chicago: Moody, 1966), 52–53.

to conclude that two churches out of seven are fulfilling their calling according to the plan and purposes of God, in any era, would be suggesting too much. However, more often than not, the majority of those churches claiming Christ as head demonstrate more qualities of the less commendable churches in Rev 2–3.

Finally, note the consistent pattern in the messages to the churches. The message to each church is addressed to the city where the church resides and more specifically to the angel of that church. Then the ultimate author of the book, the Lord Jesus, reveals himself in each case in a way that is uniquely applicable to the problems and prospects of that individual local church. There follows an assessment of the church, which is sometimes positive (Philadelphia), sometimes negative (Thyatira), and sometimes mixed (Sardis). A negative assessment is followed by either counsel or threat or both, and comfort and commendation also follow when there is need. In each of the letters to the seven churches is a concluding promise accompanied by an admonition. Once again, the promises are uniquely applicable to the seven historic congregations in Asia Minor but, by extension, valuable for all generations.

The churches themselves were located in relatively well-known cities on major highways connecting the various Greco-Roman cities in what is today southwestern Turkey. In those days the land was known as Anatolia or Asia Minor. Assuming that the messenger bearing the Apocalypse came from the island of Patmos, the order of the letters in the Apocalypse would have been at least one logical way to proceed in the delivery. Ephesus was famous for its harbor. Besides, the identification of Ephesus as John's parish during his later ministry is widely held.[49]

Departing from Ephesus and moving due north along the coast of the Aegean Sea, one would arrive at Smryna. Continuing still further north, Pergamos would appear high on the mountaintop, spreading down into the plain below. From Pergamos, the mailman would have turned due east and slightly south to arrive at the lesser-known city of Thyatira. From there a relatively short journey moving still farther south and east would reveal the city of Sardis. Departing from Sardis, a turn a little farther eastward but still moving in a gen-

---

49 This, however, is contested by some. H. Koester points to the fact that in Ignatius' epistle to the Ephesians, written around AD 107, there is no mention of John of the Revelation. Neither does Polycarp, martyred bishop of Smyrna show familiarity. Papias is thought by Koester to be ambiguous on the subject. See H. Koester, "Ephesos in Early Christian Literature," in *Ephesos Metropolis of Asia: An Interdisciplinary Approach to Its Archaeology, Religion, and Culture*, ed. H. Koester, HTS 41 (Valley Forge, PA: Trinity Press International, 1995), 135–37.

erally southward direction finds Philadelphia. A little farther inland and mostly to the south, the city of Laodicea emerges, located close to and as part of a tri-city grouping including Colosse and Heirapolis. At this point the post would have returned far enough south to be almost even with Ephesus, which could be reached by a straight but somewhat lengthy journey to the west.

Mystery surrounds the question as to why these seven churches were chosen. As mentioned, for example, known congregations existed at Colosse (see Paul's letters to the Colossians and Philemon) and at Hierapolis (Col 4:13); and there were certainly churches that had been established by the early missionary expansion of the church in the late first century at multiple locations in Asia Minor. Speculation as to why these particular seven were chosen includes the possibility that John himself had some special relationship to these churches. Perhaps these were Johannine churches in the sense that John was involved either in the founding of the churches or in some pastoral assignment for the churches of that area. Other conjectures have to do with the suitability of the particular assets and liabilities associated with these seven churches in order to give a general message to whatever New Testament churches throughout the burgeoning Christian world might read the Apocalypse. However, information is probably insufficient to make such a determination other than to note the Spirit of God as guiding the human author John to select those seven recipients as ideal for the purposes of God's communication of truth to his people.

1. To Ephesus (2:1–7)

[1]"To the angel of the church of Ephesus write,

'These things says He who holds the seven stars in His right hand, who walks in the midst of the seven golden lampstands: [2]"I know your works, your labor, your patience, and that you cannot bear those who are evil. And you have tested those who say they are apostles and are not, and have found them liars; [3]and you have persevered and have patience, and have labored for My name's sake and have not become weary.

[4]Nevertheless I have *this* against you, that you have left your first love. [5]Remember therefore from where you have fallen; repent and do the first works, or else I will come to you quickly and remove your lampstand from its place—unless you repent. [6]But this you have, that you hate the deeds of the Nicolaitans, which I also hate.

[7]He who has an ear, let him hear what the Spirit says to the churches. To him who overcomes I will give to eat from the tree of life, which is in the midst of the Paradise of God.'"

2:1 Two essential matters constitute the greeting to the first of the seven congregations. First, the recipient is identified as the church of Ephesus. Second, the instigator of the message describes himself as the one who has the seven stars in his right hand and who walks among the seven golden lamps. Specifically, the message is directed to the angel of the church in Ephesus. Hemer has indicated at least five reasonably prominent understandings of the meaning of the angel. He speaks of these as (1) heavenly guardians of the church, (2) human representatives of those churches, generally identified as their bishops or pastors, (3) personifications of the churches themselves, (4) literally human messengers who were perhaps the postmen, or (5) usage of the term in "some complex and elusive way or at differing levels" so that no lexical equivalent tells the whole story.[50] Hemer sees problems with all these views and suggests that the problem is that of attempting to use the logical categories of the modern mind to handle the symbolism of the ancient world.

As indicated previously (see chap. 1), Hemer is right to be cautious since no one has been able to present irrefutable or even compelling evidence in favor of any of the above. Nevertheless, this author believes that some actual evidence does exist for views one and two, whereas views three to five apparently constitute little more than conjecture. The first view can garner support from 1 Cor 11, in which women who prophesy or pray in the assembly "ought to have a sign of authority" on their heads "because of the angels."[51] The passage

---

50 C. J. Hemer, *The Letters to the Seven Churches of Asia in Their Local Setting*, The Biblical Resource Series, JSNTSup 11 (Sheffield, England: Sheffield Academic Press, 1989), 32.

51 H. Alford strongly supports this position and attempts to discredit the idea that pastors or bishops may be in view. *The Greek Testament* (Chicago: Moody, 1958), 4.560–61. Richard Trench finds Alford's arguments unconvincing and presents a strong case for the idea that the angel of each church is its "bishop." He states, "I am very far from affirming that bishops were commonly called Angels in the primitive Church; or called so at all, except with a more or less conscious reference to this use of the word in the Apocalypse. There is a certain mysteriousness, and remoteness from the common language of men, in the adoption of this term, and such there is intended to be. It belongs to the enigmatic symbolic character of the Book, elevated in its language throughout above the level of daily life. Those to whom this title is ascribed are herein presented to the Church as clothed with a peculiar dignity, and are herein themselves reminded that they stand before One, whose ministries of grace and love they should be swift to fulfil [sic] on earth, even as those whose names they bear are swift to fulfil [sic] them in heaven. There is then a certain, though very partial right in what Origen taught; and 'Angel' *is* a heavenly title here; but a heavenly title which has been borrowed by earth, which has been transferred and applied

suggests that angels were not uncommonly present at times when the church gathered for worship. And that particular angels were given assignments to specific churches is certainly conceivable. Of course, this is limited evidence for supporting such an exegesis and is confounded by the logical problem of why a human messenger, John, would be responsible for bringing the message of God to an angel. The further difficulty has to do with the means by which such angels would then communicate the full messages to the churches. Although angelic messengers often communicate to the people of God, there is no other case in Scripture of this being done in epistolary fashion or to the extent found in the letters to the seven churches.

While the evidence favoring the view that the messengers here are to be equated with the pastors of the churches is also scant, hinging upon use in classical Greek literature and the Septuagint where the word *aggelos* is used to represent a human messenger rather than a spirit messenger,[52] nevertheless, such an exigency in the use of language would not be out of character in the Apocalypse. After all, lamps are churches, and beasts are kingdoms. Why would it then be thought out of character for John to choose the word "angel" to denote the pastor? The word would accord the pastors of the seven churches a modicum of protection and at the same time communicate relatively clearly to anyone who had some background in Old Testament imagery. In addition, the logical expectation of John would have been for the letters to make their way to the one individual in the church who would be most responsible for reading and interpreting the letter to the congregation. How that could have been anyone other than the pastor is difficult to imagine.

The above argument does not establish any certainty as to the identification of the angel of each of the congregations but does constitute the rationale for the hypothesis that the angel may have been the pastor. Accordingly, the angels of the churches will be thus understood in the commentary that follows.

---

to men; a transfer not without its analogies in the Old Testament (Eccles. v. 6; Hagg. i. 13; Mal. ii 7; iii. 1); and rendered more easy by the fact that Angel is a name not designating the *personality*, but only the *office*, of those heavenly beings by whom it properly is borne" (R. C. Trench, *Commentary on the Epistles to the Seven Churches in Asia: Revelation II. III* [Minneapolis: Klock & Klock Christian Publishers, 1978)], 59–60).

52 W. Grundmann (*TDNT* 1:74–76) cites, for example, Plato and his reference to Hermes, the messenger of the gods, as an angel. He also notes a general protection provided for the ἄγγελος since each viewed his task as essential. Birds are even sometimes presented as ἄγγελοι. Hecate who is linked to Artemis is said to be an "ἄγγελος." Similar uses are found in Josephus.

The letter is addressed to the angel of the church in Ephesus. By the close of the first century, the word *ekklēsia* had apparently been widely accepted as standard nomenclature for the assembled body of Christ in a given location. The nuances of the word can be found in discussions elsewhere.[53] At this point the etymology of the word itself, meaning "called out," as well as the historical use of the term, lend additional insight to the concept of the New Testament church. In the Greco-Roman city-states, the men of military age constituted the voting public; and when matters were to be decided, they were initially called outside the city to form the *ekklēsia* and to hear the matter before them. The emphasis in *ekklēsia* seems to be both on the nature of God's people as a group called out from former worldly pursuits and on the assembling together of that group for purposes of worship, teaching, and preparation for evangelization and missions.[54]

Ephesus, located at the mouth of a beautiful harbor where the Cayster River flowed into the Aegean, was the chief city of this section of proconsular Asia.[55] Its harbor was relatively easy to defend and had a certain beauty as one approached from the sea and noted the city cradled between the slopes of Pion and Coressus, the two prominent mountains in the area. However, what looked to be a perfect harbor at the mouth of the Cayster was sowing seeds of its own dissolution. City engineers were unsuccessfully doing all they could to stem the tide of the silting of the harbor prior to the time of the writing of the book of Revelation. Today's visitor to the city of Ephesus will likely dock at the city of Kusadasi and approach the city of Ephesus from that point. The untrained eye will be unable to discern the location of the harbor. From the uppermost row of the theater,

---

53 See P. Patterson, "The Church in the Twenty-First Century," in *Baptist Why and Why Not Revisited*, Library of Baptist Classics 12 (Nashville: B&H, 1997), 99–125. Also, J. M. Pendleton, *Church Manual* (Philadelphia: Judson Press, n.d.), 7. Concerning all conclusions about the nature of the church, H. Küng observed, "All commentaries and interpretations, all explanations and applications must always be measured against and legitimized by the message contained in Holy Scripture with its original force, concentrated actuality, and supreme relevance. Sacred Scripture is thus the *norma normans* of the Church's tradition, and tradition must be seen as the *norma normata*" (*The Church* [New York: Sheed & Ward, 1967], 16).

54 Some authors contest the idea of drawing conclusions about the nature of the church based on the etymology of the word. See E. D. Radmacher, *The Nature of the Church* (Portland, OR: Western Conservative Baptist Seminary, 1972), 110–13.

55 Major sources for the description of Ephesus and something of its storied history include Strabo, *The Geography of Strabo*, trans. H. L. Jones, LCL 196 (Cambridge, MA: Harvard University Press, 1988), 4:221–31. See also, S. Erdemgil, *Ephesus* (Istanbul, Turkey: NET Turistik Yayinlar, 1986).

one can better appreciate the place from which the sea receded and the harbor's former location. Just a few miles to the south, the city of Miletus where Paul met the Ephesian elders toward the end of his third missionary journey provides a far more spectacular perspective of the silting of harbors and the receding of the sea. At Miletus one can stand and look over a huge alluvial plain, once an enormous harbor that almost completely surrounded the city of Miletus.

However, other features contributed to the fame of Ephesus. Foremost among them was the Artemision, or the Temple of Artemis or Diana of the Ephesians. This structure, built in phases over a long period, had by the time of the writing of the Apocalypse become known as one of the wonders of the ancient world. The temple itself was 425 feet long by 220 feet wide and boasted 60 foot columns. In addition to being something of an architectural wonder, the temple served as the center for the localized worship of Artemis, to whom the citizens of Ephesus were probably more devoted than were the citizens of almost any other ancient metropolis. Beyond being a center of devotion for Artemis, the temple was a haven for those who fled from the law. The actual Temple of Diana sat approximately a mile from the edge of the city and was the first thing viewed when a ship came into the harbor. However, so frequent were its visitors seeking asylum that eventually the emperor extended the precincts to include even a portion of the city. This proved to be so disruptive to the life of the city that eventually the precincts were shrunk and asylum given only to those within the actual *hieron* of Artemis. Strangely enough, temples such as that of Artemis also tended to be banking centers so that riches were harbored where accused felons were also protected.

The cult of Artemis was a part of the mystery religions of the Greco-Roman world. Gritz notes that they are called "mysteries" because of the injunction to silence imposed on their respective followers, especially concerning the rites and ceremonies practiced in the inner sanctum of the temples. She also mentions that two features of these religions, notably asceticism and sensuality, were in contrast to one another. Gritz says, "With the emphasis on feeling rather than thought, these cults utilized many different means to affect the emotions and imaginations of their followers: drama, acts of purification, processions, fasting, and esoteric liturgies."[56]

The rites associated with the cult of Cybele, an earlier manifestation of

---

56 S. H. Gritz, *Paul, Women Teachers, and the Mother Goddess at Ephesus: A Study of 1 Timothy 2:9–15 in Light of the Religious and Cultural Milieu of the First Century* (Lanham, MD: University Press of America, 1991), 33.

the Phrygian Mother Goddess, were violent, orgiastic, and ecstatic. Self-inflicted wounds reminded them of Cybele's sorrows at the death of her consort Attis and called him back to life. By contrast, the Roman form of Mother Goddess Artemis is depicted by Homer as a chaste huntress.[57] In fact, Xenophon's novel *Ephesiaca* describes the local festival of Artemis involving a procession moving from the city to the sanctuary and featuring all girls of marriageable age and boys entering military training. Following the sacrificial offerings came horses, dogs, and hunting equipment. Anthia, at the head of this group, would be wearing a knee-length purple tunic. A fawnskin covered this garment, and she carried javelins and was followed by dogs. She was sometimes worshipped as the goddess in person.[58] In contrast to this chaste young huntress, the usual image of Artemis was the rather grotesque image of the goddess displayed with a headdress, necklaces, strange multiple round protuberances between the necklaces and waistband. She wore a skirt with animal motifs.[59] Most of the literature describes these apparent sacks on the statues as multiple breasts, an indication of her fertility. That popular wisdom has been challenged by two other options. One suggests that they have little resemblance to female breasts and are probably just a portion of the goddess's ceremonial garment. Another view suggests that they are the testicles of bulls offered in sacrifice. Whatever the case, the business of silversmiths and perhaps others in Ephesus in producing these figurines was an economic bonanza. The perceived threat to this business as a result of Paul's preaching of the Christian gospel led to the riot in the theater described in Acts 19:21–41.

As to the nature of the Artemis cult, Gritz believes that the cult was generally more circumspect than most. However, "virgin," as used of Artemis and other priestesses, is not in the sense of having experienced no intimacy with a man but rather in the sense of "not married or committed to one man." Hence, there almost certainly was a degraded and sensual aspect to the rites of the Artemision.[60]

The current archaeological investigation of the ancient city of Ephesus is probably the finest example of a massive project in archaeology anywhere in the

---

57 Gritz, *Paul, Women Teachers, and the Mother Goddess at Ephesus*, 37–39.

58 C. M. Thomas, "At Home in the City of Artemis: Religion in Ephesos in the Literary Imagination of the Roman Period," in *Ephesos Metropolis of Asia: An Interdisciplinary Approach to Its Archaeology, Religion, and Culture*, ed. H. Koester, HTS 41 (Valley Forge, PA: Trinity Press International, 1995), 85–86.

59 Ibid., 86–87.

60 Gritz, *Paul, Women Teachers, and the Mother Goddess at Ephesus*, 38–39.

world. The street coming from the harbor has been completely excavated, and as one approaches that famous broad thoroughfare, he becomes instantly aware of the magnificent theater looming ahead. This structure, which at one time would seat 24,000 people, is mentioned in the book of Acts. Luke records that the silversmiths of Ephesus and other citizens, who felt their economy endangered by the spiritual message of the apostle Paul, stood and shouted for hours, "Great is Diana of the Ephesians." At the theater the major thoroughfare turned to the south past a large agora and culminated at the library of Celsus, which not only has been excavated but also has undergone considerable reconstruction from existing materials. The library was one of the three most extensive collections in the Roman world. Bathhouse facilities, well known to any Greco-Roman city, are found directly across from the library of Celsus. The major street at that point heads north once again and begins rising up along the slope of the hill. A brothel has been identified next to the bathhouse and a slab in the street about a block removed points the way to the brothel, though most believe this inscription was not there in Roman times. Traveling in the northerly direction up that street, one passes many other public buildings, not the least of which is the important Temple of Domitian. This temple had significance for the entire book of Revelation.

While the social life of the city of Ephesus was probably no more degrading than that of any other large Greco-Roman city, and perhaps not as degenerate as Corinth, nonetheless, temple prostitution and mutilation in rituals were reasonably common in the city. Heracleitus, who was known as the weeping philosopher of Ephesus, lamented the vileness of the city. Clement of Alexandria said,

> Rites worthy of the night and of fire, and of the great-hearted, or rather of the idle-minded people of the Erechthidae, or even of the other Greeks, for whom there awaits after death what they do not hope. . . . Against whom, indeed, does Heraclitus of Ephesus prophesy? Against night-roamers, Magians, bacchanals, revelers in wine, the initiated. These he threatens with things after death and prophesies fire for them, for they celebrate sacrilegiously the things which are considered mysteries among men.[61]

When the Apocalypse was penned, the city of Ephesus probably boasted a population of somewhere between 100,000 and 250,000.

---

61 Clement of Alexandria, *Exhortation to the Heathen* (ANF 2:177), as quoted for "Fragment 124" in *The Fragments of the Work of Heraclitus of Ephesus on Nature*, trans. G. T. W. Patrick (Baltimore: N. Murray, 1889) [online]; accessed 12 August 2011; available from http://www.classicpersuasion.org/pw/heraclitus/herpate.htm; Internet.

In each of the letters to the seven churches, the Lord identifies himself in a particular way. To the church at Ephesus, he presents himself as the One who holds the seven stars in his right hand and walks up and down in the midst of the seven golden lampstands. The words "hold" (*kratōn*) and "walk" (*peripatōn*) are both present active participles, indicating that the action of the Lord is continual. The verb *krateō* has the nuance of not merely holding but also grasping or exercising power, whereas *peripateō* gives the sense of walking about. Since the discussion of 1:20 has already identified the seven stars as the angels of the seven churches, the message of the passage is clear. The angels, whoever they may be, are firmly in the control of the Lord. Furthermore, he walks about in the midst of the seven lamps, which have been identified as the seven churches. He is fully cognizant of all that is transpiring in the churches, and there is nothing hid from his view. Perhaps here is even more evidence to suspect that the "angels" are, in fact, "pastors." The Lord walks among his churches, knowing them thoroughly and grasping the lives and ministries of the pastors firmly in his own hand.

2:2-3 Commendation for the church at Ephesus is more assuring than has often been granted by commentators. From the perspective of candidates for a pastoral position, the information provided in vv. 2-3 would suggest Ephesus as one of the most hopeful assignments to be drawn. Having assured the church that the omniscient Lord is fully aware of their works, since after all he walks up and down in the midst of the seven golden lampstands, he goes on to describe precisely the nature of the works that he commends. There are four such affirmations: the church is commended for its labor, its patience, its inability to bear those that were evil, and for the fact that it had put to a test certain ones who claimed to be apostles and had found them to be liars. *Kopos*, translated as "hard work," refers to strenuous labor that induces weariness. However, the Ephesian church, in Jesus' name, had "endured hardships" (*kopiaō*, derived from *kopos*) but had not "grown weary" (*kamnō*). "Patience" translates *hupomenō*, which by way of derivation comes from *hupo* meaning "under" and *menō* meaning "remain" or "abide." The picture, therefore, is of one who, not wishing to shirk responsibility, bears the burden of it with determined zeal.

The church at Ephesus evidently had a penchant for purity and found that those who were evil were unbearable. The word "bear" in the NKJV text is a rendering of the aorist active infinitive of *bastazō*, meaning "bear" or "endure." The church of Ephesus finds the burden excessive to bear or carry; hence, she cannot tolerate those who are *kakous* or evil. The word carries connotations of harm and corruption.

Finally, undoubtedly because Ephesus was the chief city of proconsular Asia, the apostle Paul visited the city, and John himself ministered there. This cultural center and emporium would be a magnet for those claiming apostolic authority but who were embracing positions inconsistent with New Testament Christianity—most certainly the Nicolaitans mentioned in v. 6. By the concluding years of the first century, apostolic authority in the churches was coveted by some who observed the authority and what they believed to be the power vested in men like John, Paul, and Peter, who were called apostles. The precise identity of these false apostles is impossible to determine. Sweet supposes that their teaching bore resemblance to that of the Nicolaitans (v. 6) and comments that their "outward credentials would have made their falseness harder to discern."[62]

The church had demonstrated its unwillingness to tolerate such heresy. This lack of tolerance did not manifest itself only in terms of an attitude. Understanding the necessity for doctrinal purity, the Ephesian church tried or tested these teachers. "Tested" is a translation of the aorist active indicative of *peirazō*, suggesting a thorough examination. Since this is almost always an unpleasant pursuit, the Ephesian church appears all the more remarkable.

Painting a picture of church life in Ephesus on the basis of v. 2, one can possibly affirm that the church at Ephesus was a diligent, hardworking church characterized by great patience in the apostolic endeavor, a love for moral purity, and an unquestioned orthodoxy, which made the congregation quite different from her sister churches in Pergamos or Thyatira. Some of these issues are reemphasized in v. 3 where the author, once again, utilizes the concepts of patient endurance and the enduring of hardships in the name of Christ. Here, the word for endure, *bastazō*, is used rather obviously in contrast to its understanding in v. 2 where the indication is that the church could not bear or tolerate those who were wicked. While they could not bear or tolerate the wicked, they did bear and tolerate hardships in Christ's name. The particular method of that toleration is explicitly illustrated, "You . . . have not become weary." Both persecution and the pursuit of doctrinal purity wear down those of weak faith and commitment. Once again the picture is of the near perfect congregation.

2:4-6 Verse 4 introduces the most enigmatic portion of the letter to the first of the seven churches. Having commended the Ephesians for so many features in their ecclesiastical life, the Lord of heaven now says that he has one thing against them: They have forsaken their first love. The problem in interpreting the

---

62 J. P. M. Sweet, *Revelation* (Philadelphia: Westminster, 1979), 81.

verse is partly due to the fact that, unlike many of the other commendations or condemnations of chaps. 2 and 3, there is currently no known historical precedent in the city or church at Ephesus for this allusion. Consequently, commentators have felt the necessity to speculate. Accordingly, some have speculated that the reference is to loss of love for the brethren, with a censorious spirit characterizing the life of the church.[63] Those who favor this position point out that in churches such as Ephesus where orthodoxy is emphasized, a divisive spirit often develops. Others of a more evangelistic persuasion have sought to see a loss of love for lost people, but such a view seems without any real foundation in the text.

The speculation of the present commentator is that the reference is probably to a loss of love for Christ. How, someone may ask, could a church as perfect as that of Ephesus possibly fail to love Christ or God appropriately? But to ask the question is almost to answer it. What is in view in the church of Ephesus is a question of motivation and priority. Certainly, one can do all the right things and yet do them for an inadequate or ignoble reason. One can even do the right things for some of the right reasons but fail in the service of the Lord in terms of the noblest reasoning. Perhaps Ephesus had succeeded well in many areas, but the maintenance of that success had become more important than the motivation for service—namely, the love for Christ.

Two factors favor such an interpretation. First, the expression "first love" has biblical precedent since the highest commandment explicitly declared in both the Old and New Testaments is to "love the Lord your God with all your heart, with all your soul, with all your mind, and with all your strength" (Deut 6:5; Mark 12:30). Christian readers, and perhaps even Gentile readers, would instantly have taken the "first love" statement to refer to the need to love God.

The second reason favoring such an interpretation arises out of the admonitions for remedying the situation. The church is called first, to remember; second, to repent; and third, to activate themselves in terms of what they did at "first" or in the earliest days of the church in Ephesus. Here repentance is conditioned upon remembering. One finds difficulty in repenting of something for which he feels no guilt. The Ephesian Christians are asked to remember the lofty perch of the early development of the church when most and perhaps all of them had experienced the new birth, the release of the burden of the guilt of sin, and the elation of knowing that one is right with God. Those immediate postconversion days are, for the vast majority of new converts, days of service

---

63 Sweet, *Revelation*. See also W. J. Harrington, *Revelation*, SP 16 (Collegeville, MN: Liturgical Press, 1993), 55.

to the King motivated by gratitude and pure hearts of love. The Ephesians are to remember those days; and, having assessed the difference between their present habitual pursuits versus the love-motivated pursuits of the early years, they are to repent. Repentance turns from one way in order to embark on a new way. To repent is to seek the forgiveness of God and then be motivated to embrace the last part of the command, which is to "do the first works." This command is to pursue all of the activities above: adjudication in matters of heresy, endorsement of moral good, perseverance, and copious labor for the proper reason— the love of Christ. It is the love of Christ that "compels us" (2 Cor 5:14).

A significant threat hangs over the church at Ephesus like the proverbial sword of Damocles. If they refuse to repent, then the Lord himself will come and remove the lampstand from its place. How the auditors at the church of Ephesus responded when they heard this particular threat is difficult to imagine. In the midst of what seemed to be such a successful evangelistic and missionary foray into the most prestigious city of that part of Asia Minor, the congregation has been threatened with removal because of improper motivation. For the church in any era, this should give significant pause. Neither history nor appropriate activity is sufficient to demand the continued blessings of God; rather, the only motivation must be love for Christ.[64]

The threat for removal of the lampstand illustrates the justice, providence, and intention of God. Neither God nor his kingdom is endangered by the removal of a church, even one as successful and strategic as Ephesus. Improper motivation for noble work can only precipitate judgment. After refocusing on the exciting, initial days of service to Christ, these Ephesian believers are commanded to "repent" (metanoeō). The word is employed twice in the verse. This first use is in the imperative mood or mode. The imperative invokes an action that does not exist at the time of the command.

---

64 R. M. M'Cheyne catches the pathos of the passage when he says, "Now, do you know what it is to have been in an agony, when awakened by God—to have seen your corruptions? and do you remember what you felt when you saw an unveiled Christ—when you saw first a crucified Christ? and do you remember when your sins accused you, and when you said, *Behold, my Surety, who shall condemn*?" And again, "And do you remember when first you were introduced to Christ—when first you entered into the presence of God—when you were enabled to say, he *is mine*? You had often heard of him before; but do you remember the time when you first could say, 'My Beloved is mine'? What a burning love you had then in your breast!—do you remember the leap of joy that came into your bosom? This was *first love*, this *was the love of espousals*; and this is what you have left" (*The Seven Churches of Asia* [Fearn, Scotland: Christian Focus Publications, 1991], 10–11).

The second use of the term is an aorist active subjunctive. The subjunctive is the mood of a doubtful statement according to Robertson. He states, "I have ventured in my *Short Grammar* to call the subjunctive and optative the modes of doubtful statement, while the indicative is the mood of positive assertion and the imperative that of commanding statement."[65]

The Lord of the lampstands commands repentance, but the subjunctive use of the verb suggests two important truths. First, the outcome is not assured. The command is present, but what the Ephesians do about it, while not unknown to God, is according to their own choice. Second, there is the possibility that they will repent and not suffer the removal of their witness.

Verse 6 retraces the question of dealing with false teachers. The Lord reports that he is favorably disposed toward the church at Ephesus because they "hate the deeds of the Nicolaitans," which he also hates. Several important features need to be noticed here. First, the Lord does not say that the church at Ephesus hates the Nicolaitans or, for that matter, that he hates the Nicolaitans. Specifically, "the deeds" of the Nicolaitans merit that hatred. Here again is a lesson in every era for the church concerning her response to heresy. While the heresy and its practice must be despised, the heretic himself remains an object of God's love and potential candidate for redemption. In any era of the church of Christ, responding to heresy with hate for the heretic has not earned the blessings of God but rather his judgment.

Second, to hate everything God hates is altogether appropriate. Consequently, for churches in any era to entertain heresies such as those of the Nicolaitans in the name of tolerance or love is a clear violation of Scripture. The Ephesians are commended for hating what God hated, for testing those who claimed to be apostles and were not, and for revealing the deceit of these pseudo-apostles to all. On the surface these actions may not appear to be loving; but if the attitude and motive of the church is proper, such practices are the most loving conceivable response that one can make toward the heresy.

What was the nature of the Nicolaitan heresy? Again, inadequate information, in terms of literary discoveries or other biblical references, leaves one unable to speak with certainty about the Nicolaitans. Any number of solutions have been suggested, and those will be the subject of discussion regarding the church at Pergamos. Thomas suggests three general approaches to the identity of the Nicolaitans. The majority of the patristic evidence supports the

---

65 A. T. Robertson, *A Grammar of the Greek New Testament in the Light of Historical Research* (Nashville: Broadman, 1934), 927–28.

view that the Nicolaitans were followers of Nicolas, one of the seven deacons appointed in Acts 6. According to this view, Nicolas became an apostate and, according to most, adopted a form of incipient Gnosticism. Irenaeus, Tertullian, Hippolytus, Jerome, Augustine, and others embrace this view, though it is not universal among the Fathers.[66] This conjecture, if correct, might also explain why in the letter to Ephesus, the "deeds" or "works" of the Nicolaitans are hated, while the church of Pergamos is cautioned about the "teaching" of this group, which may spawn the despicable "works." Thomas thinks this interpretation is the best.[67]

A second view sees the Nicolaitans as relating to Gnosticism but not necessarily associated with Nicolas. A third view notes the similarity of the Greek name to "Balaam," which means "devourer of the people." As such, the heretical group may be the same or related to the followers of Balaam or Jezebel or both as mentioned in the letters to Pergamos and Thyatira. This view is articulated at some length by Stefanovic.[68]

---

66 Irenaeus identifies Nicolaitans as "the followers of that Nicolas who was one of the seven first ordained to the diaconate by the apostles. They lead lives of unrestrained indulgence. The character of these men is very plainly pointed out in the Apocalypse of John, [when they are represented] as teaching that it is a matter of indifference to practice adultery, and to eat things sacrificed to idols. Wherefore the Word has also spoken of them thus: 'But this thou hast, that thou hatest the deeds of the Nicolaitanes, which I also hate'" (*Against Heresies* [*AH*] 1.26.3, trans. A. Roberts and W. H. Rambaut, *ANF* 1:352). Hippolytus agrees: "But Nicolaus has been a cause of the wide-spread combination of these wicked men. He, as one of the seven (that were chosen) for the diaconate, was appointed by the Apostles. (But Nicolaus) departed from correct doctrine, and was in the habit of inculcating indifferency of both life and food. And when the disciples (of Nicolaus) continued to offer insult to the Holy Spirit, John reproved them in the Apocalypse as fornicators and eaters of things offered unto idols" (*The Refutation of All Heresies* 7:24, trans. J. H. MacMahon, *ANF* 5:115).

67 R. L. Thomas, *Revelation 1–7: An Exegetical Commentary* (Chicago: Moody, 1992), 147–51.

68 R. Stefanovic says: "It could be that the Nicolaitans were the same people as those in Pergamum. Nicolas and Balaam seem to be parallel terms; Nicolaos is a compound Greek word (*nikaō* and *laos*) and means 'the one who conquers the people.' Balaam can be derived from two Hebrew words—*am* ('people') and *baal* (from *bala*', 'to destroy' or 'to swallow'), meaning 'destruction of the people.' Thus *Nicolaos* could be the Greek version of the Hebrew *Balaam*, meaning exactly the same thing. So it could be that these two heretical groups were propagating the same error.

"According to Numbers 31:16, Balaam was the instigator of idolatry and fornication among the Israelites (Num. 25:1-6). When Balak, the king of Moab, realized that he could not

Criswell's perspective depended on the etymology of the word (*nikaō* and *laos*, meaning "people conqueror") wedded to his view of the seven churches representing seven eras of church history. For him, the Pergamian age of the church begins with Constantine's Edict of Milan (AD 313) and chronicles the marriage of the church to the world (state) resulting in an order of ecclesiastical prelates who ruled over the people of the church as an earthly sovereign might.[69]

At this point to suggest that regardless of identity they were at least organized enough to have representative presence in Ephesus and Pergamos and perhaps elsewhere as well is sufficient. The author of the Apocalypse clearly conceives them to be outside the parameters of orthodox Christianity and indeed the object of God's total rejection (see 2:14–15 for further discussion).

2:7   Finally, there is a promise immediately following the formulaic expression, "He who has an ear, let him hear what the Spirit says to the churches." Each of the seven letters concludes with this admonition. The formula raises the question of the incomprehensibility of anyone who would not want to benefit from the promises God offers to each of these seven churches. Nowhere is that more true than in the promise to the church at Ephesus.

As in each of the letters, the Spirit begins with the expression, "To him who overcomes." The word "overcome" could easily be misunderstood in the context. Some might wish to suggest that the word relates specifically to the problem mentioned in the particular church. A better approach is to understand each of the promises for overcoming in the light of Rev 12:11, "They overcame him / by the blood of the Lamb / and by the word of their testimony; / they did not love their lives so much / as to shrink from death." There the concept of overcoming is given definition. The one who overcomes does so based on two things. First is the blood of Jesus Christ, which alone makes it possible for God to be both just and the justifier of them who are saved (Rom 3:24).

---

fight against Israel militarily, he hired Balaam, a prophet of God, to curse Israel, hoping that God would forsake Israel and that Balak could conquer them. Instead of cursing Israel, however, from Balaam's mouth came only blessings. When Balaam saw that he could not curse Israel, he advised Balak to use sexual immorality and the glamor of pagan feasts—involving the eating of food sacrificed to the Moabite gods—in order to tempt many Israelites into sin. Thus, Balaam in the New Testament is regarded as a predecessor of the corrupt teachers in the church. Similarly, the false teachers in Pergamum, the ones 'who held the doctrine of Balaam,' enticed some of their fellow Christians 'to eat the things sacrificed to idols and to commit fornication' (Rev. 2:14)" (*Revelation of Jesus Christ: Commentary on the Book of Revelation* [Berrien Springs, MI: Andrews University Press, 2002], 111–12).

69   Criswell, *Expository Sermons on Revelation*, 2:34–44.

However, as Paul also says in Rom 10:9–10, an appropriation of that atonement must be made in the life of the believer, and hence one must "confess with your mouth . . . and believe in your heart that God raised him from the dead," which results in his salvation. Therefore, the second, appropriating basis for overcoming is the "word of their testimony."

Even the word "overcome" (*nikaō*) is instructive, derived from the name of the Greek goddess of victory—Nike. Of course, subsequently this name has been appropriated as the name of a missile in the United States arsenal as well as a name brand of athletic footwear. That same word *nikos* occurs as the first syllable in the word Nicolaitan (see v. 6). In any event, if one wishes to conquer, he does so on the basis of the blood of the Lamb and the word of his testimony.

To this individual God promises that he will give the right to eat from the tree of life that is in the midst of the paradise of God. Numerous aspects of this verse will interest the interpreter. First, there is the apparent connection to the Artemesion, which was the jewel of Ephesus. Excavations, as well as examination of historical sources, have led to the discovery that a large garden area was a part of the temple of Artemis in Ephesus. In the heart of that garden, there was a tree, either an oak or an elm. Hemer notes:

> For the Christian in Domitianic Ephesus these thoughts would, I suggest, have come to a focus in a contemporary reality. The words of the epistle contrasted with a shocking parody which the pagan cult of the city offered. At the heart of its changing fortunes was the theocratic power of the Artemis temple, marked by the fixed point of the ancient tree-shrine which was the place of "salvation" for the suppliant, surrounded by an asylum enclosed by a boundary wall. But this "salvation" for the criminal corrupted the city. The Ephesian who had to live with this problem understood the promise of a city-sanctuary pervaded by the glory of God. Of that city it was said: "There shall in no wise enter into it anything that defileth, neither whatsoever worketh abomination, or maketh a lie" (Rev. 21.27).[70]

This "tree-shrine" was a special holy place for the worship of Artemis. Evidence suggests that it was, in fact, the most sacred of all the parts of the famous temple shrine and may even have been spoken of as a "tree of life." The image appears in some form on most of the coinage from ancient Ephesus along with the additional symbols of the stag and the bee, which were associated with the worship of

---

70 Hemer, *Letters*, 51.

Artemis. John's readers in the church at Ephesus knew well that this tree could provide no life at all, but there was a tree with which the Scripture writers were familiar from the earliest biblical stories in Gen 1–3. This tree of life to which our first parents had access had been lost to them as a result of sin and their exclusion from the garden. John suggests that just as that tree of life was found in the midst of the initial paradise of Eden, so it has been somehow transplanted to "the paradise of God."

Paradeisos is the transliteration of a Persian loan word, which originally meant a beautiful garden. It occurs only three times in the New Testament. Elaborate explanations making paradise distinct from heaven are common among biblical interpreters, but usually these are given without actual biblical reference. There is a good reason. The three occasions in which paradise does occur suggest that "paradise" is synonymous with the unique dwelling place of God or heaven. The first occurrence is in the gospel narrative when the convicted felon on the cross with Christ is told by Jesus, "Today you will be with me in paradise" (Luke 23:43). Since according to the text, upon our Lord's physical demise his Spirit was with God ("into your hands I commit my spirit") and since a promise of some inferior destination would hardly have been great comfort to the felon, the place he was promised was probably none other than the presence of God.[71]

A similar situation occurs in Paul's description in 2 Cor 12 of his temporary transfer to "the third heaven" (v. 2), which is also identified as "paradise" (v. 4). Here is a clear indication that paradise and the third heaven, or the dwelling place of God, are viewed synonymously. All of the above is in perfect keeping with the understanding of the tree of life as being in the midst of the paradise of God in 2:7. In fact, such a remarkable tree is again in view in 22:2. The overcomer is promised that he will have the right to eat of the tree of life, which is in the midst of the paradise of God.

One final word needs to be said about the language of the text. What is promised to the believer is that there is a *xulon* of life in the midst of the paradise of God. Almost inevitably the word used for "tree" in Greek is *dendron*. *Xulon* by comparison generally means simply "wood" and is not infrequently used as a reference to the cross. Is it possible that in John's mind, the *xulon* of life mentioned here is none other than the cross of the Lord? Whatever the case, the promise is rich with the potential of a life eternal in the presence of God himself.

---

71 For further discussion of this and other related issues, see P. Patterson, *A Pilgrim Priesthood: An Exposition of the Epistle of First Peter* (Nashville: Thomas Nelson, 1982), 195-99.

2. To Smyrna (2:8–11)

[8]"And to the angel of the church in Smyrna write,

'These things says the First and the Last, who was dead, and came to life: [9]'I know your works, tribulation, and poverty (but you are rich); and *I know* the blasphemy of those who say they are Jews and are not, but *are* a synagogue of Satan. [10]Do not fear any of those things which you are about to suffer. Indeed, the devil is about to throw *some* of you into prison, that you may be tested, and you will have tribulation ten days. Be faithful until death, and I will give you the crown of life.

[11]He who has an ear, let him hear what the Spirit says to the churches. He who overcomes shall not be hurt by the second death.'"

Ismir, the third largest city in modern Turkey, is literally built on the rubble of ancient Smyrna. A visit to the sprawling, modern city formerly gave little opportunity for the inquiring Bible student to have much of an insight concerning how the city of John's era might have appeared. A small excavation, roughly the size of a football field, is all that one could view. However, recently that excavation has been extended; and the visitor is now able to visit several levels of ancient occupation and even to note that a long tunnel beneath the present city has been opened, leading to the heights of Mount Pagus, modern Kadifekale. Although there is sufficient danger in following the tunnel, the tourist, nonetheless, can see clearly its path and can thus get a better grasp of the extent of the first-century metropolis itself.

In all of Asia there was no more beautiful city than Smyrna—at least, if one wishes to accept the judgment of the citizens of Smyrna.[72] Possessing a

---

72 W. M. Ramsay waxes eloquent in his assessment. "And history has justified the prophetic vision of the writer. Smyrna, the recipient of the most laudatory of all the Seven Letters, is the greatest of all the cities of Anatolia. At the head of its gulf, which stretches far up into the land, it is at present the one important seaport, and will remain always the greatest seaport, of the whole country. But the same situation which gives it eternal importance, has caused it to suffer much tribulation. It has been the crown of victory for many victors. It has tempted the cupidity of every invader, and has endured the greed and cruelty of many conquerors; but it has arisen, brilliant and strong, from every disaster. No city of the East Mediterranean lands gives the same impression of brightness and life, as one looks at it from the water, and beholds it spread out on the gently sloping ground between the sea and the hill, and clothing the sides of the graceful hill, which was crowned with the walls and towers of the mediaeval castle, until they were pulled down a few years ago. The difference in the beauty of the city caused thereby shows how much of the total effect was due to that 'crown of Smyrna'" (*The Letters to the Seven Churches of Asia*

land-locked and protected harbor, the city began at sea level and climbed, even as it does today, up the slopes of Mount Pagus. What accounted for the beauty of Smyrna, however, was not its location topographically or geographically. Unlike many of the cities that developed without purpose and forethought, the city planners of Smyrna had obviously done their homework. There was a cohesiveness and a pattern about the architecture that made it blend together; and as one stood at the sea harbor looking up toward the top of Mount Pagus, he could see a panorama that led it to be called "a crown." Others referred to it as "a flower" or "a statue." There was a winding thoroughfare ascending Mount Pagus and passing the magnificent temples to Cybele, Apollo, Aesculapius, Aphrodite, and toward the top a notable shrine to Zeus himself. In addition to this plethora of religious sentiment, there is also evidence that Smyrna had become the center of Caesar worship for all Asia.

Other reasons accounted for the fame of Smyrna, not the least of which was its claim to be the birthplace of Homer. In addition, Lysimachus had restored the city to greatness after a period of nearly 400 years of decline. There are evidences, in fact, that Smyrna had lost its status as a city and had degenerated into a series of disorganized settlements only to be revived into urban status by Lysimachus. The suffering that had taken place in Smyrna, leading to its demise and then its rejuvenation, are noted by some writers from antiquity with a reference to the phoenix, the famous bird of Egypt, which died and was rejuvenated of its own strength.[73]

For Christians, Smyrna also became well known as the place of the execution of Polycarp, one of its most famous early martyrs. This bishop of the church in Smyrna was executed there on February 23, AD 155. The story of his martyrdom is recorded in a letter from the church of Smyrna to fellow believers in Philomelium, a city of Phrygia.[74] Part of his story seems to contain historically reliable material, while other parts seem to have included local and somewhat fanciful piety regarding some of the events surrounding the incident. The history of the city, together with its Christian persecutions and the ultimate martyrdom of Polycarp, provides some reason for assuming that Smyrna was actually a name for *myrrh*, the fragrant plant used in the anointing oil prescribed in the book of Exodus (Exod 30:22–33) and used in the process of embalming in Egypt and elsewhere. Its association with death (though not its

---

and Their Place in the Plan of the Apocalypse [Grand Rapids: Baker, 1963], 279–80).

73   Strabo, *Geography*, LCL 211, 5:421; LCL 223, 6:201–247.

74   *The Encyclical Epistle of the Church at Smyrna* 1–22, ANF 1:39–44.

only use) and suffering are well documented. Smyrna then was famous for two things: first, its beauty and, second, its suffering. Those two things will then be observed prominently in the letter to the church at Smyrna.

The widely publicized martyrdom of Polycarp adds pathos to the promise of suffering for the church of Smyrna. Trench suggested that Polycarp was probably the angel of the church at Smyrna, the pastor to whom this circular letter of the Apocalypse came.[75] Since his martyrdom is thought to have been in AD 155 and the Apocalypse delivered possibly as early as AD 95, a difference of sixty years, this conclusion at first blush may seem unlikely. However, it is not so unlikely when Polycarp's words are cited. At the time of his execution, Polycarp spoke of serving Christ for eighty-six years. Even if Polycarp meant that he was eighty-six years old at that point, his birth would have been about AD 69 or 70. Therefore, he conceivably could have been pastor of Smyrna at age twenty-five or twenty-six. If, on the other hand, the eighty-six years to which Polycarp refers is counted from his conversion to Christ, then he may have been a centenarian; and, if so, he probably was pastor of the Smyrnan church when the Apocalypse was delivered.

Irenaeus (AD 130–200) confirms that Polycarp knew John. In turn Irenaeus knew Polycarp and says:

> But Polycarp also was not only instructed by apostles, and conversed with many who had seen Christ, but was also, by the apostles in Asia, appointed bishop of the church in Smyrna, whom I also saw in my early youth, for he tarried [on earth] a very long time, and, when a very old man, gloriously and most nobly suffering martyrdom, departing this life, having always taught the things which he had learned from the apostles, and which the church has handed down and which alone are true.[76]

2:8 The Lord identifies himself to the angel of the church at Smyrna by saying that he is the First and the Last, an expression not differing radically from another found in the Apocalypse, when the Lord refers to himself as the Alpha and the Omega. The intent of both statements is relatively clear. The One who speaks to the angel of the church at Smyrna is the One who precedes all creation and will remain when all else is gone. The statement is in keeping with the high Christology provided the reader in the prologue to John's Gospel and moves along the same lines in suggesting both the preexistence and the eternity

---

75 Trench, *Commentary on the Epistles to the Seven Churches in Asia*, 59–60.
76 Irenaeus, *AH* 3.3.4, *ANF* 1:416.

of Christ. It serves as a providential reminder that whatever intervenes in the process of life and death is presided over by One who knew about all from its inception and ultimately controls it all.

Finally, the Lord identifies himself to the church in Smyrna in a way that undoubtedly recalled the history of the city as well as the history of the Christ. He describes himself as the One who "died and came to life again." The expression in the Greek New Testament is especially poignant. A literal translation would be "the one who became dead and is alive again."[77] The use of the aorist middle indicative of *ginomai* seems to stress that his death was neither an expected part of his existence as with all of the known forms of life, nor was it something that overtook him by surprise. There is certain purpose that seems to be written into the expression "who became dead." Whatever the case, the fact that he came back to life again is even more refreshing news to saints facing possible persecution and death than the story of the death and revival of the city could possibly have been to a Smyrnan citizen, though the allusion would not have been lost on the first-century reader.

Boring notes that each of the ascriptions to Christ in the letters to the churches establish a high Christology:

> We see that these Christological statements at the beginning of each letter are neither casually chosen nor mere decorations, but they serve a theological purpose. The Letters contain ethical instructions and warnings, the commands of the risen Christ for living a faithful Christian life in a trying situation. Such commands cannot stand alone; they are not general or obvious moral truths. Their truth is bound up with the truth of the vision 1:9–20, that the crucified one is the exalted Lord vindicated by God and made Lord of all. Here, as elsewhere, the ethical imperative is founded on the Christological indicative, the Christian life is founded on the fact and reality of Christ.[78]

MacArthur captures the mystery of the declaration:

---

77 R. H. Charles notes that ἔζησεν refers to Christ's resurrection and should be contrasted with that of the "demonic caricature in the case of the Antichrist: xiii. 14, ὃς ἔχει τὴν πληγὴν τῆς μαχαίρης καὶ ἔζησεν" (*A Critical and Exegetical Commentary on the Revelation of St. John*, ICC [Edinburgh: T&T Clark, 1920], 1:56).

78 Boring, *Revelation*, 88.

Here is a profound mystery: How can the ever-living One who transcends time, space, and history die? Peter reveals the answer in 1 Peter 3:18: Christ was "put to death in the flesh, but made alive in the spirit." He died in His incarnate humanness as the perfect sacrifice for sin, but now has come to life (by His resurrection) and lives forever "according to the power of an indestructible life" (Heb. 7:16; cf. Rom. 6:9).[79]

2:9-11 The remainder of the message to the church at Smyrna focuses as clearly on the events that probably called forth the writing of the Apocalypse as any other passages in the book (see the Introduction). Reference is made to the afflictions and to the poverty of the Smyrnan Christians. Further, the author refers to the slander of those claiming to be Jews, who, in his persuasion, do not qualify but actually belong instead to the synagogue of Satan. Rather than offering to the Smyrnan Christians a reprieve from this, the letter seems to anticipate the worsening of conditions but with the promise that God, being faithful to walk with them in the experience, will reward them.

As indicated in the Introduction, though the circumstances developing immediately following the fall of the city of Jerusalem in AD 70 may have initially looked hopeful to Christians, in the final analysis they actually created a more hostile climate, particularly for those who were Jewish Christians. Obviously the rebellion of the Jews in Palestine, which culminated in the war against Rome, the fall of the city of Jerusalem in AD 70, the mass suicide at Masada in the wake of Roman troops in AD 72, and eventually the further attempted rebellion of Bar Kochba—all had the effect of considerably diminishing confidence in Jewish people throughout the Roman world.

Even though a sense of well-being among Jews of the Diaspora was certainly wavering, the Jews were themselves increasingly concerned about the inroads of the new faith in the Nazarene within their own ranks. The fact that some Christians continued to associate closely with the synagogues was apparently not a matter of great comfort to Jewish leaders. The whole situation continued to decline with growing hostility of Jews toward Christians and fostering an increasing determination not to allow them to be identified with the synagogues. Apparently all came to a crisis point about AD 90 with the so-called "Curse of the Minim" in the *Shemoneh 'Esreh*. This document produced by the Jews is apparently to be understood primarily as an official effort to

---

79 J. MacArthur, *Revelation 1-11*, The MacArthur New Testament Commentary (Chicago: Moody, 1999), 69.

divest synagogue worship everywhere of those Christians who claimed also to be Jewish.[80]

The conflict was not dissimilar to the one faced in the modern state of Israel, not just regarding Israelis who become Christians but even the question as to whether anyone other than orthodox Jews would be considered Jewish. Shortly after the issuing of the curse of the Minim, the Emperor Domitian, who had come to the throne in AD 81, intensified his own determination to extend emperor worship and to bring to bay any unruly elements in the empire. The combination of all of these events left Christians in a serious predicament. Though they had never been granted the status of an approved faith in the empire, they had existed without serious discrimination and persecution by virtue of their identification as a sub-Jewish sect. The curse of the Minim generally brought that to an end; and Christians, especially Jewish Christians, found themselves facing the unhappy alternatives of either denying Christ and embracing Judaism entirely or else preparing themselves for serious persecution at the hands of both the Romans and the Jews. The latter were now seriously alarmed as to what might become of them if they allowed association with Christians in any way. There were certain centers—apparently Smyrna, Philadelphia, and perhaps to some extent Thyatira—where the persecutions faced by Christians at the hands of both Romans and Jews were particularly ominous.

The NKJV translation "I know your . . . tribulation, and poverty" is not inaccurate, but neither does it quite plumb the pathos of the words translated "tribulation" and "poverty." In the case of tribulation (*thlipsis*), the word has the sense of *extensive* tribulation rather than mere affliction. Poverty (*ptōcheia*) is not just general poverty but denies even the basics of life. The situation for believers in Smyrna was grave indeed, yet there remains the Lord's added assessment, "but you are rich!" Although sometimes difficult for humans to appreciate adequately, the Scriptures seem to make clear that for every injustice and evil suffered by believers on the earth, there is significant reward in heaven. Here is a promise that because of the conditions of poverty and tribulation through which Smyrnan believers were walking, their value in God's eyes was exponentially increasing.

A particular problem for these Christians was the slander of those who claimed to be Jews and who doubtless would have been thus identified by the community in Smyrna. The NKJV translation of "blasphemy" is true to the col-

---

80 Hemer developed this idea, which clarifies the warnings about Jews in the last decade of the first century. Again, the wording is, "May the Nazarenes and the Minim suddenly perish, and may they be blotted out of the Book of Life and not enrolled along with the righteous" (*Letters*, 149).

orful and expressive Greek term for which it is actually a transliteration. The NIV translators recognized that the word "blasphemy" generally has a relatively narrow technical meaning as it relates to God. Since apparently the blasphemy here is toward Christians, they have chosen to render it "slander." Though the exact nature of the slander is not revealed in the text, some of the characteristic accusations hurled at first- and second-century Christians are fairly well known. These included the charge of cannibalism since Christians were heard to talk about "eating the body" and "drinking the blood" of Christ. Because they had "love feasts," they were accused of immorality, specifically of an orgiastic nature. Because they did not accept the Greek gods, they were accused of atheism; and because they spoke so much about the fire of the Spirit and the fires of divine judgment, they were accused of being arsonists or incendiaries. In addition to that, their unwillingness to pay homage to Caesar as lord earned them the accusation of disloyalty to Rome. The intense loyalty they tended to demonstrate toward one another once they had embraced Christianity and the fact that particularly Jewish families would often virtually disown those who did become Christians were sufficient to have them charged with the splitting of families. Indeed, some of the words of Jesus might have been interpreted that way as when Jesus said that he had come to set "father against son and son against father, mother against daughter" (Luke 12:53). That Jews in Smyrna and elsewhere either developed or borrowed some of these slanderous accusations is easy to imagine.

At this point John makes an accusation, which, if read by any Jew, would have been one of the most astonishing accusations of the book. The Jews perpetrating this slander, in fact, are not Jews but "are a synagogue of Satan." However, John is not questioning their ethnic derivation; rather he is indulging in the same argumentation the apostle Paul used when he said, "For not all who are descended from Israel are Israel" (Rom 9:6–8). Paul's argument that "a spiritual Israel" exists is designed to suggest that the real essence of Jewry (i.e., the business of being the people of God) is bound up not with ethnic derivation but with spiritual obedience to God. This is not the same argument amillennialists have traditionally used in their effort to substitute the church for Israel in interpreting future promises made to Israel.[81] Those Jews who had been guilty of the slanderous accusations against the Christians had not only rejected the Jewish Messiah but had also indulged in behavior

---

81 For excellent recent discussions of "Replacement Theology," also known as supersessionism, see M. J. Vlach, *Has the Church Replaced Israel? A Theological Evaluation* (Nashville: B&H Academic, 2010) and Ronald E. Diprose, *Israel and the Church: The Origins and Effects of Replacement Theology* (Downers Grove: InterVarsity, 2004).

clearly forbidden by Jewish law in order to guarantee their own physical and financial well-being. Consequently, John did not hesitate to say that though they claimed to be Jews, they were not the people of God and were, in fact, a part of the synagogue of Satan.

Ford, in the Anchor Bible Commentary, calls attention to the interjection of "synagogue" in a book in which references to "church" abound:

> The use of the word "synagogue" is significant for it stands out in sharp contrast to "church" (or community, *ekklēsia*) employed elsewhere in these prophecies. The statement may indicate either that the speaker is a Jew who, like the covenanters at Qumran, regarded those not following his rigid way of life as the "assembly of Satan." In confirmation of this, we may refer to Ramsay, p. 272, who cites an inscription of the second century A.D. in which the *quondam* Jews are mentioned as contributing ten thousand denarii to the city. Bockh understood this enigmatic phrase to refer to persons who had forsworn their faith and placed themselves on the same level as the ordinary pagan Smyrnians. On the other hand, if the speaker were a Jewish Christian he would have seen the "genuine" Jew as one who found the messianic expectation fulfilled in Christ and the "pseudo-Jew" as one who persecuted those of the Christian way. According to tradition, in Smyrna the Jews joined the heathens in inciting the people towards the martyrdom of Polycarp. See Martyrdom of Polycarp 12. Thus the warning about accusation and imprisonment in vs. 10 may be linked with the Jews mentioned in the previous verse.[82]

The Smyrnan Christians are encouraged not to fear any of these sufferings. However, rather than following this prohibition against fear by the promise of alleviation of difficulty, the Lord offers instead the promise that some of them were going to be sent to prison as a part of testing and that they were going to experience tribulation "for ten days." Further, some were to anticipate martyrdom since the Lord urges them, "Be faithful, even to the point of death, and I will give you the crown of life."

Various views concerning the possible meaning of "ten days" have been offered by different interpreters. The truth is that this remains another one of those passages awaiting further light. The possibility that "ten days" was a numerical means indicating the thoroughness of persecution to befall them is cer-

---

82   J. M. Ford, *Revelation*, AB (Garden City, NY: Doubleday, 1975), 395.

tainly a possibility.[83] That any code was needed on that particular point, however, is unlikely. The suggestion of other commentators that the "ten days" referred to ten distinctive persecutions that would come and be felt at Smyrna across the succeeding years is also speculative at best. More recently, with some merit Hemer has argued, based on inscriptions and ancient literature, that the "ten days" was a period in which those who were to be sent forth in gladiatorial combat were imprisoned.[84] If Hemer's interpretation is right, then it is conceivable that Christians in Smyrna were actually being forced to enter gladiatorial combat or, at least, to be the targets of such combat. Prior to their appearance in the arena, they experienced a ten-day incarceration followed by almost certain death. Ramsay had a similar view:

> The State would not burden itself with the custody of criminals, except as a preliminary stage to their trial, or in the interval between trial and execution. Fine, exile, and death constituted the usual range of penalties; and in many cases, where a crime would in modern times be punished by imprisonment, it was visited with death in Roman law.[85]

The promise to the church is that if they are faithful unto death, the Lord will give them a crown. First, recall that the famous golden street that wound up Mount Pagus was studded like a crown with various public edifices and temples of notable architectural achievement. Therefore, for Smyrnans to speak of the city itself as "the crown" was not unusual. But the Lord's message to the suffering saints of Smyrna is that the city itself may be a crown in the aesthetics of the builder and the beholder; but a permanent crown of life, a crown enduring forever, would be the gift of the risen Christ to those who were faithful even to death.

The crown promised here is the *stephanos*, the victor's crown, as opposed to the *diadēma* or diadem. The *stephanos* was not worn by royalty, at least not as a sign of that position, but rather was awarded to the athlete who had won an athletic event. In other words, it was a "winner's crown," and the Smyrnans are invited to see themselves, whatever their sufferings, not as losers but as winners.

---

83 Criswell, *Expository Sermons on Revelation*, 2:34–44.

84 Hemer, *Letters*, 69. Charles suggested that the designation simply meant "a short time" and cited Gen 24:55 as an example (*Critical and Exegetical Commentary*, 1:58). Ford, following Charles, arrives at the same conclusion but cites Daniel's testing (Dan 1:12–14) as the probable background (Ford, *Revelation*, 395).

85 Ramsay, *The Letters to the Seven Churches*, 279–80.

The final promise coming in v. 11 is that those who overcome will not be hurt at all by the second death. Notably no one is excluded from being hurt by the first death. Smyrnan Christians would certainly have read this promise as a two-edged sword. On the one hand, they could anticipate that some would be martyred. On the other hand, no matter what happened about the first death, those who overcome would not be hurt by the second death. Exactly what John intends by this "second death" only becomes apparent in 20:6, 14. Those who participate in the first resurrection are promised that "the second death" has no power but that they shall be priests of God and of Christ and shall reign with Christ for a thousand years (20:6). On the other hand, those who are judged at the Great White Throne judgment and found guilty by virtue of both their works and the fact that their names are not written in the Lamb's Book of Life are cast into the lake of fire, and this is "the second death." Consequently, the first death is defined as the separation of the soul from the body, whereas the second death is the separation of the soul from God and its confinement in the place the Bible denominates as hell. Overcoming saints at Smyrna may have to face physical death, but they will have no fear of the second death and by it will be untouched and unhurt.[86]

3. To Pergamos (2:12–17)

[12]"And to the angel of the church in Pergamos write,

'These things says He who has the sharp two-edged sword: [13]'I know your works, and where you dwell, where Satan's throne *is*. And you hold fast to My name, and did not deny My faith even in the days in which Antipas *was* My faithful martyr, who was killed among you, where Satan dwells.

[14]But I have a few things against you, because you have there those who hold the doctrine of Balaam, who taught Balak to put a stumbling block before the children of Israel, to eat things sacrificed to idols, and to commit sexual immorality. [15]Thus you also have those who hold the doctrine of the Nicolaitans, which thing I hate. [16]Repent, or else I will come to you quickly and will fight against them with the sword of My mouth.

---

86 Hemer interestingly observes: "A further facet merits notice. The theme of the imminent Parousia of Christ is explicitly mentioned in every letter of the seven except the present. Its absence in this case invites explanation. The answer may be that the Parousia was expected to terminate the church's interim period of suffering. That would be the occasion when Christ would bestow the crown of life. There was no need to stress it as a warning or threat" (*Letters*, 74).

[17]He who has an ear, let him hear what the Spirit says to the churches. To him who overcomes I will give some of the hidden manna to eat. And I will give him a white stone, and on the stone a new name written which no one knows except him who receives *it*.'"

Second only to the extensive archaeological investigation at Ephesus, Pergamos offers at least a whole day of intriguing discovery for those interested in history, archaeology, and interpretation. The citadel of Pergamos rises more than 1,000 feet above the plain of the river Caicus and is recessed from the Aegean coast by approximately ten miles. The winding road by which the citadel is gained not only provides a delightful view of the valleys below but also allows the observation of the construction of a major dam, creating a large lake nearby and enhancing the beauty of what was already a salubrious location.

The modern town of Bergama sits beneath the watchful eye of the citadel, and the city in Roman times was apparently large enough to occupy much of the space where the modern city sprawls below. In fact, the famous hospital and temple of Aesculapius is located on the plain close to a large modern military compound. The neuter form of the name Pergamos is found in Strabo and Polybius, whereas Pausanias and some others use the form Pergamos. Earliest written records of the existence of the city of Pergamos come from the fifth century before Christ. From that time until the relative stability of the last half of the first century and the *Pax Romana*, Pergamos, the scene of periodic resistance to the regimes that held sway in the area, was often embattled. The fortress itself, located atop the mountain and looking to the south, was formidable; and even today much of the fortification of the citadel and some of the vestiges of the military stratagems in use for the defense of the citadel are still clearly discernible, even to the untrained eye.

The most prominent feature on the citadel was the gleaming temple structure and altar dedicated to Zeus Soter, or Zeus the Savior. Attalus I, who ruled from 241 to 197 BC, also referred to himself as Attalus Soter, apparently a title that he took after defending the city against the marauding Gauls. This temple and the altar to Zeus were unquestionably the most spectacular features to greet the eye of the visitor coming through the valleys from any of three directions. To some, the great altar appeared to be something of a throne. In 88 BC Mithridates VI came into possession of the realm and was greeted as both *theos* and *sōtēr* (god and savior). This title was nothing new since Eumenes II, who ruled from 197 to 159 BC, had also desired to be referenced as both god and savior. All of this description is sufficient to establish the prevalence of the worship of rulers in the environment of Pergamos.

The additional feature giving fame to the city was the hospital and temple of Aesculapius, who was also called Aesculapius Soter. The symbolic serpent in the worship of Aesculapius has passed through time and today may be found in the intertwined serpents that are a prominent medical symbol even in the modern era.[87] The cult of Aesculapius Soter not only dealt with physical healing (though much of the effort was psychological in nature) but also developed a doctrine of personal salvation, which was almost certainly known by the residents and viewed as a contrast to the salvation in Christ. Galen, the famous physician, had perfected his medical expertise in the care of wounded and dying gladiators and had then expanded that medical practice through the hospital in the temple of Aesculapius.

The temple of Aesculapius itself has been extensively preserved and offers insight into the combination of the practice of medicine and psychology in the first century. Present in the temple complex is a theater and various baths, some of which were rather unique engineering achievements enabling the raising or lowering of the water so that those immersed in the bath were unable to account for the phenomenon. Some suggest this entered into the healing process so that the rising of the waters would be an indication that Aescula-

---

87 Visitors to Pergamos are given the story of the patient who came to be treated at the temple of Aesculapius. Galen ostensibly turned him away, seeing that he was terminally ill. On the way home the sufferer encountered two snakes drinking milk from a bowl. Availing himself of what he thought would poison him, the man drank from the bowl and was healed by the brew. Galen then adopted the sign of the two serpents as the signet for Aesculapius. See S. Gökovali, *Pergamum* (Izmir: Ticaret Matbaacilik, 1965), 15. Galen (AD 129–199) was a physician for gladiators. By the time he arrived at Pergamos, he was gaining a considerable reputation as an anatomist and philosopher, especially invoking the thought of Plato and Hippocrates. His pharmacological and dietetic writings constituted a summary of what was known up to this time. See L. Edelstein, "Galen," *OCD*, 454–55. See in the same source an entry on "Asclepius" (129–30). Actually, the caduceus or the symbol of medicine and healing with a wand and the two snakes intertwined has a fascinating history. The word caduceus is Latin, derived from the Greek term *kērukeion*, which in turn comes from *kērux* or herald, one of the terms used to describe a preacher. This *kērukeion* designated the wand carried by Hermes, the messenger of the gods. According to mythology Hermes had thrown his wand between two fighting snakes who became entwined around it. Some say that the snakes are copulating so that Hermes brought love out of hostility. Historically, however, there seems to be no connection between the wand of Hermes and that of Aesculapius and the medical profession. For a fascinating account of this, see W. J. Friedlander, *The Golden Wand of Medicine: A History of the Caduceus Symbol in Medicine*, Contributions in Medical Studies 35 (New York: Greenwood Press, 1992), 5–21.

pius had honored the request for healing. A long tunnel connected the bath-house area with the solarium, which was a large round building boasting what amounted to a track. Small apertures in the top of the tunnel enabled priests of Aesculapius to speak promising words to devotees walking through the tunnel in search of healing. Arriving in the solarium, some sources indicate the presence of hundreds of nonpoisonous snakes, whose permanent residence was the solarium. With the assistance of certain drugs, a participant in the activities of the solarium might sleep for a period of time, during which contact with one of the serpents could result in instant healing. Of course, in a study of ancient sources, determining the extent to which such psychological measures were mixed with actual practice of medicine is difficult, but at least what was possible from a medical perspective in that particular era was known in one of its advanced forms at Pergamos.[88]

2:12–13   The Lord identifies himself to the church at Pergamos as the One who has the sharp, double-edged sword, a reference to the previous identification of the risen Christ where the sharp sword came from the mouth of the risen Lord (1:16). The sword here is the *rhomphaia*, a long, flat, heavy sword. Even though the sword is probably to be identified with the words of the risen Christ at the beginning of the letter, nonetheless, this identification carries a rather ominous tone. The omniscient Lord continues by indicating that he is cognizant that the church lives "where Satan has his throne." The reference here has numerous possibilities. Hemer, once again, mentions five plausible interpretations: (1) an allusion to Pergamos as the center of pagan religion in general; (2) the acropolis itself, which looked like a great throne when viewed by a traveler approaching from Smyrna; (3) a reference to the throne-like altar of Zeus Soter previously mentioned; (4) a reference to the Aesculapian occult, particularly because of its identification of Aesculapius as "the savior;" and (5) the city's reputation as a center for emperor worship.[89] Hemer concludes that the fifth answer is best.

However, is that choice necessary in this particular situation? Generally, a particular text speaks to a specific situation, but seemingly for this author's view to imagine that all of these features in the perspective of the church contributed to a general sense of the presence and power of Satan is not far-fetched. This being the case, the Lord may simply be indicating through John

---

88   Further information about Roman Pergamum and its antecedents can be found in Strabo, *Geography*, 6:163–71. Also, see Hemer, *Letters*, 78–105.

89   Hemer, *Letters*, 84–85.

that he is well aware of the efforts of Satan to destroy the work of Christ and of Christians in the city of Pergamos through its various pagan affections.

The Lord has a strong commendation to make of the Pergamian church by observing that they had remained true to his name and had not renounced the faith even in the days when Antipas was put to death in the city where Satan lives. Nothing is known of Antipas. Indeed, even the spelling of the name is the subject of some disagreement since some conjecture Antipa, where texts read Antipas.[90] While nothing is known of this particular Christian, he had paid for his faith with his life. An interesting question is raised about the expression "martyr." The Greek word, *martus*, normally means "witness." However, most interpreters have seen the developing use of the word in this passage as coming to mean one whose witness for Christ led to his death. Thus the term gradually assumes an extended significance, which seems to be the appropriate interpretation here in light of the fact that the witness is described as having been killed where Satan dwelled. In any event the church at Pergamos could obviously anticipate persecution, not so much from the Jewish sector as in Ephesus, Smyrna, and Sardis but from the Roman establishment with its focus on the worship of the emperor and the pantheon of Roman gods.

The NIV suggests that Pergamos's believers had remained true to Christ's name and did not renounce faith in Christ. As noted in our text above, the NKJV renders the first phrase as, "And you hold fast to My name" and the second phrase as, "and did not deny My faith." Either translation pictures remarkable faithfulness. The first expression literally states that "you have held on to my name." The second says, "You did not deny my faith."[91] In this more

---

90   B. M. Metzger, *A Textual Commentary on the Greek New Testament* [*TC-GNT*], 2nd ed. (Stuttgart: Deutsches Bibelgesellschaft/German Bible Society, 1994), 664. Metzger speaking for the committee of translators says, "Since the context seems to demand the genitive Ἀντιπᾶ, several modern exegetes (including Swete, Charles, Zahn) adopt Lachmann's conjecture that, after accidental dittography of the definite article (*ANTIΠAOOMAPTYC*), the first omicron was taken as a sigma. The Committee, however, regarded the conjecture as more ingenious than compelling."

91   *The Interpreter's Bible* carries the note, "Persecution had previously broken out in Pergamum, but the members of the church there had been faithful, for they held fast to Christ's name and did not deny the faith. Ἀρνέομαι translated as deny, like μάρτυς, became a technical term among the early Christians, being used to describe those Christians who denied the name and faith of Christ when confronted with the prospect of persecution. The Christians at Pergamum had remained loyal even though one of their number, a certain Antipas, had died as a faithful martyr, the only defensible rendering in this context. It is possible, in fact, that his fate had served to strengthen the faith of his fellow Christians. Un-

common reading, the initial phrase suggests personal faith in Christ while the second may include faithfulness to "the faith" (i.e., to all that Christ is and what he taught). In any case this affirmation is remarkable.

2:14-16   The concerns expressed about the church at Pergamos are set in contrast to the achievements of the church. Specifically, they are more than one as denoted by the expression "few" (*oligos*), which generally carries the meaning of small in number or stature. But, if the few items, namely, the teaching of Balaam and the Nicolaitans, are not numerous, they are nevertheless serious enough to command one of the more serious threats to any of the churches.

Two items are specified as problematic: The church allows people to function who have the teaching of Balaam, and they also allow the teachings of the Nicolaitans. Hemer comes to the conclusion that the two are essentially the same.[92] At least two considerations seem to mitigate against Hemer's conclusion, however. First, the use of the word *oligos* here does imply more than one problem. That is more explicable if the teachings of Balaam are viewed in some sense as distinct from that of the Nicolaitans. A second reason for not accepting Hemer's view is found in the distinct mention of both problems. It would have been easy enough for the apocalyptic writer to give some indication that the two were connected. While this argument is from silence and consequently a weaker argument, its conclusion in a sense is rather obvious based on the inclusion of the two separate items in the text.

This analysis, of course, gives little explanation for the nature of the two problems, so one must now turn his attention to an assessment of these. Doubtless, the Christian residents of Pergamos would have had no difficulty identifying that about which the apostle spoke; but the distance in time, history, and culture has made the identification of the two problems much less certain. Of the two, in fact, identifying the teachings of Balaam seems easier.

Here, however, the problem is exacerbated somewhat by the fact that the Old Testament passages in view, while extensive, are less than explicit as to the exact nature of the offense of Balaam. As a matter of fact, Balaam, while certainly not commendable, comes off looking better in the Numbers account than he does in subsequent interpretations of that passage in both the New Testament and rabbinical literature. In any event the reference is to Num 22–24. The account of Israel's harlotry in Moab follows in Num 25.

---

fortunately nothing else is known concerning this early martyr." Lynn Harold Hough, "The Revelation of St. John the Divine: Exposition," *IB* 12 (Nashville: Abingdon Press, 1957), 385.
    92   Hemer, *Letters*, 87–94.

The book of Numbers devotes a long section to the incident involving Balaam and Balak, covering chaps. 22–24 and portions of chap. 31. Moab is terrified at the prospect of the obvious success of Israel, even as she marches her vagabond horde through the territory of Moab. So, Balak, who at that time is the king over Moab, becomes convinced that he cannot make a successful battle out of a direct confrontation. Thus, he determines to bring Balaam, who claims to be a prophet, to curse Israel. In a long and strange incident, Balaam receives clear indication from God that he is not to go to Moab or curse Israel. His violation of the mandate of the Lord places him in the position of experiencing a confrontation with an angel and receiving a rebuke from the donkey that provided his conveyance. Eventually, Balaam does reach the overlook where he is to observe two million plus children of Israel. Balak who has invested heavily in the enterprise waits triumphantly for Balaam to curse Israel. Rather than cursing, however, Balaam repeatedly blesses the children of Israel, each time explaining that he cannot curse that which God has blessed. After the fourth such failure, Balak refuses to invest any further in Balaam. Balaam returns to his own place, and Balak goes his way.

Based on chaps. 22–24, Balaam would not get a failing grade for his obedience to God—even though his presence made his actions less than commendable. However, the early verses of chap. 25, after Balaam left, record that Israel committed harlotry with the women of Moab. Little in chap. 25 suggests that Balaam had anything to do with this. However, Moses speaks in chap. 31:

> "Have you allowed all the women to live?" He [Moses] asked them. "They were the ones who followed Balaam's advice and were the means of turning the Israelites away from the LORD in what happened at Peor, so that a plague struck the LORD's people" (15–16).

Here the reader is introduced to the fact that before Balaam departed, he had given to Balak counsel, which perhaps can be reconstructed as follows: "I cannot curse what God has blessed; but you have paid me handsomely, and I do know people very well. These folks have been in the wilderness a long time, and you have many beautiful women in Moab. I suggest you send your women among them, and my guess is that with their behavior they will bring down God's curse upon themselves." Balak followed this advice; Israel did exactly what Balaam had anticipated, and the children of Israel brought the plague and curse on themselves with their own actions.

This incident in the history of Israel had come to represent, along with Aaron and the golden calf, the two most despicable moments in the history of the exodus and subsequent wilderness wanderings. Every child growing up in a Jewish home was introduced to the failure of the Jewish people in this incident and the danger of being seduced by Balaamite teachers. Interestingly, cases in post-Christian Jewish literature are substantiated where Jesus of Nazareth is compared to Balaam with the insinuation that the teachings of Jesus are the teachings of Balaam.[93] Such could even have been taking place in the city of Pergamos. If so, John's reference to the teachings of Balaam would be even more explicit than otherwise.

More probably, however, the apostle has simply taken an ignominious incident in the life of Israel to focus on the fact that rampant immorality was being tolerated in the church at Pergamos. However, the reference is not merely to the practice of sexual immorality (*porneuō*) and eating meat sacrificed to idols but also specifically to those who were presenting the teaching (*didachē*) of Balaam. Hemer has once again suggested the difficulty in imagining how this can be interpreted in any way other than as an antinomian emphasis, which may well have been a misrepresentation of the teaching of the apostle Paul, as (found in 1 Corinthians), in the church in Pergamos. Hemer has appropriately alleged that the apostle Paul had to war against two opposite philosophies during his own ministry: legalism and antinomianism. He further suspects that both the Nicolaitians and those who were promoting the doctrine of Balaam may have been part of an early or incipient Gnosticism, making itself known primarily in the ethics of antinomianism.[94]

In Acts 15 at the Jerusalem Conference, the participants, after having sought the mind of the Holy Spirit, reported that Gentiles were not to be asked to keep the law, including circumcision, in order to be recognized as having been genuinely saved and consequently as being a part of the church. To the contrary, they were to be asked only to be faithful in three areas of "separation" from their Gentile counterparts. They were (1) not to eat anything that had been strangled or to eat blood, (2) not to eat things sacrificed to idols, and (3) to abstain from fornication. However, by the time the apostle Paul addresses the specific question of the eating of the meat sacrificed to idols in 1 Cor 8, he does not reference the Jerusalem Conference or the apostolic agreements. Instead, Paul develops the theme that eating meat sacrificed to an idol in itself is not an endorsement of the way of the gods since everyone knows that idols actually do not exist as gods in the world (1 Cor 8:4). On the other hand, the apostle Paul

---

93 Hemer, *Letters*, 90.
94 Ibid., 91.

warned against using liberty as an occasion to bring about stumbling of weaker brothers and urged a series of practical considerations to be employed by believers before they partook of meat that had been offered to idols.

The situation in Corinth, of course, may not have been the exact situation to which the apostles had spoken in Acts 15. Even if the situation is identical, however, conceivably Paul, in dealing principally with the Gentile church at Corinth, has not felt referencing the apostolic mandates of Acts 15 advisable but has chosen to attack the problem from the perspective of "Christian responsibility." Hemer is certainly not out of line to speculate that what may have happened at Pergamos and elsewhere is that the antinomian fringe may have seized upon the apostle Paul's failure to cite the decision of the church fathers in Jerusalem and misconstrued Paul's approach as being open to such practices. They may actually have cited the apostle as support for their position. However, while such a position is entirely possible, the explanation could also be considerably less complicated. What was going on at the Pergamos church may simply have been that there were people advocating and practicing an antinomian lifestyle, which included the "freedom" to eat that which had been sacrificed to idols.

John, knowing well the traditions associated with Balaam, simply attaches Balaam's name and intention to make the practice appear as opprobrious as possible to the church at Pergamos. The church in every era has difficulty in dealing with heresy and immorality. A portion of the reason for this can even be remotely construed as noble. Often the church does not want to deal with those problems because most people in the church are very much aware of their own sinfulness and cite passages such as the instruction of Jesus "to take the plank out of your own eye" before you attempt to "remove the speck from your brother's eye" (Matt 7:4). Who are we to sit in judgment on another? Furthermore, invariably dealing with either heresy or immorality in the church never wins friends, introducing as it does a measure of confrontation, conflict, and uncertainty into the life of the congregation. This may well have been exactly the case at Pergamos. Therefore, John characterizes the teaching and practices of these people as being that of Balaam and argues that the church must take action if it wishes to be the recipient of the blessings of God.

Still to be determined is the nature of the teachings of the Nicolaitans. Of many conceivable suggestions for the meaning of Nicolaitanism, the following three may be noted. One of the earliest references attempting to define them is that of Irenaeus, who in *Adversus Haereses* suggests that they were the followers of Nicolas, one of the seven originally set aside ostensibly to serve as the first deacons of the New Testament church in Jerusalem (see Acts 6:1–6). According to Irenaeus, Nicolas and his followers had fallen into the error of Cerinthus of Ephesus, who apparently had adopted a gnostic cosmology. This view had also led him to embrace a form of adoptionism in his Christology, which claimed the divine Christ came on a human Jesus, perhaps at his baptism, and left him prior to his crucifixion.[95] In favor of Irenaeus' position are two things. First, his proximity to the events themselves and his many ties to the situation in Asia Minor place him as the best of all possible sources for understanding the passage. Furthermore, the present commentator tends to attach great significance to the perspectives of Irenaeus, especially regarding the origin and meaning of the Apocalypse.

On the other hand, even though Irenaeus does have proximity to the time of the writing of the Apocalypse, the actual intervening time is approximately 90 years because *Against Heresies* was not penned before AD 182. Furthermore, clearly Irenaeus had no opportunity to quiz the apostle John as to the meaning. Consequently, even his relative proximity to the time of the writing of the book is insufficient to render his interpretations certain.

A second possible view sees the Nicolaitans as a group seeking to impose a unique authority over the people of God in the Pergamian and Ephesian congregations and perhaps throughout Asia Minor. This view derives from breaking the word *Nicolaitan* into its two parts: *nikos* meaning "conqueror" and *laos* meaning "people." Hence, according to this view, they were people conquerors. The view has generally been held by Protestants who manifested the greatest paranoia about the Roman church. Seizing upon this view, they attempted to argue that this movement was the beginning of priesthood in the early church, which ultimately resulted in the practices described favorably by Ignatius in literature written only a short time after the Apocalypse itself.[96] Thus, the Nico-

---

95   Irenaeus ties the Nicolaitans to Cerinthus (*AH* 3.11.1, *ANF* 1:351–52). "John, the disciple of the Lord, . . . seeks, by the proclamation of the Gospel, to remove that error which by Cerinthus had been disseminated among men, and a long time previously by those termed Nicolaitans, who are an offset of that 'knowledge' falsely so called."

96   Ignatius, probably the third bishop of Antioch, was martyred in AD 107. Not too long before that he wrote to the church at Smyrna saying, "Let no man do anything connected with the Church without the bishop. Let that be deemed a proper Eucharist, which is [administered] either by the bishop, or by one to whom he has entrusted it. Wherever the bishop shall appear, there let the multitude [of the people] also be; even as where Christ is, there does all the heavenly host stand by, waiting upon him as the Chief Captain of the Lord's might, and the Governor of every intelligent nature. It is not lawful

laitans move from a priesthood of all believers to a segregated and authoritarian ecclesiastical priesthood in which all the authority of the church would be vested. Divested of its anti-Romanist polemic, the view is not totally without value since it is inevitable that people would be arising within the early church who would make every attempt to solidify their own authority and rule.

The third view is that of Harnack who flatly advocated that the Nicolaitans were essentially a gnostic sect.[97] Hemer concludes that some of Harnack's reasoning did not follow; but by the same token he arrives at essentially the same position, divested of the nomenclature of Gnosticism by simply concluding that "Nicolaitanism was an antinomian movement whose antecedents can be traced in the misrepresentation of Pauline liberty and whose incidence may be connected with the special pressures of emperor worship and pagan society."[98] As indicated, he goes on to identify Nicolaitanism as being the same as the teaching of Balaam.

One can only conclude, as is often necessary with obscure references in the Apocalypse, that the best option is to hazard a guess. I do not think Hemer is correct about equating Nicolaitanism with the teachings of Balaam, and I certainly suspect that the Nicolaitans advocated some special authority, or at least insight, as putting them in a privileged position over the common people of the church. Nevertheless, they probably shared with those maintaining the teachings of Balaam a rigorous disdain for anything they considered to be legalism. The result was for them to embrace the opposite tendency or antinomianism. Even more conceivable is that Harnack is right about the development of Gnosticism and that there was actually a form far more prevalent at the close of the first century than contemporary scholars have been willing to allow. With its basic overemphasis on Platonism (i.e., diminishing the physical and invoking the spiritual), this Gnosticism would have impacted both the theology of the incarnation and the ethics of the early church communities, especially in Asia Minor.

---

without the bishop either to baptize, or to offer, or to present sacrifice, or to celebrate a love-feast. But that which seems good to him, is also well-pleasing to God, that everything ye do may be secure and valid" (*Epistle of Ignatius to the Smyrnaeans* 8, ANF 1:89–90). Many have contested the authenticity of the epistles ascribed to Ignatius arguing that they represent conditions that existed in the churches of a much later date. If genuine, these epistles do demonstrate a changing role for pastors at an earlier stage of Christian history than usually posited.

97 A. Harnack, "The Sect of the Nicolaitans and Nicolaus, the Deacon in Jerusalem," *JR* 3 (1923): 413–22.

98 Hemer, *Letters*, 94.

So one may conclude that both those "advocating" the teaching of Balaam and the Nicolaitans represent the "few" concerns that the Lord had about the church at Pergamos. They are serious, for he promises that unless repentance is immediately forthcoming, the Lord himself will become their opponent and will fight against them with the sword of his mouth. Whether the mandate to repentance is addressed to the antinomians themselves or to the church is not clear in the text. Perhaps the best option is to see the warning as addressed to both but with not much hope of repentance on the part of the antinomians. Consequently, the church is to act by way of church discipline and exclude them from the fellowship of the church. Otherwise, they will face the judging hand of God.

2:17 If there have been difficulties in identifying those who held the teaching of Balaam and the Nicolaitans, the three promises offered to the overcomers may be even more challenging. First, those who overcome are promised that they will be given hidden manna. Second, they are promised a white stone. And, third, a new name will be written on that stone, which will be known only to those who receive it.

The reference to manna is easily identifiable since in Exod 16:32–34 God miraculously fed the children of Israel daily with manna from heaven. What makes the reference obscure is the reference to hidden manna. The solution could be as simple as arguing that just as the Egyptians and other surrounding people had no idea how the children of Israel sustained themselves in the wilderness, so the whole world will be amazed at the sustaining providence of God for his churches and for those who overcome. However, there is also a possible reference to incidents reported in Jewish literature relating to the fall of Jerusalem in 586 BC. The authors of *Second Maccabees* and *Second Baruch* in Jewish pseudepigraphal literature record that Jeremiah was warned to take the "tent of meeting," the ark, and all of its contents out of the temple just prior to the fall of the city, and that he took them to Mount Sinai where they were hidden underground until the time when the Messiah would come. The ark, according to Heb 9:4, contained not only the tablets of the covenant but also Aaron's rod, which miraculously budded, and a pot of manna—all wonderfully preserved. The ark and the tabernacle furnishings have thus been hidden and remain secluded until the Messiah, who alone knows their location, arrives. At that time the pot of manna would again be unveiled, and the hidden manna would be available.[99] If

---

99 *Second Baruch* 6:7–9 records the interruption of Baruch's lamentation over the pending loss of Jerusalem in 586 BC: "And I saw that he descended in the Holy of Holies and that he took from there the veil, the holy ephod, the mercy seat, the two tables, the holy raiment of the priests, the alter [sic] of incense, the forty-eight precious stones with which

the reference is to such Jewish tradition, it almost certainly does not anticipate a literal fulfillment of the prediction in the pseudepigraphal texts but rather utilizes such as a method of suggesting that the overcomers will experience the manna of heaven uniquely prepared for them in that day.

The possibilities associated with the white stone are much more numerous. No explanation has proven strong enough to convince even a majority of the commentators. Hemer's listing of possibilities include the following: (1) a jewel in Old Testament or Jewish tradition; (2) the judicial *calculus Minervae*, the casting of a vote for acquittal; (3) a token of admission, membership, or recognition; (4) an amulet with a divine name; (5) a token of gladiatorial discharge; (6) an allusion to a process of initiation into the service of Aesculapius; or (7) simply as a writing material whose form or color was significant.[100]

Hemer himself provides lengthy discussion of the evidence favoring each of the propositions. However, he does conclude with the view that holding the white stone as a jewel in the Old Testament or Jewish tradition is likely unsus-

---

the priests were clothed, and all the holy vessels of the tabernacle. And he said to the earth with a loud voice: Earth, earth, earth, hear the word of the mighty God, and receive the things which I commit to you, and guard them until the last times, so that you may restore them when you are ordered, so that strangers may not get possession of them. For the time has arrived when Jerusalem will also be delivered up for a time, until the moment that it will be said that it will be restored forever. And the earth opened its mouth and swallowed them up" (J. H. Charlesworth, ed., *Apocalyptic Literature & Testaments*, vol. 1 of *The Old Testament Pseudepigrapha* [Garden City, NY: Doubleday, 1983], 1:623). *Second Maccabees* 2:4–8 speaks similarly: "Further, this document records that, prompted by a divine message, the prophet gave orders that the Tent of Meeting and the ark should go with him. Then he went away to the mountain from the top of which Moses saw God's promised land. When he reached the mountain, Jeremiah found a cave-dwelling; he carried the tent, the ark, and the incense-alter [sic] into it, then blocked up the entrance. Some of his companions came to mark out the way, but were unable to find it. When Jeremiah learnt of this he reprimanded them. 'The place shall remain unknown,' he said, 'until God finally gathers his people together and shows mercy to them. Then the Lord will bring these things to light again, and the glory of the Lord will appear with the cloud, as it was seen both in the time of Moses and when Solomon prayed that the shrine might be worthily consecrated'" (*The New English Bible: The Apocrypha* [New York: Cambridge University Press, 1970], 250). These passages plus references to the copper scroll from Qumran have given rise to fascination with the missing ark of the covenant, which in the Maccabean source is said to be at Sinai but is also variously reported at Nebo, a cave near Qumran, Ethiopia, and at the Vatican—to name only a few. Speculation and efforts to locate the ark and its "hidden manna' have become common.

100 Hemer, *Letters*, 96.

tainable. Various degrees of likelihood are assigned to the others. According to some, there is an allusion to those who had been involved in gladiatorial games and had been spared the necessity of further risk of life. They were given a kind of *tessera*, which exempted them from any further obligation. Most examples of this belong to the first century BC or AD and come from Rome, but that such a practice would have been known in Pergamos also—especially when one remembers that Galan the physician had learned much of his medicine as a result of working with the gladiatorial games—is not inconceivable. In his concluding statements, Hemer was struck when visiting Pergamos by the fact that the acropolis and most of the buildings there show a darker, less beautiful granite in contrast to the blocks of gleaming white marble that are occasionally seen, especially at the reassembled altar of Zeus on the summit. White stone may well have been one of the first things the visitor to Pergamos noticed, and the impression may have been an indelible one. However, the color white is often associated with holiness, and more probably the white stone may merely be John's reference to the imputed holiness and righteousness of the overcomer. Scott sums up the matter, "It is the expression of the Lord's personal delight in each one of the conquering band."[101]

The question of the new name is somewhat more easily decided. In Rev 19:12, the returning Lord is said to have "a name written that no one knew except Himself." He also carries recognition as the Word of God, King of kings, and Lord of lords; but this one new name that no one knows save He Himself is a similar avowal to what is found in the promise to the overcomers at Pergamos.

Since in antiquity the power of a name was de facto an exercise of authority, the unknowableness of the name Christ carries seems to be a reminder that whatever one may know of him, he being God transcends anything ever communicated to humans. This is part of who God is. To assign to the overcomers at Pergamos a name that no one but the recipient of the name knew is not only to suggest the authority of the divine Christ over the believer but also to establish a personal intimacy with the individual believer.[102] Whereas the idea of real inti-

---

101 W. Scott, *Exposition of the Revelation of Jesus Christ*, 4th ed. (Westwood, NJ: Revell, 1968), 79.

102 J. Newport says, "The new name is either the name of Christ Himself, now hidden from the world but to be revealed in the future as the most powerful of names (3:12; 14:1), or the believer's new name or character changed through redemption (Isa. 62:2; 65:15). If this refers to a new name for the believer, it speaks to the identity crisis. He can have a new identity to fulfill the identity distorted by sin" (*The Lion and the Lamb* [Nashville: Broadman, 1986], 151). Ramsay offers, "Equally difficult is the allusion to the

68

macy with the gods in most other faiths would be unthinkable, in Christianity it is altogether to be anticipated. So the promises for the overcomers at Pergamos include sustenance with heavenly manna, holiness indicated by acquittal and recognized by a white stone, and a certain intimacy given by the authority of Christ himself to the individual believer.

4. To Thyatira (2:18–29)

18"And to the angel of the church in Thyatira write,

'These things says the Son of God, who has eyes like a flame of fire, and His feet like fine brass: 19"I know your works, love, service, faith, and your patience; and *as* for your works, the last *are* more than the first.

20Nevertheless I have a few things against you, because you allow that woman Jezebel, who calls herself a prophetess, to teach and seduce My servants to commit sexual immorality and eat things sacrificed to idols. 21And I gave her time to repent of her sexual immorality, and she did not repent. 22Indeed I will cast her into a sickbed, and those who commit adultery with her into great tribulation, unless they repent of their deeds. 23I will kill her children with death, and all the churches shall know that I am He who searches the minds and hearts. And I will give to each one of you according to your works. 24Now to you I say, and to the rest in Thyatira, as many as do not have this doctrine, who have not known the depths of Satan, as they say, I will put on you no other burden. 25But hold fast what you have till I come.

26And he who overcomes, and keeps My works until the end, to him I will give power over the nations—

27'He shall rule them with a rod of iron;

They shall be dashed to pieces like the potter's vessels'—

As I also have received from My Father; 28and I will give him the morning star. 29He who has an ear, let him hear what the Spirit says to the churches.'"

New Name. We take it as clear and certain that the 'new name' is the name which shall be given to the conquering Christian; and the words are connected with the already established custom of taking a new name at baptism. The name acquired in popular belief a close connexion [sic] with the personality, both of a human being and of a god. The true name of a god was kept secret in certain kinds of ancient religion, lest the foreigner and the enemy, by knowing the name, should be able to gain an influence over the god. The name guaranteed, and even gave, existence, reality, life: a new name implied the entrance on a new life" (*The Letters to the Seven Churches of Asia*, 305-6).

The modern city of Akhisar spreads across the surface of what was once the first-century city of Thyatira. A small excavation approximately sixty yards long and forty yards wide represents all that may be seen of the excavations at Thyatira. Indeed, extensive excavations have not taken place at Thyatira in part because of the presence of the modern city and in part because Thyatira is seldom mentioned in any of the sources of the ancients. Although located on a vast plain and serving as a military arsenal and the first line of defense for Pergamos, the city was poorly adapted to such military purposes and found itself repeatedly overrun by marauding soldiers across the centuries. Even this letter faces difficulties of interpretation in part associated with how little is known about the city. However, the city was not a failure. The city of Thyatira was well known for the development of its trade guilds or *collegia* to which Lydia, the seller of purple mentioned in Acts 16:14, may have belonged. From what can be pieced together, the trade guilds, which consisted of clothiers, metalsmiths, and others, became such a predominant feature in the city that they eventually took on both political and religious significance. That political and religious significance may well be reflected in some of the avowals to the church at Laodicea.

One additional feature was the activity of a famous oracle named Sambathe, who was apparently prominent in this city during the latter part of the first century. A significant portion of the city seemed to give credence to Sambathe, and some feel there may be a connection between Sambathe and Jezebel, whose work is condemned in the letter to the church at Thyatira.[103]

2:18–19 The Lord addresses the angel of the church in Thyatira and identifies himself as the Son of God, referencing eyes like a "flame of fire" and feet like "fine brass." Commentators have long basically agreed that the intent of the reference of the blazing eyes is to focus on the incisive comprehension of the Christ who knows precisely and exactly what is transpiring among all the churches in general and in Thyatira in particular. Feet like "fine brass" seem to represent strength. Both ideas definitely owe themselves in part to a similar expression in Dan 10:6, Daniel's description of the Ancient of Days. Both un-

---

103 The Sibylline oracles were written from approximately the second century BC to the seventh century AD, although mythology from Ovid relates that the first Sybil was an aged woman who uttered ecstatic prophecies. Because Apollo promised her many years, she lived for thousands of years as a shrunken old lady. Two of the most famous Sybils were Erythrea and Marpessus in Asia Minor. There may also be a connection to the famous Oracle at Delphi. The Sibylline oracles are often cited by the patristic authors. Sambathe, whose shrine was in Thyatira, was thought by many to be a Sybil. See Charlesworth, *The Old Testament Pseudepigrapha*, 317–19.

derscore the initial identification of the Lord as the Son of God. Here is John's explicit claim for the deity of Christ.

Of interest is the unusual expression that has been rendered "fine brass" (*chalkolibanon*) in the NKJV. The word, as it stands, is found only in 1:15 and 2:18 and nowhere else in Greek literature in precisely this form. Hemer's extensive discussion of a possible understanding of the word depends on passages in Strabo, which have been questioned by some but which Hemer shows may have been more accurate than scholars had previously believed. In any event, he finally concludes that one of the Thyatiran guilds had learned how to distill zinc; and in the mixing of the zinc with copper, they had developed a strong, valuable metal both for instruments of war and for coinage. He suggests the translation "copper-zinc" as appropriate with the latter part of the word *libanos* being an unrecorded word due to the fact that it was probably a peculiar trade name, perhaps derived there at Thyatira from the Greek word *leibō*.[104] Whatever the solution to that particular problem, seemingly John has taken something with which every Thyatiran would be familiar to use as an expression denoting the strength and ability of the Savior to deal with whatever situation must be faced in Thyatira.

The accomplishments of the church at Thyatira are not unimpressive. Love, faith, service, and perseverance are all mentioned; and then the phrase is added that the saints in Thyatira were achieving more now in these areas than they did even at first, which suggests growth in Christian maturity—a reasonably unusual situation since the tendency is for spiritual entropy to assert itself in the churches. "Service" is a translation of the Greek term *diakonian*, from which the English word "deacon" is derived. Coming from a rich vocabulary of terms used to describe slaves, in this case the word usually suggests a butler or table waiter. The term, however, had moved beyond that and often meant, as it does here, simply gracious hospitality and service. Like the church at Pergamos, Thyatira had much to commend it; but just as the church at Pergamos, Thyatira had tolerated the intolerable and thus shared guilt.

2:20-25 Specifically, the sin at Thyatira was the sin of tolerance. To contemporary ears, to say such a thing sounds strange since in the present climate, intolerance is about the only universally recognized sin.[105] But the church in Thy-

---

104 Hemer, *Letters*, 116.

105 Rare is the reference to a sin of tolerance. But in a remarkable sermon by Perry Webb entitled, "The Sin of Tolerance," the San Antonio pastor said, "But no survey of Christ's matchless life is complete that does not take knowledge also of his noble severity and regal austerity. We cannot but be impressed by his inflexible adherence to the principle of righteousness and by his corresponding revulsion with respect to all

atira was tolerating a woman named Jezebel, who spoke of herself as a prophetess, teaching the servants of Christ to eat things sacrificed to idols and to become involved in sexual promiscuity. Numerous questions arise at this point.

First, was Jezebel the woman's actual name? Since there is no occurrence of the name Jezebel in Greco-Roman literature of the time, doubtless the apostle John is referencing the wife of Ahab, the daughter of Ethbaal the king of Sidon, who served as queen in Israel in the days of the divided monarchy. That any Jew would name a daughter Jezebel is no more likely than for Christians to name a child Judas or for Jews to name a child Jesus in eras subsequent to the first century. So, while the risqué teacher of the Thyatiran church possibly was actually named Jezebel, more likely John has assigned her this name in order from the outset to characterize her for his readers. If so, he would have dealt a telling blow even before he proceeded to describe her behavior.[106] Some validity for this position can also be derived from the fact that in the previous letter to the church at Pergamos he had spoken of those who had the teaching of Balaam, thus showing a certain propensity to link contemporary situations with ancient occurrences whenever the author needed to focus on similar character.

Two uncial manuscripts, A and 046 from the tenth century, and a number of other versions have inserted the words "of you" (i.e., "that woman [of you] Jezebel"),

---

sham, pretense, hypocrisy, and ungodliness. While he was tender, he was also firm. His meekness was not weakness, and it was a thousand miles from that idle and amiable Laodiceanism that so often marks the lives of his liberal followers today. The sweetness of Jesus was not insipid; his patience was not indifference, nor did it arise from lack of concern. He refused to compromise with error or to violate truth in order to gain popularity. While his overtures of grace were broad, his requisitions of righteousness were exact and unyielding" (P. F. Webb, *Doves in the Dust* [Nashville: Broadman, 1953], 50–51).

106 Kistemaker focuses on this comparison noting, "The woman in Thyatira is referred to by the name of the wife of King Ahab and called herself a prophetess. The New Testament reveals that women prophesied (Luke 2:36; Acts 21:9; 1 Cor. 11:5). This woman held an influential post in the church because she was a teacher, but her instruction was deceptive. She persuaded the church to engage in illicit sexual relations at the pagan temples and there to eat the food that had been offered to an idol. No wonder that this woman is given the name Jezebel, because her namesake in the Old Testament persuaded Israel to worship Baal, the god of fertility, and Asherah, the goddess of fertility. Under the guise of religion, the people fell into the sin of sexual immorality with all its dire consequences and into the sin of apostasy by eating food in pagan temples. Notice that the order of committing fornication and eating food offered to an idol is the reverse of the sequence in the letter to Pergamum (2:14)" (*Exposition of the Book of Revelation*, New Testament Commentary [Grand Rapids: Baker Academic, 2001], 137–38).

giving rise to the interpretation by some that Jezebel was the wife of the pastor of the church in Thyatira. However, this is rendered highly unlikely by the fact that the better textual evidence is strongly against that reading. More probable, though clearly not certain, is the theory advanced by some that the Sibyl Sambethe is to be identified as the Jezebel of the Thyatiran letter. In the final analysis, inadequate evidence is available to identify Jezebel much beyond what has already been stated. There is no inherent evil in the fact that she "calls herself a prophetess," since prophetesses are clearly accepted in both the Old and New Testaments. Additionally, there is nothing inherently destructive about the fact that she is teaching in the church, since Titus 2:2 makes clear that mature women not only may but must instruct the younger women of the church. Further, clearly Timothy, as a child, was instructed by both his mother and his grandmother (2 Tim 1:5).

On the other hand, in Paul's first letter to Timothy, there is a clear prohibition forbidding women to teach or have authority over men (1 Tim 2:12). From the text itself one cannot establish that Jezebel was in violation of such a prohibition, but it does seem probable. However, the most serious problem with Jezebel was not *that* she taught but *what* she taught. Since she taught the servants of Christ to eat food sacrificed to idols and led them into sexual immorality and since those are the precise accusations made against those in Pergamos who had the doctrine of Balaam, a connection—at least in thought—to those in Pergamos who possessed the antinomian disposition seems probable. Paul's discussion of the problem of the Christians in Corinth eating meat that had been sacrificed to idols is important to understand this passage and also instructive for adjudicating most moral and ethical dilemmas not directly commanded or forbidden by commandment of God. Paul's point in 1 Cor 8 is that since idols are not actually gods, eating meat purchased at the shrine of the idol was not inherently evil (1 Cor 8:4). But participation is circumscribed by other Christian obligations (8:9; 8:13; 6:12; 9:22; 10:23). Jezebel constitutes a case in point by illustrating harm to the body of Christ in Thyatira by clouding the line between idolatry and the Christian faith.

Possibly Jezebel even went a step beyond them in claiming to be a prophetess, which would suggest that her teachings were not merely based on deductions from the material received from the apostles and prophets but that she considered her own utterances on a par with or superior to the writings of the apostles and prophets. In other words, she added to false teaching the authority, as it were, of God himself.

Regarding the enticement of the people into sexual immorality, not a few interpreters have suggested that actual sexual promiscuity is unlikely since surely this would have been intolerable in the church. Rather, the reference is to spiritual and/or doctrinal unfaithfulness. But, while such an interpretation is possible and the symbol of adultery or unfaithfulness is sometimes employed by Old Testament prophets to describe doctrinal and spiritual compromise, more likely the antino-mianism at Pergamos and Thyatira favors a rather literal rendering of *porneuō*. This would indicate a tolerance of the morays of society and the religious estab-lishment in which the Thyatiran congregation dwelt. To understand that such an interpretation is hardly preposterous, one need only to view the problems of the church throughout history and observe the success of Satan in causing almost in-terminable problems for the church in the area of sexual ethics.[107] Prov 5 may help in understanding that many of the sins visited on the human race are quite unnat-ural and must be learned. However, the heterosexual appetites are a part of the created order and become problematic only when employed outside the bounds God set for them and within which he intended them to function.

One of the lengthier passages in any of the letters to the seven churches in which the all-knowing and powerful Lord announces impending judgment upon Jezebel now follows. Initially, the Lord indicates that he had given her space to repent. The expression itself probably indicates that she had received a previous warning and had chosen to disregard it. Hence, she is deemed "unwilling" to re-pent. As a result, the Lord says that he will cast her on a "sickbed." Here is a case where the NKJV translators have moved from translation to interpretation. Even though I concur with what they have given as a probable interpretation, the fact is that the text itself only says, "I will cast her into a bed." Some variant readings, including one that adds "sickness," do occur, but these are rare and unimpressive. The text simply speaks of the bed, *klinēn*. Consequently, there have been interpre-tations of this *klinēn* that would make it a funeral bier or even a "dining couch" with the idea that this was somehow an indication of the nature of her sin. That the NKJV translators are probably right in their interpretation, however, will be discovered in the succeeding phrase, which simply elaborates the judgment of God upon her by including those also who have committed adultery with her and who will be apparently cast into great tribulation or suffering. This will happen to them unless they repent of these works. Furthermore, her children are going to be killed so that all the churches will know that the Lord is indeed the One who "searches the minds and hearts" and repays each according to his or her deeds. The expression "kill . . . with death" is literally "kill in death." This is not merely

---

107 See Betty Radice, ed. and trans., *The Letters of Abelard and Heloise* (London: Penguin Books, 1974), for an infamous faux pas of ecclesiastical history.

a tautology but has parallels in Ezek 33:27 and Jer 21:7. The phrase seems to emphasize that in this case death did not simply occur naturally, but it is the actual act of God Himself.[108]

The NKJV translators have also translated a significant phrase in the passage as the One "who searches the minds and hearts." Actually, the expression here does involve the word "heart" (*kardia*), but the word translated "mind" is *nephrous*, more accurately kidneys, which were regarded as the seat of the emotions in the ancient Near East. The Lord presents himself as the One who is continually searching (the present active participle of *eraunaō*), suggesting a continual action on the part of the Lord to evaluate both the affections and thoughts (common meaning of the Greek *kardia*) and even the emotions (*nephros*) of the Thyatiran church. Just as one will reap what he sows, the Lord promises to pay each according to his deeds.

There follows an interesting word of promise to some at Thyatira who have clearly abstained from listening to the teachings of Jezebel. The Lord promises that those who "have not known the depths of Satan" will have no other burden imposed on them. They are simply to hold fast to what they have until the Lord comes. The reference to "the depths of Satan" is especially interesting. That this prophetess Jezebel would actually have made an appeal to the deep secrets of Satan is improbable. Rather this characterization is one in which John demarcates the work of Jezebel as having to do with the deep things of Satan. However, the gnostic heresy that developed in the ancient world did claim a super knowledge and often spoke of the deep things that only gnostic initiates generally comprehended.[109] The expression "the depths of Satan" has been thought by many interpreters to indicate, once again, a connection between the doctrines of Jezebel and perhaps the teachers of the doctrine of Balaam in Pergamos to a burgeoning gnostic perspective. This idea has value, even if one cannot say for certain that this was the seer's intention.

2:26–29 The overcomers receive an interesting promise. They are told that they will have "power over the nations" and that as a part of this they will "rule them with a rod of iron" and they shall be "dashed to pieces like the potter's vessels" just as the Lord had received authority from the Father. The imagery here is not difficult to follow; and, in fact, the citation arises directly from a combination of Ps 2:9; Isa 30:14; and Jer 19:11. The word "rule" translates the Greek *poimainō*, which is the word for shepherd or pastor. But, just

---

108 Hemer, *Letters*, 121.
109 Thomas, *Revelation 1–7*, 226–28.

as the shepherd has decisive authority over his sheep and the pastor exercises spiritual authority with the flock of God, so to use the word associated with the concept of a rod of iron is proper. The humble servants of Christ who serve the church at Thyatira will someday be given enormous authority over all the nations in keeping with what the Lord Himself promised when He said, "[He that is] faithful over a few things, I will make ruler over many" (Matt 25:21). However, to assign this as a promise merely for the ultimate eternal heavenly realm also reduces to insignificance the reference to *tōn ethnōn* or "the nations." More probable would be a view that would associate this promise with assignments in the millennial kingdom discussed in chap. 20.

More problematic is the reference to the gift of the "morning star." Some considerable support for this as a reference to Christ Himself is found in Rev 22:16, where He is called "the bright Morning Star." Others have seen a reference to both the star and the scepter as emblems of messianic authority in the prophecy of Balaam discussed in Num 24:17. Still others have thought that there might be an echo of Dan 12:3 where a star is emblematic of the immortality of the righteous. While all of these views are interesting and, once again, certainty eludes the interpreter; nonetheless, on the basis of Rev 22:16, the reference is probably to Christ Himself.[110] The promise is then that the church at Thyatira, faithful to the calling of God, will eventually receive "the morning star" that is the abiding, close, imminent, and eternal fellowship with the Lord Himself.

5. To Sardis (3:1–6)

[1]"And to the angel of the church in Sardis write,

'These things says He who has the seven Spirits of God and the seven stars: "I know your works, that you have a name that you are alive, but you are dead. [2]Be watchful, and strengthen the things which remain, that are ready to die, for I have not found your works perfect before God. [3]Remember therefore how you have received and heard; hold fast and repent. Therefore if you will not watch, I will come upon you as a thief, and you will not know what hour I will come upon you.

---

110 As D. E. Aune explains, "The phrase ὁ ἀστὴρ ὁ λαμπρὸς ὁ πρωϊνός, 'the morning star' (an allusion to Num 24:17 and perhaps Isa 60:3), is referred to in 2:28 as something received by the exalted Jesus from his Father, which he in turn will give the Christian who conquers. Here [Rev 22:16b] it is a predicate of Jesus himself in the context of an ἐγώ εἰμι, 'I am,' self-disclosure formula" (*Revelation 17–22*, WBC 52c [Nashville: Thomas Nelson, 1998], 1226).

⁴You have a few names even in Sardis who have not defiled their garments; and they shall walk with Me in white, for they are worthy. ⁵He who overcomes shall be clothed in white garments, and I will not blot out his name from the Book of Life; but I will confess his name before My Father and before His angels. ⁶"He who has an ear, let him hear what the Spirit says to the churches."'

Of the churches addressed in the cities of Asia Minor, no city was as legendary as Sardis. Colorfully, Ramsay begins his description of the city by alleging that

> its situation marks it out as a ruling city, according to the methods of early warfare and early kings; it was however more like a robber's stronghold than an abode of civilized men; and in a peaceful and civilized age its position was found inconvenient. In the Roman period it was almost like a city of the past, a relic of the period of barbaric warfare, which lived rather on its ancient prestige than on its suitability to present conditions.[111]

Located in the middle of the Hermus River (or Gediz) basin, a large fertile plain broken by minor hill ranges, the citadel of the ancient city of Sardis occupied a long ridge on Mount Tmolus (modern *Bozdağ*), which rose about 1,500 feet above the area below. The acropolis was clearly the most significant feature when viewed from almost anywhere on the plain below. The city occupied a large portion of the valley below; and the acropolis, to which threatened citizens could repair in time of war, served primarily for the defense of the city. The approach to the acropolis was sheer at any point except across the saddle of Mount Tmolus, which was also steep and difficult. Hence, Sardis was considered to be almost impregnable for opposing armies.

Excavations have been reopened and are continuing at Sardis. The excavations include rather extensive Byzantine structures on the side of the highway closest to the citadel. On the other side of the highway is found the discovery and reconstruction of an enormous gymnasium with a Jewish synagogue. The presence of the synagogue, especially in some connection with the gymnasium, establishes rather strong evidence in Sardis for a large Jewish community that was widely accepted by the Sardian population.

The history of the city was no less spectacular than the citadel itself. Even if some accounts of its history are fanciful and if relatively straightforward accounts chronicle some unlikely features, Sardis, nevertheless, had a remarkable

---

111 Ramsay, *The Letters to the Seven Churches*, 354.

history. First, Sardis is conceivably the place of Jewish exile, namely, Sepharad, mentioned in Obad 20. This designation eventually was assigned to Jews from Spain, who were called Sephardic Jews. The importance of the occurrence of the term suggests that Jews from the Diaspora were living in this city early in the history of Sardis. Jewish settlement in Sardis is further confirmed by the discovery of an Aramaic inscription, which appears in bilingual form involving both Lydian and Aramaic, and by the fact that Josephus speaks of Antiochus III as having located 2,000 Jewish families from Mesopotamia in the area of Phrygia and Lydia.[112] Further biblical references to Lud or Ludim found in Gen 10 and 1 Chron 1 could be references to the Lydians and are so identified by Josephus.

In addition to the probability of a resident Jewish population, the city was famous because of its better known kings. For example, the Pactolus River, which was a tributary of the Hermus River, was early discovered to contain gold dust. This discovery gave rise, in time, to the partially mythical history of Midas of Phrygia, who divested himself of the golden touch by having cleansed himself in the springs of the Pactolus. Herodotus and Strabo both testify to the fact that gold dust was found in the Pactolus and that this contributed to the immense wealth of Sardis.[113]

Sometime after 700 BC, Gyges, the first king of the Mermnad line, became the next Lydian monarch to gain fame. The wealth of Lydia is thought to

---

112 Josephus bears witness to the character of the Jews by noting a letter from Antiochus to Zeuxis in which the former says, "Having been informed that a sedition is arisen in Lydia and Phrygia, I thought that matter required great care; and upon advising with my friends what was fit to be done, it hath been thought proper to remove two thousand families of Jews, with their effects, out of Mesopotamia and Babylon, unto the castles and places that lie most convenient; for I am persuaded that they will be well-disposed guardians of our possessions, because of their piety towards God, and because I know that my predecessors have borne witness to them, that they are faithful, and with alacrity do what they are desired to do. I will, therefore, though it be a laborious work, that thou remove these Jews, under a promise, that they shall be permitted to use their own laws." Josephus, *Antiquities of the Jews* 12.3.4, in *The Life and Works of Flavius Josephus* (Philadelphia: John C. Winston, 1957), 356. Later he cites the letter from Sardis seeking approval of the Roman Senate for relative Jewish freedom in the environs of Sardis (14.10.24, 426–27).

113 Strabo has a strange note in his discussion of the building of the city. Referencing the work of Herodotus, Strabo suggests that the city was built "by common people" and that "most of the work on which was done by prostitutes," and that "all women of that country prostituted themselves; and some call the tomb of Alyattes a monument of prostitution" (Strabo, *Geography*, 6:178–79). While doubtless a bit of an overstatement, this does suggest another unfortunate background of Sardis.

have dated from that period, and probably the appearance of the name Gugu in Assyrian inscriptions is a reference to this king. Some authors have even suggested that he serves as the historical prototype for Ezekiel's Gog and that (through Ezekiel) Gog becomes, in Jewish tradition, a type of the forces of evil in the last days. Typical of the history of Sardis, seemingly Gyges was surprised by a raiding party of Cimmerians and was about to be executed when a miracle from Apollo enabled him to escape his death.[114]

By far, however, the most important king of Sardis was Croesus, the son of Alyattes, who felt threatened by the burgeoning Persian Empire to the east. As a result, Croesus consulted the famous oracle at Delphi as to whether he should encounter the Persians head on. He was told by the oracle that if he crossed the Halys, which was the frontier, he would destroy a great empire. Unfortunately, Croesus did not consider all the possibilities in this ambiguous utterance and took the oracle to mean that he would destroy the Persians. The first encounter with Cyrus of the Persians was a defeat but not ultimately decisive, and Croesus decided to winter in the stronghold of Sardis, dismissing allies and urging them to reassemble in the early spring. However, Cyrus, who was the ultimate opportunist as a general, sensed the situation and pursued Croesus right into the city of Sardis. An initial confrontation involving the Lydian calvary proved disastrous because the horses were spooked at the sight and smell of the camels Cyrus had posted at the front of his troops. The siege of Sardis followed, and on the fourteenth day the city fell.

The story, popular at the time, was that a path up the precipitous slope was not apparent at all, and the Persian troops were not encouraged about the prospects of taking the city. Early one evening, however, a guard on the wall of the citadel lost his headpiece and a Mardian soldier observed carefully as the Lydian soldier made his way down the precipitous slope by an approach almost invisible to the Persian army below, retrieved his helmet, and went back to the city. That night the Mardian soldier led a group up that same path and discovered that the Lydians were so overconfident of their safety in the citadel that they had left that side of the city completely unguarded. The route of the Lydians and the capture of Croesus was the tragic result. Croesus was then placed on a bier to be burned, but Apollo sent a providential rainstorm and saved him.

A still further tragedy of similar note occurred when the city was captured by Antiochus III in 214 BC, once again through the negligence of the defenders of the city. The point of all this in interpreting the letter to the church at Sardis

---

114 Hemer, *Letters*, 131.

is not that all of the events thus painted happened in exactly this way but rather that these were the legends in the midst of which the Sardian populous lived. Add to that the devastating earthquake of AD 17, described by Pliny as the greatest disaster in human memory. Tacitus further affirms that Sardis and Philadelphia were the two places most severely hit, with Sardis receiving the worst of it. The picture of unanticipated, quick tragedy emerges. While it is true that the citadel of Sardis was never large, this earthquake, as well as normal weathering process-es of such precipitous cliffs, has obviously exercised a diminishing effect. The citadel of Sardis itself is generally suggested as not being more than a third of its original size in the Roman period, let alone the time of Croesus.[115]

3:1-3 To the church at Sardis, the Lord addresses himself as the One who "has the seven spirits of God and the seven stars." "Has" is the NKJV translators rendering of *echō*. The NIV translates the word as "*holds*," which is certainly one of the accepted meanings. Here, however, the NKJV translation, "has," is preferable since it is difficult to speak of the risen Christ as "holding" the Holy Spirit. The purpose of the identification seems to be relational. The risen Christ maintains relationship with both the seven spirits (i.e., the Holy Spirit; see 1:4) and with the seven stars identified as the angels of the seven churches. Once again, the deeds of the church at Sardis are clearly known to the One who has both the Spirit and the seven stars.

The problem at Sardis is also a matter of relationship. In Sardis the question is the relationship between reputation and reality. The reputation of the church at Sardis was life, but the reality was that they were dead. Here there is probably a reference to the fabled history of the city with the cita-del, which though "impregnable," had fallen at least twice (and maybe three times). This is to say nothing of the earthquake of AD 17. Precisely what John intended in speaking of the church at Sardis as in reality being dead is more difficult. Is the intent to suggest that the church was in decline due to a fail-ure in evangelism, which would eventually issue in the total demise of the congregation? Does it mean that the church was successful numerically but spiritually had become quiescent to the point that nothing significant was happening in the spiritual life of the congregation? Or does it mean that the church had died theologically and embraced some heretical belief? The third seems unlikely in the description except for the fact that later in the message there are "a few names even in Sardis who have not defiled their garments." This phrase might suggest that Sardis was not just a spiritual failure but that

---

115 Hemer, *Letters*, 130–32.

its death throes were occasioned by the deliberate activities of some members of the fellowship.

Osborne says, "It is a sad thing when the only accomplishment ('deed') of a church is what it names itself, especially if the reality shows the name to be a lie, as here."[116] Aune focuses on the word *kai* in the text, noting that "the author uses the antithetical device of paradox and indicating that the *kai* linking the two parts of the statement is adversative. The contrasting metaphors are 'life' and 'death' which represented moral and spiritual vitality morbidity."[117] Smalley takes special note of the lack of any commendation for Sardis, thus abandoning the pattern of message to the first four congregations.[118] Whatever the exact meaning and the cause of this omission may have been, the consequences are, in this case, what really matters. The church is not brokering life but death, and its prospects for the future are as dim as those of the citadel's overconfident defenders in the sordid history of Sardis.

The mandate for Sardis is "be watchful," a present active Greek participle with the sense of "awake." This is preceded by a present middle imperative of *ginomai*, which means "become." The church, then, is told to "wake up" or "be watchful" and strengthen whatever remains that is also close to death. The Lord's judgment is that He has not found the deeds of the church at Sardis to be perfect in His sight. "Perfect" is a translation of the perfect passive participle of *plēroō* and is one possible rendering. The word often carries the idea of being "full" or "filled." The offense is that Sardis has not filled the standard expected by the risen Lord.

Further counsel urges the saints of Sardis to remember two things—that which they received and that which they heard—and to be obedient to that heavenly vision through repentance. That which had been received would have to reflect the word of God, salvation, and all the manifestations of the grace of God. That which they had heard probably represents the message of redemption—the gospel.

The prospect of a visitation from the resurrected Christ would normally be viewed with pleasant anticipation. But like the day of the Lord, for which some hoped, a visitation from God is a threat to the church at Sardis. If the people of Sardis fail to stir from their slumber immediately, then the Lord will come as a thief (*kleptēs*), and the church will never realize the hour in which he came. Allusion to the fate of the city of Sardis in days long past is obvious here.

---

116 G. R. Osborne, *Revelation*, BECNT (Grand Rapids: Baker Academic, 2002), 174.

117 Aune, *Revelation 1–5*, 219.

118 S. S. Smalley, *The Revelation to John: A Commentary on the Greek Text of the Apocalypse* (Downers Grove, IL: InterVarsity, 2005), 81.

Just as the overconfident city, unaware of the enemy scaling its walls, fell when least expected; so, too, the church at Sardis, with its reputation for life, stood at that moment imperiled by a thief-like visit from God, which would result in its destruction. The threat suggests that dead and dying churches are frequently oblivious to either their condition or to the imminent threat.

3:4-6 Churches with reputations for life but who, nonetheless, harbor primarily death are common enough in any age. One feature of many of these is the presence within the church of saints who have not succumbed to the death that is all around them. Sardis was no exception. Singled out in Sardis is a group that is said not to have "defiled their garments." J. Massyngberde Ford references an inscription found in Asia Minor, which cautioned anyone from appearing in soiled garments for the worship of the gods since this would dishonor the god.[119] Sardis itself was the center of the dyeing industry; and hence, the clothing industry throughout Lydia was prominent. Soiled garments would be noticed by a citizen of Sardis. The fact that some in Sardis had not defiled their garments is probably an indication of righteous and holy living and might suggest that part of the problem at Sardis was similar to that found at Thyatira and Pergamos. Those, however, who had participated in separated and holy living were promised that they would be ambulatory with the Lord himself. This walk would continue in holiness since they would be dressed in white. This promise has special significance for these who "hunger and thirst after righteousness." Paul gave expression to the profound frustration of his heart, lamenting that "When I want to do good, evil is right there with me. . . . What a wretched man I am!" (Rom 7:21–24). Finally, to walk in white is precious to the true lover of God.

The reason for this walk in white with Christ is because these are worthy (*axios*). However, this achievement is not the accomplishment of the overcomer but is a bestowed or imputed worth based on the sacrifice of the worthy Lamb. Rev 12:11 declares, "They overcame him / by the blood of the Lamb." This is the same Lamb who alone is found "worthy" to open the seven-sealed book (Rev 5:9).

Next is a promise that the names of those who had not defiled their garments would not be blotted from the Book of Life, but rather their names would be acknowledged before the Father and his angels. This particular promise occasions a bit more debate. The Old Testament background for such a promise is found in Exod 32:32–33 and in Ps 69:28. Pseudepigraphal books reference the Ps 69 passage and speak of an actual register of Israelite citizens. In Athens the name of a condemned person was deleted from the town registers prior to the

---

119 Ford, *Revelation*, 409.

execution of that individual. However, the more probable background for the promise made here once again concerns the curse of the Minim, which read, "May the Nazarenes and the Minim suddenly perish and may they be blotted out of the book of life and not enrolled along with the righteous." Hemer believes the majority of those in the Sardis church "had found a *modus vivendi* perhaps in the synagogue on Jewish terms"[120] in order to avoid Jewish and pagan pressure relating to the curse of the Minim. However, such a threat would have no effect on those who had not soiled their garments since the Lord promises them that their names will never be blotted out of the Lamb's Book of Life.

The historical background of the curse of the Minim is probably more important for this interpretation than for others. Such a prospect will help avoid a common error made by interpreters who look at the verse "I will never blot out his name from the book of life" as a threat. Those who see the verse as a threat will inevitably raise the question about the prospect of forfeiting salvation. For example, if a name could be blotted out of the Lamb's Book of Life, seemingly a person might be saved, have his name recorded in the Lamb's Book of Life, and then have his name erased and lost due to some heinous sin. But the verse is not a threat; it is a promise made to those who have been faithful in Sardis. The promise is that whatever the threat involved in the curse of the Minim, in actuality their names will never be blotted out of the Lamb's Book of Life. When the verse is properly viewed as a promise and not a threat—and that is certainly the way a first-century reader would have read it—then verses like these do nothing to suggest the possibility of forfeiting salvation once for all received.

A final portion of the promise to the conquerors is that Christ will confess their names in the presence of His Father and before His angels. Clothed in the white of holiness, the overcomer walks as worthy into the presence of God and the angels, unafraid of his name having been removed from the Book of Life; and he listens as Jesus confesses his name before all the cosmos. The usual formula concludes the message: "He who has an ear, let him hear what the Spirit says to the churches."

6. To Philadelphia (3:7–13)

[7]"And to the angel of the church in Philadelphia write,
'These things says He who is holy, He who is true, "*He who has the key of David, He*

---

120 Hemer, *Letters*, 149.

who opens and no one shuts, and shuts and no one opens": [8]"I know your works. See, I have set before you an open door, and no one can shut it; for you have a little strength, have kept My word, and have not denied My name. [9]Indeed I will make *those* of the synagogue of Satan, who say they are Jews and are not, but lie—indeed I will make them come and worship before your feet, and to know that I have loved you. [10]Because you have kept My command to persevere, I also will keep you from the hour of trial which shall come upon the whole world, to test those who dwell on the earth.

[11]Behold, I am coming quickly! Hold fast what you have, that no one may take your crown. [12]He who overcomes, I will make him a pillar in the temple of My God, and he shall go out no more. I will write on him the name of My God and the name of the city of My God, the New Jerusalem, which comes down out of heaven from My God. And *I will write on him* My new name. [13]He who has an ear, let him hear what the Spirit says to the churches.'"

Ancient Philadelphia is marked by the modern town of Alaşehir, located roughly 30 miles to the east, southeast of Sardis on the small Cogamis River. The ancient site of Philadelphia is largely unexcavated. Prospects for future archaeological endeavors here are probably greater than at Thyatira but, once again, will be severely inhibited by the modern city, which is literally built on top of the ancient one. The name of the city apparently came about as a memorial to the loyalty of the brothers Eumenes and Attalus. One of the two may indeed have founded and named the city.

Ramsay's work features Philadelphia as a missionary city for the export of Hellenism to Phrygia and beyond.[121] Such a suggestion does apparently catch something of the city's self-understanding and is doubtless reflected in the letter to the church at Philadelphia as found in the Apocalypse. The philosophically minded Greeks often considered their language and culture to be superior to all others. More than a passing hint of this perspective is introduced in the New Testament. Paul opines that he is "obligated both to Greeks and non-Greeks" (Rom 1:14). Paul may not be championing Hellenistic superiority, but he is clearly aware of the perspective. Further, a case could be made for the

---

121 Ramsay notes, "The intention of its founder was to make it a centre of the Graeco-Asiatic civilization and a means of spreading the Greek language and manners in the eastern parts of Lydia and in Phrygia. It was a missionary city from the beginning, founded to promote a certain unity of spirit, customs, and loyalty within the realm, the apostle of Hellenism in an Oriental land. It was a successful teacher. Before AD 19 the Lydian tongue had ceased to be spoken in Lydia, and Greek was the only language of the country" (Ramsay, *The Letters to the Seven Churches of Asia*, 391–92).

Greek language as the most perfectly prepared for the expression of Christian truth. The Romans gradually abandoned Latin in favor of Greek as the *lingua franca* of the agora.

Geographically and topographically the location of Philadelphia, in close proximity to the Catacecaumene, the volcanic Burnt Land, which stretched along the frontier between Lydia and Phrygia, left something to be desired. This area was particularly susceptible not only to volcanic eruption but also to earthquake. The notable earthquake of AD 17 had a devastating effect on the city as it also did on Sardis. Evidences compiled, particularly from Strabo, give witness to aftershocks, oftentimes on an almost daily basis, and the continued cracking of the walls. There is even an allusion to the fact that for this reason few lived in the actual town, but the vast majority of the city's inhabitants were actually farmers in the countryside. Indeed, there is evidence that Philadelphia was the epicenter of the great earthquake of AD 17 and suffered tremors for years to come. A similar earthquake in Laodicea in AD 60 would have been a sober reminder to the inhabitants of Philadelphia of their dangerous location. Strabo remarks,

> . . . the city of Philadelphia, ever subject to earthquakes. Incessantly the walls of the houses are cracked, different parts of the city being thus affected at different times. For this reason but few people live in the city, and most of them spend their lives as farmers in the country, since they have a fertile soil. Yet one may be surprised at the few, that they are so fond of the place when their dwellings are so insecure; and one might marvel still more at those who founded the city.[122]

However, if urban life was a terror, the farmers in the countryside had long since found the volcanic soil of their region to be unusually hospitable, especially to the growth of grapes. If there were a paucity of trees, there certainly was no shortage of vines. However, the vineyards, too, became problematic when in AD 92 Domitian issued an edict demanding that at least half of the vineyards in all of the provinces be cut down and that no new ones be planted. Two different conceivable interpretations of this edict may not be in conflict. One interpretation saw the edict as an effort to protect the vine growers of Italy, while other interpreters noted the inadequacy of the corn production and argued that the elimination of the vineyards was to encourage the production of corn.[123]

---

122 Strabo, *Geography*, 6:181.
123 Hemer, *Letters*, 155–56.

Imperial response to the earthquake of AD 17 and the decree of Domitian regarding vineyards was eventually to have the effect of bringing the city to something of a dilemma. The city of brotherly love had shown its political sagacity in a willingness to appropriate for the city new names honoring the emperors. Particularly is it interesting that the city named itself, at one point, Neo-Caesarea and possibly, at another time, even called itself Flavia after the wife of Domitian. However, this gratitude to the imperium for its intervention in behalf of Philadelphia must have melted away quickly with the edict of Domitian regarding the vineyards. Hemer notes that probably no city in Asia was as heavily dependent on viticulture as the city of Philadelphia. In fact, Dionysus was the principal deity, and even until today vines are extensively grown in the area. Furthermore, if corn were a suitable substitute in some places, the volcanic soil of the region around Philadelphia, while adaptable for vines was certainly not good for corn.[124] Consequently, Domitian's act would have had a potentially devastating economic effect on the city and could have been viewed by its inhabitants as fickleness toward the city on the part of Domitian.

One remaining matter of interest concerning the church at Philadelphia is the question of its possible relationship to the development of the Montanist heresy of the third century. While that would have no impact on this particular letter, Calder suggested that Montanism owed its origin to Philadelphia and more especially to the influence of the Apocalypse. That Montanism definitely had influence in the area is beyond dispute, and the impact of the book of Revelation in developing Montanism is also well known. However, Calder's evidence for the Book of Revelation as being the trip wire for the development of Montanism is a matter that would need much greater demonstration than is presently possible. The Montanists expected the descent of the new Jerusalem to take place near Pepuza, which is definitely related to Philadelphia. Though these matters have little to do with the interpretation of the letter to the church at Philadelphia itself, they do add an interesting twist for viewing the use of the Apocalypse little over a century later.[125]

---

124 Hemer, *Letters*, 159.

125 Montanism was a movement with origins in Phrygia around AD 172. A wide following included Tertullian. Montanus, together with prophetesses Prisca and Maximilla, was known for his prophecies and ecstatic utterances, claiming to be led by the voice of the Paraclete similar to John and the Revelation. Most leaders of the churches rejected Montanism as heretical. The movement functioned as something of a paradigm for various later expressions of what, in the present day, would be termed charismatic theology. D. F. Wright, "Montanism," in *Evangelical Dictionary of the Theology* (Grand

3:7-10 The Lord of the lampstands identifies Himself to the church at Philadelphia with three affirmations. He presents Himself as the One who is holy, the One who is true, and the One who retains the key of David. The first two identifications are self-evident as to meaning. But a word should perhaps be added concerning the identification of the Lord as the One who is holy. First, the essential significance of "holy" (Heb. *qâdôsh*; Gk. *hagios*) is that of distinction from all else that exists in the created order. Some interpreters have described the attribute of God to be holy or distinct from all else in the cosmos as the quintessential aspect of his character. Men, of course, may be holy also; but their holiness is imputed, coming as a result of the work of Christ. In an ontological sense, holiness belongs only to God Himself. Hence, once again, the Lord establishes the claim for His own deity. Furthermore, He also describes Himself as the One who is true. This contrasts with the generally unreliable character of the human family. The Lord, however, is true both in terms of that which may be known but also in terms of His own witness.

The phrase "who holds the key of David" is somewhat more enigmatic. However, the expression evidently had definite connection to Isa 22:20-23, where Eliakim as the steward of Hezekiah is said to possess the key of David, which seems to be in the Isaianic passage a reference to the accessibility to the king and to the king's presence available in and through Eliakim. Of course, other approaches could be made to Hezekiah, but Hezekiah's steward, possessing the key of David, was unquestionably the most favorable venue if one wished to curry the favor of the sovereign.

This allusion is almost certainly what was in the mind of John when he identified the risen Lord as the One who holds the key of David.[126] Access to God is ultimately through Jesus alone. Contemporary discussions regarding the possibility of salvation outside of Christ or Karl Rahner's idea of "the anonymous Christian" (i.e., the person for whom the merits of Jesus are applicable even though he may have no knowledge of Jesus or even his name) are ideas

---

Rapids: Baker Academic, 2001), 790. For more extensive assessment, see W. Tabbernee, *Montanist Inscriptions and Testimonia: Epigraphic Sources Illustrating the History of Montanism* (Macon, GA: Mercer University Press, 1997).

126 R. H. Charles says, "The expression τὴν κλεῖν Δαυείδ has apparently a Messianic significance. Cf. v. 5, xxii. 16; ῥίζα Δαυείδ. The words teach that to Christ belongs complete authority in respect to admission to or exclusion from the city of David, the New Jerusalem. The admission referred to may primarily have to do with the Gentiles and the exclusion with unbelieving Jews (see 9). But their scope is universal" (*Critical and Exegetical Commentary*, 1.86).

enjoying current popularity.[127] However, this hope cuts across the grain of New Testament teaching, which suggests that "there is no other name under heaven given to men by which we must be saved" (Acts 4:12) and that Jesus is "the way and the truth and the life" and that "no one comes to the Father except through him" (John 14:6). Here the mediatorial office of Christ is stressed again.

Keys are obviously instruments that unlock and therefore make available the contents of that which is beyond the lock or else prevent access to those same assets. The emphasis in the passage is accessibility to God Himself through Jesus who, as the steward of God, holds the key of David. Specifically, however, the reference here has by derivation another application. They are informed that the particular issue for the church at Philadelphia, which was apparently involved in a degree of suffering and relative poverty, is not a permanent condition. Rather, the One who has the ability to open so that no man can shut and shut so that no man can open looks with favor on them and has placed before the church an open door that no man can shut. The understanding of most commentators has been that the phrase should be interpreted as an open door for missionary expansion. Beckwith offered an eschatological turn and chose to view it as a promise to the church, but its location in the letter suggests otherwise since the major promises to the churches tend to come, as they do in this letter, in the concluding statements.[128] On the other hand, understanding the phrase as an encouragement to the church (i.e., God's intention for them is to fulfill the missionary mandate for a far nobler cause than for the spread of Hellenism) is certainly in keeping with the whole purpose of the founding of the city of Philadelphia.

This open door has been set before the church at Philadelphia because of a specific problem apparently associated with the pressures arising from a particular group. Though the church at Philadelphia had little strength, which is an allusion either to the small number of believers or to the church's limited influence or both, they nevertheless had kept the word of the Lord and had not denied his name. For the second time in the letters to the seven churches, a church is commended for "remain[ing] true to my name" (Rev 2:13). Once again, that particular phrase, coupled with a second mention of those who are a part

---

127 K. Rahner, "Anonymous Christians," in *Theological Investigations* (London: Longman & Todd, 1969), 6:390–93 and James Beilby, *Postmortem Opportunity: A Biblical and Theological Assessment of Salvation after Death* (Downers Grove: InterVarsity, 2021).

128 I. T. Beckwith, *The Apocalypse of John: Studies in Introduction, with a Critical and Exegetical Commentary* (New York: Macmillan, 1919), 480.

of the "synagogue of Satan," not real Jews but liars, underscores the probable accuracy of Colin Hemer's thesis regarding the pincer pressures of Judaism and imperial religious fervor existing in Asia Minor. Compromise among many believers during the reign of Domitian had been caused by a combination of increased pressure from the state regarding the cult of the emperor, worsening relationships between Jews and Christians (particularly Jewish Christians as found in the curse of the Minim), and burgeoning pressure on the Christians of the late first century (particularly in Asia Minor) to compromise either by denouncing Christ and returning to the synagogue as bona fide Jews or by embracing, at least publicly, the cult of the emperor. Apparently, however, a small and uninfluential cadre of disciples in Philadelphia had decided they would succumb to neither of those options, but rather they would keep the Lord's word and not deny His name. In all probability this decision had brought still greater antagonism from Jews in the city of Philadelphia, but these are identified by Christ as representatives of the "synagogue of Satan."

Concerning these persecutors of believers in Philadelphia, John cites the Lord: "I will make them come and fall down at your feet and acknowledge that I have loved you." The question here lies in the time of fulfillment. Should this promise be viewed eschatologically or as a reference to something that was to transpire in the immediate future, which would humble the Jews of the city of Philadelphia before the Christian minority and show God's particular love for them? This possible understanding has in its favor the natural understanding of the relationship of this prophecy with the promise of the open door being given to the church at Philadelphia. On the other hand, there is no record of such an event.

The influence of the Old Testament on the mind of the apostle John must never be far from the thinking of the interpreter of the Apocalypse. A possible eschatological background for this passage could be found in Ezek 36:19–24, 32:

> I dispersed them among the nations, and they were scattered through the countries; I judged them according to their conduct and their actions. And wherever they went among the nations they profaned my holy name, for it was said of them, "These are the LORD's people, and yet they had to leave his land." I had concern for my holy name, which the house of Israel profaned among the nations where they had gone.
>
> Therefore say to the house of Israel, "This is what the Sovereign LORD says: It is not for your sake, O house of Israel, that I am going to do these things, but for the sake of my holy name, which you have profaned

among the nations where you have gone. I will show the holiness of my great name, which has been profaned among the nations, the name you have profaned among them. Then the nations will know that I am the LORD, declares the Sovereign LORD, when I show myself holy through you before their eyes.

"For I will take you out of the nations; I will gather you from all the countries and bring you back into your own land. . . . I want you to know that I am not doing this for your sake, declares the Sovereign LORD. Be ashamed and disgraced for your conduct, O house of Israel!"

In this important passage Ezekiel previews God's plans for His ancient people, the Jews, in the period that will follow the Diaspora. Jews will eventually be regathered from all of the nations where God has scattered them but not due to any particular favoritism for the Jews—even though God chose Abraham and although He "loved" Jacob and "hated" Esau (Rom 9:13). The language of neither of those assertions should be understood to imply any lack of devotion to all the earth's tribes that have been created by God. In fact, elsewhere in the Old Testament, God makes clear that the ultimate redemptive purpose includes the nations as well as Israel (Isa 19:23–25).

The purpose then for the regathering of Israel is faithfulness to sanctify God's holy name. The Jews "profaned . . . [God's] holy name" wherever they went. However, God will "show the holiness of [His] great name" (Ezek 36:20, 23). When Israel is regathered, God's name is hallowed before the eyes of the Jews; therefore, all nations come to understand that he is, in fact, the one true God. Again, God does not do this for the sake of Israel but for His holy name's sake.

Consequently, this passage is best seen as eschatological in nature, reflecting the end times when it will become apparent not only to Jews but also to all the nations of the earth that Jesus is the Lord's Christ. This does not preclude the possibility of an incident unknown to modern believers whereby the Christians in Philadelphia received unique affirmation from God, but it does suggest that the total fulfillment of the prophecy looks to the future.

So, too, does the next promise made to the church, which is, "Since you have kept my command to endure patiently, I will also keep you from the hour of trial that is going to come upon the whole world to test those who live on the earth." Some features of this promise are clear and undebatable. Others have been the cause of almost endless discussion among advocates of two different views relating to the nature and presence of the church during the tribulation period. First, note the portion of Scripture that hardly seems debatable.

Christians are told in the Bible to anticipate tribulation in the world. "In this world you will have trouble" (John 16:33). Jesus indicated that just as the world hated Him, so it would hate His followers (John 15:18) and that persecution and martyrdom would always be a part of the life of the church. One cannot read the central message of chaps. 6–19 of the Apocalypse without concluding that incredibly difficult times await prophetic fulfillment in the present world. Indeed, the Bible speaks of a period that is called the "tribulation" and sometimes "the great tribulation." In the words of Jesus: "For then there will be great tribulation, such as has not been since the beginning of the world until this time, no, nor ever shall be. And unless those days were shortened, no flesh would be saved, but for the elect's sake those days will be shortened" (Matt 24:21–22). The words of Jesus speak of a tribulation in the last days that will surpass any that the world has ever experienced and promises that there will never be another like it. The severity of this stress is chronicled by the Lord in suggesting that "those days were shortened." From other texts the period is limited to seven years (Dan 9:20–27).

Some interpreters of the New Testament would understand the words of the promise to the church at Philadelphia as a reference to this great tribulation of which Jesus spoke. Specifically, Rev 3:10 refers to it as "the hour of trial," the extent of which will be "upon the whole world" and the purpose of which will be "to test those who dwell on the earth." One may conclude then that a reprieve is being promised to the church at Philadelphia concerning a worldwide judgment of God that will be an "hour of trial," throughout the earth. Explanations that have sought to localize the extent of this trial and make it applicable only to the Christians in the region of Philadelphia are not attractive in light of the rather clear language of the text.[129] The text speaks of an hour of trial coming on "the

---

129 For example, R. G. Bratcher, struggling with the implications of the promise, concludes, "This is a promise that the believers in Philadelphia will not be harmed by the suffering that will soon come upon all the people in the world. This is the time of calamity and distress which, in apocalyptic theology, will precede the coming of Christ. It would not seem that they alone, of all the world's population, would be exempted from those sufferings; rather the promise is that they will successfully go through that period of distress and hardship (see the similar thought in John 17.15). So it may be better to translate 'I will keep you safe in the time of trouble that is coming on the world'" (*A Translator's Guide to the Revelation to John* [London: United Bible Societies, 1984], 36). G. K. Beale admits the universal nature of this time of testing but follows Gundry in his insistence that there is promise only of protection in the midst of tribulation (*The Book of Revelation: A Commentary on the Greek Text*, NIGTC (Grand Rapids: Eerdmans, 1999),

whole world," and the cohesiveness that the text has with the other literature of tribulation throughout Scripture makes a strong case for universal upheaval.

The problem arises at two points. First, what exactly was the value of God's promise to keep them from the hour of trial to come upon the whole world? Was the promise only for suffering Christians at Philadelphia, or does it include believers in some distant eschaton? In fact, even if the early church believed in the imminency of the Lord's return, as seems to be the case, doesn't this promise take the form of "clouds without water" in that all of the Christians to whom the promise was made at Philadelphia have long since perished and the day of that great tribulation from which they were promised an egress has not yet dawned?

The second difficulty is a grammatical one, but the consequences of it are anything but insignificant. The basic question relates to the verb *tereō*, having the sense of "keep," and the preposition *ek*, meaning "out of" or "from." The promise is that because the Philadelphians have kept the word of Christ and have persevered, Christ promises to "keep . . . [them] from the hour of trial that is going to come upon the world." Is this a promise that believers will be removed from the world prior to the great tribulation or a promise that believers, while enduring the tribulation, will be kept miraculously by God from the most serious effects of that tribulation?

Concerning the initial issue, the strategy of amillennialists and other non-millenarians has long been to discredit the futurist perspective of the Revelation. They reasoned that if much of the content of the book is made future, then it was of no value to suffering Christians in the day in which it was received. But this method of reasoning, which sounds convincing on its initial hearing, fails for two specific reasons. First, if the Apocalypse was intended only to comfort the first-century church, then what is its enduring value for the church for the next nineteen centuries? Certainly, the book could continue to have relevance in recording a history of God's intervention in behalf of His people; but in terms of any eschatological hope, the book is then lost entirely to the church of subsequent generations. More important, the logic behind the position fails also.

Eschatological promises made to the churches, such as the church at Philadelphia, many of which would never be actually experienced in their own

---

290-91). See also R. Gundry, *The Church and the Tribulation* (Grand Rapids: Zondervan, 1973). This monograph represents the most extensive attempt to refute the possibility of a pretribulation rapture of the church.

lifetime, were, nonetheless, the cause of great comfort. The church today reads those same promises and is comforted by them. Death is conceivable for any believer prior to the beginning of events described in the Apocalypse. Nonetheless the people of God are both comforted in their sorrows and encouraged in their task by the ability to read and know that their work is not in vain and that the forces of Christ and righteousness eventually prevail over the tragic evils that have scarred the landscape of human history. Consequently, even if the promise to the church at Philadelphia involves a deliverance that neither they, their children, nor their grandchildren actually experience, a promise of God for the ultimate triumph of those in Christ remains for the future.[130]

This leads to the second question, which focuses on the nature of the escape being offered. Pretribulationists, who believe the church will be taken from the world prior to the great tribulation and will return with Christ seven years later as a part of His millennial kingdom maintain that to "keep you from the hour of trial that is going to come upon the whole world" is a promise that the church will not be present for the tribulation. Posttribulationalists and midtribulationalists believe believers will have to go through all (posttribulationalism) or part (midtribulationalism, pre-wrath rapturists) of the tribulation but the church will be in, but not the object of, the great tribulation. Commentators supporting the theory that believers remain in the world for the tribulation have sought to argue on the basis of the grammar that nothing is said here about taking the church out of the world. All that is said is that Christians will be "kept from" the hour of trial.[131]

An honest assessment of the text leaves us with no ability to resolve the question based on vocabulary, grammar, and syntax alone. From a strictly grammatical position, it would be possible to read with the posttribulationalists that believers will remain in the world but will be "kept from the hour of trial" by

---

130 Hemer follows the argument of protection rather than exemption. However, in recognizing the universal nature of the coming trial, he finds it necessary to reemphasize the doctrine of the imminency of the return of Christ. He comments, "If the church then believed it was living in the last times it made no distinction between immediate and eschatological fulfillment" (*Letters*, 165).

131 In addition to the monographs already mentioned, see G. E. Ladd, *A Commentary on the Revelation of John* (Grand Rapids: Eerdmans 1972); D. Moody, *The Hope of Glory* (Grand Rapids: Eerdmans, 1964); R. Jewett, *Jesus Against the Rapture: Seven Unexpected Prophecies* (Philadelphia: Westminster, 1979); G. L. Archer, *Three Views on the Rapture: Pre-, Mid-, or Post-Tribulation?* (Grand Rapids: Zondervan, 1996); M. J. Rosenthal, *The Pre-Wrath Rapture of the Church* (Nashville: Nelson, 1990).

some miraculous intervention of God. An example of this is often given relating to the plagues of Egypt, some of which were experienced by Israel along with the Egyptians while some plagues were limited to the Egyptians. On the other hand, a pretribulational interpretation is the most obvious way to "keep you from the hour of trial." Since the problem cannot be resolved strictly on a grammatical basis, how is the promise to be taken?

First, given the descriptions in the Apocalypse of the nature and extent of the judgment of the tribulation under such figures as the four horsemen, the seven-sealed book, the seven trumpets, the seven thunders, and the seven bowls of wrath to account for how the church could be living in a world in which those things were happening and be kept from that trial becomes difficult. This is not to question the ability of God, who can certainly do anything that he wills, but a fair reading of the texts from the words of Jesus previously cited through the Apocalypse suggests that the worldwide consequences of the tribulation judgments will be such that perhaps as much as three quarters of the world's population will die in a seven-year period.

The Scriptures picture a time of unparalleled natural upheaval, of war and rumors of wars, and of political and economic instability and disaster. How exactly could believers expect to be in the world under those kinds of conditions, and how could any significant understanding of being kept "from the hour of trial" be meaningful? Add to the other matters mentioned in the introduction, such as the strange omission of the word "church" from the text of the Apocalypse following chap. 3. Apparently, evidence exists to suggest the possibility that believers are removed prior to the tribulation and that consequently the promise made to the church at Philadelphia in behalf of the Lord's church everywhere is that when God's judgment is unleashed on this earth in unprecedented form, the reward of the church, in part, will be that it is spared from enduring that experience.

3:11–13 To the church at Philadelphia, the Lord indicates, "I am coming quickly," which follows closely the promise that "I also will keep you from the hour of trial which shall come upon the whole world." This promise, plus the general belief of the first-century church in the imminency of the Lord's return, give further impetus to the view that the church will be removed from the world. On the other hand, the expression "I am coming soon" (see discussion 1:1–3) seems to be not only a promise of the certainty of the Lord's return but a promise that in terms of cosmic time, His coming is not far away. Trench cogently assesses the significance of this announcement:

94

This announcement of the speedy coming of the Lord, the ever-recurring key-note of this book (cf. xxii. 7, 12, 20), is sometimes used as a word of fear for those who are abusing the Master's absence, wasting his goods and ill-treating their fellow-servants; careless and secure as men for whom no day of reckoning is in store (Matt. xxiv. 48–51; 2 Thess. i. 7–9; 1 Pet. iv. 5; cf. Jam. v. 9; Rev. ii. 5, 16); but sometimes as a word of infinite comfort for those who with difficulty and painfulness hold their ground. He that should bring the long contest at once to an end; who should at once turn the scale, and for ever, in favour of righteousness and truth, is even at the door (Jam. v. 8; Phil. iv. 5; 2 Thess. i. 20; Heb. x. 37; 2 Pet. iii. 14). Such a word of comfort is this announcement here: "Yet a little while, and thy patience shall have its full reward; only in the interval, and till I come, *hold that fast which thou hast.*" That which Philadelphia "*had*" we have just seen—zeal, patience, with little means accomplishing not a little work.[132]

In light of this announcement, the Philadelphians are asked to keep a tight hold on that which they have so that no one will "take your crown." The crown in view here is the *stephanos* crown or victor's crown. Under no circumstances is there the threat of losing salvation, but with the intensity of persecution facing the Philadelphians, the possibility for following the pattern of the Sardian Christians, succumbing to those pressures and hence forfeiting rewards, was real. The purpose of the admonition here is not to lose the reward (see 1 Cor 3:10–17).

There follows the customary promises for the overcomers. In this case they will be made pillars in the temple of God; they will never again depart; they will possess the name of God's city, the new Jerusalem, which will be given from God in heaven; and they will also be the proud possessors of God's new name. These four promises paint an encouraging picture for the believers at Philadelphia. Some interpreters have seen the reference to the pillars as recalling the background of 1 Kgs 7:21 and 2 Chr 3:15,17 where the pillars of Jachin and Boaz are placed in the temple of Solomon. Whether that is in view, the essence of the promise seems to reflect certainty and honor for the overcomer. Furthermore, the promise "he shall go out no more" is almost certainly to be understood against the backdrop of Philadelphia's seismic history and the fact that the city often found its citizens fleeing out into the open to avoid the desti-

---

132 R. C. Trench, *Commentary on the Epistles to the Seven Churches in Asia: Revelation II, III* (Eugene, OR: Wipf & Stock, 1997), 191.

tution caused by earthquake. The promise is that the day is coming when there will be stability and permanence for the child of God, and he will never again know the kinds of uncertainties experienced by the Christians in Philadelphia.

As noted earlier, the ability to name is the ability to exercise authority and claim possession. That seems to be the significance of the names that are promised to the Philadelphian overcomers. They will receive God's written name as their possession, the new Jerusalem as their citizenship, and the new name of the Lord Jesus, probably a reference to a unique relationship sustained between them and Him. Almost certainly in the back of the apostle's mind is the memory of Isa 62:2 and Ezek 48:35, both of which reference the prospect of the new name. With such promises the Philadelphians can be imagined as eager to be the ones with ears, hearing what the Spirit says to the churches.

7. To Laodicea (3:14–22)

[14]"And to the angel of the church of the Laodiceans write,

'These things says the Amen, the Faithful and True Witness, the Beginning of the creation of God: [15]"I know your works, that you are neither cold nor hot. I could wish you were cold or hot. [16]So then, because you are lukewarm, and neither cold nor hot, I will vomit you out of My mouth. [17]Because you say, 'I am rich, have become wealthy, and have need of nothing'—and do not know that you are wretched, miserable, poor, blind, and naked—[18]I counsel you to buy from Me gold refined in the fire, that you may be rich; and white garments, that you may be clothed, *that* the shame of your nakedness may not be revealed; and anoint your eyes with eye salve, that you may see.

[19]As many as I love, I rebuke and chasten. Therefore be zealous and repent. [20]Behold, I stand at the door and knock. If anyone hears My voice and opens the door, I will come in to him and dine with him, and he with Me.

[21]To him who overcomes I will grant to sit with Me on My throne, as I also overcame and sat down with My Father on His throne. [22]He who has an ear, let him hear what the Spirit says to the churches.'"

The last of the letters to the seven churches is addressed to Laodicea, which lay in the Lycus River Valley with 8,000-foot mountains to the south and on the north a less defined range but one that has its lowest escarpment marked by what looks from a distance to be the accumulation of snow. This site of ancient Hierapolis is actually modern Pamukkale, the latter of which means "the cotton castle," probably a reference to the white formations of the mineral deposits on the rocks.

Laodicea was the greatest city of the valley; and though marked by a previous history, it was given new life when Antiochus II (261–246 BC) established the city and named it after his first wife Laodice, whom he eventually divorced in 253. Previously it had been known as Diospolis and Rhodes. The city was located at a strategic crossroads where the route from Ephesus to the east crossed the route running from Pergamos and Sardis and on to the southern coast of Asia Minor. Since these major roads were crucial to commerce, they were maintained well by both the Attalids and especially the Romans after them. Consequently, Laodicea's strategic location made it a place of considerable importance. Beasley-Murray paints the following picture of Laodicea's prosperity:

> Laodicea's position at an intersection of three imperial trade roads favoured its development as a commercial and administrative centre. In Roman times it became the wealthiest city in Phrygia, so that when it suffered all but total destruction by earthquake in AD 60–1 it refused the offer of imperial aid, which other similarly afflicted cities were glad to accept.[133]

Actually, there were a number of cities in the area, two of which are prominent in the Scriptures. Ten miles to the south nestled against the 8,000-foot Mount Cadmus (modern Honaz Dagi) was the city of Colosse. By the close of the first century, Colosse had lost much of its population and importance. Nevertheless, its prominence for biblical studies is known from Paul's letter to the church at Colosse, or Colossians, and his personal letter to Philemon, who was a resident of Colosse. Lightfoot suggested that Archippus (possibly the son of Philemon) may even have been pastor of the church at Laodicea for a period of time.[134] To the northwest about five miles away was the city of Hierapolis. This city must have originated as the religious center of the area, since its name "Hierapolis" means the city of the *hieron* or temple. There was a church not only at Colosse but also at Hierapolis, which is mentioned in Col 4:13.

Hierapolis was also a spa famous for its hot mineral baths and medical remedies. The mineral deposits from the waters have caked the cliffs for several hundred yards in a display probably not duplicated anywhere else in the world. From the valley floor below, it almost looks as though snow has fallen along

---

133 G. R. Beasley-Murray, *The Book of Revelation*, NCBC, rev. ed. (Grand Rapids: Eerdmans, 1981), 103.

134 Hemer, *Letters*, 181.

the ridge. In antiquity as now, people flocked to Hierapolis and to the healing springs available to them there.

The bishop of the church in Hierapolis was Papias (c. 60–130). While little is known about Papias, he is described by Irenaeus as a man of long ago who was a disciple of John and companion of Polycarp.[135] *Expositions of the Oracles of the Lord*, a five-volume treatise survives only in citations from Eusebius and Irenaeus. Like Irenaeus he was an early chiliast, anticipating the reign of Christ on the earth for 1,000 years.[136] In the second century Claudius Apollinarius was bishop in Hierapolis and distinguished himself as an apologist writing a *Defense of the Faith* to Marcus Aurelius (c. 172) and writing against the Montanists. He is to be distinguished from Apollinarius the younger (310–390), who was bishop of Laodicea (c. 360) and who became controversial in the Christological debates, culminating in the condemnation of his views by the second Constantinopolitan Council in 381.[137]

Philip and two of his virgin daughters were also at Hierapolis, according to Eusebius. The same passage implies that the apostle John was recalled from Patmos and died and was buried at Ephesus.[138]

Colosse, on the other side, may never have recovered from the earthquake of AD 60 and its loss of status to the rapidly growing Laodicea. However, a cold spring of water that issued forth from the side of the nearby mountain was boasted to be the finest supply of water in the region. Until this day visitors may slake their thirst at this spring.

On the other hand, Laodicea was in sharp contrast to the three cities along the Aegean coast—Ephesus, Smyrna, and Pergamos. While the Aegean cities had openly courted the favor of Rome and exercised considerable dependence upon Rome, Laodicea had always taken pride in its relative independence and self-sufficiency. Though the archaeological work done at the Tel of Laodicea is considerably less extensive than what has been done at Pergamos and Sardis, several important discoveries have been unearthed. Among those discoveries were some of the remains of the system by which water was brought into the city a considerable theater or stadium with an arena about 900

---

135 Irenaeus, *Against Heresies* 5.33.4, trans. A. Roberts and W. H. Rambaut, *ANF*, American reprint of the Edinburgh edition (Grand Rapids: Eerdmans, 1973), 563.

136 "Papias," *ODCC*, 1216.

137 "Apollinarius, Claudius," *ODCC*, 85–86. See also Eusebius of Caesarea, *The Ecclesiastical History of Eusebius Pamphilus: Bishop of Caesarea, in Palestine* (Grand Rapids: Baker, 1988), 165.

138 Eusebius, *Ecclesiastical History*, 116.

feet long, which can probably be dated to AD 79 and a large Adrianic building, which was probably a gymnasium. All these discoveries will prove to be of consequence in the interpretation of the message to the church at Laodicea.

From the historical sources, numismatics, and inscriptions, certain other helpful information can easily be deduced. First, Laodicea boasted citizens such as the Zenonid family and others who were fabulously wealthy. Not surprisingly, Laodicea then became a banking center, which Cicero cited as the place where he cashed his bills of exchange upon his arrival from Cilicia in 51 BC. Contributing to the generally optimistic economic picture was the success of the hillside shepherds who had bred a sheep famous for black, glossy, and soft wool. Additionally, the city had become a medical center of no mean consequence, particularly as it related to ophthalmic therapy. The fertility of the countryside in general and the prosperity of its citizens is depicted in the coinage of the era where cornucopia containing corn and fruit are regularly exhibited.[139]

3:14-18 The Lord of the lampstands identifies Himself to the church at Laodicea in three ways. He is "the Amen," "the Faithful and True Witness," and "the Beginning of the creation of God." "Amen," a loan word from Hebrew, carried the essential meaning of affirmation. For example, in the book of Jonah, when Jonah began to preach in Nineveh, the men of Nineveh "believed God" (Jonah 3:5). The word "believed" is a form of the Hebrew word, *aman*.[140] The immediate background in John's mind is probably Isa 65:16. By referring to Himself as the Amen, the reference seems to be to the fact that Christ is the affirmation of God. He is also the Faithful and True Witness. Some witnesses may tell the truth but prove unreliable because they do not faithfully appear to testify. Others might faithfully appear but, because they are false witnesses, mislead. Jesus, however, is both the Faithful and the True Witness. He will always be faithful to give testimony, and He will perpetually speak truth.

The last expression is "the Beginning of the creation of God." The question here is the meaning in this context of the Greek *archē*, which in some situations can mean "beginning" or "first," and in others, by derivation, "ruler." If the NKJV translation is accepted, which reads "the Beginning of the creation of God," then those who embrace an Arian Christology, such as contemporary Mormons,

---

139 Hemer, *Letters*, 178–82.

140 Jepsen notes the absence of cognates for אִי in Akkadian, Ugaritic, or Canaanite—Phoenician languages, suggesting that the word may be unique to the Hebrew language. He concludes that the general idea is "security, rest, peace, reliability or faithfulness." He also mentions the use of the word for adding credibility to a messenger and his message, citing the Jonah passage as a case in point (*TDOT* 1.292–323).

would want to argue that there was a time when the Son was not and that He was the first of the creations of the Father. Clearly enough, however, that is not what is intended in the verse. Even if the verse is translated as the NKJV has rendered it, the emphasis is not on the beginning of the Christ, but on the beginning of everything else in Christ. Clearly He is God's agent in creation, and this is consistent with what is said by the apostle John: "All things were made through Him, and without Him nothing was made that was made" (John 1:3).

The NIV translators have avoided the problem altogether by simply rendering *archē* as "ruler" and stating that Christ is the ruler of God's creation. Certainly nothing is wrong with the translation or the theology involved in this rendering. Either way the message is the same: Christ is the Affirmation of God, the Faithful and the True Witness, and the One who rules preeminently over all God's creation. He is, in the final analysis, in a position to know and to speak. Beasley-Murray notes that the expression "while echoing Prov 8:22, does so in the sense of the developed Christology which appears in the hymn of Col 1:15–20."[141]

Having identified Himself, the Lord now identifies the problem with the church at Laodicea. Affirming once again that He knows all of their deeds, He also explains that He knows that they are neither cold nor hot and then expresses the desire that they would be either cold or hot. Because they are lukewarm and neither cold nor hot, the Lord's response is to "vomit [them] out of [His] mouth." Commentators have frequently lamented the lukewarm (*chliaros*) nature of the church and suggested that the Lord's purpose would be better served if the Laodicean Christians were either hot (*zestos*) or cold (*psuchros*). The ingenious efforts of multiplied commentators to explain exactly why God would prefer a cold condition in the church to lukewarmness have occupied endless pages of commentary. The present commentator even admits to having made the same attempts in his early preaching of the book. All such attempts have one thing in common. They do not square with the text as given.[142]

That the Laodiceans needed to generate heat in their devotion to Christ and

---

141 Beasley-Murray, *The Book of Revelation*, 104.

142 Neither does Jürgen Roloff's suggestion approach an understanding of the nature of the problem. He makes it a question of the permanence of salvation: "The Christians in Laodicea were living in the self-satisfied certainty that they had already received salvation as a sure possession. In this respect, they were forgetting that this gift of salvation required radical obedience, which shows itself within the church by a love that serves and outside the church by courageous public testimony" (*The Revelation of John*, CC [Minneapolis: Fortress, 1993], 64).

to the cause is understandable. Lukewarmness as a generally pallid expression is also somewhat self-explanatory, but to suggest that the living Lord preferred the church to have ice cold aloofness in its reaction to the things of God rather than lukewarmness is clearly preposterous. Rudwick and Green first argued a different solution to the passage, and Hemer has expanded their explanation into one which this author believes fits all the conditions mandated by the text.[143]

The explanation has to do with the water supply of the three cities of the Lycus plain previously mentioned. First, Colosse initially had risen to prominence in the area because the city had a defensible position crouched up against an 8,000-foot mountain and second because it had a perpetual supply of water. This most crucial of all factors for cities in antiquity, and even today in many parts of the world, proved in the case of Colosse not only adequate but also ideal. The water flowing in a torrent out of the mountain and into the spring was actually cold water with an excellent taste. Since most of the springs in the area were hot or warm springs, this was indeed a most fortunate occurrence. On the other hand, Hierapolis, fifteen miles away on the hillside, may have had potable water, but it was certainly not so palatable as that in Colosse. As a matter of fact, the primary purpose of the waters in Hieropolos seems to have been quite different. As a resort area the warm and hot springs with their heavy mineral content provided the ideal place for those seeking relief from certain kinds of ailments to come and find relief basking in those hot mineral baths.

By comparison to both Hierapolis and Colosse, the situation in Laodicea was a contrast. While Laodicea was wonderfully blessed with prosperity and prestige, the water supply was a problem. Remains of an ancient aqueduct have been discovered and in those pipes that brought water to the city of Laodicea the evident meaning of the verse lay concealed for generations. Examination of the pipes, however, led to the discovery that large mineral deposits had accumulated in the pipes across the years, indicating that the water arriving for use in Laodicea was mineral laden and hence nauseating, not very tasty. But the strong possibilities are also present that the transfer of that water through the long aqueduct from sources in the area that were almost universally warm springs would have meant that the water arriving in Laodicea was similar to the waters at Hierapolis, only instead of being hot and mineral laden, they were lukewarm and mineral laden. Consequently, Laodicea became reasonably well known for its tepid and revolting water, which almost everyone found repulsive. With this information in view, an understanding of the verses would have

---

143 Hemer, *Letters*, 186-91.

made perfect sense to the Laodiceans and are transferrable concepts for the modern reader as well.

The Lord of the lampstands says to the church at Laodicea that like your own water supply you are lukewarm and disgusting to My taste. I wish that you were either a fresh, life-giving drink of cold water or else a healing, hot mineral bath. But, because you are neither refreshing and life giving nor healing, you are simply disgusting; and I will spew you out of My mouth.

The term translated "wretched," *talaipōros*, is used only one other time in the New Testament. In Rom 7:24 Paul speaks of the wretchedness of his own sin. Liddell and Scott provide definitions ranging from "distress" or "trouble" and including "to pronounce unhappy."[144] The stark contrast between the self-sufficiency of Laodicea and the judgment of the risen Lord that they are floundering in unhappiness and distress seems painfully applicable to most of Western Christianity today.

Eleeinos is translated, "miserable," the significance of which is found in the concept of "mercy." Laodicea thinks of its merits but what is needed is mercy. "Poor" as a description of Laodicea may have surprised this congregation more than any of the epithets of opprobrium. The word *ptōchos* does not mean "simple poverty," but "grinding poverty and need". Like this wealthy city, its church had abundance but still was wallowing in spiritual squalor before the gaze of the Lord.

To complete the diagnosis, Laodicea may have boasted about its "Phrygian powder," but the church had no vision. It had become spiritually blind. Discernment of its own condition or vision of its assignment was no longer to be found. Small wonder that, despite its rich woolen industry, the church was exposed and humiliated before God.

Pausing to reflect on this judgment may well suggest to the reader that it is the harshest of all the critiques offered to the seven churches. In some sense this may appear strange since one would expect churches involved in sexual misconduct, idolatry, and compromise of other kinds to receive the Lord's strongest caution. One cannot help but be moved to ask why the Lord would have such a strong reaction to the church at Laodicea, suggesting, in effect, that the church was to Him disgusting. The answer is doubtless to be found in the following paragraphs where the key to the problem is the awful self-sufficiency of the church, which evidently had patterned itself after the pride of the city. What is now to be confronted is a contrast between the church's opinion of itself and the

---

144 LSJ, 1753.

Lord's judgment of the church. The contrast between the two should also serve as a wake-up call for the church in any era as it tries to assess its own health.

The Lord said that the church at Laodicea had an opinion about itself—namely, that it was rich and had need of not one thing. Contrasted with that view is the Lord's judgment, which faults them for failing to realize that they were, in fact, wretched, miserable, poor, blind, and naked. Once again, the reader cannot help but be struck with the nature of the Lord's critique. What a devastating judgment to suggest to a church with a high view of itself that it is in a wretched condition and the object of pity, poverty stricken in everything that really matters, blind as to vision and discernment, and naked as to its exposure before God and the world. Whereas once in fable a little boy cried, "The Emperor has no clothes," here the eternal creator God of the universe says to the Laodicean church, "You have no clothes;" you are naked and exposed before the world and before God.

Even though the Lord finds the church repulsive, He does take time to offer counsel. His counsel itself alludes to the remarkable history of the city at Laodicea. The first counsel given is that the church purchase from Christ gold refined by fire. The reference is to the process of subjecting gold to intense heat until it liquifies the impurities, which rise to the top and are scraped away by the goldsmith. What remains is a purer gold of higher carat. The purchase price is not stated but almost certainly involved faith and intercession on the part of the Laodicean Christians. Acquiring this refined gold, they would then be genuinely rich. Faith is sometimes referenced in the Bible as being like fine gold (1 Pet 1:7). What is apparently in view here is a strike at the heart of the pride of the city and the church. Unlike Smyrna and other cities that had come to depend heavily on Rome, the great earthquake of AD 60 had found Laodicea so sufficiently blessed that not only did they not seek help from Rome, but also they evidently rejected proffered help from the Imperium. With their own resources they rebuilt the city of Laodicea. Among the inscriptions found in the excavations was a reference to a building having been constructed as a project financed totally by one man, again pointing to the evident pride of the Laodiceans in their self-sufficiency.

As concerned the church, self-sufficiency is the direct opposite of faith. The church is urged to recognize its inadequacy and in faith to seek the face of God, where alone there is adequate understanding, love, and power.

Next the church is invited to secure white clothing so that the shame of their nakedness would no longer be apparent. The shame of unexpected public nakedness is something that has been part of almost every civilized society and even, to some degree, among primitive Indians like some South American tribes, whose leaders have confessed that they knew wearing no clothing was offensive to a God they did not know. This continues to be the case, despite the promiscuous nature of much of the world. For the church at Laodicea to be informed that they stood naked before God was to say that they had nothing available to hide their shame from God or the world. Without a doubt this must have been a revelation to the proud, self-sufficient Laodiceans. After all, weren't they famous for their clothing? Didn't the black sheep on the hillside produce a wool that was sought all over the world?

The concluding part of God's counsel was to procure salve that you may see. The city of Laodicea, as indicated above, was noted by Galen the physician of Pergamos as a center of the treatment of opthalmia. References not only in Galen but also elsewhere speak of the various eye salves that had been developed from the minerals prevalent in the area. The development of the ocular sciences and observation of vision problems was apparently further advanced at Laodicea than any place else in the Greco-Roman world. But now the church residing in a place famous for vision is informed that they are actually blind. They need to buy a heavenly eye salve that will give them both discernment and vision. Once again, of course, the physical problem of blindness is here used as a metaphor for the spiritual condition. The church at Laodicea had already illustrated its failure in discernment. However, to suggest that in its self-sufficiency, the church at Laodicea manifested very little vision is probably safe. What is demanded is an intervention of the risen Christ with a healing medication for spiritual vision, which would grant to the church both discernment and vision.

3:19–22 For all of the lugubrious analysis by the Lord concerning the church at Laodicea, there follows one of the most tender warnings, including an expression of love, that one could possibly have anticipated in a message to a church that had so ignominiously failed its Lord. "As many as I love, I rebuke and chasten." "Rebuke" is a translation of *elegchō*, which means "to reprove" or "to rebuke." Standing alone, the term would suggest a certain harsh quality about it, even though the word is also sometimes used for the convicting work of the Holy Spirit (see John 16:8).[145] But, attached as it is in the text to the word *paideuō*,

---

145 F. Büchsel observes the philosophical use of the term, noting that "for Plato ἐλεγχειν as the controverting of propositions is essentially the work of the philosopher. In Aristotle ἔλεγχος is the negative conclusion which his theory of logic and rhetoric treats alongside the ἀπόδειξις or demonstration. . . . He devoted a special treatise to the correction of sophistical ἔλεγχοι. . . . In Zeno ἔλεγχος is the title of two treatises. . . . The ἔλεγχος plays an important role in Epictetus. For him ἐλεγχειν is to take from someone his δόγμα, i.e., the basic principle of his life rather than a philosophical theory." *TWNT*, 2:475.

the sense of it is softened since *paideuō* is translated by the NKJV translators as "chasten" and may mean "instruct, train, whip, scourge," or "beat." In any case the sense is discipline with the objective of obedience and is linked with the tender word *paidion*, which means child.[146] Consequently, its basic meaning references training a child. Because the Lord loves the Laodiceans, he has rebuked them and seeks to give them disciplined training as he would give to a child.

This heavenly explanation is important also as an index to the spiritual state of many in Laodicea. Despite their deplorable condition and their rebuke, they are, nonetheless, the object of Christ's affection; and he deals with them as though they were his children. Such discipline serves two purposes in the New Testament. First, discipline is a corrective. The author of Hebrews also suggests that such discipline constitutes proof that one is a child of God and not illegitimate. One disciplines only his own children, but all such children do receive this discipline (Heb 12:4–11).

Verse 20 might qualify as the most misused verse in the entire New Testament. The verse has been preached enumerable times as an evangelistic text. In one sense this is no crime. What is depicted in v. 20 is certainly a situation exactly corresponding to what happens in the life of the unredeemed. Christ, never resorting to coercion, stands at the heart's door and knocks. If the individual hears the voice of the Lord (indicating that in addition to knocking the Lord is calling out) and opens the door, the Lord will come in and have the most intimate fellowship with him. While this image can portray what occurs evangelistically in the process of salvation, the verse itself is addressed not to the lost but to the church at Laodicea. The travesty in this picture is that the Lord "loved the church and gave Himself for her" (Eph 5:25). Indeed, the church is the "Lord's church" by initiation and by sustenance. What happens, then, when the inexplicable takes place and Jesus is found not on the inside of the church but on the outside, knocking to get in?

This unconscionable scenario seems to have been precisely the problem at Laodicea. The reason the church has encountered such sharp criticism at the hand of the Lord is that it was so self-sufficient as to become an end within itself. The purpose was no longer defined by God's will but simply by maintaining the excellent fellowship that they assumed existed in Laodicea. Consequently,

---

146 For example, Bertram remarks, "As in Hb. and Rev. God's loving will as Father stands behind this use of *paideia* along the lines of OT proverbial wisdom, so the subject of the saying in Tt. 2:12 points in the same direction. This is the grace of God, which has shown itself to be to man's salvation and which subjects the Christian community to its education and discipline" (*TWNT*, 5:623).

Jesus had to say to the church, "Behold, I stand at the door and knock. If anyone hears My voice and opens the door, I will come in to him and dine with him, and he with Me." Oecumenius, writing in the early sixth century the first full Greek commentary on Revelation notes in this verse the character of the risen Christ:

> "Behold," he says, "I stand at the door and knock. If anyone hears my voice and opens the door, I will come in to him and dine with him and he with me." Here the Lord reveals his own humble and peaceful nature. The devil with an axe and hammer smashes the doors of those who do not receive him, as the prophet said, but the Lord even now in the Song of Songs says to the bride, "Open to me, my sister, my bride."[147]

The prospect of entering a home and dining with the family in the ancient Near East was the ultimate expression of human friendship, depicting the desire for an intimacy of relationship surpassed only by those relationships existing within an actual family. In this case the relationship involving the Lord may even be thought to exceed familial or filial relationships. G. B. Caird thinks the reference to the supper is Eucharistic in tone. He says,

> The promise that Christ will come in and have supper has a eucharistic flavor about it. The mention of a supper with Christ could hardly fail to conjure up pictures of the last supper in the upper room and of subsequent occasions when that meal had been re-enacted as the symbol of Christ's continuing presence. This reference to the Lord's Supper is of peculiar importance for our understanding of John's theology: for that sacrament is a clear indication that the early church believed in a coming of Christ which was an anticipation of his Parousia.[148]

While the Lord's Supper is the fellowship meal of the church and while this interpretation is not impossible, a reference to the Eucharist is not likely here. Broken fellowship is the theme, along with possible restoration.

---

147 *Revelation*, ACCS (Downers Grove: InterVarsity, 2005), 55.

148 G. B. Caird, *A Commentary on the Revelation of St. John the Divine*, HNTC (San Francisco: Harper and Row, 1966), 58. J. P. M. Sweet is of the same opinion. He says, "In eat (*deipnein*) there is inescapable reference back to the Last *Supper* (*deipnein*, John 13[2ff.], 1 Cor. 11[20,25]) and forward to 'the marriage *supper* of the Lamb' (19[9]). As before, John is recalling Christians to what they already *have* and the imminent fulfillment of all it prefigures. See on 22[17, 20]" (*Revelation*, 109–10).

A final word may be permissible. In every era the ultimate adjudication about the value of an individual church is not the question of the name of the church on the shingle at the entrance or the history of the church's liaisons and relationships or even an analysis of the history of a particular congregation. The question to be answered is always the relationship of Christ to the local church. Is He on the inside embraced, loved, honored, enthroned, and followed? Or is He on the outside knocking and calling for entrance to the entity that bears His name?

Though the other six churches had their problems, at least they appear to have some cognizance of their needs and consequently sought in various ways to honor the Lord. The Lord's perspective remained important. Apparently the church at Laodicea, self-sufficient in attitude and deficient in judgment, had effectively excluded the Lord, who had paid the price for its redemption. This passage remains the strongest warning for churches in any era.

3:21-22 For all of the sorrows that characterize the Laodicean congregation, the prospect of overcoming remains, and a wonderful promise from the One who has overcome is included. To those who overcome, Christ will give the right to sit with Him on His throne, just as He Himself has overcome and is sitting with His Father on His throne. The promise here refers to the session of our Lord. According to the Scriptures, Christ had finished the work of redemption, which He came to accomplish on the earth. He Himself had cried from the cross, "It is finished" (John 19:30), and the author of Hebrews suggests that having completed that work He is seated "at the right hand of the Majesty on high" (Heb 1:3). Though His work continues, especially regarding intercession for the saints of God (Rom 8:26), nevertheless, being seated at the right hand of the Father is a posture of rest and a position of honor. This is precisely what the Lord promises to the church at Laodicea. The day would come in the providence of God when they, too, would have a position of honor and a posture of rest. The rest does not imply inactivity. The Jewish *shabbât* never meant ceasing labor for the sake of a siesta. It always meant turning from normal pursuits, especially to seek the face of God. Hence, it was a rest and a reprieve. The heavenly *shabbât* is not inactivity in which a believer becomes a cloud potato, floating around the heavenlies forever; rather, this rest is a reprieve from the difficulties involved in the present age.

One other aspect of this promise to the church at Laodicea is of great consequence. For the Lord to invite Laodicean overcomers to join Him sitting on His throne is genuinely to extend to them the privileges of a member of the family of God. Here is a recognition that they have become through Christ "heirs" and "co-heirs" (Rom 8:17) of all that belongs to Him by virtue of His unique relationship as the only begotten Son of the Father. Consequently, all involved in being invited to sit with Christ on His throne is beyond human speculation. Paul, who caught a glimpse of it in 2 Cor 12, says that what he did see was unlawful to utter in human words (2 Cor 12:4). Once again, the admonition closes with the challenge that he who has ears is to hear what the Spirit says to the churches.

III. An Unveiling of the Future
4:1–22:6

SECTION OUTLINE

1. A Heavenly Scene (4:1–5:14)
2. The Seal Judgments (6:1–8:1)
3 The Trumpet Judgments (8:2–11:19)
4. An Interpretive Interlude (12:1–14:20)
5 The Bowls of Wrath Judgments (15:1–16:21)
6. The Judgment of Apostate Religion (17:1–18)
7. The Judgment of Great Babylon (18:1–24)
8. The Return of Christ (19:1–21)
9. The Millennial Age (20:1–10)
10. The Judgment of the Great White Throne (20:11–15)
11. The Heavenly Kingdom (21:1–22:6)

Chapters 4 and 5 comprise a transitional unit connecting the message of the glorified Christ to the seven churches and the litany of tribulation events making up most of the remainder of the Apocalypse. As such, these two chapters, in which the scene abruptly switches from earth to heaven, should really be considered together. The heavenly scene described by John is designed to provide the backdrop and understanding for the beginning of the judgments that God unleashes on the earth. The heavenly throne room vision poses unique problems for the modern reader. Because of the fact that many of the participants in this heavenly division are not specifically defined, the contemporary interpreter is left (as he often is in the Apocalypse) to look for hints as to meaning, especially in the Old Testament text, which saturated the mind of John.

However the various figures are identified, the general significance of the vision is evident. John intends to portray a magnificent heavenly throne room where God appears in his glory with all the hosts of heaven and where the council of God sets in motion all the events God has scheduled for the eschaton. The characters who participate in the massive throne room vision include the Lord Himself, the Holy Spirit, four living beings, twenty-four elders, and innumerable hosts of angels. The adoration and worship of God is presented as exhibiting the most stirring emotional and volatile atmosphere imaginable. The reader can literally sense the excitement and the grandeur of the scene unfolded by John, even though apparently John himself is groping for language adequate to describe what is presented to him by way of heavenly vision.

1. A Heavenly Scene (4:1–5:14)

A. The Twenty-Four Elders (4:1–4)

[1]After these things I looked, and behold, a door *standing* open in heaven. And the first voice which I heard *was* like a trumpet speaking with me, saying, "Come up here, and I will show you things which must take place after this." [2]Immediately I was in the Spirit; and behold, a throne set in heaven, and *One* sat on the throne. [3]And He who sat there was like a jasper and a sardius stone in appearance; and *there was* a rainbow around the throne, in appearance like an emerald. [4]Around the throne *were* twenty-four thrones, and on the thrones I saw twenty-four elders sitting, clothed in white robes; and they had crowns of gold on their heads.

4:1 The fourth chapter begins with the phrase *meta tauta*, and the expression again occurs at the end of v. 1. The phrase has been observed previously in the critically important 1:19 where John is told to write what he has seen, the things that presently are, and the things that shall be *meta tauta* or "after these things" (NASB). Though interpreters differ as to the significance of these words, the prominence of the phrase suggests that it had particular meaning for John and, therefore, for modern readers as well. John reports now that "After these things I looked" (as translated by both the NKJV and NASB). The obvious question to ask is to what does the text refer when it says, "After these things"?[149] The answer corresponds to what has already been observed in 1:19, namely, *tauta* (or "these things"); it refers both to what John has seen in the initial vision and to "what is now." John writes concerning what shall take place later or after these things. The NIV translators' rendering of *meta tauta* as "After this" is clearly inadequate. *Tauta* is plural and not singular, and here the plural must be reflected in the translation since the reference is to the "things" of the churches in chaps. 2 and 3. Furthermore, the device is used to indicate the initiation of a totally new phase of the book, which now casts the vision to those things that will take place after the church era.

---

149 G. K. Beale is typical of those who find little significance in the expression, other than that John is moving on to a new vision (*The Book of Revelation: A Commentary on the Greek Text*, NIGTC [Grand Rapids: Eerdmans, 1999], 316).

As John views the situation, he finds a door standing open in heaven; and he hears a voice like the first trumpeting voice he had heard, which said, "Come up here, and I will show you things which must take place after this." Here the NKJV and the NIV inadequately translate *meta tauta* as "after this." To do so is an interpretation rather than a translation. The phrase, properly translated, should read "after these things." Several important features of the text should be noted. First, the door open in heaven makes use of a perfect passive participle in Greek and could be rendered appropriately, "There was a door having been opened." John did not see the opening of the door. He simply observed a door that had been opened and remained opened for his ease of transport. Furthermore, he heard a powerful voice calling him upward and promising that he would be shown that which must surely take place in the future. The translation of the NKJV, "which must take place," does capture the mandatory nature of the Greek particle *dei*, which carries the sense of necessity and thus unavoidability.

Common among dispensational interpreters is the perspective that 4:1 symbolizes the rapture of the church. For example, A. C. Gaebelein says,

> The scene changes suddenly. We are no longer on earth but are transported into heaven. The true church is gone and the apostate Church while still on earth to pass into the judgments of the great tribulation, is no longer owned by the Lord and therefore not mentioned. That is why the word "church" disappears entirely from this book after the third chapter. The open door and the voice which calls "come up hither" and John's presence in glory in the spirit, clearly indicate symbolically the fulfillment of 1 Thess. iv: 15–17.[150]

Walvoord is more cautious. He notes,

---

150 A. C. Gaebelein, *The Revelation: An Analysis and Exposition of the Last Book of the Bible* (New York: Publication Office "Our Hope," 1915), 44. J. A. Seiss says, "I have said that this open door in heaven, and this calling up of the Apocalyptic seer through that door into heaven, indicate to us the manner in which Christ intends to fulfill His promise to keep certain of His saints 'out of the hour of temptation;' and by what means it is that those who 'watch and pray always' shall 'escape' the dreadful sorrows with which the present world, in its last years, will be visited (*The Apocalypse: Lectures on the Book of Revelation* [Grand Rapids: Zondervan, 1962], 98)." W. A. Criswell devotes two full chapters to the thesis and concludes, "That is a type and a picture of the door of the ascension of God's sainted people, the door opened wide to receive God's children from the earth. 'And I heard a trumpet voice . . . .' That trumpet voice is the type and symbol of the voice of the archangel of God, sounding like a trumpet, that raises the dead from their graves and that, according to the word of our Saviour, gathers His elect from the four winds of the earth" (*Expository Sermons on Revelation: Five Volumes Complete and Unabridged* [Grand Rapids: Zondervan, 1969], 3:17).

The invitation to John to "come up hither" is so similar to that which the church anticipates at the rapture that many have connected the two expressions. It is clear from the context that this is not an explicate reference to the rapture of the church, as John was not actually translated; in fact he was still in his natural body on the island of Patmos. He was translated into scenes of heaven only temporarily. Though there is no authority for connecting the rapture with this expression, there does seem to be a typical representation of the order of events, namely, the church age first, then the rapture, then the church in heaven.[151]

And finally, he says,

> From a practical standpoint, however, the rapture may be viewed as having already occurred in the scheme of God before the events of chapter 4 and following chapters of Revelation unfold. The word *church*, so prominent in chapters 2 and 3, does not occur again until 22:16, though the church is undoubtedly in view as the wife of the Lamb in Revelation 19:7.[152]

The Latin word translated *rapture* refers to the taking away of every true believer at the time of the *parousia* or coming of Christ. Pretribulation premillennialists, who believe that this event takes place prior to the tribulation, see in this visionary transfer of John from earth to heaven an indication of the rapture of the church. While the present commentator holds to the view that the church does not enter the tribulation period and is taken from the world prior to the outbreak of the events described in the tribulation, he does not agree with other dispensational interpreters that any evidence of that can be found in 4:1. In this author's perspective the evidence for a coming worldwide great tribulation of seven years, to be followed by a kingdom era of 1,000 years in which Christ reigns from Jerusalem, is the obvious anticipation of both Old and New Testament authors. The question of the relationship of the church to the tribulation, in fairness, is much less clearly delineated in the text of Scripture. Endorsing the rapture of the church as prior to the tribulation should be done on the basis of passages other than 4:1 (see Introduction). At most, 4:1 may be seen as John's personal visionary experience of what will happen to the church when the Lord returns. To read more than that into the verse would be to miss the point intended here, namely, that John is transported in his vision

---

151 J. F. Walvoord, *The Revelation of Jesus Christ* (Chicago: Moody, 1966), 103.
152 Ibid.

from the island of Patmos and the things of the churches into the presence of the heavenly throne room so that he can be prepared for the unfolding of the events that will transpire on earth during the great tribulation.

4:2–4 Immediately John found himself again "in the Spirit;" and when he looked, he saw before him a throne on which someone was seated. Most commentators believe the expression, *en pneumati* suggests that John was in an ecstatic trance. While this is possible, even probable, the first use of the expression in 1:10 may mean no more than that John, when the events unfolded, was seeking God through worship. The same is possible here, though without question what follows has much in common with Paul's experience recorded by the apostle in 2 Cor 12:1–6. Paul confessed that he was unable to delineate his exact state, in or out of the body. John's situation seems similar.

At this point the apostle made no attempt to describe the facial features or other physical attributes of the figure but contented himself with saying that he had the appearance of jasper and carnelian. Here an unexpected turn occurs in the text, when a description something like that of the Ancient of Days in the book of Daniel (Dan 7:9–10) might have been expected. Instead, two stones, the jasper stone and the sardius stone named for the city of Sardis, where apparently it was frequently found, were the two stones mentioned. Sardius or carnelian is a blood-red stone, whereas jasper (*iaspis*) refers to some form of translucent rock crystal or perhaps even a diamond. Some commentators have attempted to assign significance to the two stones, such as, for example, the blood-red carnelian as representing judgment. While that might be the case, John himself draws no such distinction from the description, and this conclusion is not necessary to carry the effect of the vision. If one assumes the jasper is a reference to the diamond, what John saw seated on the throne would be a rather spectacularly beautiful contrast between the sparkling clear diamond on the one hand and the blood-red carnelian on the other. The sparkling beauty of such a vision would be sufficient to impress any viewer with the impressive royalty of the One who sat on the throne. Walter Scott says of this theophany, "His essential glory cannot, of course, be communicated even to the most exalted of creatures. God dwells in light unapproachable: 'Whom no man hath seen, nor can see' (1 Tim. 6.16). But what can be witnessed by creatures is displayed."[153]

One other factor is mentioned. A rainbow, which resembled an emerald, encircled the throne. The description does not say whether the resemblance to the rainbow was to the shape of the bow or to the kaleidoscopic colors of the rainbow, perhaps the most prominent of which was the appealing bright green

---

153 W. Scott, *Exposition of the Revelation of Jesus Christ* (Westwood, NJ: Revell, 1968), 121.

of the emerald stone. If it is merely the shape in view here, then one can imagine that around the throne was a rainbow-shaped glow, something of a penumbra effect, contrasting the bright green of an emerald stone with the sparkle of the jasper and the blood red of the carnelian of the One that sat on the throne. The contrast of color could hardly be more dramatic than those presented here.

Next, John observes that surrounding the throne were twenty-four additional thrones, and seated on these thrones were twenty-four elders. Whether these twenty-four thrones on which the elders were seated were in a circle surrounding the entire throne, a semi-circle with all facing forward, or the word *kuklothen* is to be understood in a more general sense of just "being around" cannot be discerned from the passage. Likely the vision John saw had symmetry to it, but that is not discernible from the text itself.

The twenty-four elders themselves are dressed in white (again almost certainly a color representing purity and holiness) and had *stephanous*, "crowns" or "victor's crowns," which, nonetheless, were like diadems in the sense that they were made of gold. Issuing forth from the throne, John beheld flashes of lightning, peals of thunder, and voices. The NIV translators chose to render this last word as "rumblings" (see Rev 4:5). "Rumblings" translates the Greek *phōnai*, which is normally a word translated "voices, sounds, or languages." Perhaps the NIV translators have caught its sense in rendering the word "rumblings," since "voices" would not clearly fit with lightning and thunder. "Rumblings" would be distinct from the sharp clap of thunder occurring immediately after the bolt of lightning. Whatever the case, apparently just as a spring thunderstorm can exhibit enormous energy and power and inspire awe through the potentials associated with it, so John hears the sounds and experiences the awe.

What remains from these verses is to ascertain the identity of the twenty-four elders, but this is not so simple. Many of the considerations relating to the appropriate identification of these elders are considerations that arise in 5:9–10. Accordingly, the final effort at identification will be handled there. Sufficient for the present time is to recount the various ways the elders have been identified by commentators. Some have interpreted them to be twenty-four angels that make up a heavenly council. Although only two orders of angels are named in Scripture—the cherubim and seraphim—to see these twenty-four elders as the archangels of twenty-four orders of angels is possible. A second perspective connects them all to the church and views the twenty-four elders as representative of the entire church of God. On this explanation the number twenty-four represents a doubling of the complete number twelve and ostensibly would represent the church in its fullness. A third perspective would note the twenty-four as symbolic of the redeemed of all time represented by the twelve tribes of Israel and the twelve apostles of the Lamb. Though there are variations, these appear to be the major viable positions for identifying the twenty-four elders.

Thomas organizes the major possible interpretations in a concise manor. He notes,

> Attempts to identify the elders have fallen into two broad categories, one saying that they are men and the other that they are angels. Each category has three variations, the former one saying that the men are either representatives of Israel, representatives of the church, or representatives of both. The latter category sees the angels as representatives either of the OT priestly orders or of the faithful of all ages, or as a special class or college of angels.[154]

Beale suggests the same possibilities, adding one and depicting two others a bit differently. His list is as follows:

> Now a heavenly entourage around the throne is pictured. The elders have been variously identified as (1) stars (from an astrological background), (2) angels, (3) OT saints, (4) angelic, heavenly representatives of all saints, (5) patriarchs and apostles representing the OT and NT saints together, and (6) representatives of the prophetic revelation of the twenty-four books of the Old Testament.[155]

In the end Beale combines some of these but essentially concludes that they are angels.[156] Anticipating the explanation of chap. 5, I do not believe an angelic identification of the twenty-four elders carries a high degree of probability. Knowing of no case in which angels are presented as elders or wear victor's crowns, as well as for additional reasons presented in the following section, these elders must in some way represent redeemed and glorified humans. As will be noted, this also best explains the nature of their song.

B. The Cherubim (4:5–11)

⁵And from the throne proceeded lightnings, thunderings, and voices. Seven lamps of fire *were* burning before the throne, which are the seven Spirits of God.

---

154 R. L. Thomas, *Revelation 1-7: An Exegetical Commentary* (Chicago: Moody, 1992), 344–45.

155 Beale, *The Book of Revelation*, 322.

156 Ibid.

⁶Before the throne *there was* a sea of glass, like crystal. And in the midst of the throne, and around the throne, *were* four living creatures full of eyes in front and in back. ⁷The first living creature *was* like a lion, the second living creature like a calf, the third living creature had a face like a man, and the fourth living creature *was* like a flying eagle. ⁸*The* four living creatures, each having six wings, were full of eyes around and within. And they do not rest day or night, saying:

> "Holy, holy, holy
> Lord God Almighty,
> Who was and is and is to come!"

⁹Whenever the living creatures give glory and honor and thanks to Him who sits on the throne, who lives forever and ever, ¹⁰the twenty-four elders fall down before Him who sits on the throne and worship Him who lives forever and ever, and cast their crowns before the throne, saying:

> ¹¹"You are worthy, O Lord,
> To receive glory and honor and power;
> For You created all things,
> And by Your will they exist and were created."

4:5 John views the sparkling throne and the throne's awe-inspiring occupant; he also sees and hears the phenomenon of a magnificent thunderstorm minus the actual physical phenomena normally accompanying it, such as clouds, rain, and hail. The spectacular vision is designed to impress John and his readers with the irresistibility of heaven's power. Before the throne (probably an indication that the elders are recessed a little and not surrounding the throne, but immediately before it) are seven lamps blazing. These are to be distinguished from the lamps as they reflected the churches in chaps. 2 and 3 but are like the seven spirits of 1:4 and indeed according to the text are the seven spirits or the Holy Spirit presented in his fullness to the churches. Conceivably the seven lamps of v. 5 are to be considered the seven churches now in their heavenly abode and still possessing the fullness of the Spirit. Whatever the case, the Spirit is clearly in view.

Finally, before the throne there spreads an enormous expanse of what appeared to John to be a sea of glass like crystal. Here the word "sea" almost certainly has no reference to the undulation of the wave action but simply to the vast expanse. As far as he could see, this crystalline sparkling glass sea spread before the throne. This is likely identical with the "sea of glass mingled with fire," referenced again by John in 15:2.

4:6-11 The expression "in the midst of the throne, and around the throne" seems to mean "closest to the throne;" and on all four sides of it are four living creatures. "Living creatures" is the NKJV translation of the Greek word zōa and does not improve substantially on the Authorized Version's "beasts." Clearly enough, these are not "beasts," but to characterize them as "creatures" probably does not suggest to the contemporary mind simply beings who owe their existence to creation but rather some sort of ominous biological life form, which to look upon would be rather repulsive. That is anything but the way these zōa appear. A better translation might simply be "living beings" or "living ones." The tendency to see them as rather hideous in nature is perhaps exacerbated by the description that follows, namely, that they were covered with eyes both in front and behind. One of the living ones was like a lion, the second like an calf, the third had the face of a man, and the fourth was like a flying eagle. Furthermore, each had six wings. John, impressed with the multiplicity of ocular possibilities, refers once again to the fact that they were covered with eyes all around, and within. The NIV mysteriously translates this last word as "even under his wings." The NIV translators chose to render esōthen, which means "within, inside, or inwardly," as "under his wings," probably because the translators were struggling with how exactly there could be eyes looking inwardly.

What John sees in these "living creatures" has its background in Ezek 1–10. Marked differences occur in the living creatures that appear in Ezekiel as compared to those here (see chart on next page). However, the similarities are such that there can be little question of the identification. This is fortunate since the living creatures observed by Ezekiel are expressly said to be cherubim (Ezek 10:1), members of a specific angelic order. The differences in the description in chap. 4 of the Apocalypse and chap. 1 of Ezekiel may be accounted for in one of two ways. First, perhaps neither seer—Ezekiel or John—is able to take in every detail of what he sees. Consequently, Ezekiel provides some of the details, while John speaks similarly but adds or omits other particulars. As to those places where there are apparent contradictions (i.e., Did the living creatures have six wings as in the Apocalypse, or did they have four as in Ezekiel?), there is no specific contradiction. Ezekiel saw four of the six; John noted two more. This leads to the second possibility: Since angels are ministering spirits (see Heb 1:14), they may assume at any time whatever visible manifestation is appropriate, which may explain why occasionally angels have no wings at all (see Gen 18:2) while at other times they have either four or six wings. Whatever the case, the prophetic background of Ezek 1–10 is helpful in identifying these living ones with the cherubim.

Comparison Chart of the Cherubim		
Category	*Ezekiel's Cherubim* *(1:4-25; 10:1-20)***	*John's Living Beings* *(Rev 4:6)*
Basic description	"four living creatures" (Ezek 1:5)	"four living creatures" (vv. 6,8)
Wings	four (1:6; 10:21)	six (v. 8)
Faces*	lion ox* man eagle (1:10; 10:14)	lion calf man eagle (v. 7)
Eyes	multiple (1:18; 10:13)	multiple (vv. 6,8)
Torso	like a man (1:5	
Feet	like a calf (1:7)	
Hands	like a man (1:8; 10:8,21)	
Movement	rapid, like a flash of lightning (1:14)	
Sound	like the rushing of many waters (1:24)	
	wheels within wheels for each (1:15-21; 10:9-13)	
	*But in Ezek 10, the face of a cherub rather than an ox	*In Revelation each of the cherubim seem to have one face while in Ezekiel, each had four faces.

** For a full discussion of these cherubim, see L. E. Cooper Sr., *Ezekiel*, NAC 17 (Nashville: B&H, 1994), 64–69.

Ezekiel and John agree on their features. One looked like a lion, one like a calf, one like a man, and one like a flying eagle. J. Massyngberde Ford observes concerning these multiple eyes,

> They are probably not only for the purpose of sight, but for sparkling, as in Ezek 1:18. They represent the sleepless vigilance and secret energies. John notes that the living creatures do not pause; contrast Exod 16:23, the holy rest of the sabbath. This indicates that the divine activity in nature never rests. The essence of their ceaseless activity is to praise God; cf. I Enoch 39:12, 40:2, 71:7, II Baruch 51:11.[157]

She finds that these living beings are symbolic of creation and the divine immanence. They are what is noblest (lion), strongest (calf), wisest (man), and swiftest (eagle).[158]

Beale is probably on safer ground since Ford demonstrates some ignorance of the animal kingdom. Elephants, for example, are stronger than oxen and lions may appear noble, but that is about where it ends. Beale's conclusion is more general:

> This section also tells why the four living beings represent the whole of animate life. They are performing the function that all creation is meant to fulfill. That is, all things were created to praise God for his holiness and glorify him for his work of creation. 5:13 bears out that this is not only the ideal purpose for all creatures but also that someday this purpose will actually be fulfilled, not only in heaven but also on earth, since it is an anticipation of the consummation.[159]

Interpreters usually have evaluated this description as four segments of biological life: a lion representing untamed species, a calf representing domesticated animals, an eagle representing avian life, and man representing human life. Seemingly no place is allowed for the abundant life forms of the oceans; but, despite that, the interpretation is probably correct. The cherubim in some way represent all of God's created species.

---

157 J. M. Ford, *Revelation*, AB (Garden City, NY: Doubleday, 1975), 75.
158 Ibid.
159 Beale, *The Book of Revelation*, 332.

If portions of their descriptions seem to defy explanations, their purpose in the throne room vision is clear. Day and night they never stop saying, "Holy, holy, holy / the Lord God Almighty, / who was, and is, and is to come!" The purpose of the cherubim is to praise God continually and, as the Greek text says, "without rest." The point of having no pause or rest is simply that this is perpetually what these winged cherubim do. The chant to the thrice holy God has a clear background in Isa 6. Interestingly, while Daniel and Ezekiel are generally considered to be the major books on which John is dependent, Isaiah forms the backdrop for much of the book. In fact, as mentioned above, one conceivable explanation for the difference in four-winged versus six-winged angels is the possibility that the four-winged angels of Ezekiel are cherubim, while the six-winged angels that are found in Isa 6 are specifically said to belong to the seraphic order. Similarities between the cherubim and seraphim would be expected and would account for the similarities between John's seraphim and Ezekiel's cherubim. The witness of the angels to the holiness of God in Revelation is clearly borrowed directly from the phraseology of Isa 6.

The Isaianic formula of *qâdôsh, qâdôsh, qâdôsh*, ("holy, holy, holy") was almost certainly seen by John as a trinitarian expression. Holiness as the central attribute of God has no need for triple expression, since distinction of God from all the created order is endemic to the term. Consequently, the repetition of the term three times must have seemed to John to have been the same as saying, "Holy is the Father, Holy is the Son, and Holy is the Spirit." This is followed by the emphasis on the unity of the Godhead, "Holy, holy, holy, Lord God Almighty." Further, the eternity of God is expressed in the words, "who was, and is, and is to come." Once again, such lofty expressions of theology are not characteristic of most apocalyptic literature and separate John's Apocalypse and make it distinct. The apostle's understanding of the triunity of the Godhead is thus clearly restated in the shouts of the angels.

Calvin's view of the thrice-holy antiphonal angelic anthem is cautious but clear.

> The ancients quoted this passage when they wished to prove that there are three persons in one essence of the Godhead. I do not disagree with their opinion; but if I had to contend with heretics, I would rather choose to employ stronger proofs; for they become more obstinate, and assume an air of triumph, when inconclusive arguments are brought against them; and they might easily and readily maintain that, in this passage, as in other parts of Scripture, the number "three" denotes perfection. Although, therefore, I

have no doubt that the angels here describe One God in Three Persons, (and, indeed, it is impossible to praise God without also uttering the praises of the Father, of the Son, and of the Spirit,) yet I think that it would be better to employ more conclusive passages, lest, in proving an article of our faith, we should expose ourselves to the scorn of heretics.[160]

A question arises concerning the statement that the four living beings "do not rest day or night." The Greek term is *anapausis*. The NIV translates the word as "never stop." Apparently, this translation was chosen to suggest that the action of the living beings does not continue uninterrupted but rather goes on periodically, which seems to be the sense of what happens next. Whenever the living creatures give glory, honor, and thanks to Him who sits on the throne and who lives forever and ever, an interesting response is evoked among the twenty-four elders. When the living creatures begin to shout about the holiness of God, the twenty-four elders immediately fall from their thrones before the One who sits on the major throne, and they worship Him forever without interruption. Reaching for their victor's crowns, they lay them tenderly at the feet of Him who sits on the throne, and they join the praise of heaven by their own affirmation of the worthiness of God. Particularly, He is said to be worthy to receive glory, honor, and power because He created all things and, as a result of His own sovereign will, all things that have being continue to exist.

Several important features of this are worthy of comment. First, they worship Him who lives for ever and ever, a translation of the Greek words *tous aiōnas tōn aiōnōn*. A more literal translation would be that they worship Him "who lives to the ages of the ages." This constituted the best method for expressing in the Greek language the concept of "forever." Notably, "forever" is

---

160 J. Calvin, *Commentary on the Book of the Prophet Isaiah*, vol. 1, trans. W. Pringle, vol. 7 of *Calvin's Commentaries* (repr., Grand Rapids: Baker, 1979), 205. Gregory Nazianzen is less clear but seems to endorse the same idea (Oration 34: "On the Arrival of the Egyptians," *NPN* 2, 7:337). H. C. Leupold is even more cautious but urges that the trinitarian possibilities of the text be neither overestimated nor underestimated (*Exposition of Isaiah* [Grand Rapids: Baker, 1968], 130–31). F. Delitzsch is more bold based in part on John's identification of Isaiah's theophany of Jesus (John 12:41). He concludes, "The fact that three is the number of developed and yet self-contained unity, has its ultimate ground in the circumstance that it is the number of the Trinitarian process; and consequently the trilogy (*trisagion*) of the seraphim (like that of the cherubim in Rev. iv. 8), whether Isaiah was aware of it or no, really pointed in the distinct consciousness of the spirits themselves to the triune God" (*Biblical Commentary on the Prophecies of Isaiah*, trans. J. Martin [Grand Rapids: Eerdmans, 190], 1:193).

exactly what is intended by the writer, not only in this text but also wherever the expression occurs in the New Testament. The eternal nature of heaven and hell and the activities of both are in no way temporally limited but simply continue forever. That can be also noted in v. 9 where the same expression occurs with regard to God Himself, who is said to live until the ages of the ages or forever.

The "living creatures" are said to give glory, honor, and thanks to the One who sits on the throne. And when the twenty-four elders join the worship of heaven, they say that God is worthy to receive glory, honor, and power. Glory and honor occur in both adulations; but thanksgiving is a part of the doxology of the angelic beings, while power is ascribed to God by the twenty-four elders. The four Greek terms are *doxa* (glory), *timē* (honor), *eucharistia* (thanksgiving), and *dunamis* (power).

The question may be raised: How exactly does one give glory or power to God when those are already a part of His ontological being and possession? How the living creatures could offer thanksgiving to God and how both could offer honor to God is perfectly obvious. Nevertheless, glory and power need explanation.

The answer seems to be that there is a certain glory and power inherent in all the created orders. For example, in 1 Cor 11:7, man is the image of the glory of God and woman is the image of the glory of man. The point of the text seems to be that the living creatures and the twenty-four elders bring their created glory to God in the same way the elders bring their victors' crowns. Whatever glory belongs to all the created orders is rightly attributable to God. The same is true of power. Whatever authority or dynamic in life is available to the created orders owes its idea, origin, and continuance to God and, therefore, is brought back to Him and ascribed properly to Him at this point.

Timēn is a vivid word referring to that which is precious and rare. The word is often used with rare stones that are of great value and hence honored. Therefore, to ascribe honor to God, as both groups do, is to recognize His uniqueness in all creation and to ascribe that totally to Him. Thanksgiving (*eucharistia*) is understandable since the living creatures owe their origin and continuance to the creative and providential oversight of God. The elders also owe that to God and perhaps more. If they represent redeemed humanity, they owe also thanksgiving for their redemption to the living God.

Careful note should be made of the particular expression of faith generated by the twenty-four elders. Their claim is that God is worthy to receive glory, honor, and power because He created all things, and all things owe their being directly to His will. Once again, from the pen of John comes an intensely theological statement relating to the nature of God and creation, accomplishing several important agendas. First, there could not be a more clearly imagined separation between God and His creation, which, of course, provides something of a timeless quality to the Bible since most of the new age emphases of the contemporary era are pantheistic or panentheistic in nature. For example, Tillich says,

> The being of God is being-itself. The being of God cannot be understood as the existence of a being alongside others or above others. If God is *a* being, he is subject to the categories of finitude, especially to space and substance. Even if he is called the "highest being' in the sense of the "most perfect" and the "most powerful" being, this situation is not changed. When applied to God, superlatives become diminutives. They place him on the level of other beings while elevating him above all of them. Many theologians who have used the term "highest being" have known better. Actually they have described the highest as the absolute, as that which is on a level qualitatively different from the level of any being—even the highest being. Whenever infinite or unconditional power and meaning are attributed to the highest being, it has ceased to be *a* being and has become being-itself.[161]

The contemporary religious scene tends to regard God as somehow a part of the created order or perhaps the created order as a part of the "body or being of God." Over against this is the stark declaration of Scripture that God has no beginning and that He is to be kept clearly distinguished from His creation, which owes its initiation and continuance totally and completely to His sovereign will.

By the same token, the statement must have been felt rather pointedly by any incipient Gnosticism that might have been present in the Asian context. Gnosticism regarded all that was physical as evil, or at best of limited value, and only the spiritual as that which was good. In a recent small monograph, Walter Wink provides a more sympathetic insight into Gnosticism but nevertheless concludes,

> I love this created world, life in the body, sexuality, my wife, my children, and the God I encounter in them all. I look for the redemption of the body,

---

161 P. Tillich, *Systematic Theology* (Chicago: University of Chicago Press, 1951), 1:235.

this planet, and the whole of creation, not their dissolution. I agree with the Gnostics that humanity is alienated from both nature and nature's Creator, but I believe that this estrangement is not caused by matter and the body but by idolatry and rebellion. I agree with them that the Powers are real, that the God-image has been corrupted by the human lust for power, that all too few people seem to be aware of their divine origin and the soporific effects of the world; but I do not find it necessary to dismiss the Hebrew Bible, or take flight into solipsism, asceticism, self-absorption, or social irresponsibility. Above all, I cannot stomach the Gnostic hatred of the body and creation. The Gnostic litany of body-loathing and world revulsion sometimes sounds like a case of metaphysical anorexia nervosa, a refusal to be incarnated or to make a home in this world.[162]

Tillich says that Gnosticism does not have knowledge resulting from analytic or synthetic research but is a knowledge "by participation."[163]

In gnostic cosmogonies, commonly intermediary aeons are put between the exalted God and the created order since God Himself could not become in any way involved directly in creating materiality that was viewed as essentially evil. Over against that the Johannine theology of 4:11 that God did directly create everything that has "thingness" could not be clearer. Everything that exists owes its origin to him and that not by accident. Each comes about as a result of the determinate will of God. Whatever the essence or being of that entity might be is bound up in the creative genius of the Almighty. This lofty theological reflection is not ancillary to the Apocalypse but goes to the heart of all that John is attempting to say to the seven churches and all readers of the Apocalypse.

One final observation is worth noting. Another translation distinction should be noted here. The translators of the NIV say that the twenty-four elders lay their victors' crowns before the One who sits on the throne. The word translated "lay" is a rendering of the Greek term *ballō*, which in varying contexts means anything from "put down" to its more common meaning of "cast." Theologically, there is no high ground for either the NKJV's translation of "cast their crowns before the throne" or the NIV translation of "lay their crowns before Him." If one follows the NIV, the picture would be of ten-

---

162 W. Wink, *Cracking the Gnostic Code: The Powers in Gnosticism*, SBLMS 46 (Atlanta: Scholars Press, 1993), 49.

163 P. Tillich, *A History of Christian Thought*, ed. Carl E. Braaten (New York and Evanston: Harper & Row, 1968), 33.

derness and humility as the twenty-four elders lay their victors' crowns before Him. If one follows the NKJV, "cast[ing] crowns" would suggest spontaneity generated by the heavenly pathos of the situation, a response on the part of the elders generated by the sudden shouts of the living creatures ascribing holiness to the triune God.

Perhaps this dramatic moment suggests to the present interpreter that the NKJV's description of the twenty-four elders "cast[ing] their crowns" might be more in line with what John actually witnessed than with the gentler laying of the crowns advocated by the NIV. Whatever the case, clearly the worship of heaven is focused not on the created order but on the uncreated and eternal God; and worship is spontaneous, moving, exciting, and literally rung from the hearts of the participating entities out of their gratitude to God for creation, providence, and redemption. When the saints assemble, the worship of every church ought always to be nothing less than a rehearsal for the day when we enter the heavenly worship described here.

A Pastoral Excursus: Worship

Almost interminable discussions of worship have become a part of the landscape of culture and "worship wars." These assessments are often valuable, but some degenerate into little more than expressions of personal preference. The "throne room vision" of chap. 4 provides insight into heaven's worship and, as a consequence, is a salubrious place to begin a contemporary discussion on worship.

Here one finds color, variety, focus, significant theological content, and a recognition of God's holiness. The One who sits on the throne is like jasper and carnelian with a rainbow like an emerald above His head. As for variety, there are elders, "living creatures," and the One on the throne. In heaven, worship and reverence are apparently not defined as silence. Lightning flashes, thunder peals, seven blazing lamps, and the shouting or singing of the seraphim and the elders are all part of the heavenly scene. The focus, despite all the accoutrements, is on the One who sits on the throne and on Him alone. Theologically, He is said to be Lord God Almighty—holy, existing, formerly existing, and always existing in the future. He alone is worthy to receive glory and honor because he is the One who both created all things and sustains all things.

The most important lesson here is that worship should focus on God, not the surroundings, however beautifully appointed, or on the whims of the worshiper's preferences. Worship, though heartfelt, experiential, and motivating, can and must function in this way while emphasizing the most profound theological insights. The attribution of "holiness" to God is clear recognition on the part of all creation that God is distinct from His creation in all the best ways. The emphasis on God as Creator invokes the first declaration of Scripture, "In the beginning God created the heavens and the earth" (Gen 1:1). Thus, by virtue of creation, He is sovereign Lord, owner and sustainer of all.

His beauty is indescribable (even though John extended his best effort) and unfathomable except as He chooses to make Himself known. So exalted is he that the only posture appropriate for the twenty-four elders is to prostrate themselves in humble recognition before him and to offer Him all that they have, both praise and the victors' crowns that adorn their brows.

Accompanying the "sound theology" is the variety of beings, the triumphant signs, glorious colors, and the sounds of praise. The crescendo of heavenly worship is such that it drowns out all else—yet, I suspect, does this without being painful to the ears. Both the redeemed (the twenty-four elders) and the angels have common ground in joining in the worship in heaven. While nothing ever attempted on earth can challenge, whether in grandeur or purpose, the worship of heaven, the best approximation of that worship ought always to be the goal. The standard of maximum participation in the worship experience, together with the centrality of Christ and a theological comprehension of him, must be the theme of genuine worship.

C. The Seven-Sealed Book (5:1–4)

¹**And I saw in the right *hand* of Him who sat on the throne a scroll written inside and on the back, sealed with seven seals. ²Then I saw a strong angel proclaiming with a loud voice, "Who is worthy to open the scroll and to loose its seals?" ³And no one in heaven or on the earth or under the earth was able to open the scroll, or to look at it.**

⁴**So I wept much, because no one was found worthy to open and read the scroll, or to look at it.**

5:1–2 Chapter 5 is a continuation of the throne-room vision begun in chapter 4 so that the chapter division added here is essentially disruptive. The focus moves from the central figure on the throne and the worshippers to an inscribed book in the hand of God. The pageantry of the vision becomes so intense that John finds himself weeping over the search to find one worthy to open the book. The introduction of the Lamb is both startling and comforting and provides the solution for the heavenly search.

John's next observation, as he looks more closely at the One seated on the throne, is to acknowledge in His right hand a scroll that is written on both sides. The English word, *Bible*, is derived from the Greek term *biblion*, translated here as "scroll," which can refer to several different kinds of writing material—papyrus, leather, skin, or parchment. Almost certainly here, regardless of its material, is the form of a scroll. John speaks deliberately of the fact that the scroll has writing "on both sides." The significance apparently is that the author of the scroll had much to say. In antiquity an author was often limited to whatever could be contained in a particular sized scroll. The similarity of length in the New Testament books of Matthew, Luke, John, Acts, Romans, 1 and 2 Corinthians, Hebrews, and Revelation is testimony to some limitations in availability and size of writing materials. In this case, the author had exhausted one side of the scroll and had to turn it over to the back to complete his message.

Having completed the writing, the scroll had been sealed with seven seals. The perfect passive participle of the Greek *graphō*, as well as the perfect passive participle of *katasphragizō*, bears witness to the completed activity of writing and sealing the scroll. In Roman law, according to some evidence, a testament was sealed with seven seals by seven witnesses before its legality could be established. Clearly, the authority of heaven itself rests on this book thus written and sealed. The sealing of the document would have employed a substance such as clay, wax, or some other soft material on which an imprimatur could be placed. When the seals begin to be opened in chap. 6, the impression is that the scroll is only partially opened with the breaking of each of the seven seals. This being the case, seemingly the scroll had been sealed at particular places, probably across the top, so that the breaking of one seal would allow the scroll to be unrolled only to a point.

Simultaneously, John sees a mighty angel who is shouting with a loud voice the question, "Who is worthy to open the scroll and to loose its seals?" Interestingly, the word John employs to describe the action of the strong angel is *kērussō*, one of the two major words used in the Greek New Testament to describe preaching. Actually, the *kērux* was a relatively common character in Greco-Roman society, particularly in the day of the Greek city-state.[164] The *kērux* almost always possessed an unusually good vocal instrument, which like the "town crier," he used to assemble people for whatever reason or to deliver important messages to courts or to the people in general. He was responsible for pacifying large crowds and for establishing peace and order. Here the word probably has the sense of announcing. So the angel announces the question, "Who is worthy to break the seals?" The nature of the question suggests that most will be precluded from opening the book due to their lack of worthiness. Oecumenius explains why no one is worthy. "For how could anyone of those filled with the mist of sin look into it in the presence of the divine throne, on which the scroll was laid?"[165]

5:3 Apparently, John retains his position as spectator while a considerable search ensues. But the results of the search are negative. There is no one found in heaven, no one from the earth, and no one from under the earth worthy to open the scroll or look inside it. The reference to no one under the earth is probably a reference to Hades or to the realm of the dead. It is tantamount to saying that no one in the heavenly entourage—God Himself obviously excluded—and no one among the living or among the dead was found to open it. One interesting feature here is that a search would even be conducted among those who are "under the earth." Osborne describes the two possible but similar meanings. "Those 'under the earth' could refer to those in the grave, possibly the OT saints. In Jewish cosmology, however, it almost certainly refers to the underworld regions, the 'abyss' of 9:2, 11; and 11:7, where the demonic forces dwell."[166] More liberal biblical exegetes have often argued that in the Old Testament there is no concept of any continuing life in Sheol. The very fact that a search was made "under the earth" for a possible seal-opener is rather vivid evidence to the contrary.

5:4 At this point John discovers that he has become emotionally involved in his own vision. The NKJV translators rendered the text, "I wept much," because no one was found worthy to open the scroll or look inside. This literal rendering seems to indicate not only extended weeping but also the nu-

---

164 Friedrich, *TDNT* 3:683–96.

165 Oecumenius, *Commentary on the Apocalypse*, FC 112, trans. John N. Suggit (Washington, DC: Catholic University of America, 2006).

166 G. R. Osborne, *Revelation*, BECNT (Grand Rapids: Baker Academic, 2002), 251.

ance of this word as focusing on the loud wailing of profound bitterness. This must have gone on for a while, for the emphasis is on the continuation of the weeping. The imperfect tense of *klaiō* in the middle voice suggests this. The further and the more futile the search became, the more deeply John wept.

Aside from the interesting turn of the author of the book as being so captivated by his own vision as to become an emotional participant in it, the fact of his weeping is probably designed to carry with it the implication that he felt an alarming urgency to know exactly what was written in that book.

Caird is to the point when he remarks as follows:

> These are not the tears of the prophet, thwarted in his expectation of seeing into the future. His frustration goes deeper than that. Until the scroll is opened, God's purposes remain not merely unknown but unaccomplished. John has been brought up on the messianic hope of the Old Testament, which promised that one day God would assume his kingly power and reign openly on earth, punishing the wicked and redressing the wrongs of the oppressed. Especially in persecution God's people had longed for that day to bring an end to their sufferings, but also to vindicate their faith. For there is a limit to the capacity of faith to survive in the face of hostile fact; unless in the end right obviously triumphs over wrong, faith in a just God is utter illusion. God must "vindicate his chosen who cry out to him day and night" (Luke xviii.7). John weeps with disappointment because the hope of God's action appears to be indefinitely postponed for lack of an agent through whom God may act.[167]

Seeing the book in the right hand of the One who sat on the throne was, in essence, an invitation to grasp its message, which was clearly the communication of the One who held it. Yet there remained the question of how it could ever be known, since no one even in the heavenly entourage was considered worthy to open the book. The plaintive cry of John is doubtless a literary device to impress on the reader the cruciality of comprehending exactly how God's plans, programs, and purposes will be as recorded in the pages of the book.

---

167 G. B. Caird, *The Revelation of St. John the Divine*, HNTC (San Francisco: Harper & Row, 1966), 73.

D. The Lion of Judah (5:5–14)

[5]But one of the elders said to me, "Do not weep. Behold, the Lion of the tribe of Judah, the Root of David, has prevailed to open the scroll and to loose its seven seals."

[6]And I looked, and behold, in the midst of the throne and of the four living creatures, and in the midst of the elders, stood a Lamb as though it had been slain, having seven horns and seven eyes, which are the seven Spirits of God sent out into all the earth. [7]Then He came and took the scroll out of the right hand of Him who sat on the throne.

[8]Now when He had taken the scroll, the four living creatures and the twenty-four elders fell down before the Lamb, each having a harp, and golden bowls full of incense, which are the prayers of the saints. [9]And they sang a new song, saying:

"You are worthy to take the scroll,
   And to open its seals;
For You were slain,
   And have redeemed us to God by Your blood
   Out of every tribe and tongue and people and nation,
[10]And have made us kings and priests to our God;
   And we shall reign on the earth."

[11]Then I looked, and I heard the voice of many angels around the throne, the living creatures, and the elders; and the number of them was ten thousand times ten thousand, and thousands of thousands, [12]saying with a loud voice:

"Worthy is the Lamb who was slain
To receive power and riches and wisdom,
And strength and honor and glory and blessing!"

[13]And every creature which is in heaven and on the earth and under the earth and such as are in the sea, and all that are in them, I heard saying:

"Blessing and honor and glory and power
   Be to Him who sits on the throne,
   And to the Lamb, forever and ever!"

[14]Then the four living creatures said, "Amen!" And the twenty-four elders fell down and worshiped Him who lives forever and ever.

5:5 Suddenly John's sorrow is interrupted by one of the twenty-four elders who instructs him to cease weeping. The present imperative form with the negative particle *mē* attached to the word forbids the continuance of an action presently in progress. "Do not weep" is the command of the elder, which is followed by an invitation to John to look or "see" the Lion of the tribe of Judah, who is also the Root of David. He, according to John, has prevailed; and, as a result, he is worthy and able to open the scroll and its seven seals. The Lion was the symbol for the tribe of Judah and is usually reckoned in diverse cultures to be the "king of the beasts," an emblem of strength, majesty, courage, and intellectual excellence.[168]

That this One is also the Root of David is referenced in Isa 11:1, 10 where messianic prophecy foretold the rising of One who is both the Root and the offspring of David. The clear messianic message of Isa 11, applied here to Jesus, is no accident. The reference constitutes still another clear messianic statement concerning Jesus as well as a claim for His deity. In the important Christological passage recorded in Matt 22:41–46, Jesus stumped the Pharisee inquisitors with a question of His own. Whose son is the Christ? Since any first-century Jew found such a query elementary, they replied quickly that the Messiah would be the son of David. This fascinating exchange concludes with part two of the question as Jesus asks, "How is it then that David, speaking by the Spirit, calls him 'Lord'?" Jesus cited Ps 110:1, "The Lord says to my Lord 'Sit at my right hand.'" Then Jesus concluded, "If then David calls him 'Lord,' how can he be his son?" The Pharisees apparently had never thought of it and could frame no answer. In this text the answer is provided in the doctrine of the preexistence of Christ and His incarnation. Hence, Messiah is at once the root from which David himself arises, and He is the offspring of David through His incarnation. That He is both the Root and the offspring of David is possible because of the Lord's preexistence. Furthermore, as the offspring of David, He, in His incarnation, was born into the Davidic line. He has prevailed and here, John utilized *nikaō*, the very same word used for overcomers in the letters to the seven churches in chaps. 2 and 3. The reference is surely to the atonement and resurrection; and because of those accomplishments He has, been deemed entirely able and worthy to loose the seven seals.

5:6–10 The thoughtful reader, perusing the throne room vision of chaps. 4 and 5, might have asked the question: Where is the risen Christ? He has been prominent in the first three chapters. And, in chap. 4, One seated on the throne is in view, evidently to be identified with the Father and the seven

---

168 J. M. Ford, *Revelation*, AB (Garden City, NY: Doubleday, 1975), 85. Such views are cultural, aided no doubt by the regal appearance of male lions to say nothing of power and ferocity. But zoology would paint a different picture since no single lion would, under anything like normal circumstances, challenge a healthy adult elephant, rhino, or cape buffalo. Nevertheless, the power, quickness, and ferocity of an adult lion is more than merely impressive. See also M. E. Boring's discussion of "Jesus as the Lion and the Lamb," in *Revelation*, IBC (Louisville, KY: Westminster John Knox, 1989), 108–11.

blazing lamps, which were described as "the seven Spirits" or the Holy Spirit. At this dramatic moment the Second Person of the Trinity, the Lamb, makes His appearance. John says, "Then I saw a Lamb."

There are a number of critical features involved in John's description. First, he does not use the word *amnos*, which would usually describe an adult lamb. Instead, he uses *arnion*, which speaks of a very young lamb.[169] The second matter to be observed is that this *arnion* has all the marks of having lost its life as a sacrifice. The Greek word, *esphagmenon*, is a perfect passive participle and emphasizes a past action, the results of which are enduring and permanent. This *arnion* has been slain in the past, but the significance of that sacrifice is unabated. Furthermore, the Lamb is not lying on the ground without life but is standing at the center of the throne, encircled by four living creatures and the twenty-four elders. Therefore, apparently the elders' word to John that the Lion of Judah has "prevailed" is exactly the case. Though He was dead, He is now very much alive. Not only is He alive and standing, but He is also the center of heaven's adoration. He stands in the midst of the throne surrounded by the living creatures and the twenty-four elders.

Finally, the Lamb is said to possess seven horns and seven eyes, which are said to be the Spirits of God sent out into all the earth. Ford says that the horn is proverbially a symbol of courage, strength, and might.[170] Beckwith concurs, noting that the horn is a common symbol of power occurring frequently in the Apocalypse. Concerning the multiple eyes, Beckwith says, "This trait is taken from Zec. 4[10], and denotes, as there explained, omniscience—the eyes of Christ behold and scrutinize all things."[171]

Certainly, this is the case, but still the reader has to be struck by the strangeness of this *arnion*, which has seven eyes and seven horns. This author believes the book of Revelation, for all of its difficulties, is a closely argued unit, and that the seven horns and seven eyes, in this case, are to be relationally in-terpreted. By that he means the seven eyes are specifically said to reference the sending of the Spirit into all the earth. Previously in chap. 1 the "seven Spirits" was almost certainly a reference to the Holy Spirit given without measure to each of the seven churches. Therefore, without surprise, here is a similar ref-

---

169 Beckwith argues that "the diminutive force is not to be pressed" (I. T. Beck-with, *The Apocalypse of John* [New York: Macmillan, 1919], 509. While I agree that the diminutive form should not be pressed in terms of smallness, the sense of "young lamb" is probably intended, for example, in keeping with Passover instructions (Exod 12:5).

170 Ford, *Revelation*, 86.

171 Beckwith, *The Apocalypse of John*, 510.

erence; and a unity exists between the *arnion* and the seven eyes, which are the seven Spirits sent forth throughout all the earth. By the same token, the horns, which speak of power and authority, almost certainly relate the Lamb to the central figure, sitting on the throne, from whose hand he will shortly retrieve the scroll. Still another trinitarian allusion occurs as well as an indication of the fact that the work of the Holy Spirit throughout the earth relates specifically, and above all else, to the Lamb.

5:7   The *arnion* now approaches the throne with no reticence whatever and takes the scroll from the right hand of him who sat on the throne. A stark contrast in this heavenly scene is worth noting. Whereas all other participants of heaven (the twenty-four elders, the living creatures, and all the angels) fall on their faces and worship the One who is on the throne, the Lamb has no need of such an approach but simply approaches the throne and takes the book. At the very least, this suggests a remarkable relationship to the One who is on the throne. John must have considered the Lamb to be just as much God as the One who sat on the throne.

The contents of the book in the hand of God have also been the subject of speculation. W. A. Criswell suggests that "he lifted the title deeds of forfeiture to give back to us our lost inheritance."[172] But the idea that the book contains a title deed to the decimated earth seems alien to the text. To the contrary, the contents of the book are revealed in the opening of the seven seals in chaps. 6–8. The events of the period of the tribulation are sequentially unveiled and comprise the specific content of the scroll.

5:8   The simple act of retrieving the book from the hand of Him who sat on the throne incites another heavenly celebration. The four living creatures and the twenty-four elders now fall down before the Lamb just as they had previously fallen before the One who sat on the throne. Obviously, for one to worship any figure other than God is construed repeatedly in the Bible as idolatry (cf. Rev 19:10, 22:9). Here, however, there is no hesitancy on the part of the very ones who were worshipping the figure on the throne to fall also and worship before the Lamb. Each of these, in turn, possessed a harp or lyre; and they held golden bowls full of incense, which are said to be the prayers of the saints. Incense perennially represented, among other things, the prayers of the people of God. Just as incense is a sweet savor in human nostrils, so the supplications of God's people have always been sweet to the God of all creation. The bowls full of the incense, which are the prayers of the saints, is an indication that the Lamb is the answer to the most fervent heartfelt prayers of the people of God.

---

172 W. A. Criswell, *Expository Sermons on Revelation: Five Volumes Complete and Unabridged* (Grand Rapids: Zondervan, 1969), 3:75.

5:9   Now, for the first time, there is specific mention of singing. Israel, according to the rabbis, was to sing a new song in the advent of Messiah. Now the twenty-four elders and the living creatures join in a new song, which extols the worthiness of the Lamb to receive or take the scroll and to open its seals. That worthiness is predicated on the fact that the Lamb had been slain and had purchased salvation through his blood. Persons had been bought by his blood "out of every tribe and tongue and people and nation." The term translated "tongue" from the Greek word, *glossa*, and refers to the linguistic groupings, whereas *ethnos* is often transliterated literally into English as "ethne" and here by the NKJV as "nation." The NKJV captures the fact that the reference here is to the various national units.

The expression "have redeemed us...by your blood" is selected from a variety of rich and picturesque words describing the work of Christ on the cross. Here the verb *agorazō* appears in the aorist tense, referencing the completion of this purchase. Leon Morris traces the history of the word, which he says meant originally "to frequent the forum."[173] Of the unique emphasis of this word, Morris observes,

> When Paul says, "ye are not your own; for ye were bought with a price" (I Cor. vi. 19, 20), or again, "he that was called, being free, is Christ's slave. Ye were bought with a price; become not slaves of men" (I Cor. vii. 22, 23), he is not drawing our attention to quite the same aspect of the Christian life as when he uses the redemption words we have considered hitherto. With them the emphasis is on the final freedom of the redeemed; here it is rather on the truth that the redeemed are paradoxically slaves, the slaves of God, for they were bought with a price. This thought is a necessary supplement to the former one, for the Christian idea of redemption is not that believers are brought into a liberty of selfish ease. Rather, since they have been bought by God at terrible cost, they have become God's slaves, to do His will.[174]

Further, the price of this purchase is specific. The method of payment employs the blood of Christ. The language of vicarious sacrifice ties closely to the Day of Atonement, Passover, and to passages like Lev 17:10–11. In the Day of Atonement prescription, the blood of the sacrificial goat is carried into the holy of holies and sprinkled on the mercy seat, interposed between the just demands

---

173 L. Morris, *The Apostolic Preaching of the Cross* (Grand Rapids: Eerdmans; London: Tyndale, 1955), 54.

174 Ibid.

of the law of God and the sinful high priest (Lev 16:15–17). The Passover takes the blood of the lamb slain by each family and sprinkles it on the door facing so that the death angel passes over (Exod 12:1–13). The rationale for this is provided in Lev 17:11 where Moses is instructed that "the life of a creature is in the blood" and "I have given it to you to make atonement for yourselves on the altar." The Apocalypse abounds with high Christology and a theology of atonement commensurate with what is found in Romans, Galatians, and Hebrews. In this the book of the Revelation differs sharply from other apocalyptic literature.[175]

At this point the reader encounters several significant textual problems, which will be discussed in the text of the commentary rather than the footnotes due to their influence on the interpretation of the passage. In chap. 4, the twenty-four elders were introduced, and the statement was made that further discussion of their identity would come in chap. 5. Here the answer will be influenced to some degree by the nature of textual variants. More often than not, textual variants have little impact on crucial interpretive conclusions. On rare occasions, however, those variants may, in fact, exercise considerable impact. Here and in v. 10 are cases of possible significant impact.

The preferred reading of United Bible Societies' third edition of the Greek New Testament is "because you were slain and with your blood you purchased to God out of all nations." However, there is slight evidence favoring this reading. Far more extensive evidence favors the reading "because you have purchased us to God by your blood." The addition of the word *us*, which occurs not only in Codex Sinaiticus but also a great variety of texts from both majority sources and other earlier sources, to say nothing of the appearance of the word *us* in such varied Patristic writers as Hippolytus, Cyprian, Augustine, and others is not to be easily overlooked.[176] One may now ask: What conceivable differ-

---

175 For more extensive discussion of the significance of "blood" in the New Testament theology, see in addition to Morris, A. M. Stibbs, *His Blood Works: The Meaning of the Word "Blood" in Scripture* (London: Tyndale, 1954); and P. Patterson, "The Work of Christ," in *A Theology for the Church* (Nashville: B&H, 2007), 545–602.

176 In *A Textual Commentary on the Greek New Testament* (a companion volume to the United Bible Societies' [UBS] Greek New Testament), B. Metzger makes this rather astonishing confession: "Although the evidence for τῷ θεῷ is slight (A eth), this reading best accounts for the origin of the others. Wishing to provide ἠγόρασας with a more exactly determined object than is found in the words ἐκ πάσης φυλῆς κ.τ.λ., some scribes introduced ἡμας either before τῷ θεῷ (94 2344 *al*) or after τῷ θεῷ (ℵ 046 1006 1611 2053 *al*), while others replaced τῷ θεῷ with ἡμᾶς (1 2065* Cyprian *al*). Those who made the emendations, however, overlooked the unsuitability of ἡμᾶς with αὐτούς in the following verse (where, indeed, the Textus Receptus reads ἡμᾶς, but with quite inadequate authority)." B.

ence does it make whether the text says that Christ has "redeemed us to God" or "redeemed to God"? The difference has to do with the possible identification of the twenty-four elders.

In the previous chapter, several possibilities for the identity of the elders were discussed. Two of those possibilities involved the church in one way or another. If the text speaks of redeeming "us" as placed in the mouth of the twenty-four elders, one has almost irrefutable evidence that the twenty-four elders represent in some way or another redeemed people from the earth. The prominence in the Old Testament of the twelve tribes of Israel or the twelve sons of Jacob and in the Gospels of the twelve apostles of the Lamb, as well as the repeated prominence of both groups in the Apocalypse, would add evidence that the twenty-four elders represent all the redeemed from Israel in the Old Testament and from the church era in the New Testament. Since they are viewed in heaven, Pretribulationalists, who believe the church will not go through the tribulation, would be greatly assisted in their argument that the church has been removed from the earth prior to the outbreak of tributory events, beginning with the opening of the seals in chap. 6. On the other hand, if the word *us* is missing from the original text, then to make an identification of the twenty-four elders as some sort of an angelic group would still be possible. This is precisely what Mounce, Ladd, and others have attempted.[177] Ladd wrote,

> If this were a correct reading, the reasoning would be sound; but this is another of the numerous instances in the Revelation where the Greek text behind the old King James Version is defective. Practically all modern English translations recognize the correct form of the Greek: "For thou . . . by thy blood didst ransom men for God from every tribe and tongue and people and nation, and hast made them a kingdom and priests to our God, and they shall reign on earth." Far from supporting the identification between the

---

M. Metzger, *A Textual Commentary on the Greek New Testament* [*TCGNT*] (New York: UBS, 1971), 738. This amounts to a decision on the part of the textual committee that because of the grammatical inconsistency of ἡμᾶς and the αὐτούς of verse 10, they decided to resolve the problem by taking the reading most weakly attested. This decision is essentially a decision to resolve one problem by creating a more serious one and should be rejected in favor of the almost universally attested support in conclusion of ἡμᾶς.

177 See R. H. Mounce, *The Book of Revelation*, NICNT (Grand Rapids: Eerdmans, 1977), 147–48; and G. E. Ladd, *A Commentary on the Revelation of John* (Grand Rapids: Eerdmans, 1972), 91–92. P. R. Carrell notes that if the 24 are not angels, they are attributed with angelic functions (*Jesus and the Angels: Angelology and the Christology of the Apocalypse of John*, SNTSMS 95 [Cambridge: Cambridge University Press, 1997], 144).

elders and the church, this song of the elders clearly sets them apart from the redeemed. The elders themselves are not the redeemed, but they sing of those who are redeemed. Again, in 14:3, the elders are set over against those who have been purchased out of the earth who sing a new song which the elders cannot learn. There is no difficulty in understanding the twenty-four elders as a body of angels who help execute the divine rule in the universe.[178]

Ladd supposes he has refuted the possibility that the twenty-four elders can possibly represent the redeemed and, therefore, that they must be identified as angels. However, his admission that if they are identified as saints, then a pretribulation rapture gains credibility should be noted.

However, Mounce, Ladd, and other posttribulationalists, who conclude that believers will go through the tribulation, have not resolved their difficulties, even by following the weakly attested reading, which omits the word *us*. To account for twenty-four people described as elders (*presbuteroi*), who have victors' crowns (*stephanous*), white garments, which are most often promised to the redeemed (see Rev 4:4), and who are in some way or another distinguished from two other groups mentioned in the throne-room vision would still be necessary. The first group from which they must be distinguished are the seraphim or the "living creatures," which are given as four in number. Second, they must be distinguished from a great host of angels, which eventually join in the heavenly celebration depicted in chap. 5. Nowhere in Scripture are angels referred to as "elders," though that is fairly common terminology for leadership both in Israel (cf. Exod 3:16) and in the New Testament (cf. 1 Tim 5:17). *Stephanoi*, "crowns," are not usually found on the heads of angels but are commonly the accouterments promised to redeemed humans. The same can be said of white garments. Consequently, one can also observe that the elders are distinct from those who are martyred during the great tribulation as is noted by the involvement of one of the elders in identifying tribulation saints (Rev 7:13–17).

If the context and the description and even the textual evidence do not favor the identification of the twenty-four elders as angelic orders of some variety, then to identify the elders as representing the redeemed of both the Old and New Testaments or even, as some would do, of the church itself might be taken as reasonably certain. But, before making such a decision, a problem remains for those who would identify the twenty-four elders as the redeemed. The question might be put like this. The One who is on the throne is not just a symbol for God but is God Himself. The Lamb (*arnion*) is the Lord. The angels are the angels, and the living creatures are the seraphim. These do not merely represent something

---

178 Ladd, *Commentary on the Revelation of John*, 74–75.

symbolically but are apparently actual. Isn't it then inconsistent to speak of the twenty-four elders as symbolically representing all the redeemed of the ages? My answer is the affirmative (i.e., this would involve inconsistency in interpretive methodology). How then, under these circumstances, are the twenty-four elders to be interpreted? The answer is that the twelve sons of Jacob represent the twelve tribes of Israel, and the twelve apostles of the Lamb represent the church. This conclusion is perfectly consistent with what was promised the disciples in Matt 19:28, when Jesus said to them, "I tell you the truth, at the renewal of all things, when the Son of Man sits on his glorious throne, you who have followed me will also sit on twelve thrones, judging the twelve tribes of Israel." Exactly where could one find a council of elders more representative of the people of God than the twelve sons of Jacob and the twelve apostles of the Lamb?

What appears on the surface to be such a favorable solution (and I believe the solution to be correct), however, is not without its own problems. For example, who is the twelfth apostle? It cannot be Judas who Jesus said was "a devil" (John 6:70) and "[has gone] to his own place" (Acts 1:25),[179] apparently condemned forever. Is the twelfth apostle Matthias, or was the act of the church at Jerusalem high-handed and preliminary meaning the twelfth apostle should be identified as Paul? The same question presents itself in the identification of the twelve sons of Jacob. They are easy enough to identify, but the problem is that the listings of them in later Old and New Testament literature are not always the same. As is well known, the two sons of Joseph, Ephraim and Manasseh, are included as two separate tribal units; and Levi, with its priestly significance for all the tribes, is not always counted. Furthermore, in the seventh chapter of the Apocalypse, when each of the twelve tribes is mentioned by name, Joseph's son Manasseh is included and Joseph is included, but Levi is also included. Missing, however, are Ephraim and Dan. Dan is often thought to have been excluded, since allegedly idolatry entered Israel through the tribe of Dan; and, therefore, Dan is excluded from the promises of God. Or, perhaps the whole listing in chap. 7 of Revelation is merely symbolic and should not be taken quite so literally.

This author's own suspicion, as to the resolution of these difficulties, is that Paul is the twelfth apostle and that the final listing of the tribes as given in chap. 7 carries with it the appropriate identification of the final alignment of the twelve tribes of Israel. Such a conclusion, however, is largely speculative on the part of the author and should be treated as no more than that. On the other hand, the precise answer to the question as to who the twelfth apostle might

---

179 The Greek New Testament says, "πορευθῆναι εἰς τὸν τόπον τὸν ἴδιον," which is best translated as the NKJV correctly does, "Judas went to his own place."

be and who exactly will be counted as the twelve sons of Jacob is not essential to the correctness of the theory for the identity of the twenty-four elders. The theory could be correct without the necessity of identifying exactly who they would be. If the theory is correct, then it follows that the twenty-four elders should be identified as the twelve apostles and the twelve sons of Jacob, representing the redeemed of all time. This would be thoroughly consistent with the description of them as well as with the actions they take.

5:10 All the problems relating to the identification of the twenty-four elders have not yet been resolved because of how the NIV translates v. 10 reports: "You have made them to be a kingdom and priests to serve our God and they will reign on the earth." Two textual problems surfacing here complicate the issue. The first is that the text certainly reads, "You have made them" to be a kingdom and priests. This is inconsistent with the reading above if *hēmas* or "us" is to be included in the text. Now we would have the strange turn of events that in the song of the elders in v. 9 they sang, "With your blood you purchased us;" but in the continuation of the song in v. 10, "You have made them to be a kingdom and priests to serve our God." In brief, why the change from "us" to "them"? The problem is further extended by the next verse, which says, "And they will reign on the earth."

The translators of the United Bible Societies' Greek New Testament note that there is a reading, "We shall reign on the earth," favored by some authorities. However, they are correct in concluding that the vast majority of the textual evidence, as well as evidence that is generally considered much more reliable, favors the reading, "They shall reign." "They shall reign" would also be consistent with the previous statement, "You have made them to be a kingdom and priests." In their explanation for why they made this decision, they conjecture that "they shall reign" was changed by later commentators to "we shall reign" in order to make it consistent with the reading in v. 9, which was in the versions employed by earlier copyists, "You have purchased us with your blood."[180] This writer believes the reading, "They shall reign," is almost certainly the way the text read. Is it therefore best to abandon the viewpoint that the twenty-four elders represent the redeemed of all humanity who are praising God for their redemption and for the fact that they will someday reign with Christ on the earth?

In a book as complicated as the book of Revelation, which lends itself to a clear general perspective, the task of the interpreter remains exceedingly difficult and uncertain in such technicalities. Thus, to abandon a position that has going for it at least as much, if not more, than the position that the elders do

---

180 Metzger, *TCGNT*, 738.

not represent the redeemed of all humanity seems unnecessary. Furthermore, an observation arising out of the text has apparently been too often unnoticed. The twenty-four elders who are involved in the singing of this new song are not alone. Noting carefully v. 8, the song is apparently sung by the twenty-four elders joined in the harmony of heaven by the four living creatures. The four living creatures, if properly identified as seraphim, are not able to speak about being a kingdom of priests and reigning on the earth. Is it possible then that in the text is actually found an antiphonal song in which the elders sing, "You are worthy to take the scroll / and to open its seals, for you were slain, / and he redeemed us to God by your blood / out of every tribe and tongue and people and nation." The four living creatures answer, "You have made them to be a kingdom and priests to serve our God, / and they will reign on the earth" (NIV). Such an explanation takes most seriously the text as it apparently was originally given by John and also all the evidences relating to the various groups that are presented in the passage. The solution is at least as commendable as those who find to the contrary. Additionally, this explanation follows the reading of the strongest texts without introducing unnecessary speculation about how variant readings might have developed.

In all this discussion, one can easily overlook a more pregnant perspective, which returns the interpreter to the high Christology of the book of Revelation. The song of worthiness is sung to the Lamb because men have been purchased for God from every tribe and language and people and nation. The price of that purchase is plainly said to be the blood of Christ. Not only has the seer argued effectively in this chapter, as throughout the book of Revelation, for the deity of Christ and the triunity of the Godhead; but also he now stakes out the ground for an objective view of the atonement, indeed a penal substitutionary view of the atonement. The thesis of John is that the blood of Christ had to be shed as a penal substitutionary sacrifice in order for men to be redeemed out of all the nations of the earth.

5:11 Suddenly the seer is made aware of an additional presence in the throne room. He both sees and hears the voices of many angels, numbering thousands upon thousands and ten thousand times ten thousand. Adding up what all that means numerically probably misses the point. John has looked at them and listened to them; they were simply innumerable. They constituted a magnificent heavenly choir. They encircled the throne, the living creatures, and the elders. Probably they had been there all along, but the apostle's eyes are continuing to adjust to the spiritual depths that are needed. Like the servant of Elisha, who was unable to see the hosts of God surrounding the Syrians until Elisha prayed for him (2 Kgs 6:17), so John had missed this great heavenly choir. Probably he both sees and hears them at the same instant.

The worship of heaven is not subdued. Unfortunately, in contemporary times, churches often identify reverence with quietness. Certainly, there is a time for quietude before God. However, neither heaven nor earth are ever more reverent than when involved in a crescendo of praise to God, which is precisely what now takes place before John's eyes and ears.

5:12 In a loud voice all the heavenly choir, including angels and redeemed alike, join in the refrain, "Worthy is the Lamb who was slain / To receive power and riches and wisdom / And strength and honor and glory and blessing!" In chap. 4, the elders and the four living creatures extol and honor the Father who sits on the throne. In chap. 5, the redeemed of humanity and all the angels of heaven join in the same adoration and praise for the Lamb. The Father is praised for His creative activity in chap. 4; the Son is praised for His redemptive activity in chap. 5. Of course, the Son was involved in the creative process along with the Father, and redemption is certainly the program of the Father from beginning to end; but each is particularly praised in these passages for the accomplishment most often associated with that particular member of the Trinity. As such, chaps. 4 and 5 together effect a powerful further substantive witness to the confidence of the early church in the doctrine of the Trinity.

The Lamb is said to be worthy to receive power, riches, wisdom, strength, honor, glory, and blessing in the same way that the Father is to receive this kind of adulation. The more heaven sings, the more the doxology is extended as they search for verbiage adequate to garnish their worship before God. Certainly, the Lamb has all power, riches, wisdom, and so forth; but what is being emphasized here is that He is worthy to receive all the power, riches, strength, honor, glory, and blessing that the entire cosmos can bring to Him in gratitude for salvation.

5:13 Can the worship of heaven be extended still further? At this point John probably would have said, "This is it. This is as good as it gets." If so, he was wrong. Suddenly, he heard every creature in heaven and on earth and under the earth, even those on the sea and all that are in them singing together, "Blessing and honor and glory and power / *Be* to Him who sits on the throne, / And to the Lamb, forever and ever." This movement is extraordinary. Joining the host of heaven apparently are all the beings created by God, including not just humans but other forms of life as well. Conceivably, this chorus of glory to the Lamb even includes those who are perishing, since, after all, Paul has promised that "every knee should bow . . . and that every tongue should confess that Jesus Christ is Lord, to the glory of God the Father" (Phil 2:10–11). Redemption has no specific mention in this final chorus; simply the worthiness of the Lamb to receive praise, honor, glory, and power, and His worthiness to receive them forever.

5:14 With the whole universe having concluded the heavenly anthem, there is a final shout from the four living creatures who say, "Amen." While this commentator never objects to any response to praise and gratitude to God, such as applause; nevertheless, the most appropriate of all responses is the biblical word, "Amen." It underscores what has been said, sung, or accomplished, and pronounces the agreement of the worshipper. So, the living creatures shout, "Amen;" and the elders, as has been their practice all along, once again fall down and worship Him who sat on the throne and the Lamb. With this incredible scene, John and the reader have been prepared so that they will not be totally overwhelmed by the nature of what is about to happen on the earth. Earthly catastrophe of the magnitude of that which follows and human suffering in general are made palatable by an adequate understanding of the person and purposes of God and the perfect will and worship of God as practiced in heaven. John and the reader have now experienced and seen what they need to know as they face the information that will now be given concerning the tribulation on earth.

2. The Seal Judgments (6:1–8:1)

A. The Four Horsemen (6:1–8)

[1]Now I saw when the Lamb opened one of the seals; and I heard one of the four living creatures saying with a voice like thunder, "Come and see." [2]And I looked, and behold, a white horse. He who sat on it had a bow; and a crown was given to him, and he went out conquering and to conquer.

[3]When He opened the second seal, I heard the second living creature saying, "Come and see." [4]Another horse, fiery red, went out. And it was granted to the one who sat on it to take peace from the earth, and that *people* should kill one another; and there was given to him a great sword.

[5]When He opened the third seal, I heard the third living creature say, "Come and see." So I looked, and behold, a black horse, and he who sat on it had a pair of scales in his hand. [6]And I heard a voice in the midst of the four living creatures saying, "A quart of wheat for a denarius, and three quarts of barley for a denarius; and do not harm the oil and the wine."

[7]When He opened the fourth seal, I heard the voice of the fourth living creature saying, "Come and see." [8]So I looked, and behold, a pale horse. And the name of him who sat on it was Death, and Hades followed with him. And power was given to them over a fourth of the earth, to kill with sword, with hunger, with death, and by the beasts of the earth.

The interlude of chaps. 4 and 5 now gives way to the middle portion of the book of Revelation, which concentrates almost entirely on the events referenced as the great tribulation (Matt 24:21; Rev 7:14) or the time of Jacob's trouble (Jer 30:7; Zeph 1:15; Dan 12:1). Both Old Testament anticipation and New Testament elucidation feature this as a time of indescribable judgment on a rebellious earth. Specifically, in the book of Revelation, there are four symbols under which these judgments evolve: (1) the opening of a seven-sealed book, (2) the sounding of seven angelic trumpets, (3) the reverberations of seven thunders, and (4) the outpouring of seven bowls of divine wrath.

Serious questions as to whether these judgments should be understood as sequential, overlapping to some degree, or synonymous but employing diverse means of expression have occupied commentators who interpret the book. This commentator has taken the position that some overlapping is apparent (see 8:1-2, where the opening of the seventh seal ushers in the judgments of the seven trumpets).[181] Nevertheless, essentially two things may be clearly observed

---

181 Bauckham notes, "As seven is the number of completeness, in some sense each series completes God's judgment on the unrighteous world. In other words, the seventh of each series portrays the final act of judgment in which evil is destroyed and God's kingdom arrives. But the three series are so connected that the seventh-seal opening includes the seven trumpets and the seventh trumpet includes seven bowls. Thus each series reaches the same end, but from starting-points progressively closer to the end. This is why the three series of judgments are of progressive severity: the judgments of the seal-openings affect a quarter of the earth (6:8), those of the trumpets affect a third (8:7-12; 9:18), but those of the bowls are unlimited. Warning judgments, restrained in hope that the wicked will be warned and repent (cf. 9:20-1), are succeeded in the last series by judgments of final retribution (cf. 16:5-7). Of course, the highly schematized portrayal of the judgments depicts their theological significance. It cannot be meant as a literal prediction of events." R. Bauckham, *New Testament Theology: The Theology of the Book of Revelation* (Cambridge: Cambridge University Press, 1993), 40-41. Bauckham is correct in the majority of the paragraph, but his concluding statement constitutes nothing more than an unsupported prejudice. See also B. Witherington III, *Revelation*, New Cambridge Bible Commentary (Cambridge: Cambridge University Press, 2003), 129-30, for further evidence of the sequential view. Answering Caird (see G. B. Caird, *The Revelation of St. John the Divine*, HNTC 19 [San Francisco: Harper & Row, 1966], 105-6), he notes, "As helpful as this analysis is, it is not entirely correct. One could say these sets of sevens overlap, with the second set beginning before the end of the first and then carrying things further, and the third picking up in the midst of the second set and carrying things even further. Bauckham has pointed out that all three sets of sevens conclude with the same final judgment reached in the seventh of each of the three series. This is demonstrated by the repeated use of the terms thunder, lighting, earthquake, and heavy hail in varying order at 4:5, 8:5, 11:19, and 16:18-21. This

from the text. First, strictly speaking, the judgments are not synonymous; and, not surprisingly, the descriptions of the effects of such judgments are widely diversified. Second, one may also fairly observe that however devastating and general the seal judgments may be, the apparent intent of the author is to depict a worsening of the judgments in the progression from chap. 6 and the seals to chaps. 15 and 16, where the bowls of God's wrath reach the ultimate crescendo of Him pouring out His wrath. In fact, it might even be observed that while the seal judgments are less specifically associated with God, the trumpet judgments bear more of the actual mark of heaven since these are trumpets sounded by seven angels. The seven thunders seem to be even more associated with God, even though their message remains hidden, and the seven bowls of God's wrath are specifically associated with "the wrath of God."

The opening of the four initial seals depicts general conditions that seem to exist on the earth from the outset of the tribulation period and gradually worsen as time goes along. Also, the message of each of the seals seems to have a rather logical relationship to the opening of the seal prior to it. With this in mind, we may examine those seals.

6:1–8 From his Patmos perch, John observes the Lamb, who alone has been deemed worthy to loose the seals on the seven-sealed book and reveal its critically important message for John and his readers. The Lamb opens the first of the seven seals and suddenly John hears a voice with reverberations like a clap of thunder and understands one of the living creatures to call, "Come!" The word translated "come," an imperative form of a present tense verb, is a command. As with the NKJV, a few significant readings add the words "and see"—a translation that raises the question about to whom the command, "Come," was issued.[182] If the words "and see" should be a part of the original text, then John

---

phrase is an echo of Exod. 19.16. 'The seven seal-openings are linked to the seven trumpets by the technique of overlapping or interweaving.' But the whole sequence of bowls is a development of the seventh trumpet, and the three woes are identical with the judgments inaugurated by the last three trumpets. In other words there is recapitulation to a degree, but there is also interweaving and development in these sets of sevens as well. With the bowls being a development of the seventh trumpet, one wonders if the trumpets are not also a development of a closer look at the seventh seal. Whatever is the case, the three sets of sevens end at the same place—the culmination of history."

182 The note in *A Textual Commentary on the Greek New Testament* [*TCGNT*], reads in part, "After ἔρχου, which is well supported by A C P 1 1006 1611 1854 2053 vg cop^sa, bo *al*, several witnesses add (as though the verb 'Come!' were addressed to the Seer) καὶ ἴδε (ℵ 046 about 120 minuscules it^gig syr^ph, h eth *al*) or καὶ βλέπε (296 2049 and Textus Receptus)." See B. Metzger, *TCGNT* (New York: UBS, 1971), 739.

would have been the recipient of the command and, therefore, would have been summoned at this point to read the message revealed with the opening of the first seal in the seven-sealed scroll. There is an advantage to this interpretation. Already the nature of the scroll has been described by John as one that had writing literally on the front and back sides (see 5:1). The necessity was to open the seals so that the scroll could be unrolled and the text deciphered. Logically then, the scroll, having been opened one-seventh of the way, would make possible John's reading of the scroll, and he would be summoned to read it.

On the other hand, in dealing with apocalyptic-type genre the general rules of logic do not necessarily pertain. As a matter of fact, John mentions nothing at all about reading words but rather describes in picturesque imagery an event that seems to leap to life right out of the midst of the scroll itself. If this is a proper interpretation, it is probably best to go with the reading chosen by the NASB and NIV texts, which is simply "Come" and understand that the mandate is to the horsemen who presently appear. Whichever way one chooses to read the text at this point will have no effect on the end result of understanding what is depicted, though the latter would be favored by this commentator.

The result of the mandate to come is that there appears a rider on a white horse. The rider is described in three descriptive phrases. First, he holds a bow. Second, he has been given a *stephanos*, or victor's crown. Third, he rode out as a conqueror and with the intention to conquer. In fact, as the NIV text has translated, he is "bent on conquest." Discussions regarding the identity of this first rider and horse are about as far from one another as can be imagined. Some authors view the rider as the Messiah and point out that in rabbinical literature a rider clothed in white almost always had good connotations, if not messianic ones.[183] On the other hand, many interpreters have not

---

183 D. Chilton writes: "Amazingly, the run-of-the-mill Dispensational interpretation claims that this rider on the white horse is the Antichrist. Showing where his faith lies, Hal Lindsey goes all the way and declares that the Antichrist is 'the only person who could accomplish all of these feats.' But there are several points about this Rider that demonstrate conclusively that He can be none other than the Lord Jesus Christ. First, he is riding a white horse, as Jesus does in 19:11–16. Second, he carries a Bow. As we have seen, the passage from Habakkuk that forms the basis for Revelation 6 shows the Lord as the Warrior-King carrying a Bow (Hab. 3:9,11). St. John is also appealing here to Psalm 45, one of the great prophecies of Christ's victory over his enemies, in which the psalmist joyously calls to Him as He rides forth conquering, and to conquer:

Gird Thy sword on Thy thigh, O Mighty One,
In Thy Splendor and Thy majesty!

only argued that this is not the Christ; his identity is the opposite—namely, the Antichrist.[184]

The answer to this dilemma is contextually resolvable. Since the second, third, and fourth seals must be regarded as devastating judgments of God on the tribulation earth, one can hardly imagine the significance of the appearing of the Messiah in seal number one. Obviously, the appearance of the Messiah in seal number one would be a hopeful sign since conquering and conquest by the Lord would bring the earth into submission to Him. Such a presence, while

---

And in Thy majesty ride on victoriously,
For the cause of truth and meekness and righteousness;
Let Thy right hand teach Thee awesome things.
Thine arrows are sharp;
The peoples fall under Thee;
Thine arrows are in the heart of the King's enemies.
(Ps. 45:3–5)."

See D. Chilton, *The Days of Vengeance* (Fort Worth, TX: Dominion Press, 1987), 185–86. However, Chilton notes that some dispensationalists take a view similar to his, citing Henry Morris and Zane Hodges (185). By far the most interesting and effective advocate of this position is J. A. Seiss. See his extensive discussion in *The Apocalypse: Lectures on the Book of Revelation* (Grand Rapids: Zondervan, 1962), 125–29.

184 R. Summers concludes, "This first horseman represents conquest, militarism, armed strength with lust to subdue some new foe. The white color of the horse represents victory. A white horse was always ridden by a conqueror in a triumphal march. This horse symbolized, along with the others, one of the forces which was to bring about the downfall of the Roman Empire" (*Worthy Is The Lamb: An Interpretation of Revelation* [Nashville: Broadman, 1951], 140). W. J. Harrington voices a similar perspective saying, "It is evident that, in our passage, the four horsemen must be taken together. They represent war and its attendant evils—the war, strife, famine, and pestilence of the Synoptic apocalypse. The white horse signifies triumphant warfare; the horseman rides on his path of conquest. Though the rider is a symbolic figure, the Parthians, Rome's dreaded foe, are in mind, for John is going to focus on the fall of Rome—for him, *the foe of the Church*" (*Revelation*, SP 15 [Collegeville, MN: Liturgical Press, 1993], 91). On the other hand, A. Johnson concludes that the horseman is the Antichrist ("Revelation," *EBC* [Grand Rapids: Zondervan], 12:473). R. L. Thomas, who also provides an extensive discussion of all interpretive possibilities, views the figure as the Antichrist (*Revelation 1–7: An Exegetical Commentary* [Chicago: Moody, 418–23). G. K. Beale cannot identify the rider as the Antichrist but finds the idea that the rider represents Christ to be improbable (*The Book of Revelation: A Commentary on the Greek Text*, NIGTC [Grand Rapids: Eerdmans, 1999], 216).

understandable in initiating the millennium, is out of place and inappropriate at the outset of the tribulation.

In addition to the above, when the Lord does appear in 19:11 and following He is viewed by John rather differently than the picture of the rider on the white horse of chap. 6. In chap. 6, the Rider of the white horse carries a bow and has a victor's crown and is determined to conquer wherever He can. In chap. 19, the Lord is clearly presented with many crowns; and these are, as one would expect, *diadēma* or diadems, kingly crowns, and He fights with the sword of His mouth, which is the Word of God, not with a bow. While certainly one cannot press these particular details too far, they are perhaps sufficient to suggest, especially with the added benefit of the context, that the rider of the white horse in chap. 6 is not to be equated with the Christ.

Instead, the conqueror of the first seal should be identified with the long-awaited Antichrist, the ruler who would come and destroy the city and the sanctuary mentioned in Dan 9:26. This interpretation has the advantage of explaining the results of the opening of the first seal as seen in the conflagration that breaks out with the opening of the second seal, the famine that results in the opening of the third seal, and the widespread desolation and death as a consequence of all that is revealed in the fourth seal.

The Lamb now steps forward to open the second seal, and once again the second living creature issues his mandate, "Come!" The second horse is fiery red, and the rider of that horse is given power to take peace from the earth and to make men slay one another. As symbolic of that assignment, he is given a large sword. Obviously, the second seal anticipates resistance to the intentions of the rider on the white horse from the opening of seal number one. Jesus Himself predicted that there would be wars and rumors of wars, which has certainly been the case throughout human history. With the opening of the second seal, the reader is introduced to a worldwide involvement in such conflicts, surpassing the world wars of history, the cold war, and all other conflicts of the human family. This will become increasingly apparent as the reader is introduced to the series of judgments that follow and reads of the consequent decimation of the earth. Worthy of note is the expression that he "was granted...to take peace from the earth." Even in eras of war so widely extended as the two world wars, there has never been a time when segments of the earth did not remain essentially at peace. The uniqueness of the tribulation period seems to be that this second rider signals the taking of all peace from the earth. The most debilitating traits of greed and lust for power and money assert themselves, creating myriads of conflicts across the entire face of the globe so that conflict rather than peace becomes the rule.

At this point the Lamb opens the third seal, and the third living creature beckons, "Come!" What emerges from the seven-sealed scroll next is a black horse. The rider of this steed holds a pair of scales in his hand, such as would be found in the *agora* of all Roman and Near Eastern cities of the period. Another voice then comes to John's ears, and he is apparently unable to make out the source of this voice. He states that it seems to come from "among the four living creatures," but whether it is simply a fifth voice among them or one of the living creatures is not certain. The purpose of the voice is clear enough. The scales in the hand of the black horseman need an interpretation, which is now provided by saying that a quart of wheat would be all that could be purchased for a denarius and that three quarts of barley could be bought for that same money. The widespread practice of seeing the Roman silver denarius as the normal daily wage for a worker in the Roman Empire is widely accepted.[185] Thus, the interpretation provided by the voice is that the famine is so severe that only a small amount of wheat or barely could be purchased for a entire day of work.

The difference between wheat and barley has long been considered to be the difference between the bread of the poor and the bread of those who were better off. Barley constituted a rougher grain and was generally more readily available and less expensive than wheat. This is exactly the picture presented here since three dry measure quarts of barley are available for the same cost of one dry measure quart of wheat. This dry measure quart (*choinix*) amounted to little more than could be successfully cradled in two human hands.[186] More astoundingly, however, is the fact that it would take an entire day's wage to purchase either the barley or the wheat in such relatively small amounts. Therefore, one can imagine the conditions depicted of almost unbelievable famine, arising as a result of the opening of the second seal and the taking of peace from the earth. With fields and crops charred as a result of the conflict and with peacetime conditions necessary for husbandry largely removed, even barely enough bread for a poor man's family for one day required a full day's wage.

Remarkably, however, there does seem to be a limitation placed on the rider of the black horse. While he is permitted to decimate the grain crops, he is told for the time being not to hurt the oil and the wine. Hence, olive trees and vineyards are protected, at least for the early part of the tribulation period. The reason for this restraint is not clear. The best suggestion seems to be that

---

185 This reckoning is employed in part based on the parable of the workers in the vineyard in Matt 20:1–16. For an extensive discussion of money and coinage in the Bible see *The Illustrated Bible Dictionary* (Wheaton, IL: Tyndale, 1980), 2:1022–23.

186 Ibid., 3:1639.

a famine caused in part by drought would affect the wheat and barley crops far sooner than it would the olive orchards or, to some degree, by the difference in location for those crops—the vineyards. Some commentators also believe that vineyards and olive orchards tended to belong to wealthier people, while the wheat and barley fields would be more common throughout the land. Accordingly, the passage suggests that the lifestyles of the wealthier inhabitants of the earth are less affected by the early judgments of the tribulation.[187]

When the Lamb opens the fourth seal and the fourth living creature demands that the rider come forth, the circumstances flowing as a natural result from the opening of the first three seals are introduced in the tribulation. A pale horse gallops to light, and the rider on the horse is identified as Death, and Hades is described as following close behind him. In this case the NKJV translators have chosen to use none of the conventionally employed translations of *Hadēs* such as hell, death, or the grave but rather have simply brought the word *Hadēs* across into the English language. The meaning of *Hadēs* is never hard to establish in a general way but almost always difficult to define for specific translation. Here, if anywhere, however, the relationship of Hades as following close behind Death seems to provide good reason for rendering the word as "the grave." However, to translate *Hadēs* as "the grave" is in Western minds to associate it with the place where a corpse is interred, but the meaning for Jewish and even Greco-Roman audiences was clearly more than this understanding. The word generally is used to refer to the shadowy world of those who had passed from the visible, earthly, and biological existence, which is known at the moment. Hades is the unseen and partially unknown and unknowable world to which the dead have departed.[188]

Death parades on his horse and the realm of the departed follows like a street sweeper behind him, cleaning up the debris of the fallen and imprisoning them in that shadowy world. The various means of inflicting death on the inhabitants of the earth accord, at least in part, with seals two and three. First, people are killed by the sword as one would anticipate upon the opening of the second seal. Second, they are killed with famine and plague, precisely what is unveiled with the opening of the third seal. However, the text now adds that wild beasts of the earth also become involved in the plunder. This is also a logical outgrowth of seals two and three. First, widespread war, doubtless during the days of the tribulation, will render equally widespread burial impossible. Hence, wild beasts will do more than usual scavenging. This, in turn, seems necessary in light of conditions of famine, which will certainly affect beast as

---

187 See the discussion in Thomas, *Revelation 1–7*, 432–33.

188 For a succinct but helpful discussion of *Hades*, see Jeremias, *TDNT* 1.146–49.

well as man and necessitate not only the opportunity to feed on carrion but also the necessity of taking life where beasts with less hunger would never think of venturing. Periodically, a wild animal will take the life of a human, but it is still infrequent.[189] This will be changed by the opening of the fourth seal and conditions that, therefore, will exist during the tribulation.

B. The Martyr Seal (6:9–11)

[9]**When He opened the fifth seal, I saw under the altar the souls of those who had been slain for the word of God and for the testimony which they held. [10]And they cried with a loud voice, saying, "How long, O Lord, holy and true, until You judge and avenge our blood on those who dwell on the earth?" [11]Then a white robe was given to each of them; and it was said to them that they should rest a little while longer, until both *the number of* their fellow servants and their brethren, who would be killed as they *were*, was completed.**

6:9-11   The opening of the fifth seal at first glance seems to suggest a different direction than has been the thrust of the first four seals. The Lamb is not specifically mentioned in v. 9 but once again is assumed to be the One opening the seal. When it is opened, the scroll reveals an altar, together with souls who have been slain under that altar. The reason for the loss of their lives is statedly the word of God and the testimony that they had maintained. Even their activity is a departure from what might be expected since they cry out to the Lord to avenge their blood on the inhabitants of the earth. For this appeal they are not rebuked, and each is given a white robe and told to rest until their brothers who are yet to be killed accomplish that martyrdom.

---

189 Hippopotami and crocodiles are the most frequent killers of humans in Africa. But most of those deaths arise from encroachment of humans into their habitat. Hunters and the unwary may experience memorable encounters with Cape Buffalo. As in the case of the Tsavo lions that killed many in a few months, lions may become predators of humans; and an occasional elephant can become a rogue. Man-eating tigers were a formidable problem in the days of Jim Corbett, the famous tiger hunter and conservationist in India. Wolf packs, mountain lions, and black bears rarely kill, but brown bears are always a threat in North America. For encounters in the human domain to become frequent and for many to die as a result clearly signals monumental changes in the aggressiveness and circumstances in the animal kingdom. Rapid increases in the birth rates of venomous reptiles could also play a role. Rabid or otherwise diseased animals could be a factor in the case of the epidemics. See J. H. Patterson, *The Man-Eaters of Tsavo* (London: Macmillan, 1979). Also, J. Corbett, *The Temple Tiger and More Man-Eaters of Kumaon* (Oxford: Oxford University Press, 2008).

Part of the difficulty with the fifth seal is that with the opening of the sixth seal the reader is immediately ushered back into a recitation of the judgments of God, and this scheme continues to be characteristic of the other judgments of the tribulation. So the question arises as to the real purpose of the revelation found in the fifth seal. Some authorities have simply assessed the situation as being an interlude in the judgments, through which one is allowed to view a heavenly altar and see where the martyrs have gone. Some have even gone so far as to argue that these souls under the altar represent all those who are martyrs during the entire history of the church or even all the dead saints of God. Such explanations do not fit the context.[190]

Far more probable is that the opening of the fifth seal introduces the fact that even the elect of the tribulation period do not avoid the consequences of the far-reaching impact of the seal judgments. Quite to the contrary, those who suffer during the tribulation are singled out as being at the foot of the altar crying out to God to avenge their blood on the inhabitants of the earth. There is no way all the martyrs of all time could be thus pictured since those who martyred them would long since have come into judgment in all but the most recent cases. Furthermore, in this case, their enemies are specifically said to be still alive on the earth. Specifically, these must be determined as those who have experienced the wrath of the unbelieving earth against believers singled out for that martyrdom during the days of the tribulation. If asked where such people come from, some interpreters would see them as saints of the church age who are martyred during the tribulation. Those interpreters who anticipate that the church will be removed from the earth prior to the tribulation would insist that these are tribulation saints and would find

---

190 For the view that the martyrs observed here represent all martyrs from every age, see G. E. Ladd, *A Commentary on the Revelation of John* (Grand Rapids: Eerdmans, 1972), 104. Ladd does allow for the possibility that the end time may be particularly in view. Inveighing against the dyeing of clothes, Clement of Alexandria references the martyrs of this passage as a reason to stick with white: "The Apocalypse says also that the Lord Himself appeared wearing such a robe. It says also, 'I saw the souls of those that had witnessed, beneath the altar, and there was given to each a white robe.' And if it were necessary to seek for any other colour, the natural colour of truth should suffice. But garments which are like flowers are to be abandoned to Bacchic fooleries, and to those of rites of initiation, along with purple and silver plate, as the comic poet says:—'Useful for tragedians, not for life.' And our life ought to be anything rather than a pageant" (*The Instructor* 2.11, ANF 2:265). Tertullian argues from the visibility of the souls of these martyrs that there is a kind of spiritual corporeality to souls, at least to other souls. *A Treatise on the Soul* 8, ANF 3:187–88.

record of their unique existence in the very next chapter where 144,000 Jews are sealed and where it is specifically stated that in addition to these who are saved there is also a "great multitude that no one could count, from every nation, tribe, people and language."

Discussions about whether the altar should be identified with the altar of sacrifice or the altar of incense are probably of little consequence. Some argue that the language chosen to describe the altar using the Greek word *thusiastērion* is reminiscent of the altar of sacrifice and that just as the blood of the sacrifices would run around the altar below, so the souls of those who have been slain are pictured.[191] Others, however, argue that this would be inappropriate since one sacrifice alone has been made and that the appropriate altar is the one closest to the holy of holies—namely, the altar of incense. To identify this altar with either of the two altars in the tabernacle or temple is not necessary. It is sufficient to recognize an altar coming into view that is clearly related in some way to the heavenly scene.

The souls slain are those who have been slain during the tribulation period. Those who have vanquished them from the earth in such a fashion are still alive, and this accounts for the cry for judgment to come on the inhabitants of the earth and for their blood to be avenged. That these martyrs are presented as souls (*psuchas*) has been frequently noted. This rather remarkable and non-Jewish way of presenting them might well suggest that these martyrs are in a disembodied state, having not yet received glorified bodies. On the other hand, some interpreters believe that their being told to rest a while and being given a "white robe" is tantamount to expressing the fact that they were given glorified bodies. Since the glorification of the body is clearly promised by the apostle Paul as a gift of the Lord at his coming, such a position would be inconsistent for anyone believing that the *parousia* or coming of Christ does not occur until after the tribulation. However, even in the case of those who believe that the church has already been removed from the earth prior to the events beginning in chap. 4, to see the white robe as the bestowal of a glorified body is not necessary. The white robe is the *stolē*, which was a floor-length robe of dignity whose white color suggested holiness and purity. In all probability the souls of those who have been slain because of their testimony to Christ and because of their

---

191 J. Moffatt argues cogently for the altar of burnt offerings. See "The Revelation of St. John the Divine," in *Expositor's Greek New Testament*, ed. R. Nicoll (Grand Rapids: Eerdmans, 1951), 5:391. A. T. Robertson advances this same view in *Word Pictures in the Greek New Testament* (Nashville: Broadman, 1933), 6:343. Thomas effectively demonstrates why their positions are less than convincing (*Revelation 1–7*, 442–43).

adherence to the word of God remain in a disembodied state until all the saints who are to be killed in the tribulation have completed their destiny.

Moffatt probably rightly observes, "The white robe assigned each of these martyr-spirits as a pledge of future and final glory (vii. 9) and a consoling proof that no judgment awaited them (xx. 4–6), is a favourite gift in the Jewish heaven (*cf.* Enoch lxii. 15 f., and *Asc. Isa.* ix. 24 f.)."[192] The bigger problem in the text seems to be to explain the call for vengeance, which is less than what one would anticipate from believers who have been taught nonretaliation in kind. What is found here is more in keeping with what one would expect to find in the Old Testament imprecatory psalms. However, a closer look at the text will show that what these tribulation saints request is not an eye for an eye or a tooth for a tooth. Rather, knowing as they do the inevitabilities of the judgment of God now being visited on the earth and that it is the full purpose of God to avenge their blood on "the inhabitants of the earth," they are asking how long before all these things will be completed. There is no doubt whatsoever about the nature of what will transpire, only a question as to the timing of those judgments. Sweet responds to this concern by noting that "the spirit of the cry seems regrettably pre-Christian. This, however, is not a matter of attitudes to people in daily life, but of God's cause which seems to go by default; it is 'the language not of private revenge but of public justice.'"[193]

The response to this query is twofold. First, the white *stolē* is provided so that they are comforted and rewarded by such a distribution from the hand of God. Furthermore, they are instructed that they must wait a little longer until the killing of fellow servants and brothers, even as they had been killed, would be complete. The language, as many commentators have noted, suggests that there are a specified number of martyrs from the tribulation that God had ordained. While this seems strange to modern ears, God may well have ordained that in his providences. Or the expression may mean no more than that the final acts of God's judgment as seen in the outpouring of the bowls of wrath will not come until the closing days of the tribulation. By then all who will have faced martyrdom will have joined their brothers and fellow servants around the altar.

In any event the martyrs are told to rest, *anapausōntai* being a word sometimes meaning "stop" or "rest." Either could be in view, but the text favors the concept of "stop" in the sense that the martyrs are called upon to stop their cry

---

192 Moffatt, "The Revelation of St. John the Divine," 5:392.
193 J. P. M. Sweet, *Revelation* (Philadelphia: Westminster, 1979), 141.

to God, knowing that the full number of those who should be martyred has not yet been completed.

One last comment is worthy of note. The reason for the suffering of these martyrs is that they have been slain "because of the word of God and the testimony they had maintained." The costliness of faithfulness and testimony and of adherence to the word of God was notable in John's day even as he himself suffered exile on Patmos. Throughout history such faithfulness to the word of God and to one's testimony has often proven costly. The escalation of such difficulty awaits the tribulation period.

C. The Sixth Seal (6:12–17)

[12]I looked when He opened the sixth seal, and behold, there was a great earthquake; and the sun became black as sackcloth of hair, and the moon became like blood. [13]And the stars of heaven fell to the earth, as a fig tree drops its late figs when it is shaken by a mighty wind. [14]Then the sky receded as a scroll when it is rolled up, and every mountain and island was moved out of its place. [15]And the kings of the earth, the great men, the rich men, the commanders, the mighty men, every slave and every free man, hid themselves in the caves and in the rocks of the mountains, [16]and said to the mountains and rocks, "Fall on us and hide us from the face of Him who sits on the throne and from the wrath of the Lamb! [17]For the great day of His wrath has come, and who is able to stand?"

6:12–17   The opening of the sixth seal presents several interesting options to the interpreter. Even among millenarian interpreters who tend to take biblical passages literally, there is a tendency to treat the message of the sixth seal as more symbolic than literal. On the other hand, for consistency, others have viewed the text as presenting literal cosmic upheavals associated with the tribulation period. This author is among those who take a more literal approach out of a desire for consistency of interpretation but in the process would warn the reader against pressing even literalism so far that one says more than the text. Clearly enough, what John saw with the opening of the sixth seal was unprecedented cosmic upheaval. Most of the listed disasters are known today, but what happens with the opening of the sixth seal is beyond modern comprehension in magnitude and extent. This may be seen by the reaction of the population of the earth, who upon viewing the catastrophic consequences conclude that the magnitude is so great that it must be the hand of God and the wrath of the Lamb.

Beale describes these enumerated judgments as "stock in trade Old Testament imagery."

> The judgment of the world is depicted with stock-in-trade OT imagery for the dissolution of the cosmos. This portrayal is based on a mosaic of OT passages that are brought together because of the cosmic metaphors of judgment that they have in common. The quarry of texts from which the description has been drawn is composed primarily of Isa. 13:10–13; 24:1–6,19–23; 34:4; Ezek. 32:6–8; Joel 2:10,30–31; 3:15–16; and Hab. 3:6–11 (cf. secondarily Amos 8:8–9; Jer. 4:23–28; and Ps. 68:7–8). The same OT texts are also influential in Matt. 24:29; Mark 13:24–25; and Acts 2:19–20 (= Joel 2:30–31), which themselves likewise form part of the apocalyptic quarry influencing the dramatic portrayal in Rev. 6:12–14 (*Test. Mos.* 10:3–6 and 4 Ezra 5:4–8 [cf. 7:39–40] stand in the same OT tradition). All these passages mention at least four of the following elements, which are found here in the Revelation: the shaking of the earth or mountains; the darkening or shaking of the moon, stars, sun, and/or heaven; and the pouring of blood.[194]

Unfortunately, Beale then opts for a figurative reading of these judgments.

> The likelihood is that the portrayal is figurative, since five of the determinative OT background passages mentioned above refer to the historical end of a sinful nation's existence occurring through divine judgment, in which God conducts holy war by employing one nation to defeat another in war. Furthermore, the additionally formative texts of Matt. 24:29; Mark 13:25; and Acts 2:20 have the same figurative significance and are based on one or more of these five OT texts.[195]

The opening volley of the Lord is a great earthquake. This is followed by the sun turning black as sackcloth made of goat hair. The black goats of the Palestinian hillside are well known to any traveler. The hair of these black goats provides the ideal material for the making of Bedouin tents and many other items, not the least of which is the famous sackcloth. The black goats' hair, when woven together, provides a reasonably cool garment through which the wind can be felt.

---

194 Beale, *The Book of Revelation*, 396.
195 Ibid., 397.

However, when rains fall, the hair has a tendency to swell and, therefore, mat together, protecting what is within from rain. Consequently, this perfect material is used for both tents and sackcloth, which was famous as an indication of mourning. Whatever turned the sun black as sackcloth of hair had a corresponding effect on the moon, not turning the moon to blood but making it appear as though it were blood. By the same token the stars of the sky fell to earth similar to the way late unpicked figs eventually fall from the fig tree when it is shaken by a strong wind. Meanwhile, the sky had the appearance of receding like a scroll rolling up, and the effects of the earthquake mentioned initially seemed to be the subject of the statement that "every mountain and island was removed from its place." What exactly is to be made of the description of these cosmic upheavals?

Attempts by some modern interpreters to describe some sort of nuclear warfare producing a cloud that would blacken the sun's rays and make the moon appear red cannot be dismissed as impossible, but neither is there any necessity for such an interpretation, nor is there anything in the text to suggest it. Widespread fires or simply intense weather patterns all across the face of the globe, to say nothing of other cosmic factors such as volcanism, which could well be involved in mountains being removed from their places, could all contribute to the blackening of the sun and the making of the moon to appear reddish in color.

Insofar as stars of the sky falling to the earth, obviously the present scientific description of a star cannot be intended. This is a phenomenological reading from the perspective of John and much more probably describes meteor showers that apparently increase during the time of the opening of the sixth seal. The receding of the sky like a scroll has tended to be a greater problem to interpreters but once again need not be. Remembering John's phenomenological viewpoint, anyone who has watched the effects of a tornado in the midsections of the United States or northwest Texas could have made just such a description about its effects on the sky. Almost certainly what is being described here are meteorological storms of such increased magnitude that tornado and hurricane-like effects are created everywhere in the sky, giving the look of the rolling up of a scroll. By the same token, mountains and islands are shaken and moved from their places as would be characteristic of widespread seismic disorders and the accompanying volcanic eruptions that would take place. John's description is in keeping with natural phenomena already observable, though certainly here they increase to exponential proportions. As the heavenly scroll unrolls, the earthly scroll is rolled together.

In fact, the exponential proportions and global engulfing that seems to be pictured in the opening of the sixth seal are the factors that induce the entire population of the earth to conclude that this can only be an act of God. It is not uncommon in certain kinds of disasters even today to hear someone say, "This could only have been an act of God." How much more will that be the case in the days of the opening of the sixth seal? John goes to great lengths to indicate that no one is to be exempted from this reaction. Whether a man is a slave or a free man within the Roman Empire, whether he happens to be rich or mighty, whether he is a prince, a general, or a king, the effects are all the same. All men are reduced to a common denominator quaking in fear before the judgment of the God who alone is sovereign. In fact, v. 10 suggests that physical death is preferable to facing the Lamb in his wrath. Hence, all rankings of men call to the rocks and the mountains, pleading that these fall and hide them from the face of the One who sits on the throne and more specifically from the wrath of the Lamb. God who has always been characterized by grace in creation and the Lamb who has been characterized by grace in redemption are suddenly depicted in their eternal anger against all that is sinful and evil. The great day of their wrath has come, and John simply asks the question, "Who can stand?" John has adopted the understanding expressed in the terminology of the Old Testament prophets who foresaw a day of God's wrath coming. As the Lord had said, "My Spirit shall not strive with man forever" (Gen 6:3); there comes a day when judgment is the only remaining alternative. That day has arrived with the opening of the sixth seal.

One final matter needing consideration is the timing of the sixth seal. Some interpreters look at the cosmic portents, which are the content of the sixth seal, and conclude that this must be the end of the tribulation period and the beginning of the moment of Christ's return to the earth. These interpreters would see the six seals thus far opened as spanning the entire length of the tribulation period and would then interpret the judgments of the trumpets, thunders, and bowls of wrath as recapitulations of tribulation judgments. For example, B.H. Carroll observes:

> Now, you see that that sixth seal brings you to the end of time. Our Lord also says in his great prophecy in Matthew 24: "After the tribulation of those days the sun shall be darkened as by an eclipse, and the moon will not give her light, and the stars shall fall." It is certain that there comes a time when God does answer the long-deferred petition of his people for vengeance upon their oppressors.[196]

---

196 B. H. Carroll, *The Book of Revelation*, in *An Interpretation of the English Bible*,

However, contextual reading of the evidence does not favor this since the opening of the seventh seal will be the actual signal for the blaring of the seven trumpets. In addition to that, nothing is said in the descriptions of the judgments of the sixth seal about any conclusion to human history at this time. All events pictured with the opening of the sixth seal are perfectly consistent with conditions that may well exist early in the tribulation period and yet leave enormous devastation yet to come in the remaining three sets of judgments to be revealed. A better interpretation is to see the seven seal judgments as all belonging to the first half of the tribulation period. This persuasion is further supported by the sealing of the 144,000 Jews, which will now become the subject matter of chap. 7.

D. The Sealing of the 144,000 (7:1–8)

[1]After these things I saw four angels standing at the four corners of the earth, holding the four winds of the earth, that the wind should not blow on the earth, on the sea, or on any tree.[2]Then I saw another angel ascending from the east, having the seal of the living God. And he cried with a loud voice to the four angels to whom it was granted to harm the earth and the sea, [3]saying, "Do not harm the earth, the sea, or the trees till we have sealed the servants of our God on their foreheads." [4]And I heard the number of those who were sealed. One hundred *and* forty-four thousand of all the tribes of the children of Israel *were* sealed:

> [5]of the tribe of Judah twelve thousand *were* sealed;
>   of the tribe of Reuben twelve thousand *were* sealed;
>   of the tribe of Gad twelve thousand *were sealed*;
> [6]of the tribe of Asher twelve thousand *were* sealed;
>   of the tribe of Naphtali twelve thousand *were* sealed;
>   of the tribe of Manasseh twelve thousand *were* sealed;
> [7]of the tribe of Simeon twelve thousand *were* sealed;
>   of the tribe of Levi twelve thousand *were* sealed;
>   of the tribe of Issachar twelve thousand *were* sealed;
> [8]of the tribe of Zebulun twelve thousand *were* sealed;
>   of the tribe of Joseph twelve thousand *were* sealed;
>   of the tribe of Benjamin twelve thousand *were* sealed.

---

ed. J. B. Cranfill (Nashville: Broadman, 1947), 17:102.

7:1 Six seals have been opened. Prior to the opening of the seventh seal, an interlude that spans the totality of chap. 7 ensues. This interlude is in rather apparent juxtaposition to the judgments perpetrated on the earth as revealed in the opening of the six seals. Rather than judgment, chap. 7 reveals a program of protection and benediction for two groups of recipients. The chapter may be divided naturally into the sealing of 12,000 from each of the twelve tribes of Israel (vv. 1–8), the revelation of the great multitude of the faithful from every nation (vv. 9–12), and finally the identification of those from every nation and tongue as well as a further enumeration of the blessings of God (vv. 13–17).

The interlude of chap. 7 begins with the apocalypticist observing the four angels standing at the four corners of the earth engaged in physically restraining four winds, preventing the wind from blowing on the land, sea, or trees. The reference to the four corners of the earth is typical of passages used by those who wish to insist that there are mistakes in the Bible since the cosmology apparent in such an expression is clearly at odds with what is now known about the spherical shape of the world. Perhaps the expression "the four corners of the earth" does invoke terminology that originated in early cosmologies imagining the surface of the earth to be essentially flat. But here the expression is nothing more than a figure of speech similar to many others that, though scientifically incorrect, are a part of vocabularies even today. Such, for example, is what is intended with the phrase "the sun setting."[197] In this case John observes four angels who are actually restraining the judgments. Since to think of angels as restraining the direct retributive acts of a sovereign, omnipotent God is impossible, the judgments are better understood as a reference to restraining those who are the natural outgrowth of the rebellious and sinful nations of the world.[198]

There certainly exist judicial acts of a sovereign God in judgment. But men bring judgment on themselves, as referenced by the apostle Paul in Rom 1 and about which is said, "A man reaps what he sows" (Gal 6:7). These inevitable judgments associated with the acts of the rebellious race, nevertheless, are often restrained by a merciful God for his own purposes. In this particular case,

---

197 Other biblical passages suggest that the ancients were not unaware of the spherical shape of the earth. Isaiah's (40:22) writing in the eighth century BC spoke of the One who "sits enthroned above the circle of the earth." Job, in a presumably much older text, has Eliphaz opine about "He who walks above the circle of heaven" (Job 22:14 NKJV), and elsewhere (26:7) as the One who "hangs the earth on nothing." חוּג has possible meanings of "arch," or "vault," but the essential significance is that of "circle." BDB, 295.

198 The restraint of evil as part of divine activity seems to be the emphasis of 2 Thess 2:7 where the power of lawlessness is restrained until God's chosen time.

the inevitable results of iniquity are withheld for a particular purpose, and that purpose has to do with the sealing of the 144,000. For their sakes and until they are sealed, John clearly affirms that no wind of judgment blows on land, sea, or tree, indicating the relative immunity of the inhabitants of the land, of the sea and its creatures, and of vegetation.

7:2-3 At this point John sees a fifth angel "coming up from the east." This particular angel carries with him the seal of the living God and cries with great voice, instructing the first four angels who had been given the power to harm the land and the sea that they are not to do so until such time as the servants of God have had the seal placed on their foreheads. Several things are notable in these verses.

First, the angel who is coming from the rising of the sun possesses the seal of the living God. Here the inclusion of *zōntos* ("living") is different than what might have been expected. Certainly, it would have been sufficient simply to have said that he has the seal of God. However, the addition of *zōntos*, a present participle, emphasizes the distinction between this God and all other gods, which have no life in themselves and are manufactured either by men's thoughts or hands. By contrast God (*Yahweh*) is the only living God; and this, in turn, gives rise to the fact that He alone is able to impart that life to others. Consequently, the sealing of the 144,000 that follows receives added importance since they are to be sealed with the signet of the ever-living God.

The history of the use of seals predates the history of Israel. The Babylonians pioneered the use of the cylinder seal. These seals were anywhere from ten to twenty centimeters in height, cylindrical in shape, carefully carved—usually 360 degrees around, placed in malleable clay, and rolled across the clay. This clay seal hardened and thus carried a message of some kind. The Egyptians followed shortly thereafter with the use of scarabs, which are popularly known and seen by travelers in Egypt even in modernity.[199] Seals primarily as-

---

199 F. Rienecker and C. L. Rogers provide an explanatory note in *Linguistic Key to the Greek New Testament* (Grand Rapids: Zondervan, 1980), 828-29: "To the prophet's contemporaries 'seal' would have connoted the branding of cattle and the tattooing of slaves and soldiers, esp. those in the service of the emperor who could be recognized by this mark if they deserted; the marking of a soldier or the member of a guild on the hand, brow, or neck to seal him as a religious devotee, i.e., a member of a sacred militia. The mark in this case was a sign of consecration to the deity; it could refer to the mark prophets might have worn on their forehead, either painted or tattooed; or it could refer to the phylactery worn on the forehead and hand (s. Ford). The idea of the sealing would be to mark one's property and show ownership (Swete)."

signed ownership but were also used to tell a story, to mark for destruction or for protection. In the case of the 144,000, the text makes certain that the sealing is for protection, but interpreters disagree among themselves as to the nature of the threat that demands the sealing.

Initially, reference to sealing was visible and physical, but the Scriptures also use the concept in a spiritual manner. For example, the indwelling presence of the Holy Spirit is called a "seal." As Paul says, "And do not grieve the Holy Spirit of God, with whom you were sealed for the day of redemption" (Eph 4:30). Whereas some writers have historically wanted to make baptism the New Testament seal as a continuation of the Old Testament seal of circumcision, the New Testament writers themselves view baptism as a sign or a witness; and the presence of the Holy Spirit is the replacement for Old Testament circumcision.[200] In any event, a hierarchy of angels is also supposed in the verse since the fifth angel gives clear instructions to the first four that they are not to harm anything until such time as the servants of God have been sealed.

The precise nature of the seal given to the 144,000 is not specified. Most authors have assumed that it was the ancient Hebrew letter *tau*, which would have appeared very similar to an "x" placed on the forehead.[201] Two facts in the text would seem to support such a possibility. First, the angel actually has a seal in his hand, suggesting a physical artifice rather than simply a spiritual marking. The second is that the seal is specifically said to be placed on their foreheads. The unusual expedient of placing a given mark on the forehead of the individual seems repulsive to moderns, but the marking of the body in various ways was common in the first-century world. Still the precise nature of the sealing is not known and cannot be deduced from the passage here. That it was a mark of God for the 144,000 for the purpose of protection is sufficient information.

---

200 For examples of those who want to equate circumcision and baptism, see J. O. Buswell, *A Systematic Theology of the Christian Religion* (Grand Rapids: Zondervan, 1962), 226–66; C. Hodge, *Systematic Theology* (Grand Rapids: Eerdmans, 1970), 3:466–609.

201 See the discussion in R. L. Thomas, *Revelation 1–7: An Exegetical Commentary* (Chicago: Moody, 1992), 470. He correctly notes, "One approach to the sealing ties it to the sacrament of baptism through a reference to Ezek. 9:4–6 where 'the mark' was the Hebrew letter ת (*t*) which in its old form was shaped like a cross. The sign of the cross recalls that water baptism has replaced the Old Covenant circumcision. The connection between this seal and baptism is quite remote, however. The sacramental view could hardly be correct, because here the seal is in the hands of an angel or several of them" (Swete; Beckwith; Beasley-Murray; Mounce).

This leads to the question about the nature of this protection. Some commentators have argued that the 144,000 are protected from physical suffering and death during the awful days of the tribulation,[202] but the text does not specifically state this. Indeed other revelations to come might be rather clear indications that some or many of these 144,000 do meet death during the days of the tribulation.[203]

A second perspective emphasizes their spiritual well-being as intact—they are saved and forgiven and belong to the Lord. While that certainly seems to be the case, such a statement could easily have been made without this particular pageantry, which seems to suggest more is intended.

In a third perspective, and probably a correct one, the sealing protects them from the judgments of God that begin to unfold with the opening of the seventh seal and the sounding of the seven trumpets in chap. 8.[204] Perhaps the protection offered to these 144,000 particularly exempts them from the attacks of the demonic that become apparent in chap. 9.[205] The circumstances of the 144,000 may parallel those of the Israelites in Egypt where they were protected in various ways from most plagues but subject to others as were the Egyptians, who were the real objects of God's wrath.

7:4–8 Actually counting 144,000 people, while possible, would be time-consuming and certainly difficult. Consequently, John is given the number of those who now appear before him, and he is told that 144,000 will be sealed from all the tribes of Israel. Several interesting matters need to be considered regarding the sealing of the 144,000. Even a cursory reading of the list of the tribes would show some peculiarities about the listing. Ross E. Winkle notes the difficulty of the passage:

---

202 W. Scott thinks that "'the seal of the *living* God' implies immunity from death, and the seal upon the forehead intimates public, open acknowledgement that those who are sealed belong to God" (*Exposition of the Revelation of Jesus Christ*, 4th ed. [Westwood, NJ: Revell, 1968], 165).

203 See A. Geyser, "The Twelve Tribes of Revelation: Judean and Judeo-Christian Apocalypticism," *NTS* 28 (July 1982): 388–99.

204 This is the position articulated by Thomas, *Revelation 1–7*, 472; I. T. Beckwith, *The Apocalypse of John* (New York: Macmillan, 1919), 538; G. B. Caird, *The Revelation of St. John the Divine*, HNTC (San Francisco: Harper & Row, 1966), 96–97.

205 R. H. Charles avers, "The sealing of the faithful in our text does not mean (a) preservation from physical evil, nor (b) from spiritual apostasy, but (c) from demonic and kindred influences under the coming reign of Antichrist" (*A Critical and Exegetical Commentary on the Revelation of St. John*, ICC [Edinburgh: T&T Clark, 1920], 1:194).

The enigmatic sequence and nebulous origin of the list of tribes in Rev 7:5-8 has constantly vexed biblical interpreters during the nineteenth and twentieth centuries. For example, in 1920 the noted exegete R. H. Charles stoutly argued that "the text is unintelligible as it stands. . . ."[1] Not much later, J. Rendel Harris lamented the "extraordinary confusion which prevails in the order."[2] Such being the case, the list has engendered numerous exegetical maneuvers by creative interpreters. These interpreters have focused upon this particular list for the following basic reasons: (1) it parallels no other biblical or non-biblical list; (2) Judah—instead of Reuben—heads it; (3) it includes Levi, an unusual, but not unique, phenomenon; (4) it does not include Dan; and (5) it includes both Joseph and Manasseh, but not Ephraim.[206]

First, the tribe of Dan is missing, whereas the tribe of Levi, which is often omitted because the priesthood belonged to it, is included. Second, Joseph is also included, but one of his sons Manasseh is included, whereas the other son Ephraim is omitted. Finally, the order is interesting in that Judah rather than Reuben, the firstborn of Jacob, is listed first.

Another and even more important issue concerns the precise identity of these 144,000. While there are those who have attempted to identify them as angels, the two most prevalent views currently would be that they are (1) actually the church of the living God presented in the language of Israel and justified by the fact that the church is the Israel of God,[207] and (2) the passage should be read literally so that these who are sealed literally represent 144,000 Jewish people—12,000 from each of the tribes.

Numerous views about the identification of the 144,000 may be found in the commentaries. But when all else is considered, as is so often the case in an interpretation in the book of Revelation, the decision resolves itself into a ques-

---

206 Winkle, "Another Look at the List of Tribes in Revelation 7," *AUSS* 27 [Spring 1989]: 53. Winkle cites (n.1) R. H. Charles, *A Critical and Exegetical Commentary on the Revelation of St. John*, ICC (Edinburgh: T&T Clark, 1920), 1:207; and (n.2) J. R. Harris, *The Twelve Apostles* (Cambridge: W. Heffer & Sons, 1927), 94.

207 As examples of this position, see M. G. Reddish, *Revelation*, Smyth & Helwys Bible Commentary (Macon, GA: Smyth & Helwys, 2001), 146, where he claims: "Instead, the imagery depicts the church as the new people of God, the new Israel (cf. Jas 1:1). The entire church is the new Israel in which racial or ethnic distinctions play no part." Also, for a slightly different approach leading to the same conclusions, see Ray Summers, *Worthy Is the Lamb: An Interpretation of Revelation* (Nashville: Broadman, 1951), 146-51.

tion of whether the 144,000 are to be taken in a straightforward literal sense or whether they are to viewed figuratively. In the latter case, while representative of real individuals, the number itself and the identification of each of the twelve tribes of Israel is a reference only to the degree that 144,000, as a multiple of twelve, would suggest the number of the saved as being the complete or perfect number and the tribal identities assumed to be nothing more than a highly stylized way of indicating that these are the people of God.

The second view, in the persuasion of this commentator, is fraught with numerous problems. First, this author makes a clear distinction in his mind between these 144,000 from the twelve tribes of Israel and the great multitude who come from every nation, tribe, people, and language and who stand before the throne in vv. 9–11. The distinction between the two groups would hardly allow for any other interpretation except for one that sees the 144,000 as actually Jews. Furthermore, even commentators who do not accept this interpretation find themselves driven to admissions that constitute what are in effect rebuttals of their own position. For example, Mounce takes the position that in the accounts of both the 144,000 and of the great multitude, the church is in view—but from two different vantage points. Yet he is forced to say that "a Christian writer in identifying the church as the true Israel would probably not bother to list a detailed division of the twelve tribes (as in vv. 5–8)."[208] In order to explain this phenomenon, Mounce has to suppose that John has borrowed a Jewish apocalyptic source in which the people of Israel are protected from some calamity by receiving the seal of God on their foreheads and that John has reapplied the material to the church as it enters the period of final turmoil upon the earth.

Beckwith follows a similar line of thinking, confident that John is simply operating from Jewish sources and in this case forgot to modify one:

> The principal difficulty in the identification of Israel with the Church in our passage lies, as seen above, in the special enumeration of the tribes. But it must be kept in mind that the Apocalyptist conceivably follows his source more closely here than is his wont. In adopting the four riders from Zec. (see on 26), the four Living Creatures from Eze. (see on 46), the two olive trees from Zec., and similar imagery borrowed from the O.T., he modifies his source materially; but apparently in this instant less modifi-

---

208 R. H. Mounce, *The Book of Revelation*, NICNT (Grand Rapids: Eerdmans, 1977), 156.

cation is introduced. He may have seen in the specification of the twelve tribes, which he found in his source, a strong expression of *completeness*, which is an essential part of his purpose, having in mind the fullness of the spiritual; not the national, Israel.[209]

Ladd confesses that the identity of the 144,000 is not an easy problem: "The most natural way to interpret them is to see them as Jewish people and define in this symbolism the salvation of Israel."[210] Having confessed this as the most logical interpretation, Ladd, however, concludes, "There are good reasons to believe that by the 144,000 John means to identify spiritual Israel—the church. This view is suggested by certain irregularities in the list of the twelve tribes of Israel."[211] Or again, "John intends to say that the twelve tribes of Israel are not really Israel but the true spiritual Israel—the church."[212]

R. H. Charles admits, "For since the tribes are definitely mentioned one by one and since the number sealed in each tribe is definitely fixed (even though symbolically), the twelve tribes can only have meant the literal Israel in the original tradition."[213] Charles, of course, goes on to argue that this was not what the ultimate redactor had in mind; but he certainly does not question, based on the text itself, what was originally intended. Consequently, the contemporary reader is left with a logical conundrum for making a decision regarding the meaning of the seventh chapter, the 144,000, and the entire book of the Revelation. If the 144,000 most logically and originally were a reference to literal Israel, then why not simply take the reference at face value? If, on the other hand, they constitute a reference to "spiritual Israel" or the "church," then the reader must figure out exactly why there is such a waste of verbiage in the enumeration of the tribes. And in light of the rather peculiar arrangement and choice of tribal names, one must admit that to ascertain any meaning other than possibly the fact that Judah's first place indicates a Jewish Christian source is impossible. And then he must attempt to negotiate some type of rationale for why the author would have presented the church in two different fashions—one under the heading of Israel and the other under the heading of a great multitude from every nation, tribe, people, and language.

---

209 Beckwith, *The Apocalypse of John*, 536.

210 G. E. Ladd, *A Commentary on the Revelation of John* (Grand Rapids: Eerdmans, 1972), 112–13.

211 Ibid., 114.

212 Ibid., 115.

213 Charles, *Critical and Exegetical Commentary*, 1:193.

At the risk of making too much of a point, perhaps this is precisely where those who take the traditional amillennial or idealist view, as well as many posttribulation premillennialists, face, in this author's perspective, an insurmountable obstacle. The question seriously needs to be asked, "How would a first-century Jew have read this text?" More appropriately still, "How would a first-century Jewish Christian have read this text?" Or one may press the point even further and ask, "How would a first-century Gentile Christian have read this text?" John possessed all the vocabulary and theology necessary to state plainly what he had in mind. In fact, he did so—namely, that 12,000 of each of the tribes of Israel would be saved.

Against this is sometimes lodged the objection that no Jew today knows for sure about his tribal identity—even those who would attempt to make a case for belonging to the tribe of Levi, based on the last name of Cohen (priest) or something similar. In fact, no one can produce records of a family tree that would place him in one tribe or another. This, coupled with intermarriage with the nations in the Diaspora, has created a situation in which contemporary Jews are unaware of their respective tribal identities. Some would even say that tribal identity no longer exists. The answer is that if God numbers the very hairs of our heads, then it follows that he is able to know the genealogical descent of individuals whether a record has been kept or lost. Consequently, it is not farfetched to imagine that 12,000 from each of these twelve tribes of Israel will be sealed and saved. The issue is not so much a question of the identity of the 144,000 as to whether the Jewish people remain a significant part of the plan of God in the eschaton.

Commentators sometimes point to the similarity between the sealing of the 144,000 and the sealing of the righteous in the vision of Ezek 9. As Ezekiel contemplates the wrenching vision of the coming judgment of God on Israel, he notes that cherubim restrain the execution of the wicked while the righteous are sealed with a mark on their foreheads. Almost certainly this passage provides the background for John's apocalyptic vision, suggesting that this is Jewish ground. Furthermore, if the radiant woman of chap. 12 is to be identified as Israel (and here I anticipate that conclusion in my argument), then it becomes quite evident that Israel does have a role in the future. As in 12:17, a remnant of Israel becomes faithful to Christ during the awesome days of the great tribulation.

This idea is not limited to apocalyptic passages alone. No passage is any more compelling than Paul's anticipation of God's plan for the future of Israel revealed in Rom 9–11. In Rom 9:1–3, Paul confesses that he has unceasing anguish in his heart to the point that he wishes to be accursed and cut off from Christ for the sake of his brothers, those of his own race, the people of Israel. No one seriously questions the fact that here Israel does not mean the church but rather the actual ethnicity of Jewish people from whom Paul has descended. In Rom 10:1-2, the apostle becomes even more specific when he says that his heart's desire and prayer to God for Israel is that they might be saved since at the present time they have a zeal for God not based on knowledge. This leads him, in turn, to ask in Rom 11:1, "Has God cast away his people?" The conclusion is that by no means did he do this. Paul goes on in Rom 11:25 to explain that Israel has experienced hardening in part until the full number of Gentiles has come in. Following this, "all Israel will be saved" (Rom 11:26). Exactly what is meant by "all Israel will be saved" is another issue. What is evident is that the clear subject of chaps. 9–11 is the Jewish race. Furthermore, Paul specifies that there is an interim in which Israel is hardened against the recognition of the Messiah, but in the end there is a change of heart (Rom 11:25–26).

Interpretations of Rev 7 appear inconsistent when suggesting that 144,000 sealed Jews in the midst of the tribulation narrative, which has begun with the opening of the seals in chap. 6, are somehow to be reckoned as a representation of the church. The narrative suggests that the "times of the Gentiles" (Luke 21:24) and, with that the church age, has passed. Then back on Jewish ground, one is witnessing here the beginning of that which the apostle Paul anticipated in Rom 11.[214]

Theories about why certain tribes are included and the rationale for the order of the tribes included are also questions that have engaged scholars in every era. Most seem to agree that Judah has been placed before the actual firstborn Reuben because Christ came from the tribe of Judah. This denotes a Jewish Christian hand, which is found with John, the son of Zebedee. Although tribal listings even in the Old Testament differ somewhat, the general approach

---

214 Thomas concludes, "No clear-cut example of the church being called 'Israel' exists in the NT or in ancient church writings until A.D. 160. Galatians 6:16, where 'The Israel of God' can and probably does refer to some group other than the church as a whole, is no exception. This fact is crippling to any attempt to identify Israel as the church in Rev. 7:4. Such an attempt becomes even more ridiculous because it necessitates typological interpretation that divides the church into twelve tribes to coincide with the listing of Rev. 7:5-8, even with all the irregularities in that list. This step is even more anomalous in light of the irregularities in the listing adopted in vv. 5-8. The approach is so misconceived that it does serious violence to the context (Beasley-Murray). It cannot be exegetically sustained" (*Revelation 1-7*, 476).

is to exclude Levi since he represents the priestly tribe and then include the two sons of Joseph, Ephraim and Manasseh, in the place of Joseph: this gives a totality of twelve tribes.[215] In addition to the fact that Judah appears first in this list, the present description is further complicated by the inclusion of Levi and Joseph once again; but Manasseh, Joseph's son, remains while Ephraim has dropped out. Dan has also been excluded.

Various speculations exist as to exactly why this is true. For example, beginning at least as early as Irenaeus, there was the theory that the Antichrist would arise out of the tribe of Dan.[216] Hippolytus, the student of Irenaeus argued:

> That it is in reality out of the tribe of Dan, then, that that tyrant and king, that dread judge, that son of the devil, is destined to spring and arise, the prophet testifies when he says, "Dan shall judge his people, as (he is) also one tribe in Israel." But some one may say that this refers to Samson, who sprang from the tribe of Dan, and judged the people twenty years. Well, the prophecy had its partial fulfilment [sic] in Samson, but its complete fulfilment [sic] is reserved for Antichrist. For Jeremiah also speaks to this effect: "From Dan we are to hear the sound of the swiftness of his horses: the whole land trembled *at the sound of the neighing, of the driving of his horses.*" And another prophet says: "He shall gather together all his strength from the east even to the west. They whom he calls, and they whom he calls not, shall go with him. He shall make the sea white with the sails of his ships, and the plain black with the shields of his armaments. And whosoever shall oppose him in war shall fall by the sword." That these things, then, are said of no one else but that tyrant, and shameless one, and adversary of God, we shall show in what follows.[217]

Consequently, Dan has been omitted. Furthermore, both Dan and Manasseh were infamous because of their idolatry, and perhaps this would be the occasion of the exclusion of those two tribes. Levi appears because even though one is back on Jewish ground, all believers in Jesus are priests; hence, there is no necessity for Levi's functioning as a separate tribe of priests.

---

215 For an extensive discussion of the various approaches to this issue, see Thomas, *Revelation 1–7*, 479–82.

216 Irenaeus, *Against Heresies* 5.30.2, trans. A. Roberts and W. H. Rambaut, *ANF* 1:559.

217 Hippolytus, *The Extant Works and Fragments of Hippolytus* 2.15, *ANF* 5:207. Following Irenaeus, his teacher, Hippolytus, bases this conclusion essentially on Jer 8:10.

Others have conjectured that Dan and perhaps even Ephraim are omitted because they ceased to be tribal units. They simply died out, and by the time of the writing of the New Testament, they are not included in the listing because no Danites or Ephraimites remain. The problem with this view is that Dan, once again, is included in the tribal allotments for the millennial kingdom as provided in Ezek 48. In that particular case, the usual Old Testament practice of including both Ephraim and Manasseh as the sons of Joseph is followed, eliminating Joseph himself and omitting Levi based on the further priestly function of the Levites in the millennial temple.

The only appropriate conclusion to these difficulties is that while one can account for Judah being listed first, one cannot know precisely the mind of the Spirit in the choice of the remainder of the listing. Conceivably a far simpler explanation can be found. Possibly as a punishment for its role in idolatry, Dan is excluded from the 144,000 Jews that are specifically sealed during the tribulation period, but members of the house of Dan are saved during the tribulation; and thus, as is characteristic of the millennial goodness of God, they are reinstated in the kingdom era. Joseph is noted in the place of his son Ephraim, and Manasseh is kept to replace Dan, a tribe that does not have the benefit of the sealing.

Whether this explanation or other more complicated ones or no explanation now known is correct is impossible to know. What is clear is that 12,000 Jews from each of these twelve tribes are sealed during the days of the tribulation. The sealing does not appear to be necessarily for the purpose of protecting their lives. Above all else, this sealing seems to focus on their salvation and possibly as a result of that as a protection from the impact of the spiritual plagues that follow with the sounding of the trumpets in chap. 8.

E. The Identification of Gentile Believers (7:9–17)

[9]After these things I looked, and behold, a great multitude which no one could number, of all nations, tribes, peoples, and tongues, standing before the throne and before the Lamb, clothed with white robes, with palm branches in their hands, [10]and crying out with a loud voice, saying, "Salvation belongs to our God, who sits on the throne, and to the Lamb!"

[11]All the angels stood around the throne and the elders and the four living creatures, and fell on their faces before the throne and worshiped God, [12]saying:

"Amen! Blessing and glory and wisdom,

Thanksgiving and honor and power and might,

Be to our God forever and ever.
Amen."
¹³Then one of the elders answered, saying to me, "Who are these arrayed in white robes, and where did they come from?"
¹⁴And I said to him, "Sir, you know."
So he said to me, "These are the ones who come out of the great tribulation, and washed their robes and made them white in the blood of the Lamb. ¹⁵Therefore they are before the throne of God, and serve Him day and night in his temple. And He who sits on the throne will dwell among them. ¹⁶They shall neither hunger anymore nor thirst anymore; the sun shall not strike them, nor any heat;¹⁷for the Lamb who is in the midst of the throne will shepherd them and lead them to living fountains of waters. And God will wipe away every tear from their eyes."

7:9 While vv. 1–8 chronicle the sealing of the 144,000 Jews from the twelve tribes of Israel, the remainder of the chapter focuses on those who come from beyond the Jewish community and are yet included as the beneficiaries of the grace of God. In vv. 9–12 the focus is on their existence and actions.

John must have been delighted to discover that God's entourage included more than just the 144,000 Jews. Now he sees a multitude so great that counting is not possible. He notes that this multitude comprises people from every nation, tribe, people, and language, and they are standing before the throne in front of the Lamb. John is making the point that this group is ethnically distinct from the Jews who are sealed in the first part of the chapter, and they are further ethnically, tribally, and linguistically diverse from one another—indicating the extent to which the gospel of Jesus Christ has permeated the entire earth. They are seen standing before the Lamb and before the throne and are described as wearing white robes and holding palm branches in their hands. Most interpreters have understood the white robes to be imputed righteousness or holiness, and my own perspective affirms that judgment. Some have gone further and suggested that those white robes represent glorified bodies,²¹⁸ but this interpretation does not seem to be sustained by the text. The palm branches they hold in their hands indicate a festive season of joy and victory and were often a part of the Feast of Tabernacles. When the Lord made his triumphal entry into the city of Jerusalem, palm leaves were strewn in the way before Him as well as waved over Him as he rode into the city.

---

218 See G. B. Caird, *The Revelation of St. John the Divine*, HNTC 19 (San Francisco: Harper & Row, 1966), 254.

7:10   In v. 10, the multiethnic chorus shouts in a loud voice, "Salvation belongs to our God who sits on the throne, and to the Lamb!" Two important features of this proclamation should be noted. First, the NKJV text includes the word "belongs," which is understood but not present in the Greek text. The Greek text simply reads, "Salvation to our God." That the NKJV translators are correct to add "belongs" may be discerned in the fact that "salvation to our God," meaning "salvation proffered or accomplished for God," is neither needed nor possible. What is needed is salvation for mankind so that it is altogether proper to read the sentence as the NKJV translators have said, "Salvation belongs to our God."

Then it appears that the text proceeds to describe God in two ways: first, as the One who sits on the throne; and second, as the Lamb. Here is one of the important trinitarian or at least binitarian statements to be found in the Apocalypse. "Salvation belongs to our God, who sits on the throne," is obviously a reference to the Father. However, salvation also belongs to the Lamb, and as such the Lamb is distinguished in some way from the Father. Yet it is clear that John the monotheist has here depicted both as God, the proprietor of salvation.

Furthermore, salvation does not belong as a property to any human. Although humans are the recipients of salvation, the dispensing of that salvation is wholly and totally up to a sovereign God. Consequently, John is in complete agreement with Paul and other New Testament writers that no human work is ever sufficient.

7:11-12   The benediction of the great multitude instigates an antiphonal response from all the angels that surround the throne, the elders, and the four living creatures. All of these fall on their faces and worship God with a paeon of praise similar to that of the great multitude but expanded beyond it also. Interestingly, here the angels who are standing around the throne are clearly distinguished from the elders, and perhaps even from the four living creatures. Those who seek to identify the elders as angels face something of a difficulty where there seems to be a clear distinction here in the text. The four living creatures, on the other hand, could still qualify as angels, though distinct from those standing around the throne. But the function ascribed to the elders is distinct from either group of angels. All these together, however, are moved to the worship of God.

What is offered as praise to God begins with the expression "Amen!" *Amen*, in this case, can be interpreted both as a response to the benediction of the multi-ethnic congregation and as an introductory affirmation of what is about to be said in their own benediction (see note on 3:14 for a discussion of "amen"). The "Amen" offered by the angels, the elders, and the four living creatures is an affirmation and agreement with all the multiethnic congregation has said but also an exclamation point to their own praise. There follows the benediction of the elders, the angels, and the four living creatures when they say, "Blessing and glory and wisdom / Thanksgiving and honor and power and might / *Be* to our God forever and ever." Once again, the translators of the NKJV have added the word "be" to the text, whereas the Greek New Testament does not have a "to be" form of the word. The NKJV translators were correct in doing so, although both consistency and clarity might have been served by retaining the word "belongs" that was inserted in v. 10 in the great multitude worship.

The significance of the benediction is then a recognition that all blessing and glory and wisdom and thanksgiving and honor and power and might belong to God forever, and this is followed by a second use of the word, "Amen." The words making up this attribution of praise are interesting. The word for "blessing," *eulogia*, transliterates into English as "eulogy" and literally means "speaking well of someone." One of the most important activities of worship is always to speak well of the Lord God. Reading the Psalms will illustrate the frequency with which "praise" takes the form of recounting the mighty deeds of God (Pss. 23; 46:8-9; 48:1-8; 66:1-12).

Glory and wisdom (*doxa* and *sophia*) are also attributes of God, which though they may belong to others also are uniquely and exponentially the attributes of God. "Glory" is easier understood than explained. The term (*doxa*) seems to have initially meant "what one thinks" or "opinion." According to Deissmann, ships and women were given this name. Generally, the Greek word translates the Hebrew word *kābôd*, which carries the sense of "honor" or "weighty." Von Rad says that "if in relation to man [*kābôd*] denotes that which makes him impressive and demands recognition, whether in terms of material possessions or striking *gravitas*, in relation to God it implies that which makes God impressive to man, the force of his self-manifestation."[219]

"Thanksgiving" is a translation of *eucharistia*, which transliterates into English as "Eucharist" or the thanksgiving feast that the church practices as the Lord's Supper or the Lord's table. Since the first sin in the garden of Eden might be described as a sin of ingratitude, thanksgiving is always an especially important feature of the worship of a gracious God. Honor (*timē*) references that which is rare and valuable and is often used to describe the value of precious stones. "Power and might" (*dunamis* and *ischus*) are similar in their emphasis, but the first seems to denote more the quality of omnipotence whereas the latter perhaps fo-

---

219 *TDNT* 2.238. See 232-55 for an inclusive discussion of δόξα and its cognates as well as כָּבוֹד written by G. Kittel and G. von Rad.

cuses more on endurance. All these belong to God who remains the same forever and hence always possesses these qualities to the degree of perfection.

7:13–14 Verses 13–17 of this chapter relate to the identification of the great multitude from every nation, tribe, people, and language standing before God in praise and adoration. They are further identified as to their past, and insight is given to their future felicity.

In vv. 13–14 John once again becomes a participant in his own narrative. One of the elders addresses a question to John, and focusing on those clad in the white robes asks, "Who are they, and where did they come from?"

By this time in the development of the Apocalypse, John knows that the question is asked not with a view of securing an answer but rather with didactic intent. John therefore confesses both his own ignorance and his confidence that the elder knows the answer to his own question by simply saying, "Sir, you know." The Greek text employs the word *kurie*, which the translators of the NKJV have incorrectly rendered "sir." The Greek text not only uses the word *kurie*, but follows with the possessive pronoun, *mou*, so that to translate the whole of the text would be "my sir." The word "lord" is intended here, and the text should be read, "My lord, you know."

Of course, this view of translation raises the problem as to why John would have answered the question of the elder by addressing the Lord. There are two possibilities. First, John may have recognized that while the elder asked the question, the Lord was the ultimate source of all such knowledge. The second possibility is that the address, "my lord," does not necessarily imply deity but only superiority. Hence, the expression "my lord" could actually address the elder just as well as it could God Himself. In any event, the elder seems to answer, making the last explanation probable. The elder replies that "these are the ones who come out of the great tribulation, and washed their robes and made them white in the blood of the Lamb."

The phenomenon of 144,000 Jews and a great company of Gentiles who are actually saved during the great tribulation is thus introduced. The verse does not say exactly how they have made their exit from the great tribulation. The assumption of martyrdom might be appropriate but is not necessary in every case. The description of the great tribulation as revealed in the judgments of the seals, the trumpets, the thunders, and the bowls is sufficient to account for the deaths perhaps of the majority of the people living on the earth during that awesome period of the judgment of God. That even believers die during this period seems certain. Whatever the case, they have come out of the great tribulation, and the reference is to the *tēs thlipseōs tēs megalēs*, which means "the tribulation, the great one." Here the emphasis is on the period of time for this awesome tribulation but is also distinguished from any other such tribulation that has ever occurred by the adjectival construction "the great" tribulation. In all probability this is the exact period that Jesus had in mind in Matt 24:21–22 when he spoke of "a great tribulation" exceeding all other historic trials never to be equaled again. Indeed, Jesus says, "And unless those days were shortened, no flesh would be saved; but for the elect's sake those days will be shortened." Such language mirrors the tribulatory language of the Apocalypse and suggests that many of the elect will be overtaken by death in those days. This is an awesome period of the judgment of God, and yet there are some who during this period have washed their robes and made them white in the blood of the Lamb. Now the nature of the white robes mentioned in v. 9 becomes clearly apparent. The robes represent the spiritual attire of these tribulation saints, but they have been made white through washing in the blood of the Lamb.

In that expression the reader is introduced to one of the most salient insights to be found anywhere in the Word of the Lord. Few stains on light-colored clothing are any more difficult to remove than the stains left by blood. Yet here garments have been made white by having been soaked in the blood of the Lamb! In fact, "washed," the word employed is an indication that cleansing is involved. Here, once again, is the theology of sacrifice and the theology of substitutionary atonement. In the mind of the author of the Apocalypse there is no doubt but that one's ability to stand before God in purity is determined entirely on the basis of the shed blood of the Lamb and its application to the unholy and stained lives of those who come to the cross. Few more beautiful pictures could possibly be imagined than the remarkable contrast of men made pure through the sacrificial and substitutionary blood of the atonement of the Lamb.

7:15–17 Existence on this earth is never easy, and for the followers of Christ it is inevitably fraught with confrontation and often persecution and sorrow. This condition—exponentially heightened by the experience of the great tribulation—gives way to a new and salubrious assize in the presence of God. Now those who have come out of the tribulation find themselves before the throne of God and serve Him day and night in His temple.

Two important emphases can be found in this vision. First, these who have come out of the great tribulation are before the One who sits on the throne both day and night. To be constantly with Someone who is the object of devoted love is reward indeed. To be constantly in the presence of Someone who is not the object of one's love could be tantamount to tribulation itself. So clearly these who have come out of the tribulation, like all true blood-bought believers in Christ, love the Lord with all their hearts and are delighted to be in His presence day and night. Furthermore, they serve Him day and night. "Serve" is a translation of *latreuō*, which means more than just serve but also carries with it the implication of worship.[220] Correspondingly, the One who sits on the throne spreads His tent over them, indicating acceptance, possession, and safety. The word *skēnoō* has the sense of pitching a tent and is used, for example, in the prologue to John's Gospel where Jesus is said to have "dwelt among us" or "pitched his tent among us" (John 1:14). There is safety, protection, love, and acceptance in the presence of the One who sits on the throne.

7:16 The difficulties that encountered the saints of God during their lifetime on earth are never experienced again. Never again do they hunger, thirst, or experience the bewildering and debilitating heat of the scorching of the sun. These three immunities are only suggestive of the removal of the totality of all those things that inflict sorrow and difficulty on the saints of God during the great tribulation or any era. Now in the heavenly condition all that is removed.

Contemporary audiences in prosperous regions of the world have difficulty appreciating the promises of this verse. While millions wonder where food can be found, they alone can appreciate the promise of an adequate perennial supply of sustenance. In the Near East, ancient and modern, water can be more valuable than oil or gold. The ever-present searching sun and the paucity of fresh potable water is always foremost in the mind of the desert dweller or traveler. To imagine a circumstance of never experiencing thirst again would be heaven indeed. Doubtless, the provision of food and water portends essential spiritual satisfaction as well.[221]

---

220 H. Strathmann, after noting the classical background of the word with its essentially secular meaning of "reward" or "wages," insists that the LXX determined the religious use of the word. He further notes that the term, in this religious setting is used only of service to Deity (*TDNT*, 4:58–65).

221 For one of the most graphic and gripping accounts of the rigors, hazards, and challenges of theses arid lands in the Middle East, see W. Thesiger's chronicle of the crossing of the "Empty Quarter" of Saudi Arabia in *Arabian Sands* (London: Penguin, 1991), first published in 1959. Thesiger remembers poignantly: "We led the trembling, hesitating animals upward along great sweeping ridges where the knife-edged crests crumbled beneath our feet. Although it was killing work, my companions were always gentle and infinitely patient. The sun was scorching hot and I felt empty, sick, and dizzy. As I struggled up the slope, knee-deep in shifting sand, my heart thumped wildly and my thirst grew worse. I found it difficult to swallow; even my ears felt blocked, and yet I knew that it would be many intolerable hours before I could drink. I would stop to rest, dropping down on the scorching sand, and immediately it seemed I would hear the others shouting, 'Umbarak, Umbarak'; their voices sounded strained and hoarse" (149).

7:17 In v. 17 another of those unusual Johannine juxtapositions occurs in which the Lamb is, in fact, the Shepherd. Shepherds take care of lambs, but lambs do not take care of shepherds. Nevertheless, in this case, the Lamb who has shed His blood for them is none other than the ultimate Shepherd, and so He becomes the Shepherd of the sheep from the tribulation period. The fact that He leads them to springs of living water is an indication of His provision. Every need is met. The thirst of every legitimate and holy desire is slaked. Furthermore, sorrows are eliminated also as every tear is wiped from their eyes. Some commentators have viewed this as a wiping away of the tears of joy. While that may not be entirely impossible, the emphasis here seems to be on the available comfort coming from the Lamb as a part of the heavenly package that includes provision. In fact, the Lamb who is the Shepherd is seen as providing all that is needed through both provision and solace to those who lacked both provision and comfort in the midst of the great tribulation.

By way of practical application, every believer should note that what is presented to the eye in this passage is the promise of God—not for ultimate intervention in the present age but for perfect intervention in the age to come. The Bible makes clear that all will have tribulation and that all the godly in Christ will suffer. But while this period of time passes so quickly that it is called by the biblical writers nothing more than a vapor seen for a moment and then vanished, there is an eternal circumstance in which full provision and total solace will be provided by the Lord. Here believers labor in difficulty, there they rejoice with the Good Shepherd who cares for His sheep.

F. The Opening of the Seventh Seal (8:1)

¹When he opened the seventh seal, there was silence in heaven for about half an hour.

8:1 The opening of the seals that began in 6:1 is concluded in the first verse of chap. 8. The chapter division added at this point of the narrative might seem contrived since it occurs between the opening of the sixth and seventh seals. The appropriateness of the division was perhaps suggested by the significant departure in the progress of the opening of the six seals, whose messages are revealed essentially in chap. 6. The interim vision of the 144,000 in chap. 7 gives way to the opening of the seventh seal in chap. 8. However, the opening of the seventh seal provides an unexpected development: "silence in heaven for about half an hour."

Rather than the immediate continuation of the chaos created by the opening of the first six seals, a pregnant pause of half an hour is introduced.

Since the text does not present an exact explanation of this parenthesis, commentators are left to speculate about its significance. Thomas notes five different possibilities and includes Alford, who sees the silence as the beginning of the sabbatical rest for the millennium.[222] Walter Scott's view is that the pause is only a brief cessation of judgment and not a literal silence because the heavenly songs continue.[223] The third view is that of H. B. Swete, who argues that there was apparently a temporary suspension of heavenly revelations imposed upon John.[224] Of course, this could have been caused by any number of factors, including time for John to write what had been given to him thus far or perhaps even a period of rest before the intensity of the remaining visions unfold. The fourth view, that of R. H. Charles, links the pause with the text that follows, which focuses on the prayers of the saints.[225] This view has the advantage over the first three in that, while speculative, it nevertheless does take into careful consideration the actual text that follows. As God's people pray and their prayers are wafted aloft into the presence of God, time is given for intercession before the resumption of the judgments to follow. Thomas, following Beckwith, Seiss, Walvoord, and a host of others, opts for a fifth view. The dramatic pause is "to symbolize the awe and dread with which the heavenly hosts await the events about to happen."[226]

Perhaps choosing between these last two perspectives is unnecessary. Clearly, the pause occurs for dramatic effect and serves the purpose of alerting the reader to a significant turn in the narrative. However, since the chapter begins by highlighting the prayers of the saints, Charles also is probably not wrong to suggest the possibility of an interlude for the prayers of God's people. Certainly the significance to the opening of the seventh seal and the sounding of the seven trumpets is being tied by John in some way or another to the question of the prayers of the saints. In 6:10 the saints cried out to God to "avenge our blood" on those who were the inhabitants of the earth. The cry there, as

---

222 R. L. Thomas, *Revelation 8–22: An Exegetical Commentary* (Chicago: Moody, 1992), 2–5. See also H. Alford, *The Greek Testament* (Chicago: Moody, 1958), 4.630. Alford is following Victorinus.

223 W. Scott, *Exposition of the Revelation of Jesus Christ*, 4th ed. (Westwood, NJ: Revell, 1968), 178. "It is a calm before a storm, like a stillness in nature preceding a tempest."

224 H. B. Swete, *Commentary on Revelation: The Greek Text* (Grand Rapids: Kregel, 1977), 107.

225 R. H. Charles, *A Critical and Exegetical Commentary on The Revelation of St. John*, ICC (Edinburgh: T&T Clark), 1:223–24.

226 Thomas, *Revelation 8–22*, 2.

here, is not a vengeful cry but one frequently heard by the people of God for justice. Though the content of the prayers in 8:3 is not specified, certainly a call for justice as well as for mercy is always appropriate for the people of God.[227]

3. The Trumpet Judgments (8:2–11:19)

The sounding of the trumpets is the second of four series of judgments belonging to the period of the great tribulation. Chapters 8 and 9 compose a single unit and probably should not have been divided.

A. The First Four Trumpets (8:2–13)

[2]And I saw the seven angels who stand before God, and to them were given seven trumpets. [3]Then another angel, having a golden censer, came and stood at the altar. He was given much incense, that he should offer *it* with the prayers of all the saints upon the golden altar which was before the throne. [4]And the smoke of the incense, with the prayers of the saints, ascended before God from the angel's hand. [5]Then the angel took the censer, filled it with fire from the altar, and threw *it* to the earth. And there were noises, thunderings, lightnings, and an earthquake.

[6]So the seven angels who had the seven trumpets prepared themselves to sound.

[7]The first angel sounded: And hail and fire followed, mingled with blood, and they were thrown to the earth. And a third of the trees were burned up, and all green grass was burned up.

---

227 The Venerable Bede in his *Explanation of the Apocalypse* provides an interesting interpretation linking this silence to the difficult text in Dan 12:12. He says, "It is believed that after the destruction of the antichrist, there will be a short rest in the church. Daniel prophesied of this, 'Blessed is he who waits and comes to the thousand three hundred and thirty-five days.' The blessed Jerome commented upon this passage [of Daniel]. 'Blessed, he says, is he who when the antichrist is killed waits for the forty-five days beyond the thousand two hundred and ninety days, that is, three and a half years. For during them our Lord and Savior will come in his majesty. It is a matter of divine knowledge why there is silence for forty-five days after the death of the antichrist, unless we make the conjecture that the delay of the kingdom of the saints is a test of patience.' We should note that the greatest afflictions of the church are envisaged in the sixth period, while a rest is seen in the seventh, For the Lord was crucified on the sixth day, and he rested on the seventh, awaiting the time of the resurrection" (*Revelation*, ACCS, 118).

[8]Then the second angel sounded: And *something* like a great mountain burning with fire was thrown into the sea, and a third of the seas became blood. [9]And a third of the living creatures in the sea died, and a third of the ships were destroyed.

[10]Then the third angel sounded: And a great star fell from heaven, burning like a torch, and it fell on a third of the rivers and on the springs of water. [11]The name of the star is Wormwood. A third of the waters became wormwood, and many men died from the water, because it was made bitter.

[12]Then the fourth angel sounded: And a third of the sun was struck, a third of the moon, and a third of the stars, so that a third of them were darkened. A third of the day did not shine, and likewise the night.

[13]And I looked, and I heard an angel flying through the midst of heaven, saying with a loud voice, "Woe, woe, woe to the inhabitants of the earth, because of the remaining blasts of the trumpet of the three angels who are about to sound!"

8:2-5 Seven angels are summoned before God and are issued trumpets. The Greek word for trumpet is *salpigx*. Two primary Hebrew words translated trumpet in the Old Testament are ḥăṣōṣĕrâ and the known and more popular *shôphār*. The *shôphār*, a curled ram's horn, which subject to heat becomes malleable and is shaped by the artisan, is mentioned slightly more often than the ḥăṣōṣĕrâ. But, when New Testament literature is invoked, the *salpigx* is the instrument referenced in every case. In the LXX, the *salpigx* is used to translate *shôphār* more than forty times. On the other hand, the ḥăṣōṣĕrâ is uncertain in its derivation but according to Friedrich was a "narrow and shrill instrument."[228] He goes on to say that this corresponds to the description found in Josephus and the depiction of the trumpet found on the arch of Titus.[229] Usually the trumpet was an instrument made from silver and distinct from the *shôphār*.

On this basis one cannot be sure whether the instrument given to each of the seven angels is more like the ḥăṣōṣĕrâ or the ram's horn. Whichever the case, as the plot unfolds, the sounding of each trumpet will announce a new judgment.

At this point still another angel appears with golden censer or fire box in hand, and he comes and stands at the altar. Given much incense to offer, the angel is set to offer this sweet savor, which represents the prayers of the saints that ascend to God from the angel's hand. This action on the part of the angel is perfectly in keeping with the actions of the priest working each day with the altar of incense in the holy place. What makes the vision totally distinct is the

---

228 Friedrich, *TDNT* 7:76.
229 Ibid.

next act of the angel wherein the censer is filled with fire from the altar and hurled to the earth, resulting in thundering, lightnings, and an earthquake.

The questions presented by vv. 3–5 concern the identity of the angel, the particular altar in view, and the two acts of that angel. The natural tendency to identify this angel with the glorified Lord is understandable and not impossible. Much more likely, however, the terminology "another angel" (*allos aggelos*) generally depicts "another" of the same kind as opposed to a *heteros* or "another" angel of a different kind and suggests that this angel is not ontologically distinct from the seven angels who were given the seven trumpets. He simply is another angel with a different assignment. Like the high priest in the holy place, he has a golden censer, or fire pan, and he stands at what is apparently the altar of incense. The altar of incense was critical to the function of the holy of holies since on the Day of Atonement, the high priest, upon entering that sacred precinct, was preceded by the smoke of the incense, which provided temporary covering of the prayers of God's people until such time as he could sprinkle the blood of the sacrificial goat on the mercy seat.

As this angel stands before the altar of incense, he is given much incense mixed together with the coals of fire in his fire pan, and the incense is said to be the prayers of all the saints offered on the golden altar before the throne. Of interest to the reader here is the fact that the golden altar is no longer placed in the holy place immediately in front of the veil leading to the holy of holies but rather is now before the throne of God. Of course, there is a sense in which even in the tabernacle the altar's location is related to the throne of God. The use of incense as an analogy for the prayers of the saints is both helpful and encouraging. Two apparently antithetical aspects of the nature of God are brought together in this metaphor. First, God is transcendent and holy. As such, the approach to God is specific as to its nature and encompassed with gravity. Nevertheless, transcendence and holiness notwithstanding, the approach of God's people to commune with the eternal Creator is seen here not only as welcoming and encouraging but also as something in which God delights. Just as the smell of burning frankincense and certain other kinds of incense are pleasant to the human nostril, so the approach of God's creation to their Creator is not a matter of indifference to God.

As anticipated, the angel, functioning in much the same way that the high priest would function, offers the incense upon the golden altar; the smoke of the incense representing the prayers of the saints ascends to God. The emphasis here not only grasps the approachability of the unapproachable, transcendent, and holy God but also hints at the effectiveness of prayer. "The effective, fervent prayer of a righteous man avails much" (Jas 5:16b). Prayer is the God-ordained conduit through which he has determined to channel his sovereign power and response to the concerns of the saints. This effectiveness of prayer becomes apparent in the judgment that follows.

Now the same angel who had offered the prayers of the saints in the form of incense takes the censer and fills it with fire from the altar.[230] Once again the question is which altar? In the case of Nadab and Abihu, who offered strange fire on the altar (Lev 10; Num 3:4), there is indication that the fire offered on the altar of incense should have been ferried from the altar of sacrifice in the outer court, but they had taken a shortcut and used fire from some other source. This costly failure resulted in their immediate demise. Here, however, only the one altar is mentioned, and that is the one standing before the throne. Probably then the censer, or fire pan, in the hand of the angel is filled from that same altar that has provided the incense. Having secured the fire from the altar, the angel turns and hurls it to the earth. This act of judicial appointment seems again to be in direct response to the prayer of the martyrs mentioned previously in 6:10. In any event the coals of fire are hurled to the earth. The results come in the form of thunder, rumblings, flashes of lightning, and an earthquake. Thunder and lightning and earthquakes are common enough. What appears here, however, is clearly uncommon and is a harbinger of that which transpires next at the sounding of the trumpets.

Several times reference has been made to the prayers of the saints. Because there is still widespread misunderstanding about the "saints," a word of expla-

---

230 G. K. Beale properly notes, "The trumpets portray judgment on unbelievers because of their hardened attitude, thus demonstrating God's incomparable sovereignty and glory. These judgments are not intended to evoke repentance but to punish because of the permanently hardened, unrepentant stance of the unbelievers toward God and his people. As suggested above, although 8:3–5 primarily shows that the last judgment is God's answer to 6:10, it is possible that 8:3–5 also functions secondarily to link the trumpets with the prayer in 6:10 for the world's punishment. If this is correct, then, not only should the Last Judgment, represented by the seventh seal (and probably also the seventh trumpet), be viewed as a divine response to 6:9–11, but also the first six trumpet woes preceding that of the Last Judgment (11:15–19) should be so viewed, especially as anticipating and finding their climax in the final punishment. Another indication that the trumpets are an initial formal answer to the prayer for vindication against 'those dwelling on the earth' (6:11) is that the last three trumpets are called 'woes' against 'those dwelling on the earth' (8:13; so likewise 11:10). This would mark a progression in thought from the seals to the trumpets" (*The Book of Revelation: A Commentary on the Greek Text*, NIGTC [Grand Rapids: Eerdmans; Carlisle, UK: Paternoster Press, 1999], 472).

nation is appropriate. The word translated "saints" in the NKJV, as well as other versions, is *hagios* and means most basically "the holy ones." Once again, this is not to be understood as a separate category of Christ's followers who have some-how achieved greater sanctity or ecclesiastical recognition than others. These are men and women who have been made holy through the experience of repentance toward God and faith in the Lord Jesus Christ and the accompanying regenerat-ing ministry of the Holy Spirit. The word is used of both the departed dead who have died in Christ as well as living, regenerate individuals.

8:6-7 As the seven angels prepare to sound the trumpets, which have been given to each of them, the sound of the trumpet of the first angel peels over Patmos.[231] John sees a mixture of hail and fire mixed with blood, which is hurled down on the earth with the result that a third of the earth is burnt up. This includes especially trees and all of the green grass. The plagues associated with the blasts of the trumpets seem to echo the Exodus plagues, particularly the seventh one mentioned in Exod 9:23-27. The difference in this plague is that of intensity. While hail fell in Egypt, the combination of fire and blood heightens the devastation of this plague. As usual, those authors who want to avoid a more literal understanding of the text view this as somewhat poetic language to describe the judgment of God but do not anticipate a literal ful-fillment. Others would find it to be little more than graphic apocalyptic genre language that should not be taken in any sense to be literal.

---

231 Victorinus of Petovium says in his commentary on the Apocalypse, "He sends these seven great archangels to strike against the kingdom of the antichrist. For the Lord himself said in the Gospel: 'Then the Son of man will send his angels and will gather his elect from the four winds, from one end of heaven to the other.'" And again, "And therefore, those things written concerning the trumpets and the bowls are either the devastation of the plagues sent to the world, or the madness of the antichrist him-self, or the blasphemies of the peoples, or the variety of the plagues, or the hope for the kingdom of saints, or the ruin of cities or the ruin of Babylon, that is, of the city of Rome" (*Revelation*, ACCS, 121). Following Paulien, Beale sees the trumpets as figurative, saying, "The figurative nature of all of the first four trumpets is pointed to by at least four ob-servations: (1) The uses of ὡς ('like'), ὅμοιος ('like'), and such expressions (8:8, 10; 9:2, 3, 5, 7-10, 17, 19) indicates a lack of precision in these descriptions of what was seen in a vision and, in particular, suggests that the portrayal is metaphorical" (*The Book of Revela-tion*, 488). Tyconius, a fourth-century interpreter, offers a figurative interpretation. "He speaks of the devil as a burning mountain, for he consumed those near to him as though he were a fire. He is called 'great' because he is one angel among others and is himself a creature. . . . He calls the world a 'sea,' in which he saw the devil who had been cast down from heaven as a burning fire" (*Revelation*, ACCS, 125).

Among those who find a more literal understanding of the text, differences in precise interpretation can be expected. Whether this is to be interpreted as the result of meteor activity, volcanic activity, or simply unprecedented storms dropping hail in the midst of lightning that also takes its toll and results in a blood bath on earth, the one thing interpreters agree on is that the plague is not just a "natural occurrence" but represents the physical judgments of God on the earth. The effect is duly noted as devastating.

8:8-9 The second angel sounds his trumpet, and a huge mountain that is ablaze with fire is thrown into the sea. A third of the sea turns to blood, a third of the creatures in the sea die, and the cataclysmic upheaval at impact seems to destroy a third of the world's maritime commerce. Once again, this could be the result of a monstrous volcano, which erupts from the ocean floor devastating everything around it, or it could be a meteor. A considerable amount of time is being devoted now by the space administration and military organizations to find a way to deter a meteor of considerable size, the trajectory of which indicates an intersection with earth and corresponding devastation. Most scientists believe that these kinds of things have happened in the past and that no reason exists to believe that they cannot occur in the future. A meteor of sufficient dimension seemingly could indeed destroy all life on the earth. These predictions and precautions give v. 8 a certain viability that might not have been imaginable in John's day.

8:10-11 When the third angel sounds his trumpet, a great star comes blazing like a torch. The impact of this star when intersecting with the earth has a malevolent effect on the rivers and springs of water. The waters are turned bitter, and people who drink the bitter water die as a result.[232] The star is even named *Apsinthos*, which is translated "wormwood." The reference is to a plant especially bitter to the taste.[233] The word, found in the Old Testament in Jer 9:15 and 23:15 and in Lam 3:15,19, invariably is used in connection with the con-

---

232 Tyconius remains an interesting interpreter, saying, "The rivers and fountains of waters signify the teachers of the divine Scriptures who instruct others but turn themselves away from the way of truth. Indeed, the name Wormwood indicates either the bitterness or the sweetness of sins, which give a present sweetness to those who desire them but afterwards change themselves into bitterness" (*Revelation*, ACCS, 128).

233 M. Zohary, *Plants of the Bible* (Cambridge: Cambridge University Press, 1982), 184. "Although the whole plant is strongly aromatic and rather bitter, it is eaten by desert goats and the dried leaves are used to prepare a tea drunk by the Bedouin of the Sinai and the Negev. Wormwood is also widely used as a healing beverage against intestinal worms, a fact reflected in its name."

cept of God's judgment. Interpreters who tend to view the text as literal in its fulfillment have sometimes argued for another meteor in this case, especially because of the reference to the "great star." However, more modern commentators have sometimes noted the effect of this particular blazing star upon the waters and the fact that the waters are contaminated, resulting in the death of those that drink them.

Some years ago the author visited a lake between Pavlodar and Semipolatinsk in Kazakhstan. Though beautiful, the lake was radioactive, and, as a result, nothing lived in it. The radioactive effects of an atomic explosion found in the water are well known, and some have therefore suggested that John could have seen a missile streaking across the heaven, exploding an atomic warhead and thus generating the bitter waters. Since John would have no idea or context from which to judge what he saw, to speak of it as a "great star" would not be unnatural. In the end the exact nature or origin of this great star is impossible to determine. Reading contemporary circumstances back into a Johannine milieu, of course, is both risky and totally unnecessary. That some form of toxicity is apparently associated with the explosion that makes a third of the waters on the face of the earth undrinkable is possible to affirm.

Another thing that makes this passage especially interesting is that under normal circumstances, for a body of water that becomes radioactive to reach the point where it could again sustain life of any kind takes hundreds of years. The tribulation period is limited to seven years; and the Bible describes the kingdom period on the earth, which follows the tribulation, invariably with almost Edenic features. The Bible says that the waters of the salt sea "shall be healed" (Ezek 47:8 KJV). If that is universal, then the effect, while devastating, will be nowhere nearly as permanent as other such calamities have been.

8:12 The fourth angel now sounds his trumpet, and the sun is struck with a dimming of a third of it; correspondingly, a third of the stars and a third of the moon are turned dark. This results in a third of the day being without light and also a third of the night darkened more than usual. Whether this fourth trumpet simply chronicles the atmospheric effects of the three previous trumpets and the corresponding darkness on the earth or whether, as seems more likely, the impact of this plague is actually on the sun and the consequence of that being on the moon also and on the other luminaries of the heavens is not fully clear.

Since the relationship of planet earth is tied rather intricately to both the sun and the moon and affected perhaps more than one can know by the other luminaries of the heavens, particularly those in the Milky Way galaxy of which the earth is a part, one can only surmise that the effects of this fourth trumpet would indeed be devastating. In one sense, that life could continue (and Jesus did say that "unless those days were shorted, no flesh would be saved;" Matt 24:22) is difficult to comprehend. The possibilities of such catastrophic results on the sun and the moon, however, are not hard to imagine in light of what is known from astronomy and astrophysics. Astrophysicists have argued for some time that the sun is in the process of burning itself out. Millions of years in the future have been posited for this brilliant star at the center of our solar system actually to succeed in burning itself out. But it is also known that frequent explosions occur on the surface of the sun, creating effects of various kinds on the earth and doubtless on the other planets that are in closer proximity to the sun in our solar system. Whether such an explosion could begin the formation of a black hole or some other accompanying catastrophe is certainly not beyond the realm of possibility and is comprehensible in the text.

In conclusion, the thoughtful interpreter must admit that ascertaining the exact nature of the plagues unleashed at the sounding of the four trumpets is not possible. Having so said and with what is known about the cosmos, nothing revealed here is beyond the physical possibilities that are known to exist. Further, there is definite affirmation of monumental judgments of God on the rebellious earth and of the intensity of suffering unleashed on the inhabitants of the earth, a large number of whom obviously will perish as a result of these trumpet blasts.

8:13 The NKJV translates the expression *kai eidon*, literally "And I looked," while the NIV translators chose to refer the phrase as "As I watched." There is no real difference except that the NIV may have indeed succeeded in catching the mood intended by John. One can almost imagine John transfixed as he observes the devastation of the elements occurring as a result of the sounding of the seven trumpets. And suddenly he now hears an eagle flying in midair, calling out with a loud voice and announcing three times woe to the inhabitants of the earth. The text here contains a significant variant: *aetou*, or "eagle," was the choice of the NIV translators, while *aggelou*, or "angel," was the choice of the NKJV translators. One manuscript that has even conflated the two into *aggelou hōs aetou*, meaning "an angel as an eagle." One can safely conclude that the conflation probably is a classic case of an attempt on the part of a copyist to make sense of the word he saw in the text translated in the NIV "eagle." The action of the eagle is less in keeping with what might be expected of a great bird than what would probably be expected of an angel. However, this may also account for the reading "angel" since later copyists

might have found the term "eagle" to be as unlikely as some modern translators might think it to be.

The burden of evidence lies however with the word "eagle," which is supported by Codex Sinaiticus and Alexandrinus and most of the minuscules. The
Textus Receptus, however, follows a number of later manuscripts.[234]

Several conclusions can be drawn. First, like most of the remaining contested readings of New Testament documents, the meaning or the theology of
the text here is unscathed whether one reads the text "eagle" or "angel." Clearly
woe is determined upon the earth, and this is the judgment of God not just the
results of circumstances. Furthermore, even if one follows essentially a literal
interpretation, the language is highly poetic and figurative, and some unusual
occurrences can be expected. Observation of great eagles and the hearing of
their cry as they fly through the air could easily give John the sense of the word
"woe" (ouai).

The threefold cry of woe from the call of the eagle has nothing to do with
the four trumpets that have just sounded but rather with the trumpet blasts
sounded by the other three angels, a fact often unnoticed. The significance of
this declaration by John must have been devastating. The calamities unleashed
by the blasts of the first four trumpets are beyond anything imaginable to the
inhabitants of the earth today, but the woes announced by the eagle have to do
with the profoundly serious judgments yet to come.

The interjection "woe" (ouai) has an unchronicled origin, employed infrequently if at all in classical Greek. Moulton notes that it is common in the Septuagint and the New Testament. The interjection oua denotes wonder, real or
ironical (Mark 15:29), and not commiseration as with ouai.[235] Liddell and Scott
treat the word as an exclamation of pain and anger.[236] Whatever the genesis of
the word, the ominous overtones are apparent. John now must brace himself for
the sounding of the fifth angel.

B. The Fifth Trumpet of Demonic Oppression (9:1–12)

[1]**Then the fifth angel sounded: And I saw a star fallen from heaven to the earth. To
him was given the key to the bottomless pit. [2]And he opened the bottomless pit, and**

---

234 B. M. Metzger, *A Textual Commentary on the Greek New Testament* (New York:
UBS, 1971), 743.

235 J. H. Moulton and G. Milligan, *The Vocabulary of the Greek Testament* (Grand
Rapids: Eerdmans, 1930), 464.

236 LSJ, 1268.

smoke arose out of the pit like the smoke of a great furnace. So the sun and the air were darkened because of the smoke of the pit. ³Then out of the smoke locusts came upon the earth. And to them was given power, as the scorpions of the earth have power. ⁴They were commanded not to harm the grass of the earth, or any green thing, or any tree, but only those men who do not have the seal of God on their foreheads. ⁵And they were not given *authority* to kill them, but to torment them *for* five months. Their torment *was* like the torment of a scorpion when it strikes a man. ⁶In those days men will seek death and will not find it; they will desire to die, and death will flee from them.

⁷The shape of the locusts was like horses prepared for battle. On their heads were crowns of something like gold, and their faces *were* like the faces of men. ⁸They had hair like women's hair, and their teeth were like lions' *teeth.* ⁹And they had breastplates like breastplates of iron, and the sound of their wings *was* like the sound of chariots with many horses running into battle. ¹⁰They had tails like scorpions, and there were stings in their tails. Their power *was* to hurt men five months. ¹¹ And they had as king over them the angel of the bottomless pit, whose name in Hebrew *is* Abaddon, but in Greek he has the name Apollyon.

¹²One woe is past. Behold, still two more woes are coming after these things.

9:1 The continuation of the sounding of the seven trumpets features the two blasts of trumpets—numbers five and six. The specific plagues, which are unleashed by the reverberations of these two trumpets, involve remarkable locusts and the advance of a horde of two million invaders from beyond the Euphrates. When the sixth trumpet sounds, a great military conquest is envisioned, crossing the Euphrates River at least partially on horseback. However, when the horses and their riders are described by the seer, apparently nothing known to antiquity, or for that matter to modernity, appears in the vision. The sounding of these two trumpets presents difficulty not so much in terms of their obvious intent and extent of devastation imagined as of the impenetrable mystery regarding their precise nature, which does not underestimate the genius of interpreters in endlessly discerning various modern contraptions of war. But all are to be viewed with skepticism, even if one cannot help but appreciate the imaginative propensities of such interpreters. Now the text itself unfolds to ascertain what can be known.

With the sounding of the fifth angel, in stark contrast to the star mentioned in 8:10, John saw a star that had fallen to the earth. Whereas the star in 8:10 seems to be primarily of physical derivation (whether that be interpreted as meteor, some sort of detonated explosive, or some other physical explanation), the star of chap. 9 seems rather to be a personal being. A logical conclusion is to argue that this star from heaven should be identified as an angel, one of those who "did not keep their positions of authority" (Jude 6). That this fallen angel is presented in terms of a star with a particular reference to his fallenness, added to the fact that he clearly exercises authority, suggests him to be none other than Satan himself.[237]

Reasons for identifying this angel as Satan rest on the statement of Jesus responding to the reports of the returning disciples in Luke 10. Triumphantly Jesus noted, "I saw Satan fall like lightning from heaven" (Luke 10:18). Many commentators believe this reference is to a pre-cosmic confrontation referenced in Jude 6 and 2 Pet 2:4. I would also make the connection, which few other theologians now endorse, that the fall of Satan in view here is also the background behind the judgments on the kings of Babylon and Tyre, respectively in Isa 14 and Ezek 28. While there can be no doubt that the two kings are the immediate objects of disfavor, the text in both places offers more than can be historically sustained for these two sovereigns. If, however, they represent in their persons a more ominous event that preceded them, then one should not be surprised to hear Jesus, Jude, and Peter reference the event, which is all the more the case if the event assists in understanding the origin of evil.

"Fallen" is a translation of a perfect active participle, which may indicate not only a past action but also one with continuing results. The fall of Satan, therefore, is presented as an event, the results of which comprise a continuum essentially without hope of reversal.[238] A key is presented to this fallen star, and it is the key to the Abyss.

Two things should be noted in this regard. First, this fallen star is given the authority to unleash the horde that awaits in the Abyss. However, the key was presented to him; and although the source of the presentation of the key

---

237 R. L. Thomas is certain that the star is not Satan or any fallen angel but rather an unfallen angel bringing judgment (*Revelation 8–22: An Exegetical Commentary* [Chicago: Moody, 1992], 27). But G. K. Beale notes the similarity of this language to that of Jesus in Luke 10:18. Even so, he concludes that the reference is probably not to Satan but to some lesser fallen angel (*The Book of Revelation: A Commentary on the Greek Text*, NIGTC [Grand Rapids: Eerdmans; Carlisle, UK: Paternoster, 1999], 492–93).

238 A. T. Robertson says of the extensive perfect tense, "This comes to be the usual force of the tense. Gildersleeve has put the thing finely: 'The perfect looks at both ends of an action.' It 'unites in itself as it were present and aorist, since it expresses the continuance of completed action.' That is to say, the perfect is both punctiliar and durative. The aorist (punctiliar) represents an action as finished, the linear present as durative, but the perfect presents a completed state or condition. When the action was completed the perfect tense does not say. It is still complete at the time of the use of the tense by speaker or writer" (*A Grammar of the Greek New Testament in the Light of Historical Research* [Nashville: Broadman, 1934], 893).

is not clear in the text (perhaps it is the angel with the fifth trumpet), it is, nevertheless, a key given to him indicating the superiority of that authority to the suzerainty of the fallen star himself. Even the fallen star operates only under the ultimate authority of God.

The nature of the Abyss is nowhere plainly stated in Scripture. The word itself simply means "depth" with an alpha privative added and thus understood negatively as "without depth" (i.e., "without measurable depth"). The author obviously expects the reader to have familiarity with such concepts. Elsewhere in the Scriptures the angels who kept not their first estate were at least in part confined until the day of judgment (Jude 6). This confinement is apparently the Abyss to which John refers at this point. Most writers distinguish between a concept such as the Abyss (*abussos*) on the one hand and *Gehenna* (the lake of fire or hell) on the other. For example, Criswell notes:

> The Greek word here is *abyss*. We have taken the Greek word bodily into our language. ". . . and there was given to this principality of darkness and evil, this fallen archangel, the key of the abyss." Not only here, but throughout the Word of God, that abyss is looked upon as the darkness in which are imprisoned those fallen spirits who are reserved unto the day of judgment. For example, in the eighth chapter of the gospel of Luke, when Jesus met the Gadarene demoniac, the demons in him, vile and unclean, cried out lest the Lord come to torment them before their time, before their day of final judgment. Then they cried unto the Lord saying, "Do not command us to go into the [and it is translated in the King James Version "the deep"] into the [*sic*] abyss.["] Seven times in the Book of the Revelation is that "abyss" referred to. The last time it is mentioned is in the twentieth chapter when a mighty angel comes down from heaven and lays hands upon the devil, the dragon, the serpent, and binds him for a thousand years in that abyss. It is not the eternal home of the devil for he will be cast into the lake of fire, with all of the dupes who serve and worship him. In this abyss, in this darkness, are these spirits of evil who are reserved unto the day of judgment.[239]

---

239 W. A. Criswell, *Expository Sermons on Revelation: Five Volumes Complete and Unabridged* (Grand Rapids: Zondervan, 1969), 3:183–84. For the opposite view G. B. Caird avows, "We must not imagine, however, that John intends us to take either the fallen star or the abyss more literally than any of his other symbols. There is no place in his thinking for any precosmic fall of angels who can be blamed for subsequently corrupting the earth. He believes as firmly as any other New Testament writer that evil has its

The cosmogony of eternal states may be as simple as the new heavens and new earth, or of *gehenna* or hell, and heaven (*ouranos*). Conceivably fallen angels could be detained in a place of ongoing judgment prior to the final adjudication of their cases, just as the same thing can happen to humans, as one might note in Jesus' story of the rich man and Lazarus and their respective departures and destinations. The fact that the Abyss will be found to hold a vicious coterie is totally in keeping with what is known about the detention of fallen angels until the day of judgment, which with the advent of the tribulation is now pictured as being in its beginning stages. Satan, if he is properly identified as the fallen star, does not have the authority to unleash this horde except that authority be given of God, which apparently is done at this stage of the tribulation narrative.

9:2 As the reader would expect, the Abyss is opened by the fallen star, and John describes what appears to him to be smoke ascending out of a great furnace. The smoke is not like the luminous cloud of the presence of God in the exodus but is rather a blackening smoke as from the burning of coal, which as it spreads heavenward from the Abyss has the effect of darkening the air and the sun. Here one might reasonably ask, in anticipation of the identification of this particular "locust plague" as demonic, how can fallen angels who are presumably spiritual in nature blacken the air and obscure the noonday sun?[240] Wouldn't it be more logical to assume that the plague has a physical nature if it has such a physical effect? The answer to this objection is twofold. First, the description of the locusts and the agony they inflict is contrary to any known biological species and seems rather to be spiritual in the agony produced. Furthermore, even though these are spiritual beings, such conclusion would not

---

origin in human sin. We have already seen (I. 20) that the angels of the churches are to be understood as the heavenly counterparts of the earthly communities, and that their status before God is determined by the record of the churches they represent. Having given us this explicit clue at the outset, John expects us to be able to apply it again without reminder. It was the generally accepted view of his time, among Jews and Christians alike, that earthly institutions had their representative angels, as witness Paul's frequent mention of the principalities and powers which presided over the political, social, and religious institutions of the Roman empire. A fallen angel represents some aspect of the corporate life of men which is in open revolt against the purpose of God" (*The Revelation of St. John the Divine*, HNTC 19 [San Francisco: Harper & Row, 1966], 118).

240 Larkin speaks of them as "a kind of infernal cherubim" (*The Book of Revelation* [Philadelphia, PA: Clarence Larkin, 1919], 76). While this designation is clever, the text gives no indication as to their association with either of the two orders of angels noted in Scripture.

rule out either some sort of physical manifestation or else merely the use of vocabulary on the part of the Patmos seer to call attention to the darkening effects of such a spiritual plague in regard to light, truth, and understanding.

9:3 In v. 3 is found still another possible explanation: The locusts come from the smoke and are to be differentiated from the smoke itself. As the locusts come, the power given to them is similar to the power of the scorpions of the earth. Two things seem to be emphasized. First, they "were given power." The passage emphasizes an authority over the locusts. But even the authority of the fallen angel is subject to God's authority. Second, anyone who has had anything to do with scorpions is painfully acquainted with the numbing, aching sting induced by them. The language of the text vividly focuses on the numbing, sharp pain, and consequent ache produced in the victims of these particular locusts. Stings from scorpions are most often not fatal, though the red scorpion of India is sufficiently toxic as sometimes to be fatal. This locust plague is comprised of a heretofore unknown kind of locust that stings like a scorpion.

9:4 At this point the text takes a totally unexpected turn. John notes that these locusts are cautioned not to do harm to the grass of the earth nor to any green thing or any tree. To the contrary, humans, and a particular group of human beings—namely, those who do not have the seal of God in their foreheads, will be the only object of their assault. This verse is perhaps the first clear indication in the chapter that this phenomenon does not relate to physical locusts, which, even if they were some sort of super locusts, would generally have some difficulty inflicting such agonizing pain on a human. Also, the text clearly recalls the sealing of 144,000 from each of the twelve tribes of Israel, which was presented in 7:1–8. Although these 144,000 who are sealed must endure many of the difficulties experienced during the days of the tribulation, they, like the children of Israel in the Exodus narrative, seem to be exempt from other plagues. The exemption of those who have the seal of God is still another indication that this particular plague is spiritual rather than physical in nature and carries with it the added advantage of demonstrating the degree to which the authority of God is absolute. Although these locusts would doubtless inflict their agony on all, they are prevented by command from hurting those who have the seal of God. Once again, the seal is indicative of a protected possession of the living God.

9:5 A further indication that the locust plague should be viewed as spiritual arises from the fact that the locusts are not permitted to kill but only to torment. Again, the torment envisioned is similar to that of a scorpion, indicating once again the sharpness of the pain, followed by the numbing and aching of that portion of the anatomy thus affected, and sometimes spreading to the entire body. Specifically, the torment of the locusts of the fifth angel's trumpet is said to be five months in duration.[241] While some of the apocalyptic numbers seem to be fairly easy to explain, the precise nature of the five-month duration here is somewhat more elusive. Should the number be taken as an indication that at some point during the tribulation period there will be literally a five-month period in which the inhabitants of the earth as never before would be demonically tormented; or is John's use of "five" a case of the symbolic use of numbers? "Five" is apparently a number associated with humanity (see Introduction). Possibly, then, this is another way John has of indicating that this particular locust plague has nothing to do with any facet of nature other than human beings? The probabilities, as far as this interpreter is concerned, seem to lie with the latter interpretation. But, once again, there is no certainty.

9:6 This particular plague of scorpion-like locusts is sufficiently enervating as to evoke a most intense conceivable psychological reaction on the part of the inhabitants afflicted. The Scripture affirms that in those days men will seek death. Of course, the natural propensity of every human to seek to protect his own life above all is well known. Even with the contemporary emphasis on the "right to die" and on such entities as the "Hemlock Society," together with the well-known saga of the antiphysician Kevorkian and his efforts to enable terminally ill and profoundly suffering patients to snuff out their own lives, the overwhelming majority of the billions of inhabitants who breathe the atmosphere of the globe still seek to stay alive. The text envisions a moment when the spiritually induced agonies will be so devastating that men will actually seek the supposed relief of death.

While there is no question that physical injury or disease can become sufficiently agonizing as to induce the desire to die, pastoral endeavors have demonstrated that guilt, sorrow, addiction, and failure or perceived failure are often more devastating than physical disorders. Demonic possession often heightens such agonies exponentially. As long as these legions of demons are confined to the Abyss, spiritual and psychological pain is frequent and ominous. But when this plague is released for five months, the effects are chilling to the degree that its victims prefer death.

---

241 J. M. Ford alludes to this period saying, "The five-month period may be interpreted literally as indicating no more than the ancients' fear of locust invasions, which occurred during the last five months of the Jewish year." This idea is then rejected in favor of an historical view having to do with events in AD 70 (*Revelation: Introduction, Translation and Commentary*, AB [Garden City, NY: Doubleday, 1975], 149).

If this were not a sufficiently astonishing indication, the next insight surely qualifies. While men seek death, they are unable to find it. Although they will long to die, death will flee from them. This poignant reversal is clearly distinct from everything literature has ever imagined. Most often death is the icy monster who pursues humans across the stage of history until finally its cold fingers grasp the victim and pull him to the grave. In this normal picture, man is fleeing as rapidly as he possibly can. Now, as the result of this plague, the matter is reversed. Men are seeking death, but death flees. Whether this means that those seeking death simply failed in their courage to take their own lives or whether in the days of the tribulation those seeking what they think will be escape from agony through death will be prevented from actuating their own deaths is not clear from the text. What is abundantly evident is that their desire to die will be frustrated.

9:7-8 At this point the Patmos seer returns to his description of the locusts. He describes them as being like horses in battle array. However, unlike most horses going into battle, they have crowns on their heads, and these crowns are like gold. In this case the *stephanos* or victor's crown rather than the diadem is in view. Then, in the strangest of maneuvers, the seer notes that what began looking like a horse arrayed for battle with a gold-like victor's crown, actually has the face of a man. And if this staggering turn is not sufficiently astonishing, the creatures have the hair of women and teeth like those of lions. Since the description began using the likeness of horses, one might have expected John to speak of the mane of the horses; instead, John observes the flowing hair to be like that of women. Then leapfrogging from metaphor to metaphor, the seer takes note of the teeth of these predators and finds them to be like the teeth of lions. Locusts with the appearance of horses prepared for battle with victor's crowns on their heads, the faces of men, the hair of women, and the teeth of lions complete the picture. Such a monstrosity is clearly designed to indicate the potential devastation and possible horror induced by this locust plague, which is a part of the fifth trumpet.

9:9-10 However, the description is not complete. These locusts had breastplates of iron; and as expected of locusts but not of horses or men, they have wings; and those wings, beating as they approach, provide a sound like chariots following innumerable steeds rushing into battle. At this point John by describing these locusts as having tails that are like scorpions also returns to the question of the scorpion-like agonies inflicted. Whether John intends that these tails be the long-segmented tails expected of scorpions with the slightly scimitar-shaped sting at the end or whether he merely means to speak once again of the nature of the agony is not clear. Clearly their tails carry the authority to hurt men for five months.

9:11-12 If until now there has been any question about the appropriate identification of the star that is fallen or of the nature of the plague itself, v. 11 seems to remove all confusion. A king, who is the angel of the Abyss, rules over them. In Hebrew his name is Abaddon, and in Greek, Apollyon. To understand the text as differentiating between the king of the Abyss and the star that has fallen seems unlikely since Satan at least presently is not bound and will not be bound until the millennial period. Consequently, more likely the fallen star of 9:1 is now openly identified as the king of the Abyss in 9:11. The identification of the king as Abaddon and Apollyon make the character of the king of the Abyss apparent. The word *Abaddōn* ("destroyer") is the Hebrew name of a demon transliterated into Greek:

> This word is transliterated in Rev. 9:11 and used as the Hebrew name of the devil, called in the Greek Apollyon. This is not identical with the O.T. usage, but it is an interesting commentary on it. The word is used six times in the O.T. . . . It is obvious that the word refers to the destruction of the grave, but the contents are not clear enough to prove that it refers to external destruction.[242]

The conclusion of Harris in the *Theological Wordbook of the Old Testament*, and the author of this volume notwithstanding, more than a few commentators fail to see Abaddon as Satan. Robertson, for example, is not sure whether the reference is to Satan or just to death.[243] Newport, however, is representative of others when he says:

> The leader of these demonic forces is not Satan but an angel who presides over the bottomless pit (v. 11). This leader is called "Abaddon" in Hebrew and "Apollyon" in Greek. Apollyon appears to be an angel entrusted with authority over the abyss. The creature, his name, and his responsibility seem to be original with the author of Revelation. These creatures are part locust and part scorpion which obviously is a symbolic representation of demonic powers (vv. 7–11).[244]

---

242 R. L. Harris, "אָבַד (*'ābad*)," *TWOT* 1:3–4.

243 A. T. Robertson, *Word Pictures in the New Testament* (Nashville: Broadman, 1933), 365.

244 J. P. Newport, *The Lion and the Lamb* (Nashville: Broadman, 1986), 207.

But Walvoord is doubtless correct in his judgment:

> The Hebrew name "Abaddon" and the Greek name "Apollyon" both mean "destroyer." Such is the character of Satan and those who affiliate with him as wicked or fallen angels. Though in the modern world Satan often appears as an angel of light in the role of that which is good and religious, here the mask is stripped away and evil is seen in its true character. Satan and the demons are seen as the destroyers of the souls of men and as those who can only bring affliction. When divine restraint is released, as in this instance, the true character of the evil one is manifested immediately.[245]

Apolluon, on the other hand, is a Greek word that combines *luō*, generally meaning "loose," with the preposition *apo*, meaning "from or away from." In this case the word carries the sense of "destroy" or "loose from meaning or significance." Consequently, one can safely assume that even though men afflicted by the locust plague of the fifth trumpet may seek death and not be able to find it, they are, nevertheless, in some significant sense of the word "destroyed."

The purpose of the locust plague, including that of the king over the Abyss, is to cause widespread spiritual agony and destruction. Those who have experienced unrequited spiritual and psychological agony would be the first to attest that it can be far worse than any physical pain imaginable. This seems to be the significance of the plague associated with the sounding of the fifth angel. In this first of three woes, the apostle John is apparently saying that an unimaginable spiritual devastation will occur during the days of the tribulation. Physical woes and plagues have already been apparent but the nature of this one appears to be decidedly spiritual in nature. Though it provides little relief, the first woe is passed and two more will follow. Accessing the first should be sufficient to convince anyone that the next two will provide a more devastating picture.

C. The Sixth Trumpet of Eastern Invasion (9:13–21)

[13]**Then the sixth angel sounded: And I heard a voice from the four horns of the golden altar which is before God,** [14]**saying to the sixth angel who had the trumpet, "Release the four angels who are bound at the great river Euphrates."** [15]**So the four angels, who had been prepared for the hour and day and month and year, were re-**

---

245 J. Walvoord, *The Revelation of Jesus Christ* (Chicago: Moody, 1966), 163.

leased to kill a third of mankind. ¹⁶Now the number of the army of the horsemen *was* two hundred million; I heard the number of them.

¹⁷And thus I saw the horses in the vision: those who sat on them had breastplates of fiery red, hyacinth blue, and sulfur yellow; and the heads of the horses *were* like the heads of lions; and out of their mouths came fire, smoke, and brimstone. ¹⁸By these three *plagues* a third of mankind was killed—by the fire and the smoke and the brimstone which came out of their mouths. ¹⁹For their power is in their mouth and in their tails; for their tails *are* like serpents, having heads; and with them they do harm.

²⁰But the rest of mankind, who were not killed by these plagues, did not repent of the works of their hands, that they should not worship demons, and idols of gold, silver, brass, stone, and wood, which can neither see nor hear nor walk. ²¹And they did not repent of their murders of their sorceries or their sexual immorality or their thefts.

9:13–16 With the sounding of the trumpet by the sixth angel, the reader is introduced to another formidable assault. This one comes from the east and will be characterized by devastation of almost incomparable proportions. Once again, the descriptions of the oriental army portrayed by John defy any comparison with known military contingencies of the ancient world or with anything in the modern world. Attempts specifically to identify the horses and riders described in the latter part of chap. 9 as tanks belching forth fire and with some sort of automatic weaponry being described by their tails is far-fetched to say the least. Some have argued that since John could not have conceived of modern weaponry like a tank with a high-caliber machine gun and a large cannon affixed to it, he could not be describing such objects in vv. 13–18. Although one may respond that foreseeing such weapons in a vision might be possible, it is hardly wise exegetically to attempt to assign such specific and anachronistic meanings to an ancient text. Better is the approach that seeks to grasp the nature of the warning and the general essence of the conflict of the last days of the tribulation.

The seemingly anachronistic idea of modern employment of horses in battle is not stretching the imagination at all.[246] But again, the interpretation of the nature of the sixth trumpet is not technical specificity about the nature of warfare. The message from relatively peaceful Patmos is that of looming global conflict: Occident versus Orient and ultimately heaven versus earth in the dark days of the tribulation.

---

246 See Doug Stanton, *Horse Soldiers: The Extraordinary Story of a Band of U.S. Soldiers Who Rode to Victory in Afghanistan* (New York: Scribner, 2009) for an account of special ops' extensive use of horses in the conflict in Afghanistan.

The sounding of the sixth angel sets up a sequence of rapid events. First, the sixth angel sounds a voice from the four horns of the golden altar, which is before God. The altar, which is described as the locus of the voice, seems to be a part of the general throne room vision initiated in chap. 4 and mentioned specifically in the opening of the martyr seal, the fifth seal, where under the altar the souls of those that had been slain appear. Now from that altar comes a voice, and the voice commands the sixth angel who had the trumpet to release the four angels who are bound at the great river Euphrates. Like almost everything else in the Apocalypse, there is disagreement about the proper identity of these four angels. Roloff is certain that these are wicked angels:

> The angel that has just given the trumpet signal is to release four demonic angels that he chained in the area of the Euphrates, so that the satanic hosts, whose leaders and representatives they are, are able to fall upon the Roman Empire from its eastern borders. A motif-historical relationship with the four angels mentioned in 7:1 is certainly present, but the differences in the arrangement of details of the motif here and there are too strong to make an identification of the two groups of angels possible. In 7:1 the representatives of the four regions of the earth, or the four winds, are standing at God's disposal; here, bound by God, demonic figures are ready to exercise destructive power upon their release.[247]

Johnson, on the other hand, sees the angels as "instruments of God's judgment."[248] Since these angels appear to be restraining the onslaught of this Asian army, apparently they are best seen as restraining angels of God.

In turn these four angels, whose assignment in the tribulation has been the subject of explicit preparation, yielding for them the exact hour, day, month, and year for this task are unbound or released for the purpose of executing one third of the human family. The mention specifically of the extermination of the third of human kind raises the natural query about whether or not this third is to be seen in addition to whatever loss has been incurred in the seal judgments of chap. 6 and the first four trumpet judgments of chap. 8. This is part of a broader question involving whether the seals, trumpets, and bowls of wrath are to be understood as sequential, overlapping one another, or simply enlargements depicting the extent of the tribulation in different kinds

---

247 J. Roloff, *The Revelation of John*, CC (Minneapolis: Fortress, 1993), 118.
248 A. Johnson, "Revelation," *EBC* (Grand Rapids: Zondervan), 12:494.

of pictures. Some would also argue that choosing among those options is not necessary since all may be at work to some degree. My own perspective while its perhaps impossible to draw a firm conclusion, is that there is sequence to the judgments and consequently the third of mankind that loses life here is in addition to those who have already died. Jesus said of the tribulation period, "If those days had not been cut short, no one would survive" (Matt 24:22). Remembering that assessment, the reader will not find it strange that the world would be denuded of a substantial portion of its population by the concluding days of the tribulation period.

In addition, since the angels appear to be in some way or another directly involved in the unleashing of this judgment, the action should be seen as a judicial act of God even if the forces involved are essentially godless. A cursory reading of the Old Testament history as well as the history of the fall of Jerusalem to the Romans in AD 70 will remind the reader that not infrequently in history God has used the godless to accomplish his bidding, especially as that has to do with judgment. While the four angels who have been holding back the tide of eastern insurgency are not the ones who actually take the lives of humans, the text is clear that on the arrival of the precise year, month, day, and hour, they act in unison to release this eastern army, resulting in the carnage depicted.

The Euphrates, originating in Armenia, is the long river winding steadily across the face of the Middle East and touching Turkey, Syria, and Iraq until uniting with the Tigris and together reaching the Persian Gulf. This ageless river has long been a point of demarcation between what is sometimes referred to as the Near East on the western shores of the Euphrates and the Far East belonging to the countries on the eastern banks of the Euphrates. A second observation regards the precision in the action of the angels. The reader will note that these four restraining angels have been placed in a strategic position in order to act in a specific year, month, day, and hour. The cogent reminder here is that an omniscient God is not taken by surprise by any event of history, nor does anything proceed other than at his own choice of time. In no sense does this eliminate the freedom of human action, but it does underscore the purposes and providences of God in such a way as to comfort those who have entrusted themselves to Christ and his safekeeping through the ages.

9:17–19 Verses 17–19 provide a vivid description of the companies of troops moving across the Euphrates once the four angels release them. One of the fascinating aspects of what is presented focuses on the differences between the way the armies themselves would view the situation in contrast with God's understanding and purpose. The angels are unseen to the marauding armies, and they are consequently unaware that their decisions are in reality conditioned inevitably by the hand of God. But now that the angels release them, John looks and focuses on such an enormous movement of troops, unable to assess the number. Consider looking from a high vantage point over a mass people movement numbering 200 million. There would be no way to have any idea how many were a part of it. Accordingly, John notes that the number was told to him.

If the seer was not completely overcome by the sheer size of this numerical assault, what is displayed before him next must have held him in awe. As he looks, he discovers that there are horses, or at least something similar to steeds; those who sit on them have breastplates the color of fire, dark blue, and yellow like sulphurous stone—apparently a mixing of blue and yellow hues. The mounts are not normal horses since their heads are like heads of lions and from their mouths proceed fire, smoke, and sulphur. Despite the earlier warning in the introduction to this chapter, perhaps those suggesting that, as John notes in v. 18, a third of mankind were killed by three plagues—notably by the fire, smoke, and the sulphur that proceeded out of the mouths of the horses—one who had never seen a motorized military vehicle would describe it in this way. But it is anachronistic and unnecessary for contemporary interpreters to assign to these symbols current machinery of war. Whatever the case, clearly the deaths of a third of mankind are exacted by the unbelievable conflagration. Some of them die as a result of the initial fire, some by the contamination of the battlefield (the smoke), and others as a result of the lingering fires of the encounter.

This leads the apostle to note that the power of the horses was in their mouths and in their tails. This notion makes it improbable that John has seen an actual horse. Rather, a horse is the closest resemblance he could imagine. On the other hand, their tails are said to be like serpents' heads. Unclear from the text is whether each horse had multiple-headed tails or whether the plural "heads" refers to all of them together. Whatever the case, these hideous but effective "horsemen" making up some part of the 200-million-member hoard bring violent death to masses of humanity.

Many have raised questions about the size of the army given. Inevitably, the more cautious biblical interpreters point out that there is no such thing as a 200-million-man army in any nation or group of nations, nor is such really conceivable. Furthermore, if there even existed such a thing, imagining how such an enormous number of people could possibly be effective in confrontation with weapons of mass destruction seems impossible in a day of technological weaponry. The difficulty of the necessary lines to sustain such a movement of military personnel also exists. Such questions need not concern the reader unduly. First, John's notation that the movement of troops involves 200 million does not compel that every one of these be seen as an armed insurgent. Perhaps the number is inclusive of all who would be involved in supporting such a large movement. Second, while there is no nation with a 200-million-member army, one must remember that there are two modern nations whose populations now number more than a billion people—China and India. This is to say nothing of the large, crowded southern Asia nations surrounding India and China and containing well over half the world's population. To imagine an Asian army numbering 200-million-men is no longer preposterous at all. While such a figure may have been phenomenal to John and his early readers, no longer is such as inconceivable as it might have seemed to John. So, the Scripture can be accepted at face value even if one does not know the exact nature, circumstances, and precise origin of these people. Their purpose is clear enough.

Some interpreters do not view these horsemen as an army of humans, while others find them merely representative of clashes of history. For example, Krodel sees a historical circumstance informing an eschatological expectation:

> The **Euphrates** marked the eastern boundary of the Roman empire in Asia Minor. On the other side of the river lay the Parthian empire which had inflicted humiliating defeats on the Roman legions in 53 B.C. and A.D. 62. So it is not surprising that the Romans were quite neurotic about the Parthian menace. *1 Enoch* 56 envisions Parthians and Medes being stirred up by evil angels and invading Palestine like hungry wolves. John may allude to this widespread fear (cf. 6:2). However, as always, he reinterpreted it. He was not interested in *historical* manifestations of this plague but only in its *eschatological* dimension. Therefore he explicitly noted that these four demonic angels **had been held ready for the hour, the day, the month, and the year**. Only when God's eschatological "hour" strikes, only then will they be released.[249]

Frederick Murphy finds the same imagery to which Krodel alludes but suggests that the Parthians, instead of attacking Israel, are armies that attack the inhabitants of the earth.[250] Beasley-Murray posits the apocalyptic genre

---

249 G. A. Krodel, *Revelation*, ACNT (Minneapolis: Augsburg, 1989), 205.
250 F. J. Murphy, *Fallen is Babylon: The Revelation to John*, The New Testament in Context (Harrisburg, PA: Trinity Press International, 1998), 247.

as "political cartoon." If so, this segment of the Revelation would come close to qualifying.[251]

9:20-21 In a chapter brimful of incredible phenomena and nearly inexplicable circumstances, the most astonishing report lies not in the assault of a 200-million-man army from the east or the wrenching plague of locusts but in the assessment of life on earth at the conclusion of this enormous campaign. While the average interpreter might be almost drawn to miss vv. 20–21 and focus on the display of military prowess in the early part of the chapter, by far the most arresting statement of the chapter is John's account of the reaction of the remaining people on the earth. The anticipated response to such a holocaust as the one envisioned with the sounding of trumpets by both the fifth and the sixth angels would be a massive turn to God by all of humanity. Quite the opposite happens. The rest of mankind who managed to survive these plagues, according to John, did not repent of the works of their hands or of their worship of the demonic or of their materialism or of their idolatry of gold, silver, bronze, stone, and wood—even though these idols not only possessed no divine characteristics but were lacking even human abilities to hear and to walk.

Verse 21 continues this tragic commentary by noting further that there was no repentance for their murders, sorceries, immoralities, or thefts. "Sorceries" makes use of the Greek word *pharmakeia*, which has come into English as "pharmacy" and developed in part as a result of the ancient practice of the use of hallucinatory drugs in the practice of magic, sorcery, divination, and healing. Pliny, in his *Natural History*, discusses many of the superstitions and magical practices utilized to bring about physical changes in the body.[252] Sexual immorality (*porneia*) is the word referring to general sexual licentiousness. Less specific but inclusive of adultery, the term indicates the promiscuous nature of society including the preoccupation of the mind with sexual themes. It is inherently selfish and often abusive.

The overall picture painted is that despite the upheavals, tragedies, and overwhelming loss of life generated by the angels of the fifth and sixth trumpets, men continue to reject the one true God in favor of the gods of their own manufacturing, and worse still, even of the demonic spirits that enslave them.

---

251 G. R. Beasley-Murray, *The Book of Revelation*, NCBC (Grand Rapids: Eerdmans, 1981), 16–17.

252 Pliny, *Natural History*, Volume 8: Books 12–16, trans. W. H. S. Jones, LCL 418 (Cambridge, MA: Harvard University Press, 1963). For interesting and extensive discussion of the approaches to healing both legitimate and magical, see Books 28 and 30.

In turn, this causes them to demonstrate in their ethical and moral practices continued depravity and lack of regard for the things of God. Their lives became steeped in violence and esoteric practices of various kinds, including those induced by the introduction of foreign substances. There is a callous disregard for the will and purpose of God.

One may venture to ask then why the seer of Patmos would have recorded these last two verses. How do these verses relate to all that has gone before in the messages of the seven trumpets. The questions may be even more important than expected. I wish to argue that a statement concerning the rationale for the great tribulation is here. The outpouring of the wrath of God on humanity during the seven ominous years of tribulation demonstrates two critically important truths. First, even the threat of the imminent judgment of God is not an ultimate deterrent to the wickedness of man. Many believe that thorough, swift, and adequate punishment of criminal offenses is a deterrent. I not only respect that position but hold it to be true. On the other hand, however, the teaching of Scripture seems to be that a level of depravity, bound up in the hearts of people, so deceives and distorts as to reduce victims to insensitivity. Paul spoke of this condition saying that their "consciences have been seared as with a hot iron" (1 Tim 4:2). Even when they see the penalty of their actions, they determine to continue the practices of evil that brought about these judgments, preferring to satiate physical appetites rather then to nourish their spirits with the presence of the living God.

Second, in vv. 20–21 a justification for the judgments of God is found. In almost any generation there are those who seem to feel that a God of judgment is inappropriate. If God is to be God, they suppose, He is to be characterized by love, long-suffering, and tolerance in order to retain His claim to deity. But if He becomes a God of justice and judgment, whose patience is not unlimited, then He is somehow unworthy to continue as God. But one cannot read the reactions of the inhabitants in the great tribulation, especially in light of the onslaught of the terrible eastern horde, without coming away with the sense that there comes a point when God must act in judgment and justice. For God to fail to judge when—despite the fact that people continue in their iniquity—He has given every conceivable warning of what it means to be the recipient of divine judgment, is unthinkable. Such inaction would present to the world a God who is powerless in the face of evil. A world in which righteousness could never ultimately triumph would result. Six angels have sounded, and the devastation of God's judgments is unavoidable.

D. The Voice of the Seven Thunders (10:1–7)

¹I saw still another mighty angel coming down from heaven, clothed with a cloud. And a rainbow *was* on his head, his face *was* like the sun, and his feet like pillars of fire. ²He had a little book open in his hand. And he set his right foot on the sea and *his* left *foot* on the land, ³and cried with a loud voice, as *when* a lion roars. When he cried out, seven thunders uttered their voices. ⁴Now when the seven thunders uttered their voices, I was about to write; but I heard a voice from heaven saying to me, "Seal up the things which the seven thunders uttered, and do not write them."

⁵The angel whom I saw standing on the sea and on the land raised up his hand to heaven ⁶and swore by Him who lives forever and ever, who created heaven and the things that are in it, the earth and the things that are in it, and the sea and the things that are in it, that there should be delay no longer, ⁷but in the days of the sounding of the seventh angel, when he is about to sound, the mystery of God would be finished, as He declared to His servants the prophets.

Chapter 9 concludes with the sounding of the sixth trumpet. The seventh trumpet announcing Christ's reign over all of the cosmos will not be heard until the fifteenth verse of chap. 11. Consequently, Rev 10:1–11:14 constitutes one of the interludes that occur periodically in the Apocalypse of John. The two events composing this interlude do not appear to be intimately connected. The first event is a vision in which John himself becomes a player, while the second focuses on the appearance of two remarkable witnesses and the bizarre events that encompass their lives and ministries. But perhaps this initial appearance of unrelatedness is not the case. Although the subject matter of the tenth chapter concerns John, apparently the vision involving the seer himself serves as a bridge to introduce the two witnesses whose work is the proclamation of the coming judgment of God (see chap. 11). Since this assigned ministry obviously occurs during the midst of the tribulation period, the tenth chapter should be viewed as an explanation for events transpiring during the tribulation period, which makes this period more than just the judgment of God on the earth.

Chapter 10 chronicles the appearance of the mighty angel, the sounding of seven peals of thunder, the beginning of the end and an encounter of John with the angel bearing the little scroll. The unique feature of the participation of John in his own vision is not without precedence in the Bible or even in the dreams of humans in any era.

10:1–4 The first section of chap. 10 focuses on the appearance of a mighty angel who comes down from heaven. The depiction of his appearance suggests high rank, a position of honor, and a radiant glory. The description indicates that this angelic being is swathed with a cloud. The verb "clothed" (*periballō*) here occurs as a perfect passive participle, giving indication that the angel has been permanently clothed with this adornment. Meantime, the rainbow is about his head as though it were a crown. When John looked at the angel's face, he found it to be like the radiance of the sun itself. In all probability, one look at his face forced the eyes of the seer down in humility from the radiant gaze, calling attention immediately to the great angel's legs, which John observes were like pillars of fire. Recalling the problem encountered when the children of Israel gazed on the face of Moses as he descended from the presence of God, the Israelites requested that a veil be placed over the face of Moses so they could look in his direction. One can imagine something of the same reaction now on the part of the seer of Patmos.

The question to be answered by commentators is the proper identity of the angel. Not a few commentators have chosen to identify the angel with Christ, while others have argued that the terminology "angel," while certainly not ruling out its larger usage as "messenger" and thus possibly being applicable to Christ, favors either the archangel or a powerful, but otherwise unidentified, member of an angelic order.[253] Nothing in this verse or the verses to follow will enable the interpreter to make a certain identification; fortunately, the unequivocal identification of this angel is not necessary to the significance of the chapter. My own suspicion, since the appearance of the Lord elsewhere in the book is largely undebatable, is that this angel is one of great prestige and authority. That he is called an angel is not determinative one way or another but must favor the

---

253 A. C. Gaebelein says flatly, "It is Christ Himself" (*The Revelation: An Analysis and Exposition of the Last Book of the Bible* [New York: Publication Office "Our Hope," 1915], 66). G. R. Osborne provides a litany of possibilities but concludes that there is insufficient proof to argue that the angel is Christ (*Revelation*, BECNT [Grand Rapids: Baker Academic, 2002], 393). L. Morris concedes that certain points favor a Christological interpretation but finds the view ultimately in error: "Each of the points mentioned has elsewhere some connection with God or with Christ, so this angel is clearly important. Some (*e.g.* Stoffel) have identified him with Christ, but this is not justified. Christ is never called an angel in this book (let alone 'another angel') and this angel is not accorded divine honours. He is not worshipped, for example. The swearing of an oath 'by him who lives for ever and ever' (v. 6) does not look like an action of Christ" (*The Book of Revelation: An Introduction and Commentary*, 2nd ed., TNTC [Leicester, England: InterVarsity], 133–34). Based on the meaning of the Greek word ἄλλος, meaning "another of the same kind" of angel, H. Alford is even more certain saying, "And this consideration may serve to introduce the assertion, to me hardly admitting of a doubt, that this angel is not, and cannot be, our Lord himself" (*The Greek Testament* [Chicago: Moody, 1958], 4:649).

view that this is not the Christ. The oath the angel placed in his mouth, while once again not impossible for Christ, appears improbable but fits naturally in the mouth of even an archangel. Whatever the case, the passage emphasizes the strength, the glory of his countenance, and the contents of his hand.

John notes that the angel has in his hand a little scroll (*biblaridion*, a diminutive form of the word "book"). The stature of the angel may have been sufficient to make the scroll look small; but because this scroll will be eaten, the scroll is probably small in size, not merely in comparison with the angel who holds it. By the same token the angel has his right foot on the sea and his left foot on the land. Some interpreters eager to explain every symbol will inevitably see mention of the land as a reference to Israel and the mention of the sea as a reference to the Gentile nations. Better is the view that simply recognizes the authority of the angel as encompassing all the earth—namely, the dry land and the seas (i.e., the cosmos). The angel speaks with a loud voice as when a lion roars. The word for "roar" (*mukaomai*) is onomatopoetic and references the sound like that made by the celebrated felines. The unnerving effect of the roar of a male lion close at hand can be fully appreciated by those who have experienced from an unprotected camp in the African Savannah the bone-chilling, night-rending call of this beast.

Still, such a roar, probably another indication of the overwhelming prowess of the angel, is clearly differentiated from the seven peals of thunder, which make an antiphonal response to the roaring cry of the mighty angel. These seven peals of thunder are apparently each clearly identifiable, hence indicating sequence. This, of course, is exactly what the interpreter would expect in light of the sequential breaking of the seven seals and sounding of the seven trumpets and pouring out of the seven bowls, the seventh of which is yet to come. The seer was about to write when he is arrested by a heavenly voice forbidding him to record what the seven thunders uttered.

Two or three important observations seem warranted by this action. First, the seven thunders constituted more than just the rumble of the distant crashing of molecules. Each peal of thunder must have carried with it a discernible message such as those revealed with the opening of the seals and the sounding of the trumpets. Second, one may legitimately inquire about the report of the seven thunders and what would demand the sealing of their message in contradistinction to the revelation of the seals, trumpets, and bowls. While this question must be bracketed since certainty eludes the interpreter, possibly at least one conclusion may be ventured and perhaps a hypothesis considered about a second. The first conclusion that seems warranted is that the tragic nature and the overwhelming consequences of the judgments of God poured out on earth in the days of the great tribulation is portrayed for us in poignant and extensive detail throughout these middle chapters of the Apocalypse. Yet there remains a depth and an extent of the judgments of the great tribulation, which while shared with John are sealed against further revelation to the reader. While John understood clearly what the seven thunders said, he is also informed that their messages are sealed unless the Lord opens the seal, since "when the Lord shuts no man opens."[254] But then the interpreter may possibly address the text, asking why the message of the seven thunders would be revealed to John and not permit him to provide this information to his audience. Here once again possibly God is acting to reveal through His apostle much but not all of what he is intending to do in terms of the judgments of the tribulation period. That some of those judgments remain recondite as far as the reader is concerned is a literary device functioning as an ominous threat, having the effect of saying, "You have

---

254 S. S. Smalley recounts various reasons for the nondisclosure of the voices of the thunders but finally concludes, "The clearest, and to my mind most convincing, interpretation is offered by Bauckham (*Climax of Prophecy* 259-61), who reminds us that the image of sealing in this passage is used to contrast the thunders, which are sealed and do not become part of John's prophetic revelation, and the scroll (verse 2), which has been unsealed so that it may become the content of the seer's remaining disclosures. The incident of the seven thunderclaps, therefore, makes clear that 'there are to be no more warning judgements, but *instead* there is to be what the scroll will reveal' (ibid. 260). The process of judgement, in Johannine theology generally, and certainly in the Apocalypse, is ongoing (see Smalley, *Thunder and Love*, 150-52). We have already discovered in Revelation the end as imminent, but not realized (6.17; 8.1-5; et al.). So now, the rumbling thunders point towards the dénouement of the drama, and share in its character; but they do not precipitate it (against Caird; Mounce; Beale). The announcement of God's purposes of judgement and love for his creation (as contained in the small scroll) is to continue, both in history and in John's Revelation; and the time for these to be gathered up in Christ is always imminent, but also relentlessly future (despite the promise in verse 6 [q.v.] that there will be 'no more time of waiting')" (*The Revelation to John: A Commentary on the Greek Text of the Apocalypse* [Downers Grove, IL: InterVarsity, 2005], 262-63). E. W. Bullinger also has an interesting perspective, "John heard what the thunders said, and understood; for he was about to write. Some would have us believe that these seven thunders are the Papal Bulls issued against Luther and the Reformation. If this be so, then God sealed the book in vain! for all know what those thunders uttered. No, God's purpose in this book is very different from man's ideas of it. God has caused it to be written in order to make things known to us. Man treats it as though what is written is to conceal what is said, and make it incomprehensible" (*Commentary on Revelation* [Grand Rapids: Kregel,1984], 338-39).

seen a great deal, but nowhere close to all of my hand in judgment." Consequently, one must be content to leave the messages of the seven thunders with John who heard them, knowing that at the appropriate time their messages also will be clear. And John must accept the unusual experience of having heard and understood yet for the first time being forbidden to write what he knew.

10:5-7 The seven peals of thunder have concluded their aria, and now the mighty glorious angel is about to speak again. John's attention is once again drawn away from the trumpets to the angel with one foot on the land and one foot on the sea. But this time John notices not so much his feet but his hands. He holds the small scroll in one hand, which John had noted in his earlier description in v. 2. But now John sees his right hand lifted high to heaven in a gesture of authority and recognition. One may assume, at this point, that the little scroll must have been in his left hand, although the angel could have hoisted the small scroll heavenward also. Whatever the case, the gesture does not seem to have its focus on the scroll, but on the authority of the forthcoming declaration.

The declaration of the angel in v. 6 is largely the reason for this author's suggestion that the angel should not be identified as Christ. The angel lifts his hand heavenward and swears "by Him who lives forever and ever," the One who created heaven and earth and the sea, that there should be no longer any delay. Although the Scriptures do say that the Lord can swear by no greater than Himself (Heb 6:13), still that the Lord, who was God's agent in creation, would be here swearing by Himself is unlikely. More comprehensible is that this great angel acknowledges in his oath the superiority of the one true God whom he serves. Once again, the oath itself is in the name of One who is in possession of perpetual and endless life. The present active participle of living (*zōnti*) is employed in the angelic proclamation, emphasizing about as vividly as could possibly be done in language, the continuing uninterrupted life of the One in whose name the oath is uttered. The continuous existence of such a being is in stark contrast to the created order itself—not only by virtue of the temporality of the created order versus the eternality of the Creator but also by virtue of the fact that the created order is clearly the artistry of Him who lives forever and ever. Not only does John thus distinguish his own theology from any form of pantheism, but he also distinguishes it from modern forms of New Age thought, which fail adequately to make this distinction between the Creator and the created.

Specifically, the One in whose name the oath is taken is the One who created heaven and all in it, the earth and all in it, and the sea and all in it. The only question in understanding this text relates to the word "heaven" (*ouranos*).

"Heaven" may refer to the unique dwelling place of God or to the atmosphere of the earth or to the intergalactic heavens that make up the universe. While any of these options would still fall under the rubric of that which God created, nonetheless, probably in light of the following mention of the earth and the sea, the whole cosmos is here in view. God is the One who created the natural order, thus the sea and all the creatures in it, the land and its inhabitants, the inter-galactic heavens and all bodies included in it, are part of his creative genius.

The rationale for this description of God by the apostle provides partic-ular significance for the nature of the relatively simple oath itself. The oath declares in four simple words *hoti chronos ouketi estai*: there should no longer be any delay. *Chronos* is a term generally translated "time" and most often sug-gests time as humans reckon time—namely, the succession and passing of mo-ments. The English word, *chronology*, arises from it. However, the text provides a wonderful case of the importance of the context when interpreting a word. If the interpreter follows the Authorized Version and reads, "There shall be time no longer," he is faced immediately with a significant problem. At this point only half of the apocalyptic vision has been completed, and much of the book's message is yet to be unfolded. Furthermore, in terms of the sequence itself, this author's interpretation of the book would follow an interpretive tradition that would see the events unfolding here as a part of a seven-year series of events in the great tribulation to be followed by a kingdom era of a thousand years duration. This being the case, the text seems to call for one of the associated meanings of the word *chronos*. "Delay" is an acceptable translation of *chronos* and here fits the context exactly. Judgment and the outpouring of the wrath of God on iniquity have waited long enough. There will be no more delay.

Admittedly, this use of the noun *chronos* as meaning "delay" is rare. Del-ling confidently declares that Rev 10:6 does not mean time has come to an end but that the judgment of God will not be delayed any longer. He cites Heb 10:37, a quotation of Hab 2:3 as evidence for this meaning of *chronos*.[255] Of course, the word employed in Heb 10:37 is the verb *chronizō*. Liddell and Scott cite minor cases of the use of the noun as meaning "delay," but the major significance of the verb is "delay."[256] Translating the noun "delay" is justified here by the gen-eral derivation of the concept and the demands of the context as well.

---

255 *TDNT* 9:592.

256 LSJ, 2008. For the same conclusion, see also J. H. Moulton and G. Milligan, *The Vocabulary of the Greek Testament Illustrated from the Papyri and Other Non-Literary Sources* (London: Hodder and Stoughton, 1914), 693–94.

In addition, in v. 7 the oath concerning delay relates to the voice of the seventh angel, the sound of whose trumpet will be heard in 11:15. This passage relates to the final judgments of the tribulation period and the establishment of the kingdom with the coming of Christ to the earth. When the seventh angel, who is about to trumpet his message, sounds his instrument, then the mystery of God preached through the prophets will be accomplished or completed. To "complete" or "finish" is a translation of the aorist passive indicative of *teleō*, the same verb the Lord used from the cross when he cried *tetelestai* or "it is finished." The aorist tense here is the indication of complete action so that the reader is informed that the mystery known only to God and revealed to man through the revelation given by the apostles and prophets will now be brought to its conclusion. The significance of this statement can scarcely be underestimated.

Prophetic literature stretching back 750 years before Christ envisioned the coming of an awesome day of judgment. These passages of an ultimate "day of the Lord" were the warp and woof of prophetic utterance (see Isa 2:2–4; Joel 1:15; 2:1–5; and Amos 8:11, as a few examples). Nor were these prophecies merely foreseeing an ominous day of judgment. Equally and perhaps even in greater profusion, such prophets envisioned a golden daybreak, a utopian era, God's earthly reign, which would ultimately reverse and restore all that iniquity had cost the race and the cosmos (see Isa 35:1–2; 65:17–25 for examples). What all the angels and the prophets had foretold, that which has been delayed over the centuries giving rise to the prophets "trying to find out the time and circumstances to which the Spirit of Christ in them was pointing when he predicted the sufferings of Christ and the glories that would follow" (1 Pet 1:11)—no longer will these hidden things tease and intrigue the prophets. Now all that God has promised through the prophets and the apostles will not be delayed any longer but will come to pass in rapid sequence, following the sounding of the trumpet of the seventh angel.

E. The Bittersweet Scroll (10:8–11)

⁸Then the voice which I heard from heaven spoke to me again and said, "Go, take the little book which is open in the hand of the angel who stands on the sea and on the earth."

⁹So I went to the angel and said to him, "Give me the little book."

And he said to me, "Take and eat it; and it will make your stomach bitter, but it will be as sweet as honey in your mouth."

[10]Then I took the little book out of the angel's hand and ate it, and it was as sweet as honey in my mouth. But when I had eaten it, my stomach became bitter. [11]And he said to me, "You must prophesy again about many peoples, nations, tongues, and kings."

10:8-11 Now the narrative takes a turn doubtlessly unexpected by both John and the reader. The voice John had previously heard from heaven instructs him to go and take the little scroll, which was open in the hand of the angel who stood on the sea and the land. On the one hand, such an assignment must have been intimidating even in the midst of a vision. On the other hand, without question the authority that has presided over the vision from its outset is clear, and John has no choice but to obey. So, approaching the angel instead of simply taking the scroll, he asks him for the little scroll. The angel hands the scroll over but not without instruction. John is told to his astonishment to eat the scroll, which "will turn [his] stomach sour, but in [his] mouth it will be as sweet as honey." Again, following explicitly the commands, John consumes the scroll and finds it exactly as the angel said, sweet to his mouth but distressing to his stomach.

So what is to be made of this? First, the consuming of the scroll is tantamount to the assimilation of its message. Whatever the contents of the scroll may be, John must make them a part of himself. Only as the sentiments of the scroll become a part of his own life will the incarnational effect accomplish what God intends. The background for this mysterious culinary adventure is found in Ezek 2:10–3:3. The contents of Ezekiel's scroll are provided, whereas there is no mention of the nature of the contents in the Apocalypse. Also, Ezekiel's scroll was apparently only sweet. But the goal is the same. Assimilate the message so that it is a part of who you are as you declare God's message. As Collins notes, "The eating of the scroll is a symbolic action. It shows in a vivid and concrete way that the prophet does not announce his own message, but one which comes from outside himself."[257]

In this regard, there is a practical lesson for the preacher. In Aristotle's canons of rhetoric, the philosopher called for *ethos, pathos,* and *logos.*[258] *Ethos* reflected the credibility of the witness. John's venerable age, consistency of conviction, and long-term service to the Lord were sufficient *ethos.*

Logos represented the content itself; and since the content is part of divine revelation, sufficient logos is insured. *Pathos* referred, however, to the in-

---

257 A. Y. Collins, *The Apocalypse* (Wilmington, DE: Michael Glazier, 1979), 65.

258 Aristotle, *Rhetoric,* trans. W. Rhys Roberts, in *The Rhetoric and the Poetics of Aristotle,* Modern Library College Editions (New York: The Modern Library, 1984), 1356a 1–21.

ternalizing of the message of the *logos*, accentuated by the ethos of the messenger, and thus gives the persuasive power and the empathy needed in effective communication.[259] The preacher, like the prophet, can only be an effective spokesman for God when he thoroughly internalizes the message he is to bring before he attempts to communicate it to others. The *pathos* of that message not only includes understanding its message but also embraces the application of the message first to the preacher's own life.

John, therefore, is to assimilate the message, but the effect on the prophet is both pleasurable and distasteful.[260] Thus it is with the mystery of God's program for the ages. For those who have been willing to receive his promised redemption in Christ, the message of the gospel is sweeter than honey. It is the aroma of life unto life, but to those who have rejected the gospel and who have continued to be determined in their rebellion against God, it is the aroma of death unto death (2 Cor 2:15). There are doubtless those claiming the name of Christ who receive pleasure from the concept of the eternal judgment of others. John would never have been in that category. While he understood the necessity of judgment if God is to remain righteous and just, like God Himself, John is not "willing" that any should perish. For this reason, the message is sweet to his taste but bitter in his stomach.

This alternating sweetness and bitterness would have been the case had John's involvement been only that of knowing the message of God. But John now is instructed to internalize what he must now speak. He is thus informed, "You must prophesy again about many peoples, nations, tongues and kings." John, who was apparently a contemporary with Jesus, must have been approaching centenarian status. The thought that as an aged saint exiled on a barren, rocky island in the Aegean Sea, forty miles from Ephesus, he would yet be used significantly to prophesy, would on the surface seem rather improbable. Nevertheless, that is the message. Furthermore, the message he is to bring will concern people in general, the nations into which people have grouped themselves. The language groups into which they have been divided since the experience at Babel will be addressed. And kings and rulers will be a part of this prophecy.

---

259 For the development of these canons of rhetoric for contemporary preaching, see P. Patterson, "Ancient Rhetoric: A Model for Text-Driven Preachers," in *Text-Driven Preaching: God's Word at the Heart of Every Sermon*, ed. D. L. Akin, D. L. Allen, and N. L. Mathews (Nashville: B&H, 2010), 11–35.

260 J. P. M. Sweet notes, "In a rebellious world the gospel too is destructive to both hearers and proclaimers" (*Revelation*, Westminster Pelican Commentaries [Philadelphia: Westminster, 1979], 180). But surely this is not what John intended to convey.

Pastoral Excursus on 10:8–11

God's plan of salvation and blessing is the subject of uninterrupted thanksgiving on the part of the redeemed. To the saints of God, the story of God's graciousness in salvation becomes the theme of a thousand hymns of praise. The church sometimes expresses astonishment that the message of salvation is greeted by the world with a yawn and, not infrequently, with mild to vicious antagonism. The simple truth is that "the man without the Spirit does not accept the things that come from the Spirit of God" (1 Cor 2:14). The concept of spiritual helplessness and total dependence on the mercies of God charms the converted sinner's ear, but to the unconverted it ranges from preposterous to irritating.

At two points the Christian witness and especially the pastor, the evangelist, and the missionary will discover experientially the sweet and bitter tastes of announcing the plan and purpose of God. First, what is sweet to the witness (in his mouth) is often received antagonistically by the objects of his concern, causing stress and bitterness (a knot in his stomach) when confrontation develops.

Second, while the gospel is good news, it is the aroma of life unto life only to those being saved (2 Cor 2:15). To all others it is the aroma of death. Knowing this to be the case makes the proclamation of the gospel at once sweet and bitter. As Jesus said, "Unless you repent, you too will all perish" (Luke 13:3). There is good news in that short declaration, but there is also ominous foreboding. The necessity for the witness to iterate both God's mercies, which are like the dew, "new every morning" (Lam 3:23), is also to be accompanied by the promise of his justice and the threat of his judgment. This is simultaneously sweet to the palate and bitter to the stomach.

There is one other important lesson here. The seer of Patmos must consume the whole scroll! He cannot approach his assignment as though it were a cafeteria line, indulging the sweet while avoiding the "bitter herbs." Neither can he reverse his culinary habit. He must eat or assimilate the whole scroll. When it has become a part of who he is, then he must faithfully proclaim both.

Some witnesses rejoice to speak of love, grace, and the honey of God's blessings but are loath to declare faithfully God's justice and judgment. Others almost appear like school yard bullies, always ready to pound people with impending judgment while stressing infrequently, if at all, the love of the Lord. Either witness is inadequate, failing to have assimilated the whole counsel of God or, worse, having understood it, but failing to share all that God has said with his hearers.

Great preachers, faithful witnesses grasp all that they can of the words and ways of God and then faithfully proclaim all that they grasp. This was John's great assignment from Patmos. Pastors and all the saints share in this great commission.

F. Two Amazing Witnesses (11:1–14)

[1]Then I was given a reed like a measuring rod. And the angel stood, saying, "Rise and measure the temple of God, the altar, and those who worship there. [2]But leave out the court which is outside the temple, and do not measure it, for it has been given to the Gentiles. And they will tread the holy city underfoot *for* forty-two months. [3]And I will give *power* to my two witnesses, and they will prophesy one thousand two hundred and sixty days, clothed in sackcloth."

[4]These are the two olive trees and the two lampstands standing before the God of the earth. [5] And if anyone wants to harm them, fire proceeds from their mouth and devours their enemies. And if anyone wants to harm them, he must be killed in this manner. [6]These have power to shut heaven, so that no rain falls in the days of their prophecy; and they have power over waters to turn them to blood, and to strike the earth with all plagues, as often as they desire.

[7]When they finish their testimony, the beast that ascends out of the bottomless pit will make war against them, overcome them, and kill them. [8]And their dead bodies *will lie* in the street of the great city which spiritually is called Sodom and Egypt, where also our Lord was crucified. [9] Then *those* from the peoples, tribes, tongues, and nations will see their dead bodies three-and-a-half days, and not allow their dead bodies to be put into graves. [10]And those who dwell on the earth will rejoice over them, make merry, and send gifts to one another, because these two prophets tormented those who dwell on the earth.

[11]Now after the three-and-a-half days the breath of life from God entered them, and they stood on their feet, and great fear fell on those who saw them. [12]And they heard a loud voice from heaven saying to them, "Come up here." And they ascended

to heaven in a cloud, and their enemies saw them. [13]In the same hour there was a great earthquake, and a tenth of the city fell. In the earthquake seven thousand people were killed, and the rest were afraid and gave glory to the God of heaven.

[14]The second woe is past. Behold, the third woe is coming quickly.

The interlude, Rev 10:1–11:14, continues with a second remarkable event. John has been a participant in the saga of the small scroll and has learned through the consumption of the volume God's purpose for him to prophesy again concerning many peoples, nations, languages, and kings. That John is asked once again to participate in his own vision in chap. 11 is not surprising. This time he will have a limited role and will merely introduce the arrival of two of the most enigmatic figures in the book of the Revelation. Many commentators have believed that making sense of the verses of chap. 11 may be the most difficult assignment for any expositor of the Apocalypse.

For example, Alford notes, "This passage may well be called, even more than that previous one, ch. x. 1 ff., the *crux interpretum*; as it is undoubtedly one of the most difficult in the whole Apocalypse."[261] And Giblin adds, "Anyone about to explain a text faces the vexing problem of how precisely to pose the state of the question. His initial option will determine the results of the inquiry and will also immediately capture the interest of his readers or lose it. Initial options in approaching an apocalyptic text like Rev. 11. 1–13 boggle the mind."[262] These two citations focus both on the strategic nature of this text and on the difficulties inevitably faced by interpreters.

11:1–14 The initial instruction from heaven is that John is to make use of a reed and measure a portion of the temple of God. John does not have to find the appropriate measuring device since a reed is given to him. This reed (*kalamos*) apparently refers to a relatively common reed, found in the marshy areas in Israel, particularly in the Jordan River valley, and which easily grew to fifteen feet and in rare cases could reach eighteen to twenty feet. The *kalamos* was a hollow reed apparently used commonly for measurement when some other carefully prepared means was not available. One could simply determine the length of consistent measurement desired by holding the reed against some object the precise size needed. The *kalamos* could be marked or chopped off and would then serve as a consistent measuring device.

---

261 H. Alford, *The Greek Testament* (Chicago: Moody, 1958), 4:655.

262 C. H. Giblin, "Revelation 11. 1–13: Its Form, Function, and Contextual Integration," *NTS* 30 (1984): 433.

However, in this case, the "measuring" (*metrēson*) appears to have nothing to do with establishing the specific size of the objects measured. Some other purpose seems to be involved when the prophet is told to measure the temple, the altar, and the worshippers. Measurement served different purposes in biblical times. Certainly, a measurement could be for the purpose of determining size, but more often in Scripture measurement served as a device for indicating divine action. Sometimes that divine action was judgment as in Amos 7:7; other times it was an indication of God's protecting providences as is apparently the case in this passage. The reed employed by the prophet is used to mark off the temple of God, the altar, and the people worshipping there, but John is told not to measure a portion of the temple—the outer court. Obviously, it does not receive the protection of God but is rather given to the Gentiles, who will trample on the holy city and presumably the outer court of the temple for forty-two months.

The mention of the temple introduces the first substantive problem fiercely debated by commentators of this chapter. Obviously, one must determine which temple is in view. The earliest temple begun by Solomon in approximately 958 BC cannot be intended since it was destroyed in 586 BC by the decimating armies of Nebuchadnezzar of Babylon. One possibility is that what is often referred to as the second temple (i.e., the temple of Herod, built from 520 to 515 BC and destroyed by Titus in AD 70) is the temple in view.[263] This could come about in one of two ways. First, if the early date for the composition of the Apocalypse is adopted, and/or the events associated with the apocalyptic drama have unfolded prior to AD 70, then the second temple could be in view. However, by way of fond memory, in retrospect the second temple may also be possible. Even if John wrote in AD 95, as commonly accepted, this provides only a twenty-five-year hiatus from the time of the destruction of the temple; and all living Jews who were thirty-five years of age or older would clearly have memory of that edifice and would likely treasure that memory. For John to make this reference as though it still existed would not be out of the question.

---

263 For example, D. S. Clark writes, "Here is so plainly the destruction of Jerusalem that it could hardly be put in plainer words. It seems evident that there is no getting away from the fact that here we are dealing with the fall of Jerusalem in the year 70,—that all that John has said hitherto was leading up to this great fact,—that here we have the culmination of these prophetic seals, and this is where the first half of the book lands us. Here, as we open this chapter, is Jerusalem, still standing. Here are the temple and altar in the midst of it. This forever and absolutely precludes the idea that these events are to happen thousands of years in the future" (*The Message from Patmos: A Postmillennial Commentary on the Book of Revelation* [Dahlonega, GA: Crown Rights Book Company, 1921], 74–75).

There remain, however, other possibilities of relatedness to Jewish temples. One possibility is that the vision is a heavenly temple. The latter is made clear in 11:19 where it is stated, "Then God's temple in heaven was opened." On the other hand, this view may be made less likely by the apparent contrast that occurs in the close proximity of the temple mentioned in v. 1 and the temple mentioned in v. 19. Still another view, not necessarily in competition with the view of the temple in heaven, would be the temple of Ezekiel, which is anticipated by Ezek 40–48. A large portion of the book of Ezekiel is focused on this temple, and the author of the Revelation is familiar with Ezekiel's prophecy. However, these temples seem impossible because of location. Further, how could the "outer court" of such an edifice be "given to the Gentiles?"

Futurists will not see Ezekiel's temple as a heavenly temple but rather as a temple that is built in Jerusalem during the millennium. Obviously from its description in Ezekiel, this temple far transcends in size and immaculate beauty anything that has gone before. If Ezekiel's temple is not the heavenly temple, then perhaps it is the millennial temple, and that may be what John has in mind in chap. 11. Other interpreters are not inclined toward understanding this temple as literal in any way but, in keeping with what has been called the idealist position, would see it as symbolic in nature. Most, though not all, who would take such a position would understand the reference to the temple here to be a reference to the church. Since the people of God would normally be found in the temple, the use of the concept of "temple" becomes merely a Semitism for arguing for the affinity of the temple as being the church.

Chilton, normally a historicist, takes more of the idealist perspective in this passage, noting that the imagery is from Ezek 40–43 "where the angelic priest measures the ideal Temple, the New Covenant people of God, the Church."[264] He adds:

> St. John is to **measure** the inner court, the Church, but he is to **cast out the court that is outside the Temple**, and is specifically commanded: **Do not measure it**. Measuring is a symbolic action used in Scripture to "divide between the holy and the profane" and thus to indicate divine protection from destruction.[265]

---

264 D. Chilton, *The Days of Vengeance: An Exposition of the Book of Revelation* (Fort Worth, TX: Dominion Press, 1987), 272.

265 Chilton, *The Days of Vengeance*, 273.

Boxall enlarges this idea, saying:

> If the sanctuary of God and its worshipers symbolize the Church protect-
> ed by God, then what does the outer courtyard represent? The imagery
> is almost certainly drawn from the Court of the Gentiles, that vast open
> space bordered by porticoes, and separated from the inner courts, acces-
> sible only to Jews, by a dividing wall and the Beautiful Gate. But in John's
> vision, it must represent a group of people.[266]

However, the Bible speaks of a period known as the great tribulation. Elsewhere this is referenced as the "time of Jacob's trouble." This tribulation extends
over a duration of seven years and is divided into two equal periods of three and
one-half years, or forty-two months, or 1,260 days, or time and times and half
a time. Those who follow the idealist interpretation of Revelation are inclined
to dismiss any literal significance to these numbers, whether they occur in the
Apocalypse or in Daniel. In the end there seems to be no good reason for that
conclusion if the seven years are understood literally and if there is to be a regathering of the Jewish people into their homeland as seems to be anticipated by
Old Testament prophecies and by Paul in Rom 9–11. A new temple, which millenarians describe as the "tribulation temple," will be constructed by the Jews in
Jerusalem. At the time of the writing of this commentary, Muslim control of the
Temple Mount in Jerusalem prevents the construction of a Jewish temple. Students of history, however, are conscious of how quickly events and circumstances
can change, and those who have frequented the modern state of Israel and visited
with the most religious of the Hasidim are well aware of the intent to build such
a temple and to do so in the relatively near future. This commentator, then, understands this as a tribulation temple that will be built either immediately prior
to the beginning of the tribulation period or else in the first three and one-half
years of that tribulation.[267] The events described here belong to the last forty-two

---

266 I. Boxall, *The Revelation of Saint John*, BNTC (Peabody, MA: Hendrickson,
2006), 161.

267 J. A. Seiss says, "What, then, is the implication, but that when this period is
once reached, Jerusalem will have been largely repopulated by the children of its ancient
inhabitants, its temple rebuilt, and its ancient worship restored. God is not yet done
with the Jews as a distinct people. In their half-faith and 'blindness in part,' they will
seek and find their way back to a revival of their ancient metropolis, temple, and ritual.
Some of the most striking passages of holy Scripture assert this with a clearness and
positiveness which no fair exegesis can ever set aside. The New Testament constantly

months of the tribulation period and immediately precede the events of chap. 12 in which Israel is divested one more time of the land God provided for them.

In order to understand what is transpiring, the reader will need to remember that there are two words that describe the temple complex in the New Testament. One is the word *hieron*, referring to the entire temple complex, which would include the inner divisions of the holy place and the holy of holies as well as the outer courts, which in the time of the Second Temple included the court of Israel, the court of the women, and the court of the Gentiles, with cautionary signs placed on the low walls forbidding Gentiles to enter on pain of death. This entire complex was called the *hieron*. The *naos*, on the other hand, most often stood for the holy of holies and may well have included its description of the holy place and the court of Israel as well. The Greek word, *naos*, helps to delineate that portion of the temple that would not be subject to Gentile incursion. The "altar" in view is the subject of debate as well. While the reference could be to the altar of incense, which was a part of the holy place and had a function (Exod 30:1-10; Heb 9:4) relating to the holy of holies, more likely this is an indication on the part of the author that the *naos* intended here included the court of Israel; the altar in view here is the altar of sacrifice. Of course, the idea of an altar of sacrifice would not be appropriate for an idealist interpretation, which would view the temple as a reference to the church since the sacrificial system was rendered void by the fulfillment of those sacrifices in Christ. However, if back on Jewish ground, the presence of the sacrificial altar would be expected. Many of the Hasidim with whom this commentator spoke in the early days of the existence of the modern state of Israel declined to anticipate again the sacrificial system, saying that the world simply would not tolerate it. But more recent visits and conversations have only registered incredulity on the faces of many as they raise the question, "If we did not intend to reinstate the sacrificial system, why would we build the temple?" Whatever the social and political difficulties involved, one should not find the presence of such an altar in this tribulation temple strange.

Since measuring in this case likely had nothing to do with "size," understandably the worshippers within were also measured and are thereby being assured of the protection of God. The survival of a remnant of the Jews will

---

assumes it" (*The Apocalypse: Lectures on the Book of Revelation* [Grand Rapids: Zondervan, 1962], 237). See also W. A. Criswell, *Expository Sermons on Revelation: Five Volumes Complete and Unabridged* (Grand Rapids: Zondervan, 1969), 4:28; and J. Walvoord, *The Revelation of Jesus Christ* (Chicago: Moody, 1966), 176.

become the subject of chap. 12 to follow and is also anticipated in Rom 9–11 and various other verses throughout the Bible.

11:2 Verse 2 places the limitation on the outer court. The Greek construction is unusual, making use of the term *ekbale*, which generally speaking would have the meaning of "throw out." While the terminology is admittedly not what one might have expected, the meaning does not appear to be recondite. To the contrary, clearly the author is to "throw out" or "exclude" the outer court from measure, and the reason is also provided, namely, that the holy city, including the court of Gentiles, will be trampled for forty-two months or for one-half of the seven-year period of tribulation. In this regard, in the seventy-week prophecy of Daniel, the final week, or seven years, is divided into two periods, the first of which anticipates relative calm for Israel.[268] This calm is determined by a compact with Israel that promises to protect her for a seven-year period. However, after three and one-half years the pact is broken by the ruling authorities, and what follows is a gradual worsening of the situation for the Jewish nation. That situation terminates as will be seen with the exit of the remaining Jews from the Promised Land at the conclusion of the tribulation period. The situation described in vv. 1–2 seems to depict a time when Israel no longer controls its destiny but is ruled by Gentiles. These Gentiles, however, do allow worship to continue in Israel, and those in the temple are therefore protected.

11:3 Verse 3 introduces the reader to two witnesses who prophesy for 1,260 days. "Clothed in sackcloth," the traditional sign of mourning in the ancient Near East, indicates something of the nature of the message they bring. They are described as being two olive trees and two lampstands before all the earth. Unlike witnesses of the church, they turn out to be lethal when there is an attempt to harm them. Fire proceeds from their mouths and devours the antagonists. In addition to this, they have power to prevent rain, to turn water into blood, and to exercise a great variety of plagues. The first task of the interpreter is to identify these two witnesses.

Generally, identification proceeds along one of seven lines. Again, many idealist interpreters would argue that the witnesses represent the church of the

---

268 See A. C. Gaebelein, *The Prophet Daniel: A Key to the Visions and Prophecies of the Book of Daniel* (Glasgow: Pickering & Inglis, 1911), 130–36. Also Sir Robert Anderson, *The Coming Prince: The Marvellous Prophecy of Daniel's Seventy Weeks Concerning the Antichrist* (Grand Rapids: Kregel, 1977) where the seventieth week of Daniel is the subject of the entire volume. But notice particularly pp. 76–105. See also similar discussions in H. W. Hoehner, *Chronological Aspects of the Life of Christ* (Grand Rapids: Zondervan, 1977), 115–42.

living God who bear responsibility for a witness in the world.[269] A second view common in the historicist school of thinking identifies them with some historical figure or group, such as the Waldenses and Albigensians.[270] A third view also embraced by many in the idealist school would be that the two witnesses are the Old Testament and the New Testament, or perhaps the Law and the Prophets.

As for these views, not only is there no evidence for the presence of the church in chap. 11 but also the actions of the two witnesses are hardly in keeping with the witness of the church. The various historical figures who might be assigned are unlikely just by virtue of the great variety of suggestions. The idea that the figures represent the Old and New Testaments seems odd when one considers that they are "clothed with sackcloth" and actually have power to unleash various kinds of plagues. Furthermore, they are eventually martyred and raised to heaven, all of which seems impossible for the Old and New Testaments.

The final four views are those assumed by futurists, who anticipate appropriately identifying these two as actual witnesses—real, living individuals in the tribulation period. However, from there, all similarity vanishes. The fourth view recognizes that there is dependence here on Zech 4, where two figures are introduced. Zechariah's readers hear the prophet's testimony that he sees two olive trees and a seven-branched lampstand. The account in Revelation differs in that there are two lampstands. The olive trees in Zechariah appear to represent the two anointed figures—Zerubbabel, the civil leader, and Joshua, the high priest of chap. 3, who is the spiritual leader. These are pictured as olive trees providing

---

269 Kistemaker says, "However, I suggest a symbolic interpretation, namely, that the two witnesses represent the church of Christ that by proclaiming the gospel calls the world to repentance. First, the witnesses must address all the inhabitants of the world: peoples, tribes, languages, and nations (v. 9), which can hardly be done by only two witnesses. Second, the pairing of the witnesses is reminiscent of Jesus' sending out his disciples two by two (Mark 6:7; Luke 10:1). The apostles also go out two by two (Acts 3:1; 8:14). Third, in Israel a verdict was confirmed on the testimony of two or three witnesses (Deut. 17:6; 19:15), and the church exerts discipline on that same basis (Matt. 18:16). Indeed, the witnesses of one man can be disregarded, but on the testimony of two men truth is validated (John 8:17)" (*Exposition of the Book of Revelation*, New Testament Commentary [Grand Rapids: Baker Academic, 2001], 329). Wilcock proposes a similar view indicating that the two witnesses represent "God's people among the heathen nations" (*The Message of Revelation: I Saw Heaven Opened*, The Bible Speaks Today [Downers Grove, IL: InterVarsity, 1975], 104–5. An interesting variation of this is D. Clark's view that the two witnesses are civil and religious authority (*The Message from Patmos*, 71–77).

270 M. Henry identifies them as faithful ministers throughout history (*Acts to Revelation*, in *Commentary on the Whole Bible* [Old Tappan, NJ: Revell, 1980], 6:1157).

the light of the lampstand. However, in the Revelation, there are two olive trees and two lampstands. Obvious dependence on Zech 4 has led some to believe that the two witnesses in Rev 11 should be identified as Zerubbabel and Joshua. Certainly, such a view is a possible, but unlikely, identification. The actions of the two witnesses do not correspond at all to the actions of Zerubbabel and Joshua as revealed in Zechariah, and there seems to be no really good reason to make this identification other than the reference to the two olive trees. Rather, the connection to Zechariah's prophecy is specifically to Zech 4:14 where Joshua and Zerubbabel are "the two anointed ones who stand beside the Lord of the whole earth." In the same manner, the two witnesses of Rev 11 are anointed specifically by God for a ministry that will be observed by the whole world.

Next is the fifth view that identifies the two witnesses represented here as Enoch and Elijah.[271] The choice of these two Old Testament characters is based partly on the Elijah-like actions they take (i.e., sealing the heavens so that it does not rain) and the fact that Enoch and Elijah have in common the fact that they were able to sidestep the inevitability of physical death. Enoch "walked with God; and he was not, for God took him" (Gen 5:24). On the other hand, Elijah was swooped off his feet in a whirlwind and taken to heaven (2 Kgs 2:11). Now, according to the Scriptures, "it is appointed for men to die once but after this the judgment" (Heb 9:27). Logically, since Enoch and Elijah never experienced death, they must do so; therefore, they are prime candidates to be the two witnesses who do then experience death at the conclusion of three and one-half years of witness. This view, however, faces serious difficulties. First, while the general rule states that it is appointed unto man once to die, God is certainly able to make exceptions to His own rules if it satisfies His purpose. Second, the Scriptures make clear that there is a significantly large group who will constitute an exception to this general law, namely, those who are alive at the time of the Lord's return. These will be immediately changed and caught up into the air. Provided with glorified bodies, they will be present with the Lord forever and apparently do not go through the experience of death (see 1 Thess 4:17). So, while it is plausible that the two witnesses could be Enoch and Elijah, probability works against that identification.

---

271 One of the earliest claims for this appears in Tertullian, who is refuting the idea that anyone ultimately avoids death: "Enoch no doubt was translated, and so was Elijah; nor did they experience death: it was postponed, (and only postponed,) most certainly: they are reserved for the suffering of death, that by their blood they may extinguish antichrist" (*A Treatise on the Soul* 50, ANF 3:227–28).

The sixth general identification is that the two are Moses and Elijah.[272] This identification makes excellent sense and is probably the most popular view of futurists. The rationale for such identification is that Moses and Elijah represent the Law and the Prophets, one of the major ways by which the Hebrew canon was divided. The Law and the Prophets witnessed to Christ, and hence Moses and Elijah would be representative of those who have borne witness to Christ across the ages. Additionally, the transfiguration narrative provides a previous appearance of the two witnessing that Christ is the fulfillment of both the Law and the Prophets and conceivably even indicating the two different kinds of circumstances that exist for the transfer of saints to glory: Moses prefigures those who die in the Lord, and Elijah represents those who are taken immediately into heaven at the return of Christ. However, the most convincing argument resides in the nature of the work of the witnesses. Like Elijah, they shut up the sky so that it does not rain; like Moses, they turn the waters into blood and strike the earth with other kinds of plagues as often as they wish. Here the correspondence seems to be the strongest and provides the best case to be made for a clear identification of the two witnesses. In addition, some also argue that Mal 4:5–6 avers that Elijah is going to return before that Great Day of the Lord. This might not explain the presence of Moses, though some have also believed that Moses, too, would return based on Deut 18:15; however, Jesus said that John the Baptist fulfilled the Elijah prophecy of Malachi if the Jews would receive it. This reply seems to settle the issue regarding when that appearance actually took place, but the clause "if your are willing to receive it" (Matt 11:14) also leaves open at least the possibility of a second fulfillment, one which might be quite literal.

However, there remains a seventh possibility, which essentially denies the possibility of precise identification of the two witnesses. In the end, no reason can be demonstrated why the two witnesses must be identified with previously known figures, whether from church history or from the Bible. Perhaps they are better seen as two remarkable Jewish witnesses who arise during the tribulation with ministries similar to those of Elijah and Moses. Their names would remain unknown to the readers of the Apocalypse since it is more important to grasp the significance of what they do. This author favors the latter position as being one that has fewer obstacles to overcome and as the more probable understanding of the text. Walvoord states the matter succinctly: "It seems far preferable to regard

---

272 See discussion in R. H. Charles, *A Critical and Exegetical Commentary on the Revelation of St. John*, ICC (Edinburgh: T&T Clark, 1920), 1:280–82.

these two witnesses as two prophets who will be raised up from among those who turn to Christ in the time following the rapture."[273]

11:4–6 In vv. 4–6, the work of the two witnesses is introduced. The reference to Zech 4 and the two olive trees and two lampstands provides insight regarding the origin of their work. They are as Zerubbabel and Joshua, especially anointed of God and empowered for their work since what is done is "not by might nor by power, but by my Spirit says the Lord of hosts" (Zech 4:6). Furthermore, resistance to their message is instant, a timely reminder that however gentle and sensitive the presentation of truth may be, a world that loves darkness rather than light will never be the willing recipient of that message. When socially and politically possible, the urge to repress and, if possible, obliterate those who bring such a message is always there. However, in this case, when malicious persons attempt to harm the witnesses, fire comes from their mouths and eats (*katesthiō*) their enemies. In the English language, the general understanding is to speak of "eating things up," but that is an anatomically challenged conclusion since normally things are eaten down. So is the case here as the fire devours or "eats down" the enemies. The use of plagues, namely, prevention of rain, turning water into blood, and other such actions, seems designed to be judicial in nature as well as a warning of things yet to come. The two witnesses bring with them a message then of impending judgment and an admonition to flee from the wrath to come.

The tribulation period is a time of God's judgment on the earth. 2 Thess 2:7 suggests that he who restrains will no longer restrain. While some have assumed that the Holy Spirit is removed from the world during the tribulation, this seems impossible, first; because the Holy Spirit of God is omnipresent and; second, because redemption is still taking place during the tribulation period, and the Holy Spirit is uniquely involved in such redemption. However, the explanation from Paul in 2 Thess 2:6-7 constitutes one of the almost unnoticed works of the Holy Spirit in the church age (i.e., the restraint of evil). During the seven years of tribulation, not only is evil rampant to an extent never before experienced but also that evil is part of God's judgment on the earth. These scriptural observations explain why the sky is sealed, the waters are turned to blood, and various kinds of plagues ensue as a part of God's judgment.

11:7-14 God's two witnesses of the tribulation period have a fixed assignment, which at some point apparently near the close of the tribulation is completed. "When they finish" is the translation of *telesōsin*, which is an aorist

---

273 *The Revelation of Jesus Christ*, 179.

active subjunctive of *teleō*, meaning "complete" or "finish." The subjunctive mood suggests that at the time of John's writing all of this lies in the future and is not yet taking place. However, upon the completion of their testimony, they are confronted with the beast arising from the Abyss. The word "testimony" (*marturian*) is a derivative of *martus*, translated "witness," and plural in v. 3. The Greek word carries the concepts of both witness and testimony and eventually came as a result of the not uncommon martyrdom of witnesses to evolve into identifying martyrs so that the English word transliterated "martyr" derives directly from the Greek *martus*.[274]

The beast who comes from the bottomless pit will attack them, overpower them, and kill them. The word translated as the "bottomless pit," simply refers to a pit and is perhaps a word best left essentially untranslated or anglicized as "abyss." The word never carries anything other than an evil connotation and, as noted in a previous chapter, seems to refer particularly to the abode of the demonic and the evil. In the book of the Revelation, this evil is occasionally loosed on the earth. For example, the sounding of the fifth trumpet in chap. 9 opens the way for the plague of locusts, which were previously identified as probably a reference to demonic hoards. Now, from the same Abyss comes the beast. Apparently, the author is anticipating the message of chap. 13 when he mentions a beast from the sea and then a second beast out of the earth.

Concerning the word "beast," Thomas explains: "For the first time and somewhat by way of anticipation, *thērion*, the beast enters the description. *Thērion* is a word for a beast of prey, one with a ravenous appetite, a carnivore, like a lion or a panther, it connotes a cunning of unreasoning violence that acts according to its own cruel nature. It differs from *zōon*, a living creature which usually refers to animals also but lacks the rapacious connotations."[275] Thomas further notes correctly that the beast is not to be identified with Satan since the latter seems to be identified with the dragon when he appears in the Apocalypse.[276]

---

274 H. Strathmann concludes that the word is derived from a root meaning "bear in mind," "remember" or "be careful." "Hence μάρτυς was probably 'one who remembers, who has knowledge of something by recollection, and who can tell about it,' i.e., the witness" (*TDNT* 4:475).

275 R. L. Thomas, *Revelation 8-22: An Exegetical Commentary* (Chicago: Moody, 1992), 92.

276 Ibid. But Chilton is certain that the beast is the common opponent of the people of God in every era, namely, the Devil: "The Christians already knew the ultimate identity of the Beast who arises from **the Abyss**. It is Leviathan, the Dragon, the Serpent of old, who comes out of his prison in the sea again and again to plague the people of God. The Abyss, the dark, raging Deep, is where Satan and his evil spirits are kept imprisoned

Therefore, the beast, whether it be the one from the sea or the one from the land in chap. 13, is probably to be identified with the coming of the Antichrist, the great opponent of the Jewish people as well as of the work of Christ in the last days. This dark figure of the tribulation is obviously infuriated by the work of the two witnesses and is allowed by God (only after "they have finished their testimony") to overpower the witnesses and kill them. The word translated "overcome" is *nikēsei*, a future active indicative tense from *nikaō*, meaning "conquer" or as in the NKJV "overcome." It also occurs in Rev 2:7, 11, 17, 26; 3:5, 12, 21.

Verse 8 declares that following the martyrdom the ultimate indignity is thrust upon the witnesses in that they are not allowed burial; rather, their bodies lie in the street of the great city, figuratively called Sodom and Egypt, where their Lord was crucified. This unwanted "viewing" continues for three and one-half days and is the subject of observation by men from every people, tribe, language, and nation. Specifically, "[They] will see their dead bodies three-and-a-half days, and not allow their dead bodies to be put into graves." One will recall Deut 21:23 at this point: "for he who is hanged is accursed of God." The body,

---

except for periodic releases in order to torment men when they commit apostasy. (Note that the legion of evil spirits in the Gadarene demoniac pleaded to be kept out of the Abyss; with divine deception, Jesus sent them into the herd of swine, and the swine rushed headlong into the sea: Luke 8:31–33). The persecution of the Covenant people is never a merely 'political' contest, regardless of how evil states attempt to color their wicked actions. It always originates in the pit of hell" (*Days of Vengeance*, 280).

For G. B. Caird, the "monster from the abyss" is a myth, but a mean one. "The Christian martyr will go to his death under sentence from a Roman judge; and John has a high enough regard for Roman administration to recognize how easily the humble believer might be brought to think that after all Rome must be right and he himself wrong. He is likely to be armed against such doubts if he knows that the real author of his condemnation is the monster that rises from the abyss. In two later chapters John will have more to say about the monster (xiii and xvii). Here he contents himself with one illuminating phrase. He does not say that the monster is going to rise from the abyss at some predictable moment of the future, or that it has risen at some datable moment in the past. This monster has a long history, and rising from the abyss is not a single episode in its career, but the permanent cast of its character (cf. xvii. 8). The four beasts of Daniel's first vision were seen to rise out of the great sea, which is another name for the abyss (Dan. vii. I ff.); and they symbolized the four empires to which Jerusalem had been successively made subject. The biblical history of the monster, then, begins in the original Babylon and ends in the latter-day Babylon, which is Rome. For wherever men lay claim to despotic power, refusing to acknowledge that they are responsible to God for the use to which they put it, there the monster arises from the abyss. The monster is a myth, but one which expresses a perennial hazard in the political life of men" (*The Revelation of St. John the Divine*, HNTC [San Francisco: Harper & Row, 1966], 137).

for all its weaknesses because of the ravages of sin, was nevertheless for the Jews a part of the artistry of God. As such, the body was viewed as something to be treated with respect and dignity, and burial was prescribed immediately so as to prevent the observation of the forces of decay that begin almost immediately upon the termination of life.[277] For one to be hanged on a tree meant that he would likely be exposed there for some time following his death. To avoid this inevitability accounts in part for why the men of Benjamin took down the bodies of Saul and his sons and gave them the appropriate burial.

Paul's reference to Deut 21:23 in Gal 3:10–14 focuses on the particular reality of the crucifixion of Jesus on the cross. Redemption from the curse of the law is provided by the vicarious substitution of Christ. In Christ's crucifixion he accepted the curse of man, who had failed to keep all the law.

Not content with the mere execution of these witnesses, the government of the beast decides to make a point of the penalty for opposition to his reign. Thus, he adds indignity and disrespect to the earthly remains of these two prophets. In addition, something of a celebration, which results not only in the inhabitants of the earth "rejoice(ing) over them" but also in the sending and receiving of gifts, seems to ensue.

Two additional considerations are noted in the text. First, there is the location of their martyrdom; specifically, they are said to be martyred in that great city, "which is spiritually called Sodom and Egypt." Some translations

---

277 E. H. Merrill notes that "hanging in a public place was practiced widely by both the Israelites and their neighbors either as a means of execution (Josh 8:23, 29; Esth 2:23; 5:14; 7:10; 8:7) or as a public display after death (Gen 40:19,22; Josh 10:26; 2 Sam 4:12; 21:12). The latter was in view in our text, for the act of hanging follows the person's having been put to death. The passage reads literally, 'If there should be with regard to a man a sin deserving of death, then he must die; and if you hang him on a tree,' etc. The purpose of such a post-mortem display was doubtless to provide a sober warning to the community of the serious consequences of the crime committed. In any event, the corpse was to be brought down and buried before sunset because the curse applied to the criminal would otherwise accrue to the community and the land as a whole. Why an individual who was put on such display was considered especially cursed is not clear. Nowhere else in the Old Testament is the linkage made; and in Gal 3:13, where crucifixion and the divine curse are related, Paul was simply quoting the Deuteronomy passage. The answer lies, perhaps, in the Hebrew abhorrence of death and the desire to provide for burial as quickly and unobtrusively as possible, especially where the wicked were concerned. To expose the body, therefore, would be to hold it up to public shame and ridicule. A greater curse than this could hardly be imagined" (*Deuteronomy*, NAC [Nashville: B&H, 1994], 296–97). C. Keil and F. Delitzsch add that a corpse hanged overnight would defile the land (*The Pentateuch*, 3:408).

render this great city as allegorically called Sodom and Egypt, but the actual expression in the Greek New Testament makes use of the word *pneumatikōs*, which literally means "spiritually." Consequently, the translation "figuratively" here in the NIV text is not wrong, but "spiritually" as in the NKJV is preferable since the word "spiritually" carries the connotation of figuratively, but adds that the definition being given denotes a spiritual failure in the city being discussed. This place, spiritually called Sodom and Egypt, is "where also our Lord was crucified." That final geographical identification leaves no doubt that the city in view is Jerusalem. Thus, one can safely surmise that this moment is one of the most startling in the entire book of Revelation. Here a Palestinian Jew, who, like most Jews of his day, would have viewed the city of Jerusalem as a holy and sacred place, has referred to it spiritually as "Sodom and Egypt." In speaking of Jerusalem as "Sodom and Egypt," the author has taken two of the most reprehensible events in Jewish history and used them to describe Jerusalem. Egypt, of course, summons the memory of slavery as well as the degradation of the Egyptian culture. Sodom stood for consummate debauchery and for ultimate moral corruption; its a term that has even given rise to the English expression "sodomy." Both marked despicable events to the average Jew, and for a sensitive Jew to refer to the holy city as spiritually Sodom and Egypt marks a departure from what the reader might expect. However, the reasons for doing so seem to be that this city is where the Messiah was crucified and where the temple will be desecrated again by the Gentiles of the tribulation period.

The second point to be noted about this text is the reason given for the hatred, martyrdom, and disrespect accorded to these two prophets. They "tormented those who dwell on the earth." The vivid Greek word *basanizō* is used in the aorist active indicative tense here in the text, indicating the kind of torment or torture to which the people of the earth are subject through the ministry of these two prophets.

Remembering the reaction of Pharaoh to the plagues of Moses, one can easily imagine the frustration of the general public at finding their water turned to blood, conditions of worldwide drought, and the visitation of various other plagues. Doubtless, all of this is blamed with some accuracy on the two witnesses since it is not readily discerned as a part of the overall judgment of God. However, equally probable is the possibility that the "torment" people experience is also due to the fact that these are "witnesses." In other words, probably they did a great deal more than simply announce the inevitability of certain plagues on the earth. They were preachers of morality, witnesses of God and Christ, and harbingers of the coming of even more severe judgments of God in the days to follow. Again, recalling Exodus, the audacity of Moses to stand before Pharaoh and command him to let God's people go and sacrifice to him in the wilderness was doubtless just as irritating as the plagues to Pharaoh. So, it would be if these two witnesses opposed the worldviews, system of morality, and violation of the laws and purposes of God. This torment was simply too great and thus engendered the wrath of the beast.

Another interesting observation concerns the information that "the peoples, tribes, tongues, and nations will see their dead bodies . . . ." The fulfillment of such an anticipated event would be incredible and even unthinkable until modern times. Certainly, there is no reason for anyone to doubt the prophet even in AD 95 since after all he is the prophet of a miracle-working God. Nevertheless, that which was unthinkable in AD 95 without a miracle of God is no longer even improbable in the era of satellite communication. Hence, events that happen in faraway places are now almost instantly available around the globe to observers with the proper equipment. Too often interpreters of Revelation and of all apocalyptic/prophetic literature read modernity back into the text in a way totally unanticipated by the author and inevitably incorrectly. Here to read modernity into the text would certainly be anachronistic, but at the same time the text may render an understanding even more comprehensible to the contemporary era than it was to the recipients of John's Apocalypse.

Now, beginning with v. 11, the global party takes an unanticipated turn. As participants celebrated the demise of these two witnesses, someone noticed that they were breathing; then they were standing to their feet. This resurrection of the two prophets is attributed directly to God and to the fact that the breath of life entered into them from God, and they then stood. Were it possible for the Bible to understate the effect of an event, it would be the way the NIV translates the response to this event: "And terror struck those who saw them." "Terror" is a translation of two Greek words *phobos* and *megas*, literally meaning "great fear," as translated in the NKJV.[278] The injustice of the circumstances of the martyrdom of the witnesses, added to the indignity to which their bodies were subjected, doubtless engendered the greatest of fears in the celebrants. They must have wondered, having been victimized through the previous unleashing of these plagues by the witnesses, what would befall them now that the witnesses were alive again? However, their fears of the two witnesses are misguided since the

---

278 The NIV, inexplicably, fails to translate the word μέγας, even though there is no textual reason for the omission. Perhaps this is a phenomenological reading based on the theory that there is no substantial difference between "terror" and "great terror."

witnesses heard a voice from heaven saying, "Come up here." Whether the voice was heard by others is unclear from the text. They are received into heaven in a cloud in much the same way the ascension of the Lord took place. Just as the disciples witnessed that ascension, so the enemies of these two prophets are allowed to gaze, doubtless stupefied, upon the ascension of the two prophets.

Their gaze is interrupted quickly by a severe earthquake that causes the collapse of a tenth of the city and the death of 7,000 people. The survivors are terrified more than ever, and at this point the text takes still a different turn than anything the reader could have anticipated. In referring to the 7,000 people who are killed, the text makes use of a rather unusual expression in the Greek New Testament, namely, the use of *onomata anthrōpōn* as literally "the names of men." While interpreters cannot be certain what to make of this unusual expression, the fact that the terminology "names of men" is employed seems to suggest that the people who lose their lives in the earthquake are known and perhaps even particularly significant.[279] As indicated, the expression that "the rest were afraid and gave glory to the God of heaven" is an unusual development in the text. Most often the text of Revelation records that whatever judgments occurred have no effect on the inhabitants of the earth. For example, in 9:20–21, "But the rest of mankind who were not killed by these plagues, did not repent of the work of their hands, that they should not worship demons, and idols of gold, silver, brass, stone, and wood which can neither see nor hear nor walk, And they did not repent of their murders or their sorceries, or their sexual immorality or their thefts."

In 16:10, the outpouring of the fifth bowl of wrath results in men "gnaw[ing] their tongues in agony and curse[ing] the God of heaven because of their pains and sores, but they refused to repent of what they have done." In 16:21, the pouring out of the seventh bowl is met with a similar response: "And great hail from heaven fell upon men, each hailstone about the weight of a talent. Men blasphemed God because of the plague of the hail, since that plague was exceedingly great." Obviously, there was something so remarkable about the events associated with the ascension of the two witnesses that the terror felt by the survivors of the earthquake in Jerusalem led them to acknowledge God as the author of all of these events and

---

279 Robertson notes similar constructions in Rev 3:4 and Acts 1:15 and also in the papyri but suggests no reason for it here (*Word Pictures of the New Testament* [Nashville: Broadman, 1933], 6:383). Alford, followed by Thomas (*Revelation 8–22*, 98), is persuaded that the peculiar verbiage is for the purpose of indicating a number that is carefully and precisely stated (*The Greek Testament*, 4:663). While this may be the case, if the divine choice of these 7,000 included powerful leaders generally supposed by the people to be invincible, then the unusual behavior of the people chronicled in the remainder of v. 13 makes perfect sense.

even give glory to God. That such an expression indicates a positive response to the work of the witnesses, even leading to repentance and salvation on the part of some, is conceivable. On the other hand, it may be nothing more than the acknowledgment of rebellious people so that eventually even the wicked will have to be a part of "every tongue confessing that Jesus is Lord." These remarkable events terminate the second woe, and the third woe is coming quickly.

G. The Seventh Trumpet (11:15–19)

[15]Then the seventh angel sounded: And there were loud voices in heaven, saying,
> "The kingdoms of this world have become *the kingdoms* of our Lord and of
> His Christ,
> And He shall reign forever and ever!"

[16]And the twenty-four elders who sat before God on their thrones fell on their faces and worshiped God, [17]saying:
> "We give You thanks, O Lord God Almighty,
> The One who is and who was and who is to come,
> Because You have taken Your great power and reigned.
> [18]The nations were angry, and Your wrath has come,
> And the time of the dead, that they should be judged,
> And that You should reward Your servants the prophets and the saints,
> And those who fear Your name, small and great,
> And should destroy those who destroy the earth."

[19]Then the temple of God was opened in heaven, and the ark of His covenant was seen in His temple. And there were lightnings, noises, thunderings, an earthquake, and great hail.

11:15–19 In 9:13, the sixth angel sounded his trumpet. The interlude of chaps. 10 and 11 gives way to the blast of the seventh angel; but unlike the first six trumpets, which were the harbingers of six judgments, the sound of the seventh trumpet peels back the veil of heaven and introduces the reader to a heartening announcement, "The kingdoms of this world have become *the kingdoms* of our Lord and of His Christ, and He shall reign forever and ever."[280] What unfolds is apparently a

---

280 Alford comments that the seventh trumpet, the seventh seal, and the seventh bowl all seem to bring the climax of history. Therefore, he concludes, "All this forms strong ground for inference, that the three series of visions are not continuous, but resumptive: not indeed going over the same ground with one another, either of time or of occurrence, but each evolving something which was not in the former, and putting

heavenly scene, featuring once again the twenty-four elders who first appeared in the throne room vision in chap. 4. The announcement is made that the kingdoms of this world have become the kingdoms of our Lord and His Christ, and He will reign for ever and ever. Apparently, multiple loud voices are combined in this celestial announcement. Two things are of note. First, in a sense there has never been a time when all the cosmos, including the kingdoms of this world, have not belonged to the Lord. But there is also a sense in which, under the overarching rule of divine providence, satanic forces have been allowed to exercise limited sovereignty in the world. This is manifest continually throughout history through rogue nations, selfish and blood-thirsty dictators, and power-hungry expansionist nations.

In the Lord's model prayer, one of the petitions is "Your will be done / on earth as it is in heaven," following appropriately the petition "Your kingdom come" (Matt 6:10). It could be argued that "on earth as it is in heaven" is the conclusive explanatory phrase of what that petition means. Heaven's announcement and celebration now focuses on the answer to that prayer and announces that in some new and obvious sense never before experienced the coming of Christ and the establishment of his kingdom will be a fulfillment of the promised reign of the Son of David. From the time that He begins his reign over all the millennial earth until that millennial kingdom is presented to the Father and the eternal reign of Christ is established, He will reign forever and ever (1 Cor 15:24). The expression "forever and ever" is a translation of *tous aiōnas tōn aiōnōn*, which might be translated more literally "unto the ages of the ages." This is a Hebraism depicting a state that simply never ceases. However long the ages of the ages lasts, Christ will reign.[281]

The second observation relating to this verse is the terminology "*the kingdom of our Lord and of His Christ*," which is distinctively binitarian language. Since the role of the Holy Spirit as God is elsewhere clearly evoked in the Apocalypse, the theology of the book of Revelation is a trinitarian theology. Here, "our Lord" must be a reference to God the Father, and the terminology "and of His Christ" must be a reference to the Messiah, or Anointed One, the Lord Jesus Christ. So, the kingdom that will have everlasting significance is a kingdom of God the Father, of the Lord Jesus Christ, and of the Holy Spirit, the one God in three Persons.

---

the course of God's Providence in a different light" (*The Greek Testament*, 4:665).

281 H. B. Swete simply notes, "That Reign is perennial; no age will see its end (Dan. ii. 44, vii. 14, 28), and the Son's re-delivery of His mediatorial power to the Father does not exclude Him from sharing the Father's kingdom" (*Commentary on Revelation* [Grand Rapids: Kregel, 1977], 142).

The celestial proclamation of the coming of Christ's kingdom has a salutary effect on the twenty-four elders. Until this moment they are pictured as seated on their thrones before God; but when the announcement comes, these twenty-four elders abandoned their thrones and fell on their faces and worshiped God. "Fell" (*epesan*) is the aorist indicative form of *piptō* and is the same word and even form of the word that appears in v. 13 where a significant part of the city of Jerusalem "fell." With this picture in mind, one can appreciate the sudden action of the twenty-four elders in abandoning their thrones to prostrate themselves before the God of the universe, whom they proceed to worship.

While there is no doubt that such actions as standing, lifting holy hands to heaven, singing, and praying all have their place in Christian worship, the contemporary scene seems to be largely unaware of the most consistent response to a worshipper's discovery in the presence of God. Isaiah appeared before God and confessed that he was a man of unclean lips dwelling in the midst of a people of unclean lips and that he knew this because his eyes had seen the Lord (Isa 6:5). Simon Peter holds onto Jesus but in an apparently contradictory confession asks that the Lord to depart from him because he is a sinful man (Luke 5:8). A sense of the holiness of God engenders the type of behavior found in these passages just mentioned, and that is exactly what happens with the twenty-four elders. Previous identification of these elders finds them to be representative of the people of God, the twelve tribes of Israel, and the twelve apostles of the Lamb (see 4:2–6 notes).

The particular expression of their praise involves thanksgiving to the Lord God Almighty and provides a checklist of at least some of the items that will be involved in such a reign of Christ. The word translated, "Almighty," is the Greek word *pantokratōr*, which has a sense of irresistible power, a word employed relatively seldom in classical Greek. Liddell and Scott, in the standard *Greek-English Lexicon*, list only a few cases of its use, and most of those are references to the Septuagint.[282] Indeed, the Septuagint employs the word, *pantokratōr*, to translate the Hebrew *ṣĕbā'ôt*. The term occurs once in Paul's writings (2 Cor 6:18) and nine times in the book of the Revelation, a fact that Michaelis, writing in *TDNT*, believes to show the strong influence of the Septuagint on the genesis of the Apocalypse. Michaelis says, "The reference is not so much to God's activity in creation as to his supremacy over all things. The description is static rather than dynamic. Hence it has only a loose connection with the dogmatic concept of the divine omnipotence, which is usually linked with the omnicausality of God."[283]

---

282 LSJ, 1300.
283 W. Michaelis, *TDNT* 3:915.

Whatever one may conclude about Michaelis' reference to the similarity of the term to omnipotence, the term as used in the book of the Apocalypse seems to indicate both the irresistible nature of God as well as his ultimately controlling influence over the course of time and eternity. There is no competition for his supremacy in the cosmos or in eternity.

One of the reasons for this attribute of almighty arises from the fact that this Lord God is the One who both is and was: "Is," the translation of the present participle of "to be" (*eimi*), while "was," the imperfect tense of *eimi*. As a present participle, the emphasis is on the continual and uninterrupted state of the Lord God's status as almighty, whereas the imperfect active indicative lays stress on the continuity of an eternally existing status. Here the added note of "the One who is to come" is not mentioned because it seems apparent in the context. The Almighty, before whom the twenty-four elders now worship and who will reign forever and ever, is the same One who is at the present time and who always was.

Furthermore, the worship of the Lord God Almighty is because this One has taken power and has begun to reign. Here the tense of the Greek term "take" or "hold" (*lambanō*) made use of the perfect active indicative, so in a matter of one short sentence are found a present participle, an imperfect indicative, and a perfect indicative—the emphasis of the perfect being an action that has taken place so that the impact will remain interminably into the future. Once again there is a sense in which this great power did not need to be "taken" since God has never abrogated his rulership of the cosmos. But there is another sense in which the divine providences allow the powers of evil temporarily to "have their day" and accumulate for themselves the wrath of God. An understanding of what is implied here is found in Halloween, which is always the day before All Saints' Day. It was originally perceived to be the last fling of the devils before they were subdued by the saints on the following day. Whatever has been allowed by the devil and his minions has now been clearly circumscribed, and the Lord God has taken all power and begun to reign.

A further circumstance for this rejoicing clearly focuses on the terminal judgments of the last day. The nations are pictured in v. 18 as angry. The Greek word *orgizō*, which means "make angry" from the word *orgē* or "wrath," is certainly appropriate to describe the condition of the nations. The history of the human family is a history of "war and rumors of war." It is a sad tale of revenge, greed, oppression, and heartlessness. In the end the anger of the nations is not directed merely against one another but is a deep-seated hostility to all the truths and virtues of God and against him personally. Now the situation is reversed. The wrath of God has come.

The word "wrath" (*orgē*) is most frequently used for the wrath of God in the New Testament. There are times when *thumos* is used to describe God's anger. More often than not though, *thumos* is a word describing the flaring and rapid receding of human anger whereas *orgē*, as it is used in the New Testament documents, is not a loss of temper but a settled disposition of God against all that corrupts and distorts his creation. Hence in Rom 1 "the wrath of God (*orgē theou*) is revealed from heaven against all ungodliness" (Rom 1:18). That wrath, which has always been manifest in some form, has come in renewed intensity and final manifestation. Paul warns, "But in accordance with your hardness and your impenitent heart, you are treasuring up for yourself wrath in the day of wrath and revelation of the righteous judgment of God" (Rom 2:5). As a part of that, the time has come for the judging of the dead. There are three aspects of this judgment. First, the time has come for judging the dead. "And as it is appointed for men to die once but after this the judgment" (Heb 9:27). Life as known on planet earth is the prelude, the proscenium for eternity. All who have died and who did not elect to accept the judgment of God against sin on Christ's cross are now to face their final judgment.

However, the time is also appointed for the rewarding of the prophets and the saints and all of those who reverence the name of God, both small and great. "Your servants, the prophets" is a reference to those sent by God to proclaim His message in both the Old and New Testament eras. The reference to "saints" or "holy ones" and the ones who "reverence" (*phoboumenois*) or fear His name employs the word "fear" but not in the sense of cringing. The fear or reverence cited here is the fear of a child for his father, while knowing the great love and concern of his father, yet nevertheless knowing to fear him when his father's will has been transgressed. Fear sends the child running to the father rather than running from the father. That fear on the part of the saints is a manifestation of their holiness and is an indication that they will be rewarded in that day.

Rewards are promised in the New Testament to believers. Of course, the greatest of all rewards is eternal life in the presence of God for all eternity. Additionally, the New Testament makes mention of other kinds of reward. Though these are notoriously difficult to define as per their precise nature, clearly some will receive great reward and others will be "saved; yet so as by fire" (1 Cor 3:15 KJV). This sometimes gives rise to the question as to how anyone could be happy in heaven if he has been given few rewards or perhaps no reward at all. The key word here is "saved." Everyone present as a servant of Christ will realize in that day the grace of God that saved him from being an object of God's wrath. That alone will be enough to produce eternal happiness. In addition, a believer should receive additional rewards for his service to Christ.

Those who are to be rewarded are both the small and the great. Lupieri laments that "trying to explain these accusatives is an almost hopeless task (and many manuscripts and editors have corrected the text). I think John meant: 'Those who fear your name—it does not matter whether they are small or great (in the church).' The phrase could be considered an irregular absolute accusative (as it is not syntactically 'absolute')."[284] However unusual the construction, Lupieri has grasped the intent. Rewards will be provided both to those who are widely known and highly respected and to those scarcely noticed by the church but highly esteemed by the Lord for going quietly and perhaps largely unnoticed about the work of the Savior.

Finally, v. 18 contains the rather peculiar phrase "and should destroy those who destroy the earth." The destroying of those who destroy the earth appears to be a reference to the beast, the false prophet of chap. 13, the scarlet woman of chap. 17, and ultimately Babylon the Great. The connection of this destruction relates to the earlier statement that the time of God's wrath has come. In addition to judging the dead, as well as rewarding the prophets and the saints, He will also in that day destroy those who are destroying the earth. In this passage the reader is provided with some understanding of the nature of the wrath of God. God's fury towards sin occurs because sin is ultimately a destructive force that destroys lives and destroys all that is godly. Those who perpetrate this must also be judged and will be in that last day.

The concluding verse of the oracle provides the reader with a spectacular opportunity to look into the temple of God in heaven. That temple is said to be opened, and within the temple is seen the ark of the covenant. Following this, there are cosmic manifestations of the incredible power and authority of the God of this temple with flashes of lightning and thunder, a great hailstorm, and even a foundation-shaking earthquake. The presence of the temple in heaven is surprising to some and especially a temple containing the ark of the covenant. The author of Hebrews in chap. 9 of his epistle provides a lengthy explanation of the tabernacle, its furnishings, and their significance. In Heb 9:23 he concludes, "Therefore it *was* necessary that the copies of the things in the heavens should be purified with these, but the heavenly things themselves with better sacrifices than these." The indication is thus given that while there is one sense in which the Lamb is the temple (Rev 21:22), in another sense there is a temple that is open in heaven and within that temple is found the ark of God.

---

284 E. F. Lupieri, *A Commentary on the Apocalypse of John* (Grand Rapids: Eerdmans, 1999), 186.

The ark of the covenant has a storied history, which began with the furnishings for the tabernacle built under Moses and culminated in 586 BC with the destruction of the city and the temple under Nebuchadnezzar. Legends abound regarding what happened to the strange box containing Aaron's rod that budded, a pot of manna miraculously preserved, and the tablets of the Law, and having as its lid the mercy seat overshadowed by cherubim. Strong Jewish tradition argued that Jeremiah absconded with the ark weeks or days before the fall of the city and hid it either somewhere on Mount Zion or else, as some would have it, in the vicinity of what has become known as the Dead Sea Caves at Qumran or perhaps even on Mount Nebo. However, the Ethiopian Christians claim that they have the ark and show visitors the building where it is housed. No outside verification of this has ever been forthcoming, giving rise to substantial doubt about the claims. The ark has also been rumored to be somewhere in the Vatican and probably eight or ten other places in the world. The truth, while not verifiable, is probably that the ark, along with all of the other furnishings of the tabernacle, was melted for the gold and destroyed at the time of the Babylonian invasion.

In any event the ark is now seen in heaven. This appearance of the ark in heaven is particularly important because the ark was the symbol of the promises of God, and particularly the mercy seat was the focus of the ritual of the Day of Atonement, which foreshadowed the ultimate atonement of Christ. To the Jewish mind, the ark of the covenant within the holy of holies was where God uniquely dwelled. They recognized the omnipresence of God but also believed that in some unique way He dwelt in the holy of holies and manifested Himself in His promises to Israel. Now the ark of the covenant, symbolizing both the promises of God and the atonement available in his divine providences, is seen in heaven.

The difficulty in 21:22 is with John's description of the heavenly city: "I did not see a temple in the city, because the Lord God Almighty and the Lamb are its temple." The dilemma, avoided by most commentators, is to explain why there is a temple in chap. 11 with an ark of the covenant and there is not a temple in John's vision of the heavenly city in chap. 21. The idealist interpretation finds its highest ground here since advocates of that perspective can quickly maintain that neither the temple in chap. 11 nor the heavenly vision of chap. 21 is to be taken in any sense as literal.[285] If what is being conveyed is simply a spiritual mes-

---

285 For example, G. E. Ladd, unlike many commentators, tackles the issue: "Here again we find symbolic language which suggests the coming of the Kingdom of God. At the death of our Lord, the curtain which separated men from the presence of God was rent in

sage, then there is no problem about certain symbolism in chap. 11, which seems to be in violation of that in chap. 21. The emphasis is simply different.

The second possibility is that two different edifices are in view, one that is present in heaven at the conclusion of the tribulation period and perhaps throughout the millennium, while the temple of chap. 21 belongs entirely to the heavenly kingdom when the earth has "melted with fervent heat" and there has emerged "a new heaven and a new earth" (2 Pet 3:12–13)

A third possibility for understanding the change is that the temple of chap. 11 is the expected answer to the Heb 9 passage. The author of Hebrews indicates that the earthly tabernacle and temple were built on the pattern of a heavenly one. There is a similarity here to Plato's doctrine of the existence of universals in the mind of God, which in turn have their particulars worked out in the material world. The absence of the temple then in Rev 21, or rather the revelation that "the Lord God Almighty and the Lamb are its temple," would constitute the actual state of affairs and be coincident with the heavenly pattern that could still remain as a testimony in heaven.

In Israel today there is a large reproduction of the city of Jerusalem and another of the entire land of the Bible. In the Wilderness of Timnah exists an actual reproduction of the tabernacle in the wilderness. None of these constitute the real things but are copies. Granting the point of the idealist that the book of Revelation is full of imagery, dismissing all of this as imagery is inadequate. Doubtless, it is better to understand that what is seen in chap. 11 is the original divine plan for tabernacle/temple and in chap. 21 the actual state of affairs existing in heaven forever where God Himself is the place of worship and, therefore, the temple.

---

two (Matt. 27:51), signifying that now because of the fulfillment of the Old Testament sacrificial rites in the death of Jesus, the presence of God was no longer limited to Israel but is open to all men (see Heb. 9:8; 10:20). This, however, was only a spiritual fact, not yet a visible reality. All men now have access in spirit to God through Christ. They remain in their mortal bodies on earth, while God's temple is located in heaven. God has revealed himself to men through Jesus of Nazareth, but his own dwelling remains in heaven (3:12; 7:15; 15:5); he does not yet dwell among men. The point of the present passage is a symbolic representation of the opening up of the presence of God in the eschatological consummation. God's temple in heaven was opened that men may henceforth enter into unmediated fellowship with him. This is a symbolic way of proclaiming what is fulfilled in Rev. 21:3: 'Behold, the dwelling of God is with men.' That this is a proleptic vision is seen from the fact that the temple is conceived as continuing to be in heaven (14:15, 17; 15:5; 16:17). The opening of the temple is a proleptic, symbolic act of the consummation which does not itself occur until chapters 21–22. In the consummation God himself dwells among his people and there will be no need of a temple" (*A Commentary on the Revelation of John* [Grand Rapids: Eerdmans, 1972], 163).

4. An Interpretive Interlude (12:1–14:20)

A. A Woman, a Child, and a Dragon (12:1–17)

¹Now a great sign appeared in heaven: a woman clothed with the sun, with the moon under her feet, and on her head a garland of twelve stars. ²Then being with child, she cried out in labor and in pain to give birth.

³And another sign appeared in heaven: behold, a great, fiery red dragon having seven heads and ten horns, and seven diadems on his heads. ⁴His tail drew a third of the stars of heaven and threw them to the earth. And the dragon stood before the woman who was ready to give birth, to devour her Child as soon as it was born. ⁵She bore a male Child who was to rule all nations with a rod of iron. And her Child was caught up to God and His throne. ⁶Then the woman fled into the wilderness, where she has a place prepared by God, that they should feed her there one thousand two hundred and sixty days.

⁷And war broke out in heaven: Michael and his angels fought with the dragon; and the dragon and his angels fought, ⁸but they did not prevail, nor was a place found for them in heaven any longer. ⁹So the great dragon was cast out, that serpent of old, called the Devil and Satan, who deceives the whole world; he was cast to the earth, and his angels were cast out with him.

¹⁰Then I heard a loud voice saying in heaven,

"Now salvation, and strength, and the kingdom of God,
    And the power of His Christ have come,
For the accuser of our brethren,
    Who accused them before our God day and night,
    has been cast down.
¹¹And they overcame him by the blood of the Lamb
    and by the word of their testimony,
and they did not love their lives to the death.
¹²Therefore rejoice, O heavens,
    and you who dwell in them!
Woe to the inhabitants of the earth and the sea!
    For the devil has come down to you, having great wrath,
    Because he knows that he has a short time."

¹³Now when the dragon saw that he had been cast to the earth, he persecuted the woman who gave birth to the male *Child*. ¹⁴But the woman was given two wings of a great eagle, that she might fly into the wilderness to her place, where she is nourished for a time and times and half a time, from the presence of the serpent. ¹⁵So the serpent spewed water out of his mouth like a flood after the woman, that he might cause her to

be carried away by the flood. ¹⁶But the earth helped the woman, and the earth opened its mouth and swallowed up the flood which the dragon had spewed out of his mouth. ¹⁷And the dragon was enraged with the woman, and he went to make war with the rest of her offspring, who keep the commandments of God and have the testimony of Jesus Christ.

In many ways the twelfth chapter of the Apocalypse represents the most pivotal of all the book's paragraphs from a hermeneutical point of view. Doubtless one of the most profound verses in the entire book is v. 11. The key to understanding chap. 12 is the ability to identify the persons or the signs in its paragraphs. If one properly identifies these "signs," then the understanding of the chapter follows with relative ease. More important, chap. 12 will operate as something of a key to the understanding of the rest of the Apocalypse and, by virtue of that insight, an understanding of the plan of God for the ages.

12:1-6 The seer of Patmos now beholds a sign that appears in the heavens.[286] "Appeared" is the aorist passive indicative of *horaō* and emphasizes the fact that the sign appeared against the backdrop of the vault of the heavens. The sign, further described in the NKJV as "great," indicating its importance, includes three individuals who must be identified.[287] The first is a woman clothed with the sun (v. 1). She is about to give birth to a child. The second person to be identified is the male child whom she bears (v. 5). Standing before her is an ominous red dragon waiting to devour her child upon birth.

---

286 The Greek term σημεῖον is one of three words most frequently employed to speak of the miraculous in the New Testament. One of those, τέρατα, often appears in conjunction with σημεῖον, while the third, δύναμις, more often stands alone. While it is an oversimplification, the emphasis of δύναμις tends to focus on the power or authority producing the miracle. τέρατα calls attention to the effects of the miracle, while σημεῖον invokes the meaning of the miracle. Johannine literature makes frequent use of σημεῖον. K. H. Rengstorf, writing in the *TDNT* traces the early development of the idea in Homer where a woman hears thunder on a cloudless day and surmises that it is a σῆμα, an omen from God. He concludes that in every case, "someone or something is to be recognized and a fact or object perceived with a view to conceptual assimilation and correct classification" (7:205). Specifically in the Johannine corpus, Rengstorf says that "John knows the uses of σημεῖον in the sense of 'sign,' 'pointer,' 'mark' in such a way as to do justice to the formal character of the word" (7:243). He continues, "Furthermore the basic thrust of the term is clear in John, for no matter what specific nuances are given by the context the essential reference here again is to visual perception and the assurance this gives" (7:243).

287 The NIV's addition of "wondrous" does not represent the word-for-word text since it is absent altogether in the Greek manuscripts. This interpretation of the sign as "wondrous" may well be true, but it is not textually represented.

Since both the male child and the great red dragon will be easily identified, the interpreter is left with the problem of identifying the radiant woman. Once again, a wide variety of interpretations have been held throughout Christian history. However, the three major ones are that the woman represents Mary, the mother of our Lord; the woman represents the church; and, finally, the woman represents the offspring of Abraham (i.e., the Jewish people). The idea that the radiant woman is Mary, the Lord's mother, is understandably popular among Roman Catholic interpreters, indeed, carrying a certain appeal and natural understanding since the New Testament cannot be clearer that Jesus is the virgin-born son of Mary of Nazareth. Hence the Messiah is the child to be born.[288] However, this identification also exhibits significant problems. First, Mary is always presented in the Scriptures as a peasant girl from the town of Nazareth in Galilee, and nowhere does she appear clothed with the sun, the moon under her feet, stars on her head. Only later in church history does one find the development of Marian piety and begin to see Mary gloriously displayed in iconography. Neither does Mary flee into the wilderness where she is kept "for 1,260 days" as seen in v. 6, or "a time, times and half a time" in v. 14. These last two references might be taken by some to reference the flight to Egypt of Joseph and Mary, following the attempt of Herod to kill all the babies in Bethlehem (Matt 2:13–18), but the three and one-half years, 1,260-day reckoning cannot be made to fit with this; and the other details provided simply do not favor the possibility that Mary is in view.[289]

The idea that the radiant woman is the church must be dismissed as even less plausible. Christ gives birth to the church; the church does not give birth to the Lord. Nowhere is the church presented in such pageantry, and some of the same objections to identifying the radiant woman with Mary are also applicable to the idea that this radiant woman is the church.[290]

---

288 Oecumenius is typical, saying, "He is speaking of the mother of our Savior, as I have said. Naturally the vision describes her as being in heaven and not on the earth, as pure in soul and body, as equal to an angel, as a citizen of heaven, as one who came to effect the incarnation of God who dwells in heaven ('for,' he says, 'heaven is my throne'), and as one who has nothing in common with the world and the evils in it, but wholly sublime, wholly worthy of heaven, even though she sprang from our mortal nature and being. For the Virgin is of the same substance as we are" (*Commentary on the Apocalypse*, trans. J. N. Sugget, FC 112 [Washington, DC: Catholic University of America Press, 2006], 107).

289 For a brief but helpful discussion of the development of Marian piety in the Roman Church, especially as it developed with Bernard of Clairvaux, see R. P. McBrien, *Catholicism: New Edition* (New York: HarperCollins, 1994), 1085–89.

290 This view, however, is popular among both Catholics and Protestants. On

What can be asked, given the fact that many of John's readers would be Jewish, is what identification would a Jewish individual immediately make with the radiant woman clothed with the sun, the moon under her feet, and a crown of twelve stars on her head? For any Jewish reader this would call to mind the dream of Joseph recorded in Gen 37, a dream that failed to endear Joseph to his eleven brothers. The second of Joseph's two dreams, recorded in Gen 37:9, saw the sun, moon, and eleven stars bowing down to Joseph; and the similarity of the two visions would be brought to any Jewish mind, especially given the propensity of John to be influenced by the Old Testament. The woman is clothed with the sun, the moon is under her feet, and she has a crown of twelve stars on her head, evidently representing the twelve tribes of Israel. In 12:2 she is pregnant and in travail or labor; she is about to give birth. A dragon awaits the

---

the Catholic side of the ledger, Hippolytus, Victorinus of Petovium, and Tyconnius invoke this view. Typical is Victorinus (*Commentary on the Apocalypse* 12, *ANF* 7:355), who notes that "the woman clothed with the sun, and having the moon under her feet, and wearing a crown of twelve stars upon her head, and travailing in her pains, is the ancient Church of fathers, and prophets, and saints, and apostles, which had the groans and torments of its longing until it saw that Christ, the fruit of its people according to the flesh long promised to it, had taken flesh out of the selfsame people. Moreover, being clothed with the sun intimates the hope of resurrection and the glory of the promise. And the moon intimates the fall of the bodies of the saints under the obligation of death, which never can fail. For even as life is diminished, so also it is increased. Nor is the hope of those that sleep extinguished absolutely, as some think, but they have in their darkness a light such as the moon. And the crown of twelve stars signifies the choir of fathers, according to the fleshly birth, of whom Christ was to take flesh." Contemporary Catholic scholars are more cautious but still hold the view. See W. J. Harrington, *Revelation*, SP 16 (Collegeville, MN: Liturgical Press, 1993), 128. Among Protestants, Chilton follows this view saying, "The central symbol is a Woman, a familiar Biblical image for the Church, the people of God. (Specifically, as we shall see, the Woman here stands for *the Church in the form of Old Covenant Israel*.) St. John's first readers would immediately have thought of previous prophetic uses of the Woman as representing the Church (see, e.g., Isa. 26; 49–50; 54; 66; Jer. 3–4; Lam. 1; Ezek. 16; Hos. 1–4; Mic. 4)" (*The Days of Vengeance: An Exposition of the Book of Revelation* [Fort Worth, TX: Dominion Press, 1987], 297). R. C. H. Lenski also voices this view: "To seek the meaning in the appointment of sun, moon, and stars to *rule* the day and the night, is to obtain something that is incongruous. John sees the church in her real glory, for which reason also she is here seen in heaven and not on earth where her splendor is hidden by her lowliness as was the majesty of Jesus when he walked on earth in his humiliation" (*The Interpretation of St. John's Revelation* [Minneapolis: Augsburg, 1963], 362–63. See similarly J. Roloff, *The Revelation of John*, CC (Minneapolis: Fortress, 1993), 145.

birth of this child also; and the woman gives birth to a male child, who will rule all nations with an iron scepter (v. 5). The woman flees into a desert place in the wilderness where God takes care of her for 1,260 days.

The earliest promises to Abraham included a posterity numbered as the stars of the heavens and the sands of the seashore, a land to call his own, but most important of all, a messianic promise that "In you all families of the earth will be blessed" (Gen 12:3). While in some sense of the word most of the nations, if not all of them on the face of the earth, have been blessed by various Jewish individuals and their contributions, the universality of this promise can only be fulfilled in the Messiah, so clearly God's plan for redemption through the Messiah is to be realized as one of the promises to Abraham.[291] The Messiah will be born to the offspring of Abraham. He will be a Jewish Messiah. The only effective and appropriate identification of the radiant woman, then, is to see her as the ethnic offspring of Abraham—the Jewish people. This accounts for the fact that many scholars have claimed that the radiant woman is representative of the Jewish nation, which gives birth to the Messiah.[292]

---

291 A quick guide to the remarkable general impact of Jewish people on the world can be found in books like M. Shapiro, *The Jewish 100: A Ranking of the Most Influential Jews of All Time* (New York: Citadel, 1994) and Abba Eban, *Heritage: Civilization and the Jews* (New York: Summit Books), 1984.

292 Ladd, Mounce, and Beale support the position that this radiant woman is "Ideal Israel." Mounce says, "The woman is not Mary the mother of Jesus but the messianic community, the ideal Israel. Zion as the mother of the people of God is a common theme in Jewish writings (Isa 54:1; II Esdr 10:7; cf. Gal 4:26). It is out of faithful Israel that Messiah will come. It should cause no trouble that within the same chapter the woman comes to signify the church (vs. 17). The people of God are one throughout all redemptive history" (R. H. Mounce, *The Book of Revelation*, NICNT [Grand Rapids: Eerdmans, 1977], 236). G. E. Ladd identifies the woman the same way (*A Commentary on the Revelation of John* [Grand Rapids: Eerdmans, 1972], 166). G. K. Beale has a characteristically extended explanation in which he appears to invoke part of several views, but in the end he eliminates the possibility that the woman represents ethnic Israel. "It is too limiting to view the woman as representing only a remnant of Israelites living in trial at the last stage of history, since the following verses show that the woman symbolizes a believing community extending from before the time of Christ's birth to at least the latter part of the first century A.D. (see on vv 6, 13–17). Furthermore, in the following verses the persecution is not directed against a nation of believers *and unbelievers* but a pure community of faith" (*The Book of Revelation: A Commentary on the Greek Text*, NIGTC [Grand Rapids: Eerdmans; Carlisle, UK: Paternoster Press, 1999], 631). Interestingly, E. F. Lupieri, a Catholic, takes a similar position but seems to recognize a closer relationship of the woman to ethnic Israel, though he makes this "a heavenly representation"

In v. 3 the third sign, the dragon, is introduced.[293] He is warlike, fiery red in color, and has seven heads, ten horns, and seven kingly crowns, which will identify him with the final form of imperial suzerainty that John will watch as

---

(*A Commentary on the Apocalypse of John* [Grand Rapids: Eerdmans, 1999], 189). For an interesting defense of the radiant woman as ethnic Israel, see W. A. Criswell, *Expository Sermons on Revelation: Five Volumes Complete and Unabridged* (Grand Rapids: Zondervan, 1969), 4:65–89.

293 A fascinating note appears in *The New Interpreter's Bible* at this point. The author, C. C. Rowland says, "Talk about Satan is avoided by some liberally minded people. It seems to reflect the beliefs of simple-minded believers or the fantasies of infancy, which mature adults should have grown out of. The demonic world, particularly when it dwells on destruction, is one we may find distasteful—even pathological. We may find ourselves reacting negatively to images of hostility and polarization or, rightly, reluctant to 'demonize' others. The symbolism of evil in the Bible is a problem, and yet it is a potent resource to help us to comprehend the forces that upset and subvert our managed lives. Satan symbolizes that which stands between humans and the divine presence, and the personification of him as a dragon or a serpent is a sign of the reality of evil. As Revelation indicates, the manifestation of Satan's power is complex. It is institutional and social as well as personal. Thus the beast is a concrete embodiment of evil power. Evil does not take the form of a single king but an imperial institution or structure; it is a way of operating, and its agents of propaganda take many shapes (13:1 ff.). Likewise, Babylon is not an individual but a city with its whole network of relationships and institutions contributing to a pattern of life, involvement in which John calls 'fornication.' Revelation beckons us to broaden our horizons to understand the scope of evil by not confining it to what we can manage (e.g., the person who is before us or who may seem a threat to us), just as it refuses to allow us to confine the horizon of hope and salvation to the individual person's destiny" (*The Book of Revelation*, in *NIB* [Nashville: Abingdon, 1998], 12:653). Similarly, M. G. Reddish finds it necessary to address the figure of Satan: "Many modern readers may feel somewhat uneasy with this chapter. In some circles, any talk of the reality of evil is considered naïve and unsophisticated. As Walter Wink has observed, 'Our culture resolutely refuses to believe in the real existence of evil, preferring to regard it as a kind of systems breakdown that can be fixed with enough tinkering.' This aversion to speaking about evil is particularly true if one speaks of evil in terms of a Satan figure. But this chapter, indeed all of Revelation, forces us to face squarely the problem of evil in our world. Whether one chooses to retain the traditional imagery of Satan and demons to speak of the presence of evil in the world, or to demythologize the language of evil and recast our understanding in modern terminology, one cannot remain true to the biblical witness if he does not recognize that evil is a reality, indeed a force, threatening to overwhelm us. What is important is not the imagery depicting evil, but rather the resolve to resist evil and align ourselves with God (*Revelation*, Smyth & Helwys Bible Commentary [Macon, GA: Smyth & Helwys Publishing, 240).

the rising of the dragon-inspired beast from the sea in chap. 13. An additional item that helps still further in identifying the dragon, however, is added to the text at this point. The dragon's tail swept a third of the stars out of the sky and flung them to the earth. This is an apparent reference to the pre-cosmic fall of Satan from heaven. This heavenly conspiracy was led by Satan, but a significant number of angels were cobelligerents with him and so forfeited their "home" (Jude 6) in heaven. This fall is plainly mentioned in 2 Pet 2:4; Jude 6; and perhaps Rev 12:7–10; and many interpreters believe that Isa 14 and Ezek 28 in the lamentations on the kings of Tyre and Babylon say more than can adequately be said, even granting poetic license, about those two earthly kings. These interpreters suggest that while the lamentations of Isaiah and Ezekiel are indeed about those kings mentioned, the text goes beyond those earthly monarchs to the power that stands behind them, namely, an anointed cherub who lifted up his heart in pride against God and therefore was relieved of his position and cast out of heaven in a pre-cosmic conflict. He had a following, and those angels that kept not "their positions of authority" (Jude 6), most of whom were imprisoned until the day of judgment, followed Satan in his rebellion and also were flung from the heavens to the earth. The dragon is seen postured in front of the woman who is in labor and about to give birth. His purpose is not hidden. His intention is to "devour" (*kataphagē*) her child upon its birth. In other words, the purpose of the dragon is to frustrate the redemptive purpose of God and if possible, to destroy the work of God.

Excursus on the Fall of Satan

Contemporary interpreters almost uniformly reject the idea that laments in Isa 14 and Ezek 28 have anything at all to do with the fall of Satan. But patristic confidence in the idea that Satan, as well as the monarchs of Tyre and Babylon, is in view is recorded as almost unanimous. For example, Origen says, "Most evidently by these words is he shown to have fallen from heaven, who formerly was Lucifer, and who used to arise in the morning. For if, as some think, he was a nature of darkness, how is Lucifer said to have existed before? Or how could he arise in the morning, who had in himself nothing of the light? Nay, even the Saviour Himself teaches us, saying of the devil, 'Behold, I see Satan fallen from heaven like lightning.' For at one time he was light."[294] Jerome adds, "Lucifer fell, Lucifer who used to rise at dawn; and he who was bred up in a paradise of delight had the well-earned sentence passed upon him, 'Though thou exalt thyself as the eagle, and though thou set thy nest among the stars, thence will I bring thee down, saith the Lord.' For he had said in his heart, 'I will exalt my throne above the stars of God,' and 'I will be like the Most High.'"[295] Augustine joins them in concluding, "For example, what is said in Isaiah, 'How he is fallen from heaven, Lucifer, son of the morning!' and the other statements of the context which, under the figure or the king of Babylon, are made about the same person, are of course to be understood of the devil; and yet the statement which is made in the same place, 'He is ground down to earth, who sendeth to all nations,' does not altogether fitly apply to the head himself."[296]

Again, regarding Ezek 28, Cyril of Jerusalem claims, "The devil then is the first author of sin, and the father of the wicked: and this is the Lord's saying, not mine, *that the devil sinneth from the beginning*: none sinned before him. But he sinned, not as having received necessarily from nature the propensity to sin, since then the cause of sin is traced back again to Him that made him so; but having been created good, he has of his own free will become a devil, and received that name from his action. For being an Archangel he was afterwards called a devil from his slandering: from being a good servant of God he has become rightly named Satan; for 'Satan' is interpreted *the adversary*. And this is not my teaching, but that of the inspired prophet Ezekiel: for he takes up a lamentation over him and says, *Thou wast a seal of likeness, and a crown of beauty; in the Paradise of God wast thou born*: and soon after, *Thou wast born blameless in thy days, from the day in which thou wast created, until thine iniquities were found in thee*."[297] Tertullian says plainly, "Now, whence originated this malice of lying and deceit towards

---

294 Origen, *De Principiis* 1.5.5, *ANF* 4:259.

295 Jerome, *The Letters of St. Jerome* 22.4, *NPNF*² 6:23.

296 Augustine, *On Christian Doctrine* 3.37.55, *NPNF*¹ 2:573.

297 Cyril of Jerusalem, "Lecture II: On Repentance and Remission of Sins, and Concerning the Adversary" 4, *NPNF*² 7:8–9).

man, and slandering of God? Most certainly not from God, who made the angel good after the fashion of His good works. Indeed, before he became the devil, he stands forth the wisest of creatures; and wisdom is no evil. If you turn to the prophecy of Ezekiel, you will at once perceive that this angel was both by creation good and by choice corrupt. For in the person of the prince of Tyre it is said in reference to the devil: 'Moreover, the word of the Lord came unto me, saying, Son of man, take up a lamentation upon the king of Tyrus, and say unto him, Thus saith the Lord God: Thou sealest up the sum, full of wisdom, perfect in beauty' (this belongs to him as the highest of the angels, the archangel, the wisest of all); 'amidst the delights of the paradise of thy God was thou born' (for it was there, where God had made the angels in a shape which resembled the figure of animals."[298]

With this agree other church Fathers such as Origen and Augustine. A few recent commentators venture timid agreement with the Fathers. C. Feinberg says, "The author cannot follow those views which inject without support a foreign and false mythology, a legendary atmosphere or a hypothetical ideal personality. It cannot be conceded that Ezekiel was following a free imagination which admittedly was not ideal with him. Instead, he appeared to have the situation of his day in mind with his attention riveted upon the ruler of Tyre, the embodiment of the people's pride and godlessness. But as he viewed the thoughts and ways of that monarch, he clearly discerned behind him the motivating force and personality who was impelling him in his opposition to God. In short, he saw the work and activity of Satan, whom the king of Tyre was emulating in so many ways. Recall the incident in Matt 16:21–23 where Peter was rebuked by our Lord Jesus. No sterner words were spoken to anyone in Christ's earthly ministry. But He did not mean that Peter had somehow become Satan himself; He was indicating that the motivation behind Peter's opposition to His going to Calvary was none other than the prince of the demons. This appears to be a similar situation. Some liberal expositors admit that it would appear that Ezekiel had in mind some spirit or genius of Tyre

---

298 Tertullian, *The Five Books Against Marcion* 2.10, ANF 3:305.

comparable to the angelic powers and princes in the book of Daniel who are entrusted with the affairs of nations."[299]

In v. 5 there can be little doubt about the identification of her child. She gives birth to a son, and this son is going to rule the nations "with a rod of iron" (Rev 2:27). Interestingly, however, before the dragon can act to devour the child, the child is "caught up" to God and to His throne. The word in the Greek text is *harpazō*, which is also used for the taking up of the saints into heaven (see 1 Thess 4:17). Here the aorist passive indicative suggests that the ascension is into heaven itself. What is presented in the text is the birth and the ascension of the Lord. If asked the question, "Where is his sinless life, His death, His resurrection?" all is included; but the first and the last events of the Lord's initial advent, the bookends of His first advent, are here described.

Verse 6 anticipates the fury of the dragon as a result of his failure to interfere successfully with the redemptive program of God. Knowing that the woman is beloved of God, the dragon will now direct his anger toward her. Therefore, the woman flees into the desert to a place prepared for her where she should receive care for 1,260 days. This temporal period described in Scripture as forty-two months (Rev 11:2; 13:5), or as "a time, times and half a time" (Rev 12:14), and sometimes as three and one-half years (Dan 9:27), is a consistent reference to the final three and one-half years of the seventy-week prophecy in Dan 9.

Antichrist apparently enters into a covenant with the nation Israel at the outset of the tribulation period. However, the truth is that the final world system is even more anti-Semitic than the kingdoms of Hitler, Stalin, or other anti-Semitic leaders. The covenant made with the people of God at the outset of the tribulation is broken halfway through; and the dragon, unable to do anything about the Messiah himself, turns his fury on the woman. Therefore, the woman is taken to a safe place in the wilderness where she is miraculously preserved by God for the last 1,260 days. Were it not for this miraculous preservation, the long-standing antagonism of Satan against the Jewish people would lead to their annihilation. But God intervenes miraculously to preserve and protect a remnant.

12:7–9 In a war in heaven, Michael and his angels are the major protagonists. They fight against the dragon and his angels, who are now defined as demons (v. 7). However, the dragon and his angels lost their place in heaven

---

299 C. Feinberg, *The Prophecy of Ezekiel: The Glory of the Lord* (Chicago: Moody, 1969), 161–62. See also L. E. Cooper, *Ezekiel*, NAC 17 (Nashville: B&H, 1994), 264–65.

(v. 8). The great dragon is hurled down, and in the process, he is identified with final clarity for the reader (v. 9). He is that ancient serpent who is called the Devil (*diabolos*, "one who casts through," "accuser") and Satan, which means "adversary." The Devil (i.e., Satan) leads the whole world astray. That simple statement of purpose will be critical in understanding the information provided in chap. 13. The fallen angel, the Devil or Satan, is responsible for the deception visited on the entire world. He and all his angels with him are subsequently hurled to the earth.

The vast majority of interpreters see this occurrence as Satan's final assault on heaven. It will take place during these latter days of the tribulation, perhaps at the end. There is some reason for that interpretation, which is found in the general rejoicing that follows in heaven and in the greater fury of Satan magnified in v. 12 as well as the statement that "he knows that he has a short time." Furthermore, the sequential reading of the text favors such a view.

For example, Bullinger has a protracted discussion of the futile attempts of Satan to sabotage God's program of redemption through the ages. He notes that Michael initiates this final conquest, which is resisted unsuccessfully by Satan.[300] Walvoord favors this view as do most premillennialists.[301]

However, there is another possibility. Perhaps this event is not future but past, designed to provide explanation not only for the present experiences of John's readers but also for all that would happen in the last days. As such, its nature is like an instant video replay whereby a viewer observes an event that took place only minutes before or maybe even days or weeks before and later is replayed on the screen for the observer. My own sense of the passage is that this is still further evidence of the pre-cosmic move of Satan to try to displace God, which in his plan and its failure provides the explanation for the upheaval experienced by earth dwellers and all the creation of God since that day. There was in fact a confrontation in heaven. Michael, the leading angel of God, along with his angels, fought against the dragon. While there was a legitimate conflict, Satan finds himself arrested and hurled to the earth. He then inaugurates his program of deceiving the whole earth, but in heaven there is rejoicing.[302]

---

300 E. W. Bullinger, *Commentary on Revelation* (Grand Rapids: Kregel, 1984), 385–409.

301 J. Walvoord, *The Revelation of Jesus Christ: A Commentary* (Chicago: Moody, 1966), 191–92.

302 Alford thinks the casting down of Satan came at the hour of Christ's triumph on the cross (*The Greek Testament* [Chicago: Moody, 1958], 4:669). Oecumenius, however, in his *Commentary on the Apocalypse*, adopts the position of this commentator. Writing between AD 500 and 600, perhaps following the recapitulation theory popularized by Ire-

12:10-12   A loud voice in heaven signals the triumph. The salvation, strength, and kingdom of God, and the power of His Christ have come. The work of Christ on the cross provided the basis for salvation in Christ's atoning death, but salvation is not ultimately finished until Satan and evil are destroyed, the saints are glorified, and the heavenly state in its purity is established. So, with the defeat of Satan and his angels and with the death of Christ on the cross, the power and the kingdom of God and the authority of Christ begin to affect not only heaven but also earth. The accuser of the brethren, the Devil, who delighted to accuse them before God, day and night, has been cast down.[303]

The loud voice from heaven announces the era of salvation, of the strength and kingdom of God, and of the power of His Christ. There is certainly a sense in which all this is inaugurated with the first advent of Christ. But the Apocalypse brings the reader to the fulfillment, the consummation of the plan and purpose of God. The salvation of mankind is center focus in the Apocalypse as in all the New Testament. Accomplished in the atoning death and triumphant resurrection of Jesus and appropriated by faith, this salvation awaits a final touch of God's grace, the glorification of the body, and ushering in the final, eternal state. This consummation is now in full view.

---

naeus, Oecumenius says, "As though in a continual return to the starting-point, as already described, the vision now plans to describe an earlier beginning which had indeed been partly mentioned previously, as it prepares to tell us about the Antichrist; for the first beginning of the acts of the Antichrist was Satan's fall from heaven. The Lord, too, says of this, 'I saw Satan fall like lightning from heaven.' (2) What, therefore, does it mean, *And war arose in heaven*? The divine Scripture says that Satan raised up his neck against God, that is stretched up an arrogant and stubborn neck against him and planned to revolt. But God, inasmuch as he is naturally good and long-suffering, was forbearing towards him. The divine angels, on the other hand, did not put up with the arrogance of their master; and drove him out of their company. He now says that Michael, one of the great rulers among the angels, made war against Satan and those under him. (3) And Satan *did not prevail* in the war against him, *nor was there any place* of refuge found for him, or any dwelling *in heaven, and he was thrown down to the earth*. He either actually suffered this, or because he had been stripped of angelic and heavenly rank, he was brought down to an earthly frame of mind. (4) Then, as though taking vengeance on God because of his fall, as he could not injure God, he injures God's servants, human beings, and leads them astray and tries to get them to revolt from God, thinking that in this way he would injure the master himself" (113).

303 For a surprisingly succinct and perceptive assessment of διάβολος, see W. Foerster, *TDNT* 2:79–81. He concludes, "But in faith the community is in every respect freed from his power, so that even the blows of the angel of Satan (2 C. 12:7) and delivering to Satan (1 C. 5:5; 1 Tim. 1:20) are comprehended in the gracious operation of God" (80).

That eternal expression is an exhibit of the strength of God and of the kingdom of God. God's strength (*dunamis*) is mentioned followed by Christ's power (*exousia*). Both words are frequently rendered "power," but the former emphasizes the overwhelming irresistibility of the omnipotent God, while the latter focuses on the propriety of Christ's reign. The concept of kingdom has been the subject of frequent debate. Suffice it to say that for a kingdom to exist there must be both a king and a realm over which he rules. The point here is that the reign of God over all things has with the fall of Satan become more public and obvious.

The use of God (*theos*) here refers to the Father since He is distinguished from "His Christ." The power and the kingdom belong to the Father, but the authority to rule that kingdom is ceded to his anointed one (*christos*). This reign, according to 1 Cor 15:24, is apparently the millennial reign, at the conclusion of which Christ gives the kingdom to the Father. At least one expression of the kingdom is the reign of Christ on the millennial earth.

Contemporary pictures of the Devil tend to focus on his role as tempter, and certainly that activity, while serious, is no more devastating than his accusations against the brethren. Accusations (usually half-truths but sometimes untruths) are employed by Satan to discourage the saints and dissuade them from faith in the purposes and providences of God. The progress of the church is often more impeded by this than anything else Satan does. Thus, rejoicing is engendered by the announcement that this has been curtailed.

Verse 11 notes that "they overcame him." The antecedent of "they" is the brethren who are being accused in v. 10. The accusations prove ineffective because the brothers have what they need to overcome, or conquer, the accuser. The interesting weapon of choice in this conflict is the blood of the Lamb. They overcome Satan "by the blood of the Lamb and by the word of their testimony." Because the topic of redemption is frequently absent from most apocalyptic literature, especially redemption that comes by means of the blood of the Lamb, some suggest that Revelation does not strictly belong to the apocalyptic genre, although it certainly makes use of that mode. Here is superb testimony in the book of the Revelation that the atoning death of Christ on the cross is the only weapon sufficient to defeat Satan. However, that weapon must be appropriated, and so the author observes that they overcame Satan "by the blood of the Lamb"—the effective means of redemption—and by the word of their testimony (i.e., each of the brethren confessed Christ and his atonement alone as sufficient for his salvation). On the basis of Christ's work on the cross and their personal confession of that, the brethren overcome the accusations of Satan.

Objections to a substitutionary perspective on the atonement, especially when assigning salvific significance to the blood of Christ, are never difficult to find. Recent repudiations of the blood atonement see such a preposterous notion as substitutionary atonement as sanctioning violence.[304] But C. H. Dodd, the most famous critic of blood atonement in the modern era, has been thoroughly answered by Leon Morris and others.[305] The tie to Lev 17:11 ("For the life of a creature is in the blood, and I have given it to you to make atonement for yourselves on the altar") as well as to the whole sacrificial system of the Old Testament prefiguring the shedding of Christ's blood, is strongly attested.

The salutary effects of this are expressed not merely in the eternal, spiritual condition of the redeemed but also in the fact that the attitude of the brethren with regard to the possibility of martyrdom and of death is changed. There is no suggestion that a follower of Christ should seek death, but rather he should adhere to the providences of God. However, the threat of death is removed as Paul said, "O death, where is your sting? / O Hades, where is your victory?" (1 Cor 15:55). Therefore, death no longer is problematic for those who know the Lord of the resurrection.

Consequently, there is rejoicing in the heavens. All who dwell there join in the rejoicing. However, things are not so well back on the earth. In fact, John hears the voices from heaven announcing woe to the earth and the sea because "the devil has come down to you, having great wrath." The precise reason for this great fury is that the Devil is cognizant of the fact that he has only a short time. Not only is his time short, but in the Greek text the very use of the word *kairos* rather than *chronos*, as one might have expected, suggests that the matter is not simply that time is running short but that God has set a particular time for the final judgment of Satan.

12:13–17 In the closing verses of this chapter, an explanation is given both for the particular fury of Satan toward the Jews and also for his general fury toward all who follow Christ. In v. 13, when the dragon sees that he has been hurled to the earth and cannot have access or victory over the male child who has been born, he instead pursues the woman who gave birth. Few seem to reflect on the strange circumstance existing in the contemporary world and continuing,

---

304 For full discussion of these issues see P. Patterson, "The Work of Christ," in *A Theology for the Church*, ed. Daniel L. Akin (Nashville: B&H, 2007), 545–602. Recent objections to blood atonement include J. B. Green and M. D. Baker, *Recovering the Scandal of the Cross* (Downers Grove, IL: InterVarsity, 2001).

305 L. Morris, *The Apostolic Preaching of the Cross* (Grand Rapids: Eerdmans, 1965) and A. M. Stibbs, *The Meaning of the Word "Blood" in Scripture* (London: Tyndale Press, 1954).

in fact, for millennia. Jews today make up an infinitesimal portion of the world's population. The national and geographical entity called Israel is a small piece of real estate where to date few natural resources have been discovered. Water supply is always a problem; and unlike many of her neighbors, she does not appear to have extensive oil deposits or other wealth-bearing commodities. Doubtless the Dead Sea contains invaluable mineral deposits, but these have been notoriously difficult to extract; and other than rather large potash products, not that many assets are available to Israel in the land. Nevertheless, she is the object of almost worldwide opposition. Indeed, even the United States and certain other European countries, like Great Britain, who have attempted to be allies with Israel, have discovered that the general anti-Semitic hatred of Israel extends quickly to other nations who befriend her.

The interesting question to be raised from all this is why a piece of relatively unprofitable real estate and a small population of ethnic Jews, even if the worldwide Jewish population is counted, would generate such antagonism toward the Jewish people?[306] There is no conceivable explanation. Even if one posits atrocities rarely committed by Jews, all the other nations of the world are equally guilty and many of them more so. So it is impossible to provide a rational explanation for the almost universal practice of anti-Semitism. On the other hand, this chapter makes that understanding crystal clear. Satan, the ruler of this age, has put in the hearts of people to hate the Jews and therefore to pursue them. His ancient antipathy for God and for God's purposes in redemption flowers into hatred for every person or entity chosen of God for a role in that plan. Properly identifying the woman of chap. 12 as Israel is the hermeneutical move that renders the actions of Satan understandable in the chapter, in the Apocalypse, in the Bible, in all of history, and in the contemporary malaise. God chose Israel as the object of his love and the vehicle of his salvation. Consequently, Satan, unable to launch a successful assault on God, chose Israel as the object of his wrath.

However, in v. 14, the woman is given two wings as a great eagle so that she can fly away to a place prepared for her in the desert where she is protected out of the serpent's reach for a time, and times and half a time. How exactly this miraculous preservation takes place is not stated, nor is the precise location given. Across the years some Bible students have speculated that this safe

---

306 Although notoriously difficult to reckon, estimates suggest there are about thirteen million Jews worldwide with five million of those in Israel and five million in the United States.

harbor would be in the area of Petra where the Nabatean caravans crossed and some settled in what is now the southern part of Jordan, south of the Dead Sea. That may be a possibility, but all such conjecture is unsupportable on the basis of the text itself. The seer simply states that a remnant of the Jewish people will be protected for this forty-two-month period.[307]

Verse 15 declares every effort on the part of the serpent to overtake the woman. A torrent of water like a river is spewed out of his mouth that he might sweep her away, but the earth helps the woman and swallows the river that the dragon spewed out of his mouth. Efforts to interpret what precisely is meant by the river of water and the earth swallowing the river seem doomed in terms of precision, but the interpreter can certainly say that God has provided the means by which the woman is protected.

Understandably then, v. 17 provides the information that the dragon is enraged with the woman; and having been unable to defeat either the Messiah or the woman, he turns to make war on the rest of her offspring. The rest of her offspring are defined as those who obey God's commandments and maintain the testimony of Jesus. Is it proper to see the Christian faith as in some sense the offspring of Judaism? The answer to that question must be emphatically "yes." Again, the promise to Abraham was that "And in you all the families of the earth shall be blessed" (Gen 12:3). Jesus is a Jewish Messiah, and those who follow him are indebted to the Jewish people for being used of God in providing both the Messiah and the Messiah's salvation. Understandably then, the dragon seeks not only the demise of the woman but of all those who are the recipients of the goodness and mercy of God through her.

Unnoticed by many is the distinction in the final verse. The "offspring" of the woman and their identification as those who "have to the testimony of Jesus Christ," make it virtually certain that two separate groups are intended. The radiant woman, representing ethnic Israel is one object of Satan's fury. But the saints of the church—every follower of Jesus who bears his testimony—become the final object of satanic hatred. Since God remains beyond the reach

---

307 Ladd again avoids any literal association with ethnic Israel and inserts the church in Israel's place: "No historical equivalent is to be sought for the rescue of the woman. This is John's way of assuring the church of their ultimate safety, even in the face of martyrdom" (*Commentary on the Revelation of John*, 174). And again, "This continues the imaginative picture of Satan's effort to destroy God's people. We have no known parallels in ancient literature upon which John could have drawn his vivid pictures. Nor are we to seek historical counterparts. The message conveyed is simple and clear: Satan will do everything in his power to destroy God's people, but in vain" (174).

of Satan, the devil's wrath against God is transferred to the two objects still partially within his sphere; Israel and the church of Jesus the Christ.

B. The Beast out of the Sea (13:1–10)

Then I stood on the sand of the sea. And I saw a beast rising up out of the sea, having seven heads and ten horns, and on his horns ten crowns, and on his heads a blasphemous name. [2]Now the beast which I saw was like a leopard, his feet were like *the feet of* a bear, and his mouth like the mouth of a lion. The dragon gave him his power, his throne, and great authority. [3]And I saw one of his heads as if it had been mortally wounded, and his deadly wound was healed. And all the world marveled and followed the beast. [4]So they worshiped the dragon who gave authority to the beast; and they worshiped the beast, saying, "Who *is* like the beast? Who is able to make war with him?"

[5]And he was given a mouth speaking great things and blasphemies, and he was given authority to continue for forty-two months. [6]Then he opened his mouth in blasphemy against God, to blaspheme His name, His tabernacle and those who dwell in heaven. [7]It was granted to him to make war with the saints and to overcome them. And authority was given him over every tribe, tongue, and nation. [8]All who dwell on the earth will worship him, whose names have not been written in the Book of Life of the Lamb slain from the foundation of the world.

[9]If anyone has an ear, let him hear. [10]He who leads into captivity shall go into captivity; He who kills with the sword must be killed with the sword. Here is the patience and the faith of the saints.

Chapter 12 introduced the reader not only to the radiant woman but also to the dragon, whose opposition toward the Creator motivated his efforts to dispense with the radiant woman and her offspring. In 12:9 John's readers are left with no doubt about the identity of the dragon, who is plainly said to be the Devil/ Satan. The cosmic conflict of the ages, which apparently owes its origin to a period following the creation of the angelic orders but perhaps prior to the creation of the earth, is the subject of chaps. 12 and 13. Although Satan cannot be unaware of his forecast destiny, he nonetheless is focused on disrupting the work and worship of God to whatever extent possible. John's observation is that Satan's evil machinations intensify in anticipation of the arrival of the eschaton "because he knows that his time is short" (12:12). Chapter 13 engages the discussion of two means by which the dragon attempts to disrupt the work and worship of God and to inflict on his followers such hardship and sorrows as to cause them, if possible, to abandon allegiance to Christ or, at least in the case of unbelievers, to prevent their acquiescence to the gospel message.

The intrinsic potential of religion and the incurable spiritual nature of man has always been known and utilized by the powers of evil. The reader then will not be surprised to find an apparent effort to reduplicate the godhead as a part of the diabolical deception unveiled in chap. 13. Just as the Christian faith is a trinitarian faith, so there is something of a trinity of evil involving the dragon and the two beasts of chap. 13. In addition, a deathblow is given to one of these members, from which resuscitation is a miraculous mimicking of the work of the Second Person of the Trinity. Moreover, omens, signs, and wonders are given in order to astonish and deceive those who live on the earth. In this regard, the second beast seems to function in some ways like the Third Person of the Trinity. The two beasts of chap. 13, the first primarily political and the second more essentially religious, together mark the agenda for what appears to be the triumph of evil in the tribulation period—particularly the concluding forty-two months of that period.

13:1–10 The NIV begins verse 1, "The dragon stood on the shore of the sea," while the NKJV begins the verse, "Then I stood on the sand of the sea." With the NIV reading one would note that as chap. 12 concludes with the dragon enraged against the woman and pursuing her offspring, so he is pictured in v. 1 as standing expectantly on the shore of the sea. Some versions that follow the same textual reading as the NIV place the chapter division after 12:18, but logically the NIV is correct to make that last statement a part of 13:1 because the beast that will arise from the sea is intimately connected to the dragon. Indeed, he is summoned by the dragon, who waits expectantly for him to surface. For further information about the different renderings of the NKJV and NIV at this point, see the note below.[308]

In any event, the connection is that the dragon now unveils his efforts to frustrate the kingdom of Christ. John watches, doubtless with amazement, as a beast (*thērion*) comes out of the sea. The first beast is from the sea, and the second is from the land. Commentators through the centuries have speculated

---

308 Some manuscripts read ἐστάθην, or "I stood," leading the NKJV to translate the word as though the author John were standing. In a way this makes better sense in the flow and transition from chap. 12. But the manuscript evidence strongly supports the reading adopted by the NIV, ἐστάθη or "he stood." While this problem provides an interesting exegetical dilemma, as usual, no point of theology is in question. The appearance of the word *dragon* is not in any text and is imported by the NIV translators.

about the possible meanings of these two expressions. Generally, the seas often represent the teeming, chaotic movements of Gentile humanity, whereas reference to the land is not infrequently a reference to Israel.[309]

If these two beasts are to be identified with actual persons, as will be argued in the following section, then the interpretation of some that the first beast is of Gentile origin while the second is of Jewish origin certainly remains a possibility. Nevertheless, the beast that rises from the sea seems clearly to represent the emergence of an eschatological force of almost irresistible character. The description of the beast is heavily reminiscent of Daniel's fourth beast in Dan 7. In Daniel's vision, he watched the emergence from the sea of a lion-like beast (Babylonia), a bear (Medo-Persia), and a leopard (Graeco-Macedonian); and this is followed by a fourth beast altogether different from those that went before. This fourth beast, unlike the three previous ones, belongs yet to the future for Daniel's audience, and its suzerainty will far exceed that of the other three (Dan 7:7).

As John watches the emergence of a similar beast, he notes that the beast has ten horns, seven heads, and ten crowns on his horns. He further observes that each head has a blasphemous name, and then he notes characteristics not unlike Daniel's first three beasts. The beast in some ways resembled a leopard but had the feet of a bear and the devastating mouth of a lion. Such a formidable

---

309 Walvoord states, "The fact that the beast rises out of the sea is taken by many to indicate that he comes from the great mass of humanity, namely the Gentile powers of the world" (J. Walvoord, *The Revelation of Jesus Christ: A Commentary* [Chicago: Moody, 1966], 198). Beckwith adds the view that the vision, "though taken directly from Dan.7³, is doubtless ultimately derived from the earlier form of the myth of the beast as a sea-monster (a Leviathan); similarly the eagle-monster in 2 Es. 11 comes up from the sea. Since the figure as used by the Apocalyptist refers first of all to the Roman power, the coming from the sea would be especially appropriate in the view of one looking from the coast of Asia Minor across the Mediterranean, and most com. regard the language as chosen with that thought; but the representation is more probably purely traditional" (I. T. Beckwith, *The Apocalypse of John* [New York: Macmillan, 1919], 633). Beale concludes similarly, "This tradition may come into use here in the Apocalypse because people in Asia Minor thought of whatever came 'from the sea' as foreign and whatever came from the land as native. That is, one of the initial expressions of the first beast was Rome, whose governors repeatedly came by sea to Ephesus. Roman ships literally seemed to be rising out of the sea as they appeared on the horizon off the coast of Asia Minor. The second beast represented native political and economic authorities" (G. K. Beale, *The Book of Revelation: A Commentary on the Greek Text*, NIGTC [Grand Rapids: Eerdmans; Carlisle, UK: Paternoster Press, 1999], 682).

beast itself would seem to have sufficient power; but, as John is informed, the source of its power (*dunamis*) and authority (*exousia*) was bestowed on the beast by the dragon who stands behind him in the background. He is the source of all opposition to God and His kingdom. In addition, one of the heads of the beast received a fatal wound, but this had been somehow healed (*therapeuō*), and so the beast miraculously lived, suggesting a deliberate imitation of the Christ, though the wound, death, and resurrection prove real. The response of men is to worship the dragon because apparently, they recognized that no one would be able to oppose him successfully since he was the source of the beast's authority. The time of the particular exercise of his power was said to be forty-two months, and his reign was characterized by blasphemy against God. The only exceptions to those who worship the beast are those whose names have been written in the Book of Life, and they will either be taken into captivity or experience death or both. Such is the vision John experiences.

Assigning interpretation to all these details is a formidable task and, while essential, undoubtedly serves only to underscore the major point made in the preceding paragraphs regarding the difficulty of the chapter. Nevertheless, the interpreter gains understanding by assessing even these details. In v. 1, the beast is said to have seven heads, ten horns, and apparently ten crowns—one for each of the horns. Dan 7 helps with the interpretation of the ten horns. There Daniel is instructed that these ten horns represent ten kingdoms, which make up the power of the beast. This ten-kingdom coalition, which will manifest itself at the eschaton, is now also part of John's perspective. John does not see the uprooting of three of those horns by another little horn as Daniel did, but he does see the ten horns and notes that each of them carries a crown. Here the crown is the *diadēma*, which almost invariably refers to a kingly crown in contrast to the *stephanos* crown, which sometimes has regal implications but is more accurately seen as a victor's crown. Further evidence is therefore provided to see these as actual kingdoms.

Efforts, however, to identify these kingdoms have inevitably proven embarrassing to premillennial interpreters. During the years of the development of the European Common Market (now the European Union), some interpreters followed the line of thinking that with seven or eight participants and more surely to come, the ten kingdoms ultimately emerging as a part of the European Union would constitute the ten kingdoms mentioned here. Suddenly that movement boasted more than ten nations, and the futility of attaching national entities in the present milieu to these horns became evident. The book of Revelation gives no insight into the identity of these kingdoms, and such hypothesizing will not prove helpful. Given the geography and the sociopolitical realities of the world, a safe guess would be to imagine that the ten kingdoms encompass far more territory than just the European continent. Efforts, however, to identify the United States or any other such entity with this text are neither helpful nor warranted.

The nature and the purpose of this seven-headed, ten-horned beast are made apparent by the fact that each has ascribed to him a name of blasphemy. The Greek word *blasphēmeō*, the basic sense of which is "speak against," carries more than that basic understanding. "Blasphemy" includes ideas such as "despise," "taunt," "reproach," and even "curse." As White observes, "Blasphemy is one of the most serious of all spiritual iniquities in the Old Testament because it denies and makes sport of the overwhelming concept of all Old Testament history and law, namely, the sovereignty of the Creator. More than any other act of man, it eradicates the fundamental creator/creature distinction, upon which all the cosmic law orders are based."[310]

The concept of blasphemy is more than failure to believe in God and endorse his programs and ways; it is active repugnance and open opposition to the Creator God. Consequently, the motives and intentions of each of these ten kingdoms are explicitly noted.

Successfully identifying the seven heads is dependent to some degree on the consideration of 17:9–11. The scarlet woman rides on this beast from the sea and the seven heads are specifically stated to be seven kings ruling over seven kingdoms. The apparent identification of these seven heads associates them with the seven great kingdoms of world history: Egypt, Assyria, Babylon, Medo-Persia, Greece, Rome, and the final empire of the last days. Some interpreters have concluded that the head ruined to the point of its death but then living again is a reference to the Nero *redivivus* myth that was common in the late first century.[311] However, the death of Nero did not bring about the end of the empire, and one is forced to conclude that the wounded head was the sixth and greatest of the empires, namely, Rome. Like all the other empires, it eventually expired; but in the case of Rome, all evidence in chaps. 13 and 17 points to a resuscitation of that empire in the last days. Why the Roman Empire should be singled out among all

---

310 W. White, "Blasphemy," in *The Zondervan Pictorial Encyclopedia of the Bible* (Grand Rapids: Zondervan, 1975), 1:624.

311 For a discussion of how the early Christians developed the idea of Nero *redivivus*, see R. Summers, *Worthy Is the Lamb: Interpreting the Book of Revelation in Its Historical Background* (Nashville: B&H, 1951), 173–77. See also C. H. Talbert, *The Apocalypse: A Reading of the Revelation of John* (Louisville, KY: Westminster John Knox, 1994), 51–53.

the others for reconstitution in the end times probably has to do with its being the empire faced by the church and the power under which it had to operate.[312]

13:3–4 Because of the wound to the beast, which had been clearly fatal and yet was now healed, the whole world is astonished and follows the beast. However, even though they are amazed at the beast, clearly men intuitively know that the beast embodies something more than what is natural (v. 4). Therefore, they worship the dragon because he had given authority to the

---

312 Gaebelein notes, "The beast which John sees rising out of the sea is the Roman empire. This Daniel saw as a great nondescript, a dreadful beast with iron teeth and with ten horns. And John also sees this beast having ten horns with crowns and seven heads and these heads had names of blasphemy. Daniel had seen Babylonia, Medo-Persia and Greco-Macedonia under the emblem of the lion, the bear and the leopard. John sees this beast here like a leopard, with bear's feet and lion's mouth. This revived Roman empire is an amalgamation of parts of the previous world empires. The preceding ones are absorbed by the last, the Roman empire. Therefore the revived Roman empire will contain the different elements in one great monster. This Roman empire will be revived in the first part of the final seven years. We saw this under the first seal. Here is the beginning of the forty-two months the Dragon gives to him his power, and his throne and great authority. It becomes now fully possessed by Satan. The ten horns are the ten kingdoms which will exist in that empire. We are told later that these ten kings 'have one mind and shall give their power and strength unto the beast' (xvii:13). In the same chapter the beast is also seen coming out of the abyss (xvii:8) denoting its Satanic origin. The heads resent the seven forms of government which have characterized the empire in the past, the seventh becomes the eighth. One of the heads is especially mentioned; later we read 'he is the eighth, and is of the seven, and goeth into perdition' (xvii:11). It was as it were wounded to death, and his deadly wound was healed, and all the world wondered after the beast. This head denotes the imperial form of government, which had died, and now is revived in the person of the leader, the Prince of Daniel ix:27, the little horn, which Daniel saw in the midst of the ten horns. This will be Satan's man, one of his masterpieces. The whole earth will wonder after that beast and its Satan possessed head" (A. C. Gaebelein, *The Revelation: An Analysis and Exposition of the Last Book of the Bible* [New York: Publication Office "One Hope," 1915], 78–80). Scott's handling of the passage is similar: "This Beast is without doubt the ancient Roman empire reappearing upon the prophetic scene. It arose in a similar way to the three preceding empires. 'Four great beasts came up from the sea' (Dan. 7.3); that is, out of the unsettled, restless masses of mankind. The four universal empires, Babylon, Persia, Greece, and Rome are represented both as metals (Dan. 2) and beasts (chap. 7), and not only in the rise and initial stages of their history but at the end they are there when the Lord comes. The first three powers, shorn of their strength, are at the end merely existing, but the fourth (the Roman) will be, as in the past, the dominant power on earth. Rome originally rose out of the throes of revolution and anarchy" (W. Scott, *Exposition of the Revelation of Jesus Christ*, 4th ed. [Westwood, NJ: Revell, 1968], 269).

beast, so both the beast and the dragon become the object of worship in the last day, a worship conditioned doubtless more by fear than by faithfulness.

13:5-10 Forty-two months are allotted for the beast to utter his words of blasphemy and to exercise authority. Forty-two months (1,260 days, or times and time and half a time) is equal to three and one-half years or one-half of the tribulation period. Since the judgments seem to intensify from the opening of the seals to the sounding of the trumpets and finally to the sounding of the seven thunders and the outpouring of God's bowls of wrath, apparently the forty-two months are the last forty-two months of the tribulation period. The blasphemy uttered by the beast is not only against the person of God, but even God's dwelling place in heaven and those who are associated with Him in that presence. As for the saints who remain on earth, the text says, "It was granted to him to make war with the saints and to overcome them." The question of who provided this authority begs an answer. Some commentators have said that the dragon, or the Devil, stands behind him, while others have pointed to the fact that ultimately God wields all authority, and hence God provides this authority. The case is probably similar to what is seemingly a contradiction occurring in 2 Sam 24:1 and 1 Chr 21:1, in which this second text says that Satan stirred up David to number Israel while the first text affirms that God did it. To imagine a contradiction of the two is certainly possible, but faithful interpreters through the years have merely pointed out that it is entirely possible for both to be true. Ultimately, God is not the author of evil. He neither tempts nor can he be tempted (Jas 1:13). On the other hand, as Luther once observed, "The devil is 'God's devil.'" By that, the Reformer was merely taking note of the fact that ultimately whatever Satan does, while not caused by God, is allowed by God for the ultimate outworking of his own purposes. Doubtless, in this passage the dragon lies behind the power to make war against the saints and to conquer them, but God in his wisdom allows it for the moment. The extent of the authority is said to be over every tribe, people, tongue, and nation. Thus, whatever method of assessing people groups, the text affirms that all are there. If tribalism is in view, then every tribe is subject to his suzerainty. If ethnicity or people groups are in view, none can escape. If we assess people on the basis of language or national allegiance, the answer is the same. All the inhabitants of the earth end up worshiping the beast, including all those whose names have not been written in the Lamb's Book of Life. Here the concept of the Lamb's Book of Life and of the Lamb who was slain from the casting down of the ages is introduced.[313]

---

313 J. R. Yeatts notes two possible understandings of the word order. "The pas-

Several observations are important. First, the presence of one's name in this Book of Life is the one factor that provides an exemption from the expression, "All who dwell on the earth will worship him." Clearly there are exceptions to this statement, and they consist of only one category—those whose names are recorded in the Book of Life.[314] The second observation is that there

---

sage can be read in one of two ways. First, it may mean the names were written in the book of life before the foundation of the world, which would lend credence to the argument that the passage is a statement of predestination (Eph. 1:4; see Beale, 1999: 702–3). Second, the sense may be that the Lamb was slaughtered from the foundation of the world, a common idea in the biblical tradition (Acts 2:23; 1 Pet. 1:18–21; 1 Enoch 62; Test. Moses 1:14) that seems to have been accepted by Menno Simons (1956:109) and other sixteenth-century Anabaptists (van Braght, 1950:470, 1033). To paraphrase the words of Barclay, redemption is older than creation (1960:2.125; see also Matt. 25:34). The word order of the passage clearly favors the latter interpretation" (*Revelation*, Believers Church Bible Commentary [Scottdale, PA: Herald Press, 2003], 245). H. B. Swete shares this perspective, noting, "The reference of ἀπὸ καταβολῆς κόσμου is somewhat ambiguous; the order suggests that the words should be taken with τοῦ ἐσφαγμένου, in the sense indicated by I Pet. i. 8f." (*Commentary on Revelation* [Grand Rapids: Kregel, 1977], 167). H. Alford arrives at the same conclusion saying that "these last words are ambiguously placed. They may belong either to γέγραπται, or to ἐσφαγμένου. The former connexion is taken by Hammond, Bengel, Heinr., Ewald, Züllig, De Wette, Hengstb., Düsterd. But the other is far more obvious and natural: and had it not been for the apparent difficulty of the sense thus conveyed, the going so far back as to γέγραπται for a connexion would never have been thought of. See this remarkably shewn in the Catena: ὧν γέγραπται, ἀπὸ καταβολῆς κόσμου γέγραπται· οὕτω γὰρ δεῖ νοεῖν, οὐχ ὡς ἡ γραφὴ ἔχει· ὅτι μηδὲ ἀπὸ καταβολῆς κόσμου ἡ τοῦ ἀρνίου σφαγή. The difficulty however is but apparent: 1 Pet. i. 19, 20 says more fully the same thing. That death of Christ, which was foreordained from the foundation of the world, is said to have *taken place* in the counsels of Him with whom the end and the beginning are one" (*The Greek Testament* [Chicago: Moody, 1958], 4:677–78).

314 G. R. Osborne explains that "these are the true people of God. Moreover, this is the *Lamb's* book of life. It was the 'blood of the Lamb' that won the victory over the dragon for the saints (12:11), and this is the major title in the book for Christ, occurring twenty-eight times. The phrase τοῦ ἀρνίου τοῦ ἐσφαγμένου (*tou arniou tou esphagmenou, the Lamb that was slain*) is taken from the first appearance of the title in 5:6, which stressed the great victory of the Lamb and his worthiness to open the seals. The cross made the book of life possible, for it was the slain Lamb that became the sacrifice for sin and enabled the people of God to have 'life'" (*Revelation*, BECNT [Grand Rapids: Baker Academic, 2002], 503). The Venerable Bede observes that "they who serve the author of death should not be written in the book of life, and that they who are deluded by the fictitious death of the beast, should be without the fellowship of 'the Lamb, Who has

is an interesting contrast. Those whose names are written in this book are in a Book of Life, and yet clearly in vv. 9–10 as well as throughout the Apocalypse, many of those whose names are in fact inscribed in that book will die a martyr's death. But this fact only underscores what the Scriptures teach—namely, that the life of this earth is transitory and unpredictable, but God's children will someday experience a life that is bound by neither the transitory nor the unpredictable. And this life is the only life whose possession ultimately matters.

A third observation is that in a definite way, those whose names are written in this Book of Life are related to the Lamb, for it is the Lamb's Book of Life. Rev 5:6 introduces this Lamb, and from the outset the text is clear: He had been slain and yet was alive. However, that His death was no mere coincidence is confirmed by the text that he was slain from the casting down of the cosmos (*apo kataboles kosmou*). The presence of those names written in the Book of Life is related then to the Lamb, whose program of death and resurrection in behalf of the objects of His love was known before the actual creation of the world. The text then confirms a plan and a purpose of God in all these things.

The seer's usual admonition, to which the reader was conditioned in chaps. 2 and 3, is invoked in 13:9: "If anyone has an ear, let him hear." Verse 10, however, is less certain as to its meaning. Some have argued that the reference is intended to encourage the saints by assuring them that those who take them captive will themselves go into captivity and ultimately be killed with the sword. This general truth was articulated by Jesus, who said, "All who take the sword will perish by the sword" (Matt 26:52). The better understanding here, however, seems to embody an effort to prepare the saints of the tribulation period for submitting to the providence of God in the two fates awaiting many. Some will be taken into captivity and others are to be killed with the sword, regardless of the effort they may make to present the justice of their respective cases.[315] In the light of these inevitabilities, the saints must prepare themselves to exercise patient endurance and faithfulness to God regardless of these circumstances. Patience (*hupomone*)

---

taken away the sins of the world'" (*The Explanation of the Apocalypse*, trans. E. Marshall [Oxford: James Parker and Company, 1878], 18).

315 Textual variants in 13:10 cause Metzger to choose a reading that lacks the best attestation. Rejecting p47, ℵ, C, P, and others, Metzger concludes, "The epigrammatic style of the saying has perplexed the scribes. The reading εἰς αἰχμαλωσίαν, εἰς αἰχμαλωσίαν ὑπάγει (A vg Ps-Ambrose) best accounts for the origin of the others. The absence of one of the two instances of εἰς αἰχμαλωσίαν, although rather widespread (p47 ℵ C P 046 1006 1611 2053 *al*), appears to be the result of accidental oversight in transcription" (B. Metzger, *A Textual Commentary on the Greek New Testament* [*TCGNT*] [New York: UBS, 1971], 749).

is derived from the word "remain" (*menō*), coupled with the preposition "under" (*hupo*), picturing a man bearing an indescribably heavy load and yet making no effort to divest himself of its burden.[316] Faith is actually a translation of the Greek word *pistis*. In any age the two things essential for Christ's followers in persecution, and even martyrdom, are endurance coupled with faith. Faith in the purposes and promises of God makes endurance possible. Endurance, on the other hand, is the sure, visible outworking of the inner faith that provides the impetus for obedience to God even under intractable circumstances.

C. The Beast Out of the Land (13:11–18)

[11]**Then I saw another beast coming up out of the earth, and he had two horns like a lamb and spoke like a dragon. [12]And he exercises all the authority of the first beast in his presence, and causes the earth and those who dwell in it to worship the first beast, whose deadly wound was healed. [13]He performs great signs, so that he even makes fire come down from heaven on the earth in the sight of men. [14]And he deceives those who dwell on the earth by those signs which he was granted to do in the sight of the beast, telling those who dwell on the earth to make an image to the beast who was wounded by the sword and lived. [15]He was granted *power* to give breath to the image of the beast, that the image of the beast should both speak and cause as many as would not worship the image of the beast to be killed. [16]He causes all, both small and great, rich and poor, free and slave, to receive a mark on their right hand or on their foreheads, [17]and that no one may buy or sell except one who has the mark or the name of the beast, or the number of his name.**

[18]**Here is wisdom. Let him who has understanding calculate the number of the beast, for it is the number of a man: His number *is* 666.**

The second beast John now observes arises out of the earth, not out of the sea. This beast, while much more appealing to the eyes, is ultimately just as evil as

---

316 In a commentary written from the perspective of the "Believers Church," Yeatts adds, "As has been noted before, the word for endurance (*hypomonē*) is not a passive bearing of persecution, but its courageous acceptance and transformation into victory. Yet the saints are called to faithful endurance rather than to vengeance. Jesus showed how to accept peacefully and without retaliation the persecution that inevitably follows the decision to choose the Lamb (John 18:11). So God's faithful are called to accept tribulation without violent resistance because justice for their persecutors will be enacted by God" (*Revelation*, 246).

the dragon and the first beast.[317] In fact, in some ways, this beast may be more devastating because clearly his purpose is to deceive, and everything about him from his appearance to his actions is designed to provoke religious deceit.[318]

The beast out of the earth has been thought by some to be of Jewish ethnic origin. This is thought to be the case because he rises out of the earth rather than out of the seas, which are often pictured as the raging Gentile na-

---

317 Oecumenius explains that this beast is the Antichrist: "After many digressions and after reverting from these starting points to previous beginnings, he came to the serious business. This was to explain to us the facts about the impious and abominable Antichrist. So it is he who is now brought into the forefront; see what he says about him: . . . *Then I saw another beast rising up from the earth*, from where all human beings have their origin. For the Antichrist is a human being, 'whose advent occurs by the action of the Devil,' as Paul in his great wisdom believes. . . . *It had two horns like a lamb, and it spoke like a serpent.* He rightly said not that it had the horns of a lamb, but *like those of a lamb*, and he did not say that it was a serpent, but that it spoke like a serpent. Since the wretch pretends to be the Christ (though he is not), he has given him *horns like those of a lamb.* And although he tells of all kinds of profanity like the Devil (but he is not the Devil), he did not say that he was a serpent but that he spoke like a serpent. This being so, the account retained the image in the vision, and attributes to him the form not of a lamb, but like a lamb, nor of a serpent, but like a serpent. For Christ is said to be a lamb, and the Devil is said to be a serpent, but he was neither the one nor the other" (*Commentary on the Apocalypse*, trans. J. N. Sugget, FC 112 [Washington, DC: Catholic University of America Press, 2006], 123).

318 G. E. Ladd notes, "He is a parody of Christ—religion prostituted for evil ends. The second beast had the appearance of a lamb, but his voice belied his appearance: he spoke like a dragon. That the second beast represents religion employed in support of the worship of the beast is seen from the fact that hereafter he is called the false prophet (16:13; 19:20; 20:10). The first beast represents civil power, satanically inspired; the second beast represents religious power employed to support civil power" (*Commentary on the Revelation of John* [Grand Rapids: Eerdmans, 1972], 183). R. H. Mounce says similarly, "This priestly role identifies the second beast as a religious power. In John's day the reference would be either to the local priests of the imperial cult or to the provincial council responsible for enforcing emperor worship throughout Asia. In the final days of Antichrist the false prophet stands for the role of false religion in effecting the capitulation of mankind to the worship of secular power. It is the universal victory of humanism" (*The Book of Revelation*, NICNT [Grand Rapids: Eerdmans, 1977], 259). J. Walvoord suggests, "The identification of the second beast as the head of the apostate church is indicated in many ways in the book of Revelation. It is obvious that he is associated with the first beast in a religious way in that his miracles and activities tend to cause men to worship the image of the first beast (cf. 13:13–17). It is also clear that he shares prominence and leadership with the first beast throughout the great tribulation as they both are cast alive into the lake of fire at its close (19:20)" (*The Revelation of Jesus Christ: A Commentary* [Chicago: Moody, 1966], 205).

tions. However, this speculation is impossible to establish. Whoever he is and from wherever he comes, the text is lucid that he is not what he seems to be. On the one hand, he has two horns like a lamb; but when he speaks, his speech betrays him, and he sounds like a dragon. This beast exercises the authority of the first beast as a mediator to the people and is specifically involved in causing the earth and its inhabitants to worship the first beast, whose fatal wound had been healed. In order to achieve this feat, he is able to perform great miracles and signs—even to the extent of causing fire to come down from heaven to the earth in the full view of men. Of the three major words employed to describe miracles in the New Testament, the word *sēmeia* is the word most often employed by John in his writings. This word more than any of the others has the indication of purpose associated with it. In other words, a miracle happens in order to achieve a particular response or understanding. Fire falling from heaven, on the other hand, is a relatively frequent occurrence in the biblical narrative and is almost always associated with an act of God's judgment (Gen 19:24; Lev 10:2; Num 11:1; 1 Kgs 18:38; Rev 20:9).

The ability to employ these signs and wonders is stated for the purpose of deceiving those who live on the earth. Observation of religious life, even in the era of the church, is sufficient to establish the believability of this text.[319] Paul observed that it was the natural tendency of people to desire the spectacular in religious expression. Paul noted that the Jews seek a sign and the Greeks called for wisdom (1 Cor 1:22). Jesus observed, "An evil . . . generation seeks after a sign" (Matt 12:39). Again, the Master warned in Matt 24:24 that the "false christs and false prophet" of the last days would perform great signs and miracles to deceive even the elect of God, if it were possible. That which Jesus anticipated now unfolds to a degree never before duplicated. Those who are without discernment will conclude without reservation that fire dropping from heaven to earth is bound to be the act of God, and therefore the vast majority of the inhabitants on earth are deceived.[320]

The next act is full-fledged idolatry. The false prophet orders that those dwelling on the earth make "an image to the beast, who was wounded by the sword and lives." Whether ventriloquism or some other methodology is em-

---

319 See Pastoral Excursus at the end of this chapter.

320 G. R. Beasley-Murray provocatively suggests, "But whereas the Lamb of God is and speaks the Word of God (19:13, and chs. 2–3), the beast from the land is the 'Lamb' of Satan, and it is and speaks the word of Satan. It looks *like a lamb*, but its speech betrays its origin" (*The Book of Revelation*, NCBC [Grand Rapids: Eerdmans, 1981], 216).

ployed, the image seems to take on life and speak and even mandate death for all who refuse to worship the image. In addition to that, economic measures are taken, mandating that everyone receive a mark on his right hand or on his forehead. The word "mark" is a translation of the Greek word *charagma*, which appears infrequently in the New Testament. It is used by the apostle Paul in Acts 17:29 where he remonstrates with the Athenians about the possibility of an "image" (*charagma*) made by man's design and skill being in any way like the divine. The origin of the word can mean anything from the telltale sign of the snake's bite to a brand or an etching. Since the word is not explained in the text, almost infinite interpretations have resulted. Some have to do with the particular kinds of marks that might be placed on people even to the imbedding of computer chips that would read the identity of individuals.[321] The point to be made is that the text nowhere says what the mark will be. All suggestions offered show the variety of possibilities, but based on the text its exact identity cannot be made. In whatever form, its purpose is to restrict economic exchange for those who do not invoke "the name of the beast" or "the number of his name."

This final expression, "the number of his name," gives rise to the concluding verse of the paragraph. Here is wisdom. Let him who has understanding calculate the number of the beast, for it is the number of a man; His number is 666.[322] Here the text makes clear that this second beast is indeed one human being. But just as six falls short of the ideal number "seven," this false prophet who deceives the whole earth in this way is hopelessly compromised; and the repetition of the "six" in its trifold form 666 is clearly intended to underscore the intrinsic evil bound up in this individual. At this point some of the saints are killed, others taken into captivity, and all the earth is forced into an economic circumstance allowing only those faithfully serving the purposes of the beast to enact trade. Thus, the pressure and tribulation descending on the

---

321 For a popular, sermonic illustration of this, see A. Rogers, *Unveiling the End Times in Our Time: The Triumph of the Lamb in Revelation* (Nashville: B&H, 2004), 168-70. For example, speaking of the VeriChip, Rogers says, "An instrument smaller than an insulin syringe will inject it under your skin. You won't need a watch or a credit card. *You will be the card*" (170).

322 The *Oxford English Dictionary* defines "gematria" as "a cabbalistic method of interpreting the Hebrew Scriptures by interchanging words whose letters have the same numerical value when added" ("Gematria," *OED*, 6:424). In the case of the final verse of chapter 13, some interpreters have sought through numerical values of letters to discover the precise figure intended in the 666 designation. For a discussion of how this is attempted, see Yeatts, *Revelation*, 249-53.

saints afflicts them in every conceivable way. The unholy trinity of the dragon, the political beast, and the false prophet are now fully revealed to John and through him to his readers.

Pastoral Excursus

That Jesus and the apostles employed "signs and wonders" in the authentication of the primitive introduction of the age of the gospel is the clear testimony of Scripture (Acts 5:12; 14:3; 2 Cor 12:12). Nor is the Old Testament lacking in God's miraculous intervention (Deut 6:22). Yet Jesus and Paul warn about "signs and wonders," and John appears to present them here as the vehicle of deceit in the eschaton. How then is the disciple of Christ to respond to this apparently contradictory evidence (Matt 16:4; 1 Cor 1:22)?

Some, in the spirit of the Enlightenment, handle the issue by debunking the miraculous both then and now as impossible, the mythological trappings of ancient religious superstition. Hence, Bultmann and others attempted to strain the mythological elements from the texts in order to discover the didactically helpful spiritual nuggets.

On the other hand, fortunes have been made and thousands deceived in almost every era by "evangelists" who pander to the gullible and desperate with assurances that they have been granted apostolic powers for the working of "signs and wonders." One noted missionary affirmed to this author that he saw a man whose leg was engulfed in cancer healed. He cited another case of a girl in India who died, came back to life to urge people to see the Jesus film, and then died again a few days later. Ironically, the missionary failed to get the names of these people, the names of any witnesses, or even the precise location of these remarkable events. Not only was there no verification; there was also no evidence.

How is an evangelical disciple of Jesus to read all this? First, never under any circumstances doubt the power of God to do anything that is not inconsistent with His own nature. Second, there is no reason to question the accounts of the miraculous in Scripture. These events seldom occurred in isolation and were witnessed by many. The resurrected Jesus was observed by more than 500 who knew about His death (1 Cor 15:6).

Third, with the lone exception of the resurrection of Jesus, the sign pointed to something more important that lay beyond the miracle. Each testified to the mercy, power, authority, wisdom, control, or judgment of Almighty God. This is why they are called "signs." They signal the attributes and person of God.

Fourth, "signs," unlike the significance of that which is "signed," are easily imitated by those with less than noble intentions. Jannes and Jambres were able to duplicate the miracle of Moses, casting down their rods and making them become Egyptian cobras with the sole apparent difference being that Moses' rod proved to be hungrier, ingesting the other snakes (Exod 7:8–12; 2 Tim 3:8)! But the magicians of Egypt lacked the character of Moses, to say nothing of God, and they were not in pursuit of Moses' holy mission.

Finally, susceptibility of "signs and wonders" to satanic appropriation and deceit, together with ample scriptural warnings, should render churches and Christians cautious of the motives and intentions of men but never skeptical of the power and purposes of God. What happens in Rev 13 is powerful and persuasive deceit. Jesus says that even the elect are in danger of being deceived. To avoid such deceit, the following are essential:

1. Focus on Christ and his incarnation, atonement, and teaching.

2. Always determine the doctrinal positions of "miracle workers." If they are in violation of Scripture at any point, reject them.

3. Be especially alert to "signs and wonders" that hinge on or involve the exchange of money or goods (2 Kgs 5:1–27; Acts 3:6).

4. Remember that regeneration, conversion to Christ, or the new birth is always the greatest miracle and the sure manifestation of the power of God.

5. When uncertain, always seek discernment from the biblical text and from the guidance of the Holy Spirit.

6. Remember that the Scriptures teach that deceit and false miracles will increase as the world moves toward the eschaton.

D. The 144,000 in Heaven (14:1–5)

[1]Then I looked, and behold, a Lamb standing on Mount Zion, and with Him one hundred *and* forty-four thousand, having His Father's name written on their foreheads. [2]And I heard a voice from heaven, like the voice of many waters, and like the voice of loud thunder. And I heard the sound of harpists playing their harps. [3]They sang as it were a new song before the throne, before the four living creatures, and the elders; and no one could learn that song except the hundred *and* forty-four thousand who were redeemed from the earth. [4]These are the ones who were not defiled with women, for they are virgins. These are the ones who follow the Lamb wherever He goes. These were redeemed from *among* men, *being* firstfruits to God and to the Lamb. [5]And in their mouth was found no deceit, for they are without fault before the throne of God.

Having fully identified malignant forces of evil in chaps. 12 and 13 as the dragon, the beast from the sea, and the beast from the land, John turns in chap. 14 to a discussion of God's response to this diabolical attack. First, the intervention of God in the lives of His people is demonstrated in the reappearance of the 144,000 who were first introduced to the reader in chap. 7. Then the seer moves to the response of the living God in terms of the judgment of God on all those who by their own willful act have become the pawns of the malignant trinity. Interpreters who have argued that a futurist reading of the Apocalypse is of no comfort to Christians enduring persecution in the latter decade of the first century point to the future judgments of God as evidence that little comfort could have been derived in behalf of suffering first-century Christians. However, even those who see the book in preteristic or historical terms have to admit that the judgments in this chapter appear to be eschatological in nature. Far from failing to comfort, they do provide the promise of God's ultimate hand of justice and his hand of providence in history, thus encouraging Christians in any era of persecution. The first-century readers would no doubt be fortified by the pictures of providence and justice unveiled in chap. 14.

14:1-5   Some interpreters have supposed that the 144,000 of chap. 14 is a different group than the 144,000 of chap. 7.[323] This conclusion, however, seems

---

323 Oecumenius, for example, has the view that Israel will be regathered; but since the 144,000 listed here are celibate and since celibacy was only characteristic of Gentile Christianity, these must represent both Jews and Gentiles, a mixed company with the majority made up of the latter (*Commentary on the Apocalypse*, 127). No explanation is ventured for their similarity to the 144,000 who appear earlier. Scott has the un-

ultimately unlikely. To the contrary, much greater information about these 144,000 is now provided. In chap. 7, the reader observes them as 12,000 from each of the twelve tribes of Israel and is informed that they received the seal of God on their foreheads. The seal, which is normally a mark of ownership, is also generally an indication of protection, though in some cases the sealing might be for judgment. In this case almost certainly protection is in view. In 7:9 and following, information is provided concerning those who are martyred for the cause of Christ, but this seems to be distinct from the 144,000 who are sealed for their protection. These 144,000, including 12,000 from each of the twelve tribes of Israel, have a particular function via the tribulation period, which now is the focus of chap. 14.

As revealed in chap. 7, their Father's name is written on their foreheads, indicating that they are especially chosen of God for their task. Furthermore, in v. 1, they are standing on Mount Zion. There are basically three possibilities for an understanding of this geographical setting. The first understanding is that of the allegorists, who would take this as having a spiritual meaning and therefore another referent to the fact that they belong to God.[324] The second theory understands this Mount Zion to be a heavenly "Mount Zion," the counterpart of the earthly one—only relieved of all the inadequacies associated with the earthly Mount Zion.[325] The third view, most often held by futurists, is that Mount Zion is actually that portion of the holy city, Jerusalem, which is referenced as Mount Zion. One is not surprised to find these Jews active in the city of Jerusalem. The time once again is the period of the great tribulation, and no specific time is given within that general designation. The fact that John sees

usual interpretation that these 144,000 are all of the tribe of Judah (W. Scott, *Exposition of the Revelation of Jesus Christ*, 4th ed. [Westwood, NJ: Revell, 1968], 291).

324 This is the essential view of G. K. Beale, who notes that, "against this OT and Jewish background, 'Mount Zion' in Rev. 14:1 is to be seen as the end-time city where God dwells with and provides security for the remnant, the '144,000 who have been bought out from the earth.' Possibly this is a symbol of Christ's presence with his people on earth throughout history (cf. 3:12)." And again, "Accordingly, Zion could be the ideal, heavenly city to which saints aspire during the course of the church age (Gal. 4:25–27; Heb. 12:22–23). Therefore, deceased, glorified saints who have attained standing in that city may be in view here. This is supported by the fact that all the other references to the Lamb place him in heaven (in 7:9–14, with the redeemed multitudes). Furthermore, when Christ is associated with his people on earth elsewhere in the Apocalypse, it is only through his prophetic word" (*The Book of Revelation: A Commentary on the Greek Text*, NIGTC [Grand Rapids: Eerdmans; Carlisle, UK: Paternoster Press, 1999], 732).

325 See H. B. Swete, *Commentary on Revelation* (Grand Rapids: Kregel, 1977), 177.

them on Mount Zion has more to do with the identity than it does with permanent residence or with their labor. To pursue their task, they would almost certainly have had to move afield from Mount Zion, but they are here identified as standing on Mount Zion.

Verse 2 is interesting not only due to the phenomenon recorded but also because the distinction between heaven and earth is blurred in this passage, and John sees the totality of reality at once. The 144,000 are standing on Mount Zion sealed with God's name on their foreheads and are therefore protected by him as heaven "strikes up the band" in recognition of their assignment. The sound that John hears from heaven is like that of the roar of rushing waters. On several occasions I have had the opportunity to stand at the foot of Iguaçu Falls where Brazil, Paraguay, and Argentina come together and also at Victoria Falls where Zambia and Zimbabwe meet. The deafening roar of the sound of those rushing waters precludes any communication that is less than a shout. This is exactly like the sound John hears from heaven. Grasping for words to describe what he hears, the apostle says it was like a peel of thunder. In the midst of this, he begins to hear what sounded like harpists playing their harps. Under normal circumstances one hears only a single harp or maybe two and that usually in the presence of a whole orchestra. The soothing music of a harp is in some contrast to the sound of the rushing waters or the peal of thunder, but out of all the cacophony of sound comes the harmonious and comforting notes of the harp. In a significant way John is being prepared for the twin messages of providence and justice about to unfold. On the one hand, God's justice and judgment are overwhelming; but on the other hand, His providences, as well as His justice, are like the soothing and comforting tones of a choir of harps.

In v. 3, "They sang as it were a new song before the throne, and before the four living creatures, and the elders; and no one could learn that song except the hundred *and* forty-four thousand who were redeemed from the earth." The pronoun "they" raises a question about the actual singers. Was the song being sung in heaven and being taught to the 144,000 who were redeemed from the earth, or are the 144,000 singing it? The matter can be argued either way, but apparently the 144,000 are the antecedent for "they," and the 144,000 are singing this new song. This song was unique to the 144,000; no one else was able to learn the song. The strange limitation seems not to be a limitation of ability but rather of appropriateness. Their unique assignment from God is such that only they appropriately employ the lyrics of this beautiful song. Although they are on Mount Zion, the closeness of the throne, the four living creatures, and the twenty-four elders are noted so that they hear the intonation of the anthem. In chap. 7, doubtless that 144,000 should not be identified as angels but rather as humans in that they are said to be Jews, each one belonging to one of the twelve tribes of Israel. That now becomes even more explicit in that they are specifically identified as the object of redemption. These 144,000 have been redeemed from the earth.[326]

Additional information is provided about these remarkable men in vv. 4–5. This information provided about these 144,000 redeemed from the earth includes the fact that (1) they have not defiled themselves with women; (2) they were purchased from among men and offered as first fruits to God and to the Lamb; (3) they are notable for their truthfulness and for their general blamelessness. The evident peculiarities in these verses focus on the fact that they are said to be "virgins," and they are offered as firstfruits to God and to the Lamb. The Greek word *parthenos* most often refers to a mature, young woman who has not yet been intimately involved with a man. However, there are cases where the word *parthenos* has an expanded use, which may extend to men. This possibility leads to two conceivable understandings. Some have argued that this passage should be taken in a spiritual manner, simply referencing the fact that these 144,000 are pure in their general spiritual virginity.[327] Against this inter-

---

326 Origen, however, thinks they are not simply Jews: "But also, if those 'from the tribes' are the same as the virgins, as we showed previously, and a believer from Israel according to the flesh is rare, so that one might perhaps dare to say that the number of the 144,000 is not filled up with believers from Israel according to the flesh, it is clear that the 144,000 is composed of those gentiles who come to the divine Word, who are not defiled with women. Consequently, he who declares that the virgins of each tribe are its firstfruits would not be wrong" (*Commentary on the Gospel According to John: Books 1–10*, trans. R. E. Heine, FC 80 [Washington, DC: Catholic University of America Press, 1989], 32). Cyprian thought that women might be in doubt. "Again, also by this word of the angel the gift of continency is set forth, and virginity is preached: 'These are they which have not defiled themselves with women, for they have remained virgins; these are they which follow the Lamb withersoever He goeth.' For not only thus does the Lord promise the grace of continency to men, and pass over women; but since the woman is a portion of the man, and is taken and formed from him, God in Scripture almost always speaks to the Protoplast, the first formed, because they are two in one flesh, and in the male is at the same time signified the woman also" (*The Treatises of Cyprian*, Treatise 2: "On the Dress of Virgins" 4, *ANF* 5:431).

327 R. Summers avers, "They are with him and victorious because they had kept themselves undefiled 'with women,' symbolical of freedom from the spiritual fornication of idol worship" (*Worthy Is the Lamb: Interpreting the Book of Revelation in Its Historical Background* [Nashville: B&H, 1951], 180). Jerome, however, took them literally saying,

pretation, however, is that there are considerably less specific ways to express this idea than this verse's descriptive phrase "did not defile themselves with women." Also the verse speaks of their "without fault," *amōmoi*, before God; that expression alone would be enough to cover their general sanctification without the additional statement relating to celibate lifestyle.[328]

"These follow the Lamb withersoever He goeth: for they were redeemed from among men, first-fruits to God and to the Lamb, and in their mouth was found no guile, and they are without spot.' Out of each tribe, the tribe of Dan excepted, the place of which is taken by the tribe of Levi, twelve thousand virgins who have been sealed are spoken of as future believers, who have not defiled themselves with women. And that we may not suppose the reference to be to those who know not harlots, he immediately added: 'For they continued virgins.' Whereby he shows that all who have not preserved their virginity, in comparison of pure and angelic chastity and of our Lord Jesus Christ Himself, are defiled. 'These are they who sing a new song which no man can sing except him that is a virgin. These are first-fruits unto God and unto the Lamb, and are without blemish.' If virgins are first-fruits, it follows that widows and the continent in marriage, come after the first-fruits, that is, are in the second and third rank: nor can a lost people be saved unless it offer such sacrifices of chastity to God, and with pure victims reconcile the spotless Lamb. It would be endless work to explain the Gospel mystery of the ten virgins, five of whom were wise and five foolish. All I say now is, that as mere virginity without other works does not save, so all works without virginity, purity, continence, chastity, are imperfect" (*Against Jovinianus* 1.40, *NPNF*2, 6:378–379).

328 Fulgentius notes, "Therefore, because Christ is power (*virtus*), just as the Church has taken the word virgin from virtue, so it has received the name Christian from Christ. She, though she has in her diverse members different gifts, according to the grace which has been given to her, still she has received the greater grace of a gift in those members, in whom she is spiritually called a virgin so that she also gains the integrity of bodily virginity. For in other faithful members, who believe in God correctly according to the rule of the Catholic faith and observe conjugal and widow's chastity, who are not splattered by any stain of any act of fornication and remain exempt from any illicit sexual act of infidelity, the Church gains a spiritual virginity only; but in these members in whom he guards the correct faith in such a way that they keep the flesh untouched by any sexual intercourse, the more the Church has a fuller virginity, the more fully and perfectly it possesses the name of the same virginity" (*Fulgentius: Selected Works*, trans. R. B. Eno, FC 95 [Washington, DC: Catholic University of America Press, 1997], 316–17). Caesarius of Arles notes that purity of mind is more important than virginity of the body and that it is this purity which is principally in view. "Truly, dearest brethren, of what profit is it for a man or woman, whether cleric or monk of religious, if bodily virginity is preserved, as long as purity of heart is violated by evil desires? Of what benefit is it to show chastity in one member and to keep corruption in all the rest? For if you notice carefully, those virgins who follow the lamb do not do so merely because of the fact that they have preserved only

Consequently, one is driven to a conclusion that these 144,000 are in fact celibate and therefore properly presented here as *parthenoi* or virgins.[329] Within itself this is not so surprising since the apostle Paul in 1 Cor 7 mentions that he personally wishes all Christian men could be in this state in which he finds himself being unmarried and probably never married (1 Cor 7:8). Jesus also spoke of eunuchs who had made themselves such for the kingdom of God and commends this kind of commitment (Matt 19:12). Even one of the reasons provided by the apostle Paul, namely, that a married man must care for the things of his household and please his wife where the unmarried man may devote himself totally to the things of God seems germane to the discussion here.

These 144,000 are living during the great tribulation in the most troubled times in the history of the earth. For them to have family concerns would only seriously complicate God's assignment to them. So apparently the 144,000 constitute an order of men who choose to abstain from marriage in order to give themselves wholly to the task that is before them during the great tribulation. The one feature of this interpretation that troubles some is the nature of the expression that they "did not defile themselves with women" and they had "kept themselves pure," all of which seems to cast marriage in something of a negative light. But, as the author of Hebrews has well noted, "Marriage should be honored by all, and the marriage bed kept pure" (Heb 13:4). This judgment

---

bodily virginity. Finally, when He had said: 'These are they who did not defile themselves with women,' He continued and added: 'and in their mouth there was found no lie; they are without blemish.' Listen carefully that if anyone boasts about bodily virginity alone, as long as he loves deceit he will not be able to follow Christ along with those holy virgins. For this reason let no virgin presume only upon her physical virginity, because if she is disobedient or gossiping she knows that she will have to be excluded from the bed-chamber of her Heavenly Spouse. Although a virgin possesses a hundredfold and a married woman the thirtyfold, still a chaste and humble married woman is better than a proud virgin. For that chaste woman who serves her husband in humility possesses her thirtyfold, while not even one will remain for the proud virgin; in both of them is fulfilled what the psalmist says: 'Lowly people you save, but haughty eyes you bring low'" (*St. Caesarius of Arles: Sermons, Volume 2: 81-186*, trans. M. M. Mueller, FC 47 [Washington, DC: Catholic University of America Press, 1964], 346).

329 Tertullian suggests, "We have also in the Scriptures *robes* mentioned as allegorizing the hope of the flesh. Thus in the Revelation of John it is said: 'These are they which have not defiled their cloths with women,'—indicating, of course, virgins, and such as have become 'eunuchs for the kingdom of heaven's sake.' Therefore, they shall be 'clothed in white raiment,' that is, in the bright beauty of the unwedded flesh" (*On the Resurrection of the Flesh* 27, ANF, 3:564–65).

is sustained by the entire witness of Scripture, including the Genesis account of creation where the author makes clear that the purpose of God in creating Adam and Eve was that they should be fruitful and multiply and fill the earth. It is impossible to conclude that God's purpose could ever be construed as wrong. Rather the seer is here indicating that not only are these 144,000 unmarried but they have also maintained their deportment in such a way as not to defile themselves with women and have kept themselves pure. Rather than constituting a negative pronouncement about marriage, the degree to which they have kept themselves holy for God is underscored.

The expression that they are "firstfruits [aparchē] to God and to the Lamb" poses an exegetical problem to the interpreter. Thomas notes that the word represents a contribution without any connotation of a larger harvest to follow in two out of three occurrences of aparchē, which is used sixty-six times in the Septuagint.[330] Consequently, he believes the emphasis should not be so much on "firstfruits" as on "contribution."[331] While that is certainly true, the events belonging to the end time do provide reason for the understanding of many interpreters that these are merely the first of many to come. The position of this interpreter is that the periods of the great tribulation and the millennium belong to an era subsequent to that of the church age. These events inaugurated by the return of Christ for the church are divided into the seven-year tribulation and the 1,000-year millennial reign, but they together constitute the "end times." The description of life during the millennium seems to be one in which the earth is not only repopulated after the terrifying years of the tribulation but is also a time in which multitudes will come to Christ. Hence these firstfruits uniquely protected of God in the great tribulation are the firstfruits unto God of the coming response to Him that will occur during the millennial reign of Christ.

One final consideration regarding the 144,000 is the expression, "These are the ones who follow the Lamb wherever he goes." This expression more than any other provides information about the character of these disciples. In the end to be a Christian is to be "a little Christ." Certainly, this means one who is redeemed and regenerate, but the church often forgets that a decision to follow the Lord is a part of that commitment. The 144,000 are characterized by their faithfulness in following Christ.

---

330 R. L. Thomas, *Revelation 8–22: An Exegetical Commentary* (Chicago: Moody, 1992), 198.

331 Ibid.

E. The Announcement of the Demise of Babylon (14:6–13)

⁶**Then I saw another angel flying in the midst of heaven, having the everlasting gospel to preach to those who dwell on the earth—to every nation, tribe, tongue, and people—⁷saying with a loud voice, "Fear God and give glory to Him, for the hour of His judgment has come; and worship Him who made heaven and earth, the sea and springs of water."**

⁸**And another angel followed, saying, "Babylon is fallen, is fallen, that great city, because she has made all nations drink of the wine of the wrath of her fornication."**

⁹**Then a third angel followed them, saying with a loud voice, "If anyone worships the beast and his image, and receives *his* mark on his forehead or on his hand, ¹⁰he himself shall also drink of the wine of the wrath of God, which is poured out full strength into the cup of His indignation. He shall be tormented with fire and brimstone in the presence of the holy angels and in the presence of the Lamb. ¹¹And the smoke of their torment ascends forever and ever; and they have no rest day or night, who worship the beast and his image, and whoever receives the mark of his name."**

¹²**Here is the patience of the saints; here *are* those who keep the commandments of God and the faith of Jesus.**

¹³**Then I heard a voice from heaven saying to me, "Write: 'Blessed *are* the dead who die in the Lord from now on.'**

"Yes," says the Spirit, "that they may rest from their labors, and their works follow them."

Still another angel now enters the panorama of the seer, and this angel, wafted along in midair, is the harbinger of the eternal gospel to be proclaimed to those who live on the earth, including every nation, tribe, tongue, and people. This vision is an example of many reasons more and more scholars deny that the book of the Revelation is strictly speaking a book of apocalyptic genre. The genre of apocalypse seldom includes the gospel message, and yet the good news of salvation in Christ and of the sacrifice of the Lamb on behalf of all people occurs repeatedly on the pages of what must be described more accurately as a prophecy. Notable here is the fact that the gospel is called "the everlasting gospel" (v. 6). The word "everlasting" (*aiōnion*) is used to describe God Himself.[332] As such, clearly a writer could focus on unending perpetuity with this

---

332 Consequently, Origen wondered if the reference were not directly to Christ Himself: "Because Christ is called the power of God and the gospel also is called the power of God, the following ought to be considered: whether Christ, as he is many other

word. While there will come a day when no one else will be able to respond to the gospel, even in the eternal state, the good news of salvation in Christ will be a perpetual reminder of the love of God in the hearts of those who live with Him in the eternal city. The universality of the availability of the gospel is here stated and is to be proclaimed to all who live on the earth irrespective of national entity, tribe, language, or people group.

However, the eternal gospel of v. 6 must be understood in light of v. 7. The urgency of this final appeal of the eternal gospel is based on the need for men to fear God and give Him the glory, and that is particularly true because the hour of God's judgment has come. Men are called upon to worship Him who is the Creator God. There is a sense in which Gen 1:1 is the most important verse in the Bible. The simple statement, "In the beginning God created the heavens and the earth," establishes not merely the origin of all things but as such establishes both the ownership and the purposes of Him who is the Creator. If that verse is unreliable and does not represent the truth about human origins, then all moral and spiritual mandates are rendered tentative at best and are little more than personal (existentialism) or community (postmodernism) ethic and spirituality. If, on the other hand, God is the Creator and owner of all that exists, then the only appropriate response of any human is to worship God, fear Him, and give Him glory.

Since the focus of the material in the heart of the book of Revelation is essentially the tribulation on earth, the situation is more pressing than ever. The judgments already revealed in the opening of the seven-sealed scroll and the sounding of the seven trumpets will soon be followed by the outpouring of the bowls of God's wrath. Judgment is at hand, but even in judgment God is merciful and loving; and this fact is poignantly portrayed in the angel's crossing the heavens once again with the eternal gospel for all who live on the earth.

In v. 8 a second angel follows and announces the fall of Babylon the Great. This Babylon made all nations drink of the "wine of the wrath of her fornication." This revelation anticipates the rich imagery to follow in chaps. 17–19 where an unusually large amount of discussion is devoted to "Babylon the Great." The expression "fallen" is an aorist active indicative form of the Greek verb, *piptō*, meaning "fall." Its doubling or repetition is no scribal error

---

things, ought also to be understood as the gospel. Indeed perhaps what is called the 'eternal gospel' should be interpreted with reference to him" (*Commentary on the Epistle to the Romans: Books 1–5*, trans. T. P. Scheck, FC 103 [Washington, DC: Catholic University of America Press, 2001], 86.

but rather serves to underscore or put an exclamation point to this announcement. The aorist indicative in this case may be what is known as a *futuristic* or *proleptic* aorist, which views an action, while future, as so certain that one can speak of it as complete. Or it might be viewed as a case of the *culminative* or *effective* aorist (i.e., an aorist tense that views the action from the point of view of its results).[333] If "fallen" is a futuristic aorist, then the author is emphasizing the inevitability of its demise. If culminative, then the author has anticipated the end of Babylon portrayed in chaps. 16–18.

The added emphasis of the repetition of the word can only be understood in light of the expression of "Babylon the Great" and the description that follows, namely, that this "Babylon the Great" has thrust upon all the nations the wine of her impurity. The identification of Babylon the Great, then, becomes the key to understanding chaps. 17–19 and to some degree the entire book of the Revelation. More attention will be devoted to that identification in those chapters; but, anticipating that, the possible interpretations should be noted.

Some interpreters view this reference to Babylon as symbolic for the existence of the evil machinations of men, the world system in rebellion against the Creator God of the previous verse.[334] These interpreters see no necessity for a literal correspondence to any entity formerly existing or coming to be in the future.

A second view takes a literal approach and views Babylon to be a reference to the ancient Babylonian Empire's capital located on the banks of the Euphrates River in what is today modern Iraq. Futuristic interpreters usually insist on the literal meaning of the text and are consistent in reading this text in such a way. Babylon exists today only as a relatively small town; hence, an understanding of a literal Babylon on the Euphrates, which would again be a significant force in the world of political intrigue, would necessitate the rebuilding of such a city and

---

333 A. T. Robertson's discussion of the aorist tense views the aorist as the basic tense of Greek and cites Broadus as noting that Greek is "an aorist loving language." Robertson suggests that this basic tense was the one through which all the other tenses developed (*A Grammar of the Greek New Testament in the Light of Historical Research* [Nashville: Broadman, 1934], 831–35).

334 M. Wilcock says, "But all is not well, and the second angel has to say why. The Babylon he mentions has an entire Scene to herself later on, and will be dealt with fully in her place. Suffice it to say for the present that Babylon is another picture of the beast from the sea, the world system which is in rebellion against God. This angel's message is that the spirit of Babylon has infected all nations, and rendered men incapable of responding to the first angel's gospel; but for all her power, she is doomed to destruction" (*The Message of Revelation: I Saw Heaven Opened*, The Bible Speaks Today [Downers Grove, IL: InterVarsity, 1975], 134).

a reconstitution of its suzerainty. While certainly not impossible, at present this seems somewhat improbable. Those who have advocated this position with the rise of modern-day Iraq have not developed much of a following.[335]

A third possibility is that Babylon the Great is cryptic speech referencing Rome. Evidences exist that Christians in the late first century sometimes identified the Roman Empire by referring to it as "Babylon." Such references were occasioned by the godlessness and immorality that characterized the two and even beyond that by the propensity of both to persecute the people of God.[336] Due to the anticipated rise of the fourth beast, a world kingdom that has similarities to all the great kingdoms but in the end is a reconstitution at some level of the ancient Roman Empire, this interpretation has enjoyed considerable support among futurist interpreters of the book of Revelation.

A fourth view, combining elements of views one and three, might be ventured here. This view would hold that Babylon, which is announced as being fallen, is indeed the last-day focus on a world empire that in some way roughly approximates the ancient Roman Empire. This empire corresponds perfectly with the feet of Daniel's colossus in Dan 2 and to the fourth beast of Dan 7. What is then in view is the capital of this empire, perhaps Rome, but probably not Babylon on the Euphrates. However, as in view one, the character—more than the geography of the last day literal entity—is here in view. From the earliest chapters of Genesis, the building of the tower at Babel represents an anthropologically centered religion concocted by Satan in contradistinction to the theocentric faith of the people of God in any generation (Gen 11). This Babylonian faith is syncretistic and inclusive of anything other than the legitimate faith and allegiance to God. Inevitably it weds church and state as will be observed in chap. 17. Its hostility to true faith and its willingness to employ the power of the state and the motivation of anthropocentric religion to persecute

---

335 In 1991 amid international concerns about Saddam Hussein and war-threatening Iraq, C. Dyer published *The Rise of Babylon: Sign of the End Times* (Wheaton, IL: Tyndale, 1991), forecasting the rebuilding of Babylon on the Euphrates and its return to a world power broker status.

336 W. A. Criswell notes that, "when the Christian in John's day was martyred with the sword or was crucified or was thrown into a boiling cauldron of oil or was fed to wild beasts, it was pagan Rome that crucified him or slew him or fed him to the wild and ferocious animals. But in this vision that God gave to John, the blood of the saints and the blood of the martyrs of Jesus is shed by that rich and scarlet idolatrous church. John 'ethaumasa thauma mega' he wondered with great wonder" (*Expository Sermons on Revelation: Five Volumes Complete and Unabridged* [Grand Rapids: Zondervan, 1969], 4:186).

true faith has been exhibited repeatedly in the great empires of the world but initially in Babylon and finally in this reconstituted form of a world empire.

Now the angel announces the fall of this incredible challenge to the sovereignty of God. Emphasizing that fallenness, the angel speaks of it twice and identifies the character of the fallen kingdom as being one that brought the nations to the table to drink the wine of unfaithfulness to God.

A third angel follows almost immediately and with a loud voice proclaims exactly what will be involved individually for those who have imbibed this wine of unfaithfulness to God. Those who worship the beast and his image and receive his mark on their foreheads or hands initially appear to be the ones who are safe and secure during the tribulation on earth. In the end, however, the opposite is the case. The 144,000 are sealed and protected, but those who have followed the beast end up drinking the wine of God's fury that is poured forth full strength into the cup of his wrath.

The image of drinking an undiluted cup of God's wrath is already known in the Bible. Wine was most frequently diluted with the presence of water. Without that dilution a heavily fermented wine could be a powerful drink. When that drink is not wine at all but God's wrath, and that undiluted in any fashion, God's fury is unleashed. Generally, the wrath of God is depicted by the use of the word *orgē*, which references a constant and determinative attitude toward sin. This word also occurs in the text; but the word *thumos* also occurs here and is the word most often used in the New Testament to describe the anger of humans. Here the words are used together, establishing not only an attitude God has toward sin, but also indicating the fury with which that wrath makes itself known in the last days of the tribulation.

The state of those who are the recipients of this cup of wrath is said to be that of being tormented (*basanizō*) with fire and brimstone in the presence of the holy angels and the Lamb. "Tormented," (*basanizō*) describes agonizing upheaval and belongs to the same word group used to describe the rich man in the torments he experienced in Hades following his physical death.

The expression, "in the presence of the holy angels and in the presence of the Lamb," is not intended to denote any fiendish delight on the part of the angels, let alone the Lamb; it only establishes the full justice of that which transpires. Furthermore, in v. 11 clearly the smoke of their torment rises forever and ever. Once again, the expression "forever," in the Greek *aiōnas aiōnōn*, is a strong expression indicating unceasing perpetuity. Those who find themselves in such a predicament experience no rest from this excruciating circumstance, and these are they who have worshipped the beast or received the mark of his name.[337]

Once again, as if anticipating the objection that such a look at future judgment might be of little comfort to the late first-century Christian community suffering persecution, the seer of Patmos interprets exactly what this means for those who suffer not only in that end time but also even now. All these circumstances call for patient endurance on the part of the saints of God, and those saints of God are the ones who obey God's commandment and remain in the faith of Jesus even amid all those circumstances that occur. Certainly, if that is true of those who live through these apocalyptic days of the

---

337 Not a few find these images far too harsh to anticipate literal fulfillment. M. G. Reddish says, "What will 'the wrath of God' entail? John describes it in imagery borrowed from God's judgment upon Sodom and Gomorrah (Gen 19:24). The worshipers of the beast will be tormented with fire and sulfur (brimstone). Fire serves as a common instrument of divine punishment in Jewish apocalyptic writings (cf. *1 En.* 10:13–14; 21:1–10; 90:22–27; *Sib. Or.* 2:196–213, 252–310) as well as in the writings from other cultures and religions. By this point in the Apocalypse, the reader should be well aware that John's language here is metaphorical. Divine punishment will no more be actual fire and sulfur than Christ will literally be a lamb." And again, "The rhetorical purpose of John's depiction of the punishment of the wicked is to call the church to faithful endurance, to impress upon his readers the serious consequences of rejecting God" (*Revelation*, Smyth & Helwys Bible Commentary [Macon, GA: Smyth & Helwys, 2001], 278–79). W. J. Harrington sees it the same way by objecting, "What is one to make of such language and imagery? We must recall that, in John's view, even Christians (so the messages to the Churches) may become worshipers of the beast, and John is writing to *Christians*. His book is pastoral in purpose. He is conscious of the seductive side of Rome. His terrible picture of eternal torment is meant to alert his readers, to awaken them, brutally, to what he perceives to be a deadly threat. 'As objectifying language about what will happen to our enemies, it is cruel beyond imagination; as confessional language, intended not to describe the fate of outsiders but to encourage insiders to remain faithful, it functions precisely like the language of Jesus in the Gospels (Matt 10:28; 25:30, 46)'" (*Revelation*, SP 16 [Collegeville, MN: Liturgical Press, 1993], 152). M. E. Boring is still more explicit in his rejection of such an interpretation, comparing it to Auschwitz. "Anyone who tries to imagine this infinitely-worse-than-Auschwitz picture as somehow objectively real must ask whether God or John does not here overdo it. Such a picture calls in question both justice and the character of God. (For general principles in interpreting such language, see the 'Reflection: Interpreting Revelation's Violent Imagery.' Here, we might only note that such language does not function to give an objective picture of what shall in fact happen to God's enemies, the outsiders. To even ask whether Revelation 'teaches' eternal torment for the damned is to misconstrue the book as a source of doctrines, to mistake its pictures for propositions" (*Revelation*, IBC [Louisville, KY: Westminster John Knox, 1989], 170).

end time, even so it would be true for Christians in any age. In fact, there is a universal promise for all.

Suddenly a voice from heaven speaks in v. 13, though no angel is identified as the source of that voice. The voice pronounces an additional apocalyptic beatitude—those who die in the Lord from that point forward are blessed. The Spirit of God affirms this and promises that they will "rest from their labor" and that their "works will follow them." The Greek word translated "labor" (kopos) refers to "diligent and difficult work." This word is appropriate to describe the experience of those who attempt to live for Christ during this tribulation period. That these are the ones who are primarily in view in the text is indicated by the words "from now on." Nevertheless, surely the promise to them at that specific time is also applicable to all believers who die in the Lord.

In the Scriptures, death is presented as the final enemy, the result of the initial iniquity of the pristine couple in the garden and the entrance to the unknown from which no one has returned. Consequently, what may be known of whatever exists on the other side of death is neither the subject of a historical report nor a scientific enquiry. In addition to the fear of the unknown, the loss of all that is known and the clear weakness and decadence of the body leave death as an unassailable and irresistible terror. However, the eyes of faith see beyond all this and accept the revelation of God. A part of that revelation is the promise that those who die in the Lord are in fact not in a pitiable state but are the objects of incredible blessing. Nor is this state of blessing some sort of nirvana where there is no further suffering and an absorption into the cosmic order. Rather rest from labor inspires positive results, which follow in a known and beneficial way.

The "rest" in view here is not a picture of a siesta but follows the understanding of Sabbath rest. God created the world in six days, and on the Sabbath day he rested. There is no indication here that God was "tuckered out" and needed to have a nap. The idea is rather that he rested from his creative labor in order to take up the new task of sovereign maintenance of that which he had created. So the rest of heaven, as some Christians have indicated, is not to be portrayed as a passive "cloud potato" existence of inactive slumber but rather as a cessation of the difficulties associated with life on the earth and a new and exciting order with the contributions made to the kingdom of God on earth following as their reward.

F. A Vision of Armageddon (14:14–20)

¹⁴Then I looked, and behold, a white cloud, and on the cloud sat *One* like the Son of Man, having on His head a golden crown, and in His hand a sharp sickle. ¹⁵And another angel came out of the temple, crying with a loud voice to Him who sat on the cloud, "Thrust in Your sickle and reap, for the time has come for You to reap, for the harvest of the earth is ripe." ¹⁶So He who sat on the cloud thrust in His sickle on the earth, and the earth was reaped.

¹⁷Then another angel came out of the temple which is in heaven, he also having a sharp sickle.

¹⁸And another angel came out from the altar, who had power over fire, and he cried with a loud cry to him who had the sharp sickle, saying, "Thrust in your sharp sickle and gather the clusters of the vine of the earth, for her grapes are fully ripe." ¹⁹So the angel thrust his sickle into the earth and gathered the vine of the earth, and threw *it* into the great winepress of the wrath of God. ²⁰And the winepress was trampled outside the city, and blood came out of the winepress, up to the horses' bridles, for one thousand six hundred furlongs.

The final portion of chap. 14 is devoted to a scene of the harvesting of the earth. Seated on a white cloud is one "like the Son of Man" with a crown of gold on his head and a sharp sickle in his hand. Another angel appears out of the temple and calls with a loud voice to Him who was sitting on the cloud to take His sickle and reap because the time of the reaping and the harvest of the earth had come. The one seated on the cloud proceeds to do so. Once again, the problem with the Apocalypse is the identification of its figures, and characteristically interpreters differ over those interpretations. Some view the reaping angel on the cloud as the exalted Christ and point out that the terminology "like the Son of Man" favors that identification since it was certainly the Lord's favorite delineation of himself.³³⁸ Others prefer to identify this figure as an angel and point to what they consider to be the inappropriate command of one angel to the Son of God to thrust in his sickle and reap.³³⁹ However, such would not be

---

338 H. Alford is characteristic of those who opt for the understanding that this is the Lord, saying, "This clearly is the Lord Himself" (*The Greek Testament* [Chicago: Moody, 1958], 4:690). R. C. H. Lenski is even stronger: "In view of 1:13 one cannot mistake this person—he is Jesus" (*The Interpretation of St. John's Revelation* [Minneapolis: Augsburg, 1963], 445).

339 D. E. Aune provides extensive analysis of both views but in the end concludes against the position that the angel represents Christ. He lines up a number of "weighty arguments" against the position but draws no final conclusion. In fact, he

inappropriate communication among angels. For this interpreter, the "Son of Man" identification is sufficient to establish that the one doing the reaping is indeed the Christ. The angel is not so much commanding the Son of God to do something as he is announcing that the time for the harvest has come. The imagery of a reaper with a sharp sickle would be commonly understood in any first-century context. Christ is seated in a position of rest and has a crown of gold, which in this case is the *stephanos* or victor's crown. The temple from which the angel comes is apparently the heavenly temple observed by John, and the angel announces that the day of harvest has come.

Some interpreters see this as a harvest of the earth's elect, but the context of judgment both before and after the passage of the chapter suggest otherwise. The action appears to come at the end of the tribulation, and that part of earth's population surviving the rigors of the tribulation period and continuing to follow the beast are now to be reaped and cast into judgment.

Verses 17–20 delineate the results of that harvest. Another angel comes out of the temple in heaven, and he, too, has a sharp sickle. Still another angel who is in charge of the fire on the altar came from the altar and called with a loud voice to the one with a sharp sickle to take his sickle and gather all the clusters of grapes from the earth's vine because its grapes are ripe. The harvest of vv. 14–16 is depicted in terms of the harvesting of wheat. The harvest of vv. 17–20 is from a vineyard, and the sickle is used to gather the clusters of ripe grapes. The angel swings his sickle, and the grapes are thrown into the great winepress of the wrath of God. These are in turn trampled in the winepresses outside the city, which must surely be a reference to the city of Jerusalem. Then comes a difficult-to-interpret passage stating that blood flowed out of the press rising as high as the horses' bridles for a distance of 1,600 furlongs (in Greek, *stadia*) or approximately 184 miles (one furlong would be about 670 feet). This figure corresponds roughly to the length of the land of Israel from the Wadi el-Arish in the south to the northernmost extremities of Israel. Here literalists are faced with a considerable problem. The text appears to show a river of blood flowing for 200 miles to the depth of a horse's bridle, which would be approximately five feet from the surface of the ground. A river of blood 200 miles long and to a depth of five feet seems virtually inconceivable even as a result of the battle of Armageddon. Even a literal rendering of the text does not predispose a river

---

notes the possibility that since the Son of Man did not know the precise time of the end (Mark 13:32), perhaps he had to be told, explaining the other angel's command (*Revelation 6–16*, WBC 52b [Dallas: Word Books, 1997], 800–1).

of blood and that terminology, in fact, is not used. Verse 20 only mentions that the blood flows like grape juice from an overflowing winepress over an area of 1,600 stadia. The violence of the carnage of this bloodbath, which appears to be a reference to the battle of Armageddon, is such that blood like juice overflowing a winepress is spattered everywhere even as high as horses' bridles.[340] This picture, of course, is wholly conceivable and is in keeping with those who interpret this last conflict to be the bloodiest of history and to cover wide-ranging territory. Megiddo is about fifty miles north of Jerusalem and seems to be the center of the conflict. While the battle takes its name from that central valley, its expanse extending far beyond this valley would be no surprise.

5. The Bowls of Wrath Judgments (15:1–16:21)

A. The Presentation of the Bowls to the Angels (15:1–8)

¹Then I saw another sign in heaven, great and marvelous: seven angels having the seven last plagues, for in them the wrath of God is complete.

²And I saw *something* like a sea of glass mingled with fire, and those who have the victory over the beast, over his image and over his mark *and* over the number of his name, standing on the sea of glass, having harps of God. ³They sing the song of Moses, the servant of God, and the song of the Lamb, saying:

"Great and marvelous *are* Your works,

Lord God Almighty!

Just and true *are* Your ways,

O King of the saints!

⁴Who shall not fear You, O Lord, and glorify Your name?

For *You* alone *are* holy.

For all nations shall come and worship before You,

For Your judgments have been manifested."

---

340 Flavius Josephus provides a description of the tragic events surrounding the fall of Jerusalem in AD 70: "But although they had this commiseration for such as were destroyed in that manner, yet had they not the same for those that were still alive, but they ran every one through whom they met with, and obstructed the very lanes with their dead bodies, and made the whole city run down with blood, to such a degree indeed that the fire of many of the houses was quenched with these men's blood" (*Wars of the Jews* 6.8.5, in *The Life and Works of Flavius Josephus* [Philadelphia, PA: John C. Winston, 1957], 831).

⁵**After these things I looked, and behold, the temple of the tabernacle of the testimony in heaven was opened. ⁶And out of the temple came the seven angels having the seven plagues, clothed in pure bright linen, and having their chests girded with golden bands. ⁷Then one of the four living creatures gave to the seven angels seven golden bowls full of the wrath of God who lives forever and ever. ⁸The temple was filled with smoke from the glory of God and from His power, and no one was able to enter the temple till the seven plagues of the seven angels were completed.**

Chapter 15 constitutes an interlude, as well as an introduction to the final plagues, which will be enumerated in chap. 16 as part of the tribulation period. However, the interlude is replete with importance for adequate comprehension of what follows in the outpouring of the bowls of wrath. The reader is first introduced to a scene of triumph in heaven where specifically those who withstood the siren songs and the threats of the false prophets are gathered. These extol the majesty of the King. The way is prepared for the introduction of the angels who are divine agents executing the wrath of God.

15:1–4 From his perch on the island of Patmos, John now sees another sign, which he describes with two words: "great" and "marvelous." The Greek word for "marvelous" (*thaumastos*) emphasizes the quality of astonishment.[341] What John astonishingly beholds are seven angels who have the seven last plagues. The NIV text emphasizes the culmination of the plagues by repeating the word "last" (*eschatos*), even though the word actually only appears in the Greek text once. However, the NKJV translators doubtless noted the *hoti* clause

---

341 Bertram has a fascinating description of the history of the term in *TDNT*. Noting that the word group is prominent in philosophy, particularly in Plato, Bertram suggests that it denotes philosophical doubt that must be overcome. He also notes its use among the gods: "Naturally the deities themselves have the attribute of θαυμαστός, e.g., Serapis and Aesculapius. A healing formula can also be described as an ἔργον τοῦ θεοῦ θαυμαστόν" (*TDNT*, 3:28). Noting further its use in the NT regarding the miracles of Jesus, he says, "Here, as in similar cases, it is obvious that the purpose of the narrator and author is not to describe the historical and psychological impression made by Jesus on the crowd but rather to use the motif of astonishment as a provisional means to direct the interest of the reader to the significance of the event. Thus exegesis cannot be content merely to interpret the expression of astonishment: οὐδέποτε ἐφάνη οὕτως ἐν τῷ Ἰσρήλ, from the standpoint of those who experienced this history as Jews. It has rather to adopt the standpoint of the Christian community considering the whole history of salvation" (3:37). All of these qualities are effectively captured in the use of the word in this passage. The "sign" that John sees is great and marvelous. Whatever doubt the seer might have is overcome by the origin and significance of the sign.

of the text, which says, "for in [the seven last plagues] the wrath of God is complete," as settling the issue at hand.

"Complete" is a translation of the aorist passive indicative of *teleō*, meaning "bring to a conclusion." The aorist passive emphasizes the fact that the wrath of God has now been brought to a conclusion. The tenor of the statement gives considerable impetus to the idea of the sequential nature of these judgments. This apparent finality of the seven bowls of wrath suggests that they came last and are the culmination of the wrath of God. Indeed, the word for wrath in the text is once again *thumos*, or "fury," where one might have expected to find *orgē*, the settled disposition of God against evil. Instead, unmitigated fury in response to the injustice in the world seems to be the theme of the bowls of wrath in chap. 16. The extremities of conditions thus evoked seem to be the reason for John's use of the word "marvelous" or "astonishing" to describe what he sees.

As John continues to note the surroundings, he sees a sea of glass mixed with fire. The sea of glass has been viewed once before in the apocalyptic vision in 4:6. However, that particular sea of glass was not noted for the mixture of fire. Since fire often accompanies God's judgment, the crystal sea of glass now mixed with fire may well denote the just judgment of God. As Thomas notes, "The intermingling of fire suggests the punitive providence to materialize shortly as the seven angels pour out the terrible contents of their bowls."[342] Beside that sea, John noticed those who had victory over the beast and his mark and over the number of his name. "Victory" is once again the present active participle of *nikaō*, meaning essentially "overcome," or, as the NKJV translates, "have the victory over." The vast majority of the earth's population during the closing days of the tribulation succumb to the two beasts of chap. 13, and those who do not capitu-

---

342 R. L. Thomas, *Revelation 8–22: An Exegetical Commentary* (Chicago: Moody, 1995), 232. Oecumenius notes the same interpretation, remarking that "the very wise Paul in one of his writings, says, 'If anyone builds on this foundation with gold, silver, precious stones, wood, hay, stubble, the quality of each person's work will be tested by fire, because it will be revealed in fire.' So then when the sinners with their offerings of inflammable loads of sin are put to the test, will the righteous also be tested in fire although they bring along gold and their precious materials? . . . He is now speaking of those who have conquered the beast through thick and thin: they *are standing beside the sea of glass mingled with fire*—glass because of the brightness and purity of the righteous in it, but mixed with fire because of the purging and cleansing of all uncleanness, since even the righteous need to be cleansed. 'For we all frequently stumble,' as Scripture says, 'and who will be free from uncleanness? no one, not even if their life on earth is but one day" (*Commentary on the Apocalypse*, trans. J. N. Sugget, FC 112 [Washington, DC: Catholic University of America Press, 2006], 134–35).

late to them, other than the 144,000 who seem to be especially protected of God, pay in many cases with martyrdom. Now they are seen beside this crystal sea with justice and judgment imminently impending on those who have been deceived by the two beasts, particularly the latter one or the false prophet.

At this point harps are given to them. The expression in the Greek New Testament is literally "the harps of God." The expression seems to mean that harps were given to them by God. With them in hand, they sing a new song, which was the song of Moses, the servant of God, and the song of the Lamb. The word "song" is repeated twice, indicating the possibility that two different songs actually are being sung here. Since the imagery of the text, including the outpouring of the bowls of wrath and the delivery of the people from judgment, takes its background from the delivery of God's people in the exodus, what may be in view here is a historical song regarding the deliverance of Moses, the servant of God, and of the people of Israel. The song is sung as a prelude and enactment of this greater deliverance to be effected with the Lamb and his victory. Although the Old Testament abounds with analogies and pictures of redemption to come ultimately in Christ, no historical incident, metaphor, or illustration is more poignant than that of the exodus. Hopeless bondage gives way to miraculous deliverance followed by a journey terminating in the land of promise. The experience with Moses foreshadows salvation in Christ in just about every way. While we are not told how many stanzas were in the heavenly oratory, it clearly began with the mighty acts of God in Egypt and concluded with the still more remarkable intervention of God in Christ.

The song itself, or at least the portion of it recorded, interestingly mentions neither Moses nor the Lamb as such; so it is possible that the song should simply be understood as one that encompasses all the redemptive acts of God through history.[343] Great and astonishing (*thaumasta*) are the works, or deeds, of the Lord God. *Pantokratōr* is translated appropriately as "Almighty." The word is derived from *krateō* and *pan*, more literally "ruler of all."

Two titles are then assigned to God. He is called just and true in His ways. Already he has been described as Lord (*kurie*), as Almighty (*pantokratōr*), and as

---

343 Oecumenius avers of this song that "this was the one he sang when Pharaoh and all his army had been drowned, saying, 'Let us sing to the Lord, for he has triumphed gloriously; the horse and his rider he has thrown into the sea; he has become my help and protector for our deliverance.' The song is a paean of victory for the punishment of the ungodly and the victory over the Devil and his lawless son, the Antichrist. . . . He says, *And the song of the Lamb*, that is the appropriate song for the Lord and his righteous judgment against the ungodly; that is why they wonder at the truth and righteousness of the Lord" (Ibid., 135).

God (*theos*).[344] Now he is also said to be the "King of the saints ('*agios*" according to the NKJV, which follows the *Textus Receptus*. However, there is a major textual variant at this point. The NASB text has chosen to follow the reading "King of the nations" (*ethnōn*). The textual support for this comes from an amended reading of Codex Sinaiticus and a number of other important manuscripts, but "ages" (*aiōnōn*) also has strong evidence appearing in the Sinaiticus original and adopted by the translators of the NIV.[345] The mixed textual evidence here leaves the interpreter unable to make a decision with great finality but also illustrates the fact that the overwhelming majority of such examples of uncertainty leave a word choice that does not affect the truthfulness of the text one way or the other. Whether God is the King of the saints, King of the ages, or the King of the nations makes no difference, for all three would be emphatically true.

This gives rise to the question and its answer, which in all reality is really a rhetorical question, "Who shall not fear You, / O Lord, and glorify Your name?" Fear is *phobeō*, an aorist subjunctive, suggesting that there might be someone who would not fear God but that such a thing is unthinkable. *Phobeō* is fear in the sense of awe or reverence. The Greek word for "glorify," *doxazō*, originally indicated something heavy. "Glory" in the Bible comes to be understood as the outward manifestation of something of tremendous significance, and the expression anticipates that all will bring glory to His name.[346]

Another attribute is added to those of justice and truth in v. 3 as a reason is given for reverencing God and bringing glory to Him, namely, that He alone is holy. Again, an unexpected turn occurs in the text since generally the word used to describe the holiness of God is *hagios*, but here it is *hosios*, which also

344 W. Michaelis traces the concept noting that the last part of the word κράτος carries both a legal sense of having the right of the use of power as well as the active sense of "exercising force." Regarding the compound term παντοκράτωρ, he observes, "This liturgical usage has obviously influenced Rev. Yet the term has also a philosophical character, and in patristic lit. it was used to express the universalist claim of Christianity. With this eschatological orientation, it thus carries with it a strong religious accent" (*TDNT*, 3:914). And again, "The reference is not so much to God's activity in creation as to His supremacy over all things. The description is static rather than dynamic. Hence it has only a loose connection with the dogmatic concept of the divine omnipotence, which is usually linked with the omnicausality of God" (*TDNT*, 3:915).

345 The United Bible Societies' Greek New Testament ventures no more than a "C" rating for the probability that the text reads ὁ βασιλεὺς τῶν ἐθνῶν, indicating limited confidence in the reading. p47 provides possibly the strongest unmixed evidence against the reading. However, Ambrose and Primasius, among others, support it.

346 See discussion of δόξα in chap. 7.

references purity and worth.[347] God alone has this particular quality, and this is even more for the worship by the cosmos. Furthermore, the song concludes with the note that all nations will come and worship before the Almighty God because in all of these transactions His righteous acts have been made manifest or have been revealed. The mention that "all nations" will "come and worship" could give some evidence for the textual reading "King of the ages" in v. 3, but other interpreters believe that a copyist, being aware of that reading, may well have changed "ages" to "nations" to make it agree. The idea that God is the King of the nations suggests both His preeminence in creation and His sovereignty over the nations of the world. John echoes Paul in Phil 2:9–11:

> Therefore, God has highly exalted Him
> and given Him the name which is above every name,
> that at the name of Jesus every knee should bow,
> of those in heaven and of those on earth and of those
> under the earth, and every tongue should confess
> that Jesus Christ is Lord,
> to the glory of God the Father.

At this juncture, the text stresses God's judgments that have been manifested. The words for "judgments" and "manifested" are not unusual, nor are they what the reader might have expected. "Judgments" translates *dikaiōmata*. According to Moulton and Milligan, the idea carries overtones of litigation such as in cases like the people of the city of Prieve demonstrating their "immemorial possession of certain territory," or where a man is sent to Alexandria "having with him papers to justify his case."[348]

---

347 The unusual nature of this use of ὅσιος as an attribute of God is underscored by F. Hauck, who notes that the word has little history of reference to deities in the Greek pantheon, nor is it used often in the LXX for God. Never is it a translation of *qādôš*. Predominantly it is used of men regarding "actions which by ancient sanction are regarded as sacred." Its second use seems to reflect "a quality of inward awe before God and his eternal laws" (*TDNT*, 5:489–92). The New Testament also follows this pattern of employing the word mostly for men. But there are a few exceptions such as in this text in the Apocalypse. In Heb 7:26, Jesus is called ὅσιος as the perfect high priest. This could reflect the fact of the incarnation of the eternal God in Jesus and perhaps provide an explanation for the use of the term here.

348 J. H. Moulton and G. Milligan, *The Vocabulary of the Greek Testament: Illustrated from the Papyri and Other Non-Literary Sources* (Grand Rapids: Eerdmans, 1930), 163.

"Manifested," on the other hand, is not *apokalupsis* as might be expected, but instead an aorist passive indicative of the verb *phaneroō* with the sense here of "make clear." Colin Brown notes that the word is frequently used in the New Testament as a synonym for *apokalupsis*, but he calls attention to Rev 3:18 and to the *bēma* in 2 Cor 5:10–13 where the word carries more the sense of "make known" in a court of law.[349]

As such, the prose seems to be a Johannine theodicy. In the present era, postmoderns are fond of viewing antiquity as rather barbarous in contrast to the fastidious and forgiving nonviolence of the present era. As inconceivable as such a posture may be, the ancients, too, often demonstrated a sense of justice and a repugnance to violence. Aware of this concern, John explains that when the nations observe the judgments of God revealed in these plagues, all protests are effectively curtailed. Rather, recognizing that God is eminently righteous in His acts of judgment, the nations both fear God and bring glory to His name.

15:5-8 The familiar Greek phrase, *meta tauta*, literally "after this," introduces a heavenly vision. John turns his gaze into heaven and sees there the temple. The word for temple is *naos* rather than *hieron*. The former references the sacred things particularly, whereas the latter word covers the entire temple complex. So, what he sees is that portion of the temple considered most holy. Indeed, it is further identified as "the tabernacle" or the tent "of the Testimony." This particular identification is especially fascinating since the vision of heaven is not described in terms of the semipermanent buildings of the temple of Solomon or of Herod but rather the analogy is to the original movable tabernacle in the wilderness. However, its significance is that it contains the Testimony. The holy of holies, the *naos*, contained only one item of furnishing—the ark of the covenant. It, in turn, contained the tablets of the Law and therefore is properly referred to as "the tabernacle of the Testimony." Just about everything about the holy of holies could be appropriately regarded as the "tent of the Testimony." First, so sacred were its precincts that only the high priest could enter and only once a year on Yom Kippur, and that only in a prescribed way (among other things carrying a basin of blood from the sacrificial goat). The "Testimony" was a clear witness of the holiness and unapproachableness of God except on His timetable and in His prescribed way.

The *naos* also contained the ark of the covenant and within it the tablets of the Law—God's communication of Himself, His purposes, demands, and promises for the people of God. Aaron's rod that budded and a pot of miraculously preserved manna witnessed the saving competency of God and His

---

349 *NIDNTT* 3:321–22.

providential oversight of His people. And finally, the *qodesh qodeshim* was the location in which God gave witness to the people of His presence and power in the *shekinah* cloud of glory that descended first on the tent of the Testimony (Exod 33:9) and later on the Solomonic temple (1 Kgs 8:10).

John sees that this *naos* is open, and the angels with the seven plagues came from the presence of the holy God (v. 6). The identification of holiness on the one hand and the seven plagues on the other is further commentary on the character of God. The usual word to describe God's holiness distinguishes Him from all of his creation. He is the transcendent being who rises above all, but as a part of that holiness God's justice and judgment cannot be dismissed.

John describes the raiment of the seven angels as being that of "pure bright linen," and "having their chests girded with golden bands." Like the worship prescribed in the Old Testament, the heavenly entourage appears to model holiness in cleanliness and appropriate dress.

In v. 7 one of the four living ones who was first observed in 4:6 now reenters the drama. Each of the seven angels was presented with a bowl that is filled with a distinct manifestation of the wrath of God. Again, the word in the text is not the anticipated *orgē* but once again *thumos*, which signals the fury of a righteous God against the contamination of His entire creation through sin. God is further described as the One "who lives," a present active participle, stressing the uninterrupted continuity of His existence. This is then accentuated with the phrase often rendered in English, "forever and ever," but actually *aiōnos tōn aiōnōn* in Greek, meaning until the "ages of the ages." This particular expression underscores the righteousness and the justice of God in proceeding with the judgments. He is the Creator, sustainer, and owner of the universe; His judgment on the forces that have sought to destroy the goodness and kindness of God as manifested in His creation is an inevitable consequence.

At this point the entire temple is filled with smoke from the glory of God, rendering it impossible for anyone to enter the temple until after the seven plagues are completed. Twice before a manifestation of the *shekinah* glory of God was seen—first, upon its completion in the tabernacle and then at the dedication of the Solomonic temple. In both cases, as in this one, what John apparently observes is not a dense, black cloud associated with a fire or the acrid grey smoke arising from such a blaze but rather a luminous cloud, which, in its brightness, so obscured everything so as to make it impossible for anyone to enter or effectively work within the temple. The *shekinah* glory has been through all time a unique method of signaling the appearance of God. The glory cloud is not to be identified as a part of God but functions something as the spectacular train of a royal robe worn by a king. The *shekinah* cloud simply shrouds everything around it in brightness and signals the presence of the One who is almighty, completely just, and worthy of glory. Now the stage is set for the last plagues of the tribulation period.

Pastoral Excursus

While the heavenly scene depicted in chap. 15 is preparatory to the judgments of God unleashed on the world in the following chapters, the teaching and preaching of themes of retribution remains always an uncomfortable assignment. On the one hand, there is the counsel of Scripture to proclaim "the whole counsel of God." On the other hand, a number of problems confront a sincere, sensitive exegete and preacher. First, there is the prevailing awareness of his own sinfulness. The sense that for one sinner to proclaim judgment to another always surfaces the self-allegation of hypocrisy. Second, there is the question of theodicy. People know about the God of love and grace and find these concepts contradictory to a God of wrath and judgment. Then, of course, there is the essentially redemptive message for which individuals are most responsible. Deciding how much judgment or talk of God's wrath enters that discussion can be agonizing. Finally, most have known the "sin-fighter" preachers who are constantly entering the moral lists to joust with sinners and appear on the surface to enjoy the challenge. Such are repulsive to most followers of Christ.

This passage in Revelation assists the teacher/pastor in his dilemma. First, what is in view here are the "last plagues." The proclaimer may assure his listener that God's graciousness and love are so long-suffering as to wait until the concluding days of the great tribulation before a massive visitation of justice begins. And when that comes, it will be justice. The bowls of wrath will be neither too much nor too little. They will be just.

One of the ways this justice is emphasized in chap. 15 is the fact that the seven angels appear from "the tabernacle of the Testimony." Not only ample but also extraordinary witness has been repeatedly offered so that those who are the objects of

God's wrath know in advance of the consequences associated with their choices.

Finally, even though the angels appear with the bowls of wrath, no doubt is left in the passage but that these judgments are from the Almighty God. As God, He is just and true in all His ways and is marvelous in His deeds. His righteous acts have been and will yet be revealed in such a way that all nations will eventually acknowledge the rightness of his ways.

Armed with such insights from the passage, one who expounds both this chapter and the judgments to follow must still do so with a keen awareness of his own failures and limitations. He may even proceed with some agony of soul, but proceed he will. He will speak that which God has commissioned him to share with the confidence that his message is the declaration of a just God. Further, he will press the issue of God's wrath, knowing that those whose hearts God opens will attend to the business of "fleeing from the wrath to come."

B. The First Five Bowls of Wrath (16:1–11)

¹Then I heard a loud voice from the temple saying to the seven angels, "Go and pour out the bowls of the wrath of God on the earth."

²So the first went and poured out his bowl upon the earth, and a foul and loathsome sore came upon the men who had the mark of the beast and those who worshiped his image.

³Then the second angel poured out his bowl on the sea, and it became blood as of a dead *man*; and every living creature in the sea died.

⁴Then the third angel poured out his bowl on the rivers and springs of water, and they became blood. ⁵And I heard the angel of the waters saying:

"You are righteous, O Lord,

The One who is and who was and who is to be,

Because You have judged these things.

⁶For they have shed the blood of saints and prophets,

And you have given them blood to drink.

For it is their just due."

⁷And I heard another from the altar saying, "Even so, Lord God Almighty, true and righteous are Your judgments."

⁸Then the fourth angel poured out his bowl on the sun, and power was given to

him to scorch men with fire. ⁹And men were scorched with great heat, and they blasphemed the name of God who has power over these plagues; and they did not repent and give Him glory.

¹⁰Then the fifth angel poured out his bowl on the throne of the beast, and his kingdom became full of darkness; and they gnawed their tongues because of the pain. ¹¹They blasphemed the God of heaven because of their pains and their sores, and did not repent of their deeds.

In rapid succession, the bowls of God's wrath are poured out on the earth. Some interpreters believe chaps. 17–19 are all included in the seventh bowl of wrath, which is not impossible in light of the content and the location of those chapters. However, neither is this conclusion necessary, and the entire contents of the seven bowls of wrath may be understood as occurring in chap. 16. The monumental devastation and extent of these apocalyptic visitations of God's wrath, if taken literally, almost defy human imagination. In addition to the sheer scale of the catastrophe, there is the underlying theme of the origin of these events as belonging to God and His purposes. Etiology is not located in natural upheaval but in divine action. The crass rebellion of the human heart is also displayed since through all these tragedies—men do not repent.

16:1-2 A loud voice from the temple, which can be presumed to be the voice of God Himself, instructs the angels to go and pour out the seven bowls of wrath on the earth. This final manifestation of the judgment of God on the rebellious earth inaugurates the final days of Daniel's seventieth week, especially the last three and one-half years of the tribulation. The plagues themselves have an unmistakable similarity to the plagues of the exodus, being distinct in some ways but remarkably consistent in others.

The first angel pours out his bowl on the land, and a kind of ulcer broke out on the people who had demonstrated allegiance to the beast and worshiped his image. In the NKJV text, these sores are described with the words "foul" (*kakos*) and "loathsome," (*ponēros*). *Kakon* has a range of possible meanings that include "corrupt," "ugly," "wicked," "harmful," and "injurious." *Ponēros*, on the other hand, has similar possibilities, including "unsound," "evil," "malignant," and "malevolent." Whatever way one chooses to translate these two terms, clearly the abscesses that afflicted the worshipers of the beast were both unsightly and agonizingly painful.

Note that this plague has specified recipients. Those who formerly had accepted the mark of the beast for economic and physical protection now discover that the beast is unable to provide security for them in face of the wrath of God. The sixth plague of boils, which fell on the Egyptians and which the magicians could not mimic (Exod 9:8–12), as well as the fascinating case of the Philistines' problem with "tumors" as a result of their theft of the ark (1 Sam 5:1–6), are similar to this first bowl of wrath.[350]

16:3-7 The next two angels reduplicate the same kind of miracle that happened in the plagues of Egypt. The second angel pours out his bowl on the sea. As a result, the sea turns to blood like that of a dead man and causes every living thing in the sea to die. The debate as to the nature of these "bloody seas," whether the precise chemistry of human blood or something more similar to a "red tide," notorious in some places for killing marine life but never on such a wide scale as this, cannot be completely resolved. Those who believe that actual blood is in view, of course, point to the expression that the blood is "like that of a dead man." Those who see it as an expression indicating a blood-like substance reminding the seer of blood point to the word "like" in the text to indicate only that the texture of the sea appeared to be blood, and that the effects of this noxious condition were such as to destroy all marine life. Clearly, whatever the exact nature of the blood may have been, the loss of all marine life brings wide-scale destruction and the dismantling of the natural order on the planet.[351]

---

350 J. Roloff is characteristic of interpreters who apply this passage to the destruction of the Roman Empire of antiquity: "Second, in association with that stands the popular effort to historicize more strongly the plagues that were sketched in the prototype predominantly as cosmic catastrophes. There will be, above all, historical events that will destroy the Roman Empire—whether surging cavalry forces from countries in the east (v. 12), or the impulse of unrestrained warlike expansion that comes from within (v. 14). In precisely these events God, the Lord of history, will carry out his judgment" (*The Revelation of John*, CC [Minneapolis: Fortress, 1993], 188). B. H. Carroll adds, "Whatever the meaning of the symbols, 'the earth, sea, rivers and fountains, sun, the throne of the beast, the great river Euphrates, the air,' on which in succession the bowls of wrath were poured, they represent exhaustively the whole resources of Satan's kingdom under its apostate forms of a Holy Roman Empire, its papal head, and its harlot counterfeit church. While we may not be dogmatic in the interpretation of these symbols, the meanings given are the expression of sincere and thoughtful judgment" (*The Book of Revelation*, in *An Interpretation of the English Bible*, vol. 17, ed. J. B. Cranfill [Nashville: Broadman, 1947], 173–74).

351 Irenaeus, in a famous passage, remarks that "the whole exodus of the people out of Egypt, which took place under divine guidance, was a type and image of the exodus of the Church which should take place from among the Gentiles; and for this cause He leads it out at last from this world into His own inheritance, which Moses the servant of God did not [bestow], but which Jesus the Son of God shall give for an

Just as the second angel's bowl of wrath had been poured out on the sea, a third angel turns to the springs of water and the rivers—the fresh water supply of the earth, which is poisoned and also becomes blood. The entire population of the planet is now threatened since most of the conventional supplies of fresh water seem to be afflicted by this plague. At this point John hears the "angel of the waters" provide the rationale for this particular plague. The expression "the angel of the waters," may be understood as "the angel in charge of the waters," as the NIV translators chose to render the phrase. While this is an expansion of the text, it probably does get the point. A portion of the work of angels, as hinted in Scripture, is the care of the cosmos; and to find an angel responsible for these waters is not surprising.

The judgment offered relates to the habits of the world system as embodied in the dragon and the two beasts, who have done all within their power to persecute the people of God and wreak havoc on the purpose and plan of God for the universe. God's judgments are declared to be entirely just, coming as they do from the hand of One who exists and has always existed as the Holy One. His holy character mandates that His actions be just. The justice of His action is iterated in v. 6. Because the inhabitants of the earth in following the dragon have shed the blood of the saints and the prophets, God is justified in giving them blood to drink. "Just due" (*axios*) interestingly is the word used to describe the worthiness of the Lamb in Rev 4:11.[352] Just as the Lamb is worthy of adoration, so are the enemies of God entirely worthy of the justice they receive.

Two principles are at work here. First, "a man reaps what he sows" (Gal 6:7). However, in addition to that, the expression *axios*, referring to the ontological worth of the Lamb, also depicts the worthiness of all men to receive judgment. This concept is one of the most difficult for contemporaries of the present age to comprehend. The tendency is to believe that if people are innately religious and demonstrate morality in some ways, if they have a religion and pray, they therefore are certainly going to be safe in the judgment. To the

---

inheritance. And if any one will devote a close attention to those things which are stated by the prophets with regard to the [time of the] end, and those which John the disciple of the Lord saw in the Apocalypse, he will find that the nations [are to] receive the same plagues universally, as Egypt then did particularly" (*Against Heresies* 4.30.4, trans. A. Roberts and W. H. Rambaut, *ANF* 1:504).

352 Liddell and Scott trace the roots of the ἄξιος where it appears originally as a word emphasizing a counterbalancing weight. After Homer the word gains the moral connotation of worthy or estimable. Eventually, the idea, which is featured in the text here, simply means "deserving" (LSJ, 171).

contrary, the only thing that men are worthy to receive is judgment, as revealed herein. This is avoided by anyone totally on the basis of God's grace. Having refused God's grace and followed the beasts, now men on the earth receive their just judgment. The appropriateness of these two plagues, turning various bodies of water to blood, focuses on the long history of the suffering and bloodshed of God's people. Now the persecutors must drink blood.

From the altar there is a response in v. 7. Once more the phrase Lord God Almighty makes use of the three terms "Lord," "God," and *pantokratōr*, meaning "altogether mighty." His judgments fall into two important categories. First, they are true; second, they are absolutely just. The two concepts hold naturally together. There could be every intention for justice; but without truth, how could justice be known and accomplished? Likewise, one could know truth but fail to reveal it, making justice impossible. God's judgments embrace both truth and justice.

16:8–10 The fourth and fifth angels pour out their bowls, and the effects are interesting in contrast one to the other. When the fourth angel pours out his bowl, the sun is the target. Earlier, in Rev 8:12, the sun was deprived of a portion of its light and heat-giving capacities, which could have been due to atmospheric problems on the earth or likely an effect on the sun itself. Now, however, as the angel pours out his bowl on the sun, apparently the effects of the rays of the sun are greatly strengthened so that the sun is given power to scorch people with fire. Massive explosions on the solar surface have been chronicled by astronomers, and the effects of those titanic explosions can be traced to some degree throughout the solar system. Similar features of other stars have also been observed even to the point of flame-outs and the apparent development of black holes. Whatever the case, seemingly God causes this to happen so that the temperature on the earth is greatly increased and the intensity of the heat is a devastating blow to the population.

The inhabitants of the earth seem to know the precise cause for all this, attributing it properly to an act of God; they proceed to curse the name of God, who had control over these plagues. In addition, they refuse to repent or glorify Him. Only in chap. 11 was there a case of God's judgment that caused people to give glory and honor to Him. Strangely, every other place where the obvious judgments of God are manifest, the opposite seems to be the case. Men refused to repent or glorify Him as God, and in this case, they heaped up blasphemous accusations toward the name of God. Again, the natural tendency among humans is to suppose that once the inevitability of judgment is properly assessed, repentance surely will follow. In Luke 16, when the rich man died and found himself in Hades, he asked that Lazarus be sent by God to his brethren because he assumed that if one went to them from the dead, then they would believe and would not pursue their godless course of activity. Therefore, they could avoid coming to the place where he had been sent. This answer is appropriate. Abraham responded, "If they do not hear Moses and the prophets, neither will they be persuaded though one rise from the dead" (Luke 16:31). In other words, the strange circumstance of the human family is that their rebellion against God has nothing to do with the evidence. In this case, the inhabitants of the earth are precisely aware of the reason for their judgments, and yet their fury against God only increases.

In v. 10 the fifth angel pours out his bowl of wrath, and this is directed specifically to the throne of the beast. His kingdom is plunged into darkness. This seems to be the antithesis of what likely would have been the case with the fourth angel and gives further evidence to the fact that these judgments are in fact sequential rather than contemporaneous or overlapping. Since essentially the beast rules the entire kingdom, the extended period of darkness may be considered global. The peculiarity of this particular plague is the result—men are said to gnaw their tongues in agony. Schneider, commenting on the use of this *hapax legomenon* (*masaomai*), translated "gnaw" or "chew," offers the following observation:

> It can hardly be assumed that the darkness and pain are results of stinging scorpions which darken the sun (9:1 ff.), or that the darkness alone is πόνος [*ponos*], or that there is textual confusion. It seems rather that there is reflected here the genuine experience of the divine. In hallucinations men bite their own tongues in circumstances of great excitement; the confusion of images shows that the sense of pain on experiencing the vision was so strong that it could not find adequate plastic expression.[353]

To determine from the text what about the darkness results in this kind of agony is impossible. Usually, one might expect the painful boils that were part of the first plague or the scorching heat of the third angel to create such agony, but darkness would not generally have such a result.[354] However, this darkness

---

353 From C. Schneider, *TDNT* 4:515. H. Alford calls attention to the fact that μασάομαι was confined to the comedians and later Greek prose (*The Greek Testament* [Chicago: Moody, 1958], 4:700).

354 Responding to both preterist and historicist interpreters of the Apocalypse,

produces not only this reaction but also the continued cursing of the God of heaven because of all of their pains and their sores. Furthermore, they still refuse to repent.

C. The Sixth Bowl of Wrath—an Unholy Trinity (16:12–16)

[12]Then the sixth angel poured out his bowl on the great river Euphrates, and its water was dried up, so that the way of the kings from the east might be prepared. [13]And I saw three unclean spirits like frogs *coming* out of the mouth of the dragon, out of the mouth of the beast, and out of the mouth of the false prophet. [14]For they are spirits of demons, performing signs, *which* go out to the kings of the earth and of the whole world, to gather them to the battle of that great day of God Almighty.

[15]"Behold, I am coming as a thief. Blessed *is* he who watches, and keeps his garments, lest he walk naked and they see his shame."

[16]And they gathered them together to the place called in Hebrew, Armageddon.

The sixth angel now pours out his bowl on the great river Euphrates, and the water is dried up to prepare the way for the kings of the East. The Euphrates River, running for approximately 1,728 miles from the northwest to the southeast, has always been seen as one of the lines of demarcation between the East and the West as well as the fuel for ancient rivalries between Occident and Orient. Beyond the Euphrates River the desert stretches for a way and then gives way to the Zagros Mountains in what is modern Iran. With its ultimate boundary, the land of Israel was to stretch to the river Euphrates. The greatest extent of the Solomonic Empire extended only to Tadmor in the wilderness, which

---

E. W. Bullinger observes, "Great is the vexation caused by this awful darkness. And yet we are asked to believe that this is nothing more than the Suppression of the Monasteries, etc., in France, in 1789, by Napoleon. Is this what all the prophets have been occupied with? Even symbols must symbolise something that is congruous. But, here, the bringing on the gross darkness is made to symbolise the suppression of what is *the cause of darkness!* If it were taken to symbolise the *setting up* of monasteries, it would be more relevant. No wonder that darkness has come over this book—when imagination is substituted for faith" (*Commentary on Revelation* [Grand Rapids: Kregel, 1984], 485). But Moffatt is typical of those who see it otherwise: "The ninth Egyptian plague of darkness (due to the eclipse, *cf.* viii. 12?) falls on Rome, aggravating the previous pains of the Romans (ver. 2) and driving them into exasperation and fresh blasphemy instead of repentance" ("The Revelation of St. John the Divine," *Expositor's Greek New Testament*, ed. R. Nicoll [Grand Rapids: Eerdmans, 1951], 5:447).

remains approximately 100 miles west of the river Euphrates and is the location of the later Roman city of Palmyra. Its excavated ruins may still be visited in the country of Syria. The point of the pouring of this bowl of wrath to dry up the river is to expedite the approach of the kings from the East. One might suppose that the coming of the kings from the East is related to antagonism to the beast and his government in the West. However, more likely there is a unifying of all of these kingdoms against the work of God, and so the kings of the East are merely coming to join with the beasts of chap. 13 in their nefarious project.

At this point John beholds another phenomenal development. Three evil spirits, which to him appeared like frogs, came out of the mouth—one from the dragon, a second from the beast that came out of the sea, and the third from the false prophet or the beast out of the land. Frogs were unclean animals in the Bible and were always viewed with a certain loathing by most civilizations (Exod 8:2–15). Frogs constituted one of the plagues on Egypt and may be the background for these frogs, although clearly from the text the frogs only have the despicable nature of these amphibians and, in fact, are evil spirits.[355]

The spirit world is a real world. Angels themselves are "ministering spirits," and the demonic world, insofar as one can determine from Scripture, is inhabited by fallen angels who "did not keep their positions of domain" (Jude 6). The source of these three evil spirits, one from the dragon and the other two from the beasts, depicts the nature of this unholy trinity. They represent "spirits of demons," but they are nonetheless able to perform miraculous signs. The Signs and Wonders movements within orthodox Christianity have been

---

355 Early interpretations of the Apocalypse are interesting in their assessment of these frogs. Primasius notes, "Perhaps for this reason he adds the horrible filthiness of frogs as a comparison with their impudence. For like frogs living in the sewers at night, these false prophets make a great noise through the damnable ranting of their error. Just as frogs are loathsome in the places they inhabit, in their appearance and in their annoying croaking, so the devil with his followers is recognized to be abominable to the truth and is deservedly and justly damned to eternal fire" (*Revelation*, ACCS, 257). Oecumenius is equally vivid: "The demons are compared to frogs because they rejoice in the muddy and slimy life of human beings, and because the present murky and flabby life of sinners is preferred by them to the restrained and austere life of the righteous, since the demons are very envious and rejoice in the destruction of the living. . . . The assembling of the kings to make war against each other at the time of the end is a form of trickery on the part of the demons. He calls the day *great*, which means 'that moment.' For it is truly great and fearful, as Joel also calls it in the words, 'before the great and indisputable day of the Lord comes'" (*Commentary on the Apocalypse*, trans. J. N. Sugget, FC 112 [Washington, DC: Catholic University of America Press, 2006], 142).

slow to recognize the warnings of the Bible about such movements. While certainly there were signs and wonders associated with the developments of the early church in the book of Acts, also the Jews are rebuked by Christ because they look for "a miraculous sign" (Matt 16:4). Furthermore, repeatedly Scripture warns of the ability of the existence of satanically inspired signs and wonders, which are there for the purpose of deceiving, as it were, the elect. Here the deception, however, is not of the elect but rather to draw all of the kings of the whole world so that they are brought together in one place for "that great day of God Almighty," which is thus denominated because the patience and long-suffering of God has ended. Now evil will be dealt the final blow, and the day of God and His reign on earth will be ushered in.

At this point the writer interjects a warning for the saints of God, "Behold, I come like a thief!" The Greek word for "thief" is *kleptēs*. The question in the verse relates not so much to the coming of Christ as a thief as to the audience hearing the remark. Some interpreters believe that this is an interjection for John's audience and for all succeeding believers in the ages of the church to follow.[356] This position is held by many who believe that there will a thief-like coming of Christ prior to the tribulation period and then an obvious return of Christ at the end of the tribulation period, ushering in the millennium. Some of these interpreters note that as the thief comes unexpectedly and may be virtually unknown until after his theft has been accomplished, so it is that there is a warning to John's readers in the first century that Jesus is coming as a thief. Other interpreters prefer to see this as a reference to His actual return at the beginning of his millennial reign.[357] While that would not be a secretive return,

---

356 An occasional commentator will actually discount any "return of Christ" in the passage. Blount reckons that "the great day of God's rule is described as an appearance; it is a person, not merely an event. That appearance will come suddenly, just as the one like a child of humanity had already explained in 3:3. The connection between the two verses suggests that it is the same son, the Lamb, who is speaking here. The metaphor also counts against using Revelation as a kind of temporal road map whose writings are a code that, when read correctly, can predict the movement of the end of days" (B. K. Blount, *Revelation*, NTL [Louisville, KY: Westminster John Knox, 2009], 305). J. Walvoord sees the emphasis of the passage as "a unifying factor . . . that the coming in view results in loss for those who are not ready" (*The Revelation of Jesus Christ: A Commentary* [Chicago: Moody, 1966], 238).

357 For example, J. A. Seiss comments, "What means this strange announcement here? It is plainly the voice of Jesus, and the word is like to that so often given to the Church with reference to His coming again; but how does it apply here, after so many classes, including the great body of the saved, are already in heaven, with all

certainly the return would be unannounced as to its precise moment; hence, the warning may be for those who are urged to constancy despite the incredible sorrows that they are experiencing on every hand in the tribulation period.

Now occurs the third of seven beatitudes in the book of Revelation, the others occurring in 1:3; 14:13; 19:9; 20:6; 22:7; and 22:14. The Greek word *makarios* is a reference to anyone who is especially favored of God. One is blessed who "watches" and "keeps his garments." The reference here is meant to encourage the readers to maintain purity and righteousness before God so that one does not end up naked and therefore experience great shame (*aschēmosunē*). Even in the modern immoral age there is still an inherent reticence about being exposed in public and the shame that would be a part of that. Here, however, the shame in view is not physical nakedness but the revelation of the sinful heart and its rebellion against God. Those, then, who are aware of the fact that Christ could come at any moment and therefore stay and maintain watchfulness and vigilance remain clothed in the righteousness bestowed on them by Christ, and they are blessed.

In v. 16 is found one of the major problems of interpretation in the book of Revelation. All the kings of the earth are gathered together in a place that in Hebrew is called Armageddon. Precisely identifying this location presents the interpreter with some major difficulties. This is strange because the concept of the last great battle of history, or Armageddon, has become so impressed on the vocabulary of world inhabitants that even people who have no claim to Christianity are frequently aware of the concept; and it is not uncommon to find it mentioned almost any place in the world. The word "Armageddon" is actually a combination of the Hebrew words *har*, meaning "mountain," and *Megiddo*, a city located in the Valley of Esdraelon, also called the Plain of Jezreel. Insofar as interpreters have been able to discover, there is not a mountain of Megiddo. The present-day ruins of Megiddo, which have been extensively excavated, lie on the south side of the Valley of Esdraelon, not far from the beginning of Mount Carmel, which then stretches toward the sea, ending at the modern city of Haifa.

At the other end of the valley are the mountains of Gilboa where King

---

their anxious watching past? By referring to the vision interjected at the opening of this account of the seven last plagues, we may perhaps come upon the true explanation. . . . Somewhere about this time, then, Christ comes for this last band of the children of the resurrection, whether dead or yet living. Of course, it is a coming of the same kind and character as his coming for those saints who were taken earlier; for it is the completion of that one coming for his people which is everywhere set forth" (*The Apocalypse: Lectures on the Book of Revelation* [Grand Rapids: Zondervan, 1962], 379).

Saul and his son Jonathan were slain. On the south side of the valley beyond Megiddo are the mountains of Samaria. To the north of the valley stretches the hill country of Galilee; and Mount Tabor, a rounded mountain protruding upward from the plains of Esdraelon to a height of about 1,843 feet and is believed by some to have been the mount of the transfiguration—a major site in that area. The valley below, as well as the slope of the mountains, form a path that runs between Megiddo and Mount Carmel to pick up the Via Maris.

The Highway by the Sea is a strategic military point as evidenced by the frequency of significant battles in biblical as well as other times. Various interpreters have attempted different solutions to explain the mountain of Megiddo but none with any stellar success.[358] For all of this, almost all interpreters who tend to advocate a literal understanding of the text have looked to this famous Valley of Esdraelon as the proper location for the battle. Obviously, a battle of the immense proportions that are presented in the Apocalypse could not be

---

358 For instance, Blount avers, "The place of assembly is called in Hebrew *Harmagedōn*. Since the term is used only here in the entire Bible, it should not attract the kind of interpretive attention that many church traditions have given it over the centuries. More than likely John had conflated two Hebrew words, *har měgiddôn*, which means 'mountain of Megiddo.' 'Megiddo was an ancient city that guarded the pass through the Central Highlands at the Jezreel Valley. Because of its strategic location, Megiddo was an important military site' (Reddish 312). It was the site of several notable battles in Jewish history. According to Judg 5:19, Deborah and Barak defeated the Canaanite army of Jabin there. In 2 Kgs 9:27 King Ahaziah of Judah died there while fleeing Jehu. The tragic death of the reformist king of Judah, Josiah, also occurred there during a battle with Pharaoh Neco of Egypt (2 Kgs 23:29–30; cf. 2 Chr 35:22; 1 Esd 1:29–31). Because the area was associated with significant battles in the history of Israel, it is not odd that John would locate the assembly in preparation for apocalyptic conflict there. The difficulty is that Megiddo was not actually located on a mountain but on a plain. Scholars who suggest that John is mixing his images so that the familiar name could fit into the prophetic expectations for an eschatological mountain conflict are no doubt correct. In any case, what is most important to remember is that John does not intend a literal but symbolic battle, whose result will be the realization and recognition of the lordship of God and the Lamb" (*Revelation*, 306–7). D. E. Aune notes the possibility preferred by Oecumenius and Andrew of Caesarea that the meaning does not include the concept of a mountain at all: "Both Oecumenius (Hoskier, *Oecumenius*, 180) and Andreas of Caesarea (Schmid, *Studien*, 1/1:175) claim that Ἀρμαγεδών means διακοπή or διακοπτομένη, i.e., 'cutting' or 'cut through' because it is the place where the hostile enemies of God will attempt to 'cut through' and conquer" (*Revelation 6–16*, WBC 52b [Dallas, TX: Word, 1997], 899). See also discussion of the theological significance of the expression in Hans K. LaRondelle, "The Etymology of *Har-Magedon* (Rev 16:16)," *AUSS* 27, no. 1 (Spring 1989): 69–73.

contained within this one valley, though it is large. More probably, the conflict covers the 200 miles or so mentioned in Rev 14:20, where the blood of the conflict is spattered to the height of the horses' bridles due to the violence of the conflict. But the site of the ancient city of Megiddo and the hill country and mountains surrounding the Valley of Esdraelon may well be the staging point for either the initiation or the culmination of that great conflict.

D. The Seventh Bowl of Wrath—Consummation (16:17–21)

[17]Then the seventh angel poured out his bowl into the air, and a loud voice came out of the temple of heaven, from the throne, saying, "It is done!" [18]And there were noises and thunderings and lightnings; and there was a great earthquake, such a mighty and great earthquake as had not occurred since men were on the earth. [19]Now the great city was divided into three parts, and the cities of the nations fell. And great Babylon was remembered before God, to give her the cup of the wine of the fierceness of His wrath. [20]Then every island fled away, and the mountains were not found. [21]And great hail from heaven fell upon men, *each hailstone* about the weight of a talent. Men blasphemed God because of the plague of the hail, since that plague was exceedingly great.

The seventh angel now pours out the final bowl of God's wrath. He pours it out into the air.[359] At this point there comes a voice from the throne declaring, "It is done!" This is a translation of *gegonen*, the perfect tense of *ginomai*, which stresses the fact that something has been done with effects that linger into the future. Verification of this comes in terms of flashes of lightning, rumblings, peals of thunder, and an earthquake of such severity that the author states, "such a mighty and great earthquake as had not occurred since men were on the earth."

"The great city" split into three parts, and the earthquake was of such

---

359 The Venerable Bede comments on the fact that this bowl is poured into the air: "Above, the blood of vengeance went forth as far as the bridles of the horses, namely, the unclean spirits; and so here, when the same final vengeance was poured upon the same aërial powers, it is said that 'it is done,' that is, that the end is come, when, as the Apostle says, 'the last enemy, death, shall be destroyed.' Thus far, under the name of 'plagues,' the last persecution is described, all which Tichonius will have to be understood in a contrary way. It is, 'the plague which cannot be healed,' he says, and 'the great wrath,' to receive the power of sinning in an especial manner against the saints, and not as yet to be overtaken by the greater wrath of God" (*The Explanation of the Apocalypse*, trans. E. Marshall [Oxford and London: James Parker, 1878], 114–15).

worldwide dimensions that the cities of all the nations collapsed (v. 19). This great city almost certainly refers to Jerusalem. The text had observed a previous earthquake in that city, but this one splits it into three parts and is anticipated by the vision of Zechariah (Zech 14:1–5). The devastating effects of serious earthquakes are observable in earthquake-prone zones throughout the world. The ability of earth dwellers to prepare an adequate defense for themselves against hurricanes and tornadoes and other such storms is notably more efficient than the ability to prepare for the effects of an earthquake where there seems to be virtually no defense available.[360] Earthquakes are often caused by the movement of the earth's tectonic plates but are usually limited to a fairly small region. Apparently here the many constantly adjusting tectonic plates of the earth are caused to move simultaneously, creating the worldwide earthquake and the devastating effects described.

Specifically, the text says that God remembered Babylon the Great and "[gave] her the cup of the wine of the fierceness of His wrath." Once again, the discussion of the identity of Babylon is before the interpreter. And once again, the geographical reference is most likely to Babylon on the Tiber or the reconstituted form of the last-day Roman Empire. However, it is not unrelated to Babylon on the Euphrates since the religion and the morality spawned from Babylon on the Euphrates becomes incorporated in the Babylon on the Tiber of John's day and the final expression of a world empire in the last day.

The effects of this earthquake on islands and mountains alike is memorable. Not infrequently in earthquakes, islands that were formerly relatively prominent simply disappear as the plates move and the island is submerged beneath the surrounding seas. Mountains, too, can be violently affected. Conceivably the effects of this earthquake are so great as to obliterate some of the great mountains of the world.

A final part of the outpouring of this seventh angel's bowl of wrath is that hailstones weighing between 100 and 130 pounds begin to plummet from the heavens. Obviously, anyone hit with one of these stones would not survive. In

---

360 C. C. Rowland does not think of the passage as anything more than myth, but he does provide a vivid reflection on the passage: "Revelation may be seen as an imaginative commentary on the world, a prophetic critique of human delusion and the terrible consequences of social upheaval. It summons us to read the signs of the times with the visionary imagination and insight of prophecy and, at the same time, to recognize that the prophetic words are addressed to people with minds and habits so formed by culture and human interests that they cannot understand and repent. They need to be jolted from the slumber of incomprehension caused by the idolatrous habits of oppression, violence, and hedonism" ("The Book of Revelation," *NIB* [Nashville: Abingdon, 1998], 12:678).

Middle America, to hear a weather reporter speak of baseball-sized hail or even rarely softball-sized hail is not uncommon. Such can be incredibly destructive to property, animals, and even people. A hailstone weighing a hundred pounds, however, would be roughly a hundred times larger than a softball-sized piece of hail. The destruction is unfathomable.

For the third time in one chapter, men cursed God because the plague of the hail was so terrible. The picture here is of an earth convulsed with the judgments of God. For the entire history of the human family, rebellion against God has been escalating. The temporary and local judgments in which He manifested His fury against sin have all been warnings. Now, at the end of the great tribulation and the outpouring of the seven bowls of wrath, God's judgment escalates to such an extent that the world witnesses the incredible wrath of God.

Pastoral Excursus: Demonic Possession

The pouring of the sixth bowl of God's wrath on the earth features, among other things, three evil spirits reminding John of frogs, which suddenly appeared from the mouths of the dragon, the beast, and the false prophet. Confrontation with the world of the demonic was almost routine in the ministry of Jesus as recorded in the Gospels and also noted in Acts. The beast and the false prophet in the Apocalypse are humans; therefore, one is not surprised to find that they are demonically possessed. That the dragon, identified in the text as the Devil, should be pictured as being thus possessed when he is himself a spirit is unusual. Three important questions for pastors are generated by the text. First, is it possible for a person to be indwelt or "possessed" by a demon or, in biblical parlance, "demonized"? Second, can this happen to a believer? Third, how should this malady be identified and addressed?

Regarding the first query (i.e., can one be "demonized"), commentators have often denied the possibility as being nothing more than the arcane perspective of superstitious antiquity. Medical disabilities, according to some, were attributed to the demonic by prescientific authors. But this perspective contradicts the witness of the Scriptures and seriously repudiates the testimony of Jesus Himself. The biblical milieu conceived of a physical world that was complemented and expanded by a spiritual dimension, which included spirits both malevolent and benevolent. That a person, in fact, may be indwelt by a wicked spirit is as certain as the truth of the Holy Spirit's permanent indwelling of the individual believer (John 14:17). If the indwelling of God the Holy Spirit is possible, then so must demonic possession be a tragic reality.

However, there is no evidence that this can happen to a believer. No case exists in Scripture that indicates either by precedent or prescription that such a thing is possible. Further, the permanent indwelling of the Holy Spirit in a regenerate soul seems to preclude such a possibility. Spiritual wickedness can certainly be oppressive to believers and to churches, but this is external and not in the temple (the Greek word *naos*) of the Holy Spirit, the body of the believer.

When confronting the demonic, the follower of Jesus must recognize the serious consequences of such encounters. Christ, not the believer, is the only power sufficient for such encounters. Numbering or naming the evil spirits or carrying on conversations with them is absent from Scripture except for the brief encounter of the Lord with the Gadarene demoniac (Matt 8:28–34). The three evil spirits confronting the world of the great tribulation are powerful and knowledgeable, make use of miracles, and influence even the titular heads of state. Only God and the hosts of heaven are adequate to deal with thrones, powers, rulers, and authorities (Col 1:16). Consequently, the returning Christ ultimately defeats all evil powers. Prayer for the intervention of God and appeal to the name that is above all names constitute the only methods for demonic encounters.

6. The Judgment of Apostate Religion (17:1–18)

The identification of the beasts out of the sea and the earth in chap. 13 receives greater definition in chap. 17, which has a long history in the story of the church, especially beginning in the Reformation period when it became the focus text to identify the Roman Catholic Church as the scarlet woman. Protestants, suffering from the persecutions generated by the church at Rome, from that time until the present age, have identified the scarlet woman of chap. 17 as

308

the church at Rome.[361] This has been the case regardless of the interpretation of the text in relation to whether it is a part of the history of the church or belongs to the last days. As such, this text also becomes pivotal in the full identification of the two beasts.

Interpreting the Apocalypse involves above all else the ability to identify properly the diverse figures to whom John introduces the reader. In addition to the woman and the two beasts, there are seven hills and ten horns—all of which must be deciphered in order to determine the mind of the seer. By far, however, the scarlet woman, who is the central figure of these paragraphs, is the most important. The chapter provides at least ten observations, which, as a unit, assist in her identification: (1) She is a prostitute; (2) she sits on many waters; (3) the kings of the earth are her paramours; (4) she rides a seven-headed, ten-horned scarlet beast; (5) she carries a golden cup filled with abominations; (6) she has the title "mystery;" (7) she bears an identity with Babylon; (8) she is dressed in purple and scarlet and is fabulously wealthy; (9) she is drunk, having imbibed extensively the blood of the saints; and (10) she is identified with a great city that rules over all the kings of the earth. This impressive resumé becomes the focus and clue to the pericope that follows.

A. The Scarlet Woman (17:1–6)

[1]Then one of the seven angels who had the seven bowls came and talked with me, saying to me, "Come, I will show you the judgment of the great harlot who sits on many waters, [2]with whom the kings of the earth committed fornication, and the inhabitants of the earth were made drunk with the wine of her fornication."

[3]So he carried me away in the Spirit into the wilderness. And I saw a woman sitting on a scarlet beast *which was* full of names of blasphemy, having seven heads and

---

361 Colorful Luther, for example, speaks of the attempt of the Russian church to affiliate with Rome: "It is a notorious fact that the Russians desired to come into the Roman fellowship, but then the holy shepherd of Rome 'fed' those sheep of Christ in such a manner that they would not receive them unless they first bound themselves to a perpetual tax of I know not how many hundred thousands of ducats. Such 'food' they would not eat, and so they remain as they are, saying, if they must buy Christ, they would rather save their money until they come to Christ Himself, in heaven. Thus thou doest, thou scarlet whore of Babylon, as St. John calls thee—makest of our faith a mockery for all the world, and yet wouldest have the name of making every one a Christian" ("The Papacy at Rome: An Answer to the Celebrated Romanist at Leipzig" (1520), in *Works of Martin Luther* [Philadelphia: A. J. Holman, 1915], 1:392).

ten horns. ⁴The woman was arrayed in purple and scarlet, and adorned with gold and precious stones and pearls, having in her hand a golden cup full of abominations and the filthiness of her fornication. ⁵And on her forehead a name *was* written:

MYSTERY,

BABYLON THE GREAT,

THE MOTHER OF HARLOTS AND OF THE ABOMINATIONS OF THE EARTH

⁶I saw the woman, drunk with the blood of the saints and with the blood of the martyrs of Jesus. And when I saw her, I marveled with great amazement.

17:1-6 The fact that one of the seven angels, who had one of the seven bowls, invites John to view the punishment of the great prostitute evidences that in some way or another the vision of chaps. 17 and 18 relates to the seven bowls of wrath. Whether this is viewed as an actual part of the judgment of the seventh angel's bowl or is taken to be a further explanation for the materials beginning in chap. 13 and including the seven bowls of wrath cannot be decided with certainty. This commentator leans toward the first conclusion since especially the seventh bowl of wrath, which is poured out into the air, is said to involve God's memory of the crimes of Babylon the Great.[362]

In the Apocalypse the key to interpretation is always proper identification. In order to identify the scarlet woman of chap. 17, the author provides ten distinguishing marks. Verse 1 contains two of those marks. First, John is told that he will view the judgment of "the great prostitute." The word translated "prostitute" (*porneia*) denotes general sexual licentiousness. The usual word for "adultery" (*moicheia*) gives way here to the morally encompassing term that sim-

---

362 F. J. Murphy notes, "Chapters 17 and 18 are sometimes called the 'Babylon Appendix,' a usage we follow here, but this should not give the impression that the passage is less central than it is. Since the focus of the entire book is the defeat of Rome and Satan and the establishment of God's kingdom, chapter 17 elaborates on one of the most important themes in Revelation. The relationship between the defeat of Rome and the consummation of the church's relationship with Christ is conveyed by the fact that the fall of Rome in chapters 17 and 18 leads to the announcement of the marriage feast of the Lamb, where the bride is the church (19:6-9). This implies a contrast between the whore and the bride. The contrast is made clearer still in 21:9 when a vision of the Lamb's bride is introduced in precisely the same way as is the vision of Babylon in chapter 17" (*Fallen is Babylon: The Revelation to John*, The New Testament in Context [Harrisburg, PA: Trinity Press International, 1998], 348).

ply refers to reckless and immoral behavior in the sexual realm. In the history of Israel, idolatry and general unfaithfulness to God are always presented in terms of spiritual adultery, and here this unfaithfulness is profound. The woman has established a way of life, which is the path of rebellion against God. Second, she is said to sit on many waters. Some interpreters take the *epi*, translated here "on," to be "beside many waters;" however, the NKJV's translation is preferred because the usual use of the term is "on" or "upon." Verse 15 specifically interprets this allegation by saying that the waters upon which she sits represent peoples, multitudes, nations, and languages. Verse 3 contains an expansion of her unfaithfulness but also constitutes a third point of identification. The kings of the earth have specifically committed adultery with the scarlet woman, and as a result of that union the inhabitants of the earth are intoxicated with the wine of her adulteries. As will be determined later, the woman who is riding the beast is dependent on that beast and, as a religious system, is in union with the beast. Consequently, the fact that the kings of the earth have committed fornication with her suggests an unwholesome union of church and state, which results in the intoxication of all the peoples of the earth.

At this point the angel carries John into a wilderness. Those who would argue for a literal reestablishment of the ancient city of Babylon in the last days might find some assistance in this designation. However, this is not an essential interpretation, and the reference may only be to the devastation involved in the actions of this woman.[363] John now sees that this woman is sitting on a scarlet beast covered with blasphemous names and with seven heads and ten horns. This beast, of course, is the one rising from the sea in chap. 13 and represents the political entity of the last days, providing a fourth hint as to the woman's identification. The fifth insight arises from the ostentation of her wealth. In v. 4, the woman is dressed in purple and scarlet, the colors of royalty, and she is bedecked with gold, precious stones, and pearls. This fifth mark of identification focuses on the incredible wealth in her possession.[364]

---

363 For Oecumenius, "The wilderness symbolizes her coming desolation" (*Commentary on the Apocalypse*, trans. J. N. Sugget, FC 112 [Washington, DC: Catholic University of America Press, 2006], 146).

364 Cyprian, typical of many church fathers, seizes the opportunity to address the modesty issue: "In the Apocalypse: 'And there came one of the seven angels having vials, and approached me, saying, Come, I will show thee the condemnation of the great whore, who sitteth upon many waters, with whom the kings of the earth have committed fornication. And I saw a woman who sate upon a beast. And that woman was clothed with a purple and scarlet robe; and she was adorned with gold, and precious stones, and

The sixth identification focuses on the golden cup in her hand, noting that it is filled with abominable things and with the filth of her adulteries. While the chalice is gold, the contents are the filthy contaminants of her licentiousness. This leads to the title written on her forehead and the seventh identification, which is simply "mystery" or *mustērion* in the Greek New Testament. Some believe that the title is "Mystery, Babylon the Great," but there does seem to be a distinction being made in these identifications. Generally, in Scripture the word "mystery" refers not to a crime scene or an unresolved occurrence but rather to a fact that could not have been discerned by human ingenuity and had to be revealed by God (Matt 13:11; Rom 11:25; 1 Cor 15:51; Eph 5:32, etc.). However, another use of the term was known to the ancients, referring particularly to the mystery religions, which were well known in the first century and had a history reaching all the way back to the genesis of false religion.[365] Here there

---

pearls, holding a golden cup in her hand full of curses, and impurity, and fornication of the whole earth.' Also to Timothy: 'Let you women be such as adorn themselves with shamefacedness and modesty, not with twisted hair, nor with gold, nor with pearls, or precious garments, but as becometh women professing chastity, with a good conversation.' Of this same thing in the Epistle of Peter to the people at Pontus: 'Let there be in a woman not the outward adorning of ornament, or of gold, or of apparel, but the adorning of the heart.' Also, in Genesis: 'Thamar covered herself with a cloak, and adorned herself; and when Judah beheld her, she appeared to him to be a harlot'" (*The Treatises of Cyprian*, Treatise 12: "Three Books of Testimonies Against the Jews," 3.36, *ANF* 5:544–45).

365 Commenting on the somewhat amorphous nature of these "mysteries," W. Burkert says, "The general lack of organization, solidarity, and coherence in ancient mysteries, which may appear as a deficiency from a Jewish or Christian point of view, is outweighed by some positive aspects with which we may easily sympathize. The absence of religious demarcation and conscious group identity means the absence of any rigid frontiers against competing cults as well as the absence of any concept of heresy, not to mention excommunication. The pagan gods, even the gods of mysteries, are not jealous of one another; they form, as it were, an open society. If Mithras is somehow a stranger, he still keeps good company with familiar divinities such as Helios, Kronos, and Zeus. The findings in the sanctuaries and the texts of the inscriptions are eloquent, though confusing to scholars who look for neat systematization. It is common in sanctuaries of Sarapis and Isis, as well as those of Meter and Mithras, to dedicate statues of other gods or to make vows to them. Mithraea in particular have yielded a rich harvest of divine statues of all kinds. Cumont's attempts to find Avestan avatars in each case obviously cannot be upheld. A *mystes* initiated to a particular god is not in any way prevented from turning to another god in addition" (*Ancient Mystery Cults* [Cambridge, MA: Harvard University Press, 1987], 48–49).

is evidently a deliberate move on the part of the apostle to identify this scarlet woman in some way with those mystery religions of antiquity.

In fact, this leads to the eighth point of identification. She is called "Babylon the Great," linking her directly to the circumstances associated with the development of the substituted anthropocentric faith of ancient Babylon as recorded in Gen 10 and 11.[366] The construction of the Tower of Babel was not a clever idyll—like *Jack and the Beanstalk*, whereby a tower enables humans to climb into the heavens. The ancients were far more sophisticated than that. What does seem to be in view is the establishment of a religion with a central temple and that religion in contradistinction to the revealed faith of God.[367] Consequently, Babylon the Great is identified as the mother of prostitutes and indeed of all the abominations of the earth. In other words, Babylon the Great and the mystery religions constitute the mother of all unfaithfulness. Another mark of identification is in v. 6. John says that he saw the woman and she was drunk with the blood of the saints and the blood of those who bore testimony

---

366 Luther's description of the connection between Rome and Babylon perpetuates this view: "Next, Eck and Emser and their fellow-conspirators undertook to instruct me concerning the primacy of the pope. Here too not to prove ungrateful to such learned men, I acknowledge that I have profited much from their labors. For while I denied the divine authority of the papacy, I still admitted its human authority. But after hearing and reading the super-subtle subtleties of these coxcombs, with which they so adroitly prop up their idol (for my mind is not altogether unteachable in these matters), I now know for certain that the papacy is the kingdom of Babylon and the power of Nimrod, the mighty hunter [Gen. 10:8–9]. Once more, therefore, that all may turn out to my friends' advantage, I beg both the booksellers and my reader that after burning what I have published on the subject they hold to his proposition: THE PAPACY IS THE GRAND HUNTING OF THE BISHOP OF ROME. This is proved by the arguments of Eck, Emser, and the Leipzig lecturer on the Scriptures" ("The Babylonian Captivity of the Church" in *Martin Luther's Basic Theological Writings*, ed. T. F. Lull [Minneapolis: Fortress, 1989], 268). Luther is said to have gone further in *Table Talk*, alleging that the pope is the Antichrist. "I believe the pope is the masked and incarnate devil because he is the Antichrist. As Christ is God incarnate, so the Antichrist is the devil incarnate" (*LW* 54.346).

367 Oecumenius notes, "There was, he says, *written on her forehead*, as if it were an inscription on a monument, saying who she was, that she is *Babylon, the mother of harlots*—*Babylon* because of the turmoil and confusion in her, and the persecution of the saints (for the name 'Babylon,' signifies confusion, as has been mentioned), and she is the *mother* of fornication and of rebellion against God. For how can she not be a mother and teacher when she persecutes the gospel and those proclaiming it and persuades the nations to remain attached to their ancestral error?" (*Commentary on the Apocalypse*, 146).

to Christ. Whoever this woman is, she is a persecutor of the saints of God. This persecution is not cursory but determined and repeated with little interruption.

The result for John is unmitigated astonishment. Literally the text reads, "And I was astonished with great astonishment." The use of the verb "to be amazed" with the noun *thauma*, meaning "wonder," is then accentuated with the word *mega* or "great," underscoring the extent of the astonishment for John. The question has to be asked as to why John was so thoroughly astonished when the sixteen chapters preceding the seventeenth chapter are considered, including all of the incredible visions that he has already seen. Why at this point in time does the seer experience such overwhelming astonishment? The question is not addressed in the text; hence, no certain answer can be given. Perhaps a safe venture would be to suggest that John sees something unexpected about the character of this scarlet woman. Most of the previous visions have been known to John in some form from his reading of the Old Testament. As a prisoner of Rome on the Isle of Patmos, he would find little amazement in discovering that the rulers of the world and the world system would be in a contrarian posture to the work of God. So perhaps what takes the apostle's breath away at this point is his recognition that this is a religious system purporting to be something it is not. Hence the word "unfaithfulness" or "prostitution" is used with regard to the scarlet woman. This strong imagery converging the ideas of deceit and wickedness may suggest a religious system purporting to represent the true God while actually doing the work of Satan.

B. The Beast that Carries Her (17:7–18)

⁷But the angel said to me, "Why did you marvel? I will tell you the mystery of the woman and of the beast that carries her, which has the seven heads and the ten horns. ⁸The beast that you saw was, and is not, and will ascend out of the bottomless pit and go to perdition. And those who dwell on the earth will marvel, whose names are not written in the Book of Life from the foundation of the world, when they see the beast that was, and is not, and yet is.

⁹"Here *is* the mind which has wisdom: The seven heads are seven mountains on which the woman sits. ¹⁰There are also seven kings. Five have fallen, one is, *and the* other has not yet come. And when he comes, he must continue a short time. ¹¹The beast that was, and is not, is himself also the eighth, and is of the seven, and is going to perdition.

¹²"The ten horns you saw are ten kings who have received no kingdom as yet, but they receive authority for one hour as kings with the beast. ¹³These are of one mind,

and they will give their power and authority to the beast. ¹⁴These will make war with the Lamb, and the Lamb will overcome them, for He is Lord of lords and King of kings; and those *who are* with Him *are* called, chosen, and faithful."

¹⁵Then he said to me, "The waters which you saw, where the harlot sits, are peoples, multitudes, nations, and tongues. ¹⁶And the ten horns which you saw on the beast, these will hate the harlot, make her desolate and naked, eat her flesh and burn her with fire. ¹⁷For God has put it into their hearts to fulfill His purpose, to be of one mind, and to give their kingdom to the beast, until the words of God are fulfilled. ¹⁸And the woman whom you saw is that great city which reigns over the kings of the earth."

17:7–18   The angel who had one of the seven bowls and had taken him into the wilderness to show him the great prostitute observes his astonishment and wonders verbally why John is so astonished. Nevertheless, he says, "I will tell to you the mystery of the woman and of the beast that carries her, which has the seven heads and the ten horns." Once again, the word *mustērion* is used, but here in its frequently observable sense of something that could not be subject to the mind and intellectual prowess of humans but had to be revealed of God. As such, the word choice of the seer is in notable and stark contrast to the word "mystery" in the title of the scarlet woman. The angel promises to provide that revelation.

In 17:8, the angel begins with the beast and, observing exactly what was presented in chap. 13, speaks of the beast as the one who once was and now is not but then will come out of the bottomless pit only to go to his destruction. The reader will remember from chap. 13 that one of the heads of the beast was wounded unto death and yet the beast lived. Now the miracle of having once been alive and then perishing only to rise again from the bottomless pit is the phenomenon that John observes. However, even emerging from the bottomless pit to live again is a temporary circumstance since the beast is going to destruction.

The word the NKJV translators usually render "bottomless pit," a translation of the Greek *abussos*, is a reference to the place of the dead, not dissimilar from the meaning of Hades. Some translations simply bring the word into English as "the Abyss." The Abyss is thought of as the prison house of departed wicked spirits. "Destruction" is a translation of *apōleia*, derived from a word carrying the sense of destruction or loss. The picture is destruction in the sense of total uselessness. An unmanned boat cut free from its moorings drifts away to destruction or uselessness. This is the ultimate end to which the beast is destined.

However, awaiting that ultimate destruction, the beast does create a marvelous effect on those inhabitants of the earth whose names are not written in the Book of Life from the creation of the world. One whose name has been written in the Book of Life would have a quality of spiritual discernment and would see through the deception. The vast majority of people on the earth, however, are clearly deceived by the beast, and the most deceptive aspect of this beast is the fact that he had ceased to exist and yet once again had come to life. Its resuscitation befuddles even the most discerning.

In v. 9, the angel stresses to John that the identification of this beast has need of a mind that is possessed of wisdom. This need for wisdom is demonstrated by the numerous interpretations of the verse and the paucity of agreement even among the most scholarly. Not only facts but also understanding will be essential. The seven heads of the beast represent seven hills on which the woman sits.[368] These also represent seven kings, five of whom have fallen, one of whom exists at that time, and another who has not yet come; but when he does come, he will remain for a short while. This seventh one is also the eighth kingdom that belongs to the seventh and is going to go to destruction.[369] This complicated passage has been the ground for almost endless interpretative discussions. The tendency of many interpreters has been to try to discover a reference here to seven Roman emperors, and some have found a reference to the Nero *redivivus* myth that Nero died but had come back to life.[370] John seems to be unaware of this myth, and the reference is more probably to the seven oppressive kingdoms that constantly subjected the people of God to intense per-

---

368 Victorinus says flatly, "The seven heads are the seven hills, on which the woman sits. That is the city of Rome" (*Commentary on the Apocalypse of the Blessed John* 17.9, *ANF* 7:357–58).

369 The note in the *The Believer's Study Bible* sums up the matter: "Verses 10 and 11 are perhaps the most debated of all passages in the Apocalypse. Since 'fallen' is language more appropriate for kingdoms than for emperors, the best solution is probably to see the five fallen kings of kingdoms as Egypt, Assyria, Babylon, Medo-Persia, and Greece. The sixth kingdom ('one is') is the Rome of John's day. The last or seventh ('the other has not yet come') is the revived form of the Roman Empire first in its diversified form of ten kingdoms, eventually yielding to the eighth and final form in the beast" (W. A. Criswell et al, eds. [Nashville: Thomas Nelson, 1991], 1822–23).

370 For example, Oecumenius sees this as a reference to the Roman emperors who persecuted the church. He names Nero, Domitian, Trajan, Severus, Decius, Valerian, and Diocletian (*Commentary on the Apocalypse*, 149). Numerous other configurations have been suggested. For these, see J. M. Ford, *Revelation*, AB (Garden City, NY: Doubleday, 1975), 289–91.

secution. These kingdoms enumerated in Holy Scripture according to Thomas are as follows, "The five kingdoms of the past are the ones who have persecuted God's people: (Egypt, Ezek 29–30; Nineveh or Assyria, Nah 3:1–19; Babylon, Isa 21:9 and Jer 50–51; Persia, Dan 10:13 and 11:2; Greece, Dan 11:3–4)."[371] Added to these five kingdoms would be the sixth—the Rome contemporary to John. These evil world systems—Egypt, Assyria, Babylon, Medo-Persia, and Greece—give way to the sixth, which is the Rome of John's day. The seventh follows—the last day of persecution by a world empire; and the eighth, the final expression of that which is actually one of the seven.[372]

Verse 12 identifies the ten horns as being ten kings who have not yet received a kingdom but who will for the short duration of one hour receive authority as kings along with the beast. They are apparently part of a final confederation of kingdoms, the precise identities of which are impossible to determine based on the Scriptures. The fact that they reign for only an hour is to indicate that they have a relatively short reign. The reason for this is then provided in v. 13: They have just one purpose, which is to give their power and authority to the beast. As a confederacy, they will in v. 14 make war against

---

371 R. L. Thomas, *Revelation 8-22: An Exegetical Commentary* (Chicago: Moody, 1995), 298.

372 J. A. Seiss provides a lengthy discussion of this view. Here is only a small portion of that discussion: "But what five imperial mountains like Rome had been and gone, up to that time? Is history so obscure as not to tell us with unmistakable certainty? Preceding Rome the world had but five great names or nationalities answering to imperial Rome, and those scarce a schoolboy ought to miss. They are Greece, Persia, Babylon, Assyria, and Egypt; no more, and no less. And these all were imperial powers like Rome. Here, then, are six of these regal mountains; the seventh is not yet come. When it comes it is to endure but a short time. This implies that each of the others continues a long time; and so, again, could not mean the dictators, decemvirs, and military tribunes of the early history of Rome, for some of them lasted but a year or two. Thus, then by the clearest, most direct, and most natural signification of the words of the record, we are brought to the identification of these seven mountain kings as the seven great world-powers, which stretch from the beginning of our present world to the end of it. Daniel makes the number less; but he started with his own times, and looked only down the stream. Here the account looks backward as well as forward. That which is first in Daniel is the third here, and that which is the sixth here is the fourth in Daniel. Only in the commencing point is there any difference. The visions of Daniel and the visions of John are from the same Divine Mind, and they perfectly harmonize, only that the latest are the amplest" (*The Apocalypse: Lectures on the Book of Revelation* [Grand Rapids: Zondervan, 1962], 393).

the Lamb, but this proves not to be a fruitful enterprise. The Lamb overcomes them, and the rationale for that conquering work of the Lamb is that He is in the end both the Lord of lords and the King of kings. Joining him in the final conflict with this ten-horned, seven-headed beast are all of those who are called of God as the elect and faithful.

The doctrine of election in Holy Scripture is referenced repeatedly in one way or another. That God has acted to choose some to salvation is beyond dispute for anyone who takes the Scriptures to be the infallible Word of God. However, exactly what this means and how it is to be understood in view of the responsibility assigned to humans to respond to God in the ways mandated in Scripture is beyond present human comprehension. Who has known the mind of the Lord and who has been His counselor? All efforts to explain this achieve only limited success. On the other hand, efforts to deny it must face the inevitability of what Scripture has said. Here the ones who are faithful have been both called by God and chosen by Him. The sequence of events is not without importance. The faithful were both called and chosen of God.

While no theologian has been able to plumb the mystery of how the elective providences of God can be reconciled with the responsibility of man, some conclusions from the doctrine can be safely asserted. First, salvation from initiation to consummation is the work of God. God's gracious plan, the extension of mercy, and the vicarious substitutionary atonement of Christ on the cross recognize no human effort to satisfy the just mandates of God. Second, God's election is twice affirmed to be related to his foreknowledge (Rom 8:29; 1 Pet 1:2). Dismissal of such recognition as arguments based on "simple foreknowledge" does nothing to diminish the declaration of these verses.

Third, the book of the Revelation concludes with an invitation addressed to "whoever is thirsty" to take freely of the gift of the water of life (22:17). John's reference to election must be read in the light of his concluding appeal. What can be safely affirmed is that no one comes to God who is not drawn by the Holy Spirit. Further, all who thirst for the Lord are invited to come and slake their thirst.[373]

Now the angel has one more interpretation, and this one begins with the prostitute. The waters on which the prostitute sits are peoples and multitudes and nations and languages. Her influence and her impact are global in scope. However, while she has incredible influence both on the peoples and nations of

---

373 See notes on the doctrine of election written by this author for Rom 8 in *The Believer's Study Bible*, ed. W. A. Criswell (Nashville: Thomas Nelson, 1991), 1611.

the world and manages to do so because she is upheld by the beast upon which she also rides, the ten horns or kingdoms that make up that last-day union actually hate the prostitute. This apparent inconsistency is not surprising. Political entities have almost always reckoned with the importance of religion. Whether political leaders actually practice the faith themselves or simply use it for their own ends, inevitably religion and the course of the nations have been wed together. One might argue that under distinctively atheistic regimes, such as would be found in Marxism, religion is absent; but shrewd observers have noted the religious tones of such utopianism even if the specific absence of a deity is posited. But, in almost every case, religion has been a convenient artifice to be used by the political establishment to bring about its will in any persons who might be recalcitrant.

Once the immediate value of the scarlet woman is no longer a consideration, the hatred for her espoused by the political system asserts itself; and they bring her to ruin, leaving her naked or exposed, and they eat her flesh and burn her with fire. However, according to v. 17, this is not simply an accidental development. Rather, God has actually put it in their hearts to accomplish His purpose. And though the beast, too, will be judged and go into destruction, as has already been prophesied, he nevertheless does accomplish the purpose of God by turning against the scarlet woman and bringing about her demise. All ungodliness is ultimately judged, but heresy (prostitution in the sense of unfaithfulness) is judged first because of the magnitude of its deleterious effects. The reign of the beast then continues only until God's words are fulfilled.

One final affirmation is found in v. 18: "[T]he woman you saw is the great city which rules over the kings of the earth." Here the identification can scarcely be debated any longer. Clearly this city is Rome, the city that ruled over all the world in John's day. Any first-century reader of John's Apocalypse would have noted the reference to the seven hills, since almost every inhabitant of the empire knew that Rome was the city of seven hills. It is not surprising, then, to learn in v. 18 that the woman is the great city that rules over the kings of the earth. Efforts to try to make this into Babylon on the Euphrates, in the estimation of this commentator, fail. One must ask the question: How would first-century readers have understood the text? Doubtless, they would have understood it to be Rome.

This being the case, can one conclude with many of the Reformers and other interpreters down even to the present age that the scarlet woman is the religious side of Rome or the Roman Church?[374] From a Protestant point of view, and even from a historical view of the realities of the inquisition and the tendency of the Roman Church toward accumulation of incredible wealth and its persecution of biblical Christians, why many have made this identification is easy to understand.

While it may be tempting to identify the church of Rome and its world-wide system as the prostitute that sits on many waters, several features mitigate against this conclusion. First, there is the unquestioned identification of Rome with Babylon. This connection suggests that while the Roman Church may well be an expression of Babylonianism, it is certainly not the only expression of Babylonianism. Babylonianism seems to exist anywhere in the world where religious faith is ecumenical, primarily experiential, imperialistic, hedonistic, and generally compromised. On the other hand, the faith of the New Testament is a faith of direct revelation and is exclusivistic and theocentric in every way. One may conclude that wherever you find religion attempting to dilute the pristine faith of the New Testament, you have an expression of Babylonianism. That may happen in the Roman Church but may and also does happen in Protestant churches and in every other expression of religion known to man. Some expressions of the Babylonian deceit are more obvious than others, but they extend far more widely than just to the church in Rome.[375]

Various interpreters here called attention to the Genesis account of the construction of the tower of Babel and suggested the connection between that edifice and the origins of apostate religion. Ken Mathews states the intentions of the Babelite builders as follows:

---

374 One of the most extensive and fascinating efforts to make the scarlet woman identical to the church in Rome is a book first published in 1916, called *The Two Babylons*. In this study A. Hislop says, "Martial, in like manner, speaks of 'The seven dominating mountains.' In times long subsequent, the same kind of language was in current use; for when Symmachus, the prefect of the city, and the last acting Pagan Pontifex Maximus, as the Imperial substitute, introduces by letter one friend of his to another, he calls him '*De septem montibus virum*'—'a man from the seven mountains,' meaning thereby, as the commentators interpret it, 'Civem Romanum,' 'A Roman Citizen.' Now, while this characteristic of Rome has ever been well marked and defined, it has always been easy to show, that the Church which has its seat and headquarters on the seven hills of Rome might most appropriately be called 'Babylon,' inasmuch as it is the chief seat of idolatry under the New Testament, as the ancient Babylon was the chief seat of idolatry under the Old" (Neptune, NJ: Loizeaux Brothers, 1959, 2).

375 See the discussion in the notes of the *The Believer's Study Bible*, 1821.

The builders confess their intentions as twofold: (1) to make for themselves a "name" and (2) thereby to avoid being "scattered." They want to "empower" themselves, as we moderns say. These are independent goals, though the latter expresses their root fear, which has incited them to build. "Name" (*šēm*) and "scattering" (*pûṣ*), as we have seen, are integral ideas in the narrative. . . . They appear for the first time in the mouths of the builders themselves, echoing the antediluvian "men of renown [*name*]" in 6:4 and countering the post-diluvian command of 9:1 ("fill the earth"). "Make" and "name" are also proleptic of God's promise to "make" of Abraham a great nation and to magnify his "name" (12:2–3). The striking difference between the two examples lies in how the "name" is achieved. Reflexive "ourselves" and "for themselves" highlight the self-interested and independent efforts of the Babelites, . . . but for Abraham the Lord bestows the blessing of reputation as a gracious gift. As the Babel narrative unveils, the "name" they achieve, however, is only "Babel" ("muddle"!).[376]

The focus of Babylonianism is always on man's achievement as opposed to God's grace. Like the Babelites, most religion places the emphasis on what men can do to make themselves acceptable to God. In contrast, the faith of Abraham and the teachings of Christ and the New Testament emphasize human inability and point to the grace of God alone as the way, through faith in God's gracious saving acts, to be properly related to God. Babylon the Great stands for every human religious instigation in opposition to the revealed faith of the Scriptures.

7. The Judgment of Great Babylon (18:1–24)

[1]**After these things I saw another angel coming down from heaven, having great authority, and the earth was illuminated with his glory. [2]And he cried mightily with a loud voice, saying, "Babylon the great is fallen, is fallen, and has become a dwelling place of demons, a prison for every foul spirit, and a cage for every unclean and hated bird! [3]For all the nations have drunk of the wine of the wrath of her fornication, the kings of the earth have committed fornication with her, and the merchants of the earth have become rich through the abundance of her luxury."**

---

376 K. A. Mathews, *Genesis 1–11:26*, NAC 1a (Nashville: B&H, 1996), 482.

⁴And I heard another voice from heaven saying, "Come out of her, my people, lest you share in her sins, and lest you receive of her plagues. ⁵For her sins have reached to heaven, and God has remembered her iniquities. ⁶Render to her just as she rendered to you, and repay her double according to her works; in the cup which she has mixed, mix double for her. ⁷In the measure that she glorified herself and lived luxuriously, in the same measure give her torment and sorrow; for she says in her heart, 'I sit as queen; and am no widow, and will not see sorrow.' ⁸Therefore her plagues will come in one day—death and mourning and famine. And she will be utterly burned with fire, for strong is the Lord God who judges her.

⁹"The kings of the earth who committed fornication and lived luxuriously with her will weep and lament for her, when they see the smoke of her burning, ¹⁰standing at a distance for fear of her torment, saying, 'Alas, alas, that great city Babylon, that mighty city! For in one hour your judgment has come.'

¹¹"And the merchants of the earth will weep and mourn over her, for no one buys their merchandise anymore: ¹²merchandise of gold and silver, precious stones and pearls, fine linen and purple, silk and scarlet, every kind of citron wood, every kind of object of ivory, every kind of object of most precious wood, bronze, iron, and marble; ¹³and cinnamon and incense, fragrant oil and frankincense, wine and oil, fine flour and wheat, cattle and sheep, horses and chariots, and bodies and souls of men. ¹⁴The fruit that your soul longed for has gone from you, and all the things which are rich and splendid have gone from you, and you shall find them no more at all. ¹⁵The merchants of these things, who became rich by her, will stand at a distance for fear of her torment, weeping and wailing, ¹⁶and saying, 'Alas, alas, that great city that was clothed in fine linen, purple, and scarlet, and adorned with gold and precious stones and pearls! ¹⁷For in one hour such great riches came to nothing.' "Every shipmaster, all who travel by ship, sailors, and as many as trade on the sea, stood at a distance ¹⁸and cried out when they saw the smoke of her burning, saying, 'What *is* like this great city?'

¹⁹They threw dust on their heads and cried out, weeping and wailing, and saying, 'Alas, alas, that great city, in which all who had ships on the sea became rich by her wealth! For in one hour she is made desolate.'

²⁰"Rejoice over her, O heaven and *you* holy apostles and prophets, for God has avenged you on her!"

²¹Then a mighty angel took up a stone like a great millstone and threw *it* into the sea, saying, "Thus with violence the great city of Babylon shall be thrown down, and shall not be found anymore. ²²The sound of harpists, musicians, flutists, and trumpeters shall not be heard in you anymore. No craftsman of any craft shall be found in you anymore, and the sound of a millstone shall not be heard in you anymore. ²³The

light of a lamp shall not shine in you anymore, and the voice of bridegroom and bride shall not be heard in you anymore. For your merchants were the great men of the earth, for by your sorcery all the nations were deceived. [24]And in her was found the blood of prophets and saints, and of all who were slain on the earth."

Chapter 17 chronicles the emergence, continuance, and ultimate judgment of the scarlet woman who for a period was supported by the beast out of the sea. As part of her identification, she bore the imprimatur of Babylon the Great. She is also said to be the mistress of the great city of seven hills who ruled the whole earth. This woman is a composite of political Rome and religious Babylon.[377] The explanation and ramifications of her demise are explored in the text of chap. 18.

The economic impact of this apostate religious system which this commentator has called "Babylonianism" is another indication of the entrenched control exercised by Babylon the Great.[378] The enumeration of her variegated crimes, together with the astonishment of those whose prosperity is linked to her hegemony, provides the reader of chap. 18 with a salient perspective on just how cataclysmic is the fall of Babylon. The chapter also provides a stark contrast between the values of the secular world and the values of the people of God.

---

377 I. Boxall notes the emphasis of the chapter: "Those who know their Hebrew scriptures will hear familiar echoes in this chapter, for it is a veritable tapestry of interwoven threads from a range of Old Testament passages (especially the prophetic taunt songs of Isaiah 23–24 and Ezekiel 26–27 against Tyre, and Isaiah 47 and Jeremiah 50–51 against Babylon). Nevertheless, this is no montage of biblical quotations (that is not John's way), but a wealth of allusions and evocations rewoven into something new and creative, to speak powerfully of the arrogant and seductive Babylon that Rome has now become" (*The Revelation of St. John*, BNTC [Peabody, MA: Hendrickson, 2006], 254).

378 For an erudite history of Babylon, see G. Roux, *Ancient Iraq*, 3rd ed. (London: Penguin Books, 1992). Chapter 24 chronicles "The Splendour of Babylon" (pp. 389–404) and provides appropriate context for grasping references to Babylon in the Apocalypse. Roux describes the city having 500 acres and being home to 100,000 to a quarter of a million people. The city was bisected by the Euphrates and was home to Nebuchadnezzar's Hanging Gardens, one of the seven wonders of the ancient world. A small portion of the original wall along with a wealth of other artifacts may be profitably viewed in the Pergamon Museum in Berlin. Also for a much older description on which most contemporary ones depend, see Herodotus, *The Histories*, trans. A. D. Godley, LCL 117 (Cambridge: Harvard University Press, 1920), 1:178–87.

18:1-3 The text describes another angel descending out of heaven, apparently in distinction from the seven angels who have poured out their vials of wrath. Three affirmations are made about this messenger. He has great authority, suggesting a higher rank than that of the seven angels with the bowls. Second, his glory illuminates the entire earth. The word the NKJV translates as "glory" is the familiar Greek word *doxa*, which is most often rendered "glory." In contrast, the NIV translators chose to render the word as "splendor" which fails to grasp the full weight of *doxa* but does help to explain why the earth is brightened by his appearance.

Finally, the angel is said to shout or cry aloud with a mighty or strong voice. The crier's message announces the collapse of Babylon with a double use of the Greek aorist tense, "fallen, fallen." The repetition not only follows the pattern of the dirge in the ancient world but also emphasizes both the decisiveness and the extent of the fall of Babylon. From this judgment of God there is no redemption. The overthrow is decimating.

Babylon has now become a home (*katoikētērion*) for demons. At first this disclosure may seem strange since the subject is the destruction of the city. However, the angelic point seems to be that the judgment is so climactic that nothing good and nothing human can remain. Additionally, the destroyed city is a prison (*phulakē*), sometimes referencing a tower used for incarceration of evil (*akathartos*) or unclean spirits and also of unclean birds, consisting of pelicans, hawks, owls, ravens, ostriches, condors—all essentially birds of prey and often of carrion.[379] The NKJV text adds also the word "hated" to describe what undoubtedly are birds of carrion, gorging themselves on the carcasses of those who have perished in the mass destruction.[380] There is no reason to see a conflict between demons and evil spirits since the ruins provide both a home and a prison for them.

The reason for this destruction is now stated. The nations have drunk the wine of the wrath (*thumos*) of her adulteries. In contrast to the NKJV here, the

---

379 Considerable textual variation occurs in this listing of inhabitants for fallen Babylon. The NIV text, for example, does not include the mention of "unclean and hateful beasts" even though some manuscripts have this reading. This is only one of a number of variants, but none affect the clear intent of the passage. J. P. Newport remarks that "the 'haunt' in verse 2 is a watchtower. Here the evil spirits, watching over fallen Babylon like night birds waiting for their prey, build their nests in the broken towers that rise from the ashes of the city. She who was a great city has become a wilderness" (*The Lion and the Lamb* [Nashville: Broadman, 1986], 276–77).

380 R. L. Thomas sees this as a metaphor describing the totality of Babylon's destruction (*Revelation 8-22: An Exegetical Commentary* [Chicago: Moody, 1995], 318).

NIV translators seem to suggest that the adulteries of Babylon constitute a brew that drove the inhabitants to madness.[381] Two additional reasons for her destruction are provided. Adulterous relationships with the kings of the earth signal, as in chap. 17, an unholy union between religion and politics. Finally, the merchants of the earth also profited by her suzerainty, which demonstrated itself in love for ostentation and wealth.[382] "Luxury" (*strēnos*) is a relatively rare word speaking of insolence, arrogance, or wantonness. It is used in verb form to describe the trumpeting of an elephant.[383] Hence, the emphasis is not placed on the mere accumulation of wealth but on an obsession with wealth and the "abundance of luxury."

18:4-8   Christians are taught that God loved the world and gave His Son to make atonement for the world (John 3:16; 1 John 2:2). Followers of Christ are to imitate Him (Eph 5:1); but in a seemingly contradictory mandate, believers are instructed not to love the world (1 John 2:15) and to "come out . . . and be separate" (2 Cor 6:17). As in these last admonitions, v. 4 begins with the challenge for God's people to abandon Babylon, sharing neither in her sins nor in her plagues. Compassion, rather than condescension, for sinners is the only appropriate posture for a believer. Nevertheless, this compassion must be exercised from a position of holiness and separation to God, His purposes, and His ways. The origin of the voice from heaven is not specified, so one may conclude that the voice may well be the voice of God—especially since the call to depart from Babylon is issued to "my people."

---

381 H. Alford takes it differently than the translators of the NIV who rendered θυμός as "maddening." He notes the unusual choice of words: "The use of θυμός is even more remarkable here: of (or, by) that wine of her fornication which has turned into wrath against herself." Alford's translation seeks to preserve the general concept of θυμός as "wrath" (*The Greek Testament* [Chicago: Moody, 1958], 4:714–15).

382 Those like W. Scott who find Babylon synonymous with the Roman Church would agree with his assessment: "Love of display, of which the Romish Church boasts, is her argument and appeal to the senses, and before *this* god the nations will bow, but the kings of the earth, or leaders, are more guilty, more sober, as befits their position; they yield themselves up to the blandishments of the woman. The Church hugs the world for what of numbers and wealth she can get, and the world gladly welcomes her embrace, for has she not promised to open Heaven to all comers who pay well? The keys of St. Peter are dangled before kings and people, and so the chair of 'The Vicar of Christ' and 'Universal Bishop' will yet be exalted to a moral height far beyond that of the palmiest days of the papacy in either of the three centuries so renowned for Romish arrogance and pride, the eleventh, twelfth, and thirteenth" (*Exposition of the Revelation of Jesus Christ*, 4th ed. [Westwood, NJ: Revell, 1968], 368).

383 LSJ, 1654.

The expression "share in her sins" employs an instructive word (*sug-koinōneō*), which is constructed from *koinōnia*, often translated "fellowship" and *sun*, the preposition meaning "with," appended as a prefix to the word. The vivid picture emerging is that God's people are not to have fellowship with Babylon in her iniquities. The concept of *koinōnia* or fellowship moved a step beyond friendship and two steps beyond acquaintance. For example, in secular Greek, the term was used to describe relationship in marriage.[384] Just as Koine is the common Greek spoken in the *agora* (in English, marketplace), so the *koinōnia* word group focuses on what is held in common by one with another.

The saints are to avoid fellowship or participation in the sins of Babylon in order to avoid being the recipient (*lambanō*) of the plagues intended for her. "Receive" is from a word meaning "take" or "seize." To remain in Babylon is to be overtaken by her plagues.

Verse 5 chronicles the fact that Babylon's sins are "reached to heaven." The majority of the manuscripts employ the word *ekollēthēsan*, which is the aorist passive indicative of *kollaō*. More literally the word means "stick to" or "be joined to." The idea in the text seems to be that the sins of Babylon not only are piled one on top of another all the way to the heavens but also are related one to another as they are joined or glued together. God remembers these unrighteous acts, translated "iniquities" in the NKJV text; and, therefore, further reason is given for the people of God to separate themselves from the sins of Babylon and the plagues accompanying them. The doctrine of "separation" enjoined on the people of God here is not a condescending separation that creates legalism but rather a separation born of a love for holiness and fellowship with God. God's genuine people will find the ways of the world reprehensible. However, while having compassion for those who are caught in this world's web, they nevertheless, in their lifestyles and commitments, differentiate themselves from the world and therefore seek that separation.

The extent of the judgment of God is chronicled in the expression in v. 6 of repaying Babylon twice for what she has done. She is to be given what she has provided for others. In fact, she is to be paid back double for what she has

---

384 Hauck notes, "The group κοινων- is applied to the most varied relationships, the common share in a thing, e.g., πᾶσιν ὅσοι φύσεως κοινωνοῦντες ἀνθρω [πί] νης, common enterprises, and esp. legal relations. κοινωνός, is a tt. [i.e., title] for a business partner or associate. κοινωνία is used esp. of a close life partnership. Marriage (κοινωνία παντὸς τοῦ βίου) is closer and more comprehensive (οἰκειοτέρα μείζων) than all other forms of fellowship" (*TDNT* 3:798).

done, and a double portion is mixed for her from her own cup.[385] This expression does not imply injustice from God or that the judgment is greater than the crime demands. Anyone having read to this point, however, cannot help but be aware of the malignancy of the sins of Babylon and the corresponding world system. This is to say nothing of the scores of sorrows imposed on millions since the founding of Babylon. Therefore, giving to Babylon a double portion from her own cup is simply to accord her what she truly deserves. Specifically, torment and sorrow are meted out to her at the same level as the glory and luxury with which she favored herself (v. 7). Babylon the Great has boasted that she is no widow and rather sits as a queen that will not see sorrow.[386] The backdrop to this expression focuses on the plight of many of the widows of the Roman Empire. Patriarchalism sometimes existed in its most obnoxious form in the ancient world. The importance of marriage was affirmed because the husband thus cared for his wife and her needs were met. At the death of her husband, however, if the wife could not remarry, then widowhood often proved profoundly difficult. There is also a strong indication of this circumstance in the New Testament, resulting in (1) the directive of the early church to provide deacons (Acts 6) to care for the needs of the widows and orphans, (2) the admonitions of Paul and Timothy to the New Testament congregations to care for

---

385 S. Kistemaker addresses the issue of the plurality of the verbs in this passage: "But we still have to ask why in Greek the verbs *repay* and *give back* are written as *plural* imperatives. The broader context reveals that the plural is also used in verse 4, 'Come out of her!' and in verse 7, 'Give such torment and grief to her!' The plural in verse 4 is addressed to God's people, but interpreting the entreaty of verses 6 and 7 as addressed to God's people flies in the face of the divine admonition not to seek revenge: 'It is mine to avenge; I will repay' (Deut. 32:35; see also Rom. 12:19; Heb. 10:30). Additional suggestions are that the plural imperatives address the angels who are sent out by God to execute his judgments or that they urge the people to turn against the prostitute Babylon and ruin her (17:16–17). Both of these suggestions, however, have to account for the sudden shift from one group of addressees to another without any indication of the change" (*Exposition of the Book of Revelation*, New Testament Commentary [Grand Rapids: Baker Academic, 2001], 490). Also, see S. S. Smalley on the meaning of "double" (*The Revelation to John: A Commentary on the Greek Text of the Apocalypse* [Downers Grove, IL: InterVarsity, 2005], 447).

386 J. A. Bengel observes: "*I sit*, has the force of a perfect. Therefore Babylon displays the most unconcerned security for the past, the present, and the future. She calls herself *Queen*: and Bossuet is in error, when he thinks that we seek in Rome a corrupt church only, and not also a royal city. Both are had in view" (*Bengel's New Testament Commentary* [Grand Rapids: Kregel, 1981], 2:914).

widows (1 Tim 5:3-16), and (3) James's commendation that caring for widows and orphans is pure and undefiled religion (James 1:27).

With this in mind, Babylon the Great has boasted to herself that she will never know the rigors and sorrows of widowhood but rather the splendor and ease of monarchy. This misguided confidence is now judged, and in one day all the plagues promised by God overtake the city. Specifically mentioned are death, sorrowing or mourning, and famine. In addition to this, she will be consumed by fire because mighty, or powerful, is the Lord God who has thus judged her. Before, Babylon dealt with normal kings, but in the end she faces in judgment the irresistibility of the Lord who is God.

Lesser monarchs who cohabited with Babylon and profited by her excesses are stunned at her rapid demise. Two distinct reactions are visible to the seer. First, there is sorrow as these kings lement the fall of Babylon and with her much of their own prosperity. Second, terror sweeps across these kings as they watch Babylon's torment (*basanismos*, a word signaling the general upheaval and torment of the great city).

From the mouths of these earthly sovereigns come a lamentation, an agonizing dirge for the sudden contrast between the Babylon they once knew and the one they now behold. The NKJV reads, "that great city Babylon, that mighty city!" The word translated "mighty" (*ischuros*) is often rendered "strength." The contrast is between a city of strength and one reduced to helplessness in one hour. Doubtless, the terror they sense and the dirge they sing spring from the realization that their own destiny follows in the wake of this final world empire.

18:11-20 The reactions of various groups associated with Babylon are the subject of the next few verses of chap. 18. In v. 11 the merchants are singled out. In v. 17 the sea captains are the subject of amazement at the destruction of Babylon. The merchants in vv. 11-13 find themselves weeping and mourning over the loss of Babylon because the end of Babylon means that there is no global economic system to support the businesses that have made them wealthy. Economic chaos creates incredible stress in any social order. The list of cargo includes several categories of goods.[387]

The first focus is on those commodities to be found most prolifically among the women of the civilization and in construction projects that were luxuriously appointed. Thus, gold, silver, precious stones, and pearls are mentioned. The next

---

387 The word γόμος may refer either to a ship's freight or to the burden carried by a beast, such as the camel, the ship of the desert. LSJ, 356.

category includes the best in clothing with fine linen, purple silk, and scarlet cloth made abundantly available. The third category includes citron wood, found in North Africa which was greatly valued by the Romans because of its color and beauty.[388] In addition to the citron wood, articles made of ivory,[389] other costly woods,[390] of bronze and iron and marble were also treasured by the Romans and continue to be treasured in every era. Spices and incense included cinnamon (used in a variety of ways), myrrh, and frankincense,[391] which were used in both incense and perfume and would be employed in various forms of ancient as well as modern worship. Food products included the expected wine, olive oil, fine flour, and wheat. Livestock mentioned are sheep, cattle, horses, and carriages or four-wheeled vehicles in which wealthy Romans were often passengers along the Roman roads. Having mentioned all of these various items from which the merchants have profited, an ominous addition to all of these products is made. The merchants also trafficked in the bodies and souls of men.

Slavery was one of the most unfortunate aspects of Roman society. While the perspective of the biblical writers primarily addressed how God's people were to live successfully in a social order that was inherently evil, some people erroneously believe that there are no strong hints in the Bible that slavery was never intended by God and is wrong even in circumstances in which slaves in the Roman Empire and at other times were given good care and often assumed positions of strategic influence and importance. Nevertheless, bartering in the lives and, therefore, often with the souls of men was never God's intention and

---

388 Citron wood, θύϊνον, is described and lauded at some length by Pliny who extols its qualities as being "virtually everlasting" (*Natural History*, LCL 370 [Cambridge, MA: Harvard University Press, 1986], 4:159).

389 The word ἐλεφάντινον literally suggests belonging to elephants or ivory. Of course, there were then, as now, other sources of ivory—warthog, hippopotamus, walrus, but, as now, none so highly valued as ivory from elephants. This was harvested in both Asia and Africa.

390 In the earlier part of verse 12, λίθου τιμίου is translated "precious stone." Here the word τίμος occurs again, only this time in its superlative form, i.e. "most precious," modifying ξύλον or "wood." The sense suggests expensive woods due to limited availability, beauty, and durability.

391 A. A. Swenson notes that frankincense and myrrh are the most favored ceremonial plants because of the valuable gums derived from them. The frankincense plant can be the *Boswellia Carterii*, the *Boswellia thurifera*, or the *Boswellia papyrifera*, all of which grow in Southern Arabia, Abyssinia (modern Ethiopia), and along the coast of Africa (*Plants of the Bible and How to Grow Them* [New York: Kensington Publishing, 1995], 103). Myrrh, *Commiphora kataf*, is a related plant that grows in the same area (107).

is another indication of the sinfulness of humanity. This point is certainly observable in Paul's epistle to Philemon, and once again in this particular text the Bible makes clear that slavery was part of the wickedness of the world system.

Verses 14–16 chronicle the disappearance of certain fruit, but here the usual word for "fruit" does not occur, but rather the infrequently-used *opōra* is employed, which seems to reference a particularly refreshing summer fruit. There is mention that their souls longed for their fruit, which was now gone from them.[392] The word translated "longed for" (*epithumia*), generally rendered "lust," indicated inordinate and uncontrolled desire. Whatever this fruit may be, clearly it is greatly treasured and at the point of the fall of Babylon will no longer be readily available. In fact, all of the riches and splendor of Babylon have vanished, and they are never going to be recovered.

Verse 15 records clearly why there is such lamentation and sorrow among the merchants. These merchants have gained all their wealth from Babylon's commerce—now there is nothing for them to do but stand as far away as they can, absolutely terrified by the torment through which Babylon is passing. Again, they weep, mourn, and cry out in a sickening dirge over the demise of Babylon, "Alas, alas, that great city, / that was clothed in fine linen, purple and scarlet, / and adorned with gold and precious stones and pearls! / For in one hour such great riches came to nothing" (18:16).

In order to provide this wealth of commodities for the merchants and for Babylon, there had to be a system of transport. In John's day such a system was provided by the famous highways constructed by Rome throughout the empire. But a large portion of the delicacies enumerated above owed their origin not only to various places within the Roman Empire but also to many exotic locations far beyond. Consequently, the Roman roads themselves were not sufficient and a considerable maritime fleet was employed to ferry all the items needed by Rome. Of course, these fleets of ships and whatever other forms of transportation were employed grew wealthy by means of supplying the transportation needed. No one is surprised in v. 17 to discover that the sea captains and all of those who travel by ships, both sailors and merchants, and all who earn their living from those sea lanes, join the merchants in standing far off. What they observe is the smoke of the burning of Babylon, and this causes them to begin to reminisce? What is like this great city?

---

392 ὀπώρα references mid-July to mid-September or late summer. The fruit by this name available during that season was apparently especially palatable to the ancients and may have had some effect in curing dysentery. LSJ, 1242–43.

In the ancient Near East a person in deep distress and mourning throws dust on his head as is pictured in v. 19. They join the merchants in weeping and mourning and crying out. Their own dirge follows, "Alas, alas, that great city, / in which all who had ships on the sea / became rich by her wealth! / For in one hour she is made desolate!" Undoubtedly, John has in mind this view of Rome as he penned these words. Rome was the greatest city of all the earth at that time.

Thomas argues for a Babylon in the future since in an earlier day the Euphrates was able to take shipping from the Persian Gulf and even send it far to the north from Babylon. Therefore, Babylon on the Euphrates is more likely than Rome on the Tiber, which did not have a port of its own.[393] However, only a few miles to the west of the city of Rome, the port of Ostia in Roman times had become one of the most extensive and well-known port cities in the world. Although commerce came to the city of Rome along the Roman highways, an enormous amount of commerce also docked at Ostia.[394] So, once again, Rome on the Tiber is the proper understanding, even though certainly something even more extensive than that appears to be in the prophetic vision.

In stark contrast to the sorrow of the merchants and the terror of the sea captains, there is almost an imprecatory quality to the admonition for heaven to rejoice over the fall of Babylon. All of heaven is invited, even commanded, to rejoice over Babylon's demise.[395] The saints, the apostles, and the prophets are to rejoice over her. "Apostle" is a reference to men who were especially chosen to be the original emissaries of the gospel, who were with the Lord, and who were eyewitnesses to his resurrection (cf. Acts 1:21-22). The apostle Paul, who saw the resurrected Lord as one born out of due time (1 Cor 15:8) is the exception. Others do not qualify as apostles in that day or any other. Most of the apostles apparently died a martyr's death, and John at the time of the writing of the Apocalypse is located on the rock quarry island of Patmos as a prisoner of Rome.

---

393 Thomas, *Revelation 8–22*, 339.

394 The importance of Ostia to Rome is noted by T. Mommsen, *A History of Rome Under the Emperors* (London: Routledge, 1999), 499. L. Casson, provides a careful look at the nature of Rome's major port (*Everyday Life in Ancient Rome* [Baltimore: Johns Hopkins University Press, 1998], 72–76).

395 R. Bultmann contrasts the meaning of εὐφραίνω used here with both χαρά and ἀγαλλιᾶσθαι in the NT. He finds χαρά to be the most important term. Of εὐφραίνω he notes that it is "often used for purely secular joy," but also "as the gift of God by which even the heathen may discern the providential rule," and finally "there are the echoes of the OT demand for jubilation at God's eschatological acts of judgment" (*TDNT* 2:772–74).

The prophets of all eras, including most of the better-known prophets of Israel, likewise experienced the fury of Babylon in its various forms, being persecuted, misunderstood, abused, and tormented in various ways often to the point of death (see Heb 11). Now all these are commanded (the verb is imperative) to rejoice, but the reason for rejoicing is that God has judged Babylon for the way she treated God's people and his prophets. The rejoicing here is because justice is finally realized. The rejoicing is that God Himself proves that He is a just God. To allow sin to go unpunished would be to treat it lightly, and there is a sense in which God's justice itself is an indication of His mercy.

18:21-24 One final highly symbolic action is reported by John in the eighteenth chapter. A mighty angel picks up a boulder the size of a large millstone and throws it into the sea. Millstones came in various sizes. Some were small enough for a woman to grind meal for her family. Others were of enormous size and had to be turned by donkeys or oxen. Such a millstone would weigh thousands of pounds. This latter millstone is in view here. The angel who is able to hoist such a stone is said to be a mighty angel. The emphasis on the size and the weight of the stone seems to have two noticeable traits. The first is that when the millstone hits the water a noticeable splash would surely occur. Second, because of its weight and density and total lack of buoyancy, such a millstone would promptly sink to the bottom, disappearing from view. So, Babylon, with considerable fanfare and noticeable action falls like the millstone and disappears from view. In fact, v. 21 mentions that with this kind of violence the great city of Babylon is thrown down and the condition is permanent.

The list of events that will no longer take place in Babylon may seem almost anticlimactic and perhaps unnecessary to the reader. The styling of John's assessment perhaps underscores the picture of the total disruption of the social order. Not only is economic chaos introduced into the world with the fall of Babylon and the close of the tribulation, but all normalcy is taken from the earth with the overthrow of Babylon. For example, the musical events involving harpists, flutists, and trumpeters will never again be heard in Babylon. The guilds of workmen who plied their various trades will never again be found. The grinding of the millstones heard in many places in any ancient city will be gone, and even the twinkling light of a small lamp will never shine in Babylon again. The thoroughness of the destruction of Babylon involves not merely its economic foundation but even its most basic social life. This includes the voice of the bridegroom and the bride. Such joys and hopes are gone forever.

John notes that the merchants of Babylon have been the world's great men, honored and extolled everywhere. Based on Babylon's "sorcery," the nations had been led astray. The word translated "sorcery" is *pharmakeia*, giving the contemporary term "pharmacy." The most common translation for it is "witchcraft," or "sorcery," as rendered in the NKJV. The connection between drugs and witchcraft and sorcery seems to be found in the fact that much witchcraft and sorcery made use of various mind-expanding substances in order to create certain effects. This is doubtless why the NIV translators utilized the phrase "magic spell" here. Probably "witchcraft" or "sorcery" is indeed the better translation, though that certainly could entail "magic spells." The point is that sorcery and other forms of deceit were definitely a part of the effect of ancient Babylon on the nations.

Finally, in v. 24 is found the ultimate reason for the judgment of God on Babylon. In her was found the blood of the prophets, the saints, and literally all those who were killed on the earth. While Augustine argued that there is a "just war" and most Christian ethicists have continued to espouse that view, biblical scholars nonetheless admit that war itself is a consequence of the sinful nature of the human family.

Beginning with Cain's murder of Abel, for one to take the life of another has never been appropriate; yet the killing of people across the earth has often been used by Babylon and its associated empires as the method of removing opposition. Particularly the blood of the prophets and the blood of the saints have been taken by Babylon. Her hatred for God and for His Son Jesus led only to frustration in confrontation. Turning on Israel, annihilation proved to evade the Babylonian system and the dragon's use of it. Consequently, the prophets and the saints become the object of her wrath as indicated in chap. 17. Now a large part of the reason for the judgment on Babylon is that the blood of the prophets and saints is found there.[396]

---

396 E. Schüssler Fiorenza provides an appropriate summary of this chapter: "The narrative sequence concerning Babylon in 17:1–19:10 may be compared to a triptych with three panels. After a general introductory headline in 17:1-2, the first panel (17:3-18) describes and interprets the world capital, Babylon. The second panel (18:1-24) differs stylistically insofar as the destruction of the great city is not described but only reflected in the dirges of the kings, merchants, and ship-owners. The legal claim of the persecuted victims against Babylon is now granted. The powerful capital of the world is destroyed not just because it has persecuted Christians but also because it has unlawfully killed many other people. Rev 18:24 must therefore be understood as the hermeneutical key to the whole Babylon series of judgments. That the question of justice is at the heart of Rev's politics of meaning is also underscored by the third panel (19:9-10) which presents a heavenly liturgy praising the justice of G*d's judgments and announcing the marriage feast of the Lamb." "Epilogue,"

Pastoral Excursus on Babylon's Fall

While the information provided in chaps. 17 and 18 concerning the fall of apostate religious systems may be interesting and even helpful, the Bible teacher or preacher may wonder how this "overload" of information on Babylon may be conscripted for exposition and applied to the contemporary church. The answer lies less with the details (the laundry lists of spices, musicians) and more with the overview of what is pictured.

First, there is no spiritual failure associated with the human use and appreciation of most of the commodities enumerated in the two chapters. The problem arises whenever the accumulation of these commodities becomes an obsession. The crass materialism of most of the world constitutes a form of idolatry. Wealth, its accumulation, and the means by which it is garnered becomes the end game. Like the Sabbath, wealth was created for men and not man for wealth. Since the supreme object of one's devotion can become the god of his life, Babylon represents the enthronement of materialism as the condition prevalent in the world at the consummation of the age. An appropriate perspective regarding all things material can be contrasted with the conditions pictured in terminal Babylon.

Second, Babylon represents not merely materialism out of control but also the corruption of faith by the idolatry of materialism, including as rampant materialism always does, its willingness to barter in the "souls of men." The purpose of life is to establish and to maintain a relationship to the Creator/Redeemer God. Whenever that ceases to be the purpose of religion, injustice reigns, truth is forfeited, and what remains looks increasingly like Babylonianism. The poignant lesson here is that Babylon represents commerce and religion in unholy matrimony. Made further illegitimate by politics, this union purporting to represent God actually represents the opposite of all that God intended. Every church and every believer is subject to the siren songs of Babylonianism, and even those who proclaim the New Testament faith must constantly be aware of the danger.

Finally, Babylonianism is not immune to God's judgment,

---

in *The Book of Revelation: Justice and Judgment*, 2nd ed. (Minneapolis: Fortress, 1998), 220.

though she deceives herself into believing that she is clever enough to escape it. The judgment of Babylon is inevitable and thorough. And because all world faiths that do not follow the way of Christ and of the apostles and prophets are a part of the Babylonian system, the ultimate demise of Babylon will cause global sorrow and lamentation exactly as depicted in these chapters.

The teacher or preacher can focus effectively on these critical lessons in this text, teaching the importance of doctrinal integrity and the appropriate understanding and use of wealth. In so doing, he may enable his people to avoid conditions like those that existed in the church at Laodicea.

8. The Return of Christ (19:1-21)

The revelry of heaven, which is inaugurated in the concluding verses of chap. 18, reaches crescendo level in chap. 19. The rejoicing spills over the battlements of heaven and penetrates the environment of Patmos, from which John records his observations. The initial ten verses record the revelry of heaven but give way to an introduction to the wedding of the Lamb and to a brief sighting of the Lamb's bride, the church. Suddenly, the scene changes and the Lamb is depicted as an avenging warrior. Once again, Armageddon, the final conflict of the tribulation period, is unveiled, accompanied by an invitation to the birds of carrion to gorge themselves on the carcasses of enemies of the Lamb.

A. The Marriage of the Lamb (19:1–10)

¹After these things I heard a loud voice of a great multitude in heaven, saying, "Alleluia! Salvation and glory and honor and power belong to the Lord our God! ²For true and righteous *are* His judgments, because He has judged the great harlot who corrupted the earth with her fornication; and He has avenged on her the blood of His servants shed by her." ³Again they said, "Alleluia! Her smoke rises up forever and ever!" ⁴And the twenty-four elders and the four living creatures fell down and worshiped God who sat on the throne, saying, "Amen, Alleluia!" ⁵Then a voice came from the throne, saying, "Praise our God, all you His servants and those who fear Him, both small and great!"

⁶And I heard, as it were, the voice of a great multitude, as the sound of many waters and as the sound of mighty thunderings, saying, "Alleluia! For the Lord God Omnipotent reigns! ⁷Let us be glad and rejoice and give Him glory, for the marriage

of the Lamb has come, and His wife has made herself ready." [8]And to her it was granted to be arrayed in fine linen, clean and bright, for the fine linen is the righteous acts of the saints.

[9]Then he said to me, "Write: 'Blessed *are* those who are called to the marriage supper of the Lamb!'" And he said to me, "These are the true sayings of God." [10]And I fell at his feet to worship him. But he said to me, "*See that you do not do that!* I am your fellow servant, and of your brethren who have the testimony of Jesus. Worship God! For the testimony of Jesus is the spirit of prophecy."

19:1–10 The usual *meta tauta*, or "after these things," references the overthrow of Babylon in chap. 18. John now hears a "loud voice of a great multitude in heaven." The NIV translates the phrase as, "what sounded like the roar of a great multitude in heaven shouting." The word translated "roar" in the NIV text is *phōnēn*, which characteristically means "voice." If this is not a musical salute, then the NIV has probably characterized this voice of the great multitude in heaven correctly by utilizing "roar." On the other hand, the "roar" of a crowd is seldom comprehensible. This "roar," or more likely "voice," is understood and certain words were clearly intelligible. The heavenly voice shouts, "Hallelujah!" The word is a transliteration of the Hebrew *halal*, meaning "praise," and *yah*, the first syllable of Yahweh. As such, the text is a paean of praise to God. Six attributes ascribed to God provide the impetus for his praise. "Salvation, glory, honor, and power to our God" is the actual wording of the Greek text. The NKJV translators here, however, are correct to add the word "belong" since God has no need of acquiring glory, honor, or power, let alone salvation. Consequently, the translators properly understood that God is the only One who exercises perfect power, basks in ontological glory, deserves unmitigated honor, and provides salvation. The basic challenge of all counterfeit religion is to find some aspect of human endeavor that can be counted worthy of salvation. Salvation in biblical terms belongs only to God and is made available through His sovereign grace. However, beyond salvation, glory, honor and power, v. 2 adds that all God does as a manifestation of salvation, glory, honor, and power falls into the category of what is true and just. His judgments are accurate and inevitably just.

Periodically, newspapers introduce a solitary figure who, after years of imprisonment, is set free because of new evidence proving he was falsely indicted and convicted. While a judge or jury void of moral judgment conceivably could knowingly convict someone of a crime that they knew he did not commit, the vast majority of these cases of injustice represent errors in human judgment. Since God is omniscient, He is incapable of making an error. Though He remains the only Judge in the cosmos whose judgment is inevitably true, He is also impeccably just.

Human judges can sometimes be bought, and their own motives and commitments can thwart justice. Such is not the case with God, whose judgments are characterized by justice. This understanding is important since humans commonly raise questions about the justice of God, especially as it concerns the salvation of some and the damnation of others. The primary exhibit for this is that God has condemned the great prostitute who corrupted the earth with her adulteries.[397] That just judgment extends to the righting of the wrong that the apostate religious system visited on her enemies since God avenges on her the blood of His servants. In chap. 6, when the fifth seal of the seven-sealed scroll is opened, saints of God were revealed in heaven crying out and asking how long before justice would be provided for those who had shed their blood. At the time, they were told to wait a little while (v. 11). That little while has passed, and now the judgment is complete.

Another shout of hallelujah is followed by the simple observation that the smoke of Babylon's torment ascends forever and ever (tous aiōnas tōn aiōnōn). Literally, the translation would be "until the ages of the ages," but clearly in the Bible whatever is in view is unending. Hence, there is simply no end to the torment of Babylon.

Suddenly the twenty-four elders and the four living creatures first introduced in chap. 4 are again on stage. Falling down, they worship God who is seated on the throne, and they cry, "Amen," and a third, "Hallelujah."[398] The word "amen" is originally the Hebrew word amēn ("trustworthy"), which is a term of certainty

---

397 G. Harder notes that φθείρω means "ruin" or "destroy." Gradually it took on the sense of a curse "to be damned." The sense of the word in this text has clearly added what he terms "a special moral sense" meaning "to lead astray" into ruin. He finds this same use in Eph 4:22 and elsewhere (TDNT 9:93–106).

398 Oecumenius finds a trinitarian declaration in the three shouts of alleluia: "When the seraphim in words of the divine prophet Isaiah said 'holy' three times, they ascribed the threefold hymn of praise to the one lordship, indicating on the one hand that there were three addressed in the hymns by their peculiar attributes or persons (if it is thought proper to say so), but one in the being of the Godhead. So also here after the blessed angels had previously uttered Alleluia thrice, and had ascribed worship to each of the three holy beings, now they go on to sing Alleluia to the Holy Trinity, intimating that the holy and glorified Trinity exists in a single being and Godhead" (Commentary on the Apocalypse, trans. J. N. Sugget, FC 112 [Washington, DC: Catholic University of America Press, 2006], 158). The problem with this interpretation is the fourth alleluia of v. 6.

and affirmation. When Jonah, not so fresh from his experience with the great fish, entered Nineveh and delivered his prophecy of doom, the Bible records that "the Ninevites believed God" (Jonah 3:5). The word "believed" in that text is the verb related to *amēn*. Ps 19:7 affirms that the "statutes of the LORD are trustworthy," another use of this Hebrew word expressing certainty and reliability. The twenty-four elders and four living creatures give their full affirmation and emphasis to all that has gone before and conclude with the third shout of hallelujah.

Now a voice comes from the throne. Some have supposed that this voice is God's—certainly a possibility. What the voice utters seems unlikely to have come from God Himself, but the exact source of this vocal mandate cannot be discovered. Whatever the case, there is a command to praise God; specifically, they who are His servants are commanded to do so, and His servants are those who fear Him. "Fear" (*phobeō*) is in the form of a present middle participle and, as a word always used in reference to the appropriate response to God, does not denote so much a quaking fear as a reverential awe. As part of reverential awe, the frequent sense of fear is not missing but is rather transcended by the concept of awe and reverence. Though all human analogies break down, the observation of a child who has done wrong fleeing in tears into the arms of his father, even though he knows that his father will administer justice, is probably the closest one can get to a picture of the concept of the biblical fear of God. All the servants who fear Him are enjoined, whether they are small or great, to praise God.

The triumphant assembly erupts yet into more pronounced adulation of God. John now hears the multitudes sounding again like the rushing waters of a great waterfall and now this is accompanied by loud peals of thunder. The roar of cascading water may help identify the sound described in 19:1. For the fourth time a shout from heaven rings throughout the cosmos as all join together in the expression, "Hallelujah!" The reason provided for this particular ascription of praise is that the Lord God Omnipotent reigns. For many who struggled under the auspices of Babylon throughout the generations, there must have been times when this reality was not apparent. In fact, almost every follower of Christ has experienced moments of weakness in faith when due to the exigencies of life the sovereign reign of God did not present itself to the mind. There is no doubt now. Clearly, the Lord God Omnipotent reigns, and Babylon, which may have seemed invincible, has been destroyed. Those who are shouting in the heavens find themselves doing so antiphonally as they each urge the other to rejoice, to be glad, and to give God the glory. To "give Him glory" is to ascribe all that is noble, all that is just, all that is righteous, all that is good to Him and to Him alone. This is not to say that there is nothing good or noble

338

arising from man or angel, but that human goodness or nobility is to God like the light of the moon is to the sun. On its own the moon is dark but becomes a light-giver through the light provided by the sun. Similarly, all human and angelic goodness and nobility is ultimately a matter of the grace of God, and all heaven recognizes this truth.

However, the latter part of v. 7 provides an immediate reason for the rejoicing and the ascription of glory.[399] The marriage of the Lamb has come. His bride has made herself ready and is attired in fine linen, white and clean; the note is made that this attire was given to her to wear. The fine linen stands for the righteous acts of the saints (v. 8).

Several critically important observations should be noted here. First, the bride is presented to the Bridegroom, who is the Lamb. In the New Testament the church, consisting of every truly redeemed human, is the bride of Christ. Exactly when and where this presentation takes place is not stated. Some believe this presentation takes place shortly after the church is removed from the world at the outset of the tribulation period.[400] Others believe this will not take place until after the millennial reign of Christ and will therefore be in heaven.[401] Both of these views seem to violate the chronology of the text; and a third

---

399 In 18:20, rejoicing was mandated. The word employed in that passage (εὐφραίνου), according to Bultmann, was not as important as two other words for expressing Christian joy (*TWNT* 3:774). Here "rejoice and be glad" makes use of the more frequent words, χαίρω and ἀγαλλιάω. The verbs are both present tense, subjective mood verbs, which appear in the first-person plural and exhort others to join in a participatory act. H. E. Dana and J. R. Mantey, *A Manual Grammar of the Greek New Testament* (New York: Macmillan, 1955), 171.

400 W. A. Criswell places the event after the *Bema* but confesses that the precise time is not provided: "Concerning the marriage itself, is it not a strange narrative that God should omit to describe it? Nothing is said about it, no word is used to describe it. The Greek word here says, '*elthen* [aorist], the marriage is come . . .' and that is all. Just the fact of it. John just hears the Hallelujah chorus announcing it. He has a word to say about the wife, the bride of Christ, who has made herself ready. He describes the robe of our righteousnesses [*sic*] that shall be our reward at the Bema of Christ. But He never recounts the actual wedding itself. The event just happens and all heaven bursts into Hallelujahs concerning it, but there is no word about the ceremony itself" (*Expository Sermons on Revelation: Five Volumes Complete and Unabridged* [Grand Rapids: Zondervan, 1969], 5:31).

401 R. Summers, an amillennialist, does not believe the marriage of the Lamb is ever shown: "The book of Revelation does not reveal to us the marriage of the Lamb and the church. By the time we get to that, perhaps chapter 21, the figure has changed and the marriage is not mentioned again, even though there is perfect union between Christ and the

view, which sees this presentation as taking place at the outset of the millennium, seems to be more in keeping with the chronology of the text.[402] However, whether the presentation is on the millennial earth or in heaven is not stated. Whichever the case, just as a marriage in every culture is generally initiated with a presentation ceremony, so there is to be a presentation of the bride to the Lamb. The Lamb has purchased the bride through His atoning death on the cross. Only at the end of the church age will all who are to be added to the bride of Christ actually be present; so, the presentation awaits that moment.

A second observation has to do with the bride making herself ready. She has clothed herself in fine linen, which is bright and clean, and this fine linen stands for the righteousness of the saints (v. 8). How radiantly beautiful the bride of Christ appears as she has prepared herself to be presented to the Lamb. However, her beauty is a bestowed beauty, for John is also informed that the clean, bright linen she is wearing "was granted to her." Again, the emphasis on grace and redemption is brought to the fore. In almost every conceivable way, the Apocalypse magnifies the grace of God in salvation. The righteousness of

---

redeemed" (*Worthy Is The Lamb: Interpreting the Book of Revelation in Its Historical Background* [Nashville: B&H, 1951], 196). D. Chilton, on the other hand, apparently sees no eschatological significance at all, suggesting instead a reference to the Eucharist. "The greatest privilege of the Church is her weekly participation in the Eucharistic meal, the Marriage Supper of the Lamb. It is a tragedy that so many churches in our day neglect the Lord's Supper, observing it only on rare occasions (some so-called churches have even abandoned Communion altogether). What we must realize is that the official worship service of the Church on the Lord's Day is not merely a Bible study or some informal get-together of like-minded souls; to the contrary, it is the formal wedding feast of the Bride with her Bridegroom" (*The Days of Vengeance: An Exposition of Revelation* [Fort Worth: Dominion, 1987], 476–77). J. R. Yeatts, following Mounce, discounts an actual supper saying, "Although the marriage supper seems to be an eschatological banquet after the forces of evil are defeated and Christ's kingdom established (Matt. 8:11), the actual marriage supper of the Lamb is nowhere described. Therefore, it is likely not an event but a symbol of the joyful, intimate, and indissoluble fellowship between Christ and the faithful. The faithful saint awaits the parousia in the same way as a pure betrothed bride anticipates her wedding" (*Revelation*, Believers Church Bible Commentary [Scottdale, PA: Herald Press, 2003], 353).

402 J. Walvoord notes, "The text, of course, does not say where the marriage takes place. It merely announces that the marriage of the Lamb is come. This event is obviously subsequent to the destruction of Babylon, but, if this occurs at the end of the great Tribulation which is immediately climaxed and succeeded by the second coming of Christ, the more normal presumption would be that the supper would take place on earth in connection with the second coming to the earth itself" (*The Revelation of Jesus Christ* [Chicago: Moody, 1966], 270).

the church and those who make up the bride of Christ is not an acquired righteousness but a bestowed righteousness.

Suddenly the angel speaks to John and gives a command, introducing the fourth beatitude of the Apocalypse. That beatitude states: "Blessed are those who are invited to the wedding supper of the Lamb!" A typical approach to weddings in the ancient Near East is clearly observable in our Lord's parable of the wise and foolish virgins (Matt 25:1–13). The bridal party of the wedding is gathered at the home of the bride and awaits the coming of the groom along with his party. After the father of the bride gives the bride away, the two parties then march through the village and arrive at the home of the groom where the wedding supper is to take place. The arrival of the bridal party is about sundown, and the ceremony and the supper almost always took place after dark.

In the case of Jesus' parable, the groom delays his coming, and some of those attached to the bridal party discover that they have an inadequate supply of oil for their lamps. When the shout comes through the city streets that the bridegroom is coming, those who are unprepared awaken from slumber only to discover that they cannot light their lamps. In the middle of the night, they shuffle away into the town to find oil and find that they are excluded from the marriage supper. The groom's party arrives, the bride is given, and the steps are retraced to the home of the groom—or in the case of a large wedding to the chosen place—and the marriage supper commences. Occasionally, if it were a large wedding or a wedding involving dignitaries, the wedding feast might even continue for days. No mention of the length of this feast is made and some have argued that it is eternal in its duration. Whether that is the case, those who are invited are truly blessed, and the angel who told John to write this message ended by saying that this benediction of blessedness represents the true words of God.

Some discussion has focused on the recipients of this *makarism*. Is the reference to the bride and those who make up the bride of Christ as being blessed because they are invited, or do Old Testament saints and angelic witnesses constitute others invited to be a part of the feast, even though they themselves are not a part of the bride of Christ? A case, though not definitive, can be made for either. The present interpreter is inclined toward the view that the *makarism* would most suitably be applicable to the bride herself and those identified as that bride, but the question cannot be resolved.

At this point the apostle John is so totally overwhelmed by what he has observed that he falls at the feet of the angel to worship. Doubtless John knew better, and yet the circumstances were so momentous that he found himself prostrate at the angel's feet, probably before he thought through the whole matter.

The angel forbids the continuance of this action by explaining that he, too, is a servant, along with John and with his brothers; and his brothers are said to be those who have the testimony of Jesus. The word "testimony," or witness, references someone who has seen or experienced something to be the case. John and his brothers are therefore witnesses and the bearers of testimony to the plan and purpose of God for redemption in Jesus. Consequently, God is the only appropriate object of worship. This is explained by the somewhat enigmatic statement, "For the testimony of Jesus is the spirit of prophecy." Here the word "prophecy" (*prophēteia*), which arises from a combination of "speak" (*phēmi*) and "before" (*pro*), employs an important use of the word essentially meaning "speak for God before." "Before what?" is an appropriate question. One sense of the preposition (*pro*) would be to speak about an event before it happens. Another sense would be to speak before listeners of the purpose and acts of God. Likely in this case both of these senses are paramount. In any event, the meaning is actually reasonably clear: The spirit of both the proclamation and the telling of the future is bound up in the testimony of Jesus. Jesus the Lamb—and not just a chronology of last things—is the theme of the Revelation. As Walvoord succinctly declares, "This means that prophecy at its very heart is designed to unfold the beauty and loveliness of our Lord and Savior Jesus Christ."[403] This will become even more apparent in that which transpires next.

(2) The Triumph of Christ (19:11–16)

[11]Now I saw heaven opened, and behold, a white horse. And He who sat on him *was* called Faithful and True, and in righteousness He judges and makes war. [12]His eyes *were* like a flame of fire, and on His head *were* many crowns. He had a name written that no one knew except Himself. [13]He *was* clothed with a robe dipped in blood, and His name is called The Word of God. [14]And the armies in heaven, clothed in fine linen, white and clean, followed Him on white horses. [15]Now out of His mouth goes a sharp sword, that with it He should strike the nations. And He Himself will rule them with a rod of iron. He Himself treads the winepress of the fierceness and wrath of Almighty God. [16]And He has on *His* robe and on His thigh a name written:

KING OF KINGS AND LORD OF LORDS.

Now the Bridegroom appears. However, He does not appear as the verses immediately before might have anticipated; but rather He appears in His return to bring

---

403 *The Revelation of Jesus Christ*, 273.

judgment. Suddenly the seer observed that heaven was standing open before him, and a white horse whose Rider was called Faithful and True appeared. "Standing open" is a perfect passive participle, indicating the unchanging nature of what now happens. As John observed, the Rider on the white horse bore the designation Faithful and True. Earlier, in the message to the church at Laodicea, Jesus had identified Himself as "the Faithful and True Witness" (3:14). Now He appears as the faithful and true Judge. Consequently, with justice He now wages war.

John observes that His eyes are like the blazing of a fire, and He has on His head many diadems or crowns. Both descriptions are designed to heighten the sense of awesomeness, justice, and irresistible power and authority. The eyes like flaming fire suggest not only judgment but penetrating knowledge. Whereas many of the dragon's minions have appeared with crowns; and even though the Lamb has usually been pictured with a victor's wreath, He now appears as the Warrior-Judge, and all authority is His. Accordingly, He is crowned with multiple diadems.

John also observes that He has a name that has been written that no one knows except Himself. Again, "written" is a perfect passive participle so that the circumstance is seen as a permanent one. The name that no man knows signals the transcendent quality of this Rider. Whatever is known of Him, even by revelation, does not exhaust His essence. Though He may be known, He remains the unknowable One. And though He is the unknowable One, He makes Himself known as both Judge and Savior. Martin Luther, as well as Aquinas, called attention to the hiddenness or unknowabilty of God. The expression *Deus absconditus* (the hidden God) was overcome only by *Deus revelatus* (the revealed God).[404] But even the revelation of God is only partial. While instructing humans generally and accurately about his being and character is sufficient, the Scriptures are replete with hints that the human grasp of God remains for-

---

404 Luther said, "Diatribe, however, deceives herself in her ignorance by not making any distinction between God preached and God hidden, that is, between the Word of God and God himself. God does many things that he does not disclose to us in his word; he also wills many things which he does not disclose himself as willing in his word. Thus he does not will the death of a sinner, according to his word; but he wills it according to that inscrutable will of his. It is our business, however, to pay attention to the word and leave that inscrutable will alone, for we must be guided by the word and not by that inscrutable will. After all, who can direct himself by a will completely inscrutable and unknowable? It is enough to know simply that there is a certain inscrutable will in God, and as to what, why, and how far it wills, that is something we have no right whatever to inquire into, hanker after, care about, or meddle with, but only to fear and adore" (*LW* 33:140).

ever partial, and this is the emphasis of the declaration that He has a name written that is incomprehensible to all but Himself.

This is demonstrated in Exod 3:14 when Moses seeks information concerning the name of the God who commissioned him and is told to report that "I AM" sent him. The four transliterated Hebrew letters (that is, Yod He Waw He) translated "I AM" are referred to as the Tetragrammaton or four English letters—YHWH. The word itself both reveals who God is in contrast to pagan deities but by virtue of the fact that no one even knows for sure how to pronounce the name is a reminder of God's transcendence over all human knowledge.[405]

A similar development transpires in Judg 13:18 when Manoah, soon to be father of Samson, asks the angel of the LORD His name. Manoah is gently rebuked with the question, "Why do you ask my name? It is beyond understanding."[406] This is a translation of the word that is also used to describe Christ in Isa 9:6 where the Child to be born will be called among other things, "Wonderful Counselor." The word "wonderful" is the same term used by the angel of the LORD in Judges. God reveals all that humans can embrace, and that revelation is sufficient for salvation and happiness. Nevertheless, He remains the transcendent God.

In addition, His garment is a robe that has been dipped in blood. The garment dipped in blood once again is subject to different interpretations. Some have suggested that it represents His own blood, which has been shed for humanity.[407]

---

405 VanGemeren notes "Many scholars accept the widely held opinion that the tetragrammaton is a form of the root *hyh* ('be') and should be pronounced as 'Yahweh' ('He who brings into being'; cf. Exod. 3:12, 'I will be with you' and 'I AM WHO I AM,' v. 14). Regardless of the editorial decision of substituting Lord for *yhwh* or of using the divine name 'Yahweh,' the reader must keep in mind that LORD, Yahweh, or *yhwh* is the *name* of God that he revealed to his ancient people" ("Tetragrammaton," in *Evangelical Dictionary of the Theology* [Grand Rapids: Baker Academic, 2001], 1177).

406 The Hebrew word is פֶּלִאי.

407 Origen, while spiritualizing the entire passage, sees this blood as that of the Lamb: "Now John does not see the Word of God mounted on a horse naked. He is clothed with a garment sprinkled with blood, since the Word who became flesh, and died because he became flesh, is invested with traces of that passion, since his blood also was poured forth upon the earth when the soldier pierced his side. For, perhaps, even if in some way we attain the most sublime and highest contemplation of the Word and of the truth, we shall not forget completely that we were introduced to him by his coming in our body" (*Commentary on the Gospel According to John: Books 1–10*, trans. R. E. Heine, FC 80 [Washington, DC: Catholic University of America Press, 2000], 110). Oecumenius adds colorfully, "He says, *Clad in a robe sprinkled with blood:* for even in the

More probably, however, in this case it represents the blood of his enemies since the circumstance here involves judgment.[408]

Finally, His name is called the Word of God, reminding the reader of the prologue to John's Gospel in which he speaks specifically of Jesus as the Word of God. This declaration is an interesting contrast to the previous title that no one could know except the Lamb. Assuming that the author of the Apocalypse is also the author of the Gospel of John, this avowal would only be consistent with the theology of the second Person of the Trinity as developed in the prologue of John's Gospel. There is an important sense in which the Bible is the Word of God written, divinely inspired, and miraculously preserved. But the ultimate communication of God, whom the Scriptures reveal, is Christ, the Word of God incarnate. In Jesus one sees God and learns of His salvation. In v. 14 John observes that He is accompanied by the armies of heaven, all riding on white horses and dressed in fine linen, white and clean. Again, the testimony is to their purity as well as to their justice. However, there is actually no need for this entourage in terms of assurance of the victory because, as the Word of God, His word proves all that is necessary. Out of his mouth comes a sharp, two-edged sword, with which to strike the nations. If this two-edged sword is imagined to be an actual Roman blade (rhomphaia), it is a grotesque image. But while the imagery is strange to Western culture, it points to something that is literally the case, namely, that just as God's word was powerful enough to create the cosmos initially, so it is all that is needed to strike down the nations who rise against him. Additionally, He will rule the nations with a rod of iron.

The seer further observes that this One treads the winepresses of the fury of the wrath of God Almighty. Vats for the liberation of the juice in the grapes were sufficiently large for several workers to wade in, crushing the grapes and "thoroughly spattering their clothes with 'the blood of the grapes.'"[409] This imagery for judgment is not uncommon in the Bible. Here the Lamb is pictured as treading repeatedly through the winepress of humanity, exacting the just toll of judgment in the carnage of conflict. Finally, v. 16 declares that both on His

---

vision the Lord was bearing the marks of his passion, and was showing his all-holy body all but covered with his precious blood" (*Commentary on the Apocalypse*, 164).

408 As Walvoord says, "The spectacle, however, of Christ on a white horse with a vesture dipped in blood accompanied by innumerable heavenly beings clothed in fine linen is a demonstration that now at long last the filthy, blasphemous situation on earth is going to be wiped clean with a divine judgment of tremendous character" (*The Revelation of Jesus Christ*, 277).

409 K. H. Easley, "Ancient Winepresses," *Biblical Illustrator* (Fall 1989): 65–69.

robe and on His thigh, He is declared to be King of kings and Lord of lords. Of all kings He is *the* King. Of all lords He is *the* Lord.

C. The Demise of the Beast (19:17–21)

¹⁷Then I saw an angel standing in the sun; and he cried with a loud voice, saying to all the birds that fly in the midst of heaven, "Come and gather together for the supper of the great God, ¹⁸that you may eat the flesh of kings, the flesh of captains, the flesh of mighty men, the flesh of horses and of those who sit on them, and the flesh of all *people,* free and slave, both small and great."

¹⁹And I saw the beast, the kings of the earth, and their armies, gathered together to make war against Him who sat on the horse and against His army. ²⁰Then the beast was captured, and with him the false prophet who worked signs in his presence, by which he deceived those who received the mark of the beast and those who worshiped his image. These two were cast alive into the lake of fire burning with brimstone.²¹And the rest were killed with the sword which proceeded from the mouth of Him who sat on the horse. And all the birds were filled with their flesh.

The coming of the King of kings and Lord of lords is the impetus for the invitation of an angel standing in the sun who cries with a loud voice, inviting all the birds (*orneois*)[410] to gather together for the supper of the great God mentioned in v. 17, which is entirely distinct from the wedding supper of the Lamb in v. 9. From the vantage point of the prophet, the angel is superimposed against the backdrop of the sun, creating even greater splendor. This great supper of God is the feast of the birds of carrion consuming the flesh and the bodies of kings, generals, mighty men, horses, and the flesh of all people, whether free, slave, small, or great. The reader cannot avoid the sense of the arresting reversal depicted here. All of human history is the story of powerful monarchs or oligarchies imposing their wills on the weak. Now there is no difference any longer. Kings, generals, mighty men, all people small and great in human annals are reduced to a common denominator—the just judgment of the Creator.

The judgment of the King of kings and Lord of lords is an irresistible judgment, and these birds of prey are invited to make themselves ready to gorge on the carcasses that will remain.[411] In v. 19 the beast out of the sea

---

410 Hence the study of birds, ornithology, derives from the transliteration of this Greek word.

411 For most people vultures do not rank high in the birdwatchers' favorites list.

and all the kings of the earth and their armies gather together with the intention of making war against the Lord. However, in this last confrontation, the beast in the person of its leader is captured. So, too, is the false prophet who had been able to perform miraculous signs on behalf of the first beast. Now, however, such signs no longer succeed, and he faces inevitable defeat. The signs have been used to delude those who received the mark of the beast and worshiped his image, but now the two of them are thrown together into a lake of burning sulfur.

Two things are worthy of particular note. First, the continued emphasis on the miraculous generated by the false prophet to deceive the nations of the earth is again presented. Signs and wonders in every generation need to be subject to the keenest of spiritual discernment. Few are not deceived by them, but now no further deceit is possible.

Finally, with the beast and the false prophet thrown into the lake of fire, all opponents have been subdued except the dragon himself. The scarlet woman was deposed and executed by the first beast who no longer needed her. Now that beast and the false prophet are both defeated by the King of kings and Lord of lords. They are cast into the lake of fire. All the rest of those who served with them are killed by the sword that came from the mouth of the Rider on the horse. This is an indication that no visible sword was necessary, but the King of kings slew the enemy with simply the word of His mouth. When the carnage has been completed, the birds that have been invited to the "supper of the great God" gorge themselves on the flesh. The way is paved for the reign of the Christ upon the earth and a penultimate encounter with the dragon.

Though occasionally colorful, vultures are never aesthetically pleasing, and this initial revulsion is exacerbated by their habits, feeding, and other characteristics. But the Lord of the cosmos designed them as protection against rampant disease. The twenty-three species of vultures (sixteen in Africa alone) have remarkably designed digestive systems, which contain special acids that dissolve anthrax, botulism, and cholera bacteria. Eyesight is keen; some species are able to spot a carcass from four miles away. Rüeppell's Griffon vulture is the world's highest-flying bird, having reached a known altitude of 37,000 feet. Most vulture species mate for life and are noted for intelligent use of tools (See "16 Cool Facts about Vultures on International Vulture Awareness Day!" 5 September 2009 [online]; accessed August 14, 2011; (http://ecolocalizer. com/2009/09/05/16-cool-facts-about-vultures-on-international-vulture-awareness-day.) Here they constitute something of the ultimate judgment of God on those who are rebellious.

9. The Millennial Age (20:1–10)

Christ's judgment of the earth is complete. The beast from the land and the beast from the sea, along with the great prostitute, have all been cast into the lake of fire. There remains only one item of judgment—the dragon who lies behind it all. The judgment of the dragon will involve also the millennial reign of Christ on the earth, and so the two, together with the final judgment of all of the lost of the time of the millennium, are the subject of chap. 20.

Because of the frequent reference (six times) to a period of 1,000 years, this passage has become the most extensively debated of the entire book. The Latin terms for 1,000 years are combined in the word "millennium." From this designation, interpreters have divided themselves into three major categories with numerous variations. Futurists, or premillennialists, believe the *parousia*, or return of Christ, precedes and inaugurates a thousand-year reign of peace. Postmillennialists insist that the reign of Christ is through His church and that Christ returns at the close of the victorious age. Amillennialists take seriously the reign of Christ but generally believe that the explicit language of 1,000 years should be allegorically or spiritually understood. Many contemporary interpreters who advance this last position prefer some other designation, believing that "amillennial" is not an accurate description of their view. This commentator follows the premillennial perspective.[412]

A. The Binding of Satan (20:1–3)

[1]Then I saw an angel coming down from heaven, having the key to the bottomless pit and a great chain in his hand. [2]He laid hold of the dragon, that serpent of old, who is *the* Devil and Satan, and bound him for a thousand years; [3]and he cast him into the bottomless pit, and shut him up, and set a seal on him, so that he should deceive the

---

412 G. B. Caird is typical of commentators who take a critical view of this text: "We come now to a passage which, more than any other in the book, has been the paradise of cranks and fanatics on the one hand and literalists on the other. It bristles with questions. Why, once Satan had been securely sealed in the abyss, must he be let loose to wreak further havoc? And what claim does he have on God, that God is bound to give the Devil his due? Why the millennium? And what blessings does it confer on the martyrs that make it worth their while to wait a thousand years for the greater bliss of heaven? Who or what are Gog and Magog, and what part do they play in John's theology of history?" (*The Revelation of St. John the Divine*, HNTC 19 [San Francisco: Harper & Row, 1966], 249).

nations no more till the thousand years were finished. But after these things he must be released for a little while.

20:1–3 From his promontory on Patmos, the prophet John sees an angel coming down from heaven. Having already been tossed from his heavenly abode, Satan has become a problem for the earth (see chap. 12). Now the angel who descends from heaven to the earth to deal with Satan has the key to the "bottomless pit" and has in his hand a great chain. The Bottomless Pit or Abyss (*abusson*) is in some way distinct from the lake of fire, which will be the ultimate destiny of the dragon. The Abyss seems to be a part of the netherworld and not a savory place but certainly not as catastrophic as the lake of fire. The intention of the angel having a chain and a key to the Abyss is to apprehend Satan and confine him in chains to the Abyss. Prisoners in antiquity, as now, were bound with chains. One might reasonably ask how a spiritual being can be bound with a physical chain. However, there is no indication as to the exact nature of the chain. While a literal event is portrayed, the precise nature of the chain that binds Satan remains unknown.

The dragon, who is identified also as the ancient serpent, further as the Devil or the accuser, and finally as Satan, the adversary, is bound and thrown into the Abyss where he will remain for 1,000 years. The multiplying of names for Satan is doubtless an attempt not only to identify him clearly but to do so in a way that establishes the consummate evil of his being. He is the dragon. He is the ancient serpent, or snake, involved apparently in the initial temptations in the garden of Eden.[413] He is the one who hurls accusations (*diabolos*) and causes disruption, and as such he is the ultimate enemy and adversary (*satanas*) of all. Once he is thrown into the Abyss and it is locked, then there is one final act—the sealing of the Abyss.

When Jesus was placed in the tomb of Joseph of Arimathea, the tomb was sealed with a Roman seal. The seal was not so much an impediment to entry as it was a warning based on established authority. Anyone who broke the seal would be guilty of rebellion against Rome, so now the seal of God is on the Abyss. Since there is no higher authority than God, none is able to loose Satan from that abyss. The purpose for this sealing is important for two reasons. First, he is prevented from deceiving the nations again until the thousand years have ended. Doubtless John was surprised to hear that after that period of 1,000 years, Satan

---

413 For a provocative account of why נחש should not be understood as a "snake" in Genesis 3, see A. Clarke, *Clarke's Commentary* (New York: Abingdon, n.d.), 1:47–50. Clarke's conclusion that the culprit used of Satan in Eden is actually an "ouran outang" is novel if unlikely.

would be set free for a short time. The apparent reason for this freeing of Satan for a short time will be discussed as the second reason for this action. For the moment note that for 1,000 years he will not deceive the nations.

This period of 1,000 years mentioned twice in vv. 1–3 and four more times in vv. 4–10 clearly represents an important temporal designation. The mention of it here has made this passage among the most famous in the Apocalypse. Of course, perspectives regarding its meaning divide essentially among three positions. Perhaps the majority of scholars see it as simply a reference to a long period of time.[414] Others in a variation of that view find that the numerical significance of ten as a complete number in its multiplied form of 1,000 comes to represent the perfect or completed state. However, while numbers do have symbolic significance, the repeated numbers such as the forty-two months, 1,260 days, time and times and half a time, and the 1,000 year period emphasized here suggest that these periods are to be taken literally.[415] The viewpoint of this commentator stands with those who take the 1,000 years literally and indeed as a great emphasis because of the number of times mentioned in these first few verses.

---

414 M. Gourgues says of the passage and its interpreters, "This sparsity of data relative to the thousand-year reign contrasts sharply with the verbosity and luxuriance of certain proposed explanations. Roughly, one can distinguish two major lines of interpretation." "The Thousand-Year Reign (Rev 20:1–6): Terrestrial or Celestial?" *CBQ* 47 (1985): 677. He goes on to argue that this is not a utopian age on earth but is the language of heaven. R. Summers was more pointed: "If verses 4, 5, and 6 of Revelation 20 had been omitted, no one would ever have dreamed of a literal thousand years of Christ's reign upon the earth—his setting up a temporal throne in Jerusalem and inaugurating a millennial reign as an earthly monarch. Yet whole systems of eschatology, theology, and philosophy of history have been constructed on this precarious basis of highly symbolical verses" (*Worthy Is the Lamb: Interpreting the Book of Revelation in Its Historical Background* [Nashville: B&H, 1951], 203).

415 C. C. Rowland contrasts some of the early views of the millennium, beginning with the charismatic Montanists. "Montanist expectation was for a new Jerusalem that would descend in Phrygia. Justin looked forward to an earthly reign of the saints, where they would reign with Christ in peace and prosperity in a rebuilt and enlarged Jerusalem. This is but a prelude to judgment, however, though Justin recognizes that 'not all Christians are of this persuasion.' Irenaeus, in his refutation of Gnostic heresy, stressed the material character of salvation and supported Papias's view about the millennium. Irenaeus made reference to biblical passages that speak of peace, prosperity, and material restoration, which he refuses to spiritualize" ("The Book of Revelation," *NIB* [Nashville: Abingdon, 1998], 12:710).

B. The Reigning of Believers (20:4–6)

⁴And I saw thrones, and they sat on them, and judgment was committed to them. Then *I saw* the souls of those who had been beheaded for their witness to Jesus and for the word of God, who had not worshiped the beast or his image, and had not received *his* mark on their foreheads or on their hands. And they lived and reigned with Christ for a thousand years. ⁵But the rest of the dead did not live again until the thousand years were finished. This *is* the first resurrection.⁶Blessed and holy *is* he who has part in the first resurrection. Over such the second death has no power, but they shall be priests of God and of Christ, and shall reign with Him a thousand years.

This period of 1,000 years is to be a time when Christ shall live and reign on the earth; but there are other thrones observed by John, and seated on those thrones were those who had been given authority to judge. John also observed the presence of the souls of those who had been beheaded because of their testimony for Jesus and because of the Word of God. These are mentioned earlier as the ones who had not worshiped the beast or his image and did not receive his mark on their foreheads or hands (Rev 6:9). They were living again and reigned with Christ for 1,000 years. The text speaks of these as souls (*psuchas*), which might suggest that they had not yet received glorified bodies; however, their souls were never dead, and the word does not necessarily presuppose a disembodied state.⁴¹⁶

---

416 J. A. Seiss answers this objection decisively: "Some stumble at the word *souls* (ψυχὰς), by which these martyrs are denoted, as if that introduced a peculiarity determinative of the whole character and interpretation of the vision. But it is nothing but a metaphysical quibble, by which to obscure and get rid of a plain doctrine of the Word of God which some do not like. It is a sufficient answer to say, that one of the common uses of this word in the New Testament is to denote individual beings, and persons in the body, rather than spirits of men out of the body. So the converts on the day of Pentecost are called 'about three thousand *souls*;' and Jacob and his kindred who went down into Egypt are spoken of as 'threescore and fifteen *souls*;' and those sailing with Paul in the ship were 'two hundred threescore and sixteen *souls*;' and in the ark with Noah 'eight *souls* were saved.' In such passages disembodied souls are out of the question. Indeed, one of the rarest uses of the word by the sacred writers, if ever so used, is that which confines its meaning to the designation of that part of man capable of existence apart from the body. More commonly, it means corporeal life as distinguished from corporeal death. And as respects principles, or a mere moral influence, there is no instance in all the Word of God of its use in that sense. That the word *souls*, in John's vision of the martyrs beneath the altar, means *persons dead as to their bodies*, it is very evident, not,

John remarks that the rest of the dead did not come to life until the 1,000 years were ended. Again, debate exists over the precise group intended here. Almost certainly this is a reference to the unrighteous dead, who, as one will momentarily observe, face a judgment at the conclusion of the millennial period. That seems to be the purpose of the statement that those who are alive and reigning with Christ for 1,000 years constitute the first resurrection. Since Christ is the firstfruits of the resurrection and then those that are His at His coming and these are now joined by the resurrected righteous dead from the tribulation period, the first resurrection is not emphasizing order but life. In other words, the first resurrection is a resurrection to eternal life while the second resurrection will be a resurrection to damnation. This is exactly what is found in the fifth beatitude, "Blessed and holy are those who have part in the first resurrection" (v. 6). The negation of this would be that those who are a part of the second resurrection are neither blessed nor holy. But these who are a part of the first resurrection discover that the second death has no power over them. This, again, is not the case for those in the second resurrection or the resurrection to judgment. Their deaths become an agonizing realization of eternity.

On the other hand, those who have part in the first resurrection are identified as priests of God and of Christ and will reign with Him for 1,000 years. Under normal circumstances, a priest served as the representative between man and God. He represented God to the people in teaching, but he also represented the people to God in intercession and sacrifice. Since none of that will be necessary in the millennium or the eternal state to follow, the other aspect of priesthood must be invoked. In the Old Testament the individuals who were allowed into the holy place were the priests, and the only single individual who was allowed into the holy of holies was the high priest, and then only on Yom Kippur. The priest had access to the symbolic presence of God in a way far re-

---

however, from the meaning of the word, but from the accompanying statement that the *souls* he saw were people *slain* on account of their faith. He sees the same people, persons, *souls*, here; but this time ἔζησαν—'they lived again.' As mere souls separate from the body, they never were dead. John saw them, and heard them speaking, and beheld them invested in white robes, and recognized them as still living and waiting, though dead as to their bodies. The *living again* in which he now sees them, must therefore be a living in that in which they were dead when he first saw them, that is, *corporeally dead.* There is a resurrection of *the bodies* of dead men, but there is no such thing as the resurrection of *the spirits* of dead men. For *living* men there may be a spiritual resurrection from the death-state of sin, but there is no such spiritual resurrection for *dead* men" (*The Apocalypse: Lectures on the Book of Revelation* [Grand Rapids: Zondervan, 1962], 459–60).

moved from the common Israelite. The fact that every New Testament believer is a priest for God carries then the significance that each individual has personal access to and the experience of fellowship with the God of the universe. This realized imagery for believers is not as incredible to the western mind-set as it ought to be. Nevertheless, that the transcendent God may be known and experienced by every individual constitutes one of the great mysteries of eternity. This concept is also the essence of the doctrine of the priesthood of believers.

For many who find the idea of a literal reign of Christ on the earth to be somewhat improbable, the objection is voiced that this is the only place in the Bible where the 1,000 years is mentioned. This affirmation is correct; but even without the expressed statement of a period of time, the Old Testament prophets, particularly Isaiah, abound with kingdom age expectation. In Isa 2:2, the prophet sees a day coming when the mountain of the Lord's house will be established and all the nations shall flow into it. In Isa 11:6, the domesticity of all animals is revealed when the wolf dwells with the lamb, the leopard lies down with the young goat, the calf and a young lion feed together, and all are led by a child. In Isa 19:23–25, a day is anticipated when there will be a highway running all the way from Egypt to Assyria and, therefore, directly through the land of Israel. That will be a day when God will say, "Blessed be Egypt my people, Assyria my handiwork, and Israel my inheritance." In Isa 35:1–2, the prophet anticipates a time when the desert shall blossom like a rose. In Isa 62 he prophesies a time when Israel once again will be married to God. This latter theme is the focus of the entire book of Hosea. Multitudes of other such prophecies are found in the prophetic literature of the Old Testament. There can be little doubt that the prophets themselves, and certainly those who read their prophecies, anticipated a literal fulfillment of those prophecies. This seems to be the intent of the question by the disciples addressed to Jesus after his resurrection, when they said, "Lord, are you at this time going to restore the kingdom to Israel" (Acts 1:6)? Jesus did not tell them the question was irrelevant but rather that it was not for them to know the times or the seasons (*chronos* and *kairos* respectively), which made up the timetable of God; rather they were to be witnesses until that time came.

Therefore, the 1,000 years stipulated here should be taken literally in an anticipated fulfillment not only of what is promised here but also what is promised extensively through most of the Old Testament prophets.[417] Some people

---

417 For example, T. A. Howe, in explicating the literal nature of Christ's reign presented in Dan 7, notes, "This 'son of man' is said in Daniel's vision to come 'on

ask why this should take place on earth. That answer is not provided in Scripture. Since, however, even at the conclusion of the millennial period Satan has a following, one may hazard the hypothesis that perhaps the millennium is the final act of a gracious God to appeal to the fallen hearts in terms of what it is like to live under His compassionate rule.

C. Gog and Magog (20:7–10)

⁷Now when the thousand years have expired, Satan will be released from his prison ⁸and will go out to deceive the nations which are in the four corners of the earth, Gog and Magog, to gather them together to battle, whose number is as the sand of the sea. ⁹They went up on the breadth of the earth and surrounded the camp of the saints and the beloved city. And fire came down from God out of heaven and devoured them. ¹⁰The devil, who deceived them, was cast into the lake of fire and brimstone where the beast and the false prophet are. And they will be tormented day and night forever and ever.

20:7-10 The final doom of Satan is the subject of the next paragraph. When the 1,000 years have been completed as indicated in the earlier verse, Satan is released from his prison (*phulakēs*, the usual word for prison). He demonstrates the malignity of his character by venturing forth once again to deceive the nations from the four corners of the earth.[418] Specifically, Gog and Magog

---

the clouds of heaven.' If the expression 'son of man' refers to the *Hasidim*, how can it be said of them that they come on the clouds of heaven? There does not seem to be a convincing reason to take this reference as anything other than an appearance of the pre-incarnate Christ. It is also important to notice that the kings—in 7:17 Daniel says, 'These great beasts, which are four in number, are four kings,' using the word מַלְכִין (*malkîn*), 'kings,' not מַלְכוּת (*malkût*) 'kingdoms' as in 7:27—are portrayed as vicious and destructive animals, while this one is presented as being like a human being. The world-wide kingdom that the beasts endeavored to gain by their ferocity and destructive tactics they ultimately lose and the 'Son of Man' gains and holds forever" (*Daniel: In the Preterists' Den: A Critical Look at Preterist Interpretations of Daniel* [Eugene, OR: Wipf & Stock, 2008], 240).

418 B. K. Blount suggests, "Apparently, the combat debacle of 19:11-21 was not enough. Even after a thousand incarcerated years to mull over the rout, the dragon, perhaps delusional, harbors the hope that it can still defeat God's forces. Once liberated, the parolee goes about doing the very thing that got it imprisoned in the first place; it tries to deceive the nations—which apparently were not completely destroyed in the first 'final' battle—to join yet another ill-fated attempt to assume the lordship that be-

are enjoined to gather themselves for a great battle. Numerically they are un-
countable—like the sand of the seashore.

The reference to Gog and Magog is to the prophecy of Ezek 38–39. Gog
is the individual and Magog the geographical and political entity he represents.
Following his dry bones prophecy about the regathering of Israel, Ezekiel, in
chap. 37, sees in the last days a final assault upon Israel by Gog and Magog. The
difficulty for the interpreter of the book of Revelation is that this battle is clearly
one that occurs at the conclusion of the millennium, whereas most interpreters
have seen the battle of Gog and Magog prophesied in Ezek 38–39 as belonging to
the end of the tribulation and probably as identical to the battle of Armageddon.

Lamar Cooper, in his New American Commentary volume on Ezekiel,
chronicles seven possible interpretations of the battle but finds in the end three
major possibilities. The first is that Gog and Magog actually refers to the same
battle by that name here in Rev 20. The second views the battle as Armageddon
at the close of the tribulation period, chronicled at the end of chap. 16. The third
view is a combination of the first two, indicating that this final conflict of history
occurs at two different times with an interim period of 1,000 years.[419] Since it is
impossible to identify exactly what Gog and Magog represent, one can declare
that they are presented in Ezekiel as the perennial enemy of the people of God.
This being the case, to find the concept of Gog and Magog applied also to this
last battle of history, occurring at the end of the millennium, is not surprising.[420]

longs exclusively to God" (*Revelation*, NTL [Louisville, KY: WJK, 2009], 369).

419 L. E. Cooper, *Ezekiel*, NAC 17 (Nashville: B&H, 1994), 330–37. Cooper summarizes, "This battle probably takes place at the end of the tribulation, bringing it to a conclusion and ushering in the thousand-year reign of peace. The battle starts again, however, at
the end of the thousand years. Revelation 20:2–3 refers to the binding of Satan in the abyss
for the thousand years 'to keep him from deceiving the nations any more until the thousand
years were ended. After that, he must be set free for a short time.' Revelation 20:7–8 adds that
'when the thousand years are over, Satan will be released from his prison and will go out to
deceive the nations in the four corners of the earth—Gog and Magog—to gather them to
battle.' This seems clearly to suggest a second stage of the Gog-Magog battle that began in
Rev 19 at the coming of Messiah and conclusion of the tribulation. The purpose would be
the final defeat of Satan before the beginning of the eternal state" (336–37).

420 B. Otzen's article in *TDOT* is helpful in providing the general OT background for גּוֹג and מָגוֹג as well as showing some of the effort, though unsuccessfully,
to which they refer in prophecy. Concerning the origin of the terms, he notes, "In the
table of nations in Gen. 10, the sons of Japheth are presented 'in their lands, each with
his own language, by their families, in their nations' (10:5). The seven sons of Japheth
are: Gomer, Magog, Madai, Javan, Tubal, Meshech, and Tiras (10:2), and we encounter

The text further declares that Gog and Magog march across the breadth of the earth and surround the camp of God's people in the city he loves. This city must be Jerusalem; and although the reference to a camp may seem strange, probably the armies of the Lord would be camped around Jerusalem. However, what seems to be developing as a pitched battle among men takes a decidedly different turn when fire falls from heaven and devours Gog and Magog. Once again, of course, these have been deceived by Satan, and now the time has come to deal forever with the Devil. He has deceived them, and he is now thrown into the lake of burning sulfur where already the beast and the false prophet have been thrown. There they are tormented day and night, forever and ever.

Inevitably this raises the question of the justice of eternal punishment. In the heart of most individuals is a quasi-universalist hope. Even a few have hope for history's intolerable dictators, who have masterminded the death and enslavement of so many; but most people can see how they would be turned aside into judgment. However, Christians are widely believed to be almost sadistic in anticipating eternal punishment for most. In every generation there is a movement—even as there is presently—for the advocacy of annihilationism.[421] Such arguments involve considerable casuistry in attempting to deal with what is

---

Togarmah among the sons of Gomer (10:3; cf. 1 Ch. 1:5f.). In a series of prophecies in Ezk. 38–39, it is stated that 'after many days,' 'in the latter years' (38:8), Yahweh will lead Gog of the land of Magog, chief prince of Meshech and Tubal, at the head of a great army against Israel, returned from exile. His troops include Gomer and Beth-togarmah 'from the uttermost parts of the north,' as well as Paras (Persia), Cush (Ethiopia), and Put (Libya?) (38:1–9). Gog devises wicked plans in arrogance, and desires only to carry off plunder from Israel. But the prophet prophesies against Gog and makes it clear to him that he will be allowed to march against Israel only in order to demonstrate Yahweh's glory (38:10–16). Gog represents the enemy announced by the earlier prophets: when he comes, and earthquake will break forth upon Israel and will destroy the land (38:17–20); but in the end this destruction will also come upon Gog (38:21–23). Gog and his hordes will be brought against the mountains of Israel, and there they will be destroyed by Yahweh; the dead bodies will be devoured by the birds and the beasts (39:1–8)" (*TDOT* 2.419).

421 For an argument favoring annihilationism, see C. H. Pinnock, *A Wideness in God's Mercy: The Finality of Jesus Christ in a World of Religions* (Grand Rapids: Zondervan, 1992) and "An Inclusivist View," in *Four Views on Salvation in a Pluralistic World*, Counterpoints, ed. D. L. Okholm, T. R. Phillips, and S. N. Gundry (Grand Rapids: Zondervan, 1996), 95–123. For a thorough examination of the relationship between the thinking of Pinnock and that of K. Rahner and the conclusions of Vatican II, see K. D. Keathley, "An Examination of the Influence of Vatican II on Clark Pinnock's 'Wider Hope' for the Unevangelized," Ph.D. diss, Southeastern Baptist Theological Seminary, 2000.

abundantly clear in the text. Surely the Devil deserves eternal punishment, but the words in the text translated "eternal" with regard to Satan are identical to words used for the false prophet and the beast and indeed all the enemies of God who have chosen not to serve him. Apparently, part of what it means to be made in the image of God is to have indestructibility or immortality as a part of what it means to be a spiritual being. A choice is made as to whether one wishes to be associated with God or to be left to his own prowess. The New Testament makes clear that originally hell was not made for humans but for the Devil and his angels (Matt 25:41); but for those who do not choose the Lord, no other alternative exists. The lake of burning sulfur referred to by the Lord as *Gehenna* is the place where those who reject the Lord are tormented day and night.

Another question frequently asked relates to the lake of burning sulfur or the lake of fire and brimstone. How could the chemical combustion known as fire torment spiritual beings? Of course, there is no answer to this dilemma other than that the exact chemical makeup of what is here described as a lake of burning sulfur is not known. Clearly, the analogy points to a shattering reality in another world. Whatever it is and whatever the state of the Devil and those with him, clearly, they experience excruciating torment for eternity. How that happens is known only to God.

10. The Judgment of the Great White Throne (20:11–15)

[11]Then I saw a great white throne and Him who sat on it, from whose face the earth and the heaven fled away. And there was found no place for them. [12]And I saw the dead, small and great, standing before God, and books were opened. And another book was opened, which is *the Book* of Life. And the dead were judged according to their works, by the things which were written in the books. [13]The sea gave up the dead who were in it, and Death and Hades delivered up the dead who were in them. And they were judged, each one according to his works. [14]Then Death and Hades were cast into the lake of fire. This is the second death. [15]And anyone not found written in the Book of Life was cast into the lake of fire.

Following the judgment of Satan, John sees a great white throne and One seated on it from whom the earth and the sky fled away, and yet there was in the end no place to seek asylum.[422] The One who sits on the throne is omniscient, om-

---

422 For an excellent assessment of the theme of judgment from Jewish writings

nipotent, and omnipresent. One cannot avoid the presence of an omnipresent God nor seek asylum from an omniscient and omnipotent God. Now the dead are standing before the throne, indicating that there has been a resurrection of the ungodly. They are made up of both great and small, persons who in the eyes of the social order amounted to little and persons who were a part of the ruling aristocracies of the world. No longer a distinction between them, they all stand before the throne having in common that they died outside of Christ.

The basis of their judgment is twofold. First, books are opened, as well as another book that is called the Book of Life. All of the dead are judged out of the things that are recorded in the books. This is a judgment based on their deeds or works. Everyone is present, the sea having given up the dead who have perished there and the grave, or Hades, having given up the dead in them. Every person is judged by what he has done or what has been recorded in the books.

Thomas notes, "Scripture makes consistent reference to a register of human actions."[423] Now death, the final enemy of all mankind, and Hades, the abode of the dead itself, are thrown into the lake of fire. The lake of fire is referred to as "the second death." Just as the first death is dreaded and avoided, so the second death is the far more devastating experience, encompassing a state of continual dying. Now the second basis of judgment is provided. If anyone's name is not found in the Book of Life, he, too, is thrown into the lake of fire. This constitutes an important theological principle. Everyone who stands before the great white throne is judged from the books. The only people appearing before this Great White Throne Judgment are those who were not a part of the first resurrection, and hence were outside of Christ. No believers stand before Christ at this Judgment.

The judgment of believers is referred to as the judgment seat of Christ, or the *Bēma*. This judgment is either referenced or explained in Rom 14:10; 2 Cor 5:10; and 1 Cor 3:10-15. Only believers appear at the *Bēma*, and its description is distinct. At the great white throne judgment, only unbelievers are present, and they are judged according to their works. The fact that they are condemned on that basis bears eloquent testimony to what the Scriptures have plainly said:

---

in the same general time period of the Apocalypse, see T. F. Glasson, "The Last Judgment—in Rev. 20 and Related Writings," *NTS* 28 (October 1982): 528–39. Glasson notes that the New Testament information on judgment is unique. "Judgment in the teaching of Jesus is far too complicated a subject to embark on here. But in approaching it something is gained by recognizing that in pre-Christian Judaism no clear indication of a universal assize of living and dead can be found. Writings inevitably omitted from this survey would not, I think, affect the general conclusion" (536).

423 Thomas, *Revelation 8-22*, 431.

"For all have sinned and fall short of the glory of God" (Rom 3:23); "There is none who does good, / no not one" (Rom 3:12b); and, "The heart is deceitful above all things / and desperately wicked. / Who can know it?" (Jer 17:9). Even persons deemed good and noble by their counterparts on earth are in their hearts rebellious against God. Universally, unredeemed humanity is at enmity with God, which becomes apparent in the judgment from the books.

However, there may be one last hope. A search is made among the names found within in the Book of Life. To be found in the Lamb's Book of Life affirms that one has been forgiven of all the sins recorded in the books. To be found in the Lamb's Book of Life is to be guaranteed life on the basis of the work of Christ rather than on the basis of the deeds written in the books, by which no flesh can be justified. Those whose names are not found written in the Lamb's Book of Life are condemned.

Thomas believes every individual's name is originally written in the Lamb's Book of Life, therefore indicating his confidence in a universal atonement.[424] Those of a more Calvinistic persuasion would argue that the only ones whose names are written in the Book of Life would be the elect. The names of the non-elect would never have been recorded in it. Thomas supposed that the Book of Life would be purged of those names who do not come to Christ. This he would see as implicit in the promise to Sardis that the overcomers would not have their names "blotted out" (Rev 3:5). In whatever way this is resolved, the point of the text is that the recording of one's name in the Lamb's Book of Life is the antidote to the condemnation of God brought on men by the deeds of their hearts and lives. So, therefore, men are twice condemned. First, they are condemned by their works; and second, the condemnation of their works

---

424 Thomas, *Revelation 8–22*, 432. For a view that differs, see C. R. Smith, "The Book of Life," *GTJ* 6.2 (1985): 219–30. Concerning the threat of names being blotted out of the Book of Life, Smith notes, "Rev 22:19 is probably the most frequently cited verse in support of the view that names may be blotted from the book of life. The support wholly vanishes, however, when one examines any recognized English version other than the *KJV*. It is well known among Bible scholars that there is absolutely *no* Greek manuscript support for the *KJV*'s rendering of this verse. All of the Greek manuscripts have 'tree of life,' not 'book of life.' Rev 22:18, 19 simply affirms that unbelievers who rob this book of its authority by adding to it or by taking from it shall have the plagues of the book 'added to' them and the blessings of the book 'taken away from' them. Among the blessings to be withheld are access to the tree of life and the holy city. The tree of life symbolizes the availability of eternal life in both the opening and closing paragraphs of the Bible. Therefore, though Rev 22:19 may be difficult to understand, it cannot be used as a basis for any doctrine suggesting that names may be blotted from the book of life" (227–28).

holds because they have chosen to reject the proffered gift of God, which is eternal life. As a result, they are thrown also into the lake of fire.

11. The Heavenly Kingdom (21:1–22:6)

For all of its extensive discussion, the millennium, or the reign of Christ on the earth, is addressed in only a few verses in chap. 20. Satan's doom is pronounced and the judgment of the world's unbelievers is completed. Now the seer of Patmos comes to the salubrious conclusion of his vision. As John beholds the new Jerusalem, the new heaven, and the new earth, his frustration with human vocabulary inadequate to describe the glories he beholds is almost apparent in the text. Nevertheless, he must write what he sees.

John's description encompasses 21:1 to 22:6, at which point the text becomes a final hortatory challenge. The considerable beauty of the new Jerusalem is outlined at some length. However, these beauties pale before the relational promises and the magnificence of the vision of God himself. The vision emphasizes again the importance of having one's name in the Lamb's Book of Life.

A. Heavenly Relationships (21:1–7)

¹Now I saw a new heaven and a new earth, for the first heaven and the first earth had passed away. Also there was no more sea. ²Then I, John, saw the holy city, New Jerusalem, coming down out of heaven from God, prepared as a bride adorned for her husband. ³And I heard a loud voice from heaven saying, "Behold, the tabernacle of God *is* with men, and He will dwell with them, and they shall be His people. God Himself will be with them *and be* their God. ⁴And God will wipe away every tear from their eyes; there shall be no more death, nor sorrow, nor crying. There shall be no more pain, for the former things have passed away."

⁵Then He who sat on the throne said, "Behold, I make all things new." And He said to me, "Write, for these words are true and faithful."

⁶And He said to me, "It is done! I am the Alpha and the Omega, the Beginning and *the* End. I will give of the fountain of the water of life freely to him who thirsts. ⁷He who overcomes shall inherit all things, and I will be his God and he shall be My son.

21:1-7 The passing away of the first heaven and the first earth have been anticipated in the specific statement of Simon Peter in 2 Pet 3:10–13. Here, he predicts the disappearance of the present heavens and earth, having been destroyed by fire, and the appearance of a new heaven and a new earth, which is to be the home of the righteous. Some interpreters believe the expressions in chaps. 21 and 22 relating to the new heavens and new earth are merely a continuum of the millennium. Others see a purged heaven and earth. While this doubtless is the case, what actually occurs at the close of the millennium seems to be a somewhat more catastrophic cleansing and purging of the cosmos. The elements melt with fervent heat, and from all of that emerges a new heaven and earth. "Heaven" here almost certainly refers to intergalactic space; and, of course, the earth is a part of that arrangement. The purging of everything wicked and destructive from the entire cosmos gives rise to the new heaven and the new earth, in which righteousness will dwell.

The rather enigmatic observation that there was no longer any sea has been understood in several different ways.[425] Some have argued that John looked out every day across the Aegean Sea to where his beloved church waited for him at Ephesus. The way was barred by the sea; and, therefore, the sea, for all of its beauty, became a menace to John and stood for the separation of God's people from direct concourse with the Lord as well as with the departed dead and even many of those alive at that time. Others take the reference to the sea to be the usual metaphor of apocalyptic literature to the foment of the civil and social orders presented as a seething and unruly sea. A few others have felt that the reference is to the crystal sea before the throne, but this seems highly unlikely. Some type of combination between the first two perspectives is possible, and the hint of the expression seems to be that in the new order the painful earthly estrangements will no longer exist.

As John beheld the new heavens and the new earth, he also beheld the Holy City, a new Jerusalem coming down out of heaven from God and prepared

---

425 Maclaren has a helpful analysis: "Now what is meant by this symbol is best ascertained by remembering how the sea appears in the Old Testament. The Jew was not a sailor. All the references in the Old Testament, and especially in the prophets, to the great ocean are such as a man would make who knew very little about it, except from having looked at it from the hills of Judea, and having often wondered what might be lying away out yonder at the point where sky and sea blended together. There are three main things which it shadows forth in the Old Testament. It is a symbol of mystery, of rebellious power, of perpetual unrest. And it is the promise of the cessation of these things which is set forth in that saying, 'There was no more sea.' There shall be no more mystery and terror. There shall be no more 'the floods lifting up their voice,' and the waves dashing with impotent foam against the throne of God. There shall be no more the tossing and the tumult of changing circumstances, and no more the unrest and disquiet of a sinful heart" (*The Epistles of John, Jude and the Book of Revelation*, Expositions of Scripture [London: Hodder and Stoughton, 1910], 356).

as a bride beautifully dressed for her husband.[426] Here things may become a bit confusing since in chap. 19 is recorded an account of the wedding of the Lamb and His bride, who has prepared herself for Him and the blessedness of those who are invited to the wedding supper of the Lamb. Now the holy city, like a bride adorned for her husband, is coming down from heaven.

The question may be asked whether this is the same bride as in chap. 19, where the bride is clearly the church. Some think so, but the better interpretation seems to be that the new Jerusalem, the Holy City of the new heavens and new earth, is presented here through the metaphor of a bride prepared for her husband but not as being synonymous with the church of chap. 19.

Pulling the metaphors together, the celestial city is the eternal home for the bride of Christ. The perfect passive participle of the verb *hetoimazō*, meaning "prepare" or "make ready," calls to mind the promise of the Lord to His disciples, "I am going there to prepare a place for you" (John 14:2). The perfect passive participle indicates that this place, having been prepared, now descends, looking like a bride prepared for her husband. Another perfect passive participle coming from the word *kosmeō*, meaning "adorn" and from which have evolved the English words "cosmos" and "cosmetics," references the way in which this heavenly city was adorned.[427] The reference to the new Jerusalem coming down

---

426 Efforts to identify the new Jerusalem with some location on earth are well known and all too common. According to Epiphanius, the first such attempt was that of Montanus who supposedly located it in the region of Phrygia in two towns know as Popouza-Tymion. For a strong argument against this tradition, see W. Tabbernee, "Revelation 21 and the Montanist 'New Jerusalem,'" *ABR* 37 (1989): 52–60.

427 Jerome, with decisive language, questions whether the city should be taken literally: "Evidently this description cannot be taken literally (in fact, it is absurd to suppose a city the length, breadth and height of which are all twelve thousand furlongs), and therefore the details of it must be mystically understood" (*The Letters of St. Jerome: Letter XLVI* 7, *NPNF*[2], 6:63). B. K. Blount, however, says, "The new holy city is, finally, a city. John signals a salvific identity that is neither individualized nor spiritualized but concretized in the communal relationships that exist in an urban environment. John's view of eschatological relationship with God is not some tranquil, idyllic, one-on-one encounter in a sanctuary of eternal solitude, cloistered away from the hustling, bustling interaction with others that is so much a part of civic life on the old and apparently the new earth. Eschatological living is envisioned instead as a complex, other-connected and no doubt other-oriented relationship that brings with it all of the social and political ramifications that life in any city engenders. John's view of the future is that the believing community will find its ultimate meaning and life in urban rapport. For many contemporary Christians, this part of his vision is as scary as the segments that deal with

from heaven prepared as a bride adorned for her husband captures the awe of the moment of the presentation of a bride to a groom. In addition to the beauty of the bride, there is the anticipatory union that is about to take place in the midst of the general excitement of all who are a part of the moment.

However, v. 3 and following demand the greatest attention. John is now informed that the dwelling of God is with men. The word "dwelling" is *skēnē* in Greek, which carries the sense of "tent" or "tabernacle." It is used in its verbal form in the latter part of the clause when *skēnoō*, which literally means "live in a tent," is employed. This choice of verbiage, referencing a tent rather than a colossal structure like the temple may have seemed strange to John's readers. However, the tabernacle, or the tent in the wilderness, was not only the model for the temple when Solomon finally constructed such but also was a sign to all Israel that God dwelt among them. The *shekinah* glory of God that winged its way into the tent when it was dedicated was a sign of the presence of God dwelling within the *qodesh qodeshim*, the holy of holies in that tent.[428] Further-

---

the dragon and the plagues. Cities are inclusive, teeming, often dangerous and riotous places, where resources can be stretched to the breaking point and success—indeed, even survival—comes only when citizens work interdependently, negotiate strenuously, and compromise sincerely. Knowing all this, John believes that the city represents the most appropriate 'heaven' metaphor available to him" (*Revelation*, NTL [Louisville, KY: WJK, 2009], 378).

428 B. Witherington III provides a helpful note here: "**Vs. 3** is striking in several respects. It reads literally, 'behold the tent of God is with humanity, and he will tent with us and we will be his peoples.' The Greek word **skene** is regularly used to render the Hebrew **mishkan**, which means tent (it is a derivation of **shakan**, 'to dwell,' from which the word **Shekinah**, referring to God's glorious presence, comes). Our text is a paraphrase of such texts as Lev. 26:11 ff. and Ezek. 37.27. By a stroke of sheer luck, the Greek and Hebrew words for tent have the same consonants, so the allusions to Hebrew are more obvious, and the similar sound would conjure up various things for Jewish Christians listening to this being read" (*Revelation*, New Cambridge Bible Commentary [Cambridge: Cambridge University Press, 2003], 255). Also, Irenaeus insists on the literal nature of the city. "When these things, therefore, pass away above the earth, John, the Lord's disciple, says that the new Jerusalem above shall [then] descend, as a bride adorned for her husband; and that this is the tabernacle of God, in which God will dwell with men. Of this Jerusalem the former one is an image—that Jerusalem of the former earth in which the righteous are disciplined beforehand for incorruption and prepared for salvation. And of this tabernacle Moses received the pattern in the mount; and nothing is capable of being allegorized, but all things are stedfast, and true, and substantial, having been made by God for righteous men's enjoyment. For as it is God truly who raises up man, so also does man truly rise from the dead, and not allegorically, as I have shown repeatedly" (*Against Heresies* 5.35.2, ANF 1:566).

more, if all the other deities imagined by the human family had residences and permanent dwelling places and therefore were lords only of given geographical areas, the God of Israel was the omnipresent God who moved with His people wherever they went.

That the tabernacle of God is now with men and that He dwells among them has in one sense been true for the history of the human family. For Adam and Eve, prior to their sin, the voice of the Lord God walked in the garden in the cool of the day (Gen 3:8). The Spirit of God came upon men in the Old Testament and permanently indwelled believers in the New Testament. The doctrine of the omnipresence of God is well-known throughout holy Scripture, but there is clearly some sense in which the book of Revelation now declares that God dwells uniquely among men, the text adding several observations. First, God Himself will be with them (v. 3). Second, He will wipe away every tear from their eyes (v. 4). Third, death will be abolished (v. 4). Fourth, as a result, there shall be no more mourning or crying (v. 4). Further, there will be no pain, and generally speaking the former things will have passed away (v. 4). The doctrines of the omnipresence of God and the indwelling of the Holy Spirit throughout the history of the church have been doctrines of great comfort and an assurance of the providences of God. Believers long for the opportunity to walk visibly with Christ as was the privilege of the first-century apostles. "God is Spirit," and they that worship Him "must worship in spirit and in truth" (John 4:24). It is not clear whether a simple visual presence or a visual presence contained in the second Person of the Trinity (the glorified Lord) or whether what is intended here is not visual but rather a unique sense of God's presence transcending anything that redeemed humans have ever experienced.

For God to be so knowingly present obscures even the beauty of the new Jerusalem and of the bride, for in this case the Bridegroom is more breathtaking. Specifically, He is known by his actions. First, every tear is wiped from their eyes. Of course, tears come for reasons other than sadness. What seems to be in view here is that every tear of sadness is wiped from the eyes of God's people. One of the reasons men weep is the cold cruelty of the hideous triumph of death in the human family. Even for believers, who do not "grieve like the rest of men, who have no hope" (1 Thess 4:13), the sense of separation felt at the loss of a saved loved one is still profound. When death comes, our precious ones are no longer present, and the absence of their presence induces an unquenchable loneliness. This hurt will be abolished. As a result, no more people are found mourning with hearts broken and lives shattered. Neither will there be any further agonizing pain. People who have never experienced the excruciating pain sometimes endured by the human body and who have been unable to find relief from such suffering cannot adequately appreciate this promise. However, before death comes, most do reach the point of experiencing serious discomfort. This final phrase stresses that the things associated with weeping, pain, agony, and death shall all pass away, and God's presence will make all new and fresh.

Then God speaks. The One who sat on the throne said, "I make all things new!" (v. 5). In the end only God can create. Though His angels and even redeemed humans are able to make a contribution to the work of God, no one can bring about life from nothing or resurrect life from the dead. God declares exactly what He is going to do. He is going to make all things new.[429] Then He commands John to write words that by virtue of their origin with Him are both true and faithful (v. 5). In a similar fashion to the NKJV rendering of *pistos* as "faithful," the NIV translates it as "trustworthy." Of course, "trustworthy" carries much of the same sentiment as "true," which is the previous word. The emphasis here, then, is probably best delivered as "faithfulness," meaning that God is giving not only a true word for John to write but a word that can be depended on in every way.

The phrase "It is done" translates *gegonan*, a perfect active indicative of *ginomai*, meaning "to be." Thus, He says the things that have been mentioned in v. 5, which are true and faithful, have come to pass. A part of that which has come to pass is the recognition that the God who speaks from the throne is "the Alpha and the Omega, the Beginning and the End" (v. 6). Alpha and omega, of course, are the beginning and ending letters of the Greek alphabet—a cultural but all-encompassing way of stressing that before there was anything else God was there; He is the beginning of all things. He is not only the beginning of all things, but He is also the end of all things. Here the word *telos* carries with it more than the sentiment of the ending of a sequence of events. Rather *telos* carries the sense of completion or purpose.[430] So God is the beginning of everything, but He is also

---

429 W. J. Harrington captures the significance of the declaration: "John's use of 'a new heaven and a new earth' is not arbitrary. Not only is the concept thoroughly biblical, but also his 'new world' also opens up the perspective of an eschatological future in which the cosmos is redeemed and perfected. This is not a restoration of our broken world to its imagined original state, but a transformation beyond imagining, a transformation so radical as to be a 'new creation.' In all of this, the human aspect is always firmly in mind" (*Revelation*, SP 16 [Collegeville, MN: Liturgical Press, 1993], 210).

430 Delling in *TDNT* notes something of the wide range of nuance for τέλος: achievement, completion, perfection, obligation, maturity and even offering for the gods are examples. For example, a horse that is a τέλος horse is fully grown or mature.

the purpose of all that transpires. This promise of purpose should always provide profound comfort for the saints, knowing that there is an explanation for all sorrows and tribulations—an answer that will be completely satisfying.

Another promise follows, "I will give of the fountain of the water of life freely to him who thirsts" (v. 6). The last Greek word, *dōrean*, translated as "freely" in the NKJV, emphasizes the grace of the offer. Spiritual thirst can never be slaked by what humans find, conquer, obtain, or desire. Rather, as a part of God's being with us, He provides water from the fountain of the water of life; and no payment is sought—not because the water of life is of little value. Indeed, it is the only remedy to slake human spiritual thirst. The price for this purchase has already been paid with the death of the Lamb, and consequently the water of life is now free to those who thirst for it.[431] However, men do not seek for the water of life unless they have acknowledged their thirst. As noted earlier, the contemporary man in the West has difficulty appreciating the concepts of thirst and the quenching of that thirst as is so commonly understood among desert tribes.

God's presence takes on still a further significance. Those who overcome by the blood of the Lamb and the word of their testimony have a heritage. Therefore, God is not just present with the human family, but He actually maintains a relationship as of a Father to his son. While God has but one ontological Son, namely, Jesus, the Word of God (John 3:16), He has many children by adoption (Rom 8:15, 23; Gal 4:5). The children who by faith have been adopted into the family of God are just as much the heirs and joint heirs as the supernatural Son of God. Hence, the relationship is not just one of the benefits enumerated in the previous verses but also includes the Son's inheritance bequeathed by his Father.

"For Plato the τέλεος . . . ἄνθρωπος is he who has attained φρόνησις, 'firm and true views,' insight and philosophical knowledge" (*TDNT*, 8:69).

431 R. C. H. Lenski cogently remarks, "For 'the one thirsting' is one who has already drunk of grace, and is now thirsty for glory. His the great longing to be led by the Lamb to 'life's springs of water' in the new earth, to walk beside 'the river of life's water shining as crystal, going out from the throne of God and of the Lamb' (7:17 and 22:1). His thirst Christ promises to satisfy in the new earth and to do that δωρεάν, 'gratis,' by way of gift, for also this water is pure grace. The present context makes it impossible to think of the sinner's first reception of grace on the old earth. Little help is obtained from the thought: 'Oriental thrones usually have a fountain of cool water springing up, and from this John doubtless draws his picture.' It is not *John* who is here drawing a picture, it is *Jesus*, who is making a promise" (*The Interpretation of St. John's Revelation* [Minneapolis: Augsburg, 1963], 623).

B. Heavenly Exclusions (21:8)

⁸But the cowardly, unbelieving, abominable, murderers, sexually immoral, sorcerers, idolaters, and all liars shall have their part in the lake which burns with fire and brimstone, which is the second death."

21:8 These observations, however, lead to one of the last warnings of the Apocalypse. While all of these exquisite blessings come to the one who has overcome by the blood of the Lamb, there is another class of people delivered to the lake of fire, which is the second death. The list provided in v. 8, though not intended to be exhaustive, is certainly representative. Those enumerated are the cowardly, the unbelieving, the vile, the murderers, the sexually immoral, all who practice magic arts, the idolaters, and all liars. The list once again provides a general overall look at the natures of those who deny the Lord. "Cowardly" (*deilos*) at first seems to be far less serious than the other iniquities delineated here, and perhaps even out of place. When the word *deilos* is used to describe objects, it is usually translated in classical Greek as "miserable" or "wretched." This provides insight into the use of the word here, where it is obviously used of persons. Cowardliness is a vile, wretched, and to be sure, miserable state.[432]

Contrastively, those who at the coming of Christ possess boldness or confidence (*parrēsia*, which is more literally "all speech;" see 1 John 2:28). When Christ is revealed, some will be bold or able to speak because they are right with God and are aware of the righteousness that has been bestowed on them. However, others will call "to the mountains and the rocks, 'Fall on us and hide us from the face of Him who sits on the throne'" (6:16). Thus, they would be cowardly. The second word, *apistos*, dervies from *pistis*, "faith," with the alpha privative attached, meaning "no faith," and hence "unbelieving." "Abominable" is a translation of *bdelussō*, which means "pollute" or "defile."[433]

Nothing defiled or polluted will enter God's presence in the holy realm of the new Jerusalem. "Murderers" (*phoneus*) and "the sexually immoral" (*pornos*)

---

432 LSJ, 374. δειλός is a word for cowardice from the ancient world so detestable that one guilty of this attribute was considered vile and worthless. Since one man's cowardice is not only a reflection on his character, but also often the cause of suffering for his fellows, the term becomes even more reprehensible.

433 A. T. Robertson notes that ἐβδελυγμένοις, the perfect passive participle of the old verb βδελύσσω, while common in the LXX is used only here and in Rom 2:22 in the NT. The verb emphasizes the sense of pollution. *Word Pictures in the New Testament* (Nashville: B&H, 1973), 6:469.

are added as those who will not be allowed access to heaven. The word for "sorcerers" is *pharmakos*, which references sorcery and the use of drugs to deceive. Idolatry, of course, is the most basic sin (i.e., substituting for God something that is either man-made or perhaps man himself). Liars, the opposite of truth tellers, will obviously have no place in a city that has no deceit. All these will have their part in the lake of fire with burning sulfur, which is the second death. Since heaven will also be populated by persons guilty of all these things, one must inquire as to why some are excluded and turned aside. The distinction between the two groups is to be found in the response of the individual to the revelation of God's law and his provision on grace. Most continue their practices in the face of both law and grace. Some repent and exercise saving faith and avoid this judgment. The first death clearly is the physical death, but the second death is by far the more ominous of the two deaths. As much as the first is dreaded and avoided, the second is a death that is a continual dying for eternity and is by far the more unthinkable.

C. Heavenly Beauties (21:9–27)

⁹Then one of the seven angels who had the seven bowls filled with the seven last plagues came to me and talked with me, saying, "Come, I will show you the bride, the Lamb's wife." ¹⁰And he carried me away in the Spirit to a great and high mountain, and showed me the great city, the holy Jerusalem, descending out of heaven from God, ¹¹having the glory of God. Her light *was* like a most precious stone, like a jasper stone, clear as crystal. ¹²Also she had a great and high wall with twelve gates, and twelve angels at the gates, and names written on them, which are *the names* of the twelve tribes of the children of Israel: ¹³three gates on the east, three gates on the north, three gates on the south, and three gates on the west.

¹⁴Now the wall of the city had twelve foundations, and on them were the names of the twelve apostles of the Lamb.

¹⁵And he who talked with me had a gold reed to measure the city, its gates, and its wall. ¹⁶The city is laid out as a square; its length is as great as its breadth. And he measured the city with the reed: twelve thousand furlongs. Its length, breadth, and height are equal. ¹⁷Then he measured its wall: one hundred *and* forty-four cubits, *according* to the measure of a man, that is, of an angel. ¹⁸The construction of its wall was *of* jasper; and the city *was* pure gold, like clear glass. ¹⁹The foundations of the wall of the city *were* adorned with all kinds of precious stones: the first foundation *was* jasper, the second sapphire, the third chalcedony, the fourth emerald, ²⁰the fifth sardonyx, the sixth sardius, the seventh chrysolite, the eighth beryl, the ninth topaz,

the tenth chrysoprase, the eleventh jacinth, and the twelfth amethyst. ²¹The twelve gates *were* twelve pearls: each individual gate was of one pearl. And the street of the city *was* pure gold, like transparent glass.

²²But I saw no temple in it, for the Lord God Almighty and the Lamb are its temple. ²³The city had no need of the sun or of the moon to shine in it, for the glory of God illuminated it. The Lamb *is* its light. ²⁴And the nations of those who are saved shall walk in its light, and the kings of the earth bring their glory and honor into it. ²⁵Its gates shall not be shut at all by day (there shall be no night there). ²⁶And they shall bring the glory and the honor of the nations into it. ²⁷But there shall by no means enter it anything that defiles, or causes an abomination or a lie, but only those who are written in the Lamb's Book of Life.

21:9-27 Verses 9 through 27 now undertake the description of the beauty of the new Jerusalem itself.[434] One of the seven angels who had the seven bowls of the last plagues approaches and invites John to accompany him on a journey to observe the bride, the wife of the Lamb. Here the metaphor of both bride and wife is employed in the text so that it would be conceivable to argue a metaphorical interpretation and see this as the church. More likely, however, it is a continuation of the description begun in 21:1, interrupted only by the limitation of v. 8.

In order to have the clear perspective, John, by means of the Spirit, is carried to a mountain great and high; and he sees the holy city Jerusalem coming down out of heaven from God. The phrase *en pneumati* may mean either "in the spirit" or "by means of the spirit." If the expression is viewed as instrumental, then the Holy Spirit is the means of transport to the mountain. If it is viewed as locative, then John is claiming only that his spirit is transported to the mountain; but since this is not likely an out-of-body experience, more probably the Spirit is the means by which he is transported.

When the dimensions of the holy city are provided, it becomes apparent why John had to be transported to a high mountain in order to get a panoramic view of the whole. As John views the city, the first thing he notes in v. 11 is

---

434 R. H. Gundry and others see the city only as symbolic: "But the New Jerusalem is a very large symbol. Its description occupies a whole chapter or more. Therefore we may rightfully expect that the details of the description contribute small, individual symbols to the large, overall symbol, even as contemporary interpreters of Jesus' parables have come to understand that although we must resist allegorism, the longer the story that constitutes a narrative parable, the more likely it is that some details of the parable have their own significance within the overall meaning" ("The New Jerusalem: People as Place, Not Place for People," *NovT* 29 [1987]: 254).

that the City was "having the glory of God." In contrast the NIV text states "it shone with the glory of God." The words, "it shone," are not actually in the text but are an interpretation of the Greek verb *echō*, or "have," and constitute a reference to the sparkling radiance of the city. In fact, the word "light" (*phōstēr*) references a concentrated light that sparkles or radiates before the observer. This light was like that of a precious stone. The word "precious" (*timios*) suggests "precious" as in contrast with "common." Precious stones are stones that have acquired immense value because they are not common. They are difficult to obtain and normally have an intrinsic beauty not found in more common stones. Hence, they are precious. Specifically, this is said to be like a jasper stone, clear as crystal. With this identification the reader is introduced to an elucidation on the stones that are also a part of the foundation of the heavenly city and in the process to some major problems.

The first problem occurs with regard to the jasper stone.[435] Sometimes called a horn stone, it comes in a great variety of colors but basically translates a Greek word meaning "striped" or "spotted." Sometimes it has green transparent qualities and on occasion has even been identified with diamonds. The jasper stone itself has a Mohs of only six and a half to seven, which is quite different from a diamond, the hardest of all stones that has a Mohs rating of ten. Most people think of a jasper stone in its green transparent manifestation, and that certainly is a possibility in the text. Some think that diamonds had not yet been discovered or at least were not widely known in the first century. They are probably incorrect. Some evidence exists for diamonds in India as many as 3,000 years earlier. Furthermore, the Greek word *adamas*, with an almost certain reference to "diamond," was used in classical Greek.[436] This may favor the more traditional understanding of jasper, but most commentators have favored the idea of the sparkling qualities and hardness of the diamond and understand that to be the sparkle of the city.

---

435 There is even a grammatical problem. W. W. Reader says: "This list of gems in Rev 21:19b–20 is only an apparent apposition to 21:19a (not asyndeton), but in fact is not one at all, for the grammar does not agree with that in 21:19a. According to that preceding line one would expect the stones to be listed in the dative case which would of course mean: 'The first foundation stone [was *adorned*] *with* jasper, . . .' However, from the nominative one must conclude that each foundation stone *consisted of* one single enormous gem" ("The Twelve Jewels of Revelation 21:19–20: Tradition History and Modern Interpretations," *JBL* 100 [1981]: 433).

436 Liddell and Scott give ἀδάμας the major translations of "adamant" and "unbreakable" but also clearly reference "diamond," known in antiquity for its adamant qualities (LSJ, 20).

In v. 12, John sees that there is a high wall and twelve gates. Each of those twelve gates has an angel. Here it may represent an angel sentry at each gate, or the language could describe a group of twelve angels at each gate. The former is more probable than the latter. On each of the gates are inscribed the names of the twelve tribes of Israel. In v. 14 this capital city of the cosmos for all the people of God has foundations that will be described as containing the names of the twelve apostles of the Lamb. Whether the subject is Israel or the church, the rigidity of some premillennialists in arguing that Israel is forever separate from the church might at first blush seem to get some support here but on more careful consideration must be jettisoned just on the basis of this description. It is one city stamped both with the twelve tribes of Israel and with the apostles of the Lamb.

The suggestion that Jews before the dispensation of the church would certainly remember and know of their Judaism and that those who are a part of the church—the body of Christ, both Jew and Gentile—would be aware seems obvious. But all inhabitants of heaven will be the people of God from whatever era. Since the apostles of the Lamb are not specifically named in the text, one cannot be sure what those names included. Almost certainly Judas is not there, but whether the Twelve should include Matthias (Acts 1:12-26) or Paul (Rom 1:1; 1 Cor 1:1; 9:1-2; Gal 1:1; Eph 1:1; Col 1:1) is a matter of conjecture. The gates themselves are in groups of three facing each of the directions of the compass.

Verse 15 chronicles a monologue of the angel who is carrying a measuring rod of gold with his purpose to measure the city and its gate and its wall. John notes that the city, as he observed it, is laid out like a square as long as it is wide. In effect, however, the city is more than just a square. It is apparently cubic in its construction, with all sides being equal. The city is measured with a rod and is discovered to be 12,000 *furlongs* in length and as wide as it is tall. A *furlong*, according to Rienecker and Rogers, is about 607 English feet and this would make the city at 12,000 furlongs to be 1,400 miles cubed.[437] Now the necessity for the tall mountain is apparent. Even with the highest of peaks, a view covering 1,400 miles has to be one viewed with aid from "the Spirit." The wall is also measured and turns out to be 144 cubits thick. The text itself only says that it is "144 cubits." However, the NIV translators are correct to add the word "thick" since a wall no taller than 144 cubits on a cube to a thousand *furlongs* in height, to say the least, would be dwarfed. So, understanding it to be 144 cubits thick, with a cubit understood as being approximately the

---

437 F. Rienecker and C. L. Rogers, *Linguistic Key to the Greek New Testament* (Grand Rapids: Zondervan, 1982), 860.

length of a man's arm from his elbow to the tip of his third finger, would have full plausibility.

The wall itself is made of jasper, the same word used above; but the city itself is pure gold, as pure as glass (v. 18). Literally the expression *chrusion katharon* means "gold without impurity." A goldsmith heating gold till the impurities rise to the top is able to remove with patience most of the impurities, but this gold is different in that there literally are no impurities; furthermore, the appearance is that of glass, probably indicating the transparency of this gold construction.

In vv. 19–21, John describes the foundations of the city walls. Each foundation is said to be decorated with all kinds of precious stones.[438] This raises several interesting questions. First, exactly how do these foundations function together? Are the foundations layered one on top of another? Do the foundations proceed one after another around the city as one great but varied foundation? The text does not provide this explanation.

The second problem relates to the stones themselves. Of the various stones, some are easily identifiable. Already the problem identifying the jasper stone has been mentioned. The topaz, sapphire, emerald, jacinth, chrysoprase, sardius (carnelian), amethyst, beryl, and the chalcedony do not pose great difficulties. Sardonyx and chrysolite, however, join with the jasper stone in being more difficult to identify. Making the problem still more acute is the fact that current knowledge of mineralogy and of the various precious stones identifies them on criteria other than just color. In many of these stones a much wider variety of colors than what would have been known in John's day has been chronicled. There is also a certain tendency with the more limited knowledge of John's day to identify different kinds of stone in just one way if the color was that which was thought to be the primary shade of that particular stone. Nevertheless, information can be gained, based on the understandings that are available to interpreters, to appreciate the magnificence and the spectacular nature of the city.[439]

After the jasper stone is the sapphire, one of the hardest stones with a Mohs number of nine. In Greek the word means "blue" and, along with the ruby sapphire, is a variety of corundum. The rubies, of course, are under most conditions a bright deep red, whereas the sapphire stones run the gamut from light

---

438 J. M. Ford says, "Each foundation probably was a stout oblong block like the stones which may still be seen in the lower rows of the Herodian masonry at Jerusalem" (*Revelation*, AB [Garden City, NY: Doubleday, 1975], 333).

439 For a superb introduction to these gemstones, see W. Schumann, *Gemstones of the World* (New York: Sterling Publishing, 1984).

to dark blue and sometimes even black. Here John is most probably referencing the typical medium to dark blue stone often found with a star-like glow in the middle and spoken of as a star sapphire. The third stone is called chalcedony and is a stone belonging to a group of micro-crystalline quartzes. Its color is bluish white or grey, and its hardness is only about six and a half to seven on the Mohs scale. Its name comes from Chalcedon, the city on the east bank of the Bosporus, which became the meeting place for the critically important council of Chalcedon in AD 451. The fourth stone is the emerald, which is readily known to almost everyone. With a hardness of seven and a half to eight, this green stone in various shades of green also bears a Greek name but probably one that was borrowed from the Persians. It is also the fourth stone in the breastplate of the high priest and has been highly valued in all eras.

The fifth stone, the sardonyx, seems to be a compound word for the sardias stone and an onyx. Indeed, the stone is layered, sometimes dark red and white and sometimes almost brown and white. Onyx is derived from the Greek word *onux*, which may mean "talon" or "claw" but also "fingernail" and probably references the translucent quality of the stone.[440] Most probably John is seeing here a dark red and white layered stone. The sixth stone is sardius or carnelian, a deep red stone taking its name from the kornel, which is a type of cherry. The carnelian, a fairly well-known and highly sought stone, was often worn by someone who needed to soften his anger since its blood red color was thought to have that mellowing effect on the wearer. The seventh stone is chrysolite. Interestingly, most of the chrysolites available in ancient, and for that matter in modern times, come from a Red Sea island named St. John. Of course, that name has a later origin, but the island now takes the name of the apostle John. The chrysolite stone gets its name from the Greek word for "gold" and is sometimes identified as a "peridot," or by its more popular name "olivine." It is not a hard stone, registering only six and a half to seven on the Mohs scale.

The eighth stone is the beryl, a gold or a yellow-green stone, sometimes shading almost to yellow. The name itself, however, means "green" and is usually thought to be the first stone in the fourth row of the breastplate of the high priest. The ninth stone is topaz, well known for its sparkling yellow or gold form. However, topaz is now found as smoky topaz and has a variety of colors from red-brown to pinkish-red as well as the traditional yellow. Topaz also is mined, among other places, on the island Zebirget in the Red Sea, but originally the island carried the name Topazos. Probably what John sees here is the rather spar-

---

440 LSJ, 1234.

kling yellow version, which the ancients would have immediately identified as topaz. The tenth stone, chrysoprase, is an apple-green stone in the chalcedonic group. The eleventh stone is jacinth, a yellow-red to red-brown stone normally of great brilliance and intensity, also appearing in the breastplate of the high priest. The final stone of the foundation is amethyst, also well-known in the modern period. However, its origin is interesting. It is only seven in hardness on the Mohs scale but the most valued of all the stones in the quartz group, and it is transparent to translucent blue-violet. Its origin is of great interest since the Greek word *methustos* means "drunken." The alpha privative added to the front of the word *amethustos* brings negation, meaning "not drunken;" and it was the favorite stone to be worn by those who wanted to ward off the ill effects of drunkenness.

Accentuating the twelve foundations adorned with these stones are the twelve gates, which are described as twelve *margaritai*, or "pearls." Each gate is said to be made of a single pearl. Picturing John's observation is somewhat difficult at this point. Since the gates of the city are never closed, perhaps the twelve giant pearls making up the gates are not swinging gates at all but rather the equivalent of gatehouse formations with the appearance of gigantic pearls. Pearls were often more valued than any other stone in antiquity because of their natural, unvarnished appearance as a part of the life of the sea. Finally, John concludes this part of the description by observing that the streets of the city were pure gold, like transparent glass, a similar expression to what was observed in v. 18 regarding the general nature of the entire city.

John surveys the city, noting that he sees no temple in it. This observation could be almost expected since the most prominent single observation about the city of Jerusalem was the temple of Solomon. Located as it was on the top of a mountain, identified by many as Moriah from the Old Testament, the temple looked down on the City of David to its south and over the Kidron Valley and the Mount of Olives to the east and the Valley of Hinnom immediately on the west with Mount Zion behind. To travelers coming into the city from almost any direction, Solomon's temple would have been the most arresting single feature.

In addition to the way Solomon's temple may have appeared, Judaism, in contradistinction to most of the other faiths of the world at that time, was known as a monotheistic faith. In the heart of Judaism, whatever its cultural achievements may have been, was the worship of Yahweh, the God of Israel. Consequently, the prominence of the temple suggested the most prominent single feature for the Jewish people.

John, a typical Jew, upon observing the city, looks immediately for the temple, but such is not to be found. The temple is no longer necessary because the Lord God Almighty and the Lamb constitute the temple.[441] To be in their presence is to be at the center of the worship of the universe. Furthermore, as John observes the city, he also notes in v. 23 that the typical light sources, namely, the sun and the moon, are unnecessary. Just like the temple, they have been eclipsed by the glory of God as the light and by the Lamb himself as the lamp. The radiance of the Lamb is sufficient to light the city.

In v. 25, John notes that the gates of the city are never shut because there no longer remains any threat posed by the coming of darkness. That which might stealthily approach the city under cover of darkness cannot do so in the light; besides, such has all been confined already to the lake of fire. There is no necessity for closing the gates for any reason.

In v. 26, John does record that the glory and honor of the nations will be brought into the city. Verse 27 promises that nothing that defiles will ever enter into it, nor shall anyone who causes an abomination or lies, only those whose names are written in the Lamb's Book of Life. The statement that the nations shall bring their glory into the city is enigmatic. Is this a reference to the governments existing during the millennial kingdom, which are now said to bring their glory into the city; or does this take into consideration the economy of the new heavens and the new earth? The latter seems to be the better estimate. By now, even the millennial earth has perished with fervent heat, and the new heavens and the new earth are in place.

The popular understanding of the eternal state has been detrimental to the cause of Christianity. Expressions improperly understood, such as "it is a place of rest," drum up for most people the idea of an eternal siesta. People seem to picture in the mind's eye glorified saints as cloud potatoes strumming their harps of gold and simply lounging for eternity. Actually, all the expressions of the eternal state are quite different. First, the eternal prospect of enriching and triumphant worship that can be only distantly anticipated in the present state is a constant activity of the eternal state. Second, Jesus has promised, he who is "faithful with a few things" he "will put . . . in charge of many things" (Matt 25:21). Every expression of the eternal state is one of intense activity minus the problems of illness and weariness, which due to sin prevent full accomplishment and enjoyment of work. In the eternal state there will apparently

---

441 E. W. Bullinger remarks: "No temple or 'place of worship' is needed; for the whole city is hallowed and pervaded by the presence of God. This fact separates this part of the book from the former part, where the temple is seen (iii. 12 ; vii. 15 ; xi. 1, 16–19 ; xiv. 15, 17 ; xv. 5, 6, 8 ; xvi. 1, 17); and shows that we are here carried far beyond millennial lines" (*Commentary on Revelation* [Grand Rapids: Kregel, 1984], 665–66).

be endless learning and extensive assignments. The probable interpretation is that those of responsibility throughout the cosmos bring all of the glory of the expanse of the new heavens and the new earth into the glorious city. Anything that is defiled or deceitful does not enter the city but only those whose names have been inscribed (*gegrammenoi*, a perfect passive participle of *graphō*, meaning "write") in the Lamb's Book of Life. The perfect passive participle shows that this has been done with permanent effects. Those who have overcome all the powers of evil by the blood of the Lamb have their names permanently written in the Lamb's Book of Life and therefore gain access forever to the holy city.

D. Heavenly Provisions (22:1-6)

¹And he showed me a pure river of water of life, clear as crystal, proceeding from the throne of God and of the Lamb. ²In the middle of its street, and on either side of the river, *was* the tree of life, which bore twelve fruits, each *tree* yielding its fruit every month. The leaves of the tree *were* for the healing of the nations. ³And there shall be no more curse, but the throne of God and of the Lamb shall be in it, and His servants shall serve Him. ⁴They shall see His face, and His name *shall be* on their foreheads. ⁵There shall be no night there: They need no lamp nor light of the sun, for the Lord God gives them light. And they shall reign forever and ever.

⁶Then he said to me, "These words *are* faithful and true." And the Lord God of the holy prophets sent His angel to show His servants the things which must shortly take place.

22:1-6 Rev 22 is a continuation in the first six verses of the vision of the new Jerusalem in Rev 21. The emphasis shifts to the provisions made for the perpetual blessings of God on those who follow the Lord. These blessings include regaining access to the tree of life, permanent healing, and the dispelling of all darkness. This is followed by a testimony from John concerning the rationale for the penning of the Apocalypse. Finally, the concluding paragraphs contain various admonitions, promises, and warnings to provide the reader with the appropriate conclusion to the prophecy.[442]

---

442 Johnson speaks eloquently of this final chapter: "With consummate art, the notes of the introit (1:1-8) are sounded again in the conclusion. So the book ends with the voices of the angels, Jesus, the Spirit, the bride, and, finally, John (v. 20). The book is a seamless garment. There are three major emphases in the conclusion: confirmation of the genuineness of the prophecy (vv. 6-7, 16, 18-19); the imminence of Jesus' coming (vv. 7, 12, 20); the warning against idolatry and the invitation to enter the city (vv. 11-12, 15,

The prophet Zechariah foresaw a time when, "On that day a fountain will be opened to the house of David and the inhabitants of Jerusalem, to cleanse them from sin and impurity" (Zech 13:1). Ezekiel's vision of the millennial temple included a fountain of water coming from the temple and flowing east (Ezek 47). The fountain, like the loaves and the fishes, was multiplied until what began as a trickle became a wadi, or a roaring river, in which to swim. Ezekiel had noted that on the bank of the river there were trees in great numbers and that those trees, growing on both banks of the river, bear their fruit every month, and their fruit would serve for food and their leaves for healing. Those visions, while different in time and application, are doubtless in the background of John's mind as he views the heavenly vision of a river of the water of life. In this case, the river of the water of life flows down the middle of the central street of the city, not from the temple but from the throne of God and of the Lamb. It is difficult for those who have never lived in a desert climate fully to appreciate the scene unfolded here. However, to residents of the Mediterranean world, and especially the eastern Mediterranean world, the aridity of the land, the sparseness of rainfall, and the paucity of anything to drink except what was not directly dependent on the supply of water, was a daily aspect of life. The earlier commentary on the message to the church at Laodicea is an indication of the water problem that affected so many in the eastern Mediterranean world and the deserts still further to the east and south. In the lands of the wadis, water could be prolific, even too prolific! But more often than not, survival was precarious due to its paucity.

By the same token, the great street of the city stood in stark contrast to most of the city streets of the cities and towns throughout the world. Major city streets were often filthy, strewn with garbage and animal waste. There were certainly notable exceptions, but the wide, great street and the crystal clear water of life flowing from the throne of God through the middle of that street had to be riveting for any resident of the Levant. Moderns have often known only polluted water sources and are usually startled to see the crystal-clear water that scuba divers love most. Here the water is unpolluted and clear to the bottom.

17–19). A similar word of assurance (v. 6), such as that in 19:9 and 21:5, provides the transition from the glorious vision of the Holy City to the final words of the book. An angel declares that it is 'the Lord, the God of the spirits of the prophets,' the one from whom the prophets like John receive their message, that assures the readers of the speedy fulfillment of all that has been revealed (cf. 1:1; 10:6-7). John has been the recipient of divine prophecy that will have its immediate consequences (cf. v. 10)" ("Revelation," EBC [Grand Rapids: Zondervan], 12:601).

John further notes what appears to be a perpetual oasis. On each side of the river stands the tree of life. The emphasis here is not on a single tree but on the kind of tree. Apparently, all along the bank this tree of life, which has not been observed since the garden of Eden, is there; and the tree bears its fruit every month. There is no "season" for its productivity, but its production is perpetual. Not only is the fruit available, but even the leaves of the tree are to be used for the healing of the nations. Apparently as long as the first parents were in the garden and had access to the tree of life, they would not have suffered death. Excluded from the garden, physical death was inevitable. Now, once again, however, all the nations have access to the tree of life and to its healing leaves and, therefore, rejoice in eternal life.

In v. 3 another promise is provided against the context of rich, biblical imagery. No longer will there be any curse.[443] In Genesis the judgments of God are administered to Adam and Eve for their rebellion against God. Adam receives these words, "Cursed is the ground for your sake" (Gen 3:17). Adam is further instructed that instead of bringing forth fruit prolifically the ground is going to bring forth thorns and thistles. Only with difficulty will he be able to produce the food needed.[444]

Because the Hebrews believed that the body was the artistry of God, to leave anyone's body unburied and exposed after his death was a serious curse. In fact, the Scriptures said that it was a curse to place a body on a tree. The same imagery is picked up again in Galatians when the apostle Paul speaks of

---

443 The word for "curse" here is κατάθεμα. J. Behm notes the difference between this term and the more frequent NT term, ἀνάθεμα. "The rare κατάθεμα, which is probably another and sharper form of ἀνάθεμα (the κατα- frequently indicating a hostile reference), or which may be a contraction of καταvάθεμα, is not found outside early Christian texts (Act. Phil., 28, 15, 12 Bonnet) except on a Cyprian magic tablet of the 3rd century A.D" (*TDNT* 1:355). Swete also notes that "κατάθεμα is without example in Biblical Greek." H. B. Swete believes that κατάθεμα is a somewhat stronger term than ἀνάθεμα (*Commentary on Revelation* [Grand Rapids: Kregel, 1977], 300).

444 G. R. Beasley-Murray calls attention to the fact that this "is a citation from Zechariah 14:11, and in this context it indicates a reversal of Genesis 3:14ff., 17ff. The reference is to existence in the city. Nothing in it will be cursed, for there will be within it no cause for curse. Rebellion against the will of God is unthinkable within the city's walls, therefore there are no springs of ruin among men and no judgment from God. This thought is in harmony with that expressed immediately afterwards: the throne of God and of the Lamb shall be in it. God and the Lamb dwell there in manifest glory and sovereignty, his will is everywhere acknowledged, and therefore only blessing is known within the city" (*The Book of Revelation*, NCBC [Grand Rapids: Eerdmans, 1981], 332).

the curse of God resting on anyone who fails to continue in everything written in the Book of the Law (Gal 3:10). However, the apostle goes on to say that Christ has redeemed us from the curse of the law by becoming a curse for us since it is written, "Cursed is everyone who is hung on a tree" (Gal 3:13 NLT). Thus, Christ's death on the cross constituted His becoming a curse for man in order that man might go free. Now the curse of sin is forever removed, and there is no longer a curse. To the contrary, the throne of God and of the Lamb are in the city and God's servants will serve Him and Him alone.

Verse 4 records a new level of intimacy. The saints will see His face, and God's name is on their foreheads, an indication of ownership. That indication of ownership carried with it the guarantee of safety and protection. Finally, v. 5 promises that there will be no more night. There is no more need of a lamp or the light of the sun, for the Lord God gives light, and those who serve Him will reign forever and ever. The expression, "There shall be no night there," brings to memory that "men loved darkness rather than light, because their deeds were evil" (John 3:19). However, evil deeds are no longer a part of the heavenly scene, and so there is no love of darkness and no presence of darkness. The Lord God replaces all other light givers as the supreme Light-Giver.

Finally, the observation that the saints will reign forever and ever suggests not only a kingly priesthood for all believers, but again underscores that the eternal state is one of responsibility and achievement. The angel speaks once more, and his words are faithful and true. His message is from the One who is the God of the spirits of the prophets. The meaning of this phrase seems to underscore the same general truth declared in 2 Pet 1:21: "For prophecy never came by the will of man, but holy men of God spoke as they were moved by the Holy Spirit." The point seems to be (1) that the message is directly from God and (2) that the vehicle chosen by God to convey this message is the "spirits of the prophets" (Rev 22:6 NASB).[445] In the final clause, the angel declares again the purpose of the entire book. His purpose has been to alert John and, therefore, all of John's readers to the things that must take place. Again, the aorist active infinitive *deixai* is used to show John and his readers the binding nature, the absolute essential determination of the things that are to happen quickly.

---

445 I. T. Beckwith underscores this saying, "But the words here added show that the divinely illumined spirits of the prophets are meant. The purpose of this sentence is to authenticate the book as a genuine work of prophecy; God who controls the inspiration of the prophets has inspired his angel and the Apocalyptist to show his servants what must shortly come to pass" (*The Apocalypse of John* [New York: Macmillan, 1919], 772–73).

Tachu, translated "soon" in the NIV text, but translated "shortly" by the NKJV, is one of the words that preterists have used to argue that the events outlined in the book of Revelation all began to take place immediately and were fulfilled during the time of the apostle John, with the exception of those items that clearly speak of the *parousia* or the final coming of Christ. However, this does not have to be the meaning of the word and seems here clearly to be wrong. As in the earlier verses of the Revelation, here the emphasis is not on the fact that all of these things recorded in the book would take place within a few months or years; but rather that they will happen certainly and quickly when the eschaton begins, as indicated by the NKJV translators. Several times *tachu*, in v. 7, is also translated "quickly" (cf. Luke 14:21; 16:6; Acts 12:7; 22:18). *Tachu* of v. 7 is used in the sense of "quick" in Matt 5:25; 28:7; and 28:8.[446] The emphasis of vv. 6 and 7, taken together, point to the certainty of the events described in the Apocalypse and the rapidity of their development when the events begin.[447]

---

446 R. H. Mounce observes, "The nearness of the consummation, as reflected by the clause 'which must shortly come to pass,' is not a problem peculiar to Revelation. Paul, as well, writes that the time is short and that men should adjust their manner of life accordingly (1 Cor 7:29–31). In one of his earliest letters the apostle includes himself with those who are to be alive when Jesus returns (1 Thess 4:15). One way to solve the problem of this as-yet-unfulfilled expectation is to hold that God is more concerned with the fulfillment of his redemptive purposes than he is with satisfying our ideas of appropriate timing. All the issues which find their complete fulfillment in that point in time yet future when history will verge into eternity, are also being fulfilled in the ever advancing present. The end and the beginning are but two perspectives on the same great adventure. The final overthrow of evil was determined from the beginning and has been in force ever since the defeat of Satan by the sacrificial death of Christ and his triumphal resurrection" (*The Book of Revelation*, NIC-NT [Grand Rapids: Eerdmans, 1977], 390–91). G. E. Ladd adds, "This must be taken either as a quotation by the angel of the words of the Lord, or as a new statement in which the Lord himself speaks. It reiterates what Christ said in the earlier part of the Revelation (2:16; 3:11). The word may mean 'quickly' (AV) or 'soon' (RSV). The Christian community should always live under the expectancy of the imminent coming of the Lord. No man knows the day nor hour (Matt. 24:36) and no one can set dates or calculate the time of his coming; but every generation must be awake as though the coming of Christ was at the threshold (Matt. 24:42–44). The biblical warnings involve a spiritual and moral tension of expectancy and perspective" (*A Commentary on the Revelation of John* [Grand Rapids: Eerdmans, 1972], 290).

447 For further discussion see comments at 1:1–3.

IV. Concluding Invitation
22:7-21

---

[7]"Behold, I am coming quickly! Blessed *is* he who keeps the words of the prophecy of this book."

[8]Now I, John, saw and heard these things. And when I heard and saw, I fell down to worship before the feet of the angel who showed me these things. [9]Then he said to me, "See *that you do* not *do that.* For I am your fellow servant, and of your brethren the prophets, and of those who keep the words of this book. Worship God."

[10]And he said to me, "Do not seal the words of the prophecy of this book, for the time is at hand. [11]He who is unjust, let him be unjust still; he who is filthy, let him be filthy still; he who is righteous, let him be righteous still; he who is holy, let him be holy still."

[12]"And behold, I am coming quickly, and My reward *is* with Me, to give to every one according to his work. [13]I am the Alpha and the Omega, *the* Beginning and *the* End, the First and the Last.

[14]Blessed *are* those who do His commandments, that they may have the right to the tree of life, and may enter through the gates into the city. [15]But outside *are* dogs and sorcerers and sexually immoral and murderers and idolaters, and whoever loves and practices a lie.

[16]"I, Jesus, have sent My angel to testify to you these things in the churches. I am the Root and the Offspring of David, the Bright and Morning Star."

[17]And the Spirit and bride say, "Come!" And let him who hears say, "Come!" And let him who thirsts come. Whoever desires, let him take the water of life freely.

[18]For I testify to everyone who hears the words of the prophecy of this book: If anyone adds to these things, God will add to him the plagues that are written in this book; [19]and if anyone takes away from the words of the book of this prophecy, God shall take away his part from the Book of Life, from the holy city, and *from* the things which are written in this book.

[20]He who testifies to these things says, "Surely I am coming quickly."

Amen. Even so, come, Lord Jesus!

[21]The grace of our Lord Jesus Christ *be* with you all. Amen.

22:7-11 Once again in v. 7 the imminency and the certainty of the Lord's return are emphasized. "I am coming quickly" (*tachu*) is followed by another of the beatitudes of the Apocalypse. "Blessed is he who keeps the words of the prophecy of this book." *Tēreō*, meaning "keep" or "observe," in its present participial form here stresses the continual observation of the words of the prophecy. Complicit in the command is the keeping of the moral admonitions, as well as the clear soteriology and spiritual mandate of the book; however, probably even more than that is enjoined. By promising blessedness to the one who observes the prophecies of this book, there is a hint of enormous value in the reading and the understanding of the prophecy.

Two opposite reactions seem to be prominent among Christians across the centuries. Some have become so infatuated with the book of Revelation that the remainder of the Bible has become little more than a support system for eschatology. The opposite reaction to that has been to view the book of Revelation as such a difficult book to understand as to render it worth little more than an occasional read. The vast majority of pastors make no attempt to teach their people the Apocalypse; and whenever pastors do choose to preach from the book, the messages usually end at chap. 3. In between these two extremes is the appropriate place where the book is carefully expounded and its treasures enshrined in the hearts of the people for whom the *eschaton* becomes a blessed hope as people are called to look for the appearing of the Lord. All of this seems to be a part of the promised blessedness in the verse.

In v. 8 John declares his own involvement in the message. Once again, he anticipates that the readers will know who he is and does not sense the necessity of further identification other than the mention of his name. Though this does not establish that the Lord's apostle is the author, it is strong testimony to the effect that one of the Sons of Thunder has written the words of the book. He claims two different experiences—seeing and hearing the things that he has then committed to writing. The effect of this experience on the apostle causes him to make the same mistake he made in 1:17, falling down at the feet of the angel who had been his faithful guide through the book. And, once again, the angel corrects the understandable reaction by forbidding the action, repeating once again that he himself is merely a fellow servant with John, with his brothers the prophets, and with all of those who keep the words of the book. Rather, he also is to worship God.

Verse 10, however, looks to the immediate future by forbidding John to seal up the words of the prophecy because the time for the fulfillment of these things is near. Again, the Scripture makes use of the word *engus*, meaning "near at hand," therefore emphasizing the imminency of the Lord's return and even the temporal nearness of some of the events outlined in the chapters devoted to the seven churches. The only portion of the book remaining sealed is that message spoken by the seven thunders. The seven seals, the seven trumpets, and the seven bowls of wrath are now known, but John was told not to write whatever the seven thunders uttered. There remains, even after the Apocalypse, mystery regarding the great tribulation, the millennium, and the future. But what God has revealed is not to be sealed.

Verse 11 takes an unexpected turn. The angel now calls on all who do wrong to continue doing wrong. By the same token, those who are accustomed to filthy behavior are allowed to continue in that filthy behavior. The word for "filthy" (*rhupainō*), with its accompanying verb, has the sense of "soil," "make dirty," or "defile." The disregard of impure persons because of the holiness of God soon establishes a permanent state. By the same token, those who exercise righteousness and who seek after holiness will find that eventually those aspirations are solidified and made permanent. Beale connects this difficult passage to Dan 12 and offers some assistance in comprehension of the text.[448]

22:12-17   One final time Jesus himself announces, "Behold, I am coming quickly!" *Tachu* doubtless references the imminency of the Lord's return for the church as well as the certainty of all these coming events. The One who gives assurance of His return also promises that the believer's reward is with Him and that when He comes, He will give to everyone according to what He has done. Salvation is not in view here because salvation is a matter of what God has done and not what a human can do. However, once people experience the grace of God in salvation, everything else they do is counted unto them as reward or else taken from them as loss (1 Cor 3). That which is wood, hay, and stubble and worthless will be consumed by the fiery gaze of Him who sits on the throne; that which is gold, silver, and precious stone will be purified since

---

448 G. K. Beale says, "But, as noted above, Rev. 22:11 makes explicit allusion to Dan. 12:10, following on the heels of the allusion to Dan. 12:4, 9 in 22:10. How does the Daniel allusion contribute to the theological background of dual exhortations in Rev. 22:11? The Daniel text predicts that during the latter days false members of the covenant community will not understand the dawning fulfillment of prophecy (alluded to in Rev. 22:10) and consequently will continue to disobey God's laws, whereas the godly will have insight and discern the beginning of the fulfillment of prophecy occurring around them. They will respond by obeying God's word. The change from prediction in Daniel to imperatives in Rev. 22:11 expresses awareness that Daniel's prophecy is beginning to be fulfilled in John's own time and that genuine believers should discern this revelation and respond positively to it. This tone of inauguration fits nicely with 22:10 and the repeated exhortations in the letters to the readers to 'hear with the ears'" (*The Book of Revelation: A Commentary on the Greek Text*, NIGTC [Grand Rapids: Eerdmans, 1999], 1133).

even good works are invariably tainted by human sin. However, these will be purified and counted as reward. Again, the Lord declares that He is the Alpha and Omega and stresses that He is the One with whom all things have as a beginning and he is also the last. This time the word for "last" is *eschatos*, which is the basis of the word eschatology or the study of last things. He is the One, then, that brings all things to their final conclusion.

The final beatitude of the Apocalypse occurs in v. 14. Again, the question of salvation is presented in such a way as to establish purposes broader than those found in most of the books that are called apocalyptic. "Blessed are those who do His commandments, that they may have the right to the tree of life and may enter through the gates into the city." The Alexandrian text type here reads, "Blessed are those who wash their robes..." rather than "Blessed are those who do His commandments. . . ." This commentator believes the latter to be the best reading. The washing of the robes is a recognition that the spirits of all men are contaminated by sin. This is overcome once again by the blood of the Lamb. Early in the book there is the hymn of praise, "To him who loved us and washed us from our sins in His own blood" (Rev 1:5). As indicated in that particular place, the words for "wash" and for "freed" or "loosed" are pronounced the same way, and the original text cannot be decided with certainty. Most favor "that he freed us from our sins in his own blood," but it is also true that he washed us in his own blood (1:5). Also, elsewhere in the book such a thing is mentioned. Not only is the one who has his robe washed and hence clean, blessed; such a happening also enables him to have a right to the tree of life so that he never dies, and he is given access through the gates into the city and therefore into the presence of God Himself.[449]

Verse 15 provides the last essentially threatening verse in the book of Revelation. Those who are left on the outside of the Holy City and in fact are confined to the lake of fire are those who have not washed their robes, do not have access to the tree of life, and cannot enter through the gates of the city. These are described as "dogs and sorcerers and the sexually immoral and the murderers and the idolaters and whoever who loves and practices a lie." The

---

449 G. R. Osborne favors an emphasis on continued sanctification: "As several bring out (Giesen 1997: 487; Mounce 1998: 407), the present tense πλύνοντες (*plynontes*, washing) speaks of an ongoing activity that characterizes their lives. This is a recurring theme in the book, used negatively for the church at Sardis (who had 'soiled their clothes' [3:4, with the overcomers there 'dressed in white,' 3:5]) and at Laodicea (who should purchase from Christ 'white clothes to wear,' 3:18)" (*Revelation*, BECNT [Grand Rapids: Baker Academic, 2002], 789).

intriguing feature of the verse is the mention of "dogs" (*kunos*). This tends to be an especially difficult concept for Westerners to understand since their love for canines is well known—whether in Europe or in America—but in the East such is often not the case. The dogs were unclean animals and were often the street-scavengers who had no real home or obligation. They were often viewed as dangerous; and although they fulfilled a purpose, they were granted none of the affection that many Westerners pour out on their canine companions. Still, seemingly the reference here is metaphorical and not a reference to canines, whether of an endearing or reprehensible variety. At least this much is obvious: The reference is to despicable people whose behavioral patterns are in some sense or another indistinguishable from street-roving scavengers. The probability is, however, that even greater specificity is possible. In Deut 23:18, the children of Israel are informed that they cannot bring the price of a prostitute or the price of a dog as an offering to the temple. No great explanation is necessary for explaining why the price of a prostitute would be unacceptable. But why would that sale of a dog be unacceptable?

When the children of Israel arrived in the land of Canaan, they found the practice of ritual prostitution abhorrent, and that often involved homosexuality within many of the religions of the land. Unfortunately, the vice observed therein often repulsed them at first but later seduced them. Nevertheless, there is evidence that the earliest observations of the children of Israel concerning these same-sex relationships in the honor of the gods were so reprehensible they found the behavior of the canine inhabitants to be superior to that of the human inhabitants. They may have referred to those practicing homosexual prostitution as "dogs." Consequently, the expression in v. 14 may reference ritual prostitution and be an additional item added to the sexual immorality that is mentioned.[450]

---

450 Oecumenius focuses on similar concepts: "He says, *Outside are the dogs:* it is the custom in Holy Scripture to call those who have prostituted themselves *dogs* on account of their shamelessness and impurity. For the law of the priest Moses in Deuteronomy says, 'You shall not bring the hire of a harlot or the price of a dog into the house of the Lord your God for any vow of yours,' for such people are like dogs in their shamelessness, as a heathen wise man also testifies, saying, 'Keep far from murder of every kind and a woman's adulterous couch, and swearing by the gods, and youths' shameless beds.' Therefore, *the dogs*, whoever they may be, are *outside* the holy city and the life of the righteous. For what do they have in common with the righteous folk of God?" (*Commentary on the Apocalypse*, 198–99). Johnson is more specific. "Such are 'the dogs,' i.e., those who practice magic arts, etc.—viz., those who rebel against the rule of God

In the NKJV translation, "sorcerers" again are denoted as a possible meaning from *pharmakos*, which suggests but does not mandate the use of drugs. Drugs were often a part of that behavior. Certainly, the laundry list of evils in this verse, including murder, idolatry, and the love and practices of lying, gets to the heart of rebellious behavior against God and defines the nature of iniquity as closely as any list could.

In v. 16 Jesus speaks again, "I, Jesus, have sent My angel to testify to you these things in the churches." "Testify...in the churches" is the aorist active infinitive form of *martureō*, which means "witness." Jesus is the ultimate Author of the book. He has ferried the testimony of the book through angelic messengers to John, who is to see that it is provided for the churches. Just as Jesus does in His specific messages to the seven churches, He now gives a precise identification of Himself. He is both "the Root and the Offspring of David" and also "the Bright and Morning Star." As the Root of David, He is the One from whom David himself came, and to whom David owes his existence and purpose. As the Offspring of David, Jesus became a Man in the incarnation and was born to the line of David as promised by the prophets. Had the Pharisees grasped this truth, they would not have found themselves in the difficulty of answering Jesus' question in Matt 22:42, "What do you think about the Christ? Whose Son is He?" Knowing the certainty of the prophets they answered quickly, "The Son of David." But they did not anticipate the two-part question. The second part of the question, "How then does David in the Spirit call Him 'Lord'?" The answer, had the Pharisees known it, is that Christ in His preincarnate form lived forever as God before David's existence and hence is the Root of David even as He is in His incarnation the Offspring of David. The reference to "the Bright and Morning Star" is a reference to the hope that people have only in Christ.

Verse 17 constitutes a sincere invitation to all from two sources—"the Spirit and the bride say, 'Come!'" Apparently, all who hear are asked to join in the chorus and say, "Come." Anyone who is thirsty is invited to come, and whoever wishes is asked to take the free gift of the water of life. "Come" is the present active imperative of *erchomai* and is at once both a mandate and an invitation. This invitation appears to be sincere on the part of the Spirit and the bride, joined by all who hear: "Whoever desires, let him take the water of life freely."

(cf. Deut 23:18, where a dog signifies a male prostitute; Matt 15:26, where 'dogs' refers to Gentiles; Phil 3:2-3, where 'dogs' refers to the Judaizers). There is no doubt that such people will not be admitted through the gates of the Holy City" ("Revelation," 602).

The doctrine of election is a biblical doctrine of great importance and must not be ignored. However, the issue is not whether the doctrine of election is a part of the biblical text and the faith of the Lord Jesus Christ but rather what it means. For all the history of God's people that question has been debated; and the debates have yet to produce an answer satisfactory to a significant majority of God's people in any era. Whatever election means, this verse suggests that it cannot mean that a sincere offer is not being made. If anyone has the "desire," *thelōn*, a present active participle meaning "will," and wishes to slake his thirst in the water of life, he is invited to come. The extensive warnings of the wrath to come that grace the book of Revelation on every page, as well as the gracious provisions of God for forgiveness and salvation occurring with almost equal frequency, are the grounds for extending this sincere invitation to all. The plaintive plea of the Spirit and the bride concluding the Apocalypse should be the appropriate consummation of the message of the church in every age.

22:18-21 A final warning comes from John in v. 18. The apostle warns that if anyone adds anything to the prophecy of the book, God will add to him the plagues described in the book. On the other hand, if anyone takes away from the words of the prophecy, his part in the tree of life and the Holy City, as described in this book, will be taken away from him.[451] Though *dendron* is most often the word translated "tree," here *xulon* is used (v. 14). The latter may mean "tree" but is more often rendered "wood" (e.g., Rev 18:12). This same word is employed in reference to the cross (Acts 5:30; 10:39; 13:29; 1 Pet 2:24). In any event, the serious threat associated with the manipulation of the text is almost unexpected. The precise significance of this warning is not entirely agreed on by interpreters.

At the time of the writing of the Apocalypse, the only way for multiple copies of any written material to make their way from the location of writing to the various recipients anticipated was for multiple copies to be handwritten. Some have imagined that John is concerned with the copying of the book and wants to be sure copyists do not take matters into their own hands. Perhaps a copyist would feel that something included did not make sense to him and therefore should be omitted, or perhaps a copyist might think that some other

---

451 The Authorized Version reading, "book of life," may seem to make more sense, but in this case the textual evidence for "tree of life" is so overwhelming that the 3rd edition of the United Bible Societies' Greek New Testament does not even give the reading "book of life." The slim evidence favoring "book" may be seen in H. C. Hoskier, *Concerning the Text of the Apocalypse* (London: Bernard Quaritch, 1929), 2:644.

explanation more than John had given was essential. John, according to those who hold this view, is concerned for the integrity of the text because he believes that it is not merely the imagination of his own mind but rather the Spirit of God who has inspired the text. Consequently, he wants it reproduced by copyists with maximum accuracy.

In the introduction there has been some discussion of the textual evidence for the book of Revelation, and this textual evidence is somewhat fragmented with many unresolved textual problems in the book just as would be found in other New Testament literature. This alone would provide reason for John to say this.[452]

However, the more likely cause for this expression can be seen in the beatitude when those are promised blessedness if they keep the words of the prophecy of this book (22:7). To attempt to do something other than abide by its message, either explaining it away or adding to its message, only results in a deception that makes one the recipient of the plagues who has lost any opportunity for access to the tree of life and the holy city. This seems to be the best understanding of this final warning.[453]

John provides one more testimony from the living Lord. "He who testifies to these things says, 'Surely, I am coming quickly.'" That promise rings from John two important responses. First, he says, "Amen." As previously noted, the word "amen" arises from the Hebrew and references an affirmation. When Jesus once again concludes that He is coming soon, John's response from his island

---

452 A. Y. Collins notes, "Charles argued that these verses were added to Rev by a later editor (*Commentary* 2. 222–23). His strongest argument was that since John expected the end in a short time, he hardly would be concerned about the transmission of his book over a long period of time. But the remarks in vv 18–19 say nothing about a long period. If he considered that his work contained divine revelation necessary for the faithful to prepare properly for the end, he may well have been concerned that it be transmitted accurately in the short time remaining. Another function of these remarks is to reinforce the claim made elsewhere in the book that its contents originate with God (see 1:1)" (*NJBC*, 1016).

453 Using this verse to support a cessationist perspective regarding the gift of prophecy, R. L. Thomas says, "The conclusion of this investigation accepts the inevitability of connecting the decline and cessation of the spiritual gift of prophecy to Rev 22:18. Compliance with, indeed universal knowledge of, this warning was not immediate. Nevertheless the divine intention behind the warning necessitated that it eventually be recognized and that the body of Christ move into new phases of its growth without dependence on the foundational gift of prophecy" ("The Spiritual Gift of Prophecy in Rev 22:18," *JETS* 32 [1989]: 216).

observatory is immediately one of affirmation, "Amen." There follows a prayer voiced heavenward, "Even so, come, Lord Jesus!" John's heart is ready, and he is eager for the return of Christ. In typical epistolary form not often found in apocalyptic literature, the final theme exhibited in v. 21 is the grace of God.

John prays for his readers now by saying, "The grace of our Lord Jesus Christ be with you all." The NIV translators added the words "God's people." *Pantōn*, which means "all," certainly supports this translation; but the text just uses the one word. The NJKV includes the word, "Amen," which is present in the *textus receptus* and in Codex Sinaiticus and a great variety of other texts on Revelation. Some, however, omit it, probably thinking that it would not occur in both vv. 20 and 21. The NKJV translators have probably grasped it correctly in finding its presence in the original text. The Revelation is concluded with the affirmation, "Let it be so."

BIBLIOGRAPHY

Allen, Elliot Douglas. *Armageddon: Studies in the Revelation of St. John*. Philadelphia: P&R, 1964.

Anderson, Sir Robert. *The Coming Prince: The Marvelous Prophecy of Daniel's Seventy Weeks Concerning the Antichrist*. Reprint of the 10th ed. Grand Rapids: Kregel, 1977.

Ashcraft, Morris. *Revelation*. The Broadman Bible Commentary, vol. 12. Nashville: Broadman, 1972.

Aune, David E. *The New Testament in Its Literary Environment*. LEC 8. Philadelphia: WJK, 1987.

_____. *Revelation*. WBC 52. 3 vols. Dallas: Word Books, 1997.

Backus, Irena D. *Reformation Readings of the Apocalypse: Geneva, Zurich, and Wittenberg*. Oxford Studies in Historical Theology. Oxford: Oxford University Press, 2000.

Barclay, William. *The Revelation of John*. The Daily Study Bible. 2 vols. Philadelphia: Westminster, 1960.

Barker, Margaret. *The Revelation of Jesus Christ: Which God Gave to Him to Show to His Servants What Must Soon Take Place (Revelation 1.1)*. Edinburgh: T&T Clark, 2000.

Barr, David L., ed. *Reading the Book of Revelation: A Resource for Students*. Resources for Biblical Study 44. Atlanta, GA: Society of Biblical Literature, 2003.

_____. *The Reality of Apocalypse: Rhetoric and Politics in the Book of Revelation*. SBLSymS 39. Atlanta, GA: Society of Biblical Literature, 2006.

Bass, Clarence B. *Backgrounds to Dispensationalism: Its Historical Genesis and Ecclesiastical Implications*. 1st ed. Grand Rapids: Eerdmans, 1960.

Bauckham, Richard. *The Climax of Prophecy: Studies on the Book of Revelation*. Edinburgh: T&T Clark, 1993.

_____. *New Testament Theology: The Theology of the Book of Revelation*. Cambridge: Cambridge University Press, 1993.

Bavinck, Herman. *The Last Things: Hope for This World and the Next*. Edited by John Bolt. Translated by John Vriend. Carlisle, UK: Paternoster Press, 1996.

Beale, Gregory K. *John's Use of the Old Testament in Revelation*. JSNT 166. Sheffield, England: Sheffield Academic Press, 1998.

_____. *The Book of Revelation: A Commentary on the Greek Text*. NIGTC. Grand Rapids: Eerdmans, 1999.

_____. *The Use of Daniel in Jewish Apocalyptic Literature and in the Revelation of St. John*. Lanham, MD: University Press of America, 1984.

Beasley-Murray, George R. *The Book of Revelation: Based on the Revised Standard Version*. NCBC. Grand Rapids: Eerdmans, 1981.

_____, George R., Ray F. Robbins, and Herschel H. Hobbs. *Revelation: Three View-points*. Nashville: Broadman, 1977.

Beckwith, Isbon Thaddeus. *The Apocalypse of John*. New York: Macmillan, 1919.

Bengel, John A. *Bengel's New Testament Commentary*. 2 vols. Grand Rapids: Kregel, 1981.

Beilby, James. *Postmortem Opportunity: A Biblical and Theological Assessment of Salvation after Death*. Downers Grove: InterVarsity, 2021.

Benware, Paul N. *Understanding End Times Prophecy: A Comprehensive Approach*. Chicago: Moody, 1995.

Berkouwer, G. C. *The Return of Christ*. Studies in Dogmatics. Grand Rapids: Eerdmans, 1972.

Bishop, George Manning. *The Revelation in the Light of History*. New York: Carlton Press, 1991.

Blaising, Craig A., Kenneth L. Gentry Jr., and Robert B. Strimple. *Three Views on the Millennium and Beyond*. Counterpoints: Bible & Theology. Edited by Darrell L. Bock and Stanley N. Gundry. Grand Rapids: Zondervan, 1999.

Blevins, James L. *Revelation as Drama*. Nashville: Broadman, 1984.

Bloesch, Donald G. *The Last Things: Resurrection, Judgment, Glory*. Christian Foundations. Downers Grove, IL: InterVarsity, 2004.

Bloom, Harold. *The Revelation of St. John the Divine*. Modern Critical Interpretations. New York: Chelsea House Publishers, 1988.

Blount, Brian K. *Revelation: A Commentary*. NTL. Louisville, KY: WJK, 2009.

Bock, Darrell L., and Craig. A. Blaising, eds. *Dispensationalism, Israel and the Church: The Search for Definition*. Grand Rapids: Zondervan, 1992.

Bøe, Sverre. *Gog and Magog: Ezekiel 38–39 as Pre-Text for Revelation 19, 17–21 and 20, 7–10*. WUNT 135. Tübingen: Mohr Siebeck, 2001.

Boring, M. Eugene. *Revelation*. IBC. Louisville, KY: WJK, 1989.

Bousset, Wilhelm. *The Antichrist Legend: A Chapter in Christian and Jewish Folklore*. Texts and Translations Series 24. Atlanta, GA: Scholars Press, 1999.

Boxall, Ian. *The Revelation of St. John*. BNTC. Peabody, MA: Hendrickson, 2006.

Bratcher, Robert G. *A Translator's Guide to the Revelation to John*. London: United Bible Societies, 1984.

Bray, John L. *Matthew 24 Fulfilled*. Lakeland, FL: John L. Bray Ministry, 1996.

Brickner, David. *Future Hope: A Jewish Christian Look at the End of the World*. San Francisco: Purple Pomegranate Productions, 1999.

Brower, Kent E., and Mark W. Elliot, eds. *Eschatology in Bible & Theology: Evangelical Essays at the Dawn of a New Millennium*. Downers Grove, IL: InterVarsity Press, 1997.

Brown, David. *Christ's Second Coming: Will It Be Pre-Millennial?* Grand Rapids: Baker, 1983.

Buchanan, George Wesley. *The Book of Revelation: Its Introduction and Prophecy*. The Mellen Biblical Commentary 22. Lewiston, NY: Mellen Biblical Press, 1993.

Bull, Malcolm, ed. *Apocalypse Theory and the Ends of the World.* Wolfson College Lectures. Cambridge, MA: Blackwell, 1995.

Bullinger, E. W. *Commentary on Revelation.* Grand Rapids: Kregel, 1984.

Bultmann, Rudolf K. *The Presence of Eternity: History and Eschatology.* The Gifford Lectures, 1955. New York: Harper, 1957.

Burkert, Walter. *Ancient Mystery Cults.* Cambridge, MA: Harvard University Press, 1987.

Caird, George Bradford. *The Revelation of St. John the Divine.* HNTC. San Francisco: Harper & Row, 1966.

Campbell, Donald K., and Jeffery L. Townsend, eds. *A Case for Premillennialism: A New Consensus.* Chicago: Moody, 1992.

Carey, Greg. *Ultimate Things: An Introduction to Jewish and Christian Apocalyptic Literature.* St. Louis, MO: Chalice Press, 2005.

Carrell, Peter R. *Jesus and the Angels: Angelology and the Christology of the Apocalypse of John.* SNTSMS 95. Cambridge: Cambridge University Press, 1997.

Carroll, B. H. *An Interpretation of the English Bible.* Volume 17: *Revelation.* Edited by J. B. Cranfill. Nashville: Broadman Press, 1947.

Casson, Lionel. *Everyday Life in Ancient Rome.* Baltimore: Johns Hopkins University Press, 1998.

Chapman, Charles T. *The Message of the Book of Revelation.* Collegeville, MN: Liturgical Press, 1995.

Charles, R. H. *A Critical and Exegetical Commentary on the Revelation of St. John.* ICC. 2 vols. Edinburgh: T&T Clark, 1920.

_____. *A Critical History of the Doctrine of a Future Life: In Israel, in Judaism, and in Christianity.* Jowett Lectures for 1898–99. Eugene, OR: Wipf & Stock Publishers, 1999.

_____. *Studies in the Apocalypse: Being Lectures Delivered Before the University of London.* Eugene, OR: Wipf & Stock Publishers, 1996.

_____, ed. *The Book of the Secrets of Enoch.* Translated by W. R. Morfill. Oxford: Clarendon Press, 1896.

Chilton, David. *The Days of Vengeance: An Exposition of the Book of Revelation.* Fort Worth: Dominion Press, 1987.

Clark, David S. *The Message from Patmos: A Postmillennial Commentary on the Book of Revelation.* Dahlonega, GA: Crown Rights Book Company, 1921.

Collins, Adela Yarbro. *The Apocalypse.* Wilmington, DE: Michael Glazier, 1979.

_____. *Crisis and Catharsis: The Power of the Apocalypse.* 1st ed. Philadelphia: Westminster Press, 1984.

Combs, Jim. *Rainbows from Revelation: How to Understand the Apocalypse.* Springfield, MO: Tribune Publishers, 1994.

Cook, Stephen L. *Prophecy & Apocalypticism: The Postexilic Social Setting*. Minneapolis: Fortress, 1995.

Cooper, Lamar Eugene. *Ezekiel*. NAC 17. Nashville: B&H, 1994.

Conner, Kevin J. *The Seventy Weeks Prophecy: An Exposition of Daniel 9*. Blackburn, Victoria: Acacia Press, 1983.

Court, John M. *The Book of Revelation and the Johannine Apocalyptic Tradition*. JSNT 190. Sheffield, England: Sheffield Academic Press, 2000.

_____. *Revelation*. NTG. Sheffield, England: JSOT Press, 1994.

Criswell, W. A. *Expository Sermons on Revelation: Five Volumes Complete and Unabridged in One*. Grand Rapids: Zondervan, 1969.

Davies, Philip R. *Daniel*. OTG. Sheffield, England: JSOT Press, 1985.

Davis, R. Dean. *The Heavenly Court Judgment of Revelation 4–5*. Lanham: University Press of America, 1992.

DeHaan, Martin R. *Revelation: 35 Simple Studies in the Major Themes in Revelation*. Grand Rapids: Zondervan, 1946.

Diprose, Ronald E. *Israel and the Church: The Origins and Effects of Replacement Theology*. Downers Grove: InterVarsity, 2004.

Dorman, Lucy Mary. *The Unveiled Future: An Interpretation of the Revelation Given to St. John*. London: Marshall, Morgan & Scott, 1936.

Duguid, Iain M. *Ezekiel*. NIV Application Commentary. Grand Rapids: Zondervan, 1999.

Duty, Guy. *Christ's Coming and the World Church*. Dimension Books. Minneapolis: Bethany Fellowship, 1971.

Dyer, Charles H. *The Rise of Babylon: Sign of the End Times*. Wheaton, IL: Tyndale House Publishers, 1991.

_____. *World News and Bible Prophecy*. Wheaton, IL: Tyndale House Publishers, 1993.

Easley, Kendell H. *Living with the End in Sight: Meditations on the Book of Revelation*. Nashville: Holman Bible Publishers, 2000.

_____. *Revelation*. Holman New Testament Commentary. Nashville: B&H, 1998.

Efird, James M. *End-Times: Rapture, Antichrist, Millennium: What the Bible Says*. Contemporary Christian Concerns. Nashville: Abingdon, 1986.

_____. *Revelation for Today: An Apocalyptic Approach*. Nashville: Abingdon, 1989.

Ehlert, Arnold D. *A Bibliographic History of Dispensationalism*. BCH Bibliographic Series. Grand Rapids: Baker, 1965.

Faley, Roland J. *Apocalypse Then and Now: A Companion to the Book of Revelation*. New York: Paulist Press, 1999.

Feinberg, Charles Lee. *A Commentary on Revelation: The Grand Finale*. Winona Lake, IN: BMH Books, 1985.

Fergusson, David, and Marcel Sarot, eds. *The Future as God's Gift: Explorations in Christian*

Eschatology. The Society for the Study of Theology. Edinburgh: T&T Clark, 2000.

Finger, Thomas N. *Christian Theology: An Eschatological Approach*. Vol. 2. Scottdale, PA: Herald Press, 1989.

Ford, J. Massyngberde. *Revelation: Introduction, Translation, and Commentary*. AB. Garden City, NY: Doubleday, 1975.

Fraser, Alexander. *The First Four Parables of the Kingdom of Heaven*. Scottdale, PA: Evangelical Fellowship, 1945.

_____. *The Return of Christ in Glory*. Scottdale, PA: Evangelical Fellowship, 1957.

Friesen, Steven J. *Imperial Cults and the Apocalypse of John: Reading Revelation in the Ruins*. Oxford: Oxford University Press, 2001.

Fröhlich, Ida. *Time and Times and Half a Time: Historical Consciousness in the Jewish Literature of the Persian and Hellenistic Eras*. Journal for the Study of the Pseudepigrapha. Sheffield, England: Sheffield Academic Press, 1996.

Fuller, Robert C. *Naming the Antichrist: The History of an American Obsession*. New York: Oxford University Press, 1995.

Gaebelein, Arno C. *The Prophet Daniel: A Key to the Visions and Prophecies of the Book of Daniel*. Glasgow: Pickering & Inglis, 1911.

_____. *The Revelation: An Analysis and Exposition of the Last Book of the Bible*. New York: Publication Office, 1915.

George, Timothy, Richard D. Land, and Herschel H. Hobbs, eds. *Baptist Why and Why Not Revisited*. Library of Baptist Classics 12. Nashville: B&H, 1997.

Giblin, Charles Homer. *The Book of Revelation: The Open Book of Prophecy*. Good News Studies 34. Collegeville, MN: Liturgical Press, 1991.

Glasson, T. F. *The Revelation of John*. CBC. Cambridge: Cambridge University Press, 1965.

Gökovali, Sadan. *Pergamum*. Translated by Cevat F. Noonan. Izmir: Ticaret Matbaacilik, 1965.

Goldingay, John E. *Daniel*. WBC 30. Dallas, TX: Word Books, 1989.

Goldsworthy, Graeme. *The Gospel in Revelation: Gospel and Apocalypse*. Greenwood, SC: Attic Press, 1984.

González, Catherine Gunsalus, and Justo L. González. *Revelation*. Westminster Bible Companion. Louisville, KY: WJK, 1997.

Gore, Ken. *The Faithful Witness: A Pastmillenial Study of Revelation*. New York: Vantage Press, 2001.

Govett, Robert. *The Locusts, the Euphratean, Horsemen and the Two Witnesses*. Miami Springs, FL: Conley and Schoettle, 1985.

Gregg, Steve, ed. *Revelation: Four Views: A Parallel Commentary*. Nashville: Thomas Nelson, 1997.

Grimsrud, Ted. *Triumph of the Lamb: A Self-Study Guide to the Book of Revelation.* Scottdale, PA: Herald Press, 1987.

Guimond, John. *The Silencing of Babylon: A Spiritual Commentary on the Revelation of John.* New York: Paulist Press, 1991.

Gundry, Robert H. *The Church and the Tribulation.* Grand Rapids: Zondervan, 1973.

_____. *First the Antichrist: Why Christ Won't Come Before the Antichrist Does.* Grand Rapids: Baker, 1997.

Guthrie, Donald. *The Relevance of John's Apocalypse.* The Didsbury Lectures. Grand Rapids: Eerdmans, 1987.

Haldeman, I. M. *Antichrist and the False Prophet: An Analysis of Revelation 13.* New York: Haldeman, 1900.

_____. *The Coming of Christ: Both Pre-Millennial and Imminent.* Philadelphia: Philadelphia School of the Bible, 1906.

Harrington, Wilfrid J. *Revelation.* SP 16. Collegeville, MN: Liturgical Press, 1993.

Havner, Vance. *Repent or Else!* Westwood, NJ: Revell, 1958.

Hemer, Colin J. *The Letters to the Seven Churches of Asia in Their Local Setting.* The Biblical Resource Series. Grand Rapids: Dove Booksellers, 2001.

_____. *The Letters to the Seven Churches of Asia in Their Local Setting.* JSNTSup. Sheffield: JSOT Press, 1986.

Himmelfarb, Martha. *Ascent to Heaven in Jewish and Christian Apocalypses.* New York: Oxford University Press, 1993.

Hindson, Edward E. *Approaching Armageddon: The World Prepares for War with God.* Eugene, OR: Harvest House, 1997.

_____. *End Times, the Middle East, and the New World Order.* Wheaton, IL: Victor Books, 1991.

Hislop, Alexander. *The Two Babylons.* Neptune, NJ: Loizeaux Brothers, 1959.

Hocking, David L. *The Coming World Leader: Understanding the Book of Revelation.* Portland, OR: Multnomah Press, 1988.

Hoehner, H. W. *Chronological Aspects of the Life of Christ.* Grand Rapids: Zondervan, 1977.

Hoekema, Anthony A. *The Bible and the Future.* Grand Rapids: Eerdmans, 1979.

Holwerda, David E. *Jesus and Israel: One Covenant or Two?* Grand Rapids: Eerdmans, 1995.

Hoskier, H. C. *Concerning the Text of the Apocalypse: Collations of All Existing Available Greek Documents with the Standard Text of Stephen's Third Edition, Together with the Testimony of Versions, Commentaries and Fathers; A Complete Conspectus of All Authorities.* 2 vols. London: Bernard Quaritch, 1929.

Howe, Thomas A. *Daniel in the Preterists' Den: A Critical Look at Preterist Interpretations of Daniel.* Eugene, OR: Wipf and Stock, 2008.

Hoyt, Herman A. *The End Times.* Handbook of Bible Doctrine. Chicago: Moody, 1973.

Hughes, P. E. *The Book of the Revelation: A Commentary*. Leicester, England: Inter-Varsity Press, 1990.

Hurtgen, John E. *Anti-Language in the Apocalypse of John*. Lewiston, NY: Mellen Biblical Press, 1993.

Ice, Thomas, and Timothy Demy. *The Truth About the Antichrist and His Kingdom*. Pocket Prophecy Series. Eugene, OR: Harvest House, 1996.

_____. *The Truth About the Last Days' Temple*. Pocket Prophecy Series. Eugene, OR: Harvest House, 1996.

_____. *The Truth About the Rapture*. Pocket Prophecy Series. Eugene, OR: Harvest House, 1996.

_____. *The Truth About the Tribulation*. Pocket Prophecy Series. Eugene, OR: Harvest House, 1996.

Irenaeus. *Against Heresies*. Translated by A. Roberts and W. H. Rambaut. *ANF* 1.

Ironside, Harry A. *Wrongly Dividing the Word of Truth: Ultra-Dispensationalism Examined in the Light of Holy Scripture*. Neptune, NJ: Loizeaux Brothers, 1938.

Jeffrey, Grant R. *Apocalypse: The Coming Judgment of the Nations*. New York: Bantam Books, 1994.

Johnson, Alan F. "Revelation." In *Expositor's Bible Commentary*, vol. 12, ed. Frank E. Gaebelein, 399–603. Grand Rapids: Zondervan, 1981.

_____. *Revelation: Bible Study Commentary*. Bible Study Commentary Series. Grand Rapids: Zondervan, 1983.

Kaiser, Walter C. *Back Toward the Future: Hints for Interpreting Biblical Prophecy*. Grand Rapids: Baker, 1989.

Kallas, James G. *Revelation: God & Satan in the Apocalypse*. Minneapolis: Augsburg Publishing House, 1973.

Kealy, Sean P. *The Apocalypse of John*. Message of Biblical Spirituality 15. Collegeville, MN: Liturgical Press, 1990.

Kik, J. Marcellus. *Matthew Twenty-Four, an Exposition*. Swengel, PA: Bible Truth Depot, 1948.

Kimball, William R. *What the Bible Says About the Great Tribulation*. Phillipsburg, NJ: P&R, 1984.

Kistemaker, Simon J. *Exposition of the Book of Revelation*. New Testament Commentary. Grand Rapids: Baker Academic, 2001.

Knight, Jonathan M. *Revelation*. Readings: A New Biblical Commentary. Sheffield, England: Sheffield Academic Press, 1999.

Koester, Helmut, ed. *Ephesos Metropolis of Asia: An Interdisciplinary Approach to Its Archaeology, Religion, and Culture*. Valley Forge, PA: Trinity Press International, 1995.

Kohlenberger, John R., ed. *The Parallel Apocrypha: Greek Text, King James Version, Douay Old Testament, The Holy Bible by Ronald Knox, Today's English Version, New Revised*

Standard Version, New American Bible, New Jerusalem Bible. New York: Oxford University Press, 1997.

König, Adrio. *The Eclipse of Christ in Eschatology: Toward a Christ-Centered Approach.* Grand Rapids: Eerdmans, 1989.

Kovacs, Judith L., and Christopher Rowland. *Revelation: The Apocalypse of Jesus Christ.* BBC. Malden, MA: Blackwell Publishing, 2004.

Kraybill, J. Nelson. *Imperial Cult and Commerce in John's Apocalypse. JSNT* 132. Sheffield, England: Sheffield Academic Press, 1996.

Kreider, Glenn R. *Jonathan Edwards's Interpretation of Revelation 4:1–8:1.* Dallas, TX: University Press of America, 2004.

Krodel, Gerhard A. *Revelation.* ACNT. Minneapolis, MN: Augsburg, 1989.

Kuyper, Abraham. *The Revelation of St. John.* Translated by John Hendrik De Vries. Grand Rapids: Eerdmans, 1935.

Ladd, George Eldon. *The Blessed Hope.* Grand Rapids: Eerdmans, 1956.

_____. *A Commentary on the Revelation of John.* Grand Rapids: Eerdmans, 1972.

_____. *Crucial Questions About the Kingdom of God: The Sixth Annual Mid-Year Lectures of 1952 Delivered at Western Conservative Baptist Theological Seminary of Portland, Oregon.* Grand Rapids: Eerdmans, 1952.

_____. *The Gospel of the Kingdom: Scriptural Studies in the Kingdom of God.* Grand Rapids: Eerdmans, 1959.

_____. *Jesus and the Kingdom: The Eschatology of Biblical Realism.* 1st ed. New York: Harper & Row, 1964.

_____. *The Last Things: An Eschatology for Laymen.* Grand Rapids: Eerdmans, 1978.

_____. *Rightly Dividing the Word.* Philadelphia: Clarence Larkin, 1921.

LaHaye, Tim. *Revelation: Illustrated and Made Plain.* Grand Rapids: Lamplighter Books, 1975.

Lange, John Peter. *The Revelation of John.* In vol. 12 of *Commentary on the Holy Scriptures: Critical, Doctrinal and Homiletical*, ed. and trans. Philip Schaff. Grand Rapids: Zondervan, 1960.

Larkin, Clarence. *The Book of Revelation.* Philadelphia, PA: Clarence Larkin, 1919.

Larsen, David L. *Jews, Gentiles, and the Church: A New Perspective on History and Prophecy.* Grand Rapids: Discovery House, 1995.

Lenski, R. C. H. *The Interpretation of St. John's Revelation.* Minneapolis: Augsburg, 1963.

Lewis, David Allen. *Prophecy 2000.* Green Forest, AR: New Leaf Press, 1990.

_____. *Who Will Go in the Rapture?* Springfield, MO: Menorah Press, 1986.

Lindsey, Hal. *The Late Great Planet Earth.* Grand Rapids: Zondervan, 1970.

Loane, Marcus L. *They Overcame: An Exposition of the First Three Chapters of Revelation.* Grand Rapids: Baker, 1981.

Longman, Tremper, III. *Daniel*. The NIV Application Commentary. Grand Rapids: Zondervan, 1999.

Lupieri, Edmondo F. *A Commentary on the Apocalypse of John*. Grand Rapids: Eerdmans, 1999.

MacArthur, John. *Revelation 1-11*. The MacArthur New Testament Commentary. Chicago: Moody, 1999.

_____. *Revelation 12-22*. The MacArthur New Testament Commentary. Chicago: Moody, 2000.

Maclaren, Alexander. *The Epistles of John, Jude and the Book of Revelation*. Expositions of Scripture. London: Hodder and Stoughton, 1910.

Malina, Bruce J. *The New Jerusalem in the Revelation of John: The City as Symbol of Life with God*. Zacchaeus Studies: New Testament. Collegeville, MN: Liturgical Press, 2000.

_____. *On the Genre and Message of Revelation: Star Visions and Sky Journeys*. Peabody, MA: Hendrickson, 1995.

Malina, Bruce J., and John J. Pilch. *Social-Science Commentary on the Book of Revelation*. Minneapolis: Augsburg Fortress, 2000.

Marrs, Texe, Tim LaHaye, David Breese, and David A. Lewis, with William T. James. *Storming Toward Armageddon: Essays in Apocalypse*. Green Forest, AR: New Leaf Press, 1992.

Massee, Jasper Cortenus. *The Second Coming*. Philadelphia: Philadelphia School of the Bible, 1919.

Matlock, R. Barry. *Unveiling the Apocalyptic Paul: Paul's Interpreters and the Rhetoric of Criticism*. JSNT 127. Sheffield, England: Sheffield Academic Press, 1996.

McClain, Alva J. *The Greatness of the Kingdom: An Inductive Study of the Kingdom of God*. Chicago: Moody, 1968.

McGinn, Bernard. *Antichrist: Two Thousand Years of the Human Fascination with Evil*. San Francisco: HarperCollins, 1994.

M'Cheyne, Robert Murray. *The Seven Churches of Asia*. Fearn, Scotland: Christian Focus Publications, 1991.

McLean, John Andrew. *The Seventieth Week of Daniel 9:27 as a Literary Key for Understanding the Structure of the Apocalypse of John*. Mellen Biblical Press Series 38. Lewiston, NY: Mellen Biblical Press, 1996.

Mealy, J. Webb. *After the Thousand Years: Resurrection and Judgment in Revelation 20*. JSNTSup. Sheffield: JSOT Press, 1992.

Meinardus, Otto F. A. *St. John of Patmos and the Seven Churches of the Apocalypse*. Athens, Greece: Lycabettus Press, 1995.

Metzger, Bruce M. *Breaking the Code: Understanding the Book of Revelation*. Nashville: Abingdon Press, 1993.

Miceli, Vincent P. *The Antichrist*. Harrison, NY: Roman Catholic Books, 1981.

Michaels, J. Ramsey. *Interpreting the Book of Revelation.* Guides to New Testament Exegesis 7. Grand Rapids: Baker, 1992.

_____. *Revelation.* IVP New Testament Commentary Series 20. Downers Grove, IL: InterVarsity Press, 1997.

Minear, Paul S. *New Testament Apocalyptic.* Nashville: Abingdon, 1981.

Moffatt, James. "The Revelation of St. John the Divine." *Expositor's Greek New Testament.* Vol. 5. Edited by Robertson Nicoll. Grand Rapids: Eerdmans, 1951.

Moltmann, Jürgen. *In the End, the Beginning: The Life of Hope.* Minneapolis: Fortress, 2004.

Mommsen, Theodor. *A History of Rome under the Emperors.* London: Routledge, 1999.

Moody, Dale. *The Hope of Glory.* Grand Rapids: Eerdmans, 1964.

Morris, Henry M. *The Revelation Record: A Scientific and Devotional Commentary on the Book of Revelation.* Wheaton, IL: Tyndale, 1983.

Morris, Leon. *The Apostolic Preaching of the Cross.* Grand Rapids: Eerdmans; London: Tyndale, 1955.

_____. *The Biblical Doctrine of Judgment.* 1st ed. London: Tyndale, 1960.

_____. *The Book of Revelation: An Introduction and Commentary.* 2nd ed. TNTC. Leicester, England: InterVarsity, 1987.

Mounce, Robert H. *The Book of Revelation.* NICNT. Grand Rapids: Eerdmans, 1977.

_____. *What Are We Waiting for? A Commentary on Revelation.* Grand Rapids: Eerdmans, 1992.

Moyise, Steve. *The Old Testament in the Book of Revelation.* JSNTSup 115. Sheffield, England: Sheffield Academic Press, 1995.

Mulholland, M. Robert. *Revelation: Holy Living in an Unholy World.* Grand Rapids: Francis Asbury Press, 1990.

Murphy, Frederick J. *Fallen Is Babylon: The Revelation to John.* The New Testament in Context. Harrisburg, PA: Trinity Press International, 1998.

Newell, William R. *The Book of the Revelation.* Chicago: Moody, 1947.

Newport, John P. *The Lion and the Lamb: A Commentary on the Book of Revelation for Today.* Nashville: Broadman Press, 1986.

Nogués, R. L. Serralta. *Daniel 7: How Will We Know When Is the Return of Jesus Christ Even at the Door.* n.p.: Baptist Messenger Press, 1999.

Oecumenius. *Commentary on the Apocalypse.* Translated by John N. Suggit. FC 112. Washington, DC: Catholic University of America Press, 2006.

Oliver, W. H. *Prophets and Millennialists: The Uses of Biblical Prophecy in England from the 1790s to the 1840s.* Auckland, New Zealand: Auckland University Press, 1978.

Osborne, Grant R. *Revelation.* BECNT. Grand Rapids: Baker Academic, 2002.

Pate, C. Marvin, ed. *Four Views on the Book of Revelation.* Grand Rapids: Zondervan, 1998.

Patterson, Paige. "Ancient Rhetoric: A Model for Text-Driven Preachers." In *Text-Driven*

Preaching: God's Word at the Heart of Every Sermon, ed. Daniel L. Akin, David L. Allen, and Ned L. Mathews, 11–35. Nashville: B&H, 2010.

_____. "Interpreting the New Testament for Preaching—The Apocalypse," *Faith and Mission* 12, no. 1 (Fall 1994): 67–79.

_____. "Israel and the Great Tribulation," in *The Return of Christ*, ed. D. Allen and S. Lemke, 62–74. Nashville: B&H Academic, 2011.

_____. *A Pilgrim Priesthood: An Exposition of the Epistle of First Peter*. Nashville: Thomas Nelson, 1982.

_____. "Reflections on the Atonement." *CTR* 3 (1989): 307–20.

_____. *Song of Solomon*, Everyman's Bible Commentary. Chicago: Moody, 1986.

_____. "The Church in the Twenty-First Century," in *Baptist Why and Why Not Revisited*, Library of Baptist Classics 12, 99–125. Nashville: B&H, 1997.

_____. "The Work of Christ." In *A Theology for the Church*, ed. Daniel L. Akin, 545–602. Nashville: B&H, 2007.

Payne, J. Barton. *Encyclopedia of Biblical Prophecy*. New York: Harper & Row, 1973.

Pentecost, J. Dwight. *Things to Come: A Study in Biblical Eschatology*. Grand Rapids: Zondervan, 1958.

Petersen, Rodney L. *Preaching in the Last Days: The Theme of "Two Witnesses" in the 16th & 17th Centuries*. New York: Oxford University Press, 1993.

Pettingill, William L. *Loving His Appearing, and Other Prophetic Studies*. Findlay, OH: Fundamental Truth Publishers, 1943.

Phillips, John. *Exploring Revelation*. Chicago: Moody, 1987.

Pieters, Albertus. *The Lamb, the Woman and the Dragon: An Exposition of the Revelation of St. John*. Grand Rapids: Zondervan, 1937.

Pilch, John J. *What Are They Saying About the Book of Revelation?* New York: Paulist Press, 1978.

Pippin, Tina. *Death and Desire: The Rhetoric of Gender in the Apocalypse of John*. Literary Currents in Biblical Interpretation. 1st ed. Louisville, KY: WJK, 1992.

Pitre, Brant. *Jesus, the Tribulation, and the End of the Exile: Restoration Eschatology and the Origin of the Atonement*. Tübingen: Mohr Siebeck, 2005.

Potter, David S. *Prophets and Emperors: Human and Divine Authority from Augustus to Theodosius*. Revealing Antiquity 7. Cambridge, MA: Harvard University Press, 1994.

Poythress, Vern S. *The Returning King: A Guide to the Book of Revelation*. Phillipsburg, NJ: P&R, 2000.

The Proceedings of the Conference on Biblical Inerrancy, 1987. Nashville: Broadman Press, 1987.

Ramm, Bernard L. *Them He Glorified: A Systematic Study of the Doctrine of Glorification*. Grand Rapids: Eerdmans, 1963.

Ramsay, William Mitchell. *The Letters to the Seven Churches of Asia and Their Place in the Plan of the Apocalypse.* Grand Rapids: Baker, 1963.

Reagan, David R. *Wrath and Glory: Unveiling the Majestic Book of Revelation.* Green Forest, AR: New Leaf Press, 2001.

Reddish, Mitchell G., ed. *Apocalyptic Literature: A Reader.* Nashville: Abingdon, 1990.

_____. *Revelation.* Smyth & Helwys Bible Commentary. Macon, GA: Smyth & Helwys, 2001.

Reese, Alexander. *The Approaching Advent of Christ.* Grand Rapids: Grand Rapids International Publications, 1975.

Richard, Pablo. *Apocalypse: A People's Commentary on the Book of Revelation.* The Bible & Liberation Series. Translated by Phillip Berryman. Maryknoll, NY: Orbis Books, 1995.

Richards, Edward H. *The Revelation Letters: Expository Sermons on the Seven Churches.* Nashville: Eric Publishers, 1975.

Rimmer, Harry. *The Purposes of Calvary,* Grand Rapids: Eerdmans, 1939.

Rist, Martin, and Lynn Harold Hough. "The Revelation of St. John the Divine." In vol. 12 of *IB,* 345–613. Nashville: Abingdon Press, 1985.

Robinson, John A. T. *The Human Face of God.* Philadelphia: WJK, 1973.

_____. *Jesus and His Coming: The Emergence of a Doctrine.* 2nd ed. Philadelphia: WJK, 1979.

Roloff, Jürgen. *The Revelation of John.* A Continental Commentary. Minneapolis: Fortress, 1993.

Rorem, Paul. *Pseudo-Dionysius: A Commentary on the Texts and an Introduction to Their Influence.* New York: Oxford University Press, 1993.

Rowland, Christopher C. "The Book of Revelation." In vol. 12 of *NIB,* 501–743. Nashville: Abingdon, 1998.

Rowley, H. H. *The Relevance of Apocalyptic: A Study of Jewish and Christian Apocalypses from Daniel to the Revelation.* Greenwood, SC: Attic, 1980.

Royalty, Robert M. *The Streets of Heaven: The Ideology of Wealth in the Apocalypse of John.* Macon, GA: Mercer University Press, 1998.

Russell, D. S. *The Method and Message of Jewish Apocalyptic: 200 BC–AD 100.* Philadelphia: WJK, 1964.

Ruthven, Jon Mark. *The Prophecy That Is Shaping History: New Research on Ezekiel's Vision of the End.* Fairfax, VA: Xulon Press, 2003.

Ryrie, Charles C. *Dispensationalism Today.* Chicago: Moody, 1965.

_____. *Revelation.* Everyman's Bible Commentary. Chicago: Moody, 1968.

Sanders, Carl E. *The Premillennial Faith of James Brookes: Reexamining the Roots of American Dispensationalism.* Lanham, MD: University Press of America, 2001.

Sauer, Erich. *The Dawn of World Redemption: A Survey of Historical Revelation in the Old Testament.* Grand Rapids: Eerdmans, 1951.

_____. *From Eternity to Eternity: An Outline of the Divine Purposes*. Grand Rapids: Eerdmans, 1957.

_____. *The Triumph of the Crucified: A Survey of Historical Revelation in the New Testament*. Translated by G. H. Lang. London: Paternoster Press, 1951.

Sauer, Val J., Jr. *The Eschatology Handbook: The Bible Speaks to Us Today About Endtimes*. Atlanta, GA: J. Knox Press, 1981.

Schmidt, Thomas E., and Moisés Silva, eds. *To Tell the Mystery: Essays on New Testament Eschatology in Honor of Robert H. Gundry*. JSNT 100. Sheffield, England: JSOT Press, 1994.

Schumann, Walter. *Gemstones of the World*. New York: Sterling Publishing Company, 1984.

Schüssler Fiorenza, Elisabeth. *The Book of Revelation: Justice and Judgment*. 2nd ed. Philadelphia: Augsburg Fortress, 1998.

Scott, Walter. *Exposition of the Revelation of Jesus Christ*. 4th ed. Westwood, NJ: Revell, 1968.

Seiss, Joseph A. *The Apocalypse: Lectures on the Book of Revelation*. Grand Rapids: Zondervan, 1962.

Showers, Renald. *Maranatha, Our Lord, Come! A Definitive Study of the Rapture of the Church*. Bellmawr, NJ: Friends of Israel Gospel Ministry, 1995.

_____. *The Pre-Wrath Rapture View: An Examination and Critique*. Grand Rapids: Kregel, 2001.

Sims, James H. *A Comparative Literary Study of Daniel and Revelation: Shaping the End*. Lewiston, NY: Mellen Biblical Press, 1995.

Sinclair, Scott Gambrill. *Revelation: A Book for the Rest of Us*. Berkeley, CA: BIBAL Press, 1992.

Sleeper, C. Freeman. *The Victorious Christ: A Study of the Book of Revelation*. Louisville, KY: WJK, 1996.

Smalley, Stephen S. *The Revelation to John: A Commentary on the Greek Text of the Apocalypse*. Downers Grove, IL: InterVarsity Press, 2005.

Smith, Robert H. *Apocalypse: A Commentary on Revelation in Words and Images*. Collegeville, MN: Liturgical Press, 2000.

Smith, T. C. *Reading the Signs: A Sensible Approach to Revelation and Other Apocalyptic Writings*. Macon, GA: Smyth & Helwys Publishing, 1997.

Smith, Uriah. *The Prophecies of Daniel and the Revelation*. Christian Home Library. Vol. 2. Washington, DC: Review and Herald, 1944.

Smith, Wilbur M. *The Second Advent of Christ*. Fundamentals of the Faith 10. Washington, DC: Christianity Today, n.d.

Spilsbury, Paul. *The Throne, the Lamb & the Dragon: A Reader's Guide to the Book of Revelation*. Downers Grove, IL: InterVarsity Press, 2002.

403

Sproule, John A. *In Defense of Pretribulationism*. Winona Lake, IN: BMH Books, 1980.

Stagg, Frank. *New Testament Theology*. Nashville: Broadman Press, 1962.

Stanton, Gerald B. *Kept from the Hour: Biblical Evidence for the Pretribulational Return or Christ*. Miami Springs, FL: Schoettle, 1991.

Stefanovic, Ranko. *Revelation of Jesus Christ: Commentary on the Book of Revelation*. Berrien Springs, MI: Andrews University Press, 2002.

Stibbs, Alan M. *His Blood Works: The Meaning of the Word "Blood" in Scripture*. London: Tyndale, 1954.

Strabo. *The Geography of Strabo*. Translated by Horace Leonard Jones. LCL 49–50, 182, 196, 211, 223, 241, 267. Cambridge, MA: Harvard University Press, 1988.

Suetonius. *Lives of the Caesars*. Translated by C. J. Rolfe. LCL 31, 38. Cambridge, MA: Harvard University Press, 1997.

Summers, R. *The Life Beyond*. Nashville: Broadman Press, 1959.

_____. *Worthy Is the Lamb: An Interpretation of Revelation in Its Historical Background*. Nashville: B&H, 1951.

Sweet, J. P. M. *Revelation*. TPI New Testament Commentaries. London: SCM Press; Philadelphia: Trinity Press International, 1990.

_____. *Revelation*. Westminster Pelican Commentaries. Philadelphia: Westminster Press, 1979.

Swete, Henry Barclay. *Commentary on Revelation*. Grand Rapids: Kregel, 1977.

Swindoll, Charles R. *Letters to Churches Then and Now*. Fullerton, CA: Insight for Living, 1986.

Tacitus. *Histories*. Translated by C. H. Moore and John Jackson. LCL 111, 249. Cambridge, MA: Harvard University Press, 1956.

Talbert, Charles H. *The Apocalypse: A Reading of the Revelation of John*. 1st ed. Louisville, KY: WJK, 1994.

Tchakmakjian, Kevork. *The Great Babylon, Battle of the Ages: A Prophetic Interpretation of the Bible*. Whittier, CA: Stockton Trade Press, 1980.

Tenney, Merrill C. *Interpreting Revelation*. Grand Rapids: Eerdmans, 1957.

Tertullian. *A Commentary on the Revelation of St. John the Divine*. ANF 3.

_____. *The Five Books Against Marcion*. ANF 3.

_____. *On the Resurrection of the Flesh*. ANF 3.

_____. *A Treatise on the Soul*. ANF 3.

Thomas, Robert L. *Revelation 1–7: An Exegetical Commentary*. Chicago: Moody, 1992.

_____. *Revelation 8–22: An Exegetical Commentary*. Chicago: Moody, 1995.

Thompson, Leonard L. *The Book of Revelation: Apocalypse and Empire*. New York: Oxford University Press, 1990.

Thompson, Steven. *The Apocalypse and Semitic Syntax*. SNTSMS 52. New York: Cambridge University Press, 1985.

Thucydides. *History of the Peloponnesian War*. Translated by C. F. Smith. 4 vols. LCL 108–110, 169. 4 vols. London: William Heinemann, 1956.

Torrance, Thomas F. *The Apocalypse Today*. Grand Rapids: Eerdmans, 1959.

Trench, Richard Chenevix. *Commentary on the Epistles to the Seven Churches in Asia: Revelation II. III.* Eugene, OR: Wipf & Stock, 1997.

Tucker, W. Leon. *Studies in Revelation: An Expositional Commentary*. Grand Rapids: Kregel Publications, 1980.

Van Gemeren, William A. *Interpreting the Prophetic Word: An Introduction to the Prophetic Literature of the Old Testament*. Grand Rapids: Zondervan, 1990.

Van Hartingsveld, L. *Revelation: A Practical Commentary*. Text and Interpretation. Grand Rapids: Eerdmans, 1985.

Wainwright, Arthur W. *Mysterious Apocalypse: Interpreting the Book of Revelation*. Nashville: Abingdon Press, 1993.

Wall, Robert W. *Revelation*. New International Biblical Commentary 18. Peabody, MA: Hendrickson Publishers, 1991.

Walvoord, John F. *The Final Drama: 14 Keys to Understanding the Prophetic Scriptures*. Grand Rapids: Kregel, 1998.

_____. *Daniel: The Key to Prophetic Revelation*. Chicago: Moody, 1989.

_____. *Major Bible Prophecies: 37 Crucial Prophecies That Affect You Today*. Grand Rapids: Zondervan, 1991.

_____. *The Nations in Prophecy*. Grand Rapids: Zondervan, 1967.

_____. *The Prophecy Knowledge Handbook*. Wheaton, IL: Victor Books, 1990.

_____. *The Revelation of Jesus Christ: A Commentary*. Chicago: Moody, 1966.

_____, and Roy B. Zuck, eds. *The Bible Knowledge Commentary: An Exposition of the Scriptures*. Wheaton, IL: Victor Books, 1983.

Weinrich, William C. *Revelation*. ACCS. Downers Grove, IL: InterVarsity Press, 2005.

Wenham, David. *The Jesus Tradition outside the Gospels*. Gospel Perspectives 5. Sheffield: JSOT Press, 1985.

Westcott, Brooke Foss. *The Revelation of the Risen Lord*. London: Macmillan, 1884.

Wilcock, Michael. *The Message of Revelation: I Saw Heaven Opened*. The Bible Speaks Today. Downers Grove, IL: InterVarsity Press, 1975.

Wilkinson, Paul Richard. *For Zion's Sake: Christian Zionism and the Role of John Nelson Darby*. Studies in Evangelical History and Thought. Colorado Springs: Paternoster, 2007.

Witherington, Ben, III. *Revelation*. CBC. Cambridge: Cambridge University Press, 2003.

Worth, Roland H. *The Seven Cities of the Apocalypse and Greco-Asian Culture*. New York: Paulist Press, 1999.

Yeatts, John R. *Revelation*. Believers Church Bible Commentary. Scottdale, PA: Herald Press, 2003.

Name Index

A

B

C

Subject Index

A

B

W

SCRIPTURE INDEX

www.ingramcontent.com/pod-product-compliance
Lightning Source LLC
Chambersburg PA
CBHW021656120626
46545CB00004B/1271